MathLinks 9

Authors

Bruce McAskill
B.Sc., B.Ed., M.Ed., Ph.D.
Mathematics Consultant
Victoria, British Columbia

Wayne Watt
B.Sc., B.Ed., M.Ed.
Mathematics Consultant
Winnipeg, Manitoba

Chris Zarski
B.Ed., M.Ed.
Evergreen Catholic Separate
   Regional Division No. 2
Alberta

Eric Balzarini
B.Sc., B.Ed., M.Ed.
School District 35 (Langley)
British Columbia

Blaise Johnson
B.Sc., B.Ed.
School District 45 (West
   Vancouver)
British Columbia

Emily Kalwarowsky
B.Sc., B.Ed.
Edmonton Catholic Separate
   School District No. 7
Alberta

Tricia Licorish (Perry)
B.Ed.
St. James-Assiniboia School
   Division
Manitoba

Michael Webb
B.Sc., M.Sc., Ph.D.
Mathematics Consultant
Toronto, Ontario

Assessment/Pedagogy Consultants

Bruce McAskill
B.Sc., B.Ed., M.Ed., Ph.D.
Mathematics Consultant
Victoria, British Columbia

Wayne Watt
B.Sc., B.Ed., M.Ed.
Mathematics Consultant
Winnipeg, Manitoba

Chris Zarski
B.Ed., M.Ed.
Evergreen Catholic Separate
   Regional Division No. 2
Alberta

Aboriginal Consultant

Cheryl Makokis
Kitaskinaw Education
   Authority
Alberta

Differentiated Instruction Consultant

Reg Fogarty
School District 83 (North
   Okanagan/Shuswap)
British Columbia

Gifted Consultants

Rick Wunderlich
School District 83 (North
   Okanagan/Shuswap)
British Columbia

Robert Wong
Edmonton Public Schools
Alberta

Literacy and Numeracy Consultant

Ian Strachan
Calgary Board of Education
Alberta

Problem Solving, Mental Math, and Estimation Consultant

Sandra Harazny
Regina Roman Catholic
   Separate School Division
   No. 81
Saskatchewan

Technology Consultant

Ron Kennedy
Mathematics Consultant
Edmonton, Alberta

ELL Consultant

Maureen Sims
Special Education and ELL
   Teacher
Toronto, Ontario

Advisors

Ralph Backé
The Winnipeg School
   Division
Manitoba

Scott Carlson
Golden Hills School Division
   No. 75
Alberta

Ron Coleborn
School District 41 (Burnaby)
British Columbia

Brad Epp
School District 73
   (Kamloops/Thompson)
British Columbia

Emily Kalwarowsky
Edmonton Catholic Separate
   School District No. 7
Alberta

Wanda Lloyd
Calgary Roman Catholic
   Separate School District No. 1
Alberta

P. Janelle McFeetors
River East Transcona
   School Division
Manitoba

Sam Muraca
School District 35 (Langley)
British Columbia

Vicki Park
Calgary Board of Education
Alberta

Enzo Timoteo
Mathematics Consultant
Edmonton, Alberta

Technology Advisor

Ted Keating
Thompson Rivers University
British Columbia

McGraw-Hill Ryerson

Toronto   Montréal   Boston   Burr Ridge, IL   Dubuque, IA   Madison, WI   New York
San Francisco   St. Louis   Bangkok   Bogotá   Caracas   Kuala Lumpur   Lisbon   London
Madrid   Mexico City   Milan   New Delhi   Santiago   Seoul   Singapore   Sydney   Taipei

The McGraw-Hill Companies

COPIES OF THIS BOOK
MAY BE OBTAINED BY
CONTACTING:

McGraw-Hill Ryerson Ltd.

WEB SITE:
http://www.mcgrawhill.ca

E-MAIL:
orders@mcgrawhill.ca

TOLL-FREE FAX:
1-800-463-5885

TOLL-FREE CALL:
1-800-565-5758

OR BY MAILING YOUR
ORDER TO:
McGraw-Hill Ryerson
Order Department
300 Water Street
Whitby, ON L1N 9B6

Please quote the ISBN and
title when placing your
order.

McGraw-Hill Ryerson
MathLinks 9

ISBN-13: 978-0-07-097340-4
ISBN-10: 0-07-097340-7

http://www.mcgrawhill.ca

6 7 8 9 10 TCP 7 6 5 4

Printed and bound in Canada

Care has been taken to trace ownership of copyright material contained in this text. The publishers will gladly accept any information that will enable them to rectify any reference or credit in subsequent printings.

Statistics Canada information is used with the permission of Statistics Canada. Users are forbidden to copy the data and redisseminate them, in an original or modified form, for commercial purposes, without permission from Statistics Canada. Information on the availability of the wide range of data from Statistics Canada can be obtained from Statistics Canada's Regional Offices, its World Wide Web site at *http://www.statcan.ca*, and its toll-free access number 1-800-263-1136.

Microsoft® Excel is either a registered trademark or trademarks of Microsoft Corporation in the United States and/or other countries.

The Geometer's Sketchpad®, Key Curriculum Press, 1150 65th Street, Emeryville, CA 94608, 1-800-995-MATH.

MATH PUBLISHER: Linda Allison
CONTENT MANAGER: Jean Ford
PROJECT MANAGER: Helen Mason
DEVELOPMENTAL EDITORS: Susan Till, Rita Vanden Heuval, Kelly Cochrane,
            Richard Dupuis, Maggie Cheverie
EDITORS: Laura Resendes, Sarah Rowe
MANAGER, EDITORIAL SERVICES: Crystal Shortt
SUPERVISING EDITOR: Jaime Smith
COPY EDITOR: Linda Jenkins, Red Pen Services
PHOTO RESEARCH & PERMISSIONS: Linda Tanaka
EDITORIAL ASSISTANT: Erin Hartley
EDITORIAL COORDINATOR: Jennifer Keay, Janie Reeson
MANAGER, PRODUCTION SERVICES: Yolanda Pigden
SENIOR PRODUCTION COORDINATOR: Paula Brown
INTERIOR DESIGN: Pronk & Associates
COVER DESIGN: Valid Design & Layout
ART DIRECTION: Tom Dart, First Folio Resource Group, Inc.
ELECTRONIC PAGE MAKE-UP: Tom Dart, Kim Hutchinson, Adam Wood,
            First Folio Resource Group, Inc.
COVER IMAGE: Emanuele Taroni

Acknowledgements

There are many students, teachers, and administrators who the publisher, authors, and consultants of MathLinks 9 wish to thank for their thoughtful comments and creative suggestions about what would work best in their classrooms. Their input and assistance have been invaluable in making sure that the Student Resource and its related Teacher's Resource meet the needs of students and teachers who work within the Western and Northern Canadian Protocol Common Curriculum Framework.

We would like to thank the Grade 9 students of Raymond Junior High, Raymond, Alberta, Principal, Cory Bevans, and Janet Workman for their help in coordinating the photography sessions.

Aboriginal Reviewer

Paul Paling
School District 52 (Prince Rupert)
British Columbia

Inuit Reviewer

Christine Purse
Mathematics Consultant
British Columbia

Métis Reviewer

Greg King
Northern Lights School Division
 No. 69
Alberta

Reviewers

John M. Agnew
School District 63 (Saanich)
British Columbia

Lisa M. Allen
Regina School Division No. 4
Saskatchewan

Andy Amour
Calgary Roman Catholic Separate
 School Disctrict No. 1
Alberta

Linda M. Benson
Seven Oaks School Division
Manitoba

Len Bonifacio
Edmonton Catholic Separate School
 District No. 7
Alberta

Jill Booth
Fort McMurray School District
 No. 2833
Alberta

Chris Buffie
Seven Oaks School Division
Manitoba

Mario R. Chaput
Pembina Trails School Division
Manitoba

Van Chau
School District 37 (Delta)
British Columbia

Sabine Chute
Edmonton Public Schools
Alberta

Barbara Corbett
Edmonton Public Schools
Alberta

Dawn Driver
School District 35 (Langley)
British Columbia

Karen Dunbar
Southwest Horizon School Division
Manitoba

Victor Epp
School District 5 (Southeast
 Kootenay)
British Columbia

Cheryl Evoy
The Winnipeg School Division
Manitoba

Michelle Fior
Calgary Roman Catholic Separate
 School District No. 1
Alberta

Helen J. Fulara
Edmonton Public Schools
Alberta

Barbara Lee Gajdos
Calgary Roman Catholic Separate
 School District No. 1
Alberta

Peter Gee
Parkland School Division No. 70
Alberta

Patrick Giommi
St. Margaret's School (Independent)
British Columbia

Field Testers

Craig Adair
Edmonton Public Schools
Alberta

Ralph Backé
The Winnipeg School Division
Manitoba

Kari Bergmuller
St. James-Assiniboia School Division
Manitoba

Jill Booth
Fort McMurray School District
  No. 2833
Alberta

Karen Dunbar
Southwest Horizon School Division
Manitoba

Donna Ell
Regina Roman Catholic Separate
  School Division No. 81
Saskatchewan

Paula Evoy
Edmonton Public Schools
Alberta

Barbara Lee Gajdos
Calgary Roman Catholic Separate
  School District No. 1
Alberta

Heather M. Granger
Prairie South School Division
  No. 210
Saskatchewan

Sandra Harazny
Regina Roman Catholic Separate
  School Division No. 81
Saskatchewan

Glenn Johnston
School District 35 (Langley)
British Columbia

Emily Kalwarowsky
Edmonton Catholic Separate School
  District No. 7
Alberta

Deborah Schamuhn Kirk
Edmonton Public Schools
Alberta

Dan Norman
Brentwood College School
  (Independent)
British Columbia

Vicki Park
Calgary Board of Education
Alberta

Trevor Troy
Regina Roman Catholic Separate
  School Division No. 81
Saskatchewan

Kathy Vladicka-Davies
Fort McMurray School District
  No. 2833
Alberta

Carter Watson
Calgary Roman Catholic Separate
  School District No. 1
Alberta

Brennan Yaremko
Regina Roman Catholic Separate
  School Division No. 81
Saskatchewan

Contents

Chapter 9

Chapter 10

Chapter 11

A Tour of Your Textbook

Chapter Opener

Each chapter begins with a two-page spread which introduces you to what you will learn in the chapter.

Foldables™

Each chapter includes a Foldable to help you organize what you are learning and keep track of what you need to work on. Instructions on where and how to record information on the Foldable will help you use it as a study tool.

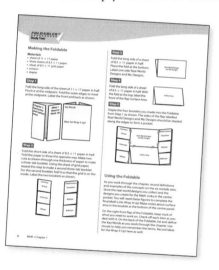

Math Link

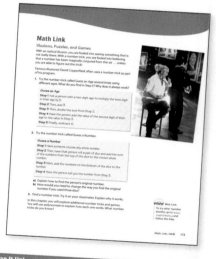

Each chapter introduces a Math Link that helps you connect math and your own personal experiences. You will often revisit the Math Link at the end of a lesson. This is an opportunity for you to build concepts and understanding. The Math Link: Wrap It Up! at the end of each chapter gives you an opportunity to demonstrate your understanding of the chapter concepts.

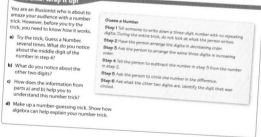

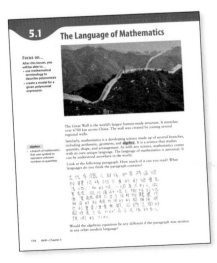

Numbered Sections

The numbered sections often start with a visual to connect the topic to a real setting. The purpose of this introduction is to help you make connections between the math in the section and the real world, or to make connections to what you already know.

A three-part lesson follows.

Explore

- An activity is designed to help you build your own understanding of the new concept and lead toward answers to the key question. This activity is often related to the opening visual and introductory text in the section.

Link the Ideas

- Some of these sections start with a piece of text that will help you connect what you did in the Explore to the **Examples**.
- **Examples** and **Solutions** demonstrate how to use the concept.

- A summary of the main new concepts is given in the **Key Ideas**.

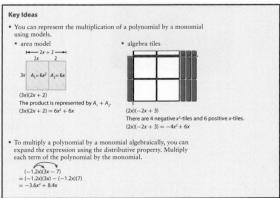

Check Your Understanding

- **Communicate the Ideas:** These questions let you talk or write about the concepts and assess whether you understand the ideas.
- **Practise:** These are questions to check your knowledge and understanding of what you have learned.
- **Apply:** In these questions, you need to apply what you have learned to solve problems.
- **Extend:** These questions may be more challenging and may make connections to other lessons.

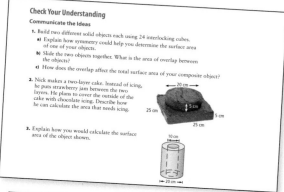

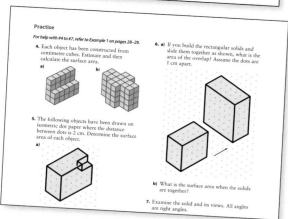

How does *MathLinks 9* help you learn?

Understanding Vocabulary

Key Words are listed on the Chapter Opener. Perhaps you already know the meaning of some of them. Great! If not, watch for these terms the first time they are used in the chapter. The meaning is given close by in the margin.

A **Literacy Link** at the beginning of each chapter provides tips to help you read and interpret the chapter content.

Other **Literacy Links** throughout the chapter assist you in reading and interpreting items in math. These tips will help you in other subjects as well.

Key Words

symmetry	rotation symmetry
line of symmetry	order of rotation
line symmetry	angle of rotation
centre of rotation	surface area

centre of rotation
- the point about which the rotation of an object or design turns

rotation symmetry
- occurs when a shape or design can be turned about its centre of rotation so that it fits onto its outline more than once in a complete turn

⊙ Literacy Link

A thematic map can help you understand and connect new terms and concepts.

Create a thematic map in your math journal or notebook. Make each shape large enough to write in. Leave enough space to draw additional lines. As you work through the chapter, complete the thematic map.

- Use the boxes to record the key ideas for each section.
- Use the lines to explain the key ideas by recording definitions, examples, and strategies.
- Where possible, include a visual to support your definition.

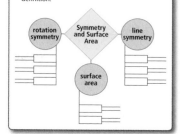

⊙ Literacy Link
Parentheses is another name for brackets. They can be used in place of a multiplication sign. For example,
$-4 \times 1.5 = -4(1.5)$

⊙ Literacy Link
Klassen's winning time of 1:55.27 means 1 min, 55.27 s.

Understanding Concepts

The **Explore** activities are designed to help you construct your own understanding of new concepts. The key question tells you what the activity is about. Short steps, with illustrations, lead you to make some conclusions in the **Reflect and Check** question(s).

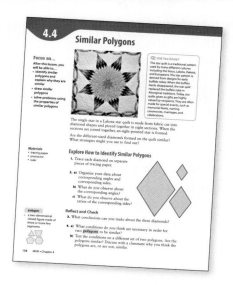

The **Examples** and their worked **Solutions** include several tools to help you understand the work.

- Notes in a speech bubble help you think through the steps.
- Sometimes different methods of solving the same problem are shown. One way may make more sense to you than the other. Or, you may develop another way that means more to you.
- **Problem Solving Strategies** are pointed out.
- Calculator key press sequences are shown where appropriate.
- Most Examples are followed by a **Show You Know**. These questions help you check that you understand the skill covered in the Example.

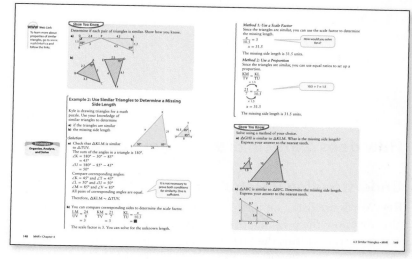

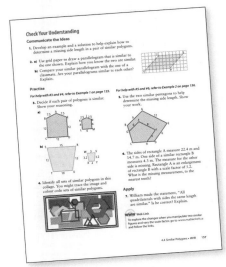

The **Check Your Understanding** exercises begin with **Communicate the Ideas**. These questions focus your thinking on the **Key Ideas** you developed in **Link the Ideas**. By discussing these questions in a group, or doing the action called for, you can see whether you understand the main points of the lesson.

The first few questions in the **Practise** can often be done by following one of the worked Examples.

Problem Solving

At the beginning of the student resource there is an overview of the four steps you can use to approach **Problem Solving**. Samples of problem solving strategies are shown. You can refer back to this section if you need help choosing a strategy to solve a problem. You are also encouraged to use your own strategies.

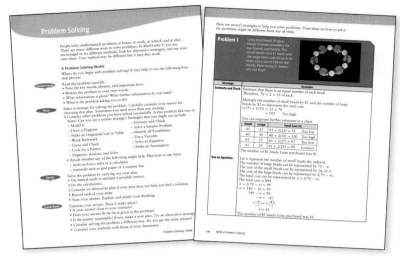

Mental Math and Estimation

This **Mental Math and Estimation** logo does one of two things:

1. It signals where you can use mental math and estimation.
2. It provides useful tips for using mental math and estimation.

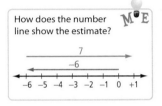

How does the number line show the estimate?

Other Features

> **Did You Know?**
> The Métis flag shown in part a) is a white infinity symbol on a blue background. The infinity symbol can represent that the Métis nation will go on forever. It can also be interpreted as two conjoined circles, representing the joining of two cultures: European and First Nations.

Did You Know?

These are interesting facts related to math topics you are learning.

> **WWW Web Link**
> To explore more about symmetry, go to www.mathlinks9.ca and follow the links.

Web Links

You can find extra information related to some questions on the Internet. Log on to **www.mathlinks9.ca** and you will be able to link to recommended Web sites.

> **Tech Link**
> The key for entering a negative sign may look different on different calculators, for example, +←→ +/− or (−). It is not the subtraction key, −. Experiment with calculations involving negative signs on your calculator.

Tech Links

Some Tech Links show what calculator keys to use for certain types of questions. Keys and key sequences may vary depending on the calculator make and model. Experiment to find out what works on yours.

> **Tech Link**
> You can use a spreadsheet program to create the graph.

Other Tech Links suggest that you could use computer applications to do certain activities.

Still other Tech Links refer you to the *MathLinks 9* Online Learning Centre where you can use software to extend your understanding of a concept.

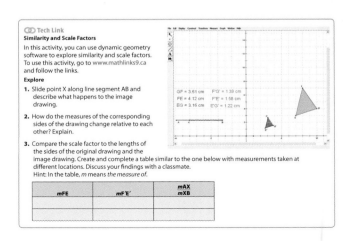

> **Tech Link**
> **Similarity and Scale Factors**
> In this activity, you can use dynamic geometry software to explore similarity and scale factors. To use this activity, go to www.mathlinks9.ca and follow the links.
>
> **Explore**
> 1. Slide point X along line segment AB and describe what happens to the image drawing.
> 2. How do the measures of the corresponding sides of the drawing change relative to each other? Explain.
> 3. Compare the scale factor to the lengths of the sides of the original drawing and the image drawing. Create and complete a table similar to the one below with measurements taken at different locations. Discuss your findings with a classmate.
> Hint: In the table, *m* means *the measure of*.

*m*FE	*m*F'E'	*m*AX *m*XB

Chapter Review and Practice Test

There is a **Chapter Review** and a **Practice Test** at the end of each chapter. The chapter review is organized by section number so you can look back if you need help with a question. The test includes the different types of questions that you will find on provincial tests: multiple choice, numerical response, short answer, and extended response.

Cumulative Review

To help you reinforce what you have learned, there is a review of the previous four chapters at the end of Chapters 4, 7, and 11. The reviews at the end of Chapters 4 and 7 are followed by a Task.

Task

These tasks require you to use skills from more than one chapter. You will also need to use your creativity.

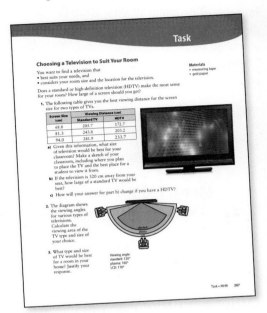

Challenges

The last two pages of each chapter provide **Challenges.** The **Challenges** provide interesting problems that show how the math you learned in the chapter relates to jobs, careers, or daily life. Some Challenges are games you can play, or make and play, with your friends and family.

Answers

Answers are provided for all Practise, Apply, Extend, and Review questions. Sample answers are given for questions that have a variety of possible answers or that involve communication. If you need help, read the sample and then try to give an alternative response. Answers are omitted for the Math Link questions and for Practice Tests because teachers may use these questions to assess your progress.

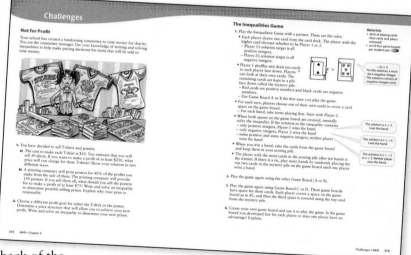

Glossary

Refer to the illustrated **Glossary** at the back of the student resource if you need to check the exact meaning of mathematical terms.

Index

If you want to find a particular math topic in *MathLinks 9*, look it up in the index, which is at the back of the student resource. The index provides page references that may help you review that topic.

Problem Solving

People solve mathematical problems at home, at work, at school, and at play. There are many different ways to solve problems. In *MathLinks 9*, you are encouraged to try different methods, look for alternative strategies, and use your own ideas. Your method may be different but it may also work.

A Problem Solving Model

Where do you begin with problem solving? It may help to use the following four-step process.

Read the problem carefully.
• Note the key words, phrases, and important facts.
• Restate the problem in your own words.
• What information is given? What further information do you need?
• What is the problem asking you to do?

Select a strategy for solving the problem. Carefully consider your reason for choosing that plan. Sometimes you need more than one strategy.
• Consider other problems you have solved successfully. Is this problem like one of them? Can you use a similar strategy? Strategies that you might use include:

– Model It	– Estimate and Check
– Draw a Diagram	– Solve a Simpler Problem
– Make an Organized List or Table	– Identify all Possibilities
– Work Backward	– Use a Variable
– Guess and Check	– Solve an Equation
– Look for a Pattern	– Make an Assumption
– Organize, Analyse, and Solve	

• Decide whether any of the following might help. Plan how to use them.
  – tools such as a ruler or a calculator
  – materials such as grid paper or a number line

Do It!

Solve the problem by carrying out your plan.
• Use mental math to estimate a possible answer.
• Do the calculations.
• Consider an alternative plan if your plan does not help you find a solution.
• Record each of your steps.
• State your answer. Explain and justify your thinking.

Look Back

Examine your answer. Does it make sense?
• Is your answer close to your estimate?
• Does your answer fit the facts given in the problem?
• Is the answer reasonable? If not, make a new plan. Try an alternative strategy.
• Consider solving the problem a different way. Do you get the same answer?
• Compare your methods with those of your classmates.

Here are several strategies to help you solve problems. Your ideas on how to solve the problems might be different from any of these.

Problem 1

Leisa purchased 70 glass beads to make jewellery for her friends and family. The small beads cost $1 each, and the large ones cost $2 each. In total, Leisa spent $99 on the beads. How many $1 beads did she buy?

Strategy	Example
Estimate and Check	Estimate that there is an equal number of each bead. Therefore, $70 \div 2 = 35$ of each.

Multiply the number of small beads by $1 and the number of large beads by $2 to determine the total cost.
$$1(35) + 2(35) = 35 + 70$$
$$= 105 \quad \text{Too high}$$

You can organize further estimates in a chart.

Small	Large	Total Cost ($)
45	25	$45 + 2(25) = 95$ Too low
40	30	$40 + 2(30) = 100$ Too high
43	27	$43 + 2(27) = 97$ Too low
41	29	$41 + 2(29) = 99$ Correct!

The number of $1 beads Leisa purchased was 41.

Use an Equation

Let n represent the number of small beads she ordered.
The number of large beads can be represented by $70 - n$.
The cost of the small beads can be represented by $1n$, or n.
The cost of the large beads can be represented by $2(70 - n)$.
The total cost can be represented by $n + 2(70 - n)$.
The total cost is $99.
$$n + 2(70 - n) = 99$$
$$n + 140 - 2n = 99$$
$$140 - n = 99$$
$$-n = -41$$
$$\left(\frac{-n}{-1}\right) = \left(\frac{-41}{-1}\right)$$
$$n = 41$$

The number of $1 beads Leisa purchased was 41.

Problem 2	In a community in northern Manitoba, $\frac{1}{4}$ of the school population is grade 9 students. Of these grade 9 students, $\frac{3}{5}$ are boys. There are 18 grade 9 boys in the school. How many students are there in the school in total?

Strategy	Example
Draw a Diagram	The rectangle represents the entire school population. The grade 9 students represent $\frac{1}{4}$ of the rectangle. grade 9 students Divide the $\frac{1}{4}$ section into five parts. Label three parts to show that $\frac{3}{5}$ are boys. boys boys boys Since 18 grade 9 boys fill three boxes, 6 students must be in each box.　$6 + 6 + 6 = 18$ The rectangle has 20 parts altogether. So, $20 \times 6 = 120$. There are 120 students in the school. 6 boys 6 boys 6 boys
Solve a Simpler Problem	First, determine the fraction of grade 9 boys in the school. The number of grade 9 students is $\frac{1}{4}$ of the school population. The number of grade 9 boys is $\frac{3}{5}$ of the grade 9 students. So, the number of grade 9 boys in the school is $\frac{1}{4} \times \frac{3}{5} = \frac{3}{20}$. Now, use $\frac{3}{20}$ to determine the school population. The number of grade 9 boys is 18. So, $\frac{3}{20}$ of the school population is 18. That means the school population is $18 \div \frac{3}{20}$. $$18 \div \frac{3}{20} = 18 \times \frac{20}{3}$$ $$= \frac{360}{3}$$ $$= 120$$ There are 120 students in the school.

Problem 3

Damien is going to cut a Saskatoon berry pie into four equal slices. If he cuts the pie into six equal slices, each slice will have a mass that is 40 g less. What is the mass of the whole pie?

Strategy	Example
Draw a Diagram	Draw two circles of the same size. Divide one into four equal sections and shade $\frac{1}{4}$ blue. Divide the other into six equal sections and shade $\frac{1}{6}$ blue. Since $\frac{1}{4} = \frac{3}{12}$, and $\frac{1}{6} = \frac{2}{12}$, divide the circles into 12 sections. Now $\frac{3}{12}$ of one circle is blue and $\frac{2}{12}$ of the other circle is blue. Shade $\frac{2}{12}$ of each circle yellow. Note that $\frac{1}{12}$ of the $\frac{1}{4}$ section is blue. This $\frac{1}{12}$ represents the difference in size between the two pieces. This difference has a mass of 40 g. So, $\frac{1}{12}$ of the pie is 40 g. $40 \times 12 = 480$ Therefore, the mass of the whole pie is 480 g.
Use an Equation	Let m represent the mass of the whole pie. The mass of a slice from a four-slice pie can be represented by $\frac{1}{4}m$. The mass of a slice from a six-slice pie can be represented by $\frac{1}{6}m$. The two slices differ by 40 g. Solve using a common denominator. $$\frac{1}{4}m - \frac{1}{6}m = 40$$ $$\frac{3}{12}m - \frac{2}{12}m = 40$$ $$\frac{1}{12}m = 40$$ $$\frac{1}{12}m \times 12 = 40 \times 12$$ $$m = 480$$ The mass of the whole pie is 480 g.

Problem 4

Two dancers start at point O on a stage. They move in a straight line to A. Then, the first dancer moves along the circumference of the circle to point B, and the second dancer moves to point C. The first dancer will now dance along BC to the second dancer. How far is this distance?

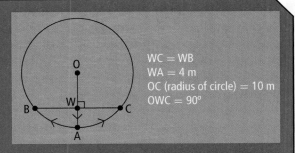

WC = WB
WA = 4 m
OC (radius of circle) = 10 m
OWC = 90°

Strategy	Example
Organize,	Sketch the circle and label the given information.

Analyse,	Develop a plan to find the length of BC.
	WC and WB are equal segments of BC. Find the length of either WC or WB. Choose WC.
	△OWC is a right triangle. Determine the length of WC using the Pythagorean relationship.
	You need to know the lengths of OC and OW.
	OC is a hypotenuse of the right triangle. OC = 10 m
	OW is a leg of the right triangle. Determine the length of OW.
	OW and WA are segments of OA.
	OA = radius of the circle, WA = 4 m
	    = 10 m
	OW + WA = OA
	  OW + 4 = 10
	      OW = 6
	
	Apply the Pythagorean relationship to find WC.
	$OW^2 + WC^2 = OC^2$
	  $6^2 + WC^2 = 10^2$
	  $36 + WC^2 = 100$
	      $WC^2 = 64$
	       $WC = 8$

and Solve	Now that you have the length of WC, determine the length of WB.
	WC = WB
	WC = 8, so WB = 8
	
	Determine the length of BC.
	BC = WC + WB
	    = 8 + 8
	    = 16
	The distance from the first dancer to the second is 16 m.

Symmetry and Surface Area

Examine this photograph of a monarch butterfly. What do you notice about it? Are there any parts that look like mirror images? The mirrored nature of the two sides of the image is called symmetry.

Symmetry is all around us. Even though it is something that we recognize, it can be difficult to define. It can be thought of as beauty, resulting from a balance in form and arrangement. Describe places where you have seen symmetry.

In this chapter, you will explore different kinds of symmetry. You will learn how to use symmetry in solving mathematical problems.

WWW Web Link

For a sampling of different places where symmetry can be found, go to www.mathlinks9.ca and follow the links.

What You Will Learn

- to find lines of symmetry in 2-D shapes and images
- to use lines of symmetry to create designs
- to determine if 2-D shapes and designs have rotation symmetry
- to rotate a shape about a vertex and draw the resulting image
- to create a design with line and rotation symmetry
- to use symmetry to help find the surface area of composite 3-D objects

Key Words

symmetry	rotation symmetry
line of symmetry	order of rotation
line symmetry	angle of rotation
centre of rotation	surface area

⊂⊃ Literacy Link

A thematic map can help you understand and connect new terms and concepts.

Create a thematic map in your math journal or notebook. Make each shape large enough to write in. Leave enough space to draw additional lines. As you work through the chapter, complete the thematic map.

- Use the boxes to record the key ideas for each section.
- Use the lines to explain the key ideas by recording definitions, examples, and strategies.
- Where possible, include a visual to support your definition.

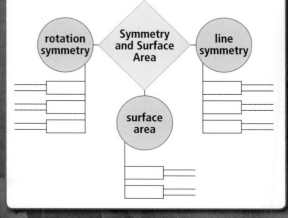

Making the Foldable

Materials
- sheet of 11 × 17 paper
- three sheets of 8.5 × 11 paper
- sheet of 8.5 × 11 grid paper
- scissors
- stapler

Step 1

Fold the long side of the sheet of 11 × 17 paper in half. Pinch it at the midpoint. Fold the outer edges to meet at the midpoint. Label the front and back as shown.

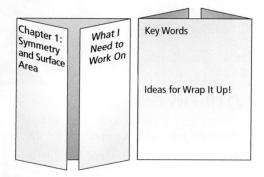

Step 2

Fold the short side of a sheet of 8.5 × 11 paper in half. Fold the paper in three the opposite way. Make two cuts as shown through one thickness of paper to make a three-tab booklet. Using the sheet of grid paper, repeat this step to make a second three-tab booklet. For this second booklet, fold it so that the grid is on the inside. Label the two booklets as shown.

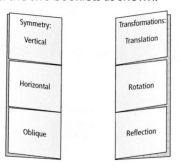

Step 3

Fold the long side of a sheet of 8.5 × 11 paper in half. Place the fold at the bottom. Label one side Real-World Designs and My Designs.

Step 4

Fold the long side of a sheet of 8.5 × 11 paper in half. With the fold at the top, label the front of the flap Surface Area.

Step 5

Staple the four booklets you made into the Foldable from Step 1 as shown. The sides of the flap labelled Real-World Designs and My Designs should be stapled along the edges to form a pocket.

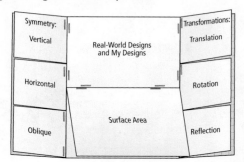

Using the Foldable

As you work through the chapter, record definitions and examples of the concepts on the six outside tabs. Store the real-world designs you collect and the designs you create for the Math Links in the centre pocket. You will need these figures to complete the final Math Link: Wrap It Up! Make notes about surface area in the booklet at the bottom of the centre panel.

On the right front flap of the Foldable, keep track of what you need to work on. Check off each item as you deal with it. On the back of the Foldable, list and define the Key Words as you work through the chapter. Use visuals to help you remember the terms. Record ideas for the Wrap It Up! here as well.

Math Link

Reflections on Our World

Symmetry is related to motion geometry and transformations. Many of the images in our world show translations, reflections, or rotations. In fact, some scientists believe that the human mind uses transformations to help visualize the world around us. This piece of art was created by Cree elder, Sally Milne. It is made by biting designs into birch bark. What reflections and rotations do you see in it?

symmetry

• an object or image has symmetry if it is balanced and can fit onto itself either by reflection or rotation

Literacy Link

A *transformation* moves a geometric figure. Examples are translations, reflections, and rotations.

A *translation* is a slide along a straight line. There are several ways to describe a translation. Here are three of them:

• Words: 3 units to the right and 2 units down

• Abbreviations: R3 and D2

• Symbols:

1. A line that divides an object or image into two identical halves is called a *line of reflection*. Use a mirror or Mira™ to help you find the line of reflection for each image. (There may be more than one.) How many do you think there are? Describe them.

a)

b)

2. In the following figure, the line of reflection is represented by a dashed line, labelled *r*. Describe the reflected image.

3. Examine the figure.
   a) Figure ABC has been translated to create image A'B'C'. What rule could describe this translation?
   b) Share with your classmates different ways to express the translation using words and symbols.
   c) Describe a translation that would place the image for ABC in quadrant III. Have a friend check your description to ensure it is correct.

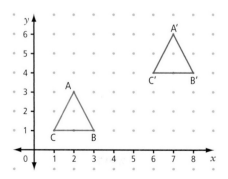

In this chapter, you will explore different types of symmetry. Find an image from a magazine, book, or greeting card, or on the Internet, that shows symmetry. Store this image in the pocket of your Foldable. You will need it for the Wrap It Up! activity.

Line Symmetry

Focus on...

After this lesson, you will be able to...

- **classify 2-D shapes or designs according to the number of lines of symmetry**
- **identify the line(s) of symmetry for a 2-D shape or design**
- **complete a shape or design given one half of the shape and a line of symmetry**
- **create a design that demonstrates line symmetry**

Materials
- scissors
- isometric dot paper
- tracing paper
- grid paper

---

line of symmetry

- a line that divides a figure into two reflected parts
- sometimes called a line of reflection or axis of symmetry
- a figure may have one or more lines of symmetry, or it may have none
- can be vertical, horizontal, or oblique (slanted)

This optical illusion was developed around 1915 by the Dutch psychologist Edgar Rubin. Like many optical illusions, this one involves a reflection. Look at the illusion. What do you see? Where is the line of reflection in this example?

Explore Lines of Symmetry

1. Fold a piece of paper in half. Mark two points, A and B, on the fold. Draw a wavy or jagged line between points A and B on one side of the paper. Cut along the line and then unfold your cut-out figure.

a) How does the fold affect the shape of the cutout?

b) Explain why it would make sense to refer to your fold line as a **line of symmetry**.

2. a) How could you fold a piece of paper so that a cutout shape would have two lines of symmetry? Use your method to create a cutout with two lines of symmetry.

b) Fold and cut a piece of paper to make a design with four lines of symmetry.

3. Draw an equilateral triangle on isometric dot paper. Then, cut it out using scissors. How many lines of symmetry are there? Explain how you arrived at your answer.

4. The diagram shows half of a shape. Line *r* represents a line of symmetry for the shape. Copy the diagram. Then, draw the complete shape.

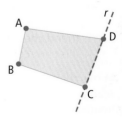

Reflect and Check

5. What are some ways to complete the shape in #4? Describe one way to a partner. See if your partner can follow your instructions.

6. Describe two different ways to find a line of symmetry for a symmetric 2-D shape. Which one do you prefer? Why?

Link the Ideas

Symmetry creates a sense of balance and, often, a sense of peace, tranquility, and perfection. A famous example of its use in architecture is the Taj Mahal, in Agra, India. Many parts of the building and grounds were designed and built to be perfectly symmetrical. Symmetry can also be seen in the pools that reflect an image of the structure. However, as with most cases of naturally occurring symmetry, the reflection in the pools is not perfect.

Example 1: Find Lines of Symmetry

Each of the following demonstrates **line symmetry**. For each part, use a different method to find the line(s) of symmetry. State the number of lines of symmetry and describe each one.

a)

 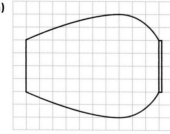

b)

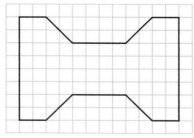

c)

 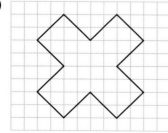

line symmetry

- a type of symmetry where an image or object can be divided into two identical, reflected halves by a line of symmetry
- identical halves can be reflected in a vertical, horizontal, or oblique (slanted) line of symmetry

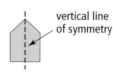
vertical line of symmetry

horizontal line of symmetry

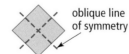
oblique line of symmetry

Solution

a) By using a Mira™, you can see that there is one horizontal line of symmetry.

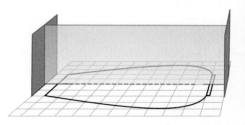

b) You can find the lines of symmetry by counting on the grid. For this figure, there are the same number of squares above and below the horizontal line of symmetry. There are the same the number of squares to the left and right of the vertical line of symmetry. You can see that there are two lines of symmetry: one horizontal and one vertical.

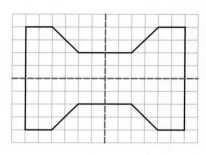

c) You can find the lines of symmetry by folding. If the shape on each side of the fold is the same, the fold line is a line of symmetry. This figure can be folded along four different lines to create mirrored shapes: one horizontal, one vertical, and two oblique.

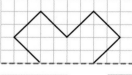

> You can sketch the complete figures to prove that the fold lines in these images are, in fact, lines of symmetry?

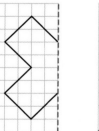 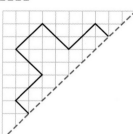 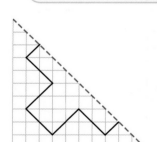

Show You Know

How many lines of symmetry are possible for each figure? Describe each line of symmetry as vertical, horizontal, or oblique.

a)    **b)**    **c)**

Example 2: Complete Drawings Using Symmetry

Each drawing shows half of a figure. The dashed brown line represents a line of symmetry for the figure. Draw a complete version of each figure.

a)    **b)**

Solution

a) *Method 1: Use Paper Folding*

Fold a piece of paper in half. Draw the figure on the paper so that the line of symmetry is along the folded edge. Cut out the figure you have drawn. Unfold the paper to reveal the complete figure.

 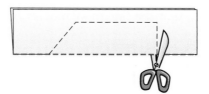 

Method 2: Use Measurement or Counting

Draw the half figure onto a grid, and label the vertices A, B, C, and D. All points not on the line of symmetry are reflected on the opposite side of the line. In this figure, this is points B and C. The reflected points are drawn the same perpendicular distance from the fold line so that BX = B′X and CD = C′D. Join A to B′, B′ to C′, and C′ to D to complete the figure.

Literacy Link

B′ and C′ are symbols used to designate the new positions of B and C after a transformation. B′ is read as "B prime."

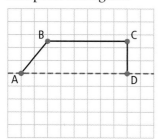 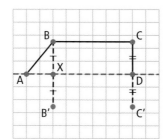

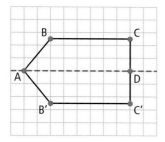

b) One method is to mark the perpendicular distance from each vertex on the opposite side of the line of symmetry. Then, connect the lines to complete the figure.

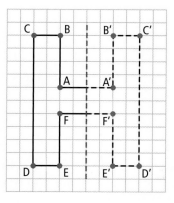

What is another method that you could use to create this figure?

The completed figure is a block-letter H.
Notice that the line of symmetry is not part of the final figure.

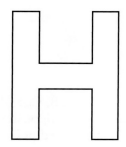

WWW Web Link

To explore more about symmetry, go to www.mathlinks9.ca and follow the links.

Show You Know

Copy each shape. Use the line of symmetry and a method of your choice to complete each shape.

a)

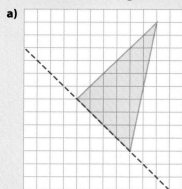

b)

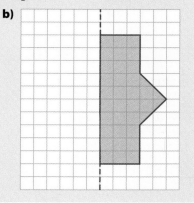

Key Ideas

- Line symmetry exists whenever a shape or design can be separated into two identical halves by a line of symmetry. The line of symmetry, also known as a line of reflection, may or may not be part of the diagram itself.

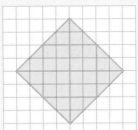 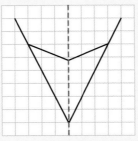

- A shape or design can have any whole number of lines of symmetry.

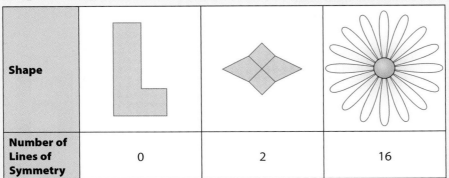

Shape			
Number of Lines of Symmetry	0	2	16

> Describe the lines of symmetry in these images.

- You can complete a symmetric drawing by folding or reflecting one half in the line of symmetry. The opposite halves are mirror images.

OT|TO

This name has one line of symmetry. If you know the first two letters you can complete the name by reflecting in the dashed line.

Literacy Link

If a shape or design has symmetry, then it can be described as *symmetric* or *symmetrical*.

Check Your Understanding

Communicate the Ideas

1. Any rectangle has only two lines of symmetry. Do you agree or disagree with this statement? Explain. Use drawings to support your argument.

2. Explain the changes you would need to make in the diagram so that the diagonal lines in the centre would become lines of symmetry. Redraw the diagram to match your answer.

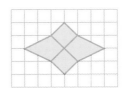

3. Three students disagree on whether a parallelogram is symmetric. Sasha claims it is symmetric and has two lines of symmetry. Basil says it is symmetric and has four lines of symmetry. Kendra argues it is not symmetric since it has no lines of symmetry. Which of the three answers is correct? Explain why.

⊂⊃ Literacy Link

A *parallelogram* is a four-sided figure with opposite sides parallel and equal in length.

Practise

For help with #4 to #6, refer to Example 1 on pages 7–8.

4. Where are the lines of symmetry for each figure? Draw a rough sketch of the figures in your notebook. Show all lines of symmetry in a different colour.

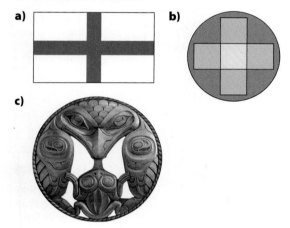

a)

b)

c)

5. Redraw each diagram, showing all lines of symmetry.

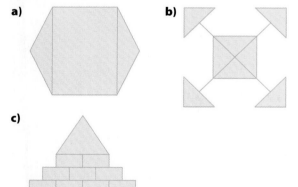

a)

b)

c)

6. Which figures have only two lines of symmetry? Explain how you know.

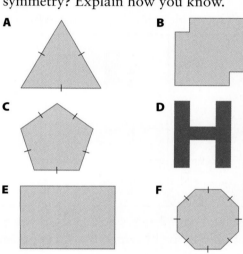

A

B

C

D

E

F

For help with #7 and #8, refer to Example 2 on pages 9–10.

7. If the dashed line is the line of symmetry, what does the complete diagram look like? Sketch your diagrams on grid paper.

a)

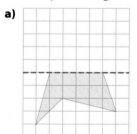

b)

8. Copy each figure. Use the line of symmetry shown to complete each figure.

a)

b)

Apply

9. Copy the figure on a coordinate grid.

a) Draw the reflection image if the *y*-axis is the line of reflection. Label the reflected vertices A′, C′, and E′.

b) What are the coordinates of A′, C′, and E′ in your drawing in part a)?

c) Do the original figure and its reflection image show line symmetry? Explain.

10. Create a figure similar to question #9, using a coordinate grid.

a) Translate the figure 4 units to the right.

b) What are the coordinates of A′, C′, and E′?

c) Do the original figure and its translation image show line symmetry? Explain your thinking.

d) Now, translate the figure you created in part a) 5 units down. Do the original figure and this new translation image show line symmetry? Explain.

11. Some regular shapes, such as an equilateral triangle, a square, or a regular hexagon, appear to show line symmetry when they are translated in one direction. Do you agree or disagree with this statement? Give examples to support your argument. Discuss your answer with a partner.

12. The Norwegian flag has a width to length ratio of 8 to 11.

a) Does the flag have line symmetry? Explain your answer.

b) What changes would be necessary in order to have exactly two lines of symmetry?

13. How many lines of symmetry does the flag of each of the following countries have?

a) Belgium

b) Canada

c) Scotland

d) Switzerland

14. The number of lines of symmetry for a square flag can vary. Create sketches of flag designs that show 0, 1, 2, and 4 lines of symmetry.

15. Consider the upper-case block letters of the English alphabet.

A B C D E F G H I J K L M N
O P Q R S T U V W X Y Z

a) Which letters have a horizontal line of symmetry?

b) Which letters have a vertical line of symmetry?

c) Which letter(s) have both horizontal and vertical lines of symmetry?

16. Using block letters, the word MOM can be written either vertically or horizontally. In each position, it has one vertical line of symmetry.

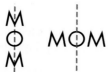

a) Write at least two other words that have one vertical line of symmetry when printed vertically or horizontally.

b) Find a word that has a horizontal line of symmetry when it is printed horizontally, and a vertical line of symmetry when printed vertically.

c) Find a word that has one line of symmetry when it is printed vertically, but that is not symmetric when printed horizontally.

17. a) Some single digits have line symmetry, depending on how they are printed. Which digits can demonstrate line symmetry?

b) Write a four-digit number that has two lines of symmetry when written horizontally.

c) What is a five-digit number that has two lines of symmetry?

18. Margaux is exploring regular polygons and line symmetry. She discovers that

- an equilateral triangle has three interior angles and three lines of symmetry

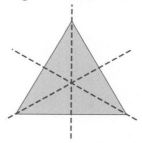

- a square has four interior angles and four lines of symmetry

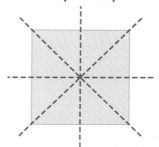

- a regular pentagon has five interior angles and five lines of symmetry

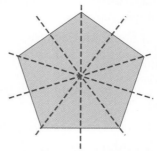

a) Work with a partner to continue Margaux's exploration for a regular hexagon, heptagon, and octagon.

b) What pattern do you discover?

c) Does this pattern continue beyond an octagon? How do you know?

19. Consider these figures.

Figure A

Figure B

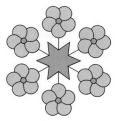

Figure C

a) Which figure(s) shows line symmetry?

b) What effect does the colour have on your answer in part a)?

c) How many lines of symmetry does each figure you identified in part a) have?

Extend

20. The triangle A(-6, 0) B(-2, 0) C(-2, -3) is first reflected in the *y*-axis. The resulting triangle is then reflected in a vertical line passing through (10, 0) to form △A″B″C″. Describe one transformation that translates △ABC directly to △A″B″C″.

21. Consider the clocks shown.

A

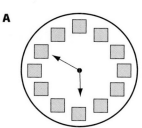

B

a) Explain whether each clock has line symmetry at some time? Ignore the different lengths of the hands on clock A.

b) At what time(s) do your choices in part a) show true line symmetry?

22. Points A(4, 3) and B(6, -4) are reflected in the *y*-axis to form a quadrilateral. What is its area?

23. The triangle A(-6, 0) B(-2, 0) C(-2, -3) is reflected in the *y*-axis. The resulting image is then reflected in a diagonal line passing through the origin and (5, 5) to form △A″B″C″. Describe one transformation that translates △ABC directly to △A″B″C″.

24. A three-dimensional object that is cut in half by a plane may be symmetric. Do you agree? Give examples.

> **Literacy Link**
>
> A *plane* is a flat, two-dimensional surface that extends in all directions.

Math Link

Imagine that you are working for a company that produces designs for many different uses, from playing cards to novelty items. Your job is to create appealing designs that can be used for a variety of products. As part of your portfolio, create a design that has at least two lines of symmetry. Draw your design on a half sheet of 8.5 × 11 paper. Store it in the pocket in your Foldable. You will need this design for the Math Link: Wrap It Up! on page 39.

Rotation Symmetry and Transformations

Focus on...

After this lesson, you will be able to...

- tell if 2-D shapes and designs have rotation symmetry
- give the order of rotation and angle of rotation for various shapes
- create designs with rotation symmetry
- identify the transformations in shapes and designs involving line or rotation symmetry

Materials
- scissors
- tracing paper

Some 2-D shapes and designs do not demonstrate line symmetry, but are still identified as having symmetry. The logo shown has this type of symmetry. What type of transformation can be demonstrated in this symbol?

centre of rotation

- the point about which the rotation of an object or design turns

rotation symmetry

- occurs when a shape or design can be turned about its centre of rotation so that it fits onto its outline more than once in a complete turn

Explore Symmetry of a Rotation

Look carefully at the logo shown.

1. The logo has symmetry of rotation. What do you think that means?

2. Copy the logo using tracing paper. Place your drawing on top of the original figure. Put the point of your pencil on the tracing paper and rotate the design until the traced design fits perfectly over the original design.

   a) Where did you have to put your pencil so that you were able to rotate your copy so that it fit over the original? How did you decide where to put your pencil? Explain why it is appropriate that this point is called the centre of rotation.

   b) How many times will your tracing fit over the original design, in one complete turn?

   c) Approximately how many degrees did you turn your tracing each time before it overlapped the original?

3. Work with a partner to try #2 with some other logos or designs.

Reflect and Check

   4. What information can you use to describe rotation symmetry?

Link the Ideas

Example 1: Find Order and Angle of Rotation

For each shape, what are the **order of rotation** and the **angle of rotation**? Express the angle of rotation in degrees and as a fraction of a revolution.

a)

b)

c)

order of rotation

- the number of times a shape or design fits onto itself in one complete turn

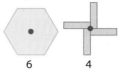

6   4

angle of rotation

- the minimum measure of the angle needed to turn a shape or design onto itself
- may be measured in degrees or fractions of a turn
- is equal to 360° divided by the order of rotation

Solution

Copy each shape or design onto a separate piece of tracing paper. Place your copy over the original, and rotate it to determine the order and angle of rotation.

	Order of Rotation	Angle of Rotation (Degrees)	Angle of Rotation (Fraction of Turn)
a)	2	$\frac{360°}{2} = 180°$	$\frac{1 \text{ turn}}{2} = \frac{1}{2}$ turn
b)	5	$\frac{360°}{5} = 72°$	$\frac{1 \text{ turn}}{5} = \frac{1}{5}$ turn
c)	1	360°	1 turn

The figure in part c) does not have rotational symmetry.

Show You Know

For each shape, give the order of rotation, and the angle of rotation in degrees and as a fraction. Which of the designs have rotation symmetry?

a)

b)

c)

Did You Know?

The Métis flag shown in part a) is a white infinity symbol on a blue background. The infinity symbol can represent that the Métis nation will go on forever. It can also be interpreted as two conjoined circles, representing the joining of two cultures: European and First Nations.

Example 2: Relating Symmetry to Transformations

Examine the figures.

Figure 1

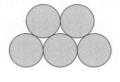

Figure 2

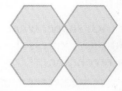

Figure 3

Visualize the translation and rotation of the figures. How does this help you determine the type of symmetry that they demonstrate?

a) What type of symmetry does each figure demonstrate?

b) For each example of line symmetry, indicate how many lines of symmetry there are. Describe whether the lines of symmetry are vertical, horizontal, or oblique.

c) For each example of rotation symmetry, give the order of rotation, and the angle of rotation in degrees.

d) How could each design be created from a single shape using translation, reflection, and/or rotation?

Solution

The answers to parts a), b), and c) have been organized in a table.

	Figure 1	Figure 2	Figure 3
a) Type of symmetry	rotation	line	rotation and line
b) Number and direction of lines of symmetry	No lines of symmetry	Total = 1: vertical	Total = 2: 1 vertical 1 horizontal
c) Order of rotation	3	1	2
Angle of rotation	$\dfrac{360°}{3} = 120°$	360°	$\dfrac{360°}{2} = 180°$

Figure 2 does not have rotational symmetry

d) Figure 1 can be created from a single arrow by rotating it $\frac{1}{3}$ of a turn about the centre of rotation, as shown.

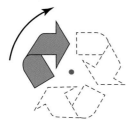

Figure 2 can be created from a single circle by translating it four times.

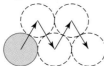

How could you use reflection to create this figure?

Figure 3 can be created from one of the hexagons by reflecting it in a vertical line, followed by a horizontal reflection (or vice versa).

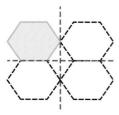

How could you use translation and reflection to create this design?

WWW Web Link

To see examples of rotation symmetry, go to www.mathlinks9.ca and follow the links.

Show You Know

Consider each figure.

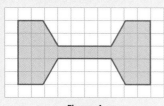

Figure A

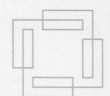

Figure B

a) Does the figure show line symmetry, rotation symmetry, or both?

b) If the figure has line symmetry, describe each line of symmetry as vertical, horizontal, or oblique.

c) For each example of rotation symmetry, give the order of rotation.

d) How could each design be created from a single part of itself using translations, reflections, or rotations?

Key Ideas

- The two basic kinds of symmetry for 2-D shapes or designs are
  - line symmetry
  - rotation symmetry

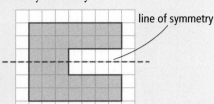

line of symmetry

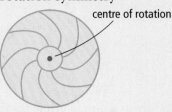

centre of rotation

- The order of rotation is the number of times a figure fits on itself in one complete turn.

  For the fan shown above, the order of rotation is 8.

- The angle of rotation is the smallest angle through which the shape or design must be rotated to lie on itself. It is found by dividing the number of degrees in a circle by the order of rotation.

  For the fan shown above, the angle of rotation is $360° \div 8 = 45°$ or $1 \div 8 = \frac{1}{8}$, or $\frac{1}{8}$ turn.

- A shape or design can have one or both types of symmetry.

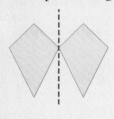

line symmetry

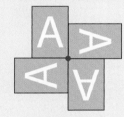

rotation symmetry

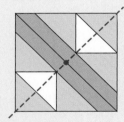

both

Check Your Understanding

Communicate the Ideas

1. Describe rotation symmetry. Use terms such as centre of rotation, order of rotation, and angle of rotation. Sketch an example.

2. Maurice claims the design shown has rotation symmetry. Claudette says that it shows line symmetry. Explain how you would settle this disagreement.

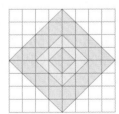

3. Can a shape and its translation image demonstrate rotation symmetry? Explain with examples drawn on a coordinate grid.

Practise

For help with #4 and #5, refer to Example 1 on page 17.

4. Each shape or design has rotation symmetry. What is the order and the angle of rotation? Express the angle in degrees and as a fraction of a turn. Where is the centre of rotation?

a)

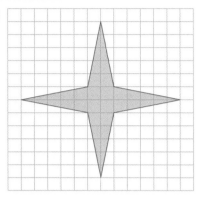

b)

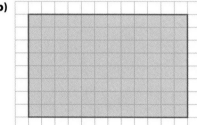

c) **1961**

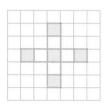

5. Does each figure have rotation symmetry? Confirm your answer using tracing paper. What is the angle of rotation in degrees?

a)

b)

c) **XOX**

For help with #6 and #7, refer to Example 2 on pages 18–19.

6. Each design has line and rotation symmetry. What are the number of lines of symmetry and the order of rotation for each?

a)  **b)**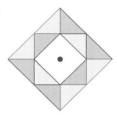

c)

7. Each design has both line and rotation symmetry. Give the number of lines of symmetry and the size of the angle of rotation for each.

a)  **b)**

Apply

8. Examine the design.

a) What basic shape could you use to make this design?

b) Describe how you could use translations, rotations, and/or reflections to create the first two rows of the design.

9. Consider the figure shown.

a) What is its order of rotation?

b) Trace the figure onto a piece of paper. How could you create this design using a number of squares and triangles?

c) Is it possible to make this figure by transforming only one piece? Explain.

10. Many Aboriginal languages use symbols for sounds and words. A portion of a Cree syllabics chart is shown.

▽ e		△ i	△̇ ii	▷̇ u	▷̇ uu	◁ a	◁̇ aa	
•▽ we			•△̇ wii			•◁ wa	•◁̇ waa	
∨ pe	•∨ pi	∧ pii	∧̇	> pu	>̇ puu	< pa	<̇ paa	•<̇ pwaa
∪ te	•∪ twe	∩ ti	∩̇ tii	⊃ tu	⊃̇ tuu	⊂ ta	⊂̇ taa	•⊂ twaa
٩ ke	•٩ kwe	ρ ki	ρ̇ kii	d ku	d̊ kuu	ხ ka	ხ̇ kaa	•ხ kwaa

a) Select two symbols that have line symmetry and another two that have rotation symmetry. Redraw the symbols. Show the possible lines of symmetry and angles of rotation.

b) Most cultures have signs and symbols with particular meaning. Select a culture. Find or draw pictures of at least two symbols from the culture that demonstrate line symmetry or rotation symmetry. Describe what each symbol represents and the symmetries involved.

11. Does each tessellation have line symmetry, rotation symmetry, both, or neither? Explain by describing the line of symmetry and/or the centre of rotation. If there is no symmetry, describe what changes would make the image symmetrical.

a)

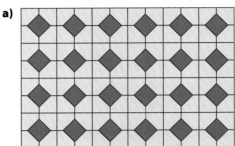

b)

c)

d)

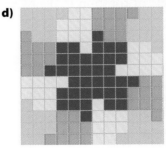

> **⊂⊃ Literacy Link**
>
> A *tessellation* is a pattern or arrangement that covers an area without overlapping or leaving gaps. It is also known as a tiling pattern.

12. Reproduce the rectangle on a coordinate grid.

a) Create a drawing that has rotation symmetry of order 4 about the origin. Label the vertices of your original rectangle. Show the coordinates of the image after each rotation.

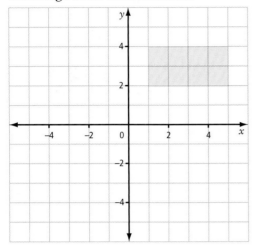

b) Start again, this time using line symmetry to make a new design. Use the y-axis and then the x-axis as a line of symmetry. How is this new design different from the one that you created in part a)?

13. Sandra makes jewellery. She created a pendant based on the shape shown.

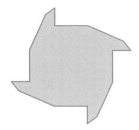

a) Determine the order and the angle of rotation for this design.

b) If Sandra's goal was to create a design with more than one type of symmetry, was she successful? Explain.

14. Alain drew a pendant design that has both line and rotation symmetry.

a) How many lines of symmetry are in this design? What is the size of the smallest angle between these lines of symmetry?

b) What are the order and the angle of rotation for this design?

15. Imagine you are a jewellery designer. On grid paper, create a design for a pendant that has more than one type of symmetry. Compare your design with those of your classmates.

16. Copy and complete each design. Use the centre of rotation marked and the order of rotation symmetry given for each part.

a)

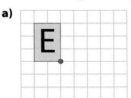

Order of rotation: 2

b)

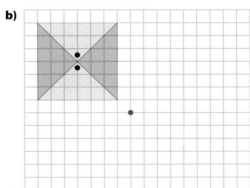

Order of rotation: 4
Hint: Pay attention to the two dots in the centre of the original shape.

17. Automobile hubcaps have rotation symmetry. For each hubcap shown, find the order and the angle of rotation in degrees.

a)

b)

c)

d)

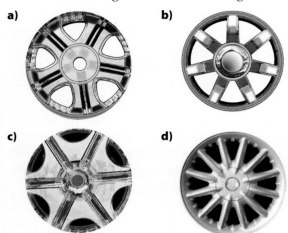

18. a) Sometimes the order of rotation can vary depending on which part of a diagram you are looking at. Explain this statement using the diagram below.

b) How would you modify this diagram so that it has rotation symmetry?

19. a) Describe the symmetry shown on this playing card.

b) Why do you think the card is designed like this?

c) Does this playing card have line symmetry? Explain.

20. Two students are looking at a dart board. Rachelle claims that if you ignore the numbers, the board has rotation symmetry of order 10. Mike says it is order 20. Who is correct? Explain.

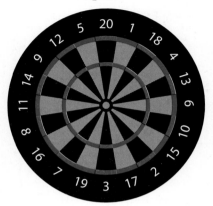

21. a) Which upper-case letters can be written to have rotation symmetry?

b) Which single digits can be considered to have rotation symmetry? Explain your answer.

c) Create a five-character Personal Identification Number (PIN) using letters and digits that have rotational symmetry. In addition, your PIN must show line symmetry when written both horizontally and vertically.

22. Some part of each of the objects shown has rotation symmetry of order 6. Find or draw other objects that have rotation symmetry of order 6. Compare your answers with those of some of your classmates.

23. Organizations achieve brand recognition using logos. Logos often use symmetry.

a) For each logo shown, identify aspects of symmetry. Identify the type of symmetry and describe its characteristics.

A   B

b) Find other logos that have line symmetry, rotation symmetry, or both. Use pictures or drawings to clearly show the symmetry involved.

Extend

24. Two gears are attached as shown.

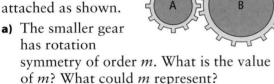

a) The smaller gear has rotation symmetry of order *m*. What is the value of *m*? What could *m* represent?

b) The larger gear has rotation symmetry of order *n*. Find the value of *n*.

c) When the smaller gear makes six full turns, how many turns does the larger gear make?

d) If gear A has 12 teeth, and gear B has 16 teeth, how many turns does B make when A makes 8 turns?

e) If gear A has *x* teeth, and gear B has *y* teeth, how many turns does B make when A makes *m* turns?

25. Examine models or consider these drawings of the 3-D solids shown.

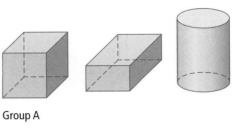

Group A

Group B

a) Select one object from each group. Discuss with a partner any symmetry that your selected objects have.

b) For one of the objects you selected, describe some of its symmetries. Use appropriate mathematical terminology from earlier studies of solids and symmetry.

26. A circle has a radius of length *r*. If a chord with length *r* is rotated about the centre of the circle by touching end to end, what is the order of rotation of the resulting shape? Explain.

Surface Area

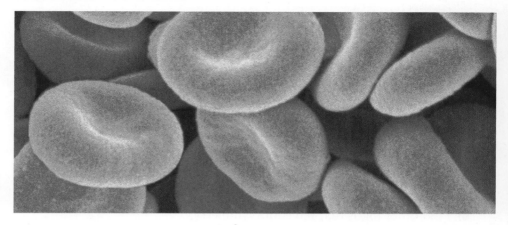

Focus on...

After this lesson, you will be able to...

- determine the area of overlap in composite 3-D objects
- find the surface area for composite 3-D objects
- solve problems involving surface area

Red blood cells are the shape of very tiny disks. They have a thickness of 2.2 microns and a diameter of 7.1 microns. A micron is another term for a micrometre—one millionth of a metre. Red blood cells absorb oxygen from the lungs and carry it to other parts of the body. The cell absorbs oxygen through its surface.

The disease multiple mycloma causes the red blood cells to stick together. How would this affect the **surface area** of the cells?

surface area
- the sum of the areas of all the faces of an object

Explore Symmetry and Surface Area

1. a) Use a small disk to represent a single red blood cell. Estimate the surface area of the disk.

b) Stack four disks. Estimate the surface area of the stack of disks.

c) How did you estimate the surface area for parts a) and b)? Compare your method of estimation with your classmates' methods.

d) How does the total surface area of the four separate disks compare to the surface area of the four stacked disks? By what percent did the total surface area decrease when the disks were stacked?

Materials

- small disks or pennies
- small boxes or dominoes

> **⬤⬤ Literacy Link**
>
> An object that is made from two or more separate objects is called a *composite object*.

2. Some medicine is shipped in small boxes that measure 1 cm by 4 cm by 2 cm. Six boxes are wrapped and shipped together. Working with a partner, use models to help answer the following questions.

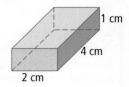

1 cm
4 cm
2 cm

a) If the arrangement of the six boxes must form a rectangular prism, how many arrangements are possible?

b) The cost to ship a package depends partly on total surface area. Would it be cheaper to ship the boxes in part a) individually, or wrapped together in plastic? If you wrapped the boxes together, which arrangement do you think will cost the least to ship? Explain.

3. You want to waterproof a tent. You need to determine the surface area of the tent's sides and ends to purchase the right amount of waterproofing spray. You do not have to waterproof the bottom. Calculate the surface area. Give your answer to the nearest tenth of a square metre.

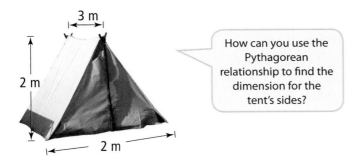

How can you use the Pythagorean relationship to find the dimension for the tent's sides?

Reflect and Check

4. How can symmetry help you find the surface area in each of the three situations? Explain.

5. How does the surface area of a composite object compare with the sum of the surface areas of its separate parts? Explain.

Link the Ideas

Different formulas can be used to find the surface area of a rectangular prism or a cylinder. There is one formula that works for both:

Surface Area = 2(area of base) + (perimeter of base) × (height)

$$SA_{prism} = 2(\text{area of base}) + (\text{perimeter of base}) \times (\text{height})$$
$$= 2(4 \times 2) + (4 + 2 + 4 + 2) \times 1$$
$$= 16 + 12$$
$$= 28$$

The surface of this prism is 28 cm².

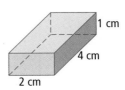

Using this same approach, the formula for the surface area of a cylinder is

$$SA_{cylinder} = 2(\text{area of base}) + (\text{perimeter of base}) \times (\text{height})$$
$$= 2(\pi r^2) + (2\pi r)h$$
$$= 2\pi r^2 + 2\pi rh$$

Example 1: Calculating Surface Area of a Solid

Consider the solid shown, in which all angles are right angles.

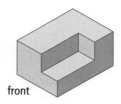

front

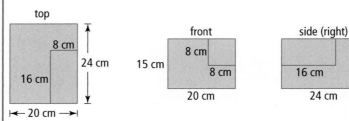

top

8 cm

24 cm

16 cm

← 20 cm →

front

8 cm

15 cm

8 cm

20 cm

side (right)

16 cm

24 cm

a) What are the dimensions of the cutout piece?
b) What is the total surface area of the solid?

Solution

a) The cutout notch is a right rectangular prism. The dimensions of the notch are 8 cm by 8 cm by 16 cm.

8 cm

8 cm   16 cm

b) *Method 1: Find the Surface Area of Each Face*
You need to find the area of nine faces, including the faces of the notch. Number the faces to help keep track of the faces you have completed. Let the left face be #7, the back #8, and the bottom #9.

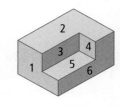

Why do you subtract 8 × 8 in the calculation for face 1?

Face	Calculation	Surface Area (cm²)
1	$15 \times 20 - (8 \times 8)$	236
2	$20 \times 24 - (8 \times 16)$	352
3	8×16	128
4	8×8	64
5	8×16	128
6	$15 \times 24 - (8 \times 16)$	232
7 (left side)	15×24	360
8 (back)	15×20	300
9 (bottom)	20×24	480
	Total Surface Area:	2280

The total surface area of the solid is 2280 cm².

Method 2: Use Symmetry
Calculate the surface area of only certain faces.
face 9 (bottom): $20 \times 24 =$ 480
face 8 (back): $15 \times 20 =$ 300
face 7 (left side): $15 \times 24 =$ 360
Total of 3 faces: 1140

Notice that, by symmetry, opposite faces match.
face 2 + face 5 = face 9
face 1 + face 4 = face 8
face 6 + face 3 = face 7
You can obtain the surface area by doubling the area for
face 9 + face 8 + face 7.
$1140 \times 2 = 2280$

The surface area of
the solid is 2280 cm².

> Why could the following be used to
> calculate the surface area?
> $SA = 2(15 \times 20) + 2(15 \times 24) + 2(20 \times 24)$

Did You Know?

If you cut a right rectangular piece out of one corner of a rectangular prism (Figure 2), the surface area does not change from that of the original prism (Figure 1). The surface area does change if the cutout extends across the solid (Figure 3). Explain why.

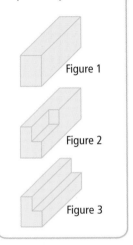

Figure 1

Figure 2

Figure 3

Show You Know

A set of concrete steps has the dimensions shown. Estimate and then calculate the surface area of the faces that are not against the ground. What is the area of the surface that is against the ground? Explain your answer.

60 cm
40 cm
80 cm
20 cm
90 cm

Example 2: Painting a Bookcase

Raubyn has made a bookcase using wood that is 2 cm thick for the frame and shelves. The back is thin plywood. He wants to paint the entire visible surface. He will not paint the back, which stands against a wall.

a) What assumptions could you make about how the bookcase is painted?
b) What surface area does Raubyn need to paint?

Strategies

Make an Assumption

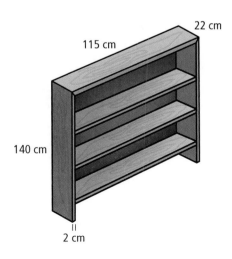

22 cm
115 cm
140 cm
2 cm

> *Solution*

a) Assumptions could include:
He paints the undersides of the three shelves.
The shelves are set inside the ends of the bookcase.
He paints the visible or inside back surface.
He does not paint the area of the base on which
the bookcase stands.
Raubyn paints the bookcase after it is assembled.

> Why would this assumption make a difference?

b) Group similar surfaces together.
Group 1: underside of top, and top and bottom of each of the
three shelves.
Surface area $= 7 \times 111 \times 22$
$= 17\ 094$

> Why is this measurement 111 cm, rather than 115 cm?

Group 2: outside of top and sides.
Surface area $= 22 \times 115 + 2(22 \times 140)$
$= 8690$

Group 3: back of bookcase that shows inside and front edges of the
three shelves.
Surface area $= 111 \times 138$
$= 15\ 318$

Group 4: front edges of top and sides.
Surface area $= 2(2 \times 138) + 2 \times 115$
$= 782$

> This measurement is 138, rather than 140, because the top piece is 2 cm thick. Notice that no surface area was subtracted to account for the back edges of the shelves, and none was added to account for the front edges. Using symmetry, explain why this works.

Total surface area:
$17\ 084 + 8690 + 15\ 318 + 782 = 41\ 884$
The surface area Raubyn needs to paint is 41 884 cm².

WWW Web Link

For information on how to calculate the surface area of different shapes, go to www.mathlinks9.ca and follow the links.

Show You Know

Consider the building shown.

a) Estimate the outside surface area of the building.

b) Calculate the outside surface area. Determine your answer two different ways.

c) Which method do you prefer? Why?

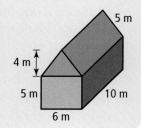

Key Ideas

- To determine the surface area of a composite 3-D object, decide which faces of the object you must consider and what their dimensions are.
- There are several ways to determine the surface area of an object.
  - Determine the area of each face. Add these areas together.
  - Use symmetry to group similar faces. Calculate the area of one of the symmetrical faces. Then, multiply by the number of like faces. This reduces the number of faces for which you need to calculate the surface area.

The top of this object has an area of 13 square units. The bottom must have the same area.

  - Consider how the shape is made from its component parts. Determine the surface area of each part. Then, remove the area of overlapping surfaces.

Check Your Understanding

Communicate the Ideas

1. Build two different solid objects each using 24 interlocking cubes.
   a) Explain how symmetry could help you determine the surface area of one of your objects.
   b) Slide the two objects together. What is the area of overlap between the objects?
   c) How does the overlap affect the total surface area of your composite object?

2. Nick makes a two-layer cake. Instead of icing, he puts strawberry jam between the two layers. He plans to cover the outside of the cake with chocolate icing. Describe how he can calculate the area that needs icing.

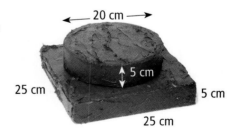

3. Explain how you would calculate the surface area of the object shown.

Practise

For help with #4 to #7, refer to Example 1 on pages 28–29.

4. Each object has been constructed from centimetre cubes. Estimate and then calculate the surface area.

a)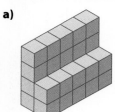

b)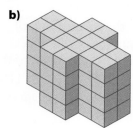

5. The following objects have been drawn on isometric dot paper where the distance between dots is 2 cm. Determine the surface area of each object.

a)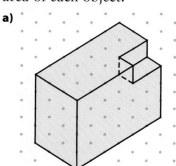

b)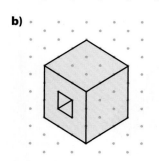

Note: The hole extends all the way through the block.

6. a) If you build the rectangular solids and slide them together as shown, what is the area of the overlap? Assume the dots are 1 cm apart.

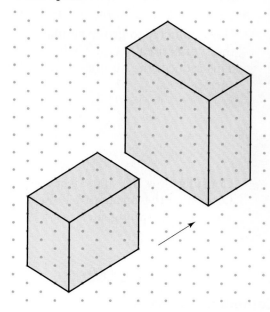

b) What is the surface area when the solids are together?

7. Examine the solid and its views. All angles are right angles.

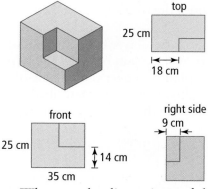

a) What are the dimensions of the cutout piece?

b) Explain how cutting out the corner piece will affect the surface area of the original rectangular solid.

For help with #8 and #9, refer to Example 2 on pages 29–30.

8. Six small boxes, all the same size, have been arranged as shown.

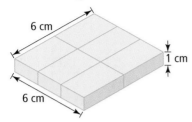

a) What are the dimensions of a single box?

b) What is the surface area for the arrangement of the six boxes?

c) What is the ratio of the answer in part b) to the total surface area of the six separate boxes?

WWW Web Link

To see how surface area changes when a composite object is broken apart, go to www.mathlinks9.ca and follow the links.

9. Examine the bookshelf. It is constructed of thin hardwood. The top, bottom, and all three shelves are the same size. There is an equal distance between the top, the shelves, and the base.

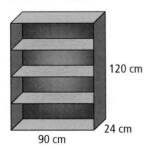

a) What is the surface area of one shelf? Include both sides, but ignore the edges.

b) What is the total surface area of the bookcase?

c) What is the fewest number of surfaces for which you need to find the surface area in order to answer part b)?

Apply

10. Use centimetre cubes to build the object shown.

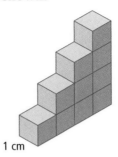

a) What is the object's surface area?

b) Take the same ten cubes and build a rectangular prism. Estimate and then calculate whether the surface area remains the same. Explain with examples.

11. List places or situations in which surface area is important. Compare your list with those of your classmates.

12. Consider this drawing of a garage. The left side of the garage is attached to the house.

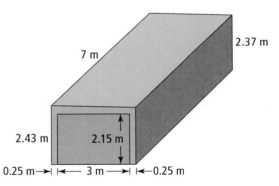

a) What is the difference in height between the left-hand and right-hand sides of the garage? Explain why you would want a slight slant to a roof?

b) Given that the house is attached to the left side of the garage, what is the surface area of the garage to the nearest hundredth of a square metre? What assumption(s) did you make in answering this question?

13. A mug for hot beverages is to be designed to keep its contents warm as long as possible. The rate at which the beverage cools depends on the surface area of the container. The larger the surface area of the mug, the quicker the liquid inside it will cool.

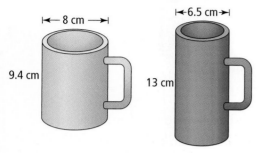

8 cm

6.5 cm

9.4 cm

13 cm

a) What is the surface area of each mug? Assume that neither has a lid.

b) Which is the better mug for keeping drinks warm? Justify your answer.

14. A chimney has the dimensions shown. What is the outside surface area of the chimney? Give your answer to the nearest hundredth of a square metre.

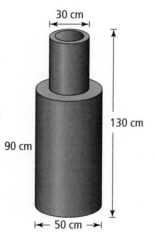

30 cm

130 cm

90 cm

50 cm

15. Twila made the object shown.

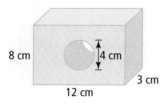

8 cm

4 cm

3 cm

12 cm

a) How can you use symmetry to help find the surface area of this object?

b) What is the surface area?

16. You are planning to put new shingles on the roof of the home shown.

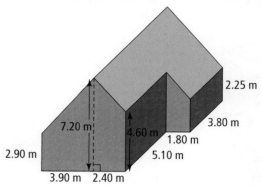

7.20 m

2.25 m

4.60 m

3.80 m

1.80 m

2.90 m

5.10 m

3.90 m   2.40 m

a) How many times would you need to use the Pythagorean relationship in order to find the area of the roof of the building shown in the diagram?

b) What is the area of the roof that you cannot see in this figure, assuming that it is a rectangular roof?

c) One bundle of shingles covers approximately 2.88 m² and costs $26.95. What does it cost for shingles to cover the roof?

17. The hollow passages through which smoke and fumes escape in a chimney are called flues. Each flue shown is 2 cm thick, 20 cm high, and has a square opening that is 20 cm by 20 cm.

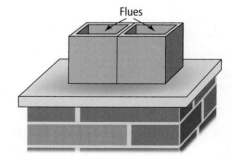

Flues

a) What are the outside dimensions of the two flues?

b) If the height of each flue is 30 cm, what is the outside surface area of the two flues? Hint: Do not forget the flat edges on top.

18. A small metal box is shown. What is the inside surface area of the box? What assumptions did you make in finding your answer?

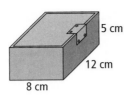

5 cm

12 cm

8 cm

19. A party planner buys two plain cakes for a meal she is planning. One cake is square and the other is round. Both cakes are 6 cm thick. The square cake measures 25 cm along each edge. The round cake has a diameter of 25 cm.

a) Sketch and label a diagram of each cake.

b) Show how to make four cuts to create eight equal pieces for each cake.

c) Estimate and then calculate how much the surface area increases after each cake is cut and the pieces are slightly separated.

Extend

20. Explain how surface area of individual grains of rice may affect the boiling of a cup of uncooked rice. Assume you have two kinds of rice. One has small grains and the other has larger ones. Consider each grain of rice to be cylindrical.

21. An elephant's ears are one of nature's best examples of the importance of surface area in heating and cooling. Research this phenomenon or another one that interests you. Write a brief report outlining the importance of surface area in heating and cooling. (Two other possible topics are why radiators have complex internal shapes and how a cactus minimizes surface area.)

22. The plan for a concrete birdbath is shown below. The bowl is a cylinder with a depth of 10 cm. If the bowl has a diameter of 30 cm, what is the exposed surface area of the birdbath, including the pillar and pedestal?

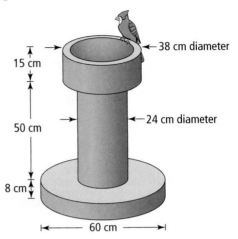

38 cm diameter

15 cm

50 cm

24 cm diameter

8 cm

60 cm

23. A swimming pool measures 25 m long and 10 m wide. It has a shallow end that is 1 m deep and gradually slopes down to a depth of 3 m at the deep end. The inside walls of the pool need repainting. Calculate the total area of the surfaces to be painted, to the nearest square metre.

25 m

10 m

1 m

3 m

Math Link

Your design company wants to create a new product that will have a design printed on it. Your project team has suggested playing cards, business cards, memo pads, and sticky notes. Choose one of these items.

a) What are the dimensions of your pack of cards or pad of paper?

b) What is the surface area of your pack of cards or pad of paper?

Chapter 1 Review

Key Words

For #1 to #6, choose the letter that best matches the description.

1. another name for a reflection line

2. type of symmetry in which the shape can be divided into reflected halves

3. what you are measuring when you find the area of all faces of an object

4. type of symmetry in which a shape can be turned to fit onto itself

5. number of times a shape fits onto itself in one turn

6. amount of turn for a shape to rotate onto itself

A line

B rotation

C angle of rotation

D surface area

E line of symmetry

F order of rotation

1.1 Line Symmetry, pages 6–15

7. How many lines of symmetry does each design have? Describe each possible line of symmetry using the terms *vertical*, *horizontal*, and *oblique*.

a)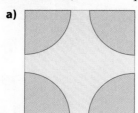

b)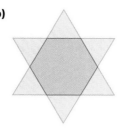

8. Half of a figure is drawn. The dashed line represents the line of symmetry. Copy and complete the figure on grid paper.

a)

b)

9. Determine the coordinates of the image of points A, B, C, D, E, and F after each transformation. Which of these transformations show symmetry? Describe the symmetry.

a) a reflection in the *y*-axis

b) a translation R6, D3

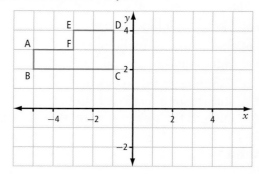

1.2 Rotation Symmetry and Transformations, pages 16–25

10. What is the order and angle of rotation symmetry for each shape? Express the angle in degrees and in fractions of a turn.

a)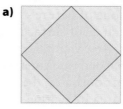

b)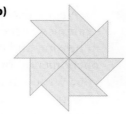

11. Write a brief description of any symmetry you can find in this square flag. Compare your ideas with those of a classmate.

12. The arrangement of Ps has rotation symmetry, but no line symmetry.

a) Show a way that you can arrange six Ps to make a design that has both types of symmetry.

b) What letter(s) could you place in the original arrangement that would have both line and rotation symmetry?

13. Examine the design carefully. Does it have rotation symmetry, line symmetry, or both? Explain.

14. Create a coordinate grid that will allow you to do the transformations. Give the coordinates for the image of points P, Q, R, U, V, and W. Are the original and each image related by symmetry? If yes, which type(s) of symmetry?

a) rotation counterclockwise 180° about the origin

b) reflection in the *x*-axis

c) translation 7 units left

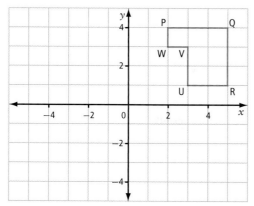

1.3 Surface Area, pages 26–35

15. The triangular prism shown has one of its triangular ends placed against a wall. By what amount does this placement decrease the exposed surface area of the prism?

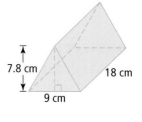

16. Two blocks are placed one on top of the other.

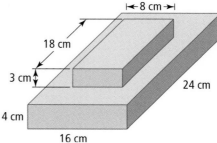

a) What is the total surface area for each of the blocks when separated?

b) What is the exposed surface area of the stacked blocks?

17. Use centimetre cubes or interlocking cubes to build the solids shown in the sketches.

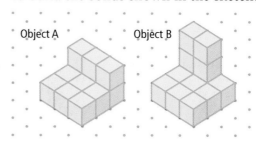

a) What is the exposed surface area of Object A?

b) What is the exposed surface area of Object B?

c) What is the minimum exposed surface area for a new object formed by sliding Object A against Object B? Do not lift them off the surface on which they are placed.

For #1 to #4, choose the best answer.

1. Which design has rotation symmetry of order 2?

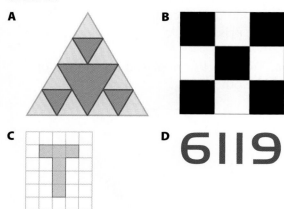

A

B

C

D

2. How many lines of symmetry are possible for the design?

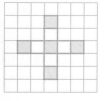

A 0   **B** 1   **C** 2   **D** 4

3. Two prisms are shown.

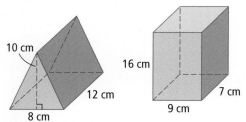

Imagine that the triangular prism is placed so that one triangular face is against the 9 cm by 16 cm face of the rectangular prism. How much less is the total surface area of this composite object than when the two objects are separated?

A 40 cm²   **B** 80 cm²

C 144 cm²   **D** 160 cm²

4. Which figure has only one type of symmetry?

A

B

C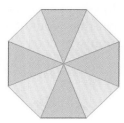

D

5. The design has rotation symmetry.

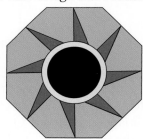

a) Its order of rotation is ■.

b) The angle of rotation is ■ degrees.

Short Answer

6. Use the upper case letters shown.

A B C D E F G H I J K L M N
O P Q R S T U V W X Y Z

a) Which letters have line symmetry? Indicate if each line of symmetry is horizontal, vertical, or oblique.

b) Which letters have rotation symmetry where the angle of rotation is 180°?

7. A rectangular prism has a 1 cm cube cut out of each of its eight corners. One of the cutouts is shown. What is the ratio of the original surface area to the new surface area? Explain.

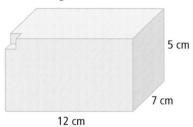

8. Imagine that the object is cut in half at the blue line. If the two pieces are separated, by how much is the surface area of each half increased?

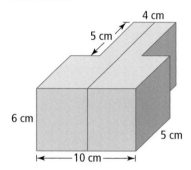

Extended Response

9. Build rectangular prisms that each use 36 one-centimetre cubes.

a) What are the dimensions of the rectangular prism that has the greatest surface area?

b) What are the dimensions of the rectangular prism with the least surface area?

c) What do you conclude from this?

10. Look at the stained glass window. Write two paragraphs describing the symmetry in the window. In the first paragraph, describe the line symmetry. In the second paragraph, describe the rotation symmetry.

Math Link: Wrap It Up!

You have been asked to present the product idea you developed in the Math Link in section 1.3.

a) Include the design for the individual cards or pieces of paper with at least one line of symmetry. Describe the type of symmetry your design exhibits.

b) Create a design for the cover of a box that will hold your product. This design must exhibit rotational symmetry, and it may also exhibit line symmetry.

c) Write a description of the dimensions of a box needed to hold the deck of cards or pad of paper. What are the dimensions and surface area of this box?

d) Your company also wants to explore the possibility of distributing a package containing six boxes of your product, wrapped in plastic. What is the total surface area of six individual boxes of your product? What would be the surface area of six of these boxes wrapped together? Explain how you would package these so that they would have the smallest surface area.

Challenges

Making a Paper Airplane

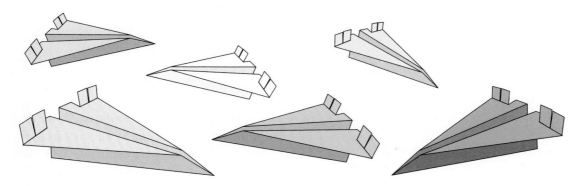

1. Make a paper airplane by following the folding instructions below. In step six, make four small cuts as indicated to create tabs. Fold the tabs up to make flaps.

Materials
- ruler
- scissors

 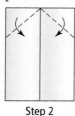 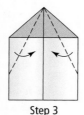 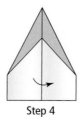  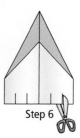

| Step 1 | Step 2 | Step 3 | Step 4 | Step 5 | Step 6 |

2. Use the airplane you made in part 1.
   a) Find the total surface area of the top view of the two wings.
   b) Fly the airplane 5 times. Record the average distance and direction travelled in each flight.

3. Design and create a second symmetrical airplane, which has a different surface area. Record the following:
   a) the new surface area
   b) the average distance and direction travelled in 5 trial flights

4. Design and create a non-symmetrical airplane. Record the following:
   a) the new surface area
   b) the average distance and direction travelled in 5 trials

5. Which of the three airplanes you constructed is the most functional? Consider surface area and symmetry when you explain your thinking.

Musical Instruments

1. Find pictures of, or draw musical instruments of your choice. Draw in the lines of symmetry. Describe any rotation symmetry present.

2. Explain the role symmetry plays in the design of your selected musical instruments.

3. Select a musical instrument that can be roughly represented as a composite shape formed by
   • right cylinders
   • right rectangular prisms, and/or
   • right triangular prisms
   Determine the surface area of the representation to approximate the surface area of the instrument. Show your thinking.

Rational Numbers

When you think of your favourite game, what comes to mind? It may be a computer game or video game. You may also enjoy playing games that have been around a lot longer. These may include the use of a game board and may involve cards, dice, or specially designed playing pieces. Examples of these games include chess, checkers, dominoes, euchre, bridge, Monopoly™, and Scrabble®.

In this chapter, you will learn more about games and about how you can use rational numbers to describe or play them. You will also design your own game.

> **⊕ Did You Know?**
>
> Canadians have invented many popular board games, such as crokinole, Yahtzee®, Trivial Pursuit®, Balderdash™, and Scruples™.

WWW Web Link

For more information about board games invented by Canadians, go to www.mathlinks9.ca and follow the links.

What You Will Learn

- to compare and order rational numbers
- to solve problems involving operations on rational numbers
- to determine the square root of a perfect square rational number
- to determine the approximate square root of a non-perfect square rational number

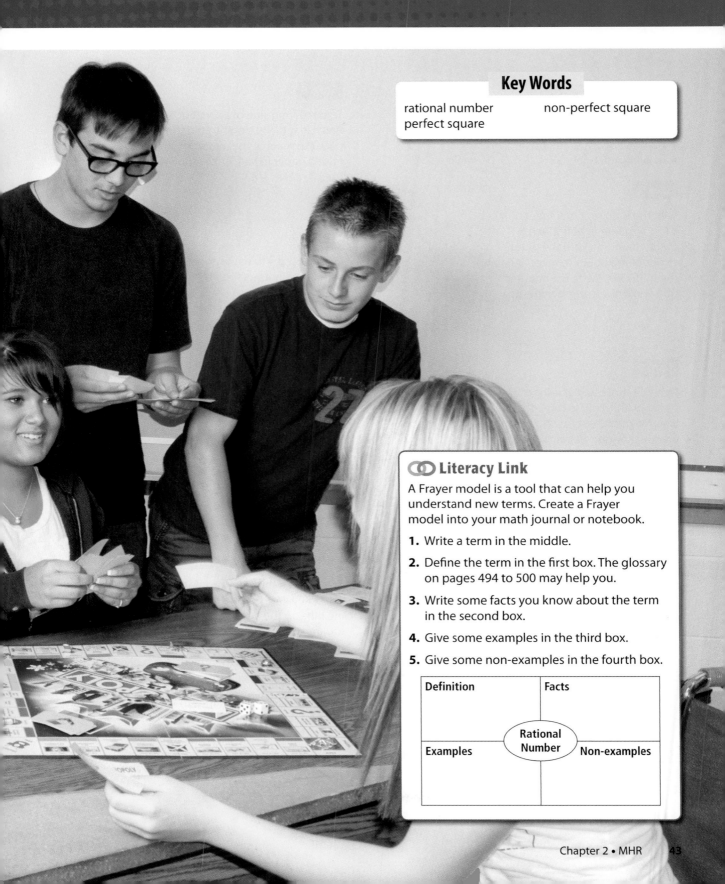

rational number   non-perfect square
perfect square

⚭ Literacy Link

A Frayer model is a tool that can help you understand new terms. Create a Frayer model into your math journal or notebook.

1. Write a term in the middle.

2. Define the term in the first box. The glossary on pages 494 to 500 may help you.

3. Write some facts you know about the term in the second box.

4. Give some examples in the third box.

5. Give some non-examples in the fourth box.

Definition	Facts
Examples	Non-examples

Rational Number

Making the Foldable

Materials
- sheet of 11 × 17 paper
- three sheets of 8.5 × 11 paper
- sheet of grid paper
- ruler
- scissors
- stapler

Step 1

Fold the long side of a sheet of 11 × 17 paper in half. Pinch it at the midpoint. Fold the outer edges of the paper to meet at the midpoint. Write the chapter title and draw a number line as shown.

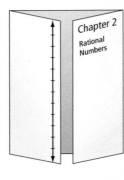

Step 2

Fold the short side of a sheet of 8.5 × 11 paper in half. Fold in three the opposite way. Make two cuts as shown through one thickness of paper, forming three tabs. Label the tabs as shown.

Step 3

Fold the short side of a sheet of 8.5 × 11 of grid paper in half. Fold in half the opposite way. Make a cut through one thickness of paper, forming two tabs. Label the tabs as shown.

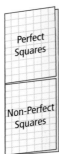

Step 4

Fold the long side of a sheet of 8.5 × 11 paper in half. Pinch it at the midpoint. Fold the outer edges of the paper to meet at the midpoint. Fold the long side of the folded paper in half. Cut as shown, forming four doors.

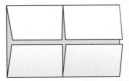

Repeat Step 4 to make another four-door book. Label the doors as shown below.

Step 5

Staple the four booklets you made into the Foldable from Step 1 as shown.

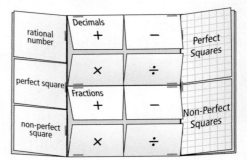

Using the Foldable

As you work through the chapter, write the definitions of the Key Words beneath the tabs on the left. Beneath the tabs on the right, define and show examples of square roots of perfect squares and non-perfect squares. Beneath the centre tabs, provide examples of adding, subtracting, multiplying, and dividing rational numbers in decimal form and fraction form.

On the back of the Foldable, make notes under the heading What I Need to Work On. Check off each item as you deal with it.

Math Link

Problem Solving With Games

Millions of Canadians enjoy the challenge and fun of playing chess. Early versions of this game existed in India over 1400 years ago. The modern version of chess emerged from southern Europe over 500 years ago.

1. If each of the small squares on a chessboard has a side length of 3 cm, what is the total area of the dark squares? Solve this problem in two ways.

2. If the total area of a chessboard is 1024 cm², what is the side length of each of the smallest squares?

3. For the chessboard in #2, what is the length of a diagonal of the board? Express your answer to the nearest tenth of a centimetre.

4. Compare your solutions with your classmates' solutions.

In this chapter, you will describe or play other games by solving problems that involve decimals, fractions, squares, and square roots. You will then use your skills to design a game of your own.

Comparing and Ordering Rational Numbers

Focus on...

After this lesson, you will be able to...

• compare and order rational numbers
• identify a rational number between two given rational numbers

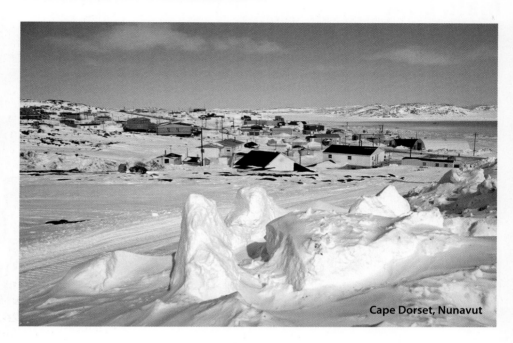

Cape Dorset, Nunavut

The percent of Canadians who live in rural areas has been decreasing since 1867. At that time, about 80% of Canadians lived in rural areas. Today, about 80% of Canadians live in urban areas, mostly in cities. The table shows changes in the percent of Canadians living in urban and rural areas over four decades.

> **Did You Know?**
>
> An urban area has a population of 1000 or more. In urban areas, 400 or more people live in each square kilometre. Areas that are not urban are called rural. What type of area do you live in?

Decade	Change in the Percent of Canadians in Urban Areas (%)	Change in the Percent of Canadians in Rural Areas (%)
1966−1976	+1.9	−1.9
1976−1986	+1.0	−1.0
1986−1996	+1.4	−1.4
1996−2006	+2.3	−2.3

How can you tell that some changes in the table are increases and others are decreases?

Explore Rational Numbers

1. How are the **rational numbers** in the table on page 46 related. Explain your reasoning.

2. **a)** Choose a rational number in decimal form. Identify its opposite. How do you know these are opposite rational numbers?

   b) Choose a rational number in fraction form. Identify its opposite.

   c) Identify another pair of opposite rational numbers.

3. **a)** Identify equivalent rational numbers from the following list.

   $$\frac{12}{4} \quad \frac{-8}{4} \quad \frac{-9}{-3} \quad -\frac{4}{2} \quad \frac{4}{-2} \quad \frac{12}{3} \quad -\left(\frac{4}{-1}\right) \quad -\left(\frac{-4}{-2}\right)$$

   b) Choose a rational number in fraction form that is not equivalent to any of the rational numbers in part a). Challenge a classmate to write four rational numbers that are equivalent to your chosen number.

Reflect and Check

4. **a)** How can you identify opposite rational numbers?

   b) How can you identify equivalent rational numbers?

5. **a)** Predict what you think the change in the percent of Canadians in urban areas from 2006 to 2016 might be. Justify your prediction.

   b) What would you expect the change in the percent of Canadians in rural areas to be for that decade? Explain.

rational number

- a number that can be expressed as $\frac{a}{b}$, where a and b are integers and $b \neq 0$
- examples include -4, 3.5, $-\frac{1}{2}$, $1\frac{3}{4}$, and 0

> **Literacy Link**
>
> When numbers are *equivalent*, they have the same value. $\frac{24}{-4}$, $\frac{-18}{3}$, $-\frac{12}{2}$, and $-\left(\frac{-6}{-1}\right)$ are all equivalent. They all represent the same rational number. What is it?

Vancouver, British Columbia

Link the Ideas

Example 1: Compare and Order Rational Numbers

Compare and order the following rational numbers.

$$-1.2 \qquad \frac{4}{5} \qquad \frac{7}{8} \qquad -0.\overline{5} \qquad -\frac{7}{8}$$

Solution

You can estimate the order.

-1.2 is a little less than -1.

$\frac{4}{5}$ is a little less than 1.

$\frac{7}{8}$ is a little less than 1.

$-0.\overline{5}$ is a little less than -0.5.

$-\frac{7}{8}$ is a little more than -1.

An estimate of the order from least to greatest is $-1.2, -\frac{7}{8}, -0.\overline{5}, \frac{4}{5}, \frac{7}{8}$.

Express all the numbers in the same form.
You can write the numbers in decimal form.

$$-1.2 \qquad \frac{4}{5} = 0.8 \qquad \frac{7}{8} = 0.875 \qquad -0.\overline{5} = -0.555... \qquad -\frac{7}{8} = -0.875$$

Place the numbers on a number line.

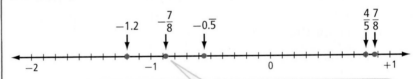

What number is the opposite of $-\frac{7}{8}$? How does the position of that number on the number line compare with the position of $-\frac{7}{8}$?

The numbers in ascending order are $-1.2, -\frac{7}{8}, -0.\overline{5}, \frac{4}{5},$ and $\frac{7}{8}$.

The numbers in descending order are $\frac{7}{8}, \frac{4}{5}, -0.\overline{5}, -\frac{7}{8},$ and -1.2.

Show You Know

Compare the following rational numbers. Write them in ascending order and descending order.

$$0.\overline{3} \qquad -0.6 \qquad -\frac{3}{4} \qquad 1\frac{1}{5} \qquad -1$$

Example 2: Compare Rational Numbers

Which fraction is greater, $-\frac{3}{4}$ or $-\frac{2}{3}$?

Solution

Method 1: Use Equivalent Fractions

You can express the fractions as equivalent fractions with a common denominator.

A common denominator of the two fractions is 12.

> How do you know 12 is a common denominator?

$$-\frac{3}{4} = -\frac{9}{12} \qquad -\frac{2}{3} = -\frac{8}{12}$$

When the denominators are the same, compare the numerators.

$$-\frac{9}{12} = \frac{-9}{12} \qquad -\frac{8}{12} = \frac{-8}{12}$$

$\frac{-8}{12} > \frac{-9}{12}$, because $-8 > -9$.

$-\frac{2}{3}$ is the greater fraction.

> How does the number line show the comparison?
>
> $-\frac{9}{12} = -\frac{3}{4}$ $-\frac{8}{12} = -\frac{2}{3}$
>
>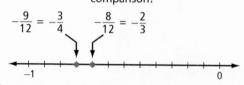

Literacy Link

The quotient of two integers with unlike signs is negative. This means that

$$-\frac{9}{12} = \frac{-9}{12} = \frac{9}{-12}$$

and

$$-\frac{8}{12} = \frac{-8}{12} = \frac{8}{-12}.$$

Method 2: Use Decimals

You can also compare by writing the fractions as decimal numbers.

$$-\frac{3}{4} = -0.75$$

$$-\frac{2}{3} = -0.\overline{6}$$

$$-0.\overline{6} > -0.75$$

$-\frac{2}{3}$ is the greater fraction.

Show You Know

Which fraction is smaller, $-\frac{7}{10}$ or $-\frac{3}{5}$?

WWW Web Link

For practice comparing and ordering rational numbers, go to www. mathlinks9.ca and follow the links.

Example 3: Identify a Rational Number Between Two Given Rational Numbers

Identify a fraction between -0.6 and -0.7.

Solution

You can first identify a decimal number between -0.6 and -0.7, using a number line.

Strategies

Draw a Diagram

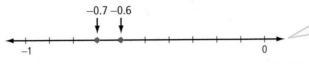

> You can also change -0.6 and -0.7 into fraction form. What would the number line look like?

One decimal number between -0.6 and -0.7 is -0.65.

Convert the decimal to a fraction. $-0.65 = -\dfrac{65}{100}$

A fraction between -0.6 and -0.7 is $-\dfrac{65}{100}$.

> What is another way to express $-\dfrac{65}{100}$ as a fraction?

Show You Know

Identify a fraction between -2.4 and -2.5.

Key Ideas

- Rational numbers can be positive, negative, or zero. They include integers, positive and negative fractions, mixed numbers, and decimal numbers.

    Examples: -6, 15, $\dfrac{3}{4}$, $-1\dfrac{2}{3}$, 3.9, $-2.\overline{3}$

- Equivalent fractions represent the same rational number.

    $-\dfrac{5}{2}$, $\dfrac{-5}{2}$, $\dfrac{10}{-4}$, and $-\left(\dfrac{-10}{-4}\right)$ all represent $-2\dfrac{1}{2}$ or -2.5.

- One strategy for comparing and ordering rational numbers is to use a number line.

    - On a horizontal number line, a larger rational number is to the right of a smaller rational number.
    - Opposite rational numbers are the same distance in opposite directions from zero.

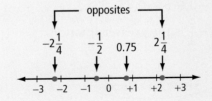

- You can compare fractions with the same denominator by comparing the numerators.

    $\dfrac{-7}{10} < \dfrac{-6}{10}$, because $-7 < -6$.

- One strategy for identifying a rational number between two given rational numbers is to use a number line.

    A rational number in fraction form between -0.3 and -0.1 is $\dfrac{-1}{5}$.

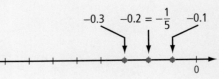

Check Your Understanding

Communicate the Ideas

1. Laura placed $-2\frac{1}{2}$ incorrectly on a number line, as shown.

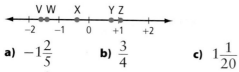

How could you use the idea of opposites to show Laura how to plot $-2\frac{1}{2}$ correctly?

2. Is Dominic correct? Show how you know.

3.1 is greater than 2.5, so -3.1 is greater than -2.5.

3. Tomas and Roxanne were comparing -0.9 and $-\frac{7}{8}$. Tomas wrote -0.9 as a fraction, and then he compared the two fractions. Roxanne wrote $-\frac{7}{8}$ as a decimal, and then she compared the two decimals.

a) Which method do you prefer? Explain.

b) Which is greater, -0.9 or $-\frac{7}{8}$? Explain how you know.

Practise

For help with #4 to #9, refer to Example 1 on page 48.

4. Match each rational number to a point on the number line.

a) $\frac{3}{2}$　　　　**b)** -0.7　　　**c)** $-2\frac{1}{5}$

d) $\frac{14}{5}$　　　　**e)** $-1\frac{1}{3}$

5. Which point on the number line matches each rational number?

a) $-1\frac{2}{5}$　　　**b)** $\frac{3}{4}$　　　　**c)** $1\frac{1}{20}$

d) $-1\frac{3}{5}$　　　**e)** $-0.\overline{4}$

6. Place each number and its opposite on a number line.

a) $\frac{8}{9}$　　**b)** -1.2　　**c)** $2\frac{1}{10}$　　**d)** $-\frac{11}{3}$

7. What is the opposite of each rational number?

a) $-4.\overline{1}$　**b)** $\frac{4}{5}$　　**c)** $-5\frac{3}{4}$　　**d)** $\frac{9}{8}$

8. Compare $1\frac{5}{6}$, $-1\frac{2}{3}$, -0.1, 1.9, and $-\frac{1}{5}$. Write the numbers in ascending order.

9. Compare $-\frac{3}{8}$, $1.\overline{8}$, $\frac{9}{5}$, $-\frac{1}{2}$, and -1. Write the numbers in descending order.

For help with #10 to #13, refer to Example 2 on page 49.

10. Express each fraction as an equivalent fraction.

a) $-\dfrac{2}{5}$ **b)** $\dfrac{10}{6}$

c) $-\dfrac{9}{12}$ **d)** $\dfrac{-4}{3}$

11. Write each rational number as an equivalent fraction.

a) $\dfrac{-1}{3}$ **b)** $\dfrac{-4}{-5}$

c) $-\left(\dfrac{-5}{-4}\right)$ **d)** $\dfrac{7}{-2}$

12. Which value in each pair is greater?

a) $\dfrac{1}{3}, -\dfrac{2}{3}$ **b)** $-\dfrac{9}{10}, \dfrac{7}{10}$

c) $-\dfrac{1}{2}, -\dfrac{3}{5}$ **d)** $-2\dfrac{1}{8}, -2\dfrac{1}{4}$

13. Which value in each pair is smaller?

a) $\dfrac{4}{7}, \dfrac{2}{3}$ **b)** $-\dfrac{4}{3}, -\dfrac{5}{3}$

c) $-\dfrac{7}{10}, -\dfrac{3}{5}$ **d)** $-1\dfrac{3}{4}, -1\dfrac{4}{5}$

For help with #14 to #17, refer to Example 3 on page 50.

14. Identify a decimal number between each of the following pairs of rational numbers.

a) $\dfrac{3}{5}, \dfrac{4}{5}$ **b)** $-\dfrac{1}{2}, -\dfrac{5}{8}$

c) $-\dfrac{5}{6}, 1$ **d)** $-\dfrac{17}{20}, -\dfrac{4}{5}$

15. What is a decimal number between each of the following pairs of rational numbers?

a) $1\dfrac{1}{2}, 1\dfrac{7}{10}$ **b)** $-2\dfrac{2}{3}, -2\dfrac{1}{3}$

c) $1\dfrac{3}{5}, -1\dfrac{7}{10}$ **d)** $-3\dfrac{1}{100}, -3\dfrac{1}{50}$

16. Identify a fraction between each of the following pairs of rational numbers.

a) 0.2, 0.3   **b)** 0, −0.1

c) −0.74, −0.76   **d)** −0.52, −0.53

17. Identify a mixed number between each of the following pairs of rational numbers.

a) 1.7, 1.9   **b)** −0.5, 1.5

c) −3.3, −3.4   **d)** −2.01, −2.03

Apply

18. Use a rational number to represent each quantity. Explain your reasoning.

a) a temperature increase of 8.2 °C

b) growth of 2.9 cm

c) 3.5 m below sea level

d) earnings of $32.50

e) 14.2 °C below freezing

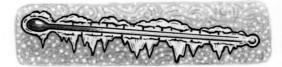

19. The table includes the melting points and boiling points of six elements known as the noble gases.

Noble Gas	Melting Point (°C)	Boiling Point (°C)
Argon	−189.2	−185.7
Helium	−272.2	−268.6
Neon	−248.67	−245.92
Krypton	−156.6	−152.3
Radon	−71.0	−61.8
Xenon	−111.9	−107.1

a) Which noble gases have a melting point that is less than the melting point of argon?

b) Which noble gases have a boiling point that is greater than the boiling point of krypton?

c) Arrange the melting points in ascending order.

d) Arrange the boiling points in descending order.

Science Link

For many years, the noble gases were known as the *inert gases*. Most chemists thought that these gases would not react with other chemicals. In 1962, Neil Bartlett, a chemist at the University of British Columbia, proved them wrong.

WWW Web Link

To learn more about Neil Bartlett and to research Canadian scientific discoveries, go to www.mathlinks9.ca and follow the links.

---

20. a) Kwasi said that he ignored the fractions when he decided that $-2\frac{1}{5}$ is smaller than $-1\frac{9}{10}$. Explain his thinking.

b) Naomi said that she ignored the integer -1 when she decided that $-1\frac{1}{4}$ is greater than $-1\frac{2}{7}$. Explain her thinking.

21. The table shows the average early-morning temperature for seven communities in May.

Community	Average Early-Morning Temperature (°C)
Churchill, Manitoba	−5.1
Regina, Saskatchewan	3.9
Edmonton, Alberta	5.4
Penticton, British Columbia	6.1
Yellowknife, Northwest Territories	−0.1
Whitehorse, Yukon Territory	0.6
Resolute, Nunavut	−14.1

a) Write the temperatures in descending order.

b) Which community has an average temperature between the values for Whitehorse and Churchill?

22. Replace each ■ with >, <, or = to make each statement true.

a) $\dfrac{-9}{6}$ ■ $\dfrac{3}{-2}$

b) $-\dfrac{3}{5}$ ■ $-0.\overline{6}$

c) $-1\dfrac{3}{10}$ ■ $-\left(\dfrac{-13}{-10}\right)$

d) -3.25 ■ $-3\dfrac{1}{5}$

e) $-\dfrac{8}{12}$ ■ $-\dfrac{11}{15}$

f) $-2\dfrac{5}{6}$ ■ $-2\dfrac{7}{8}$

23. Is zero a rational number? Explain.

24. Give an example of a fraction in lowest terms that satisfies the following conditions.

a) greater than 0, with the denominator greater than the numerator

b) between 0 and −1, with the denominator less than the numerator

c) less than −2, with the numerator less than the denominator

d) between −1.2 and −1.3, with the numerator greater than the denominator

25. Which integers are between $\frac{11}{5}$ and $\frac{15}{-4}$?

26. Which number in each pair is greater? Explain each answer.

  a) 0.4 and 0.44

  b) $0.\overline{3}$ and 0.33

  c) -0.7 and -0.77

  d) -0.66 and $-0.\overline{6}$

27. Identify the fractions that are between 0 and -2 and that have 3 as the denominator.

Extend

28. How many rational numbers are between $\frac{2}{3}$ and $0.\overline{6}$? Explain.

29. Replace each ■ with an integer to make each statement true. In each case, is more than one answer possible? Explain.

  a) $\blacksquare.5 < -1.9$

  b) $\frac{\blacksquare}{-4} = -2\frac{1}{4}$

  c) $\frac{-3}{\blacksquare} = -\frac{-15}{5}$

  d) $-1.5\blacksquare2 > -1.512$

  e) $-\frac{3}{4} < -0.7\blacksquare$

  f) $-5\frac{1}{2} > \frac{11}{\blacksquare}$

  g) $-2\frac{3}{5} = \frac{\blacksquare}{10}$

  h) $\frac{8}{\blacksquare} < -\frac{2}{3}$

30. Determine the value of x.

  a) $\frac{4}{-5} = \frac{x}{-10}$

  b) $\frac{x}{3} = \frac{6}{-9}$

  c) $\frac{5}{x} = -\frac{20}{12}$

  d) $\frac{-6}{-5} = \frac{30}{x}$

Math Link

Play the following game with a partner or in a small group. You will need one deck of playing cards.
- Remove the jokers, aces, and face cards from the deck.
- Red cards represent positive integers. Black cards represent negative integers.
- In each round, the dealer shuffles the cards and deals two cards to each player.
- Use your two cards to make a fraction that is as close as possible to zero.
- In each round, the player with the fraction closest to zero wins two points. If there is a tie, each tied player wins a point.
- The winner is the first player with ten points. If two or more players reach ten points in the same round, keep playing until one player is in the lead by at least two points.

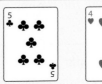

represents -5 represents 4

With a five of clubs and a four of hearts, you can make $\frac{4}{-5}$ or $\frac{-5}{4}$. Choose $\frac{4}{-5}$ because it is closer to zero.

Problem Solving With Rational Numbers in Decimal Form

Focus on...

After this lesson, you will be able to...

- perform operations on rational numbers in decimal form
- solve problems involving rational numbers in decimal form

Did You Know?

As Canada's sunniest provincial capital, Regina averages almost 6.5 h of sunshine per day. That is over 2 h per day more sunshine than St. John's, Newfoundland and Labrador. St. John's is the least sunny provincial capital.

In Regina, Saskatchewan, the average mid-afternoon temperature in January is −12.6 °C. The average mid-afternoon temperature in July is 26.1 °C. Estimate how much colder Regina is in January than in July.

Explore Multiplying and Dividing Rational Numbers in Decimal Form

1. a) Estimate the products and quotients. Explain your method.

$$3.2 \times 4.5 \qquad 3.2 \times (-4.5) \qquad -20.9 \div 9.5 \qquad -20.9 \div (-9.5)$$

b) Calculate the products and quotients in part a). Explain your method.

2. a) Suppose the temperature one January afternoon in Regina decreased by 2.6 °C every hour for 3.5 h. What was the overall temperature change during that time?

b) Suppose the temperature in Regina one July afternoon increased by 9.9 °C in 5.5 h. What was the average temperature change per hour?

Reflect and Check

3. How can you multiply and divide rational numbers in decimal form?

4. Create a problem that can be solved using the multiplication or division of rational numbers. Challenge a classmate to solve it.

Link the Ideas

> ### Example 1: Add and Subtract Rational Numbers in Decimal Form
>
> Estimate and calculate.
> **a)** $2.65 + (-3.81)$
> **b)** $-5.96 - (-6.83)$
>
> ### Solution
>
> **a)** Estimate.
> $$2.65 + (-3.81)$$
> $$\approx 3 + (-4)$$
> $$\approx -1$$
>
>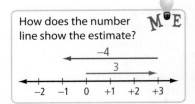
>
> How does the number line show the estimate?
>
> *Method 1: Use Paper and Pencil*
> Calculate.
> Adding the opposite of 3.81 is the same as subtracting 3.81.
> $2.65 + (-3.81) = 2.65 - 3.81$
>
> Determine the difference between 3.81 and 2.65.
> $3.81 - 2.65 = 1.16$
> However, $2.65 - 3.81$ must be negative, since $3.81 > 2.65$.
> So, $2.65 + (-3.81) = -1.16$.
>
> *Method 2: Use a Calculator*
> Calculate. `C` `2.65` `+` `3.81` `+∠−` `=` -1.16
>
> **b)** Estimate.
> $$-5.96 - (-6.83)$$
> $$\approx -6 - (-7)$$
> $$\approx -6 + 7$$
> $$\approx 1$$
>
>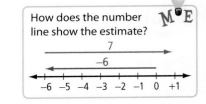
>
> How does the number line show the estimate?
>
> *Method 1: Use Paper and Pencil*
> Calculate.
> $-5.96 - (-6.83) = -5.96 + 6.83$
>
> > Why is subtracting -6.83 the same as adding its opposite, 6.83?
>
> Determine $6.83 + (-5.96)$.
> $$6.83 + (-5.96)$$
> $$= 6.83 - 5.96$$
> $$= 0.87$$
> So, $-5.96 - (-6.83) = 0.87$.
>
> > Why is $-5.96 + 6.83$ the same as $6.83 + (-5.96)$?
>
> > Is the calculated answer reasonable? How do you know?
>
> *Method 2: Use a Calculator*
> Calculate. `C` `5.96` `+∠−` `−` `6.83` `+∠−` `=` 0.87

⚙ Tech Link

The key for entering a negative sign may look different on different calculators, for example, `+∠−`, `+/−` or `(−)`. It is not the subtraction key, `−`. Experiment with calculations involving negative signs on your calculator.

Show You Know

Estimate and calculate.

a) $-4.38 + 1.52$

b) $-1.25 - 3.55$

Example 2: Multiply and Divide Rational Numbers in Decimal Form

Estimate and calculate.

a) $0.45 \times (-1.2)$

b) $-2.3 \div (-0.25)$

Solution

a) Estimate.
$0.5 \times (-1) = -0.5$

Calculate.
Method 1: Use Paper and Pencil
You can calculate by multiplying the decimal numbers.
$0.45 \times 1.2 = 0.54$
Determine the sign of the product.
$0.45 \times (-1.2) = -0.54$

> How do you know what the sign of the product is?

Method 2: Use a Calculator
C 0.45 × 1.2 +⟷− = -0.54

b) Estimate.
$-2.3 \div (-0.25)$
$\approx -2 \div (-0.2)$
≈ 10

Calculate.
C 2.3 +⟷− ÷ 0.25 +⟷− = 9.2

Show You Know

Estimate and calculate.

a) $-1.4(-2.6)$

b) $-2.76 \div 4.6$

> **Literacy Link**
>
> *Parentheses* is another name for brackets. They can be used in place of a multiplication sign. For example,
> $-4 \times 1.5 = -4(1.5)$

Example 3: Apply Operations With Rational Numbers in Decimal Form

On Saturday, the temperature at the Blood Reserve near Stand Off, Alberta decreased by 1.2 °C/h for 3.5 h. It then decreased by 0.9 °C/h for 1.5 h.

a) What was the total decrease in temperature?

b) What was the average rate of decrease in temperature?

Solution

Why are the time periods represented by positive rational numbers?
Why are the rates of temperature decrease represented by negative rational numbers?

a) The time periods can be represented by 3.5 and 1.5. The rates of temperature decrease can be represented by −1.2 and −0.9.

Method 1: Calculate in Stages
You can represent the temperature decrease in the first 3.5 h by $3.5 \times (-1.2) = -4.2$.

You can represent the temperature decrease in the last 1.5 h by $1.5 \times (-0.9) = -1.35$.

$4 \times (-1) = -4$ **M E**
$1.5 \times (-1) = -1.5$
$-4 + (-1.5) = -5.5$

Add to determine the total temperature decrease.
$-4.2 + (-1.35) = -5.55$

The total decrease in temperature was 5.55 °C.

Method 2: Evaluate One Expression
The total temperature decrease can be represented by $3.5 \times (-1.2) + 1.5 \times (-0.9)$.

$4 \times (-1) + 1.5 \times (-1) = -5.5$ **M E**

Evaluate this expression, using the order of operations.
$$3.5 \times (-1.2) + 1.5 \times (-0.9)$$
$$= -4.2 + (-1.35)$$
$$= -5.55$$

You can also use a calculator.
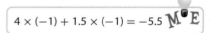
The total decrease in temperature was 5.55 °C.

Literacy Link

Order of Operations

- Perform operations inside parentheses first.
- Multiply and divide in order from left to right.
- Add and subtract in order from left to right.

b) The average rate of decrease in temperature is the total decrease divided by the total number of hours.
The total number of hours is $3.5 + 1.5 = 5$.
$$\frac{-5.55}{5} = -1.11$$

$-5 \div 5 = -1$ **M E**

The average rate of decrease in temperature was 1.11 °C/h.

Show You Know

A hot-air balloon climbed at 0.8 m/s for 10 s.
It then descended at 0.6 m/s for 6 s.

a) What was the overall change in altitude?

b) What was the average rate of change in altitude?

Key Ideas

- One way to model the addition of rational numbers is on a
  number line. One way to model the subtraction of rational
  numbers is by adding the opposite on a number line.

  $-2.2 - 1.3 = -3.5$ or $-2.2 + (-1.3) = -3.5$

- The product or quotient of two rational numbers with the same
  signs is positive.

  $-1.2 \times (-1.5) = 1.8$ $-1.5 \div (-1.2) = 1.25$

  The product or quotient of two rational numbers with different signs
  is negative.

  $1.2 \times (-1.5) = -1.8$ $-1.5 \div 1.2 = -1.25$

- The order of operations for calculations involving rational numbers
  is the same as for whole numbers, decimals, and integers.
  - Perform operations inside parentheses first.
  - Divide and multiply in order from left to right.
  - Add and subtract in order from left to right.

Check Your Understanding

Communicate the Ideas

1. a) Would you expect the subtraction $-3.5 - (-4.3)$ to give a positive
   answer or a negative answer? Explain.

   b) Evaluate $-3.5 - (-4.3)$.

2. How do the values of the following two products compare? Explain
   your reasoning.

   $2.54 \times (-4.22)$ -2.54×4.22

3. Leslie evaluated $-2.2 + 4.6 \times (-0.5)$ as -1.2. Zack evaluated the same
   expression as -4.5. Who was correct? Explain.

Practise

For help with #4 and #5, refer to Example 1 on page 56.

4. Estimate and calculate.

    a) $0.98 + (-2.91)$

    b) $5.46 - 3.16$

    c) $-4.23 + (-5.75)$

    d) $-1.49 - (-6.83)$

5. Calculate.

    a) $9.37 - 11.62$ **b)** $-0.512 + 2.385$

    c) $0.675 - (-0.061)$ **d)** $-10.95 + (-1.99)$

For help with #6 and #7, refer to Example 2 on page 57.

6. Estimate and calculate.

    a) $2.7 \times (-3.2)$

    b) $-3.25 \div 2.5$

    c) $-5.5 \times (-5.5)$

    d) $-4.37 \div (-0.95)$

7. Calculate. Express your answer to the nearest thousandth, if necessary.

    a) $-2.4(-1.5)$ **b)** $8.6 \div 0.9$

    c) $-5.3(4.2)$ **d)** $19.5 \div (-16.2)$

    e) $1.12(0.68)$ **f)** $-0.55 \div 0.66$

For help with #8 to #11, refer to Example 3 on page 58.

8. Evaluate.

    a) $-2.1 \times 3.2 + 4.3 \times (-1.5)$

    b) $-3.5(4.8 - 5.6)$

    c) $-1.1[2.3 - (-0.5)]$

◯◯ Literacy Link

In $-1.1[2.3 - (-0.5)]$, square brackets are used for grouping because -0.5 is already in parentheses.

---

9. Determine each value.

    a) $(4.51 - 5.32)(5.17 - 6.57)$

    b) $2.4 + 1.8 \times 5.7 \div (-2.7)$

    c) $-4.36 + 1.2[2.8 + (-3.5)]$

10. In Regina, Saskatchewan, the average mid-afternoon temperature in January is $-12.6\ °C$. The average mid-afternoon temperature in July is $26.1\ °C$. How many degrees colder is Regina in January than in July?

11. One January day in Penticton, British Columbia, the temperature read $-6.3\ °C$ at 10:00 a.m. and $1.4\ °C$ at 3:00 p.m.

    a) What was the change in temperature?

    b) What was the average rate of change in temperature?

Apply

12. A pelican dives vertically from a height of 3.8 m above the water. It then catches a fish 2.3 m underwater.

    a) Write an expression using rational numbers to represent the length of the pelican's dive.

    b) How long is the pelican's dive?

13. A submarine was cruising at a depth of 153 m. It then rose at 4.5 m/min for 15 min.

    a) What was the submarine's depth at the end of this rise?

    b) If the submarine continues to rise at the same rate, how much longer will it take to reach the surface?

14. Saida owned 125 shares of an oil company. One day, the value of each share dropped by $0.31. The next day, the value of each share rose by $0.18. What was the total change in the value of Saida's shares?

◯◯ Literacy Link

A *share* is one unit of ownership in a corporation.

---

15. In dry air, the temperature decreases by about 0.65 °C for each 100-m increase in altitude.

   a) The temperature in Red Deer, Alberta, is 10 °C on a dry day. What is the temperature outside an aircraft 2.8 km above the city?

   b) The temperature outside an aircraft 1600 m above Red Deer is −8.5 °C. What is the temperature in the city?

16. Bella is more comfortable working with integers than with positive and negative decimal numbers. This is her way of understanding −4.3 + 2.5.

−4.3 is $\frac{-43}{10}$ or −43 tenths.

2.5 is $\frac{25}{10}$ or 25 tenths.

−43 tenths + 25 tenths is −18 tenths.

−18 tenths is $\frac{-18}{10}$ or −1.8.

So, −4.3 + 2.5 = −1.8.

   a) Use Bella's method to determine 6.1 + (−3.9).

   b) How could you modify Bella's method to determine 1.25 − 3.46?

17. Two wooden poles measured 1.35 m and 0.83 m in length. To make a new pole, they were attached by overlapping the ends and tying them together. The length of the overlap was 12 cm. What was the total length of the new pole in metres?

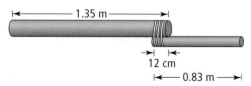

18. Determine the mean of each set of numbers. Express your answer to the nearest hundredth, if necessary.

   a) 0, −4.5, −8.2, 0.4, −7.6, 3.5, −0.2

   b) 6.3, −2.2, 14.9, −4.8, −5.3, 1.6

19. A company made a profit of $8.6 million in its first year. It lost $5.9 million in its second year and lost another $6.3 million in its third year.

   a) What was the average profit or loss per year over the first three years?

   b) The company broke even over the first four years. What was its profit or loss in the fourth year?

20. Research to find out the current price of gasoline in Calgary. It is 300 km from Calgary to Edmonton. How much less would it cost to drive this distance in a car with a fuel consumption of 5.9 L/100 km than in a car with a fuel consumption of 9.4 L/100 km? Give your answer in dollars, expressed to the nearest cent.

WWW Web Link

To find out prices of gas in Calgary, go to www.mathlinks9.ca and follow the links.

21. Andrew drove his car 234 km from Dawson to Mayo in Yukon Territory in 3 h. Brian drove his truck along the same route at an average speed of 5 km/h greater than Andrew's average speed. How much less time did Brian take, to the nearest minute?

22. An aircraft was flying at an altitude of 2950 m. It descended for 3 min at 2.5 m/s and then descended for 2.5 min at 2.8 m/s. What was the plane's altitude after the descent?

23. One week in October in Iqaluit, Nunavut, the daily high temperatures were −4.6 °C, −0.5 °C, 1.2 °C, 2.3 °C, −1.1 °C, 1.5 °C, and −3.0 °C. What was the mean daily high temperature that week?

Did You Know?

Iqaluit is the capital of Nunavut. This territory covers almost $\frac{1}{5}$ of the area of Canada but has less than $\frac{1}{1000}$ of the Canadian population. Over $\frac{4}{5}$ of the people who live in Nunavut are Inuit.

WWW Web Link

For more information about Nunavut, go to www.mathlinks9.ca and follow the links.

24. Copy and complete each statement.

a) ■ + 1.8 = −3.5

b) −13.3 − ■ = −8.9

c) ■ × (−4.5) = −9.45

d) −18.5 ÷ ■ = 7.4

25. Create a word problem that involves operations with rational numbers in decimal form. Make sure you can solve your problem. Then, have a classmate solve your problem.

Extend

26. Four points, A, B, C, and D, have the following coordinates:

A(0.75, 0.81)
B(0.75, −0.65)
C(−1.22, −0.65)
D(−1.22, 0.81)

What is the area of quadrilateral ABCD, to the nearest hundredth of a square unit?

27. The mean of six rational numbers is −4.3.

a) What is the sum of the rational numbers?

b) If five of the numbers each equal −4.5, what is the sixth number?

28. Evaluate each expression.

a) $3.6 + 2y, y = −0.5$

b) $(m − 1.8)(m + 1.8), m = 1.7$

c) $\dfrac{4.5}{q} − \dfrac{q}{4.5}, q = −3.6$

29. Add one pair of parentheses or square brackets to the left side of each equation to make a true statement.

a) $3.5 × 4.1 − 3.5 − 2.8 = −0.7$

b) $2.5 + (−4.1) + (−2.3) × (−1.1) = 4.29$

c) $−5.5 − (−6.5) ÷ 2.4 + (−1.1) = −0.5$

Math Link

Play this game with a partner or in a small group. You will need two dice and one coin.

- For each turn, roll the two dice and toss the coin. Then, repeat.
- Create numbers of the form ■.■ from the result of rolling the two dice.
- Tossing heads means the rational numbers are positive. Tossing tails means the rational numbers are negative.
- Record the two pairs of numbers.
- Choose one number from each pair so that the sum of the chosen numbers is as close as possible to zero. Record the sum of the chosen numbers.
- In each round, the player with the sum one closest to zero wins two points. If there is a tie, each tied player wins one point.
- The winner is the first player with ten points. If two or more players reach ten points in the same round, keep playing until one player is in the lead by at least two points.

gives the pair 1.2 and 2.1

gives the pair −5.6 and −6.5

The four possible sums are
1.2 + (−5.6)   1.2 + (−6.5)
2.1 + (−5.6)   2.1 + (−6.5)
Estimation shows that 2.1 + (−5.6) is closest to zero, so calculate this sum.
2.1 + (−5.6) = −3.5

Problem Solving With Rational Numbers in Fraction Form

Focus on...

After this lesson, you will be able to...

- **perform operations on rational numbers in fraction form**
- **solve problems involving rational numbers in fraction form**

A news report gives the results of an Olympic speed skating event:

Winnipeg's Cindy Klassen won the gold medal in the 1500-m speed skating event at the Winter Olympics in Turin, Italy. Her winning time was 1:55.27. Ottawa's Kristina Groves won the silver medal. She finished in a time of 1:56.74. The bronze medalist was Ireen Wust of the Netherlands. She finished only $\frac{16}{100}$ s behind Groves.

What are Klassen's time and Groves's time as a mixed number of seconds? How many seconds, in decimal form, did Wust finish behind Groves?

Literacy Link

Klassen's winning time of 1:55.27 means 1 min, 55.27 s.

WWW Web Link

To learn more about Cindy Klassen and other Canadian speed skaters, go to www.mathlinks9.ca and follow the links.

Explore Adding and Subtracting Rational Numbers

1. Determine the number of seconds by which Klassen beat Groves
   a) by using their times in fraction form to give an answer in fraction form
   b) by using their times in decimal form to give an answer in decimal form

2. Which method did you prefer in #1? Explain.

3. What was Wust's time for the event? Show your work.

4. By how many seconds did Klassen beat Wust? Use fractions to show two ways to determine your answer.

Reflect and Check

5. **a)** Use the following data to create a problem involving the addition or subtraction of rational numbers. Ask a partner to solve it.

   > Canada's Perdita Felicien won in the 100-m hurdles at the world championships in Paris, France. Her time was 12.53 s. Brigitte Foster-Hylton of Jamaica placed second at 12.57 s. Foster-Hylton was $\frac{1}{10}$ s ahead of Miesha McKelvy of the United States.

   b) Show how you could determine the answer to your problem by using a different method than your partner used.

   c) Discuss with your partner the differences between your methods. Decide which method you prefer. Explain your choice.

Link the Ideas

Example 1: Add and Subtract Rational Numbers in Fraction Form

Estimate and calculate.

a) $\dfrac{2}{5} - \left(-\dfrac{1}{10}\right)$

b) $3\dfrac{2}{3} + \left(-1\dfrac{3}{4}\right)$

Solution

a) Estimate. $\dfrac{1}{2} - 0 = \dfrac{1}{2}$ **M❂E**

Calculate.

$$\dfrac{2}{5} - \left(-\dfrac{1}{10}\right)$$

$$= \dfrac{2}{5} - \left(\dfrac{-1}{10}\right)$$

$$= \dfrac{4}{10} - \left(\dfrac{-1}{10}\right)$$

$$= \dfrac{4 - (-1)}{10}$$

$$= \dfrac{5}{10}$$

$$= \dfrac{1}{2}$$

> Subtracting $-\dfrac{1}{10}$ is the same as adding the opposite of $-\dfrac{1}{10}$.
>
> $\dfrac{2}{5}$ $\dfrac{1}{10}$
>
> 0 ———————→ 1

> A common denominator of 5 and 10 is 10.

> Is the calculated answer close to the estimate?

b) Estimate. $4 + (-2) = 2$ **M❂E**

Calculate.

Method 1: Rewrite the Mixed Numbers as Improper Fractions	*Method 2: Add the Integers and Add the Fractions*

Method 1: Rewrite the Mixed Numbers as Improper Fractions

$$3\dfrac{2}{3} + \left(-1\dfrac{3}{4}\right) = \dfrac{11}{3} + \left(-\dfrac{7}{4}\right)$$

Add.

$$\dfrac{11}{3} + \left(-\dfrac{7}{4}\right)$$

$$= \dfrac{11}{3} + \left(\dfrac{-7}{4}\right)$$

$$= \dfrac{44}{12} + \left(\dfrac{-21}{12}\right)$$

$$= \dfrac{44 + (-21)}{12}$$

$$= \dfrac{23}{12}$$

$$= 1\dfrac{11}{12}$$

Method 2: Add the Integers and Add the Fractions

$$3\dfrac{2}{3} + \left(-1\dfrac{3}{4}\right)$$

$$= 3 + \dfrac{2}{3} + (-1) + \left(-\dfrac{3}{4}\right)$$

$$= 3 + (-1) + \dfrac{2}{3} + \left(-\dfrac{3}{4}\right)$$

$$= 3 + (-1) + \dfrac{8}{12} + \left(-\dfrac{9}{12}\right)$$

$$= 2 + \left(-\dfrac{1}{12}\right)$$

$$= 1\dfrac{12}{12} + \left(-\dfrac{1}{12}\right)$$

$$= 1\dfrac{11}{12}$$

Estimate and calculate.

a) $-\dfrac{3}{4} - \dfrac{1}{5}$

b) $-2\dfrac{1}{2} + 1\dfrac{9}{10}$

Example 2: Multiply and Divide Rational Numbers in Fraction Form

Determine.

a) $\dfrac{3}{4} \times \left(-\dfrac{2}{3}\right)$

b) $-1\dfrac{1}{2} \div \left(-2\dfrac{3}{4}\right)$

Solution

a) Multiply the numerators and multiply the denominators.

$$\dfrac{3}{4} \times \left(-\dfrac{2}{3}\right) = \dfrac{3}{4} \times \left(\dfrac{-2}{3}\right)$$

$$= \dfrac{3 \times (-2)}{4 \times 3}$$

$$= \dfrac{-6}{12}$$

$$= \dfrac{-1}{2} \text{ or } -\dfrac{1}{2}$$

$1 \times \left(-\dfrac{1}{2}\right) = -\dfrac{1}{2}$ **M E**

You could remove the common factors of 3 and 2 from the numerator and denominator before multiplying.

$$\dfrac{\cancel{3}^{1}}{\cancel{4}_{2}} \times \left(\dfrac{\cancel{-2}^{-1}}{\cancel{3}_{1}}\right) = \dfrac{-1}{2} \text{ or } -\dfrac{1}{2}$$

b) *Method 1: Use a Common Denominator*

Write the fractions with a common denominator and divide the numerators.

$$-1\dfrac{1}{2} \div \left(-2\dfrac{3}{4}\right) = -\dfrac{3}{2} \div \left(-\dfrac{11}{4}\right)$$

$$= \dfrac{-6}{4} \div \left(\dfrac{-11}{4}\right)$$

$$= \dfrac{-6}{-11}$$

$$= \dfrac{6}{11}$$

Recall that $\dfrac{-6}{4} \div \left(\dfrac{-11}{4}\right) = \dfrac{-6 \div (-11)}{4 \div 4}$

$$= \dfrac{-6 \div (-11)}{1}$$

$$= \dfrac{-6}{-11}$$

Method 2: Multiply by the Reciprocal

Another strategy is to multiply by the reciprocal.

$$\dfrac{-3}{2} \div \left(\dfrac{-11}{4}\right) = \dfrac{-3}{2} \times \dfrac{4}{-11}$$

$$= \dfrac{-12}{-22}$$

$$= \dfrac{6}{11}$$

You could remove the common factor of 2 from the numerator and denominator.

$$\dfrac{-3}{\cancel{2}_{1}} \times \dfrac{\cancel{4}^{2}}{-11} = \dfrac{6}{11}$$

Determine each value.

a) $-\dfrac{2}{5}\left(-\dfrac{1}{6}\right)$

b) $-2\dfrac{1}{8} \div 1\dfrac{1}{4}$

Example 3: Apply Operations With Rational Numbers in Fraction Form

At the start of a week, Maka had \$30 of her monthly allowance left. That week, she spent $\frac{1}{5}$ of the money on bus fares, another $\frac{1}{2}$ shopping, and $\frac{1}{4}$ on snacks. How much did she have left at the end of the week?

Solution
You can represent the \$30 Maka had at the beginning of the week by 30.

You can represent the fractions of the money spent by $-\frac{1}{5}$, $-\frac{1}{2}$, and $-\frac{1}{4}$.

> Why would you represent the \$30 by a positive rational number?
>
> Why would you represent the fractions of money spent by negative rational numbers?

Calculate each dollar amount spent.

For bus fares:

$$-\frac{1}{5} \times 30$$
$$= \frac{-1}{5} \times \frac{30}{1}$$
$$= \frac{-30}{5}$$
$$= -6$$

For shopping:

$$-\frac{1}{2} \times 30$$
$$= \frac{-1}{2} \times \frac{30}{1}$$
$$= \frac{-30}{2}$$
$$= -15$$

For snacks:

$$-\frac{1}{4} \times 30$$
$$= \frac{-1}{4} \times \frac{30}{1}$$
$$= \frac{-30}{4}$$
$$= -\frac{15}{2} \text{ or } -7.5$$

Determine the total dollar amount spent.
$-6 + (-15) + (-7.5) = -28.5$

> You could also calculate the total by adding the three fractions $-\frac{1}{5}$, $-\frac{1}{2}$, and $-\frac{1}{4}$ and multiplying their sum by 30. Why does this strategy work? Which strategy do you prefer?

Determine how much Maka had left.
$30 + (-28.5) = 1.5$

Maka had \$1.50 left at the end of the week.

Show You Know
Stefano had \$46 in a bank account that he was not using. Each month for three months, the bank withdrew $\frac{1}{4}$ of this amount as a service fee. How much was left in the account after the last withdrawal?

Key Ideas

- The addition of rational numbers can be modelled on a number line. The subtraction of rational numbers can be modelled by adding the opposite on a number line.

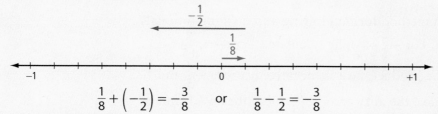

$$\frac{1}{8} + \left(-\frac{1}{2}\right) = -\frac{3}{8} \quad \text{or} \quad \frac{1}{8} - \frac{1}{2} = -\frac{3}{8}$$

- Rational numbers expressed as proper or improper fractions can be added and subtracted in the same way as positive fractions.
- Rational numbers expressed as mixed numbers can be added by
  - first writing them as improper fractions
  - adding the integers and adding the fractions
- Rational numbers expressed as mixed numbers can be subtracted by first writing them as improper fractions.
- Rational numbers expressed as proper or improper fractions can be multiplied and divided in the same way as positive fractions. The sign of the product or quotient can be predicted from the sign rules for multiplication and division.
- Rational numbers expressed as mixed numbers can be multiplied and divided by first writing them as improper fractions.

Check Your Understanding

Communicate the Ideas

1. Emma and Oleg both calculated $-\frac{1}{12} - \frac{2}{3}$ correctly.

   a) Emma used 12 as a common denominator. Show how she calculated the difference in lowest terms.

   b) Oleg used 36 as a common denominator. Show how he calculated the difference in lowest terms.

   c) Which common denominator do you prefer using for the calculation? Explain.

2. Ming and Al both determined $-\frac{7}{15} \times \left(-\frac{5}{14}\right)$ and wrote the product in lowest terms. Ming multiplied before she removed common factors. Al removed common factors before he multiplied. Whose method do you prefer? Explain.

3. a) Calculate $\dfrac{-9}{12} \div \dfrac{3}{8}$ by multiplying by the reciprocal.

b) Calculate $\dfrac{-9}{12} \div \dfrac{3}{8}$ by writing the fractions with a common denominator and dividing the numerators.

c) Which method do you prefer for this calculation? Explain.

4. Joshua suggested his own method for multiplying and dividing rational numbers in fraction form. For $-\dfrac{4}{5} \times \dfrac{2}{3}$, he calculated $\dfrac{4}{5} \times \dfrac{2}{3} = \dfrac{8}{15}$.

Then, he reasoned that the product must be negative because $-\dfrac{4}{5}$ and $\dfrac{2}{3}$ have different signs. He gave the answer as $-\dfrac{8}{15}$. Describe an advantage and a disadvantage of Joshua's method.

Practise

For help with #5 and #6, refer to Example 1 on page 64. Write your answers in lowest terms.

5. Estimate and calculate.

a) $\dfrac{3}{10} + \dfrac{1}{5}$ **b)** $2\dfrac{1}{3} + \left(-1\dfrac{1}{4}\right)$

c) $-\dfrac{5}{12} - \dfrac{5}{12}$ **d)** $-2\dfrac{1}{2} - \left(-3\dfrac{1}{3}\right)$

e) $-\dfrac{5}{6} + \dfrac{1}{3}$ **f)** $\dfrac{3}{8} - \left(-\dfrac{1}{4}\right)$

6. Estimate and calculate.

a) $\dfrac{2}{3} - \dfrac{3}{4}$ **b)** $-\dfrac{2}{9} + \left(-\dfrac{1}{3}\right)$

c) $-\dfrac{1}{4} + \left(-\dfrac{3}{5}\right)$ **d)** $-\dfrac{3}{4} - \left(-\dfrac{5}{8}\right)$

e) $1\dfrac{1}{2} - 2\dfrac{1}{4}$ **f)** $1\dfrac{2}{5} + \left(-1\dfrac{3}{4}\right)$

For help with #7 and #8, refer to Example 2 on page 65. Write your answers in lowest terms.

7. Estimate and calculate.

a) $\dfrac{4}{5} \div \dfrac{5}{6}$ **b)** $3\dfrac{1}{3}\left(1\dfrac{3}{4}\right)$

c) $\dfrac{1}{8} \times \left(-\dfrac{2}{5}\right)$ **d)** $-\dfrac{9}{10} \div \left(-\dfrac{4}{5}\right)$

e) $-\dfrac{3}{8} \times 5\dfrac{1}{3}$ **f)** $\dfrac{1}{10} \div \left(-\dfrac{3}{8}\right)$

8. Estimate and calculate.

a) $-\dfrac{3}{4} \times \left(-\dfrac{1}{9}\right)$ **b)** $1\dfrac{1}{3} \div 1\dfrac{1}{4}$

c) $-\dfrac{3}{8} \div \dfrac{7}{10}$ **d)** $-2\dfrac{1}{8} \div 1\dfrac{1}{4}$

e) $\dfrac{7}{9}\left(-\dfrac{6}{11}\right)$ **f)** $-1\dfrac{1}{2} \div \left(-2\dfrac{1}{2}\right)$

For help with #9 and #10, refer to Example 3 on page 66.

9. Lori owed her mother $39. Lori paid back $\dfrac{1}{3}$ of this debt and then paid back $\dfrac{1}{4}$ of the remaining debt.

How much does Lori still owe her mother?

10. A carpenter has 64 m of baseboard. He installs $\dfrac{1}{2}$ of the baseboard in one room. He installs another $\dfrac{3}{5}$ of the original amount of baseboard in another room. How much baseboard does he have left?

Apply

11. In everyday speech, *in a jiffy* means in a very short time. In science, a specific value sometimes assigned to a jiffy is $\dfrac{1}{100}$ s.

Naima can type at 50 words/min. On average, how many jiffies does she take to type each word?

12. In the table, a positive number shows how many hours the time in a location is ahead of the time in London, England. A negative number shows how many hours the time is behind the time in London.

Location	Time Zone
Alice Springs, Australia	$+9\frac{1}{2}$
Brandon, Manitoba	-6
Chatham Islands, New Zealand	$+12\frac{3}{4}$
Istanbul, Turkey	$+2$
Kathmandu, Nepal	$+5\frac{3}{4}$
London, England	0
Mumbai, India	$+5\frac{1}{2}$
St. John's, Newfoundland and Labrador	$-3\frac{1}{2}$
Tokyo, Japan	$+9$
Victoria, British Columbia	-8

a) How many hours is the time in St. John's ahead of the time in Brandon?

b) How many hours is the time in Victoria behind the time in Mumbai?

c) Determine and interpret the time difference between Tokyo and Kathmandu.

d) Determine and interpret the time difference between Chatham Islands and St. John's.

e) In which location is the time exactly halfway between the times in Istanbul and Alice Springs?

13. The diameter of Pluto is $\frac{6}{17}$ the diameter of Mars. Mars is $\frac{17}{300}$ the diameter of Saturn.

a) What fraction of the diameter of Saturn is the diameter of Pluto?

b) The diameter of Saturn is 120 000 km. What is the diameter of Pluto?

14. Li and Ray shared a vegetarian pizza and a Hawaiian pizza of the same size. The vegetarian pizza was cut into eight equal slices. The Hawaiian pizza was cut into six equal slices. Li ate two slices of the vegetarian pizza and one slice of the Hawaiian pizza. Ray ate two slices of the Hawaiian pizza and one slice of the vegetarian pizza.

a) Who ate more pizza?

b) How much more did that person eat?

c) How much pizza was left over?

15. Predict the next three numbers in each pattern.

a) $-1\frac{1}{2}, -\frac{7}{8}, -\frac{1}{4}, \frac{3}{8}, 1, \ldots$

b) $1\frac{1}{3}, -\frac{2}{3}, \frac{1}{3}, -\frac{1}{6}, \frac{1}{12}, \ldots$

16. Boris has $2\frac{1}{2}$ times as much cash as Anna. Charlie has $\frac{3}{4}$ as much cash as Anna. Anna has $25.60 in cash.

a) How much cash do the three people have altogether?

b) How much more cash does Boris have than Charlie?

17. To calculate $-\frac{3}{4} + \left(-\frac{2}{3}\right)$, Amy decided to convert the fractions to decimals and add the decimals on a scientific calculator.

a) Explain why she had difficulty in determining the exact answer by this method.

b) How should she calculate to get an exact answer?

18. One ninth of the height of an iceberg was above the surface of the water. The iceberg extended to a depth of 75.8 m below the surface. What was the height of the iceberg above the surface? Express your answer to the nearest tenth of a metre.

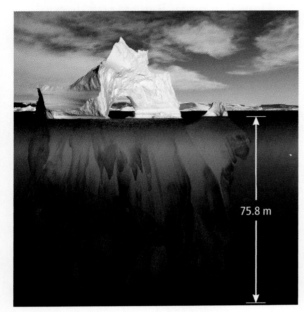

75.8 m

19. Copy and complete each statement.

a) $\frac{1}{2} + \blacksquare = -\frac{3}{4}$ **b)** $\blacksquare - 1\frac{4}{5} = -\frac{7}{10}$

c) $-2\frac{1}{6} \times \blacksquare = -1\frac{1}{3}$ **d)** $\blacksquare \div \left(-\frac{3}{5}\right) = 2\frac{1}{2}$

20. In a magic square, the sum of each row, column, and diagonal is the same. Copy and complete this magic square.

$-\frac{1}{2}$		
	$-\frac{5}{6}$	
	$\frac{1}{2}$	$-1\frac{1}{6}$

21. Calculate.

a) $\frac{1}{3}\left(\frac{2}{5} - \frac{1}{2}\right) + \frac{3}{10}$

b) $\frac{3}{4} \div \frac{5}{8} - \frac{3}{8} \div \frac{1}{2}$

c) $1\frac{1}{2} + 1\frac{1}{2}\left(-2\frac{5}{6} + \frac{1}{3}\right)$

22. Taj has three scoops for measuring flour. The largest scoop holds $2\frac{1}{2}$ times as much as the smallest one. The middle scoop holds $1\frac{3}{4}$ times as much as the smallest one. Describe two different ways in which Taj could measure each of the following quantities. He can use full scoops only.

a) $3\frac{1}{4}$ times as much as the smallest scoop holds

b) $\frac{1}{2}$ as much as the smallest scoop holds

23. a) Write a subtraction statement involving two negative fractions or negative mixed numbers so that the difference is $-\frac{4}{3}$.

b) Share your statement with a classmate.

Extend

24. Can the sum of two rational numbers be less than both of the rational numbers? Explain using examples in fraction form.

25. The following expression has a value of 1.

$$\left[-\frac{1}{2} + \left(-\frac{1}{2}\right)\right] \div \left[-\frac{1}{2} + \left(-\frac{1}{2}\right)\right]$$

Use $-\frac{1}{2}$ four times to write expressions with each of the following values.

a) -1 **b)** 0

c) $\frac{1}{4}$ **d)** 4

e) $-\frac{3}{4}$ **f)** $-1\frac{1}{2}$

26. Multiplying a fraction by $-\frac{1}{2}$, then adding $\frac{3}{4}$, and then dividing by $-\frac{1}{4}$ gave an answer of $-3\frac{3}{4}$. What was the original fraction?

27. For what values of x does $x - \frac{1}{x} = 1\frac{1}{2}$?

Math Link

Play this game with a partner or in a small group. You will need a deck of playing cards.
- Remove the jokers, face cards, and 10s from the deck.
- Red cards represent positive integers. Black cards represent negative integers. Aces represent 1 or −1.
- In each round, the dealer shuffles the cards and deals four cards to each player.
- Use your four cards to make two fractions with a product that is as far from zero as possible.
- In each round, the player with the product that is furthest from zero wins two points. If there is a tie, each tied player wins a point.
- The winner is the first player with ten points. If two or more players reach ten points in the same round, keep playing until one player is in the lead by at least two points.

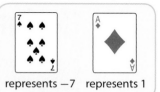

represents −7   represents 1

represent −7, 1, −3, and 8
An expression for the product furthest from zero is
$$\frac{-7}{1} \times \frac{8}{-3} \quad \text{or} \quad \frac{8}{-3} \times \frac{-7}{1} \quad \text{or} \quad \frac{8}{1} \times \frac{-7}{-3} \quad \text{or} \quad \frac{-7}{-3} \times \frac{8}{1}$$

⊙ History Link

Fractions in Ancient Egypt

A fraction with a numerator of 1, such as $\frac{1}{4}$, is called a *unit fraction*. In ancient Egypt, fractions that were not unit fractions were expressed as sums of unit fractions. For example, $\frac{5}{6}$ was expressed as $\frac{1}{2} + \frac{1}{3}$.

1. Express each of the following as the sum of two unit fractions.

   a) $\frac{3}{10}$ **b)** $\frac{9}{14}$ **c)** $\frac{9}{20}$ **d)** $\frac{11}{18}$

2. Describe any strategies that helped you to complete #1.

> ⊙ **Did You Know?**
>
> The Eye of Horus as shown below was used by ancient Egyptians to represent fractions. Each part of the Eye of Horus was a unit fraction. Egyptians believed that the parts had a combined value of 1.

Repetition was not allowed in the Egyptian system. Therefore, $\frac{2}{5}$ was not expressed as $\frac{1}{5} + \frac{1}{5}$ but could be expressed as $\frac{1}{15} + \frac{1}{3}$.

3. Express each of the following as the sum of two unit fractions without using any fraction more than once.

   a) $\frac{2}{7}$ **b)** $\frac{2}{9}$ **c)** $\frac{2}{11}$

4. Express each of the following as the sum of three unit fractions without using any fraction more than once.

   a) $\frac{7}{8}$ **b)** $\frac{11}{24}$ **c)** $\frac{3}{4}$

Determining Square Roots of Rational Numbers

Focus on...

After this lesson, you will be able to…

- determine the square root of a perfect square rational number
- determine an approximate square root of a non-perfect square rational number

The Great Pyramid of Giza is the largest of the ancient pyramids in Egypt. The pyramid has a square base with a side length between 230 m and 231 m. Estimate how the dimensions of the base compare with the dimensions of a football field.

Materials
- grid paper

Literacy Link

When the *square root* of a given number is multiplied by itself, the product is the given number. For example, the square root of 9 is 3, because $3 \times 3 = 9$. A square root is represented by the symbol $\sqrt{}$, for example, $\sqrt{9} = 3$.

Explore Square Roots of Rational Numbers

1. a) Explain how the diagram represents $\sqrt{16}$.

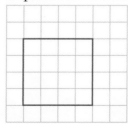

b) Draw a diagram that represents $\sqrt{25}$.

c) Explain how you could use the following diagram to identify a rational number with a square root that is between 4 and 5.

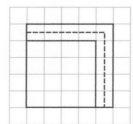

d) Describe another strategy you could use to complete part c).

2. a) Explain how the shading on the hundred grid represents $\sqrt{0.25}$.

b) Draw a diagram that represents $\sqrt{0.36}$.

c) Explain how you could use the following diagram to identify a rational number with a square root that is between 0.5 and 0.6.

d) Describe another strategy you could use to complete part c).

Reflect and Check

3. Compare your strategies from #1d) and #2d) with a classmate's strategies. How are they similar and different?

4. Use the dimensions provided in the opening paragraph of this section to estimate the base area of the Great Pyramid of Giza. Explain your method.

Did You Know?

The Great Pyramid of Giza is on the outskirts of Cairo. The pyramid is over 4500 years old. It was built as a tomb for Khufu, a king of ancient Egypt. Tens of thousands of workers took at least ten years to build the pyramid from over two million stone blocks.

Link the Ideas

Example 1: Determine a Rational Number From Its Square Root

A square trampoline has a side length of 2.6 m. Estimate and calculate the area of the trampoline.

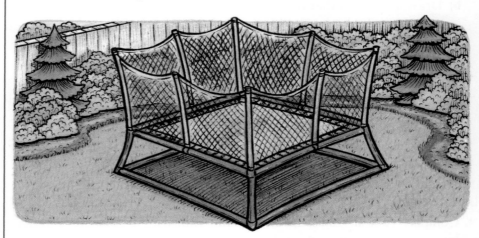

Solution

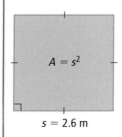

$A = s^2$

$s = 2.6$ m

Estimate.

$2^2 = 4$ $\qquad 3^2 = 9$

So, 2.6^2 is between 4 and 9.

2.6 is closer to 3 than to 2, so $2.6^2 \approx 7$.

An estimate for the area of the trampoline is 7 m².

Calculate.

$2.6^2 = 6.76$ $\quad$ **C 2.6 x^2** 6.76

The area of a trampoline with a side length of 2.6 m is 6.76 m².

Show You Know

Estimate and calculate the area of a square photo with a side length of 7.1 cm.

Example 2: Determine Whether a Rational Number Is a Perfect Square

Determine whether each of the following numbers is a perfect square.

a) $\dfrac{25}{49}$ **b)** 0.4

Literacy Link

A *perfect square* can be expressed as the product of two equal rational factors. The decimal 0.25 is a perfect square because it can be expressed as 0.5 × 0.5. The fraction $\dfrac{9}{16}$ is a perfect square because it can be expressed as $\dfrac{3}{4} \times \dfrac{3}{4}$.

> *Solution*

a) In $\dfrac{25}{49}$, both the numerator and denominator are perfect squares.

> How do you know that 25 and 49 are perfect squares?

$\dfrac{25}{49}$ can be expressed as the product of two equal rational factors, $\dfrac{5}{7} \times \dfrac{5}{7}$.

So, $\dfrac{25}{49}$ is a perfect square.

> How does this diagram represent the situation?

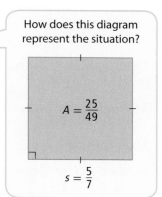

$A = \dfrac{25}{49}$

$s = \dfrac{5}{7}$

b) 0.4 can be expressed in fraction form as $\dfrac{4}{10}$.

The numerator, 4, is a perfect square.
The denominator, 10, is not a perfect square.

$\dfrac{4}{10}$ cannot be expressed as the product of two equal rational factors.

> How do you know that 10 is not a perfect square?

So, 0.4 is not a perfect square.

Show You Know

Is each of the following numbers a perfect square? Explain.

a) $\dfrac{121}{64}$ **b)** 1.2 **c)** 0.09

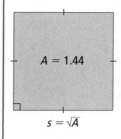

Literacy Link

Square Roots of Perfect Squares

0.25 can be expressed as 0.5 × 0.5.

Therefore, $\sqrt{0.25} = 0.5$.

$\frac{9}{16}$ can be expressed as $\frac{3}{4} \times \frac{3}{4}$.

Therefore, $\sqrt{\frac{9}{16}} = \frac{3}{4}$.

Strategies

Draw a Diagram

Example 3: Determine the Square Root of a Perfect Square

Evaluate $\sqrt{1.44}$.

Solution

$$A = 1.44$$

$$s = \sqrt{A}$$

Determine the positive number that, when multiplied by itself, results in a product of 1.44.

Method 1: Use Inspection
$1.2 \times 1.2 = 1.44$
So, $\sqrt{1.44} = 1.2$.

Since $12 \times 12 = 144$, then $1.2 \times 1.2 = 1.44$.

Method 2: Use Guess and Check
$1.1 \times 1.1 = 1.21$ Too low
$1.3 \times 1.3 = 1.69$ Too high
$1.2 \times 1.2 = 1.44$ Correct!
So, $\sqrt{1.44} = 1.2$.

Method 3: Use Fraction Form
$1.44 = \frac{144}{100}$
$\qquad = \frac{12}{10} \times \frac{12}{10}$
$\qquad = 1.2 \times 1.2$
So, $\sqrt{1.44} = 1.2$.

Check: C 1.44 √x 1.2

Tech Link

Check the key sequence for determining square roots on your calculator. Make sure that you can obtain the correct answer for Example 3.

Show You Know

Evaluate.

a) $\sqrt{2.25}$

b) $\sqrt{0.16}$

Example 4: Determine a Square Root of a Non-Perfect Square

a) Estimate $\sqrt{0.73}$.
b) Calculate $\sqrt{0.73}$, to the nearest thousandth.

Solution

a) Estimate.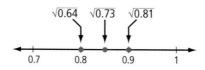

You can use the square root of a
perfect square on each side of $\sqrt{0.73}$.
$\sqrt{0.73}$ is about halfway
between $\sqrt{0.64}$ and $\sqrt{0.81}$.

One reasonable estimate for $\sqrt{0.73}$ might be about halfway
between 0.8 and 0.9, which is about 0.85.

$$\sqrt{0.73} \approx 0.85$$

b) Calculate.

$\boxed{\text{C}}\ 0.73\ \boxed{\sqrt{x}}\ 0.854400375$

So, $\sqrt{0.73} \approx 0.854$,
to the nearest thousandth.

> A calculator usually gives a closer
> approximation than an estimate does.
> Why is the value that the calculator
> shows only an approximation?

Check:
Use the inverse operation, which is squaring.
$0.854^2 = 0.729\ 316$
0.854^2 is close to 0.73.

Show You Know

a) Estimate $\sqrt{0.34}$.
b) Calculate $\sqrt{0.34}$, to the nearest thousandth.

---

non-perfect square

- a rational number that
  cannot be expressed as
  the product of two
  equal rational factors
- for example, you
  cannot multiply any
  rational number by
  itself and get an answer
  of 3, 5, 1.5, or $\frac{7}{8}$

Strategies

Draw a Diagram

Did You Know?

The square root of a
non-perfect square
has certain properties:

- It is a non-repeating,
  non-terminating
  decimal.
  For example, $\sqrt{5} =$
  $2.236\ 067\ 978\ldots$.
- Its decimal value is
  approximate, not
  exact.

Key Ideas

- If the side length of a square
  models a number, the area of
  the square models the square
  of the number.

$A = s^2$

- If the area of a square
  models a number, the
  side length of the square
  models the square root
  of the number.

A

$s = \sqrt{A}$

- A perfect square can be expressed as the
  product of two equal rational factors.

  $3.61 = 1.9 \times 1.9$

  $\frac{1}{4} = \frac{1}{2} \times \frac{1}{2}$

- The square root of a perfect square can
  be determined exactly.

  $\sqrt{2.56} = 1.6$

  $\sqrt{\frac{4}{9}} = \frac{2}{3}$

- The square root of a non-perfect square
  determined using a calculator is an
  approximation.

  $\sqrt{1.65} \approx 1.284\ 523\ 258$

Check Your Understanding

Communicate the Ideas

1. Max said that the square root of 6.4 is 3.2. Lynda claimed that the square root of 6.4 is 0.8. Jamila estimated that the square root of 6.4 should be about 2.5.

    a) Who is correct?

    b) What mistakes did the other two students make?

2. Without calculating any square roots, identify the square roots that have values between 4.5 and 5.5. Explain your reasoning.

    $\sqrt{21.3}$ $\sqrt{20.1}$ $\sqrt{31.7}$ $\sqrt{27.9}$ $\sqrt{30.5}$ $\sqrt{25.4}$ $\sqrt{30.2}$

3. Since $\sqrt{9}$ is less than 9, and $\sqrt{1.44}$ is less than 1.44, André predicted that $\sqrt{0.0625}$ would be less than 0.0625. Do you agree with his prediction? Explain.

4. a) Determine $\sqrt{2}$ using a scientific calculator. Record all of the digits that the calculator displays.

    b) Enter the decimal value of $\sqrt{2}$ from part a) into the calculator and square the value. Record the result.

    c) In part a), did the calculator display the exact value of $\sqrt{2}$? Explain how you know.

Practise

5. Use the diagram to identify a rational number with a square root between 3 and 4.

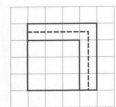

6. Identify a rational number with a square root between 0.7 and 0.8.

For help with #7 and #8, refer to Example 1 on page 74.

7. Estimate and calculate the number that has the given square root.

    a) 3.1   b) 12.5

    c) 0.62   d) 0.29

8. Estimate and calculate the area of each square, given its side length.

    a) 4.3 cm   b) 0.035 km

For help with #9 and #10, refer to Example 2 on page 75.

9. Is each of the following rational numbers a perfect square? Explain.

    a) $\dfrac{1}{16}$ b) $\dfrac{5}{9}$

    c) 0.36   d) 0.9

10. Determine whether each rational number is a perfect square.

    a) $\dfrac{7}{12}$ b) $\dfrac{100}{49}$

    c) 0.1   d) 0.01

For help with #11 and #12, refer to Example 3 on page 76.

11. Evaluate.

a) $\sqrt{324}$ b) $\sqrt{2.89}$

c) $\sqrt{0.0225}$ d) $\sqrt{2025}$

12. Calculate the side length of each square from its area.

a) 169 m²   b) 0.16 mm²

For help with #13 and #14, refer to Example 4 on page 77.

13. Estimate each square root. Then, calculate it to the specified number of decimal places.

a) $\sqrt{39}$, to the nearest tenth

b) $\sqrt{4.5}$, to the nearest hundredth

c) $\sqrt{0.87}$, to the nearest thousandth

d) $\sqrt{0.022}$, to the nearest thousandth

14. Given the area of each square, determine its side length. Express your answer to the nearest hundredth of a unit.

a) 0.85 m²   b) 60 cm²

Apply

15. Kai needs to replace the strip of laminate that is glued to the vertical faces on a square tabletop. The tabletop has an area of 1.69 m². What length of laminate does she need?

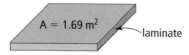

A = 1.69 m²   laminate

16. a) The label on a 1-L can of paint states that the paint will cover an area of 10 m². What is the side length of the largest square area that the paint will cover? Express your answer to the nearest hundredth of a metre.

b) What is the side length of the largest square area that a 3.79-L can of the same paint will cover? Express your answer to the nearest hundredth of a metre.

c) Nadia is applying two coats of the paint to an area that is 4.6 m by 4.6 m. How much paint will she use if she applies the same amount of paint for each coat? Express your answer to the nearest tenth of a litre.

17. Some parks contain fenced gardens. Suppose that it costs $80 to build each metre of fence, including materials and labour.

a) How much does it cost to enclose a square with an area of 120 m²? Express your answer to the nearest dollar.

b) Predict whether the total cost of enclosing two squares with an area of 60 m² each is the same as your answer to part a).

c) Test your prediction from part b) and describe your findings.

18. A frame measures 30 cm by 20 cm. Can you mount a square picture with an area of 500 cm² in the frame? Explain.

19. A square picture with an area of 100 cm² is mounted on a square piece of matting. The matting has 2.5 times the area of the picture. If the picture is centred on the matting, what width of matting is visible around the outside of the picture? Give your answer to the nearest tenth of a centimetre.

20. Leon's rectangular living room is 8.2 m by 4.5 m. A square rug covers $\frac{2}{5}$ of the area of the floor. What is the side length of the rug, to the nearest tenth of a metre?

21. A baseball diamond is a square area of about 750 m². What is the distance from first to second base. Give your answer to the nearest tenth of a metre.

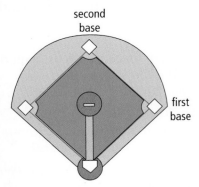

second
base

first
base

22. The hypotenuse of an isosceles right triangle has a length of 20 cm. What is the length of each leg of the triangle? Provide your answer to the nearest tenth of a centimetre.

23. A rectangular floor that measures 3 m by 2 m is covered by 384 square tiles. Determine the side length of each tile, in centimetres. State any assumptions you make.

24. The distance, d, in kilometres, that a person can see across the ocean to the horizon is given by the formula $d = \sqrt{12.74 \times h}$. In the formula h is the height, in metres, of the person's eyes above the water. Calculate the distance that each of the following people can see across the ocean to the horizon. Express each answer to the nearest tenth of a kilometre.

a) Adèle is sitting on a lifeguard station at the edge of the ocean. Her eyes are 4.1 m above the water.

b) Brian is standing at the water's edge. His eyes are 165 cm above the water.

c) Yvonne is the pilot of an aircraft flying 5 km above the coastline.

Literacy Link

Perform operations under a square root symbol before taking the square root. For example, $\sqrt{9 \times 4} = \sqrt{36}$ or 6.

25. What is the length of the longest line segment you can draw on a sheet of paper that is 27.9 cm by 21.6 cm? Express your answer to the nearest tenth of a centimetre.

26. A bag of fertilizer will cover an area of 200 m². Determine the dimensions of a square that $\frac{3}{4}$ of a bag of fertilizer will cover. Express your answer to the nearest tenth of a metre.

27. The surface area of a cube is 100 cm². Determine the edge length of the cube, to the nearest tenth of a centimetre.

28. The period, t, in seconds, of a pendulum is the time it takes for a complete swing back and forth. The period can be calculated from the length, l, in metres, of the pendulum using the formula $t = \sqrt{4l}$. Determine the period of a pendulum with each of the following lengths. Express each answer to the nearest hundredth of a second.

a) 1.6 m   **b)** 2.5 m   **c)** 50 cm

29. The speed of sound in air, s, in metres per second, is related to the temperature, t, in degrees Celsius, by the formula $s = \sqrt{401(273 + t)}$. How much greater is the speed of sound on a day when the temperature is 30 °C than on a day when the temperature is −20 °C? Express your answer to the nearest metre per second.

30. A square field has an area of 1000 m². Laura wants to walk from one corner of the field to the opposite corner. If she walks at 1.5 m/s, how much time can she save by walking diagonally instead of walking along two adjacent sides? Express your answer to the nearest tenth of a second.

31. The area of a triangle can be determined using Heron's formula, which requires the side lengths of the triangle. Heron's formula is $A = \sqrt{s(s-a)(s-b)(s-c)}$. In the formula A is the area; a, b, and c are the side lengths; and s is half the perimeter or $\dfrac{a+b+c}{2}$. Determine the area of each triangle with the following side lengths. Express each area to the nearest tenth of a square centimetre.

a) 15 cm, 12 cm, 10 cm

b) 9.3 cm, 11.4 cm, 7.5 cm

History Link

Heron's formula was determined by a Greek mathematician and inventor named Heron (or Hero) of Alexandria. Historians believe that he lived in the first century of the Common Era, but little is known of his life. Heron wrote about geometry and about his inventions, which included machines driven by water, steam, and compressed air.

WWW Web Link

For more information about Heron of Alexandria, go to www.mathlinks9.ca and follow the links.

Extend

32. This shape is made from eight congruent squares. The total area of the shape is 52 cm². What is its perimeter, to the nearest centimetre?

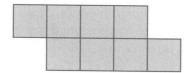

33. A square has an area of 32 cm². What is the area of the largest circle that will fit inside it? Express your answer to the nearest tenth of a square centimetre.

34. Use the formula $r = \sqrt{\dfrac{A}{\pi}}$ to determine the radius of a circular garden with an area of 40 m². Express your answer to the nearest tenth of a metre.

35. The width of a rectangle is $\dfrac{1}{3}$ its length. The area of the rectangle is 9.72 cm². What are the dimensions of the rectangle?

36. Determine $\sqrt{\sqrt{\sqrt{65\ 536}}}$.

Math Link

Sudoku is a Japanese logic puzzle completed on a 9-by-9 square grid. The grid includes nine 3-by-3 sections.

Answer each of the following questions about the sudoku grid in two different ways. Compare your solutions with your classmates' solutions.

a) If the smallest squares on the grid have a side length of 1.1 cm, what is the area of the whole grid?

b) If the whole grid has an area of 182.25 cm², what are the dimensions of each 3 by 3 section?

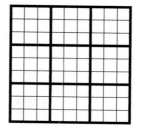

WWW Web Link

To learn more about sudoku puzzles, go to www.mathlinks9.ca and follow the links.

Chapter 2 Review

For #1 to #4, use the clues to unscramble the letters.

1. S T I S P O P O E

two numbers represented by points that are the same distance in opposite directions from zero on a number line

2. T A L I N A R O   B R U N M E

the quotient of two integers, where the divisor is not zero (2 words)

3. C R E F P E T   Q U E S A R

the product of two equal rational factors (2 words)

4. F R E N C E N T O P   A Q U E R S

a rational number that cannot be expressed as the product of two equal rational factors (2 words, 1 hyphenated)

2.1 Comparing and Ordering Rational Numbers, pages 46–54

5. Which of the following rational numbers cannot be expressed as an integer?

$$\frac{24}{3} \quad \frac{3}{24} \quad \frac{-8}{2} \quad \frac{-10}{-6} \quad -\frac{6}{4}$$

$$-\left(\frac{-21}{-7}\right) \quad \frac{82}{-12} \quad -\left(\frac{-225}{15}\right)$$

6. Replace each ■ with >, <, or = to make each statement true.

a) $\frac{-9}{6}$ ■ $\frac{3}{-2}$

b) -0.86 ■ -0.84

c) $-\frac{3}{5}$ ■ $-0.\overline{6}$

d) $-1\frac{3}{10}$ ■ $-\left(\frac{-13}{-10}\right)$

e) $-\frac{8}{12}$ ■ $-\frac{11}{15}$

f) $-2\frac{5}{6}$ ■ $-2\frac{7}{8}$

7. Axel, Bree, and Caitlin were comparing $-1\frac{1}{2}$ and $-1\frac{1}{4}$.

a) Axel first wrote the two mixed numbers as improper fractions. Describe the rest of his method.

b) Bree first wrote each mixed number as a decimal. Describe the rest of her method.

c) Caitlin first ignored the integers and wrote $-\frac{1}{2}$ and $-\frac{1}{4}$ with a common denominator. Describe the rest of her method.

d) Which method do you prefer? Explain.

8. Write two fractions in lowest terms between 0 and -1 with 5 as the numerator.

2.2 Problem Solving With Rational Numbers in Decimal Form, pages 55–62

9. Calculate.

a) $-5.68 + 4.73$

b) $-0.85 - (-2.34)$

c) $1.8(-4.5)$

d) $-3.77 \div (-2.9)$

10. Evaluate. Express your answer to the nearest tenth, if necessary.

a) $5.3 \div (-8.4)$

b) $-0.25 \div (-0.031)$

c) $-5.3 + 2.4[7.8 + (-8.3)]$

d) $4.2 - 5.6 \div (-2.8) - 0.9$

11. One evening in Dauphin, Manitoba, the temperature decreased from 2.4 °C to -3.2 °C in 3.5 h. What was the average rate of change in the temperature?

12. Over a four-year period, a company lost an average of $1.2 million per year. The company's total losses by the end of five years were $3.5 million. What was the company's profit or loss in the fifth year?

2.3 Problem Solving With Rational Numbers in Fraction Form, pages 63–71

13. Add or subtract.

a) $\dfrac{2}{3} - \dfrac{4}{5}$

b) $-\dfrac{3}{8} + \left(-\dfrac{3}{4}\right)$

c) $-3\dfrac{3}{5} + 1\dfrac{7}{10}$

d) $2\dfrac{1}{3} - \left(-2\dfrac{1}{4}\right)$

14. Multiply or divide.

a) $-\dfrac{1}{2}\left(-\dfrac{8}{9}\right)$

b) $-\dfrac{5}{6} \div \dfrac{7}{8}$

c) $2\dfrac{3}{4} \times \left(-4\dfrac{2}{3}\right)$

d) $-4\dfrac{7}{8} \div \left(-2\dfrac{3}{4}\right)$

15. Without doing any calculations, state how the values of the following two quotients compare. Explain your reasoning.

$$96\dfrac{7}{8} \div 7\dfrac{3}{4} \qquad -96\dfrac{7}{8} \div \left(-7\dfrac{3}{4}\right)$$

16. How many hours are there in $2\dfrac{1}{2}$ weeks?

17. The area of Manitoba is about $1\dfrac{1}{5}$ times the total area of the four Atlantic provinces. The area of Yukon Territory is about $\dfrac{3}{4}$ the area of Manitoba. Express the area of Yukon Territory as a fraction of the total area of the Atlantic provinces.

2.4 Determining Square Roots of Rational Numbers, pages 72–81

18. Determine whether each rational number is a perfect square. Explain your reasoning.

a) $\dfrac{64}{121}$ b) $\dfrac{7}{4}$ c) 0.49   d) 1.6

19. Estimate $\sqrt{220}$ to one decimal place. Describe your method.

20. Determine the number with a square root of 0.15.

21. Determine.

a) $\sqrt{12.96}$

b) $\sqrt{0.05}$, to the nearest thousandth

22. In what situation is each of the following statements true? Provide an example to support each answer.

a) The square root of a number is less than the number.

b) The square root of a number is greater than the number.

23. A hundred grid has an area of 225 cm².

$A = 225 \text{ cm}^2$

a) What is the side length of each small square on the grid? Solve this problem in two ways.

b) What is the length of the diagonal of the whole grid? Express your answer to the nearest tenth of a centimetre.

24. Suppose a 1-L can of paint covers 11 m².

a) How many cans of paint would you need to paint a ceiling that is 5.2 m by 5.2 m? Show your work.

b) Determine the maximum dimensions of a square ceiling you could paint with 4 L of paint. Express your answer to the nearest tenth of a metre.

25. Close to the surface of the moon, the time a dropped object takes to reach the surface can be determined using the formula $t = \sqrt{\dfrac{h}{0.81}}$. The time, t, is in seconds, and the height, h, is in metres. If an object is dropped from a height of 200 m, how long does it take to reach the surface of the moon? Express your answer to the nearest tenth of a second.

Chapter 2 Practice Test

For #1 to #7, select the best answer.

1. Which fraction does not equal $\frac{4}{-6}$?

A $-\left(\frac{-10}{15}\right)$
B $-\frac{8}{12}$

C $\frac{6}{-9}$
D $-\left(\frac{-2}{-3}\right)$

2. Which value is greater than $-1\frac{5}{6}$?

A $-1.\overline{8}$
B $-1\frac{7}{8}$

C $-1.8\overline{3}$
D $-1\frac{4}{5}$

3. Which fraction is between -0.34 and -0.36?

A $-\frac{17}{50}$
B $-\frac{9}{25}$

C $-\frac{7}{20}$
D $\frac{35}{100}$

4. Which value equals $-3.78 - (-2.95)$?

A -6.73
B -0.83

C 0.83
D 6.73

5. Which expression does not equal $\frac{3}{5} \times \left(-\frac{6}{7}\right)$?

A $-\frac{3}{7} \times \frac{6}{5}$
B $\frac{3}{-5} \times \frac{6}{7}$

C $\frac{-3}{5} \times \left(\frac{-6}{-7}\right)$
D $\frac{-3}{-5} \times \frac{6}{7}$

6. Which value is the best estimate for $\sqrt{1.6}$?

A 2.6
B 1.3

C 0.8
D 0.4

7. Which rational number is a non-perfect square?

A $\frac{1}{25}$
B 0.16

C 0.9
D $\frac{121}{4}$

Complete the statements in #8 and #9.

8. A square has an area of 1.44 m². The perimeter of the square is ■ m.

9. On a number line, you would find $-3\frac{5}{11}$ to the ■ of -3.4545.

Short Answer

10. Explain why any integer is a rational number.

11. Arrange the following in descending order.

$$-1.\overline{2} \quad -1.2 \quad \frac{19}{20} \quad \frac{9}{10} \quad \frac{9}{-10} \quad 0.94$$

12. Identify the fractions in lowest terms that are between -2 and -3 and that have 6 as the denominator.

13. Calculate.

a) $1\frac{4}{5} - 2\frac{2}{3}$
b) $-3.21 + 1.84$

c) $\frac{5}{8} \div \left(-\frac{11}{12}\right)$
d) $-2\frac{5}{7}\left(-3\frac{1}{2}\right)$

e) $-3.66 \div (-1.5)$
f) $-\frac{5}{6} + \left(-\frac{1}{12}\right)$

14. Canada's Donovan Bailey won the gold medal in the 100-m sprint at the Summer Olympics in Atlanta in a time of 9.84 s. He beat the second-place finisher, Frankie Fredericks of Namibia, by $\frac{5}{100}$ of a second.

What was Fredericks's time?

15. What is the average of a rational number and its opposite? Explain using examples in decimal or fraction form.

16. Is 31.36 a perfect square? Explain how you know.

17. Determine.
   a) the number with a square root of 6.1
   b) $\sqrt{0.1369}$
   c) $\sqrt{7}$, to the nearest hundredth

Extended Response

18. This shape is made from ten congruent squares.

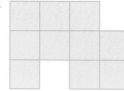

   a) If the perimeter of the shape is 40 cm, what is its area?
   b) If the area of the shape is 75 cm², what is its perimeter, to the nearest tenth of a centimetre?

19. Ron buys 75 shares in a car company. A year later, he sells the shares for $15.64 each. The result is a loss of $260.25. How much did Ron pay for each share? State any assumptions you make.

20. A Canadian quarter is made from nickel, copper, and steel. The quarter is $\frac{11}{500}$ nickel, $\frac{19}{500}$ copper, and $\frac{47}{50}$ steel.
   a) Predict the sum of the three fractions. Justify your prediction.
   b) Test your prediction by calculating the sum of the three fractions.
   c) How many times as great is the mass of the steel as the combined mass of the nickel and the copper?
   d) The mass of a Canadian quarter is 4.4 g. In a roll of 40 quarters, how much greater is the mass of copper than the mass of nickel?

Math Link: Wrap It Up!

Design a game that can be played with a partner or in a small group. The game must include
- calculations that involve at least two operations and both positive and negative rational numbers
- dice, coins, playing cards, or other materials to generate numbers

a) Describe the rules of the game, including how the winner is decided.

b) Give examples of the calculations that the game involves.

c) Play the game with a partner or in a small group.

d) Suggest alternative rules for the game. For example, you might suggest modifications to the game, such as including different operations.

Challenges

Reaction Time

An important skill drivers must have is the ability to react to obstacles that may suddenly appear in their path. You be the driver! What types of obstacles might you encounter? How quickly do you think you could react to an obstacle in the road?

You are going to calculate your reaction time.

1. Work with a partner to do the following experiment.
   - Your partner will hold a 30-cm ruler vertically in front of you, with the zero mark at the bottom.
   - Position your thumb and index finger on each side of the ruler so that the zero mark can be seen just above your thumb. Neither your thumb nor your finger should touch the ruler.
   - Your partner will drop the ruler without warning. Catch the ruler as quickly as you can by closing your thumb and finger.
   - Read the measurement above your thumb to the nearest tenth of a centimetre. This is your reaction distance.
   - Perform this procedure five more times, recording each distance.
   - Switch roles to determine your partner's five reaction distances.

   Calculate your average reaction distance.

2. The formula $d = \frac{1}{2}gt^2$ can be used to calculate reaction time, where
   - d is the reaction distance, in metres
   - g is the acceleration due to gravity, which is 9.8 m/s^2
   - t is time, in seconds

   Calculate your average reaction time. Show your reasoning.

Materials
- 30-cm ruler

3. a) Imagine you are driving a car in a residential area and a ball rolls onto the road in front of you. You move your foot toward the brake. Based on the reaction time you calculated in #2, if you are driving at 40 km/h, how far will the car travel before you step down on the brake?

b) What distance would you have travelled before stepping down on the brake if your original speed was 100 km/h?

c) What other factors might influence your reaction time and your stopping distance? Share your ideas with your classmates.

Going Up?

You be an engineer! Your job is to design an elevator. It will work alongside an existing escalator to move people between levels at a local sports and entertainment arena.

1. The escalator that is already in place can move 30 people per minute from the main level to the upper level. Based on this information, how long would it take to use the escalator to move 100 people from the main level to the upper level?

2. The design of an elevator is based on the available building space, the load capacity, and the need to allow for people's personal space. An average person represents a load of 67 kg, and needs a radius of 26 cm for personal space. The area of the floor space for the elevator you are designing will be 3.75 m².

a) To maximize the number of people that can be carried, what dimensions would you recommend for the elevator?

b) Why did you choose these dimensions?

c) What is the maximum number of people that your elevator could carry?

d) What would be its load capacity? Justify your answer.

3. a) If the average time the elevator takes to move between the main level and the upper level is 8 s, how many people could move from the main level to the upper level in 1 min?

b) What assumptions did you make?

4. There is a concert tonight. You want to minimize the time for moving 2000 concert goers from the main level to the upper level.

a) What recommendations would you have for the staff who are directing people to the escalator and elevator? Justify your thinking.

b) What assumptions did you make?

Powers and Exponents

Thrill-seekers around the world enjoy the rush of extreme sports like whitewater rafting and kayaking, kitesurfing, hang gliding, rock climbing, heli-skiing, bungee jumping, and sky diving. In some of these sports, the experience involves a free fall. During each second of a free fall, the distance a person falls increases. A formula that approximates the distance fallen is $d = 4.9t^2$, where d is the total distance, in metres, and t is the time, in seconds. In the formula, 2 is an exponent. What does this exponent represent? In what other formulas have you seen exponents?

In this chapter, you will explore the use of exponents in mathematical expressions.

What You Will Learn

- to use powers to represent repeated multiplication
- to solve problems involving powers

Key Words

power	base
exponent	exponential form
coefficient	

🔗 Literacy Link

A spider map can help you understand and connect new terms and concepts. It is designed to be used throughout the chapter.

Create a spider map in your math journal or notebook. As you work through the chapter, complete the map.

- After completing section 3.1, use the upper left leg to identify the parts of a power and the different forms in which powers can be expressed.

- After completing section 3.2, use the upper right leg to list and provide examples of the exponent laws.

- After completing section 3.3, use the lower left leg to list all rules and examples associated with the order of operations involving powers.

- After completing section 3.4, use the lower right leg to list rules and examples related to solving problems involving powers.

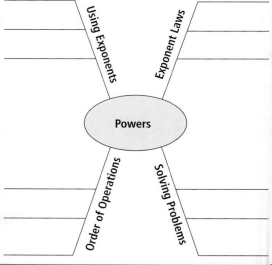

Making the Foldable

Materials
- sheet of 11 × 17 paper
- six sheets of 8.5 × 11 paper
- scissors
- ruler
- stapler

Step 1

Fold the long side of a sheet of 11 × 17 paper in half. Pinch it at the midpoint. Fold the outer edges of the paper to meet at the midpoint. Label it as shown.

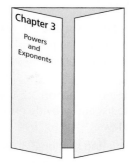

Step 2

Fold the short side of a sheet of 8.5 × 11 paper in half. Fold in four the opposite way. Make three cuts as shown through one thickness of paper, forming a four-tab book. Label the tabs as shown.

Order of Operations: Brackets

Exponents

Multiply and Divide

Add and Subtract

Step 3

Fold the short side of a sheet of 8.5 × 11 paper in half. Fold in three the opposite way. Make two cuts as shown through one thickness of paper, forming a three-tab book. Label the tabs as shown.

Repeated Multiplication Form

Exponential Form

Standard Form

Step 4

Stack four sheets of 8.5 × 11 paper so that the bottom edges are 2.5 cm apart. Fold the top edge of the sheets and align the edges so that all tabs are the same size. Staple along the fold. Label as shown.

Exponent Laws and Key Words

$(a^m)(a^n) = a^{m + n}$

$a^m \div a^n = a^{m - n}, m > n$

$(a^m)^n = a^{mn}$

$(ab)^m = a^m b^m$

$\left(\frac{a}{b}\right)^n = \frac{a^n}{b^n}, b \neq 0$

$a^0 = 1, a \neq 0$

Key Words

Step 5

Staple the three booklets you made into the Foldable from Step 1 as shown.

Repeated Multiplication Form

Exponential Form

Standard Form

Exponent Laws and Key Words

$(a^m)(a^n) = a^{m + n}$

$a^m \div a^n = a^{m - n}, m > n$

$(a^m)^n = a^{mn}$

$(ab)^m = a^m b^m$

$\left(\frac{a}{b}\right)^n = \frac{a^n}{b^n}, b \neq 0$

$a^0 = 1, a \neq 0$

Key Words

Order of Operations: Brackets

Exponents

Multiply and Divide

Add and Subtract

Using the Foldable

As you work through the chapter, write the Key Words beneath the tab in the centre panel, and provide definitions and examples. Beneath the remaining tabs in the centre, and the tabs in the left and right panels, provide examples, show work, and record key concepts.

On the front of the right flap of the Foldable, record ideas for the Math Link: Wrap It Up! On the back of the Foldable, make notes under the heading What I Need to Work On. Check off each item as you deal with it.

Math Link

Mobile Design

In 1931, Alexander Calder, a mechanical engineer and artist, created intricate sculptures that moved with the air currents of a room. These sculptures are called *mobiles*. Mobiles are known for their bright colours, variety of shapes, and interesting movements. The shapes used are often geometric shapes. Think about some mobiles you have seen. What types of geometric shapes did they contain?

One important consideration when creating a mobile is balance. The balance of a mobile is affected by the surface area and volume of the shapes used. Work with a partner to answer the following questions.

1. What is the name of each geometric shape shown?

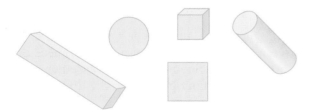

2. How could you determine the area of a square?

3. How could you determine the area and the circumference of a circle?

4. How could you determine the surface area of each three-dimensional shape?

5. How could you determine the volume of each three-dimensional shape?

6. How are the methods you suggested in #2 to #5 similar? How are they different?

7. Which shapes would you use to put on a mobile? Why did you choose these shapes?

In this chapter, you will determine the links between geometric shapes and powers by exploring mobile designs. At the end of this chapter, you will design and build a mobile using shapes of your choice.

WWW Web Link

To learn more about mobiles and how to create them, go to www.mathlinks9.ca and follow the links.

Using Exponents to Describe Numbers

Focus on...

After this lesson, you will be able to...
- represent repeated multiplication with exponents
- describe how powers represent repeated multiplication

In the story *Alice in Wonderland*, Alice could change her size dramatically by eating cake. If she needed to triple her height, she would eat a piece of cake. Imagine that she is currently 1 m tall. She needs to increase her height to 700 m in order to see over a hill. How many pieces of cake do you think she will need to eat?

Materials
- calculator

Explore Repeated Multiplication

1. Create a table that shows how Alice's height changes after eating one, two, and three pieces of cake. Describe any patterns you see in the table.

2. a) How many pieces of cake does Alice need to eat to become at least 700 m tall? Show how you arrived at your answer.
   b) What is Alice's height after eating the number of pieces of cake in part a)?
   c) How many factors of 3 do you need to multiply to obtain your answer to part b)?

3. Explore how you could use a calculator to determine Alice's height after eating eight pieces of cake. Share your method(s) with your classmates. Record the methods that work for your calculator.

Reflect and Check

4. a) The expression 3^2 can be used to represent Alice's height after eating two pieces of cake. What does this expression mean in terms of factors of 3?

  b) How could you represent $3 \times 3 \times 3 \times 3 \times 3$ as a **power**? Identify the **base** and **exponent**.

5. What is Alice's height after eating ten pieces of cake?

Link the Ideas

Example 1: Write and Evaluate Powers

a) Write $2 \times 2 \times 2 \times 2 \times 2$ in **exponential form**.
b) Evaluate the power.

Solution

a) There are five factors of 2 in the expression $2 \times 2 \times 2 \times 2 \times 2$.
$2 \times 2 \times 2 \times 2 \times 2$ can be written as the power 2^5.
The base of the power is 2 and the exponent of the power is 5.

b) The product $2 \times 2 \times 2 \times 2 \times 2$ is 32.
So, $2^5 = 32$.

> **Show You Know**
>
> **a)** Write $4 \times 4 \times 4$ as a power.
> **b)** Evaluate the power.

power

- an expression made up of a base and an exponent

base   exponent

4^2
power

base

- the number you multiply by itself in a power

exponent

- the number of times you multiply the base in a power

exponential form

- a shorter way of writing repeated multiplication, using a base and an exponent
- $5 \times 5 \times 5$ in exponential form is 5^3

⬤ Literacy Link

There are several ways to read powers.

You can read 2^5 in the following ways:
- two to the fifth
- two to the exponent five

⬤ History Link

Euclid was a Greek mathematician who lived from about 325 BCE to about 265 BCE. He was the first person to use the term *power*. He referred to power only in relation to squares.

The first time that the term *power* was used to refer to expressions with exponents greater than 2 was in 1696 in *Arithmetic* by Samuel Jeake.

Euclid

Example 2: Powers With Positive Bases

Evaluate each power.

a) 4^2 **b)** 2^3 **c)** 3^6

Solution

Strategies

Model It

a) The power 4^2 can be read as "four squared."
You can use a model of a square to represent the power.

How does the model of the square represent 4^2?

Each side of the square is 4 units in length.
The area of the square is 16 because there are 16 small squares altogether in the square.

In the power 4^2, the base is 4 and the exponent is 2.
$$4^2 = 4 \times 4$$
$$= 16$$

b) The power 2^3 can be read as "two cubed."
You can use a model of a cube to represent the power.

How does the model of the cube represent 2^3?

Each edge of the large cube is 2 units in length.
The volume of the large cube is 8 because there are 8 small cubes altogether in the large cube.

In the power 2^3, the base is 2 and the exponent is 3.
$$2^3 = 2 \times 2 \times 2$$
$$= 8$$

c) In the power 3^6, the base is 3 and the exponent is 6. You can represent 3^6 as repeated multiplication.
$$3^6 = 3 \times 3 \times 3 \times 3 \times 3 \times 3$$
$$= 729$$

C 3 y^x 6 = 729.

You could think of 3^6 as
$(3 \times 3) \times (3 \times 3) \times (3 \times 3)$
$= 9 \times 9 \times 9$
$= 9^3$
or
$(3 \times 3 \times 3) \times (3 \times 3 \times 3)$
$= 27 \times 27$
$= 27^2$
Are there other possibilities?

Show You Know

Evaluate each power.

a) 6^2 **b)** 3^4 **c)** 5^3

Example 3: Powers With Negative Bases

Evaluate each power.
a) $(-2)^4$
b) -2^4
c) $(-4)^3$
d) $-(-5)^6$

Solution

a) In the power $(-2)^4$, the base is -2 and the exponent is 4.
The exponent applies to the negative sign because -2 is enclosed in parentheses.

You can write the power as repeated multiplication.
$$(-2)^4 = (-2) \times (-2) \times (-2) \times (-2)$$
$$= 16$$

> Why is the answer positive?

b) In the power -2^4, the base is 2 and the exponent is 4.
The exponent does not apply to the negative sign because -2^4 is the same as $-(2^4)$.
$$-2^4 = -(2^4)$$
$$= -(2 \times 2 \times 2 \times 2)$$
$$= -16$$

c) In the power $(-4)^3$, the base is -4 and the exponent is 3.
$$(-4)^3 = (-4) \times (-4) \times (-4)$$
$$= -64$$

> Why is the answer negative?

d) In the expression $-(-5)^6$, the base is -5 and the exponent is 6.
The exponent does not apply to the first negative sign because the first negative sign lies outside the parentheses.
$$-(-5)^6 = -[(-5) \times (-5) \times (-5) \times (-5) \times (-5) \times (-5)]$$
$$= -(15\ 625)$$
$$= -15\ 625$$

`C ( ( 5 +/- yˣ 6 ) +/- -15625.`

Show You Know

a) Explain how $(-5)^2$ and -5^2 are different and how they are the same.

b) Evaluate $(-6)^2$ and $(-6)^5$.

Key Ideas

- A power is a short way to represent repeated multiplication.
  $7 \times 7 \times 7 = 7^3$

- A power consists of a base and an exponent. The base represents the number you multiply repeatedly. The exponent represents the number of times you multiply the base.

base   exponent

$(-3)^5$

power

Check Your Understanding

Communicate the Ideas

1. Explain why it is often easier to write an expression as a power rather than as repeated multiplication. Use a specific example.

2. Explain how the two diagrams and calculations show that 2^3 and 3^2 are different.

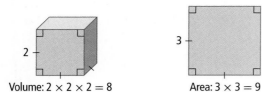

Volume: $2 \times 2 \times 2 = 8$ Area: $3 \times 3 = 9$

3. Pani says, "When you evaluate a power with a negative base and an even exponent, you get a positive value. When you evaluate a power with a negative base and an odd exponent, you get a negative value." Is Pani correct? Justify your answer.

$(-2)^4$

$(-2)^3$

Practise

For help with #4 and #5, refer to Example 1 on page 93.

4. Write each expression as a power, and evaluate.

a) 7×7

b) $3 \times 3 \times 3$

c) $8 \times 8 \times 8 \times 8 \times 8$

d) $10 \times 10 \times 10 \times 10 \times 10 \times 10 \times 10$

5. Write each expression as a power. Identify the base and the exponent in each power. Then, evaluate.

a) $1 \times 1 \times 1 \times 1$

b) $2 \times 2 \times 2 \times 2 \times 2$

c) $9 \times 9 \times 9 \times 9 \times 9 \times 9 \times 9$

d) 13

For help with #6 to #9, refer to Example 2 on page 94.

6. Evaluate each power.

a) 5^2 **b)** 3^3 **c)** 4^5

7. What is the value of each power?

a) 8^3 **b)** 2^6 **c)** 1^9

8. Copy and complete the table.

Repeated Multiplication	Exponential Form	Value
a) $6 \times 6 \times 6$	6^3	■
b) $3 \times 3 \times 3 \times 3$	■	■
c) ■	■	49
d) ■	11^2	■
e) ■	■	125

9. Does $4^3 = 3^4$? Show how you know.

For help with #10 to #13, refer to Example 3 on page 95.

10. Evaluate each power.

a) $(-9)^2$ **b)** -5^3 **c)** $(-2)^7$

11. What is the value of each power?

a) -8^2 **b)** $(-1)^5$ **c)** $-(-3)^7$

12. Copy and complete the table.

	Repeated Multiplication	Exponential Form	Value
a)	$(-3) \times (-3) \times (-3)$	$(-3)^3$	■
b)	$(-4) \times (-4)$	$(-4)^2$	■
c)	$(-1) \times (-1) \times (-1)$	■	■
d)	■	$(-7)^2$	■
e)	■	■	-1000

13. Does $(-6)^4 = -6^4$? Show how you know.

Apply

14. The volume of a cube with an edge length of 3 cm is 27 cm³. Write the volume in repeated multiplication form and exponential form.

3 cm

15. In a children's story, Double Dan the Dragonfly is growing fast. His body length is doubling every month. At the beginning of the story, his length is 1 cm.

a) Create a table to show how Dan's body length increases every month for ten months.

b) What is his body length five months after the beginning of the story? Express your answer as a power. Then, evaluate.

c) After how many months is his body length more than 50 cm?

16. Arrange the following powers from least to greatest value: 1^{22}, 3^4, 4^3, 2^5, 7^2.

17. A single bacterium doubles in number every hour. How many bacteria are present after 15 h?

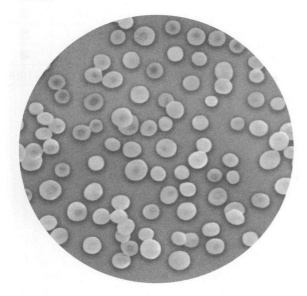

18. Express 9 as a power where the exponent is 2 and the base is

a) positive

b) negative

19. Explain what the following statement means using numerical examples:

Multiplication is a way to represent repeated addition, and powers are a way to represent repeated multiplication.

20. The power 7^3 can be read as "seven cubed." Draw a picture of a cube with a volume of 7^3 cubic units, or 343 cubic units. Label appropriate dimensions for the cube.

21. Represent 144 in three different ways using repeated multiplication.

Extend

22. Evaluate the powers of 5 from 5^3 to 5^{10}. Use only whole numbers as exponents.

a) What do you notice about the last three digits of each value?

b) Predict the last three digits if you evaluate 5^{46}.

23. Evaluate the powers of 3 from 3^1 to 3^{12}. Use only whole numbers as exponents.

a) What do you notice about the units digit?

b) Predict the units digit if you evaluate 3^{63}. Explain how you arrived at your answer.

Math Link

Some formulas use exponents. Two that you are familiar with are given below.
- $SA = 6s^2$
- $V = \pi r^2 h$

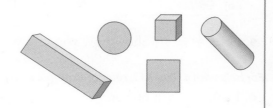

a) Rewrite each formula using repeated multiplication. Identify what the formula represents and how you would use it.

b) For the mobile you will build at the end of the chapter, you will need to use formulas. Identify two formulas that contain exponents, for the shapes shown. Write each formula using repeated multiplication.

3.2

Exponent Laws

Focus on...

After this lesson, you will be able to...

- explain the exponent laws for
  - product of powers
  - quotient of powers
  - power of a power
  - power of a product
  - power of a quotient

The environmental club has permission to use a rectangular plot of land in the school yard for composting and recycling storage. If they know the dimensions of the plot of land, how can they determine the area? If they know the area and the length of the land, how can they determine the width?

Explore Operations on Powers

1. The environmental club learns that the area of the plot of land is 64 m^2.

   a) What are the possible whole dimensions of the rectangular plot of land?

   b) What is 64 expressed as a power of 2?

   c) Show how you can express each of the dimensions in part a) using powers of 2.

2. a) Describe any patterns you observe in your expressions from #1c).

   b) Choose a base other than 2. Determine the product of a pair of powers with the base you chose. Does your observation still apply?

3. The environmental club is given another plot of land behind the school to use for a garden. The table gives some possible dimensions and the area of the rectangular plot.

Length of the Rectangular Plot (m)	Width of the Rectangular Plot (m)	Area of the Rectangular Plot (m²)
3^4	3^1	3^5
3^3	3^2	3^5
3^2	3^3	3^5

a) Describe any patterns you observe in the table.

b) Imagine that you are given only the area and length as powers with the same base. Use your patterns to describe how you can determine the width, in exponential form.

c) Choose a base other than 3. Determine the quotient of a pair of powers with the base you chose. Does your observation still apply?

> What operation do you perform to determine width when you are given the area and length?

Reflect and Check

4. a) Explain how you can write a product of powers as a single power.

b) Explain how you can write a quotient of powers as a single power.

5. Make up a problem of your own that involves multiplication or division of powers with the same base. Exchange problems with a classmate. Check each other's solution.

Link the Ideas

Example 1: Multiply Powers With the Same Base

Write each product of powers as a single power. Then, evaluate the power.
a) $2^3 \times 2^2$
b) $(-3)^2 \times (-3)^5$

Solution

a) *Method 1: Use Repeated Multiplication*
Rewrite the multiplication statement using repeated multiplication.
$$2^3 \times 2^2 = (2 \times 2 \times 2) \times (2 \times 2)$$
$$= 2^5$$
$$= 32$$

> There are five factors of 2 in the repeated multiplication.

Method 2: Apply the Exponent Laws
Since the bases are the same, you can add the exponents.
$$2^3 \times 2^2 = 2^{3+2}$$
$$= 2^5$$
$$= 32$$

b) Since the bases are the same, you can add the exponents.
$$(-3)^2 \times (-3)^5 = (-3)^{2+5}$$
$$= (-3)^7$$
$$= -2187$$

Literacy Link

Another term for repeated multiplication is *factored form*.

Literacy Link

Multiplying Powers

When multiplying powers with the same base, add the exponents to write the product as a single power.

$$(a^m)(a^n) = a^{m+n}$$

Show You Know

Evaluate each expression in two different ways.
a) $4^3 \times 4^5$
b) $(-5)^2 \times (-5)^3$

Did You Know?

Some common viruses require at least 2^{87} viral particles in the human body before symptoms occur.

ARE YOU SURE THIS IS A 'FLU VIRUS?

SEE FOR YOURSELF... ITS NOSE IS RUNNING!

Example 2: Divide Powers With the Same Base

Write each quotient as a single power. Then, evaluate the power.
a) $2^6 \div 2^2$
b) $(-5)^9 \div (-5)^6$

Solution

a) *Method 1: Use Repeated Multiplication*
Rewrite each power using repeated multiplication.
$$2^6 \div 2^2 = (2 \times 2 \times 2 \times 2 \times 2 \times 2) \div (2 \times 2)$$
$$= \frac{2 \times 2 \times 2 \times 2 \times 2 \times 2}{2 \times 2}$$
$$= \frac{2 \times 2 \times 2 \times 2 \times \overset{1}{\cancel{2}} \times \overset{1}{\cancel{2}}}{\underset{1}{\cancel{2}} \times \underset{1}{\cancel{2}}}$$
$$= 2 \times 2 \times 2 \times 2$$
$$= 2^4$$
$$= 16$$

> You can divide the common factors in the numerator and denominator.

Method 2: Apply the Exponent Laws
Since the bases are the same, you can subtract the exponents.
$$2^6 \div 2^2 = 2^{6-2}$$
$$= 2^4$$
$$= 16$$

b) Since the bases are the same, you can subtract the exponents.
$$(-5)^9 \div (-5)^6 = (-5)^{9-6}$$
$$= (-5)^3$$
$$= -125$$

⬤ Literacy Link

Dividing Powers

When dividing powers with the same base, subtract the exponents to write the quotient as a single power.

$a^m \div a^n = a^{m-n}$

Show You Know

Evaluate each expression in two different ways.
a) $2^5 \div 2^4$
b) $(-3)^{10} \div (-3)^7$

Example 3: Raise Powers, Products, and Quotients to an Exponent

a) Write the expression $(2^3)^2$ as a single power. Then, evaluate.
b) Write the expression $[2 \times (-3)]^4$ as the product of two powers. Then, evaluate.
c) Write the expression $\left(\dfrac{3}{4}\right)^3$ as the quotient of two powers. Then, evaluate.

Solution

a) *Method 1: Use Repeated Multiplication*
$$(2^3)^2 = 2^3 \times 2^3$$
$$= (2 \times 2 \times 2) \times (2 \times 2 \times 2)$$
$$= 2^6$$
$$= 64$$

> How many factors of 2 are there in the repeated multiplication?

Method 2: Apply the Exponent Laws
You can multiply the exponents.
$$(2^3)^2 = 2^6$$
$$= 64$$

Literacy Link

Raising a Power to an Exponent

When a power is raised to an exponent, multiply the exponents to write the expression with a single exponent.

$$(a^m)^n = a^{mn}$$

b) *Method 1: Use Repeated Multiplication*
$$[2 \times (-3)]^4 = [2 \times (-3)] \times [2 \times (-3)] \times [2 \times (-3)] \times [2 \times (-3)]$$
$$= 2 \times 2 \times 2 \times 2 \times (-3) \times (-3) \times (-3) \times (-3)$$
$$= 2^4 \times (-3)^4$$
$$= 16 \times 81$$
$$= 1296$$

> How do you know that you can rearrange the factors?

Method 2: Apply the Exponent Laws
You can write each factor in the product with the same exponent.
$$[2 \times (-3)]^4 = 2^4 \times (-3)^4$$
$$= 16 \times 81$$
$$= 1296$$

> How else could you evaluate this expression?

Literacy Link

Raising a Product to an Exponent

When a product is raised to an exponent, you can rewrite each factor in the product with the same exponent.

$$(ab)^m = a^m b^m$$

c) *Method 1: Use Repeated Multiplication*
$$\left(\frac{3}{4}\right)^3 = \left(\frac{3}{4}\right) \times \left(\frac{3}{4}\right) \times \left(\frac{3}{4}\right)$$
$$= \frac{3 \times 3 \times 3}{4 \times 4 \times 4}$$
$$= \frac{3^3}{4^3}$$
$$= \frac{27}{64}$$

> Why can you not divide these powers by subtracting the exponents?

Method 2: Apply the Exponent Laws
You can write each number in the quotient with the same exponent.
$$\left(\frac{3}{4}\right)^3 = \frac{3^3}{4^3}$$
$$= \frac{27}{64}$$

Literacy Link

Raising a Quotient to an Exponent

When a quotient is raised to an exponent, you can rewrite each number in the quotient with the same exponent.

$$\left(\frac{a}{b}\right)^n = \frac{a^n}{b^n}, b \neq 0$$

Show You Know

a) Write $[(-3)^4]^3$ as a single power. Then, evaluate.

b) Write $(5 \times 4)^2$ as the product of two powers. Then, evaluate.

c) Write $\left(\frac{2}{5}\right)^5$ as the quotient of two powers. Then, evaluate.

Example 4: Evaluate Quanities With an Exponent of Zero

Evaluate 3^0.

Strategies

Make a Table

Look for a Pattern

Solution

You can use a table to determine a pattern in the powers of 3.

Power	Value
3^4	81
3^3	27
3^2	9
3^1	3
3^0	■

Determine the pattern in the values.
$81 \div 3 = 27$
$27 \div 3 = 9$
$9 \div 3 = 3$

Each value can be found by dividing the value above it by 3.
$3 \div 3 = 1$

So, the value of 1 belongs in the blank.
$3^0 = 1$

Literacy Link

Raising a Quantity to an Exponent of Zero

When the exponent of a power is 0, the value of the power is 1 if the base is not equal to 0.

$a^0 = 1, a \neq 0$

Check:
You can use division to show that $3^0 = 1$.
Choose any power of 3, such as 3^4. Divide it by itself.

$$\frac{3^4}{3^4} = 3^{4-4} \qquad \frac{3^4}{3^4} = \frac{\overset{1}{\cancel{3^4}}}{\underset{1}{\cancel{3^4}}}$$

$$= 3^0 \qquad\qquad\qquad = 1$$

So, $3^0 = 1$.

You can also check using a calculator.

$\boxed{\text{C}}\ \boxed{3}\ \boxed{y^x}\ \boxed{0}\ \boxed{=}$ 1.

Show You Know

Evaluate each expression.

a) $(-5)^0$ **b)** -5^0

c) $-(5)^0$ **d)** 5^0

Key Ideas

- You can apply the exponent laws to help simplify expressions.

  - You can simplify a product of powers with the same base by adding exponents.

    $a^m \times a^n = a^{m+n}$
    $\qquad 3^7 \times 3^2 = 3^{7+2}$
    $\qquad\qquad\qquad = 3^9$

  - You can simplify a quotient of powers with the same base by subtracting the exponents.

    $a^m \div a^n = a^{m-n}$
    $\qquad 5^8 \div 5^2 = 5^{8-2}$
    $\qquad\qquad\qquad = 5^6$

  - You can simplify a power that is raised to an exponent by multiplying the two exponents.

    $(a^m)^n = a^{mn}$
    $\qquad (3^4)^5 = 3^{4 \times 5}$
    $\qquad\qquad\quad = 3^{20}$

  - When a product is raised to an exponent, you can rewrite each number in the product with the same exponent.

    $(a \times b)^m = a^m \times b^m$
    $\qquad (5 \times 6)^3 = 5^3 \times 6^3$

  - When a quotient is raised to an exponent, you can rewrite each number in the quotient with the same exponent.

    $\left(\dfrac{a}{b}\right)^n = \dfrac{a^n}{b^n}$
    $\qquad \left(\dfrac{5}{3}\right)^4 = \dfrac{5^4}{3^4}$

  - When the exponent of a power is 0, the value of the power is 1 if the base is not equal to 0.

    $a^0 = 1, a \neq 0$
    $\qquad (-10)^0 = 1$

Check Your Understanding

Communicate the Ideas

1. Explain why $(4^2)^5 = 4^{10}$.

2. Show whether the expression $(-2)^2 \times (-2)^3$ and the expression $[(-2)^2]^3$ are equal.

3. Explain why $\left(\dfrac{3}{4}\right)^4 = \dfrac{81}{256}$.

4. Is Ranbir correct? Justify your answer.

I think $-6^0 = 1$.

Practise

For help with #5 to #8, refer to Example 1 on page 101.

5. Write each expression as a single power. Then, evaluate each power.

a) $4^3 \times 4^4$

b) $7^2 \times 7^4$

c) $(-3)^5 \times (-3)^2$

6. Rewrite each expression as a single power. Then, evaluate.

a) $5^2 \times 5^3$

b) $(-6)^3 \times (-6)^3$

c) $8^1 \times 8^2$

7. Write each expression as a product of two powers, and then as a single power.

a) $(4 \times 4 \times 4) \times (4 \times 4 \times 4 \times 4)$

b) $(2 \times 2 \times 2 \times 2 \times 2) \times (2 \times 2)$

c) $(9 \times 9 \times 9 \times 9) \times$
$(9 \times 9 \times 9 \times 9 \times 9 \times 9 \times 9)$

8. Write the following expression in repeated multiplication form, and then as a single power: $3^2 \times 3^3 \times 3^4$.

For help with #9 to #13, refer to Example 2 on page 102.

9. Write each expression as a single power. Then, evaluate each power.

a) $5^5 \div 5^3$

b) $3^8 \div 3^4$

c) $(-4)^6 \div (-4)^2$

10. Rewrite each expression as a single power. Then, evaluate.

a) $7^4 \div 7^1$

b) $(-8)^8 \div (-8)^6$

c) $(-2)^6 \div (-2)^5$

11. Write each expression as a quotient of two powers, and then as a single power.

a) $(6 \times 6 \times 6 \times 6) \div (6 \times 6 \times 6)$

b) $\dfrac{3 \times 3 \times 3 \times 3 \times 3 \times 3 \times 3 \times 3}{3 \times 3}$

c) $(5 \times 5 \times 5 \times 5 \times 5 \times 5 \times 5) \div (5)$

12. Write the following expression as the division of two powers: $(-5)^{7-2}$.

13. Write the numerator and the denominator in exponential form, and then write the expression as a single power:
$\dfrac{(6 \times 6) \times (6 \times 6) \times (6 \times 6)}{6 \times 6 \times 6}$.

For help with #14 to #17, refer to Example 3 on page 102–103.

14. a) Write $(3^2)^4$ as a single power. Evaluate.

b) Write $[7 \times (-3)]^4$ as the product of two powers. Evaluate.

c) Write $\left(\dfrac{5}{6}\right)^4$ as the quotient of two powers. Evaluate.

15. a) Write $(-4^2)^3$ with one exponent. Evaluate.

b) Write $(3 \times 4)^4$ as the multiplication of two powers. Evaluate.

c) Write $\left(\dfrac{4}{5}\right)^3$ as the division of two powers. Evaluate.

16. Write the following expression as a power raised to an exponent.

$(2 \times 2) \times (2 \times 2) \times (2 \times 2) \times (2 \times 2)$

17. Copy and complete the table.

Expression	Repeated Multiplication	Powers
a) $[2 \times (-5)]^3$	■■■■	■■■■
b) ■■■■	$(9 \times 8) \times (9 \times 8)$	$9^2 \times 8^2$
c) $\left(\dfrac{2}{3}\right)^4$	■■■■	■■■■

For help with #18 and #19 refer to Example 4 on page 104.

18. a) Evaluate 2^0. Use a pattern to justify your answer.

   b) Check your answer a different way.

19. a) Evaluate -4^0. Show your thinking.

   b) Evaluate $(-4^0) \times (-4^0) \times (-4^0)$.

Apply

20. Jake's older model computer has a processing speed of 20^2 MHz. Hanna's new computer has a processing speed of 50^2 MHz.

   a) What is the ratio, in fraction form, of Jake's computer processing speed to Hanna's computer processing speed? Do not simplify your answer.

   b) Write this ratio as a single power in simplest form.

⊙⊙ Did You Know?

According to Moore's Law, computer processing power tends to increase exponentially, doubling every two years. The observation was originally made in 1965 by Gordon Moore, co-founder of Intel. This exponential growth is expected to continue for at least another ten years.

21. Express each of the following as a single power.

   a) $(3^2)^4 \times 3^3$

   b) $\dfrac{(-4)^2(-4)^4}{(-4)^3}$

22. Jenny was asked to complete the following exercise.

Write the expression as a product of two powers, and then express as a single power: $(7 \times 7 \times 7 \times 7 \times 7) \times (7 \times 7 \times 7)$.

Find and explain the mistake Jenny made in her solution.

$(7 \times 7 \times 7 \times 7 \times 7) \times (7 \times 7 \times 7)$
$= 7^5 \times 7^3$
$= 7^{5 \times 3}$
$= 7^{15}$

23. Write three different products. Each product must be made up of two powers and must be equal to 4^5.

Extend

24. Find two different whole numbers that can be placed in the boxes so that the following statement is true.
$$0.1 \le \left(\dfrac{\blacksquare}{\blacksquare}\right)^4 \le 0.2$$

25. a) Find a pair of whole numbers, excluding zero, that can be placed in the boxes to make the following equation true.
$$81^{\blacksquare} = 27^{\blacksquare}$$

   b) What is a second pair?

26. If $3^x = 11$, use exponent laws to evaluate the following expressions.

   a) 3^{2x}

   b) $3^{(x+1)}$

Order of Operations

In the game show Power of 5, contestants try to answer eight questions in their pursuit of $10 million.

Explore Order of Operations With Powers

1. How many times greater is each prize value than the previous prize value? Explain how you arrived at your answer.

2. a) What is an expression in exponential form that represents the prize value for answering the fourth question correctly? Compare your answer with a classmate's.

b) How could you find the value of this expression?

3. Write expressions in exponential form for the top prize value and for the prize value for answering the fifth question correctly. Use these expressions to write an expression that shows the difference between these prize values. Then, evaluate the expression. Compare your answer with a classmate's.

Reflect and Check

4. a) Identify the coefficient and the power in the expression 128×5^7.

> The expression 128×5^7 can also be written as $128(5^7)$.

b) What does each of these values represent in the Power of 5 game show?

5. a) What does the expression $128(5^7) - 128(5^3)$ represent in terms of prize values in the Power of 5 game show?

b) Describe the steps you would use to evaluate this expression.

Link the Ideas

Example 1: Determine the Product of a Power

Evaluate.

a) $3(2)^4$ **b)** $-3(-5)^2$ **c)** -4^4

Solution

a) *Method 1: Use Repeated Multiplication*
You can use repeated multiplication
for the power.
$$3(2)^4 = 3 \times 2^4$$
$$= 3 \times 2 \times 2 \times 2 \times 2$$
$$= 48$$

Method 2: Use Order of Operations
$$3 \times 2^4 = 3 \times 16$$
$$= 48$$

> Evaluate the power first.

Method 3: Use a Calculator
C 3 × 2 y^x 4 = 48.

b) $$-3(-5)^2 = -3(25)$$
$$= -75$$

c) $$-4^4 = -1 \times 4^4$$
$$= -1 \times 256$$
$$= -256$$

Literacy Link

The order of
operations is:
• brackets
• exponents (powers)
• divide and multiply
  in order from left to
  right
• add and subtract in
  order from left to
  right

Tech Link

The key sequence may
be different on
different calculators.
Experiment with
performing order of
operations on your
calculator. Record the
proper key sequence
for your calculator.

Show You Know

Evaluate. Use a calculator to check your answer.

a) 4×3^2

b) $6(-2)^3$

c) -7^2

Example 2: Evaluate Expressions With Powers

Evaluate.

a) $4^2 - 8 \div 2 + (-3^2)$ **b)** $-2(-15 - 4^2) + 4(2 + 3)^3$

Solution

a) *Method 1: Use Order of Operations*

$$4^2 - 8 \div 2 + (-3^2)$$
$$= 16 - 8 \div 2 + (-9)$$
$$= 16 - 4 + (-9)$$
$$= 12 + (-9)$$
$$= 3$$

Method 2: Use a Calculator

You may need to use a different key sequence on your calculator.

b) *Method 1: Use Order of Operations*

$$-2(-15 - 4^2) + 4(2 + 3)^3$$
$$= -2(-15 - 16) + 4(5)^3$$
$$= -2(-31) + 4(5)^3$$
$$= -2(-31) + 4(125)$$
$$= 62 + 4(125)$$
$$= 62 + 500$$
$$= 562$$

Method 2: Use a Calculator

C 2 +⟷− × (| 15 +⟷− − 4 x² |) + 4 ×
(| 2 + 3 |) yˣ 3 = 562.

> **Show You Know**

Evaluate.

a) $4^2 + (-4^2)$ **b)** $8(5 + 2)^2 - 12 \div 2^2$

Key Ideas

- Expressions with powers can have a numerical coefficient. Evaluate the power, and then multiply by the coefficient.

- Evaluate expressions with powers using the proper order of operations.
  - brackets
  - exponents
  - divide and multiply in order from left to right
  - add and subtract in order from left to right

Expression	Coefficient	Power	Repeated Multiplication	Value
$5(4^2)$	5	4^2	$5 \times 4 \times 4$	80
$(-2)^4$	1	$(-2)^4$	$(-2)(-2)(-2)(-2)$	16
-3^4	-1	3^4	$-1 \times 3 \times 3 \times 3 \times 3$	-81

Check Your Understanding

Communicate the Ideas

1. Using the terms *coefficient* and *base*, explain why the two expressions -2^2 and $(-2)^2$ are different and result in different answers.

2. Your classmate, Han, needs help with his homework. Explain how to evaluate $(5 - 2)^2 + (-4)^3$.

$(5 - 2)^2 + (-4)^3$

3. Identify the incorrect step in the following solution. Show how to correct it. What is the correct answer?

$(3 + 5)^2 - 4 \times 3^2$

$= 8^2 - (4 \times 3^2)$ Step 1
$= 64 - 4 \times 3^2$ Step 2
$= 60 \times 3^2$ Step 3
$= 60 \times 9$ Step 4
$= 540$ Step 5

4. Maria was asked to evaluate 128×5^3. What mistake did Maria make in her solution?

128×5^3
$= 640^3$
$= 262\ 144\ 000$

Practise

For help with #5 to #7, refer to Example 1 on page 109.

5. Evaluate each expression.

a) $4(2)^5$ **b)** $7(-3)^2$

c) $-2(5^4)$ **d)** $3(-2^2)$

6. Write each expression using a coefficient and a power. Then, find the value of each expression.

a) $4 \times 2 \times 2 \times 2 \times 2$

b) $3 \times (-2) \times (-2) \times (-2)$

c) $7(10)(10)(10)(10)(10)$

d) $-1 \times 9 \times 9 \times 9 \times 9$

7. Write the key sequence you would use to evaluate each expression using your calculator. What is the answer?

a) 4×3^2

b) $-5(4)^3$

For help with #8 and #9, refer to Example 2 on page 110.

8. Evaluate.

a) $3^2 + 3^2$

b) $(2 + 7)^2 - 11$

c) $7^3 - 3(-4)^3$

d) $9 + (-2)^3 - 2(-6^2)$

9. Find the value of each expression.

 a) $7 - 2(3^2)$

 b) $(-4 - 3)^2 + (-3)^2$

 c) $(-2)^6 \div 4^3$

 d) $24 - 2^2 + (7^2 - 5^2)$

Apply

10. For each pair of expressions, which one has a greater value? How much greater is it?

 a) $3(2)^3$ $2(3)^2$

 b) $(3 \times 4)^2$ $3^2 \times 4^2$

 c) $6^3 + 6^3$ $(6 + 6)^3$

11. Find the step where Justin made an error. Show the correct answer.

 $(-3 + 6)^2 - 4 \times 3^2$

 $= 3^2 - 4 \times 3^2$ Step 1

 $= 9 - 4 \times 9$ Step 2

 $= 5 \times 9$ Step 3

 $= 45$ Step 4

12. Find the step where Katarina made an error. What is the correct answer?

 $32 \div (-2)^3 + 5(4)^2$

 $= 32 \div (-8) + 5 \times 8$ Step 1

 $= -4 + 5 \times 8$ Step 2

 $= -4 + 40$ Step 3

 $= 36$ Step 4

13. Write an expression with powers to determine the difference between the volume of the small cube and the volume of the large cube. What is the difference?

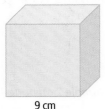

9 cm   7 cm

14. Read the following riddle and then answer the questions below.

 In downtown Victoria, there are seven pink houses. Every pink house has seven pink rooms, every pink room has seven cats, and every cat has seven kittens.

 a) How many pink rooms are there?

 b) How many kittens are there?

 c) Write an expression using powers of 7 to determine the total number of houses, rooms, cats, and kittens. Evaluate your expression.

15. Write an expression with powers to determine the difference between the area of the large square and the area of the small square. What is the difference?

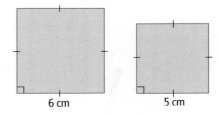

6 cm   5 cm

16. A red square with a side length of 8 cm is placed on a yellow square with a side length of 10 cm. Write an expression with powers to determine the visible yellow area. What is the visible yellow area?

10 cm   8 cm

Extend

17. What is the value of 5^{3^2}?

18. In a game show called The Pyramid of Money, a contestant must successfully answer a set of questions. The first question is worth $3125. Each question after that is worth four times the value of the previous question.

a) What is the value of question 2? question 3? question 4?

b) How many questions would a contestant have to answer correctly before becoming eligible to answer a question with a value of $3 200 000?

c) Which question is represented by the expression 3125×4^7?

d) Write an expression with powers that represents the sum of the values of the first four questions.

19. A phone tree is used to notify the players on a football team about a change in the time for their next game. Each of the three coaches calls two different players, and then each player calls two more players. Each person only makes two calls. The chart shows the number of people calling and receiving calls for each round of two calls.

Round of Calls	Number of People Calling	Number of Calls Received	Total Number of People Notified
First	3	6	3 + 6 = 9
Second	6	12	9 + 12 = 21
Third	12	24	21 + 24 = 45
Fourth	24	■	45 + ■ = 93

a) What value belongs in each unknown box?

b) Write an expression for the number from part a) as a product of 3 and a power of 2.

c) What does the 3 in part b) represent?

d) What does the exponent in part b) represent?

e) Imagine that the phoning continued. Determine an expression for the number of calls received in the sixth round and evaluate it.

f) If five coaches started the phone tree instead of three, what would be the number of calls received in the third round?

20. Use four 2s to write an expression with the greatest possible value.

Math Link

You are planning to build a mobile with a cylinder and a cube.

a) The height and radius of the cylinder and the height of the cube will all be the same measurement. Choose a whole number measurement, in centimetres.

b) Write an expression in exponential form to calculate the difference in the area of material required to make each shape. Which shape requires more material? How much more? Express your answer to the nearest tenth of a square centimetre.

c) Write an expression in exponential form to calculate the total area of material needed to make both shapes. Express your answer to the nearest tenth of a square centimetre.

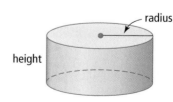

radius

height

height

3.4 Using Exponents to Solve Problems

Focus on...

After this lesson, you will be able to...

- solve problems that require combining powers
- use powers to solve problems that involve repeated multiplication

Near Alberta/British Columbia border

The mountain pine beetle has the ability to double its population in one year if conditions are right. These beetles live in mature pine trees by boring into the bark. Only 6 mm long, these small beetles can kill pine trees if their numbers are great enough.

The mountain pine beetle has destroyed thousands of pine trees in British Columbia and Alberta. It is estimated that by 2013, 80% of the pine trees in BC will be eliminated by the mountain pine beetle.

Explore Operations on Powers

A population of 10 000 mountain pine beetles doubles each year.

1. Create a table to show the growth of the population of pine beetles over three years.

2. Express the population each year as a product of 10 000 and a power of 2. Add this information to your table.

3. What patterns do you notice in your table?

4. How could you determine the number of beetles in ten years without extending the table? Show two methods.

5. How would your table be different if the beetles tripled in number each year?

Reflect and Check

6. Write an expression in exponential form to determine the number of beetles in n years. Explain what each value represents.

7. How could you determine the number of years that have passed if the number of beetles is 640 000?

Link the Ideas

Example 1: Use Formulas to Solve Problems

Write an exponential expression to solve each problem.

a) What is the surface area of a cube with an edge length of 4 cm?

4 cm

b) Find the area of the square attached to the hypotenuse in the diagram.

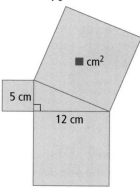

■ cm²

5 cm

12 cm

c) A circle is inscribed in a square with a side length of 20 cm. What is the area of the shaded region?

|←—— 20 cm ——→|

$20^2 - (\pi \cdot 10^2)$

Solution

a) The formula for the surface area of a cube is $SA = 6s^2$, where s is the edge length of the cube.
$SA = 6s^2$
$SA = 6(4)^2$
$SA = 6(16)$
$SA = 96$
The surface area of the cube is 96 cm².

b) The diagram models the Pythagorean relationship. The relationship between the areas of the squares on the sides of a right triangle is represented by the formula $c^2 = a^2 + b^2$, where a and b are the legs of the triangle and c is the hypotenuse.
$c^2 = a^2 + b^2$
$c^2 = 5^2 + 12^2$
$c^2 = 25 + 144$
$c^2 = 169$
The area of the square attached to the hypotenuse is 169 cm².

c) *Method 1: Calculate in Stages*
The formula for the area of a square is $A = s^2$, where s is the side length of the square.
$A = s^2$
$A = 20^2$
$A = 400$
The area of the square is 400 cm².

The formula for the area of a circle is $A = \pi r^2$, where r is the radius of the circle.
The diameter of the circle is 20 cm. Therefore, the radius is 10 cm.
$A = \pi r^2$
$A = \pi(10)^2$
$A = \pi(100)$
$A \approx 314 \dots$
The area of the circle is approximately 314 cm².

Calculate the area of the shaded region. You can subtract the area of the circle from the area of the square.
$400 - 314 = 86$
The area of the shaded region is about 86 cm².

Method 2: Evaluate One Expression
Calculate the area of the shaded region. You can subtract the area of the circle from the area of the square.
$A = s^2 - \pi r^2$
$A = 20^2 - \pi(10)^2$
$A = 400 - \pi(100)$
$A \approx 400 - 314$
$A \approx 86$
The area of the shaded region is about 86 cm².

Show You Know

Use a formula to solve each problem.

a) A right triangle has two shorter sides that measure 8 cm and 15 cm. What is the area of a square attached to the hypotenuse of the right triangle?

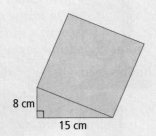

8 cm

15 cm

b) What is the surface area of a cube with an edge length of 3 m?

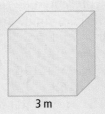

3 m

Example 2: Develop a Formula to Solve a Problem

A dish holds 100 bacteria. It is known that the bacteria double in number every hour. How many bacteria will be present after each number of hours?

a) 1 **b)** 5 **c)** n

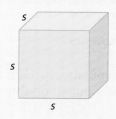

Solution

a) After 1 h, the bacteria population doubles.
$100 \times 2 = 200$
After 1 h, there will be 200 bacteria.

b) In a period of 5 h, the bacteria population doubles five times.
$100 \times 2 \times 2 \times 2 \times 2 \times 2$
$= 100(2^5)$
$= 100(32)$
$= 3200$
After 5 h, there will be 3200 bacteria.

c) After n hours, the bacteria population doubles n times.
Number of bacteria $= 100(2^n)$
After n hours, there will be $100(2^n)$ bacteria.

Strategies

Use a Variable

Show You Know

A type of bacterium is known to triple every hour. There are 50 bacteria to start with. How many will there be after each number of hours?

a) 3 **b)** 5 **c)** t

Key Ideas

- Powers are found in many formulas. When repeated multiplication is present in a formula, it is represented as a power. The use of powers keeps the formula as short as possible.
- Many patterns that involve repeated multiplication can be modelled with expressions that contain powers.

Volume of a cube $= s^3$

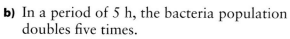

Check Your Understanding

Communicate the Ideas

1. The surface area, *SA*, of a sphere can be calculated using the formula $SA = 4 \times \pi \times r \times r$, where *r* is the radius. Rewrite the formula using powers and no multiplication signs. Identify the coefficient, variable, and exponent in your formula.

2. Explain what each number and letter represents in the following expression: Number of bacteria = $100(2)^n$.

Practise

For help with #3 and #4, refer to Example 1 on page 115.

3. What is the volume of a cube with an edge length of 6 cm? Write an exponential expression to solve the problem.

6 cm

$6^3 = 216$ cm^3

4. Which is larger, the area of a square with a side length of 14 cm or the surface area of a cube with an edge length of 6 cm? Show your work. Write an exponential expression to solve the problem. 14^2 or $6(6)^2 = 6(6)^2$

For help with #5 and #6, refer to Example 2 on page 117.

5. A colony of bacteria triples every hour. If there are 20 bacteria now, how many will there be after each amount of time?
   a) 1 h $20(3)^1$
   b) 6 h $20(3)^6$
   c) *n* hours $20(3)^n$

6. A population of 200 bacteria has the perfect conditions to double every 20 min. How many bacteria will there be after each amount of time?
   a) 20 min
   b) 60 min
   c) 4 h

Apply

46 cm^3

7. Sarah wants to send a cube-shaped package to her cousins in Pond Inlet, Nunavut. She is going to wrap the package in brown paper The side length of the package measures 46 cm. What is the minimum amount of paper Sarah will need?

8. Albert Einstein stated that $E = mc^2$. The mass, *m*, is measured in kilograms, and the speed of light, *c*, is approximately 300 000 000 m/s. The amount of energy released, *E*, is measured in joules. How much energy is released if 1 g of mass is converted to energy?

9. A true/false quiz with four questions has a total of 2^4 possible sets of answers. One possible set of answers is TFFF.
   a) What does the exponent, 4, represent?
   b) What does the base, 2, represent?
   c) List the remaining sets of possible answers.
   d) How many sets of answers are possible for a quiz with ten true/false questions? Express as a power and then evaluate.

10. A standard combination lock has 60 numbers on its face from 0 to 59. A combination consists of three numbers, and numbers can be repeated. What is the total number of possible combinations? Express as a power and then evaluate.

11. A formula that estimates the stopping distance for a car on an icy road is

$$d = 0.75s\left(\frac{c}{1000}\right)^2.$$

The distance, d, is measured in metres. The speed of the car, s, is in kilometres per hour. The mass of the car, c, is in kilograms.

a) What is the stopping distance for a 1000-kg car travelling at 50 km/h?

b) What is the stopping distance for a 2000-kg car travelling at 60 km/h?

c) Write the key sequence for solving part b) using your calculator.

Extend

12. The number 10^{100} is known as a googol.

a) Research where the term googol originated. Why do you think the founders of Google™ used that name for their search engine?

b) How many zeros would follow the 1 if you wrote 10^{100} as a whole number?

c) If you were able to continue writing zeros without stopping, how long would it take you to write a googol as a whole number? Explain why you believe your answer is correct.

13. Sometimes powers have the same bases and different exponents. At other times, powers have the same exponents and different bases.

a) Use the examples below to explain how you would compare such powers. Generate rules you could use for comparing these powers.

3^5 and 3^7

6^4 and 5^4

b) How could you use the exponent laws to alter these powers so you could easily compare them without finding their values?

32^4 and 64^3

Math Link

Stefan plans to make a mobile out of five equal-sized cubes with a side length of 3 cm. He has the exact amount of paper he needs to create his mobile. However, he then decides he would like the cubes to be larger.

a) Suggest a larger size for the cubes. Use whole number dimensions.

b) What is the minimum area of paper Stefan will need to create the five cubes that you suggest? Give your answer as an expression in exponential form. Then, evaluate.

c) How much more paper will Stefan need than the original amount he had? Give your answer as an expression in exponential form. Then, evaluate.

3 cm

Chapter 3 Review

Key Words

For #1 to #5, use the clues to unscramble the letters.

1. T F N F E E I C C O I

   a number that multiplies a power

2. N N T O E I P A X L E   M O R F

   the form for writing a number so that it is made up of a base and an exponent (two words)

3. E A S B

   the number in a power that is multiplied repeatedly

4. W R O E P

   an expression made up of a base and an exponent

5. T O X E N P N E

   the number in a power that indicates how many times to repeatedly multiply the base by itself

3.1 Using Exponents to Describe Numbers, pages 92–98

6. Write each expression as a power.

   a) $2 \times 2 \times 2$

   b) $(-3) \times (-3) \times (-3) \times (-3)$

7. Write each power in repeated multiplication form.

   a) 4^6

   b) 6^4

   c) $(-5)^7$

   d) -5^7

8. The area of a square on grid paper is 5^2. Evaluate the area. Draw the square and label its area and side length.

9. A cube has an edge length of 4 cm. Express its volume in repeated multiplication form and in exponential form. Then, evaluate.

   4 cm

10. Arrange the following numbers in ascending order:

    4^3 7^2 -3^4 9 2^5

3.2 Exponent Laws, pages 99–107

11. Rewrite each power in the following products in repeated multiplication form.

    a) $3^2 \times 5^4$

    b) $(-3)^3 \times 2^6$

12. Write each expression in parentheses as a power. Then, write the entire expression as a single power.

    a) $(2 \times 2 \times 2) \times (2 \times 2)$

    b) $\dfrac{(4 \times 4)(4 \times 4 \times 4 \times 4)}{(4 \times 4 \times 4)}$

13. Write each expression in repeated multiplication form, and then as a single power.

    a) $(-5)^2 \times (-5)^5$

    b) $(3^2)^4$

14. Write each expression as the multiplication of two powers.

a) $(6 \times 4)^3$

b) $[(7 \times (-2)]^5$

15. Write each expression as the division of two powers.

a) $\left(\dfrac{4}{5}\right)^2$

b) $\left(\dfrac{2}{7}\right)^4$

16. Evaluate.

a) -4^2

b) $(-10)^0$

c) $3^2 \times 3^3$

3.3 Order of Operations, pages 108–113

17. Write the calculator key sequence you would use to evaluate each expression.

a) $(-2)^2 + (-2)^3$

b) $(2^3)^2 - 4 \times 6^0$

c) $(-3)^4 - (-3)^3 + (2 \times 4)^2$

18. Evaluate.

a) $7^2 + (-2)^3 \div (-2)^2$

b) $(2 - 5)^3 + 6^2$

c) $\dfrac{(2)^6(2)^2 - 13 \times 2^0}{(-1 + 2^2)^5}$

d) $(-1)^{10} + (-22)^0 - \left(\dfrac{3}{5}\right)^2$

19. Explain the mistake in Ang's solution. Determine the correct answer.

$(-3)^4 + 7 \times 2^3$
$= 81 + 7 \times 8$
$= 88 \times 8$
$= 704$

3.4 Using Exponents to Solve Problems, pages 114–119

20. What is the surface area of a cube with an edge length of 5 m?

5 m

21. A population of ten bacteria doubles every hour. This growth can be represented by $N = 10(2)^t$, where N is the number of bacteria, and t is the amount of time, in hours. How many bacteria will there be after each number of hours?

a) 3

b) 6

22. A formula that approximates the distance an object falls through air in relation to time is $d = 4.9t^2$. The distance, d, is measured in metres, and the time, t, in seconds. A pebble breaks loose from a cliff. What distance would it fall in each number of seconds?

a) 1

b) 2

c) 6

Chapter 3 Practice Test

For #1 to #6, choose the best answer.

1. What is the value 3 in the power 4^3 called?

   A base
   B power
   C exponent
   D coefficient

2. What is the coefficient in the expression $-(-3)^5$?

   A -3
   B -1
   C 1
   D 3

3. What expression is represented by $(3^2)^4$?

   A $(3 \times 3)(3 \times 3 \times 3 \times 3)$
   B $(3 \times 3 \times 3 \times 3 \times 3 \times 3)$
   C $(3 \times 3)(3 \times 3)(3 \times 3)(3 \times 3)$
   D $(3 \times 3 \times 3 \times 3)(3 \times 3 \times 3 \times 3)$ $(3 \times 3 \times 3 \times 3)(3 \times 3 \times 3 \times 3)$

4. What expression is equivalent to $(5 \times 4)^2$?

   A 10×8
   B 5×4^2
   C $5^2 \times 4$
   D $5^2 \times 4^2$

5. What is $\dfrac{(-7)^3(-7)^5}{(-7)^2}$ expressed as a single power?

   A $(-7)^6$
   B $(-7)^{10}$
   C $(-7)^{13}$
   D $(-7)^{17}$

6. Evaluate $(7 - 2)^3 + 48 \div (-2)^4$.

   A 338
   B 128
   C 10.8125
   D -10.8125

Complete the statements in #7 and #8.

7. The expression $10^5 \times 5^5$ written with only one exponent is ■.

8. The expression $\dfrac{5^6}{8^6}$ written with only one exponent is ■.

Short Answer

9. Write the expression $\dfrac{4^4 \times 4}{4^2}$ in repeated multiplication form, and then evaluate.

10. The formula for the volume of a cylinder is $V = \pi r^2 h$. Find the volume, V, of a cylinder with a radius of 3 cm and a height of 6.4 cm. Express your answer to the nearest tenth of a cubic centimetre.

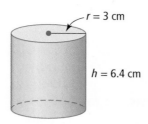

11. A skydiver free falls before opening the parachute. What distance would the skydiver fall during 7 s of free fall? Use the formula $d = 4.9t^2$, where d is distance, in metres, and t is time, in seconds.

12. Write the calculator key sequence you would use to evaluate each expression. Then, evaluate.

    a) $(1 - 3)^4 \div 4$
    b) $(-2)^0 + 4 \times 17^0$
    c) $16 - 9(2^3) + (-4)^2$

13. The prime factorization of 243 is $3 \times 3 \times 3 \times 3 \times 3$. Write 243 as the product of two powers of 3 in as many ways as possible.

14. A formula for estimating the volume of wood in a tree is $V = 0.05hc^2$. The volume, V, is measured in cubic metres. The height, h, and the trunk circumference, c, are in metres. What is the volume of wood in a tree with a trunk circumference of 2.3 m and a height of 32 m? Express your answer to the nearest tenth of a cubic metre.

Oyster River, British Columbia

Extended Response

15. Nabil made an error in simplifying the following expression.

a) Explain his mistake.

b) Determine the correct answer.

$$(12 \div 4)^4 + (5 + 3)^2$$
$$= (3)^4 + 5^2 + 3^2$$
$$= 81 + 25 + 9$$
$$= 106 + 9$$
$$= 115$$

16. A type of bacterium triples in number every 24 h. There are currently 300 bacteria.

a) Create a table to show the number of bacteria after each of the next seven days. Express each number of bacteria as the product of a coefficient and a power.

b) Determine a formula that will calculate the number of bacteria, B, after d days.

c) Use the formula to find the number of bacteria after 9 days.

d) How many were there 24 h ago? Explain your reasoning.

Math Link: Wrap It Up!

Create a mobile that uses at least three different types of regular three-dimensional shapes such as a cube, a square-based prism, and a cylinder. You may wish to choose a different type of geometric shape to build as well.

cube

square-based prism

cylinder

- Choose whole-number dimensions between 10 cm and 20 cm for each shape.
- Use a ruler and a piece of construction paper or other heavy paper to draw a net for each shape.
- Build each shape.
- Use expressions in exponential form to label the surface area and the volume of each shape.
- Evaluate each expression. Show all of your work.
- Make your mobile. Use colour and creativity!

Challenges

Develop Your Own Online Tournament

You are a game designer! You have developed an online computer game for you and your friends to play. Your goal is to make it available to a wider online audience one day. What kind of game is it?

Suppose the first tournament you hold has 16 players entered. You want to create a single-elimination draw to determine a winner.

1. Make a draw for your competition. Show your work and explain your thinking.

2. What would be the next largest number of players that would fill a draw so that no player receives a bye?

3. **a)** Your dream is to hold a huge worldwide tournament. It will be a single-elimination draw involving close to one million players. What pattern from the first tournament can help you set up a tournament for a larger number of competitors?

   b) What would be the ideal number of players closest to one million that would determine one winner fairly? Explain.

   c) How many rounds would be played, based on the number of players in part b)?

Literacy Link

A *draw* is a method to determine which players compete against each other in a tournament. In a single-elimination draw, competitors who lose a single match are knocked out of the tournament.

Literacy Link

A *bye* occurs when there is an odd number of teams or players in a tournament draw. When players are paired to compete against one another, there will be one player without an opponent. That player gets a bye, or pass, into the next round of the tournament.

Stopping the Spread of Harmful Bacteria

Health authorities encourage people to wash their hands, with good reason. If a single *Escherichia coli* bacterium finds its way under your skin, the number of bacteria can double every 20 min under ideal conditions. This means that one bacterium in a Petri dish could grow to about 500 000 bacteria in approximately 6 h and 20 min.

You are a public health official. You have been assigned the responsibility of creating a presentation about bacteria. Your presentation will inform the public about how quickly a population of bacteria can grow. It will also discuss the importance of reducing bacteria growth.

Research facts about a type of bacterium of your choice. Your presentation will include the following information:

- how long it would take for one bacterium to expand to a billion or more bacteria
- what mathematical terms you could use to describe this growth
- how you could determine the doubling rate of the bacterium you chose
- ways to reduce the growth of harmful bacteria

Use a format of your choice that would be effective for communicating your message.

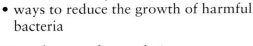

4

Scale Factors and Similarity

The Canadian Museum of Civilization in Gatineau, Québec, was designed by architect Douglas Cardinal. This Canadian of Aboriginal heritage was born in Red Deer, Alberta. Cardinal is famous for designing buildings with smooth, flowing lines that reflect the landscape. The building has been recognized, in Canada and internationally, as a world-class structure.

The scale model shown here is an exact replica of the actual building. It has the same shape but not the same size. What scale models have you seen? How is a scale model useful?

In this chapter, you will learn about scale models and their relationship to scale factors and similarity.

> **⬭ Did You Know?**
>
> The form of the Canadian Museum of Civilization represents four natural features. These include the Canadian Shield, the glaciers, the streams formed by the melting glaciers, and the plains that stretched before the melting glaciers. Try to identify each of these elements.

WWW Web Link

For more information about Douglas Cardinal and his designs, go to www.mathlinks9.ca and follow the links.

What You Will Learn

- to draw enlargements and reductions to scale
- to identify scale diagrams and interpret the scale factor
- to determine the scale factor from scale diagrams
- to determine similar triangles and similar polygons
- to solve problems using the properties of similar triangles and similar polygons

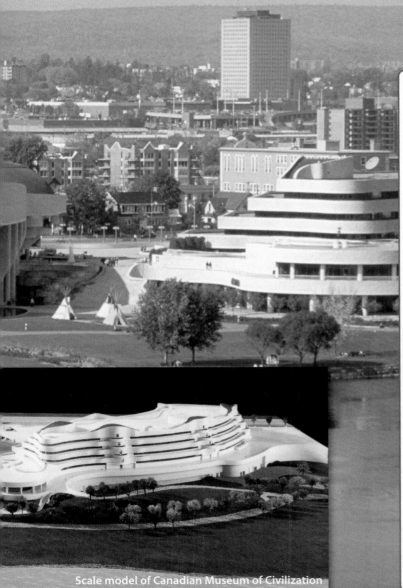

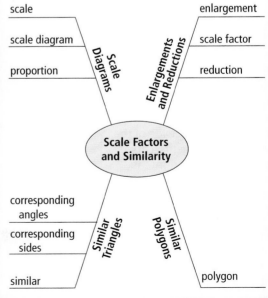

Scale model of Canadian Museum of Civilization

Key Words

enlargement	proportion
scale factor	corresponding angles
reduction	corresponding sides
scale	similar
scale diagram	polygon

⬭ Literacy Link

A spider map can help you understand and connect new terms and concepts. This spider map is designed to be used throughout the chapter.

Create a spider map in your math journal or notebook. As you work through the chapter, complete the map.

Define each term using words, a diagram, or a mathematical expression. In your definition of *polygon*, mention the sum of the angles of a polygon.

scale

scale diagram

proportion

Scale Diagrams

enlargement

scale factor

reduction

Enlargements and Reductions

Scale Factors and Similarity

corresponding angles

corresponding sides

Similar Triangles

Similar Polygons

similar

polygon

Materials

- sheet of 11 × 17 paper
- ruler
- two sheets of 8.5 × 11 paper
- scissors
- two sheets of 8.5 × 11 grid paper
- stapler

Step 1

Fold the long side of a sheet of 11 × 17 paper in half. Pinch it at the midpoint. Fold the outer edges of the paper to meet at the midpoint. Label it as shown.

Chapter 4
Scale Factors and Similarity

What I Need to Work On

Step 2

Fold the short side of a sheet of 8.5 × 11 paper in half. On one side, use a ruler to draw a line 5.5 cm from the top. Then, draw eight more lines at 2.5-cm intervals. Cut along the lines through one thickness of paper, forming ten tabs. Label the tabs as shown.

Key Words
enlargement
scale factor
reduction
scale
scale diagram
proportion
corresponding angles
corresponding sides
similar
polygon

Step 3

Fold the long side of a sheet of 8.5 × 11 grid paper in half. Fold in half the opposite way. Make a cut through one thickness to make a two-tab book. Label the outside of the left tab Enlargements. Label the outside of the right tab Reductions. Open the two-tab book. Label the inside of the tabs as shown here.

Use Grid Paper | Use Grid Paper

Use a Scale Factor | Use a Scale Factor

Repeat Step 3, using a plain sheet of 8.5 × 11 paper, to make another two-tab book. Label the outside of it as shown.

Use a Scale | Use a Proportion

Step 4

Fold the short side of a sheet of 8.5 × 11 grid paper in half. Fold in half the opposite way. Make a cut through one thickness of paper, forming two tabs. Label the tabs as shown below.

Step 5

Staple the four booklets you made into the Foldable from Step 1 as shown.

Using the Foldable

As you work through Chapter 4, define the Key Words beneath the tabs on the left. Beneath the tabs at the top of the centre panel, record notes about enlargements and reductions. Beneath the tabs at the bottom of the centre panel, record notes about using a scale factor and proportions to solve problems. Beneath the tabs on the right, record notes about the properties of similar triangles and similar polygons.

On the back of the Foldable, record ideas for the Math Link: Wrap It Up! On the back of the right flap of the Foldable, make notes under the heading What I Need to Work On. Check off each item as you deal with it.

Math Link

Designers

Many occupations require people to design projects using models or diagrams. Some examples include architecture, fashion and furniture design, web design, automotives, and tourism.

For example, architects create plans also for homes. These plans are called blueprints. Architects work with ratios and proportions to produce floor plans that represent accurate dimensions of the various areas of a home. The floor plan helps people judge if the proposed design is suitable for their lifestyle.

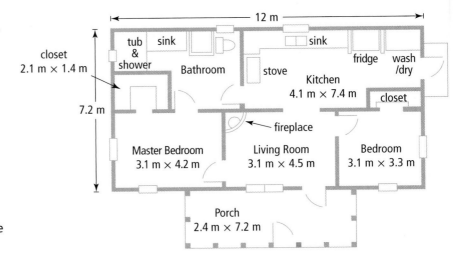

Use the floor plan to answer the following questions.

1. a) What is the area of the actual house?
   b) What is the area of the house on the blueprint?

2. a) What is the area of the actual living room?
   b) What is the area of the living room on the blueprint?

3. a) What is the ratio of the area of the actual house to the area of the blueprint house?
   b) What is the ratio of the area of the actual living room to the area of the blueprint living room?
   c) Compare the two ratios. What can you conclude about the ratios?
   d) What ratio do you expect for the areas of the actual and blueprint master bedrooms? Explain why.

4. a) Why do you think accuracy is important in developing a floor plan?
   b) Why is it important to maintain the same proportions for the dimensions of an actual object and its image?

5. Discuss with a partner other examples in which ratios are used to compare objects in daily life.

In this chapter, you will learn skills to draw diagrams that are proportional to the actual objects. You will also plan and complete your own design project.

Enlargements and Reductions

Focus on...

After this lesson, you will be able to...

- **identify enlargements and reductions, and interpret the scale factor**
- **draw enlargements and reductions to scale**

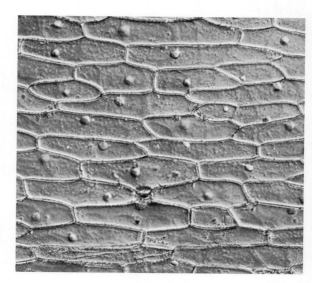

A microscope magnifies objects that are too small to be seen by the naked eye. This picture shows an enlarged view of cells in onion skin.

To calculate the factor that the onion cells are magnified by, multiply the magnification of the eyepiece by the magnification of the objective lens. The objective lens is the lens you choose to look at the object with.

Magnification of eyepiece: 10x

Magnification of objective lens: 40x

Total magnification: $10 \times 40 = 400x$

The onion cells are enlarged by 400 times their original size.

How do you think the enlarged view is the same as the actual piece of onion skin? How is it different?

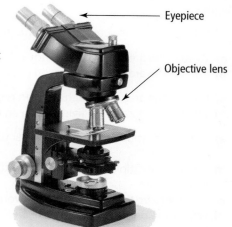

Eyepiece

Objective lens

> **Did You Know?**
>
> One of the most powerful microscopes used in high schools today can enlarge an object 1500 times.

Materials

- centimetre grid paper

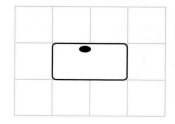

- tracing paper
- ruler

Explore How to Enlarge an Image

1. Brainstorm with a classmate how you might enlarge the onion cell. What different strategies can you develop?

2. Try out at least one of your strategies and draw an image that is twice as large as this onion cell. What will be the ratio of the lengths of the sides of the enlargement to the original?

Example 2: Draw a Reduction

Draw a **reduction** that is half as large as the original.

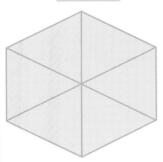

reduction

- a decrease in the dimensions of an object by a constant factor
- can be 2-D or 3-D
- each dimension of this reduction is half the length of the original

Solution

Method 1: Use Grid Paper

Trace the picture on centimetre grid paper.

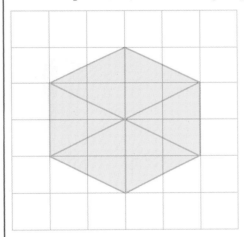

Draw the contents of each grid square into the corresponding area on a piece of 0.5-cm grid paper.

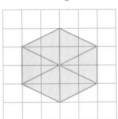

> How could you use 2-cm grid paper and 1-cm grid paper to draw this reduction? What if you have only 1-cm grid paper?

Method 2: Use a Scale Factor
Measure the length of each line segment.

What scale factor will you use? Explain why.

2 cm

⬤⬤ Tech Link

You can use a drawing program to enlarge or reduce an image using a scale factor. Or, you can drag an object to the size you want.

Multiply the length by 0.5.
$2 \times 0.5 = 1$

The length of each line segment for the reduction is 1 cm.

Use the new length of each line segment to draw the reduction.

The scale factor indicates whether an object is enlarged or reduced. What does each statement tell you?
• a scale factor greater than 1
• a scale factor less than 1
• a scale factor equal to 1

Which method do you prefer for drawing a reduction? Explain.

Show You Know

Use a method of your choice and a scale factor of 0.5 to draw a reduction of this shape.

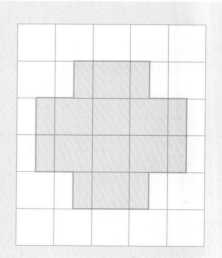

Key Ideas

- An enlargement results in an image that is the same shape but proportionally larger than the original.

- A reduction results in an image that is the same shape but proportionally smaller than the original.

- The scale factor is the constant amount that all dimensions of an object are multiplied by to draw an enlargement or reduction.
  - A scale factor greater than 1 indicates an enlargement.
  - A scale factor less than 1 indicates a reduction.
- You can use grid paper and a scale factor to draw enlargements and reductions.

Check Your Understanding

Communicate the Ideas

1. Jesse thinks many photographs in this student resource are reductions. Is he correct? Justify your reasoning.

2. Mary used a scale factor of 3 to enlarge a rectangle.

3 X 3 = 9

The length of each side for the enlargement is 9 cm.

Is she correct? If so, explain how you know. If she is incorrect, explain her mistake. Discuss your answer with a partner.

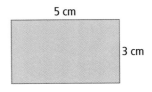

5 cm

3 cm

3. This logo was designed for a film club. Describe two different methods to enlarge the logo for a poster.

Practise

For help with #4 and #5, refer to Example 1 on pages 131–132.

4. Use a scale factor of 2 to enlarge each letter.

a)

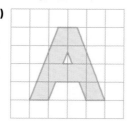

b)

5. Draw an enlargement of the flag using a scale factor of 4.

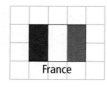

France

For help with #6 to #8, refer to Example 2 on pages 133–134.

6. Use a scale factor of 0.5 to draw a reduction of each letter.

a)

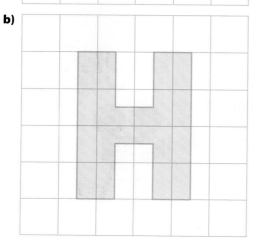

b)

7. For the image on the right in each pair of pictures, indicate if the scale factor is
- greater than 1
- less than 1
- equal to 1

Explain how you know.

a)

b)

c)

@WWW Web Link

To explore enlargements and reductions of images graphically or numerically by using a scale factor, go to www.mathlinks9.ca and follow the links.

8. Draw an image of the flag using a scale factor of $\frac{1}{3}$.

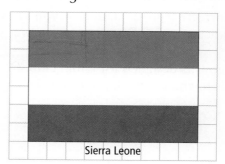

Sierra Leone

Apply

9. Melissa is observing a slide of human cheek cells under the microscope.

a) Is this an enlargement or a reduction? Explain your reasoning.

b) What is the scale factor? Explain its meaning.

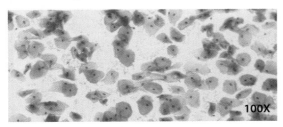

100X

10. Hassan and Mia made posters for the *Festival du Voyageur*. What is the scale factor on Mia's poster compared to Hassan's poster? Explain your reasoning.

Hassan

Mia

> ### Did You Know?
>
> In 1969, the *Festival du Voyageur* was founded in Saint Boniface. The event has grown from three days held in Winnipeg's French Quarter to a ten-day, province-wide celebration every February. This festival celebrates the *joie de vivre* of the fur traders who established the Red River colony and the growing French-Canadian community in western Canada. The Festival encourages people to appreciate the beauty of winter by participating in historical and entertaining activities.
>
>

11. How can you determine if Figure B is a true reduction of Figure A?

Figure A   Figure B

12. The ratio of the length to the width of the Canadian flag is $2:1$. Assume that you have a flag that is 9 cm wide.

a) What are the dimensions of a flag that has a scale factor of 3?

b) What are the dimensions of a flag that has a scale factor of 0.5?

13. For the Heritage Fair, Chloe wants to sew miniature replicas of traditional hunting dress. The pattern piece below is for making pants. She wants to make three different sizes of the pants using the pattern. Use a scale factor of 0.5, 2, and 3 to draw each size.

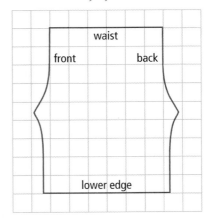

Extend

14. Draw an enlargement of the quadrilateral on grid paper using a scale factor of 2.

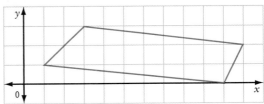

15. Keita made a new bag for her laptop. Her cousin would like the pattern so she can make one. Draw a pattern using the actual measurements. You do not have to include the flap or the strap. Then, reduce the pattern so it will fit on a piece of notebook paper.

30 cm

42 cm → 10 cm

16. Create a scale diagram of your classroom.

a) Measure the dimensions of the classroom and items that can be seen in a top view, including desks, tables, cupboards, and shelves.

b) Choose a scale factor and draw the scale diagram on grid paper.

c) What changes would you make to the layout of your classroom? Where would you place desks or tables? Draw a scale diagram of your new classroom layout.

17. Draw an image so that each line segment is

a) 40% of the original length

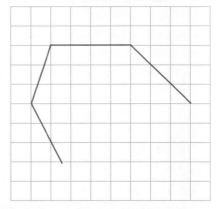

b) 2.5 times the original length

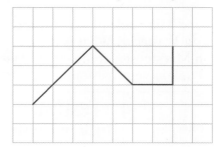

Math Link

Use what you have learned to design a project that requires a scale diagram. You may wish to choose one of the following projects:
• Design at least four different hopscotch patterns for a local recreational area.
• Design or enlarge a pattern for an outfit to wear at your school's fashion show. Assume that you have the instructions and the skills needed to construct the outfit.
• Design a modification of a car's blueprints for a project in your automotive course.
• Design a miniature version of a landmark in your province for display in a tourism project.
• Design a web page featuring a topic and related visuals of your choice. For example, you might feature contemporary drum designs.

a) What design project will you choose?

b) Research your project using the library or the Internet. Obtain or develop an initial design or drawing.

c) Using grid paper, draw an enlargement or a reduction of your design to scale.

Haida hand drum design

Scale Diagrams

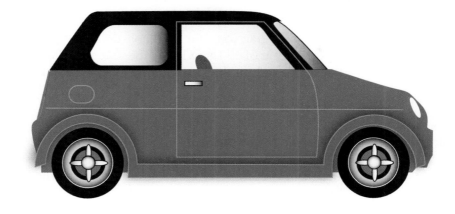

Focus on...

After this lesson, you will be able to...

- identify scale diagrams and interpret the scale factor
- determine the scale factor for scale diagrams
- determine if a given diagram is proportional to the original shape

scale

- a comparison between the size of an object's diagram and the actual size of the object
- can be expressed as a ratio, as a fraction, as a percent, in words, or in a diagram
- the scale 1 : 32 means that 1 cm on the diagram represents 32 cm on the actual car

Materials

- ruler

Car manufacturers create scale drawings that show what a new car will look like.

An actual car measures 339.2 cm in length and 163.2 cm in height. It is drawn to a **scale** of 1 : 32. Is the drawing an accurate representation of the actual model? What different strategies can you develop to find out?

Explore the Accuracy of a Diagram

1. What measurements would help you compare the diagram of the car to the actual car? Take the measurements.

2. Compare the measurements. What conclusions can you make?

Reflect and Check

3. **a)** How did you set up your calculations to determine if the diagram accurately represents the actual car?

   b) What information did you need to determine whether the diagram is an accurate representation of the actual car?

4. **a)** Choose an object and draw one view of it. Estimate the scale between your drawing and the actual object.

   b) Use the method you developed to determine how accurately the drawing represents the actual object.

5. Compare your method with the one used by a classmate. How are the methods similar? How are they different? Which method seems more efficient? Explain.

Link the Ideas

scale diagram

- a drawing that is similar to the actual figure or object
- may be smaller or larger than the actual object, but must be in the same proportions

Example 1: Use the Scale to Determine the Actual Length of an Object

The **scale diagram** of a skateboard uses a scale of $1 : 14$. What is the actual length of the skateboard?

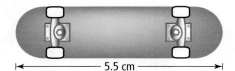

5.5 cm

Solution

Method 1: Use the Scale
The scale $1 : 14$ means that the actual dimensions of the skateboard are 14 times those of the diagram. Multiply the length of the skateboard in the diagram by 14.
$5.5 \times 14 = 77$

The actual length of the skateboard is 77 cm.

Method 2: Use a Proportion
Set up a proportion using the scale and the measurement that is given.

$$\text{scale} = \frac{\text{diagram measurement}}{\text{actual measurement}}$$

> The scale is $1 : 14$. The diagram measures 5.5 cm. The actual measurement is unknown.

$$\frac{1}{14} = \frac{5.5}{y}$$

$\times 5.5$

$$\frac{1}{14} = \frac{5.5}{77}$$

$\times 5.5$

The actual length of the skateboard is 77 cm.

Literacy Link

A *proportion* is a relationship that shows two ratios are equal. It can be written in fraction or ratio form.

For example, the ratio 1 girl to 4 students is the same as 5 girls to 20 students. As a proportion, write:
$\frac{1}{4} = \frac{5}{20}$ or $1 : 4 = 5 : 20$
The corresponding parts of each ratio are in the same units.

Show You Know

The scale for the diagram of the chinook salmon is $1 : 9.2$.

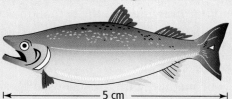

5 cm

Calculate the actual length of the salmon.

Example 2: Determine the Scale Factor

An actual Canadian quarter has a diameter of 23.88 mm. Calculate the scale factor used to create the diagram of the quarter. Express the answer to the nearest tenth.

Solution

Measure the diameter of the diagram of the quarter. It measures 1.4 cm.

> The diagram is a reduction. The scale factor will be less than 1.

Set up a proportion for the scale and the measurements.

$$scale = \frac{diagram\ measurement}{actual\ measurement}$$

$$\frac{1}{x} = \frac{14}{23.88}$$

$$\div 14$$

$$\frac{1}{1.7} = \frac{14}{23.88}$$

$$\div 14$$

> To compare items using a ratio, the units must be the same. The actual measurement is 23.88 mm. The diagram measures 1.4 cm, which is 14 mm.

Strategies

Solve an Equation

Divide to determine the scale factor.
$1 \div 1.7 \approx 0.588...$
$ \approx 0.6$

The scale factor is approximately 0.6.

This means that the quarter in the diagram is approximately 0.6 times as large as the actual quarter.

Show You Know

The flying distance from Dawson City to Whitehorse is 540 km. The distance shown on the map is 3 cm.

a) Complete the following to express the map scale in words.

scale: 1 cm represents ■ km

b) What is the scale factor?
Hint: 1 km = 100 000 cm.

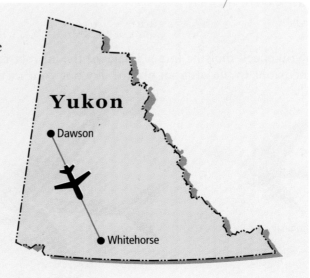

Key Ideas

- A scale diagram is a proportionally smaller or larger representation of an actual object.

- The scale is a ratio between two sets of measurements.

    The scale compares a distance on the map to the actual distance.

    If 1 cm represents 12 km, then 1 cm represents 12 × 100 000 cm.

    The scale is 1 : 1 200 000.

    The scale factor is $\dfrac{1}{1\,200\,000}$.

- You can solve problems involving scale diagrams using different methods.

A map is a scale diagram.

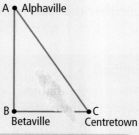

> 1 km = 1000 m and 1 m = 100 cm, so 1 km = 100 000 cm.

- **Use a scale.**

    The distance from A to B on the map is 3 cm. Determine the actual distance.

    3 × 1 200 000 = 3 600 000

    The actual distance is 3 600 000 cm or 36 km.

- **Use a proportion.**

    The distance from A to C on the map measures 4 cm. Determine the actual distance.

    $$\text{scale} = \dfrac{\text{diagram measurement}}{\text{actual measurement}}$$

    $$\dfrac{1}{1\,200\,000} = \dfrac{4}{\blacksquare}$$

    The actual distance is 4 800 000 cm or 48 km.

Check Your Understanding

Communicate the Ideas

1. Joseph is unsure about how to determine the actual length of an object using a scale diagram. List the steps to solve a problem of your choice. Discuss the steps with a classmate.

2. Kira plans to ride 150 km on her bike. This distance is 10 cm on a map. Express the scale of the map

   a) in words   **b)** as a ratio

3. How can you check that the larger image of the airliner is proportional to the dimensions in the original photo? Try out your method. Describe your results.

original

image

Practise

For help with #4 to #7, refer to Example 1 on page 140.

4. State whether you would multiply or divide to determine the missing value.

a) $\dfrac{1}{3} = \dfrac{\blacksquare}{144}$
b) $\dfrac{1}{\blacksquare} = \dfrac{5.2}{117}$

5. Determine the missing value in each proportion.

a) $\dfrac{1}{9} = \dfrac{\blacksquare}{117}$
b) $\dfrac{1}{12} = \dfrac{10.5}{\blacksquare}$

6. Calculate the actual length of each object.

a) The scale for the image of the school bus is $1:302.5$.

b) The scale for the enlarged image of a mosquito is $1:0.5$.

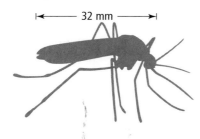

— 32 mm —

7. Determine the actual length of each object.

a) The scale for the image of Victoria's tallest totem pole is $1:972.5$.

4 cm

b) The scale for the model of the humpback whale is $1:280$.

— 5 cm —

For help with #8 to #12, refer to Example 2 on page 141.

8. What is the scale factor?

a) $\blacksquare = \dfrac{30}{200}$
b) $\blacksquare = \dfrac{21}{12.5}$

9. Determine the scale factor.

a) $\blacksquare = \dfrac{0.5}{25}$
b) $\blacksquare = \dfrac{1.6}{3.2}$

10. What scale factor was used to create the image of the snowboard if its actual length is 166 cm? Express your answer to the nearest hundredth.

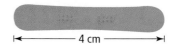

— 4 cm —

11. At the time his photo was taken for the hockey card, Ken was 152.4 cm tall. Calculate the scale factor used to create Ken's image on the hockey card. Express the answer to the nearest hundredth.

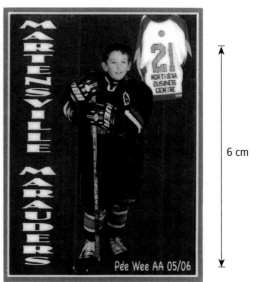

6 cm

12. A flying distance is 800 km. If this distance on a map is 5 cm, what is the scale factor? Hint: 1 km = 100 000 cm.

Apply

13. A Ukrainian decorated egg is called a pysanka. A giant version of a pysanka is located in Vegreville, Alberta. The length of the egg is 9.4 m.

   a) On a scale diagram of the pysanka, what would the length be, if you used a scale of 1:150?

   b) Could your result represent the length of an actual egg? Explain.

14. The footprint of an adult male polar bear measures 30 cm across.

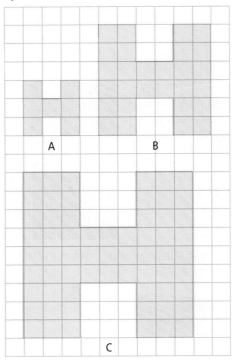

~~2 cm~~

   a) What is the scale factor of this drawing?

   b) What is the actual length of the polar bear's footprint? Show how you know.

   c) Measure your hand span by spreading your hand on a piece of paper. Write the ratio of your hand span to the span of the polar bear's footprint. What conclusion can you make?

15. Viruses are much smaller than bacteria. Some viruses measure 0.0001 mm in diameter. An artist's diagram of a virus shows the diameter as 5 mm. Determine the scale factor used.

16. For the science fair, Leanne plans to build a scale model of a communications tower that is actually 250 m in height. The model has to fit in the foyer of the school, which has a floor-to-ceiling height of 3 m. If Leanne uses a scale of 1:100 to build the model, will it fit into the foyer? Show your work.

17. A model train is a scale model created from actual measurements. The scale factor for HO or Half Zero model trains is 1:87. A typical engine, such as the one shown, is 50 mm in height and 200 mm in length. Determine the actual dimensions of the train engine.

18. Determine the scale factor for each enlargement or reduction.

   a) from A to B   **b)** from A to C

   c) from B to C   **d)** from C to A

   e) from C to B

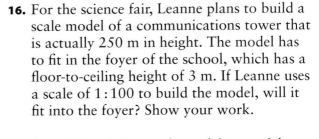

19. Tracy took a picture of a wind turbine at the wind farm in Cowley Ridge, Alberta. The height of the turbine is 45 m.

2.5 cm

a) What scale factor was used to make this reduction?

b) What is the length of a wind turbine blade?

Extend

20. △ABC has coordinates A(4, 3), B(4, 0), and C(7, 0). △DEF has coordinates D(0, −1), E(0, −2), and F(1, −2).

a) Draw the triangles on grid paper.

b) Are the two triangles proportional to each other? Justify your answer.

c) What is the scale factor of △ABC to △DEF?

d) Determine the scale factor of △DEF to △ABC.

e) Calculate the area of each triangle.

f) What is the ratio of the area of △ABC to the area of △DEF? of the area of △DEF to the area of △ABC?

g) How does the scale factor of the side lengths compare to the scale factor of the areas?

21. Elk Valley Coal uses trucks such as the one shown. The man in the picture is 1.69 m tall.

a) What is the height of the wheel of the truck?

b) What is the height of the truck?

> **Did You Know?**
>
> Elk Valley Coal operates five open-pit coal mines. The mines are in southeastern British Columbia and in west-central Alberta.

22. A rectangle has sides measuring 12 cm and 16 cm. An enlarged, similar rectangle has an area of 1200 cm².

a) What is the scale factor between
  • the smaller and the larger rectangle?
  • the larger and the smaller rectangle?

b) Is one method better than the other to express this scale factor? Explain your reasoning.

Math Link

a) Determine the scale factor for the enlargement or reduction of the design you drew for the Math Link on page 138. Show your work.

b) Choose a new feature to add to your design.
  • Draw it on your scale diagram.
  • Calculate the actual dimensions of the new feature.

c) Explain how you know the scale diagram is proportional to the actual design.

4.3 Similar Triangles

Focus on...

After this lesson, you will be able to...

- determine similar triangles
- determine if diagrams are proportional
- solve problems using the properties of similar triangles

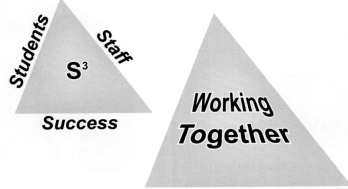

Students and Staff

Bonnie and Justin created these logos for the Student Council.

Their advisor tells them that the triangles are similar. How can she tell? What do you know about similar figures? What strategies can you develop to determine if triangles are similar?

Materials

- tracing paper
- ruler
- protractor

**corresponding angles
corresponding sides**

- have the same relative position in geometric figures

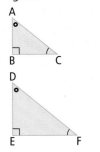

corresponding angles:
∠A and ∠D
∠B and ∠E
∠C and ∠F

corresponding sides:
AB and DE
BC and EF
AC and DF

Explore How to Identify Similar Triangles

1. Trace each logo on separate pieces of tracing paper.

2. a) Measure the angles in each logo. What do you notice about the **corresponding angles**?

b) Measure the side lengths in each logo. What do you notice about the ratios of the **corresponding sides** of the triangles?

Reflect and Check

3. a) What conclusions can you make about the corresponding angles of the two triangles?

b) What conclusions can you make about the corresponding sides of the two triangles?

4. a) What conditions do you think are necessary in order for two triangles to be similar?

b) Test the conditions on a different set of two triangles. Are the triangles similar? Discuss with a classmate why you think the triangles are, or are not, similar.

Link the Ideas

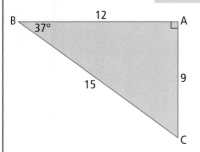

Example 1: Identify Similar Triangles

Determine if △ABC is **similar** to △EFG.

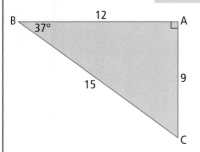

> **similar (figures)**
> • have the same shape but different size
> • have equal corresponding angles and proportional corresponding sides

Solution

Similar triangles have corresponding angles that are equal in measure and corresponding sides that are proportional in length.

Compare corresponding angles:
∠A = 90° and ∠E = 90°
∠B = 37° and ∠F = 37°
∠C = 53° and ∠G = 53°

> The sum of the angles in a triangle is 180°. If you know the measures of two pairs of angles are equal, then what can you conclude about the third pair of angles?

The corresponding angles are equal.

Compare corresponding sides:

$$\frac{AB}{EF} = \frac{12}{4} \qquad \frac{BC}{FG} = \frac{15}{5} \qquad \frac{AC}{EG} = \frac{9}{3}$$
$$= 3 \qquad\qquad = 3 \qquad\qquad = 3$$

The corresponding sides are proportional with a scale factor of 3.
△ABC ∼ △EFG

> **Literacy Link**
> The symbol ∼ means is similar to.
> △ABC ∼ △EFG means triangle ABC is similar to triangle EFG.

> **Literacy Link**
>
> Angles can be named in two ways:
> • Use three capital letters. The middle letter is the vertex of the angle.
> • Use only the middle letter identifying the vertex. Use a single letter when there is only one angle at a vertex.
>
> For example, the angle at vertex L can be named ∠KLM or ∠L.
>
>

WWW Web Link

To learn more about
properties of similar
triangles, go to www.
mathlinks9.ca and
follow the links.

Show You Know

Determine if each pair of triangles is similar. Show how you know.

a)
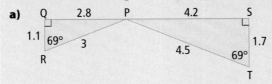

b)
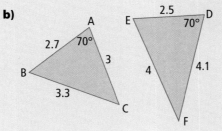

Example 2: Use Similar Triangles to Determine a Missing Side Length

Kyle is drawing triangles for a math puzzle. Use your knowledge of similar triangles to determine

a) if the triangles are similar
b) the missing side length

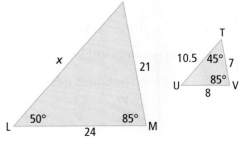

Solution

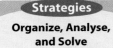

Strategies

Organize, Analyse, and Solve

a) Check that △KLM is similar to △TUV.
The sum of the angles in a triangle is 180°.
$\angle K = 180° - 50° - 85°$
$\quad = 45°$
$\angle U = 180° - 85° - 45°$
$\quad = 50°$
Compare corresponding angles:
$\angle K = 45°$ and $\angle T = 45°$
$\angle L = 50°$ and $\angle U = 50°$
$\angle M = 85°$ and $\angle V = 85°$
All pairs of corresponding angles are equal.

> It is not necessary to prove both conditions for similarity. One is sufficient.

Therefore, $\triangle KLM \sim \triangle TUV$.

b) You can compare corresponding sides to determine the scale factor.

$$\frac{LM}{UV} = \frac{24}{8} \qquad \frac{KM}{TV} = \frac{21}{7} \qquad \frac{KL}{TU} = \frac{x}{10.5}$$
$$\quad = 3 \qquad\qquad\quad = 3 \qquad\qquad\quad\; = \blacksquare$$

The scale factor is 3. You can solve for the unknown length.

Method 1: Use a Scale Factor
Since the triangles are similar, you can use the scale factor to determine the missing length.

$$\frac{x}{10.5} = 3$$

$$x = 31.5$$

> How would you solve for x?

The missing side length is 31.5 units.

Method 2: Use a Proportion
Since the triangles are similar, you can use equal ratios to set up a proportion.

$$\frac{KM}{TV} = \frac{KL}{TU}$$

× 1.5

> $10.5 \div 7 = 1.5$

$$\frac{21}{7} = \frac{x}{10.5}$$

× 1.5

$$x = 31.5$$

The missing side length is 31.5 units.

Show You Know

Solve using a method of your choice.

a) △GHI is similar to △KLM. What is the missing side length? Express your answer to the nearest tenth.

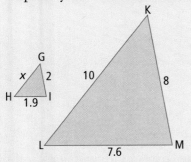

b) △ABC is similar to △EFC. Determine the missing side length. Express your answer to the nearest tenth.

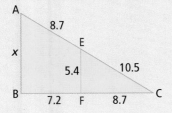

Key Ideas

- Triangles are similar if one of the following conditions holds true:
  - corresponding angles are equal in measure
  - corresponding sides are proportional in length

    △DEF is similar to △ABC.
    △DEF is not similar to △PQR.
    ∠D = ∠A, ∠E = ∠B, ∠F = ∠C

    $\dfrac{DE}{AB} = \dfrac{3}{1.5}$　　$\dfrac{EF}{BC} = \dfrac{2.2}{1.1}$　　$\dfrac{DF}{AC} = \dfrac{2.6}{1.3}$
    　= 2　　　　　= 2　　　　　= 2

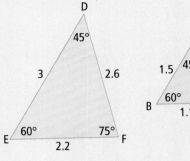

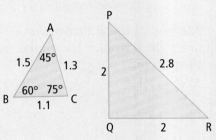

- You can solve problems related to similar triangles using different methods.
  - Use a scale factor.
  - Use a proportion.

Check Your Understanding

Communicate the Ideas

1. If two triangles are similar, what can you say about the angles of the triangles? the side lengths of the triangles?

2. Amanda is unclear about similar triangles. She drew these two triangles and states they are similar. Is she correct? Explain.

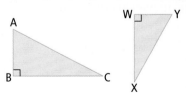

3. Are two triangles that have equal angles and equal sides similar? Use an example to support your answer.

Practise

For help with #4 to #8, refer to Example 1 on page 147.

4. List the corresponding angles and the corresponding sides for △PQR and △TUV.

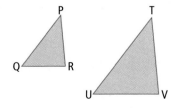

5. What are the corresponding angles and the corresponding sides in this pair of triangles?

6. Are the triangles similar? Show how you know.

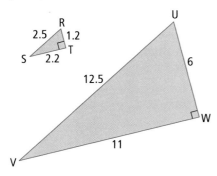

7. Determine if the triangles are similar. Show how you know.

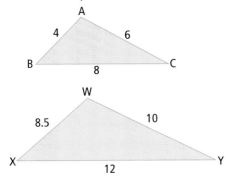

8. Determine which pairs of triangles are similar. Use a sketch to help explain how you know.

Triangle	Angles	Sides
△ABC	∠A = 90° ∠B = 45° ∠C = 45°	AB = 6 BC = 8.4 AC = 6
△EFG	∠E = 90° ∠F = 45° ∠G = 45°	EF = 3 FG = 4.2 EG = 3
△HIJ	∠H = 90° ∠I = 60° ∠J = 30°	HI = 9.2 IJ = 18.4 HJ = 15.9
△KLM	∠K = 90° ∠L = 45° ∠M = 45°	KL = 9 LM = 12.6 KM = 9

For help with #9 to #11, refer to Example 2 on pages 148–149.

9. △STR is similar to △UWV. Determine the missing side length.

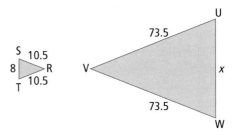

10. △CDE is similar to △GFE. What is the missing side length?

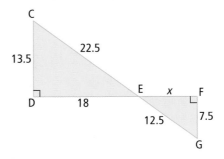

11. Draw a triangle that is similar to the one shown. Label the measurements for angles and sides on your similar triangle.

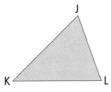

Apply

12. Sam built a ramp to a loading dock. The ramp has a vertical support 2 m from the base of the loading dock and 3 m from the base of the ramp. If the vertical support is 1.2 m in height, what is the height of the loading dock?

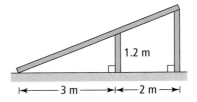

13. Two extension ladders are leaning at the same angle against a vertical wall. The 3-m ladder reaches 2.4 m up the wall. How much farther up the wall does the 8-m ladder reach?

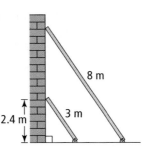

14. Erin, who is 1.60 m tall, casts a shadow that is 1.25 m long. Her shadow extends to the end of a tree's shadow when she stands 4.75 m from the tree. What is the height of the tree?

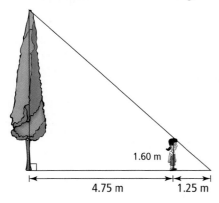

15. Sara was helping her father assemble a slide for the local park. He decides to reinforce the slide with an extra support beam. How long should the extra support beam be?

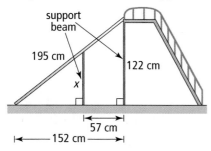

16. Peter, who is 168 cm tall, casts a 45-cm shadow. Michael, who is standing beside him, casts a 40-cm shadow. Can you tell who is taller? Use a diagram to help explain why or why not.

17. Develop a word problem that can be solved using similar triangles. Include a diagram.

Extend

18. A tourist wants to estimate the height of an office tower. He places a mirror on the ground and moves away to sight the top of the tower in the mirror.

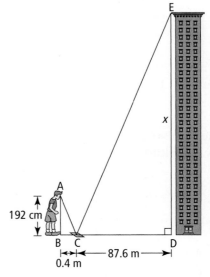

a) How tall is the tower?

b) In this situation, why is the mirror reflection a better way to indirectly measure the tower than by using shadows?

19. Is it possible for the two triangles described below to be similar? Explain your reasoning.

a) Two angles of one triangle measure 60° and 70°. Two angles of the other triangle measure 50° and 80°.

b) Two angles of one triangle measure 45° and 75°. Two angles of the other triangle measure 45° and 60°.

20. The sides of a triangle measure 3 cm, 5 cm, and 6 cm. If the side of a similar triangle corresponding to 3 cm measures 8 cm,

a) determine the lengths of the other sides

b) determine the ratio of the perimeter of the smaller triangle to the perimeter of the larger triangle

21. Using a measuring tape, your shadow, and yourself, how can you determine the height of your school without actually measuring it?

22. △WXY is similar to △ZWY. Calculate ZY to the nearest tenth.

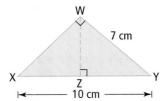

W

7 cm

X

Z

10 cm

Y

23. Use two different sets of measurements to determine the area of △KLM.

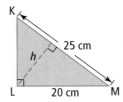

K

25 cm

h

L

20 cm

M

Math Link

For your design project report, include a signature logo that features your name.

a) On a sheet of 8.5 × 11 paper, design your logo. Include a triangle that is similar to the one shown. Measure all the angles and side lengths.

b) Draw a scale diagram of the logo to fit on your design project. Identify the scale factor you used.

Tech Link

Similarity and Scale Factors

In this activity, you can use dynamic geometry software to explore similarity and scale factors. To use this activity, go to www.mathlinks9.ca and follow the links.

Explore

1. Slide point X along line segment AB and describe what happens to the image drawing.

2. How do the measures of the corresponding sides of the drawing change relative to each other? Explain.

3. Compare the scale factor to the lengths of the sides of the original drawing and the image drawing. Create and complete a table similar to the one below with measurements taken at different locations. Discuss your findings with a classmate. Hint: In the table, *m* means *the measure of*.

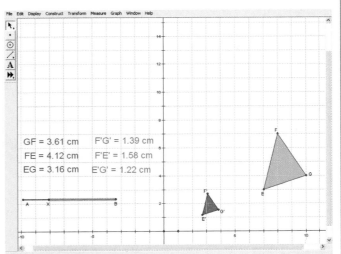

*m*FE	*m*F′E′	$\dfrac{m\text{AX}}{m\text{XB}}$

4.4 Similar Polygons

Did You Know?

The star quilt is a traditional pattern used by many different cultures including the Sioux, Lakota, Dakota, and Europeans. The star pattern is derived from designs for early buffalo robes. When the buffalo herds disappeared, the star quilt replaced the buffalo robe in Aboriginal traditions. Today, star quilts given as gifts are highly valued by recipients. They are often made for special events, such as memorial feasts, naming ceremonies, marriages, and celebrations.

Focus on...

After this lesson, you will be able to...
- identify similar polygons and explain why they are similar
- draw similar polygons
- solve problems using the properties of similar polygons

The single star in a Lakota star quilt is made from fabric cut into diamond shapes and pieced together in eight sections. When the sections are joined together, an eight-pointed star is formed.

Are the different-sized diamonds formed on the quilt similar? What strategies might you use to find out?

Explore How to Identify Similar Polygons

Materials
- tracing paper
- protractor
- ruler

1. Trace each diamond on separate pieces of tracing paper.

2. a) Organize your data about corresponding angles and corresponding sides.

b) What do you observe about the corresponding angles?

c) What do you observe about the ratios of the corresponding sides?

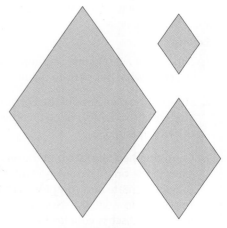

Reflect and Check

polygon
- a two-dimensional closed figure made of three or more line segments

3. What conclusions can you make about the three diamonds?

4. a) What conditions do you think are necessary in order for two **polygons** to be similar?

b) Test the conditions on a different set of two polygons. Are the polygons similar? Discuss with a classmate why you think the polygons are, or are not, similar.

Link the Ideas

Similar polygons have corresponding angles that are equal and corresponding side lengths that are proportional.

Example 1: Identify Similar Polygons

The two quadrilaterals look similar. Is M′A′T′H′ a true enlargement of MATH? Explain.

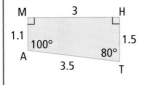 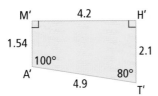

Literacy Link
M′ is read "M prime."

Solution

Compare corresponding angles:
∠M = 90° and ∠M′ = 90°
∠A = 100° and ∠A′ = 100°
∠T = 80° and ∠T′ = 80°
∠H = 90° and ∠H′ = 90°

> What is the sum of the interior angles in a quadrilateral?

Compare corresponding sides:

$$\frac{M'A'}{MA} = \frac{1.54}{1.1} \qquad \frac{A'T'}{AT} = \frac{4.9}{3.5}$$
$$= 1.4 \qquad\qquad = 1.4$$

$$\frac{H'T'}{HT} = \frac{2.1}{1.5} \qquad \frac{M'H'}{MH} = \frac{4.2}{3}$$
$$= 1.4 \qquad\qquad = 1.4$$

The corresponding side lengths are proportional with a scale factor of 1.4.

M′A′T′H′ is a true enlargement of MATH by a scale factor of 1.4.

Did You Know?

Polygons can be divided into non-overlapping triangles. The sum of the interior angles in a triangle is 180°. You can determine the sum of the interior angles in a polygon by multiplying the number of triangles by 180.

To draw the triangles, start with any vertex of the polygon, and from there draw a line to connect to each of the other vertices. The pentagon can be divided into three triangles.

3 × 180° = 540°
The sum of the interior angles in a pentagon is 540°.

Show You Know

Determine if the two trapezoids are similar. Explain how you know.

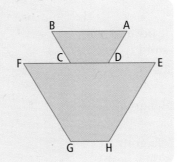

WWW Web Link
To learn more about the properties of similar polygons, go to www.mathlinks9.ca and follow the links.

Example 2: Determine a Missing Side Length

Jason wants to make an enlargement of the flag of Nunavut. He knows that the two rectangles JKLM and PQRS are similar. What is the missing side length of rectangle JKLM?

Solution

Since the rectangles are similar, the side lengths are proportional. Use corresponding sides to set up a proportion.

$$\frac{KL}{QR} = \frac{LM}{RS}$$

$$\frac{32}{5} = \frac{x}{9}$$

$$6.4 = \frac{x}{9}$$

$$x = 57.6$$

The missing side length is 57.6 cm.

> What different method could you use to solve the problem? Try it.

Strategies

Solve an Equation

Show You Know

The two trapezoids shown are similar. Determine the missing side length. Show your work.

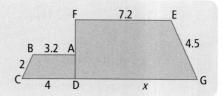

Key Ideas

- Polygons are similar if both of the following conditions hold true:
  - corresponding angles are equal in measure
  - corresponding side lengths are proportional
- You can use similar polygons to determine unknown side lengths or angle measures.

The trapezoids HIJK and LMNO are similar.

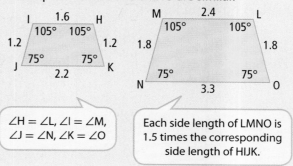

> ∠H = ∠L, ∠I = ∠M, ∠J = ∠N, ∠K = ∠O

> Each side length of LMNO is 1.5 times the corresponding side length of HIJK.

Check Your Understanding

Communicate the Ideas

1. Develop an example and a solution to help explain how to determine a missing side length in a pair of similar polygons.

2. a) Use grid paper to draw a parallelogram that is similar to the one shown. Explain how you know the two are similar.

   b) Compare your similar parallelogram with the one of a classmate. Are your parallelograms similar to each other? Explain.

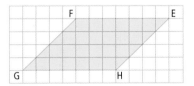

Practise

For help with #3 and #4, refer to Example 1 on page 155.

3. Decide if each pair of polygons is similar. Show your reasoning.

   a)

   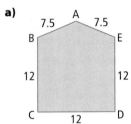

   b)

   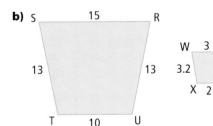

4. Identify all sets of similar polygons in this collage. You might trace the image and colour code sets of similar polygons.

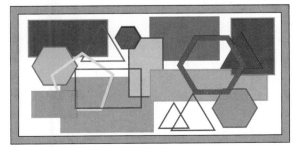

For help with #5 and #6, refer to Example 2 on page 156.

5. Use the two similar pentagons to help determine the missing side length. Show your work.

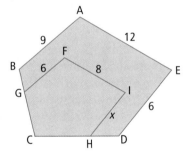

6. The sides of rectangle A measure 22.4 m and 14.7 m. One side of a similar rectangle B measures 4.3 m. The measure for the other side is missing. Rectangle A is an enlargement of rectangle B with a scale factor of 5.2. What is the missing measurement, to the nearest tenth?

Apply

7. William made the statement, "All quadrilaterals with sides the same length are similar." Is he correct? Explain.

WWW Web Link

To explore the changes when you manipulate two similar figures and vary the scale factor, go to www.mathlinks9.ca and follow the links.

8. Chicken wire is often used for building fences. It is made of flexible wire with gaps that are shaped like hexagons.

a) Use grid paper to draw and label:
   - two hexagons that are similar to one shown in the picture
   - two hexagons that are not similar to one shown

b) For each pair of hexagons, explain how you know they are similar or not similar.

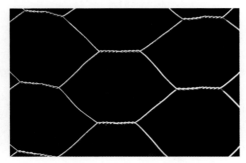

9. Michelle plans to make a game board that is a reduction of an actual baseball diamond. A baseball diamond is a square with sides that measure 27.4 m (2740 cm). Draw Michelle's game board using a scale of 1 : 182.5.

10. a) Rachel's family is making a cement deck around a pool that is a regular octagon. They want the cement deck to keep the same shape as the pool, but with sides 1.5 times as long as the pool. What do the lengths of the cement forms along the sides of the outer octagon need to be in order to pour the cement?

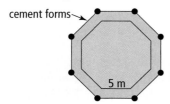

cement forms

5 m

b) What is the sum of the interior angles in an octagon? Show how you know.

11. The pattern shows the front of a birdhouse. Chris enlarged the pattern using a scale factor of 3. He needs to make it twice as large as that.

a) Draw the correct size.

b) Explain how you know the enlargement is similar to the original pattern.

12. A piece of cardboard is cut showing the inner and outer boundaries of a pair of similar quadrilaterals. Calculate the perimeter of the smaller quadrilateral.

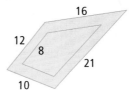

16

12

8

21

10

Extend

13. In a camera, similar figures occur as shown. Calculate the actual height of the arrow.

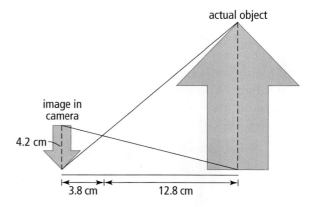

actual object

image in camera

4.2 cm

3.8 cm

12.8 cm

14. Eliza is building a model of the canvas tent her family uses in Behchoko, NWT. The model will have a peak height of 12 cm. The actual tent floor measures 2.4 m by 3 m. The walls are 1.5 m high and the peak height is 2.4 m.

   a) What scale factor will Eliza need to use for her model?

   b) The front of the tent is a pentagon. Calculate the dimensions of this polygon on the model.

   c) Calculate the other dimensions of the tent model.

15. An old rectangular tank with length 0.3 m could hold 154 L of water. A new similar tank has a length of 1.5 m. What is the capacity of the new tank?

16. How do the ratios of areas compare to the ratios of corresponding side lengths in similar polygons? Use pairs of similar polygons to help explain your answer.

17. Develop an argument showing that if two prisms have corresponding side lengths in the ratio of $3:1$, then their volumes are in the ratio of $27:1$.

18. a) Identify the similar polygons shown in the tessellation.

   b) Describe the pattern verbally. Use your description to create your own tessellation that features similar polygons.

   c) Sketch each different set of similar polygons in your tessellation. Label the dimensions of each set.

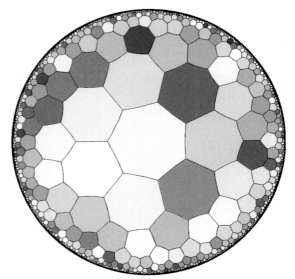

Math Link

For your design project, include a polygon.
• Use a polygon that is similar to one shown here.
• Use an appropriate scale factor and draw a scale diagram of the polygon to fit on your design project. Identify the scale factor used on your design.

Chapter 4 Review

Key Words

For #1 to #4, unscramble the letters for each term. Use the clues to help you.

1. L G Y N O P O

A ▇▇▇▇ is a closed figure with sides that are line segments.

2. I R I S L M A

▇▇▇▇ figures have equal corresponding angles and proportional corresponding side lengths.

3. C A S E L   O T C A F R

The ▇▇▇▇ ▇▇▇▇ is the constant amount by which any dimension of a shape is enlarged or reduced.

4. R R O O P P T I N O

A ▇▇▇▇ is a statement that says two ratios are equal.

4.1 Enlargements and Reductions, pages 130–138

5. Use grid paper to draw the design using each scale factor.

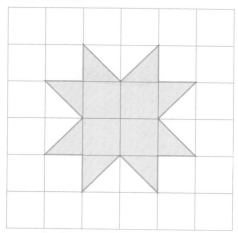

a) scale factor of 2

b) scale factor of 0.5

6. Draw an image of the egg design that is three times as large as the original.

> **◖◗ Art Link**
>
> Pysanky is the traditional Eastern European art that uses beeswax and dyes to create designs on eggs.

7. Draw a reduction of the arrow that is half as large as the original.

8. Draw an image of the square to illustrate each of the following.

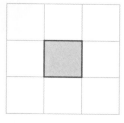

a) a scale factor equal to 1

b) a scale factor greater than 1

c) a scale factor less than 1

4.2 Scale Diagrams, pages 139–145

9. An actual CD jewel case measures 14.3 cm. Determine the scale factor used to create the image.

|←— 2.2 cm —→|

10. Determine the actual length of each object from its scale diagram.

a) spoon

Scale 1:4

3.5 cm

b) toy car

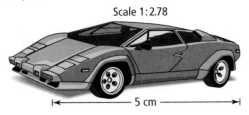

Scale 1:2.78

5 cm

11. The scale for an image of a tower is 1 cm represents 12.5 m. If the actual tower measures 108.75 m in height, what is its height on the drawing?

12. A highway is 600 km in length. If the length of the highway on a map is 6 cm, what is the scale factor? Hint: 1 km = 100 000 cm.

4.3 Similar Triangles, pages 146–153

13. Are these triangles similar? Explain.

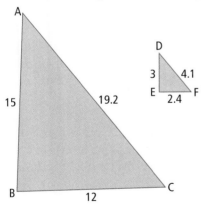

14. △UVW is similar to △UYZ. Determine the length x.

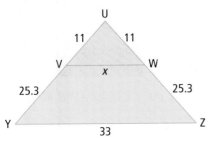

15. Given that △GHI is similar to△KLM, what is the length of side IG?

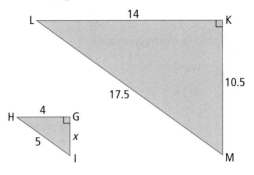

4.4 Similar Polygons, pages 154–159

16. Determine if the two polygons are similar.

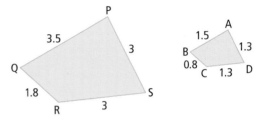

17. The sides of one quadrilateral measure 3 cm, 9 cm, 12 cm, and x. The corresponding sides of a similar quadrilateral measure 2.25 cm, 6.75 cm, 9 cm, and 13.5 cm. What is the value of x?

18. The pentagons DEFGH and JKLMN are similar. Determine the missing side lengths, to the nearest tenth.

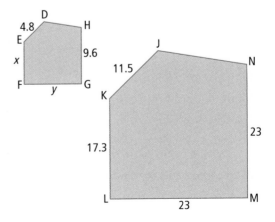

For #1 to #4, choose the best answer.

1. What is the value of x if $\frac{1}{x} = \frac{8}{32}$?

   A 2   **B** 3   **C** 4   **D** 7

2. $\triangle GHI \sim \triangle KLM$. Determine the missing length.

   A 4
   B 8
   C 10
   D 14

   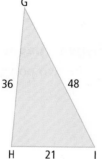
   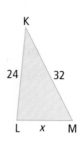

3. On a scale diagram, what does 1 in the scale 1:5 represent?

   A how many times larger the object is
   B one unit of the actual size
   C one unit of the diagram size
   D the total size of the scale diagram

4. Which pair of quadrilaterals appears to be similar?

   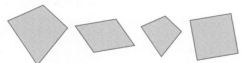

   Figure 1   Figure 2   Figure 3   Figure 4

   A Figure 1 and Figure 2
   B Figure 1 and Figure 3
   C Figure 1 and Figure 4
   D Figure 2 and Figure 3

Complete the statements in #5 and #6.

5. An umbrella is 75 cm in length. Using a scale of 1:5, the length of an image of the umbrella is ■.

6. The constant amount by which the dimensions of an object are enlarged or reduced is called the ▇▇▇ ▇▇▇.

Short Answer

7. Draw a reduction that is half the size of this figure.

8. If the actual pencil has a length of 18.8 cm, determine the scale factor used to create this image. Give your answer to the nearest tenth.

   4 cm

9. The flagpole in front of city hall is 5.5 m tall. If the height of a model of the flagpole is 6.5 cm, what is the scale factor of the model? Express your answer to the nearest hundredth.

10. An actual western spruce budworm larva can grow to 32 mm in length. Using a scale of 1:1.43, what would be the length of an image of the larva? Express your answer to the nearest tenth.

> **◑◑ Did You Know?**
>
> Western spruce budworm larvae feed mostly on the foliage, flowers, and developing cones of fir and spruce trees. These insects cause serious damage to Douglas firs in the interior of British Columbia.
>
>

11. Is the image proportional to the original shape? Explain how you know. If it is proportional, state the scale factor.

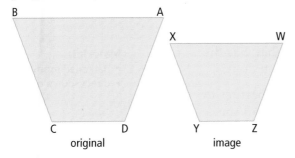

original

image

Extended Response

12. At noon one day, a 20-m vertical pole casts a shadow that is 28 m long. A nearby building casts a shadow 35 m in length. Sketch the situation. How tall is the building?

13. Determine if △ABC and △DEF are similar. Show all your work.

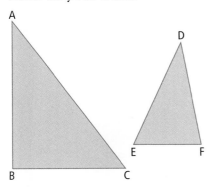

14. Bees made the hexagonal-shaped cells in the honeycomb shown here. Draw a hexagon similar to one of these cells. Explain why the two hexagons are similar.

> **Did You Know?**
>
> A honeycomb is a mass of hexagonal wax cells that contain bee larvae, honey, and pollen. The hexagonal arrangement is an efficient way to pack as many cells as possible in a limited space.

15. These polygons are similar. Determine the missing lengths x and y. Show your work.

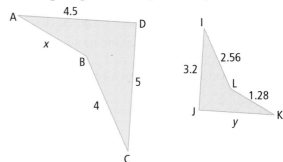

Finalize your design project.

a) Decide on the layout. Include the following elements:
   • an enlarged or reduced image of your design
   • a similar triangle for the logo
   • a similar polygon that features the title of your design project
   • a scale diagram of your design

b) Make a presentation that includes:
   • your design and the scale you used
   • a description or actual sample of the completed design project
   • what you learned about scale diagrams and similarity

Challenges

Shadow, Shadow

When was the last time you made a shadow puppet? What was the largest shadow puppet you have ever made? How did you do it?

You be the puppeteer for a children's show. Work with a partner to develop shadow puppets that can be used to explore some of the mathematics you learned in this chapter.

Materials
• darkened room
• direct source of light

1. Create a bird shadow like the one shown.
   a) What is the scale factor between the hands and the corresponding shadow? Explain how you determined the scale factor.
   b) Use a different set of dimensions to calculate the scale factor.
   c) What do you notice about the two scale factors?
   d) What is the mathematical relationship between the hands and the corresponding shadow?

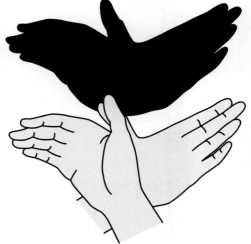

2. a) Create a shadow puppet of your own design. Do not move the light source. Instead, move your hands, changing the distance between them and the wall.
   b) How does moving your hands affect the scale factor of the shadow? Record your observations and justify your response mathematically.

3. a) Cast the shadow puppet on the wall. Keep your hands in the same location but this time move the light source closer to and farther away from your hands.
   b) How does moving the light source affect the scale factor of the shadow? Record your observations and justify your response mathematically.

Graphic Designer

You be a graphic designer. Design a logo for a community, an organization, a school, a product, or a service. Your logo must

- include a feature that sets the community, organization, school, product, or service apart. For example, you might represent
  - a community award using a symbol such as a trophy
  - a culture using a symbol such as a totem pole
  - an organization using a symbol such as an animal with qualities that reflect those of the organization
  - a service using symbols such as a computer, a calculator, or a hammer and nails
  - an industry using symbols such as an oil well or a grain elevator
  - geography using symbols such as mountains, trees, or plains
- include polygons or composite shapes made of polygons
- be scalable, meaning that it can be enlarged or reduced

1. **a)** Design the logo.
   b) Explain why you chose the particular elements of your logo.

2. **a)** Decide on the dimensions of an enlargement of the logo for a billboard or a banner.
   b) Determine the scale factor.
   c) Mathematically justify the scale factor for three measurements in your logo.

3. **a)** Decide on the dimensions of a reduction of the logo for a business card or a web site.
   b) Determine the scale factor.
   c) Mathematically justify the scale factor for three measurements in your logo.

Canadian Blood Services
Société canadienne du sang

Chapter 1 Symmetry and Surface Area

1. Sketch each shape showing its line(s) of symmetry. Describe the lines of symmetry and the type of symmetry each shape has.

   a) 　　**b)**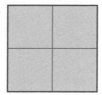

2. Describe two ways you could complete the drawing if the dashed line represents a line of symmetry. Complete the drawing.

   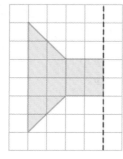

3. Create a design within a circle that shows both line and rotation symmetry.

   a) How many lines of symmetry are in your design? Describe them.

   b) What is the order of rotation in your design?

   c) Give the angle of rotation in both degrees and fractions of a revolution.

4. Draw a diagram of a square cake and a round cake. Select any dimensions you like as long as the side of the square cake is the same length as the diameter of the round cake.

   a) Find the surface area of each cake. Use all sides except the bottom.

   b) Cut each cake into four equal pieces. If the pieces of cake are separated from each other, by what percent does the surface area of each cake increase? Again, do not consider the bottom.

5. Reproduce the triangle on a coordinate grid.

   a) Complete a diagram that has rotation symmetry of order 4 about the origin.
   - Label the vertices on the original triangle.
   - Show the coordinates of their images after each rotation.

   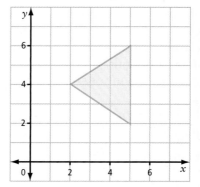

   b) Start again, this time using line symmetry to make a new diagram. Use the y-axis and then the x-axis as lines of symmetry.

6. Four cubes, each with side lengths of 25 cm, are joined as shown.

   a) Find the surface area of the solid that is formed.

   b) If the four cubes are rearranged as shown, how does the surface area change?

Chapter 2 Rational Numbers

7. Write the following rational numbers in ascending order.

$$0.\overline{6} \quad -0.9 \quad -\frac{4}{5} \quad 2.7 \quad -2\frac{3}{4} \quad -\frac{2}{3}$$

8. Identify a fraction between -6.3 and -6.4.

9. Estimate, then calculate.
- **a)** $-2.52 + 1.84$
- **b)** $-2.4 \times (-1.5)$
- **c)** $-4.37 \div (-0.95)$
- **d)** $0.76 + (-1.83)$
- **e)** $8.48 - 10.51$
- **f)** $-5.3(4.2)$
- **g)** $-2.31 - (-5.72)$
- **h)** $-5.5 \div (-5.5)$

10. Estimate, then calculate.
- **a)** $1\frac{1}{10} - \left(-1\frac{1}{10}\right)$
- **b)** $3\frac{3}{5} \div \left(-3\frac{3}{8}\right)$
- **c)** $-1\frac{1}{2} - \frac{1}{12}$
- **d)** $-\frac{1}{6} + \left(-\frac{1}{8}\right)$
- **e)** $\frac{1}{10} \times \left(-\frac{3}{7}\right)$
- **f)** $\frac{2}{3} \div \frac{4}{5}$
- **g)** $-4\frac{1}{2} + 2\frac{5}{9}$
- **h)** $-2\frac{1}{2}\left(-2\frac{1}{2}\right)$

11. Estimate and then calculate the side length of each square from its area. If necessary, round your answer to the nearest hundredth of a unit.
- **a)** 2.56 cm^2
- **b)** 0.01 km^2
- **c)** 0.048 mm^2
- **d)** 1.02 km^2

12. Mary is sewing a square quilt. If the area of her quilt is 2.89 m^2, what is its perimeter?

Chapter 3 Powers and Exponents

13. Write $4^2 \times (4^3)^5$ as a single power.

14. Evaluate the expression $(-6)^0 + 2^3 \div (7 - 5)^2$.

15. Write $\dfrac{(-4)^2(-4)^{10}}{(-4)^3}$ as a single power and then evaluate.

16. Write $(3 \times 7)^4$ as repeated multiplication without any exponents and as a product of two powers.

17. A population of 50 bacteria doubles in number every hour. The formula $N = 50(2)^t$ determines the number of bacteria, N, that are present after t hours. How many bacteria will there be after each number of hours?
- **a)** 5 h
- **b)** 9 h

18. Make an enlargement of the figure using a scale factor of 3.

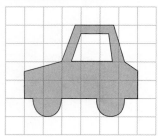

19. Determine the missing values.

a) $\dfrac{1}{3.5} = \dfrac{\blacksquare}{42}$

b) $\dfrac{1}{\blacksquare} = \dfrac{2.7}{49.95}$

c) $\dfrac{1}{0.09} = \dfrac{4.6}{\blacksquare}$

20. Determine the missing length.

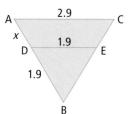

21. Use the scale to calculate the actual flying distance from Calgary to Regina. Express your answer to the nearest kilometre.

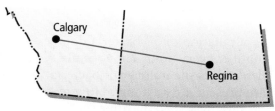

Scale: 1 cm represents 154 km

22. Are any of the rectangles similar? Justify your answer.

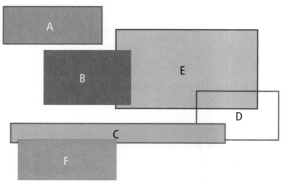

23. a) Identify the different types of polygons shown in the tessellation.

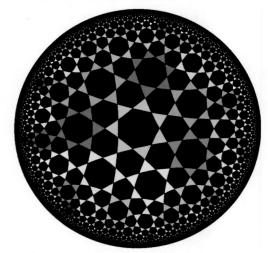

b) Identify any similar polygons. Describe the pattern verbally.

c) Create your own tessellation that features similar polygons.

How Many Times Can You Fold a Piece of Paper?

Bruce claims that no one can fold a piece of paper in half more than seven or eight times, no matter how large the sheet or how thin the paper. Check it out. Is Bruce correct?

Materials
• paper of different sizes and thicknesses

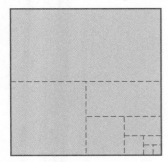

1. Use three different thicknesses of paper.
   a) For each type of paper, estimate the thickness of a single sheet.
   b) Devise a strategy to show how to determine the thickness of a sheet of paper. Support your work mathematically.

2. Use three different sizes of paper to explore the number of times in a row that a piece of paper can be folded in half.
   a) For each piece of paper, predict how many times you will be able to fold it in half.
   b) Fold each piece of paper in half as many times in a row as possible. Record your results. Compare your results with those of your classmates.

3. a) Write expressions for the thickness of the stack after each fold for a piece of paper of thickness, t.
   b) Write expressions for the area of the top of the stack after each fold for a piece of paper of area, a.
   c) Compare the patterns in the expressions you wrote. Use the patterns to help explain why it becomes difficult to fold a piece of paper after only a few folds.

5

Introduction to Polynomials

Many people have an interest in tricks, games, and puzzles. Sometimes, it is difficult to determine how puzzles work. However, with a few simple techniques you can usually figure them out.

Illusions are one type of puzzle. In the illusion shown here, there are several faces. Examine the picture. How many faces can you find?

In this chapter, you will use polynomials, a part of algebra, to help explain how games, puzzles, and number tricks work.

What You Will Learn

- to demonstrate an understanding of polynomials
- to model, record, and explain addition and subtraction of polynomials

WWW Web Link

The optical illusion shown here is not the full image. To look for faces in the full image, go to www.mathlinks9.ca and follow the links. Try to find at least 8 faces.

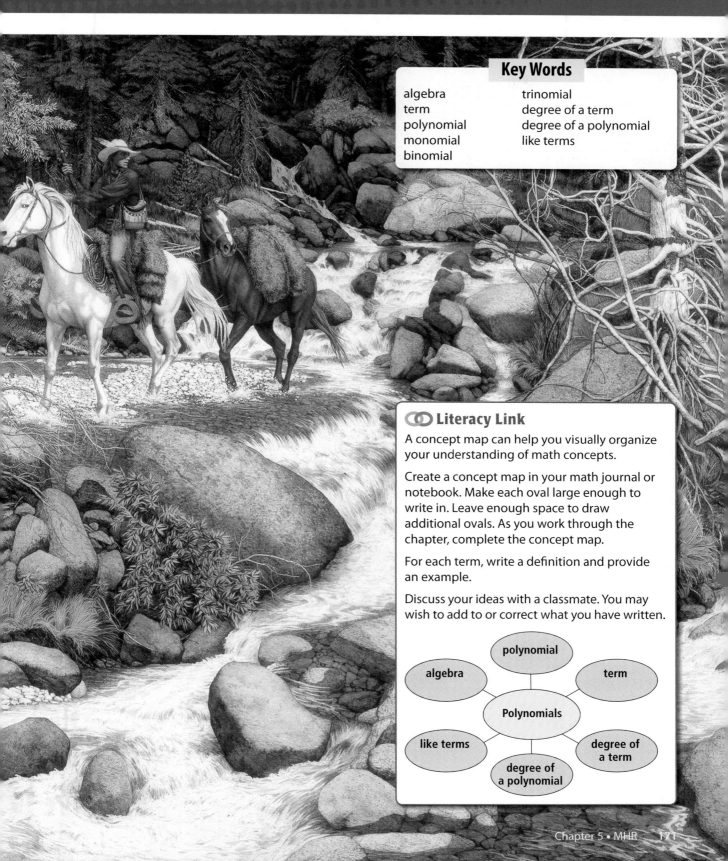

Key Words

algebra	trinomial
term	degree of a term
polynomial	degree of a polynomial
monomial	like terms
binomial	

⬮⬮ Literacy Link

A concept map can help you visually organize your understanding of math concepts.

Create a concept map in your math journal or notebook. Make each oval large enough to write in. Leave enough space to draw additional ovals. As you work through the chapter, complete the concept map.

For each term, write a definition and provide an example.

Discuss your ideas with a classmate. You may wish to add to or correct what you have written.

Making the Foldable

Materials
- sheet of 11 × 17 paper
- four sheets of 8.5 × 11 paper
- ruler
- scissors
- stapler

Step 1

Fold the long side of a sheet of 11 × 17 paper in half. Pinch it at the midpoint. Fold the outer edges of the paper to meet at the midpoint. Label it as shown.

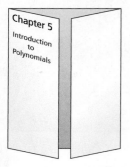

Step 2

Fold the short side of a sheet of 8.5 × 11 paper in half. On one side, use a ruler to draw a line 4 cm from the top. Then, draw seven more lines at 3-cm intervals. Cut along the lines, forming nine tabs. Label the tabs as shown.

Step 3

Fold the long side of two sheets of 8.5 × 11 paper in half. Label them as shown.

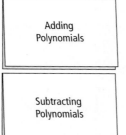

Step 4

Fold the long side of an 8.5 × 11 paper in half. Fold in four the opposite way. Make three cuts as shown through one thickness of paper, forming four tabs. Label the tabs as shown.

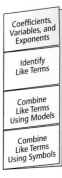

Step 5

Staple the four booklets you made into the Foldable from Step 1 as shown.

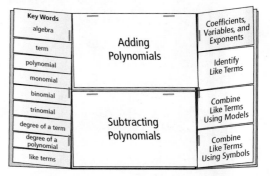

Using the Foldable

As you work through the chapter, write the definitions of the Key Words beneath the tabs on the left. Beneath the tabs in the centre panel and the tabs on the right, record notes and show worked examples.

On the front of the right flap of the Foldable, record ideas for the Wrap It Up! On the back of the centre panel, make notes under the heading What I Need to Work On. Check off each item as you deal with it.

Math Link

Illusions, Puzzles, and Games

With an optical illusion, you are fooled into seeing something that is not really there. With a number trick, you are fooled into believing that a number has been magically conjured from thin air … unless you are able to figure out the trick!

Famous illusionist David Copperfield often uses a number trick as part of his program.

1. Try the number trick called Guess an Age several times using different ages. What do you find in Step 5? Why does it always work?

> **Guess an Age**
>
> **Step 1** Ask a person with a two-digit age to multiply the tens digit in their age by 5.
>
> **Step 2** Then, add 3.
>
> **Step 3** Then, double the sum from Step 2.
>
> **Step 4** Have the person add the value of the second digit of their age to the value in Step 3.
>
> **Step 5** Finally, subtract 6.

2. Try the number trick called Guess a Number.

> **Guess a Number**
>
> **Step 1** Have someone choose any whole number.
>
> **Step 2** Then, have that person roll a pair of dice and add the sum of the numbers from the top of the dice to the chosen whole number.
>
> **Step 3** Next, add the numbers on the bottom of the dice to the number.
>
> **Step 4** Have the person tell you the number from Step 3.

a) Explain how to find the person's original number.
b) How would you need to change the way you find the original number if you used three dice?

3. Find a number trick. Try it on your classmates. Explain why it works.

In this chapter, you will explore additional number tricks and games. You will use polynomials to explain how each one works. What number tricks do you know?

WWW Web Link

To try other number puzzles, go to www. mathlinks9.ca and follow the links.

5.1

The Language of Mathematics

The Great Wall is the world's largest human-made structure. It stretches over 6700 km across China. The wall was created by joining several regional walls.

Similarly, mathematics is a developing science made up of several branches, including arithmetic, geometry, and **algebra**. It is a science that studies quantity, shape, and arrangement. As with any science, mathematics comes with its own unique language. The language of mathematics is universal. It can be understood anywhere in the world.

Look at the following paragraph. How much of it can you read? What languages do you think the paragraph contains?

古代希臘人相信, 如果將兩個物體同時抛下, 重的那個會先落地。加利略, 一個意大利人, 做實驗, 從比薩斜塔上擲球到地面。實驗顯示出不同的物體運行相同的距離所用的時間相同與它的質量/重量無關。它們之間的關係是公式 $Y = ax^2$ 而不是像許多人預測的 $Y = ax$.

Would the algebraic equations be any different if the paragraph was written in any other modern language?

Focus on...

After this lesson, you will be able to...

- **use mathematical terminology to describe polynomials**
- **create a model for a given polynomial expression**

algebra

- a branch of mathematics that uses symbols to represent unknown numbers or quantities

Explore the Language of Algebra

1. a) For the algebraic expression $5a + 4b$, what terminology can you use to describe the numbers 4 and 5, and the letters a and b?

b) What terminology can you use to describe the expression $-7x^2$ and its parts?

2. Make up a real-life situation and write an algebraic expression for it. What do the parts of your expression represent?

3. Algebraic expressions can have different numbers of **terms**.

Number of Terms	Examples
1	5 $7x$ $-3ab$ $\dfrac{y}{2}$
2	$5 + x$ $3x^2 - 2$ $7xy + z^2$
3	$1 - x + y$ $2x^2 - 3x + 5$ $a + b + c$

Write other examples of expressions with one term, two terms, and three terms.

term
- an expression formed from the product of numbers and/or variables
- $9x$ is a term representing the product of 9 (coefficient) and x (variable)
- a constant value, such as 5, is also a term

4. A study of algebra includes working with **polynomials**. They are named by their number of terms. How do the names *monomial*, *binomial*, and *trinomial* relate to the number of terms in an expression?

> What common words do you know that have prefixes of *mono*, *bi*, and *tri*?

polynomial
- an algebraic expression made up of terms connected by the operations of addition or subtraction
- $3x^2 - 4$ has two terms. $3x^2$ and 4 are connected by the operation of subtraction.

Reflect and Check

5. Look at the algebraic equations in the paragraph written in Chinese on the previous page. Use as much algebraic terminology as you can to describe them.

Language Link

The word *algebra* comes from Arabic. The word originated in Iraq. Around A.D. 830, Mohammad al-Khwarizmi of Baghdad wrote a book called *Hisab al-jabr w'al-muqabalah*. This book summarized Hindu understandings of equations and how to solve them. The whole title was too hard for some Europeans so they kept only the word *al-jabr*. We get the term *algebra* from that Arabic word.

WWW Web Link

For more information about the history of algebra, go to www.mathlinks9.ca and follow the links.

Link the Ideas

Example 1: Name Polynomials by the Number of Terms

For each expression, identify the number of terms and whether it is a monomial, binomial, trinomial, or polynomial.

a) $4xy + 3$ **b)** $7a^2 - 2ab + b^2$
c) $5x^2 + y^2 + z^2 - x - 6$ **d)** 13

Solution

Expression	Number of Terms	Name
a) $4xy + 3$	2	binomial
b) $7a^2 - 2ab + b^2$	3	trinomial
c) $5x^2 + y^2 + z^2 - x - 6$	5	polynomial
d) 13	1	monomial

> What are the two terms in $4xy + 3$?

Show You Know

For each expression, identify the number of terms and whether the expression is a monomial, binomial, trinomial, or polynomial.

a) $5j^2$ **b)** $3 - m^2$
c) $ab^2 - ab + 1$ **d)** $-4x^2 + xy - y^2 + 10$

Example 2: Identify the Number of Terms and Degree of a Polynomial

What is the number of terms and the **degree** of each polynomial?

a) $4x^2 + 3$ **b)** $7a^2 - 2ab + b^2$
c) $5x + z - 6$ **d)** 7

Solution

a) The polynomial $4x^2 + 3$ has two terms.
The term with the highest degree is $4x^2$.
Its degree is 2.
The degree of the polynomial is 2.

> What degree does the constant term 3 have?

b) The polynomial $7a^2 - 2ab + b^2$ has three terms.
Each of the three terms has a degree of 2.
The degree of the polynomial is 2.

> When a variable has no exponent, the value of the exponent is 1. How do you know $2ab$ has a degree of 2?

c) The polynomial $5x + z - 6$ has three terms.
Both of the terms $5x$ and z have a degree of 1.
The degree of the polynomial is 1.

d) The number 7 is one term that is constant.
A constant term has a degree of 0.
The degree of the polynomial is 0.

Show You Know

What is the number of terms and the degree of each polynomial?
Explain each answer.

a) $1 - 3x$

b) $4x - 3xy + 7$

c) $-27b^2$

d) 99

> **⟲ Literacy Link**
>
> When a term has more than one variable, the variables are usually written in alphabetical order.
>
> Examples: $5ab$, $-12x^2y^2$

Example 3: Model Polynomials

Model each polynomial.

a) $3x + 2$

b) $-x^2 - 2$

c) $2x^2 + 3 - x$

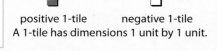

positive 1-tile   negative 1-tile
A 1-tile has dimensions 1 unit by 1 unit.

Solution

You can model each polynomial using algebra tiles.

a) $3x + 2$

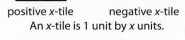

positive x-tile   negative x-tile
An x-tile is 1 unit by x units.

b) $-x^2 - 2$

c) $2x^2 + 3 - x$

> Tiles can be either horizontal or vertical.

positive x^2-tile   negative x^2-tile
An x^2-tile is x units by x units.

Show You Know

a) Model $-x^2 + 4x - 3$.

b) What expression is shown by the algebra tile model?

> **ⓦ Web Link**
>
> For practise using virtual algebra tiles, go to www.mathlinks9.ca and follow the links.

Key Ideas

- Algebra is a branch of mathematics that uses symbols to represent unknown numbers or quantities. The symbols are often letters and are called variables.
- Polynomials are made up of terms. Terms are connected by addition or subtraction.

  $3x^2 + 2x - 7$ has three terms.
- Polynomials can have one or more terms. Some polynomials have specific names.

Name	Number of Terms	Example
monomial	1	$6x^2$
binomial	2	$3a^2 - 5$
trinomial	3	$-w^2 + 5w + 1$
polynomial	more than 3	$2s^2 - t^2 + st + 7t - 4$

- Each algebraic term has a degree. You can find the degree of a term by adding the exponents of the variable(s) in the term.

  $3x$ has degree 1. $-5x^2y$ has degree 3.
- A polynomial has the same degree as its highest-degree term.

  $x^2 + 5x - 7$ has degree 2.

  12 has degree 0.
- You can use models, such as algebra tiles and diagrams, to represent some polynomials.

  $2x^2 - 4x + 3$

Check Your Understanding

Communicate the Ideas

1. Identify at least three mathematical words or phrases you could use to refer to the polynomial $-5 + x^2$.

2. Sonja and Myron are discussing the algebra tile model shown below.

   Sonja says, "The model represents the expression $3x^2 + x + 2$." Myron claims, "It represents $3x^2 - x - 2$." Who is correct? How do you know?

3. Give two examples of a polynomial that satisfies all statements.
- consists of two terms
- contains two variables
- has degree 2
- one term is of degree 1 and has a coefficient of 1

4. When is it acceptable not to write the 1 in an algebraic expression? When must you write the 1? Give examples.

Practise

For help with #5 to #7, refer to Example 1 on page 176.

5. For each expression, identify the number of terms and whether the expression is a monomial, binomial, trinomial, or polynomial.
- **a)** $3x^2 - 5x - 7$
- **b)** $-11a$
- **c)** $c^2 + cf + df - f^2$
- **d)** 8

6. What is the number of terms and what is a name for each expression?
- **a)** n
- **b)** $6 + 4x - x^2$
- **c)** 0
- **d)** $p^2 + 3pq$

7. Refer to the polynomials below to answer each question.

$6x$	-15
$3x - y$	$4c^2 - cd$
$7 + a + b$	$3m^2 - 4mn - 9n^2 + 1$

- **a)** Which ones are monomials?
- **b)** Which ones are trinomials?
- **c)** Which ones have two terms?

For help with #8 to #10, refer to Example 2 on pages 176–177.

8. For each polynomial, what is the degree and number of terms?
- **a)** $4 - b$
- **b)** $fg + 2g$
- **c)** $8x^2 - xy - y^2$

9. State the degree and number of terms for each polynomial.
- **a)** $3xy + 1$
- **b)** $11k^2 + 7k - 5$
- **c)** 6

10. Refer to the polynomials below to answer each question.

$3b^2$	$2 + p$
$4st + t - 1$	$2x^2 - y^2$

- **a)** Which ones are binomials?
- **b)** Which ones have degree 2?
- **c)** What is the variable in the monomial?
- **d)** Which polynomials have a constant term?

For help with #11 to #14, refer to Example 3 on page 177.

11. What expression is represented by each set of algebra tiles?

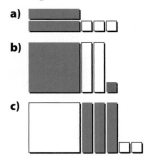

- **a)**
- **b)**
- **c)**

12. Write the expression represented by each set of algebra tiles.

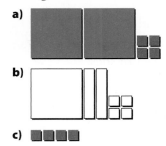

- **a)**
- **b)**
- **c)**

13. Model each polynomial.

   a) $x^2 + x - 1$

   b) $3x + 2$

   c) $-2x$

14. Use a model to represent each polynomial.

   a) $-x^2 + 3$

   b) $2x^2 - 3x$

   c) 8

Apply

15. Represent each of the following with a diagram and an expression.

   a) binomial

   b) monomial of degree 1

   c) monomial of degree 2 with a coefficient of 9

   d) polynomial with four terms that is of degree 2

16. Use your knowledge of algebra tiles to answer the following questions.

   a) How are the dimensions of a 1-tile and an x-tile related?

   b) The rectangle shown was formed using an x^2-tile and three x-tiles. What is an expression for the length of the rectangle?

17. Write an algebraic expression for each of the following.

   a) the product of 6 and x

   b) the sum of $2x$ and 3

   c) the length of the rectangle below, which is made from algebra tiles

18. Make a model of an algebraic expression that includes at least one x^2-tile, at least two x-tiles, and two 1-tiles. Use materials or a diagram. Then, use symbols to show your expression. What type of polynomial is it?

19. For the polynomial $6x^2 - 5$, state the following.

   a) number of terms

   b) coefficient of the first term

   c) number of variables

   d) degree of polynomial

   e) constant term

20. Let 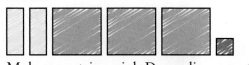 represent x^2, represent x, and represent 1. The same diagrams in yellow represent negative quantities.

   a) What is an expression for the polynomial shown?

   b) Make up a trinomial. Draw diagrams to represent your trinomial.

21. Write each statement as an algebraic expression. Include what your variables represent.

   a) Eight and a number are added together.

   b) Omar has some money in his wallet. How much money does he have after a friend gives him $5?

   c) A page is 4 cm longer than its width.

   d) The product of a number and 5 is increased by 2.

   e) The result of 3 times the number of people decreased by 21.

22. Describe a situation that could be modelled by each given polynomial.

   a) $3x + 5$ **b)** $10 - x$

23. Marion gives French lessons in the evening. She charges $20 for adults and $15 for children. The expression $20a + 15c$ represents her earnings.

a) What do the variables a and c represent?

b) How much does Marion make if she gives lessons to four adults and nine children? Show your work.

c) Write a new expression for Marion's earnings if she charges $3 more for adults and $2 more for children.

24. Tickets for a school concert are $10 for adults and $5 for students. Write an expression that shows the total income for the school concert. Tell what your variables represent.

25. A hockey league awards teams two points for a win, one point for a shoot-out loss, and no points for a loss in regulation time.

a) Write an algebraic expression to represent the total points for a hockey team.

b) What variable(s) did you use? Indicate what each variable represents.

c) In the first 20 games of the season, Team A had 12 wins and 4 shoot-out losses. How many losses in regulation time did the team have?

d) What were the total points for Team A?

e) Team A was tied with Team B after 20 games. However, Team B had a different record than Team A. Show two possible records for Team B. Use your expression to show that the two hockey teams had the same number of total points.

26. A banquet hall can be rented for parties. An expression for the rental cost is $5n + 75$, where n is the number of people.

a) What type of polynomial is $5n + 75$, and what is its degree?

b) What could the numbers 5 and 75 represent?

c) How much does it cost to rent the banquet hall for 150 people?

Extend

27. On a true/false test, there is a penalty for incorrect answers. Miranda's teacher advises the students not to guess at any of the 25 questions. The teacher awards 2 points for a correct answer, -1 point for a wrong answer, and 0 points if the question is not answered.

a) Write a polynomial to represent a student's score on this test.

b) What are the maximum and minimum scores possible on this test? Explain.

c) What are all of the possible scores if Miranda got 20 questions correct? Explain.

28. What is the degree of
$xy - abx + cdy - qr - prqz$
if x, y, and z are variables and a, b, c, d, p, q, and r are coefficients?

29. Ricardo draws the following rectangle with dimensions in metres.

$2x$

$x + 3$

a) What is an expression for the perimeter of the rectangle?

b) Write an equation showing how the length and width of the diagram would be related if the dimensions given were for a square.

c) Solve your equation in part b) to find the value of x. Show your work.

30. Create a polynomial satisfying the following conditions:
   - contains three variables
   - has three terms
   - is of degree 2
   - has a constant term, 3

31. Deidra is training for a triathlon. From her training, she knows that she can swim at 1.3 km/h, cycle at 28 km/h, and run at 12 km/h.

   a) Write the formula
   distance (d) = speed × time
   using variables of your choice for speed and time. Tell what each variable represents.

   > The distance for each leg of the competition is different. In the table, this difference is shown using subscripts.

   b) Use your formula to complete the table.

Part of Race	Distance (km)	Speed (km/h)	Time (h)
swim	d_1	1.3	$\dfrac{d_1}{1.3}$
cycle	d_2	28.0	
run	d_3	12.0	

   c) Write a trinomial to model Deidra's total time for a triathlon.

   d) A triathlon includes a 1.5-km swim, a 40-km cycle, and a 10-km run. How long will it take Deidra to complete this triathlon? What assumptions are you making?

   e) If Deidra could maintain the same speeds, how long would it take her to complete a triathlon that is a 3.8-km swim, 180-km cycle, and 42.2-km run?

WWW Web Link

The Ironman Canada Triathlon in Penticton, B.C., involves a 3.8-km swim, 180-km cycle, and 42.2-km run. The times of recent winners are impressive. Top men's times are around 8 h, while women's times are around 9 h. For information about the Ironman Canada Triathlon and about the history of the Ironman competition, go to www.mathlinks9.ca and follow the links.

Math Link

You want to be a contestant on a game show. In order to get on the show, you must show how to spend exactly $100 by choosing from the items shown.

You may purchase some or all of the six items, and as many of a single item as necessary.

a) Find at least six answers that would get you on the game show.

b) Write an algebraic expression for one of your combinations in part a). What is an equation for this same combination?

c) Is it possible to spend $100 choosing all different items? Explain.

5.2 Equivalent Expressions

Today's space program requires extensive use of algebra. Computer programs control shuttle flights and manipulate the Canadarm. They also control conditions inside the International Space Station. These programs use algebraic models, expressions, and equations. Where else in the real world is algebra used?

Focus on...

After this lesson, you will be able to...

- use algebra tiles and diagrams to show whether expressions are equivalent
- identify equivalent expressions that are polynomials
- combine like terms in algebraic expressions

Explore Combining Like Terms

The astronauts on the space shuttle have a limited amount of living space. They eat, sleep, and relax in a rectangular space with a width of only about 3.2 m and a length that is 0.8 m greater than the width.

Materials
- concrete materials, such as algebra tiles

1. What is the length of the living space? How do you know?

2. Draw and label a diagram of the rectangular living space. Find the perimeter of the rectangle. How did you find the perimeter?

3. Draw another rectangle. The length is still 0.8 m greater than the width but you have no known value for the width. What could you use to represent the width of the rectangle? What would be an expression for the length of this rectangle?

4. Write an expression for the perimeter of the second rectangle.

5. How many terms are in your expression for the perimeter?

6. Use materials or a diagram to model your expression for the perimeter.

7. Rearrange your model so similar objects, shapes, or variables are all together. Combine the similar objects, shapes, or variables. What is an equivalent expression for the perimeter?

Reflect and Check

8. What do you think *like terms* means? Give examples to support your ideas.

9. How do you combine like terms in polynomials? Explain with examples.

Link the Ideas

Example 1: Identify Coefficients, Variables, and Exponents

For each expression, identify the coefficient, the variable(s), and the exponent of each variable.

a) $3w$ **b)** a^2 **c)** $-4xy$ **d)** $-g$

Solution

Expression	Coefficient	Variable(s)	Exponents of the Variable(s)
a) $3w$	3	w	1
b) a^2	1	a	2
c) $-4xy$	-4	x and y	1 and 1
d) $-g$	-1	g	1

Literacy Link

Even if a term has two variables, it always has only one coefficient. Example: A term would be written as $-6xy$, *not* as $-2x3y$.

> **Show You Know**
>
> Give the coefficient, the variable(s), and the exponent of each variable.
>
> **a)** $3c^2$ **b)** $-x$ **c)** b **d)** $7st^2$

Example 2: Identify Like Terms

Identify the **like terms** in each group.

a) $5b^2$ $3cb$ $-2b$ $7c$ $6b$

b) $3x^2$ $4xy$ $-2x^2$ $7x^2$ $\frac{1}{2}y$

c) $3pq$ 11 $-4q^2$ -3 pq

like terms

- terms that differ only by their numerical coefficients
- examples of like terms are
  - $3x$ and $-2x$
  - $6y^2$ and $-4y^2$
  - $-5xy$ and yx
  - 17 and -8

Solution

a) $-2b$ and $6b$ are like terms. Both have a variable b with an exponent of 1. All the other terms are unlike.

b) $3x^2$, $-2x^2$, and $7x^2$ are like terms. Each of them has a variable x with an exponent of 2. The other terms are unlike.

c) $3pq$ and pq are like terms. Both have variables p and q, each with an exponent of 1. The terms 11 and -3 are also like terms.

> **Show You Know**
>
> **a)** Give an example of three like terms.
> **b)** Identify the like terms in the following group: $6t$ $3s$ $6t^2$ $6st$ $-8s$

Example 3: Combine Like Terms

Combine like terms in each expression.

a) $4x - 2x + 3 - 6$
b) $2x^2 + 3x - 1 + x^2 - 4x - 2$
c) $4 - x^2 + 2x - 5 + 3x^2 - 2x$

Solution

Method 1: Use a Model

a) $4x - 2x + 3 - 6$
You can use algebra tiles to represent each term.

Group the tiles to form zero pairs and remove the pairs.

Write an expression for the remaining tiles.
$2x - 3$

> Like terms can be combined to simplify expressions.

So, $4x - 2x + 3 - 6 = 2x - 3$.

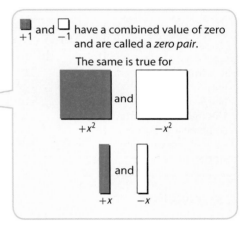

> $\square$ and $\square$ have a combined value of zero and are called a *zero pair*.
> +1   −1
>
> The same is true for
>
> $\square$ and $\square$
> $+x^2$ $-x^2$
>
> $\vert$ and $\vert$
> $+x$ $-x$

b) $2x^2 + 3x - 1 + x^2 - 4x - 2$

Group like terms and remove the zero pairs.

$$2x^2 + 3x - 1 + x^2 - 4x - 2$$
$$= 3x^2 - 1x - 3$$
$$= 3x^2 - x - 3$$

> **Literacy Link**
>
> Any term with a variable having a coefficient of 1 can be written without its numerical coefficient. However, the sign must remain. Example:
> $-1x = -x$
> $+1x = x$
> $-1x^2 = -x^2$
> $+1x^2 = x^2$
>
> Coefficients without a sign are positive.

c) $4 - x^2 + 2x - 5 + 3x^2 - 2x$

Group like terms and remove the zero pairs.

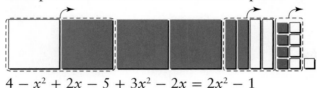

$4 - x^2 + 2x - 5 + 3x^2 - 2x = 2x^2 - 1$

Method 2: Use Symbols

a) Add or subtract the coefficients of like terms.
$4x - 2x + 3 - 6 = 2x - 3$

b) A polynomial with more than one term can be written in different orders. Rearrange by grouping like terms.
$$2x^2 + 3x - 1 + x^2 - 4x - 2$$
$$= 2x^2 + x^2 + 3x - 4x - 1 - 2$$
$$= 3x^2 - x - 3$$

c)
$$4 - x^2 + 2x - 5 + 3x^2 - 2x$$
$$= -x^2 + 3x^2 + 2x - 2x + 4 - 5$$
$$= 2x^2 - 1$$

⊕ Literacy Link

In algebra, terms are often arranged in descending order by degree. For example,
$-3y + 4y^2 - 1$
is written as
$+4y^2 - 3y - 1$
or $4y^2 - 3y - 1$.
This makes it easier to compare expressions. Answers are usually written this way.

WWW Web Link

To learn more about the parts of a polynomial and combining like terms, go to www.mathlinks9.ca and follow the links.

Show You Know

Combine like terms.
a) $5x - 3x^2 + 2x - x^2$ **b)** $2x - 6 - 2x + 1$
c) $k - 2k^2 + 3 + 5k^2 - 3k - 4$

Key Ideas

- An algebraic expression is made up of terms. Each term can have any number of variables. Each variable has an exponent. A constant term, such as 9, has no variable.

Term	Coefficient	Variable(s)	Variable's Exponent
$6p^2$	6	p	2
$-x^2y$	-1	x, y	2 for x, 1 for y

- Like terms differ only by their numerical coefficients.

  Like terms can be combined.

  Like terms:
  - $-7x$ and $3x$
  - w^2, $3w^2$, and $0.5w^2$
  - 6 and 15

  Unlike terms cannot be combined.

  Unlike terms:
  - $6x$ and $3x^2$
  - m^2n and $4mn^2$
  - 7 and $7d$

Check Your Understanding

Communicate the Ideas

1. Using models, show how you know that $s - 5s$ combines to give $-4s$.

2. Jean claimed that $3m^2 + 4m$ could be combined to give $7m^3$. Do you agree? Explain with diagrams.

3. Most people would agree that 2 cats + 5 cats = 7 cats and 7 cats − 2 cats = 5 cats. Use this information to support an argument for combining like terms and for being unable to combine unlike terms in algebra. Use examples with two different animals and two different variables.

4. Does a number in front of a variable affect whether or not you have like terms? Explain using examples.

Practise

For help with #5 to #7, refer to Example 1 on page 184.

5. What is the value of the coefficient and the number of variables for each term?

   a) $-3z^2$　　b) k　　c) 43

6. Determine the value of the coefficient and the number of variables for each term.

   a) $4d$　　b) $-prt$　　c) $-8fg^2$

7. Use the following monomial expressions to answer the questions below:

$3x$	$4t$	x^2
$-ts$	xt	$2t^2$

   a) Which have a coefficient of 1?

   b) Which have two variables?

   c) Which have only one variable with an exponent of 1?

   d) Which have a coefficient of -1?

For help with #8 and #9, refer to Example 2 on page 184.

8. Identify the like terms in each group.

   a) $2a$　5　$-7.1a$　$9b$　$-c$

   b) $3m$　$-2ab$　$\frac{4}{3}m$　$-2ad$　m^2

   c) -1.9　$6p^2$　5　$-2p$　p^2

9. Which terms are like terms in each group?

   a) $-2k$　9　$104k$　$104f$　$-f^2$

   b) $\frac{1}{2}ab$　$0.5a$　$-4b$　ab^2　ab

   c) -5　$13d^2$　5　$-10d$　d^2

For help with #10 to #12, refer to Example 3 on page 185.

10. Collect like terms.

    a) $3x - 2x^2 + x - 2x^2$

    b) $-4 - 2n^2 - 3n + 3 + 2n^2$

    c) $2q - 4q^2 - 2 + 3q^2 + 2 - 3q$

    d) $-4c + 3 + 5c - 7$

    e) $h^2 - 3h + 4h^2 + 2h$

    f) $3j - 5 + 2j^2 - 1 + 2j - 3j^2$

11. Simplify by collecting like terms.

    a) $2d - 3d^2 + d^2 - 5d$

    b) $y^2 + 2y - 2y^2 + y$

    c) $-p + 4p^2 + 3 - 3p^2 - 5 + 2p$

    d) $m - 4 + 6 + 3m$

    e) $q^2 - 3q + 2q^2 - q$

    f) $5w - 3 + w^2 - 2w - 4w^2 - 1$

12. Which expressions are equivalent to the simplified expression $-3x^2 + x - 4$?

A $-4 + 3x^2 + x$

B $x - 4 - 3x^2$

C $x^2 + 2 - 4x^2 + 3x - 6 - 2x$

D $-3 - 5x^2 + x + 1 + 2x^2$

E $2x - 2 + x^2 - x - 4x^2 - 2$

F $-4 - 3x - 3x^2 - 0 + 5x^2 + 4x - 6x^2$

Apply

13. Jessica and Taz are working on a measurement problem. Their calculations involve combining Jessica's measurement of 2 m and 32 cm with Taz's measurement of 1 m and 63 cm. Jessica claims you find the answer just like in algebra. Do you agree? Explain.

14. Describe a real-life situation that could be represented by each expression.

a) $m - 3$ **b)** $2p + 5$

15. For each of the following polynomials, write an equivalent expression with six terms.

a) $2p^2 - 3p + 2$ **b)** $-3x^2 + 5x - 4$

c) $4r^2 - 2q^2 - 3qr$

16. Write an expression for the perimeter of each figure. Then, combine like terms if possible.

a)

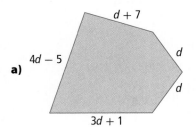

$d + 7$

$4d - 5$

d

d

$3d + 1$

b) w

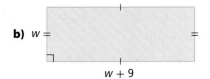

$w + 9$

17. a) Draw a figure with a perimeter that is represented by $(5s) + (3s - 2) + (s + 6)$, where each value in parentheses represents the length of one side.

b) Simplify the expression for the perimeter.

18. A student council decides to raise money by organizing a dance. The cost of a band is $700. The student council decides to sell tickets at $5 each.

a) Write an expression for the profit that the student council would make. What does your variable represent?

b) If 250 students pay to attend the dance, what is the profit?

c) Estimate, then calculate, the minimum number of students who will need to buy tickets for the student council to make a profit.

19. A heating company charges $60 per hour plus $54 for a service call. Let n be the number of hours the technician works at your house.

a) What expression represents the total cost of the job?

b) What is the cost for a job requiring 2 h?

c) The company charges half as much for a second technician. Write an expression showing the total cost if two technicians install a new furnace. Simplify your expression by combining like terms.

20. A publisher makes books for a number of distributors. For one book, the charge to the distributor is represented by a fixed cost of $3000 plus $16 per book.

a) Write an expression for the cost that a distributor is charged for b copies of this book.

b) How much do 600 books cost?

c) What is the cost per book if 600 are ordered?

d) What is the cost per book if 1000 are ordered?

21. Raj was told to write an expression equivalent to $3x - 8 - 5x + 9$.

$3x - 8 - 5x + 9$

$= 3x - 5x - 8 + 9$

$= 2x - 1$

a) What errors did he make?

b) Show the correct response.

22. The diagram represents a piece of string.

| x | $3x + 7$ | $2x - 5$ |

a) What is an expression for the total length of the string?

b) Combine like terms to get the simplest expression possible for the length of the string.

Extend

23. When would the expressions $x + y + 3$ and $x + w + 3$ be equal? How do you know?

24. A department store marks up wholesale prices 40% to get its retail or selling price.

a) Complete the following table. The first row has been done for you.

Wholesale Price ($)	Expression For Retail Price	Retail Price ($)
8.00	$8 + (0.4)(8)$	11.20
12.00		
30.00		
x		

b) How could you find the retail price if the wholesale price is $x + 10$ dollars? Show two ways to find the answer.

25. Zip Publishers will print posters for fundraising events for an initial cost of $100 plus $2 per poster. Henry's Printers charges $150 plus $1 per poster.

a) Write an expression for each company, showing the total cost for any number of posters.

b) What is the cost of 125 posters from each company?

c) What is the total cost if you print 200 posters at each company? Show two different ways to find the answer.

Math Link

Refer to the Math Link for section 5.1 on page 182. Represent each item with a variable:

a = blender b = watch c = book

d = soccer ball e = drum f = coffeemaker

a) Rewrite all your combinations that add to $100, using the letters a to f. Arrange each combination in alphabetical order. For example, $a + e + d + 3c$ would be written as $a + 3c + d + e$.

b) The example in part a) can be used to find other combinations. Notice that e has a value of $40. What other items from the list have a value of $40? By substituting into e the letter or letters that combine to a total value of $40, you arrive at another answer. Do not forget to combine like terms and arrange each expression in alphabetical order. What other combinations can you find using substitution?

c) If you were asked to find combinations of the items that add to $101, how could you use algebra to help you? Give two ways that algebra could help you.

Adding and Subtracting Polynomials

Focus on...

After this lesson, you will be able to...

- add polynomial expressions
- subtract polynomial expressions
- solve problems using the addition and subtraction of polynomials

A music store rents out a drum kit for $55 per month, plus a deposit of $30. Is there a pattern? How could you use a polynomial expression to represent this pattern?

Explore Adding or Subtracting Polynomial Expressions

1. In first semester, Kira decides to play drums for music class. To rent a drum kit, it costs $55 per month, plus a $30 deposit.

   a) What is the total cost of renting the drum kit for three months, including the deposit?

   b) Write an expression to show the total cost for any number of months, including the deposit. Tell what your variable represents.

2. In second semester, Kira decides to play electric guitar. To rent an electric guitar, it costs $22 per month, plus a $20 deposit.

   a) What is the total cost of renting an electric guitar for three months, including the deposit?

   b) Write an expression to show the total cost for any number of months, including the deposit.

> Use the same variable that you used in #1. Why might you be able to use the same variable?

3. Mark wants to learn to play both drums and electric guitar. What is an expression for the total cost of renting a drum kit and a guitar for any number of months, including deposits? Then, show how to find a simpler expression.

4. What is an expression for the difference between the cost of renting a drum kit and the cost of renting a guitar for any number of months, including deposits? Then, show how to find a simpler expression.

Reflect and Check

5. **a)** Describe how to add or subtract polynomial expressions.

   b) Why was it necessary to use the same variable for each expression?

6. Make up your own situation that involves the rental of two items. Write an expression for the total cost and for the difference in cost.

Link the Ideas

Example 1: Add Polynomials

Add $3x - 4$ and $2x + 5$. Simplify your answer by combining like terms.

Solution

Method 1: Use a Model
You can use algebra tiles to model each polynomial.

> What is another way to model the polynomials?

Strategies

Model It

Arrange the model so that like objects are together.
Remove zero pairs if necessary.

Rewrite the model in simplest form.

$(3x - 4) + (2x + 5) = 5x + 1$

Method 2: Use Symbols
You can combine like terms.
$$(3x - 4) + (2x + 5)$$
$$= 3x + 2x - 4 + 5$$
$$= 5x + 1$$

Show You Know

Use two methods to show each addition of polynomials. Give your answers in simplest form.

a) $(2a - 1) + (6 - 4a)$

b) $(3t^2 - 5t) + (t^2 + 2t + 1)$

Frank and Ernest

© 2008 Thaves. Reprinted with permission. Newspaper dist. by NEA, Inc.

Example 2: Determine Opposite Expressions

What is the opposite for each of the following?

a) $3x$ **b)** -2

c) $4x - 1$ **d)** $a^2 - 3a + 2$

Solution

a) You can use algebra tiles to represent $3x$.

> How might you use a diagram to model $3x$?

Strategies
Model It

Add three negative x-tiles to give zero.

The opposite of $3x$ is $-3x$.

You can also use inspection.   M E
$3x$ is positive. The opposite of positive is negative.
The opposite of $3x$ is $-3x$.

b) You can use algebra tiles to represent -2.

Add two positive 1-tiles to give zero.

The opposite of -2 is $+2$ or 2.

You can also use inspection.   M E
-2 is negative. The opposite of negative is positive.
The opposite of -2 is $+2$ or 2.

⊂⊃ Art Link

Opposites can be used to create interesting optical illusions.

Look at the dot in the center of the rings. Lean forward and backward. The rings appear to rotate in opposite directions.

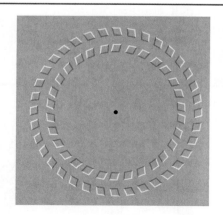

c) You can use algebra tiles to represent $4x - 1$.

Add four negative x-tiles and one positive 1-tile to give zero.

The opposite of $4x - 1$ is $-4x + 1$.

You can also use inspection.
$4x$ is positive. The opposite of positive is negative.
The opposite of $4x$ is $-4x$.
1 is being subtracted. The opposite of subtracting 1 is adding 1.
The opposite of $4x - 1$ is $-4x + 1$.

d) You can use algebra tiles to represent $a^2 - 3a + 2$.

Add a negative a^2-tile, three positive a-tiles, and two negative 1-tiles.

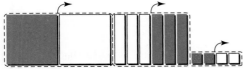

The opposite of $a^2 - 3a + 2$ is $-a^2 + 3a - 2$.

You can also use inspection.
a^2 is positive. The opposite of positive is negative.
The opposite of a^2 is $-a^2$.
$3a$ is being subtracted. The opposite of subtracting $3a$ is adding $3a$.
2 is being added. The opposite of adding 2 is subtracting 2.
The opposite of $a^2 - 3a + 2$ is $-a^2 + 3a - 2$.

Show You Know

What is the opposite of each expression? Justify your answer.

a) x

b) $5 - 3x$

c) $7x^2 + 5x - 1$

Example 3: Subtract Polynomials

Subtract $2x + 3$ from $3x - 4$. Simplify your answer by combining like terms.

Solution

$(3x - 4) - (2x + 3)$

Strategies

Model It

Method 1: Use a Model
You can use algebra tiles to model each polynomial.

From remove 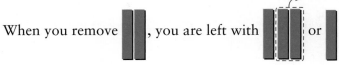   .

> What other way could you model $(3x - 4) - (2x + 3)$?

When you remove ▮▮ , you are left with ▮▮▮ or ▮ .

You cannot yet remove ■■■ since there are no positive 1-tiles.

Add three zero pairs.

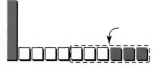

Now, you can remove ■■■ .

You are left with ▮☐☐☐☐☐☐☐ or $x - 7$.

$(3x - 4) - (2x + 3) = x - 7$

> Recall that when you subtract integers, you can add the opposite.
> $(-2) - (+3)$
> $= (-2) + (-3)$
> $= -5$

Method 2: Add the Opposite
One way to subtract a polynomial is to add the opposite terms.

$(3x - 4) - (2x + 3)$
$= (3x - 4) + (-2x - 3)$
$= 3x - 4 - 2x - 3$
$= 3x - 2x - 4 - 3$
$= 1x - 7$ or $x - 7$

> How do you know the opposite of $2x + 3$ is $-2x - 3$?

WWW Web Link

To learn more about adding and subtracting polynomials, go to www.mathlinks9.ca and follow the links.

Show You Know

a) Simplify the following expression. Model your solution.
$(2x - 3) - (-x + 2)$

b) Subtract and combine like terms.
$(5x^2 - x + 4) - (2x^2 - 3x - 1)$

Key Ideas

- You can add or subtract polynomials. You can use models to help simplify the expression.

  $(2x^2 - 3x) + (x^2 + x + 4)$

  Group like terms. Remove any zero pairs.

  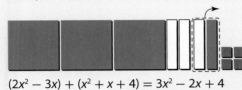

  $(2x^2 - 3x) + (x^2 + x + 4) = 3x^2 - 2x + 4$

- The opposite of a polynomial is found by taking the opposite of each of its terms.

  The opposite of $-3x^2 + x + 1$ is $3x^2 - x - 1$.

- To subtract a polynomial, you can add the opposite terms.

  $(6x^2 - 3x + 4) - (x^2 - 3x + 2)$
  $= (6x^2 - 3x + 4) + (-x^2 + 3x - 2)$
  $= 6x^2 - x^2 - 3x + 3x + 4 - 2$
  $= 5x^2 + 0x + 2$
  $= 5x^2 + 2$

  > $-3x + 3x = 0x$ or 0, so it does not need to be included in the answer.

Check Your Understanding

Communicate the Ideas

1. Jeanette and Tim find the answer to $(3x^2 - 5x) - (4 - 2x)$. Jeanette claims the simplified answer has three terms. Tim says it has only two terms. Who is correct? How do you know?

2. What is the opposite of $-x^2 + 2x - 3$? Use diagrams and then use symbols to determine the answer. Which method do you prefer? Why?

3. Identify any errors in Mei's work and correct them.

   $(-2x^2 + 7) - (3x^2 + x - 5)$
   $= (-2x^2 + 7) + (-3x^2 - x + 5)$
   $= -2x^2 - 3x^2 - x + 7 + 5$
   $= 5x^2 - x + 12$

4. Create a situation in which the polynomials $3x + 2$ and $5x - 1$ are involved. In your situation, what does $(3x + 2) + (5x - 1)$ represent?

Practise

For help with #5 to #7, refer to Example 1 on page 191.

5. Which addition statement does the diagram model?

A $(2x^2 - 3x) + (3x^2 - x)$

B $(-2x^2 + 3x) + (3x^2 + x)$

C $(-2x^2 + 3x) + (3x^2 - x)$

6. Add the polynomials.

a) $(3x - 4) + (2x - 3)$

b) $(-a^2 - 3a + 2) + (-4a^2 + 2a)$

c) $(5p + 5) + (5p - 5)$

d) $(2y^2 - 15) + (6y + 9)$

7. Perform the indicated operation and simplify by combining like terms.

a) $(-3x + 4) + (6x)$

b) $(3n - 4) + (7 - 4n)$

c) $(2b^2 - 3) + (-b^2 + 2)$

d) $(5a^2 - 3a + 2) + (-4a^2 + 2a - 3)$

For help with #8 to #12, refer to Example 2 on pages 192–193.

8. What is the opposite of the expression represented by each diagram? Express your answer using both diagrams and symbols.

a)

b)

9. Let represent x^2,  represent x, and ▨ represent 1. The same diagrams in yellow represent negative quantities Determine the opposite of the expression represented by each diagram. Use both diagrams and symbols to express your answer.

a)

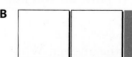

b)

10. What is the opposite of each expression?

a) $-9x$

b) $5d + 6$

c) $-2x^2 + 3x - 5$

11. What is the opposite of each expression?

a) $3x - 7$

b) $4g^2 - 4g + 2.5$

c) $v^2 + 8v - 1$

12. Which of the following represents the opposite of $2x^2 - x$?

A $-2x^2 - x$

B

C

D $2x^2 + x$

For help with #13 to #15, refer to Example 3 on page 194.

13. Draw a diagram to model the subtraction statement $(-3x^2 + 4x) - (-2x^2 - x)$.

14. Simplify by combining like terms.
   a) $(2x - 3) - (5x - 1)$
   b) $(-3b^2 - 5b) - (2b^2 + 4b)$
   c) $(5 - 6w) - (-2 - 3w)$
   d) $(m + 7) - (m^2 + 7)$

15. Subtract.
   a) $(8c - 3) - (-5c)$
   b) $(-3r^2 - 5r - 2) - (r^2 - 2r + 4)$
   c) $(y^2 - 5y) - (2y - y^2)$
   d) $(6j^2 - 4j + 3) - (-2j^2 - 5)$

Apply

16. A triangle has the dimensions shown.

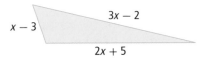

a) What does $(x - 3) + (3x - 2) + (2x + 5)$ represent?

b) Simplify the expression in part a).

c) If x has a value of 5, what is the perimeter of the triangle? Did you use the expression in part a) or part b) to find this answer? Why?

17. Complete the addition pyramid. Find the value in any box by adding the expressions in the two boxes immediately below it.

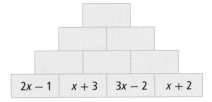

18. In Langley, British Columbia, you can rent a backhoe for \$399 per day and a bulldozer for \$550 per day. It costs \$160, round trip to move each piece of equipment back and forth to the job site.

a) Write an expression for the total cost of renting the backhoe, before tax. Include transportation to and from the job site. What does your variable represent?

b) What is an expression for the total cost of renting and moving the bulldozer? Use the same variable as in part a).

c) What is an expression for the cost of renting both a backhoe and a bulldozer? Give your answer in its simplest form.

d) What is an expression for the difference in cost between renting the backhoe and the bulldozer? Give your answer in simplest form.

19. Consider the addition pyramid shown below.

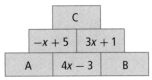

a) Write an expression for box C. Do not simplify.

b) Show how you can find the value for boxes A and B. Simplify your answers.

20. The cost to print n copies of a book is $15n + 2000$ dollars. The cost to ship n copies of the book is $2n + 150$ dollars.

   a) What is an expression for the total cost to print and ship n copies of the book?

   b) What is the actual cost to print and ship 600 copies of the book?

   c) What does $(15n + 2000) - (2n + 150)$ represent? Find a simpler expression for this subtraction statement.

21. Describe any errors in Jorge's work and how you would correct each one.

$$(4p^2 - p + 3) - (p^2 + 3p - 2)$$
$$= 4p^2 - p + 3 - p^2 - 3p - 2$$
$$= (4p^2 - p^2) + (-p - 3p) + (3 - 2)$$
$$= 3p^2 - 3p + 1$$

22. Simplify by combining like terms.

   a) $(6x - 7) + (3x - 1) + (x - 4)$

   b) $(3a^2 - 4a) + (3a - 5) - (a^2 - 1)$

   c) $(4t^2 - t + 6) - (t^2 + 2t - 4) + (2t^2 - 3t - 1)$

   d) $(2x - 1.8) - (3.4x - 2.1) - (0.9x - 0.1)$

23. Replace each question mark with algebra tiles to make a true statement.

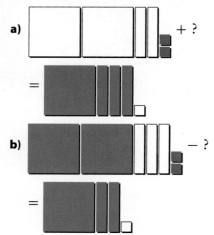

24. The perimeter of the triangle shown is $12x^2 + 6x$, in metres. Find a polynomial representing the missing side length.

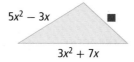

$5x^2 - 3x$

$3x^2 + 7x$

25. Your student council plans to thank 25 students and staff who have made special contributions to the school. Wooden plaques cost \$17.95. It costs \$0.12 per letter to engrave a message on the plaque. All costs are before tax.

With Appreciation To
Mark and Lise
For All Your Help

   a) Write an expression for the cost of engraving 25 plaques with the following message and the name of your school. *Thank you for your generous support.*

   b) Write an expression for the cost of buying and engraving the plaques.

   c) Write an expression for the cost of buying and engraving 25 plaques with an unknown number of letters.

   d) Show how to use the addition of polynomials to find the cost of 50 plaques if each plaque has the same number of letters and numbers.

Extend

26. Kiesha's dad is a Haisla artist. He makes his own prints and sells them on the Internet. He will ship the prints to purchasers anywhere in Canada. For large prints, he charges \$30 to ship one print plus \$7 for each additional print. For small prints, he charges \$20 for one print plus \$5 for each additional print.

   a) How much does her dad charge to ship two large prints?

   b) How much does he charge to ship four small prints?

   c) Write an expression to show how much he charges to ship an unknown number of large and small prints.

27. The length of the picture shown is 15 cm more than its width. The picture frame has a width of 4 cm. What is the minimum length of material needed to make the frame for this picture? Give your answer as a simplified expression.

28. A small manufacturer makes air quality monitoring kits for home use. The revenue, in dollars, from the sale of n kits can be shown by $-n^2 + 3600n$. The cost, in dollars, to make n kits is represented by $-3n^2 + 8600$. The manufacturer makes a profit if the cost subtracted from the revenue is positive.

a) Write an expression to find the profit. Simplify your answer.

b) Estimate and then calculate if the manufacturer will make a profit or suffer a loss after selling 20 test kits. Explain.

29. Simplify $(2x + 4x + 6x + 8x + \ldots + 2006x + 2008x) - (x + 3x + 5x + 7x + \ldots + 2005x + 2007x)$.

30. Mary is sewing two wall hangings. The length of one wall hanging is 56 cm greater than its width. The length of the other wall hanging is 15 cm greater than its width. Each of them has the same width. She is going to add a trim strip around each wall hanging. What is the total minimum length of trim she will need for both wall hangings?

"Camp, With Animals Nearby" by Annie Taipanak (1931-) of Baker Lake and Rankin Inlet, Nunavut.

"Hunting Caribou by Kayak" by Tobi Kreelak (1977-) of Baker Lake, Nunavut.

Math Link

Try this number trick several times.

a) How can you find the original number from the number in the last step?

b) Use algebra to show why this number trick works.

c) Find or make your own number trick. Use algebra to show why it works.

Guess a Number

Step 1 Pick a number.

Step 2 Add 5.

Step 3 Double the sum.

Step 4 Subtract 10.

Chapter 5 Review

Key Words

For #1 to #6, choose the letter that best matches each description. You may use each letter more than once or not at all.

1. $3w$ is a like term

2. has three terms

3. monomial

4. opposite polynomial to $3x - 1$

5. polynomial of degree 2

6. contains the constant term 3

A $-3x + 1$

B $-4d + 3$

C $1 - 3x^2$

D $-w$

E $x - 6y + 2$

F $-3x - 1$

G $3f - 1$

5.1 The Language of Mathematics, pages 174–182

7. For each expression, identify the number of terms and whether the expression is a monomial, binomial, trinomial, or polynomial.

a) $5 - p + px - p^2$

b) $3f - q$

c) $-2a$

d) $5xy - 27x^2 + 2$

8. What is the degree of each polynomial? Explain how you found your answers.

a) $6x^2$

b) $ab - 7a + 3$

c) $3 - y$

9. Provide an example of each of the following.

a) binomial

b) polynomial with three terms

c) polynomial of degree 2

d) monomial that is a constant term

10. Model each expression.

a) $1 - v$　　**b)** $3x^2 - 2x + 1$

11. What expression is shown by each model?

a)

b)

c)

12. You are selling used video games for $10 and used books for $4. The expression $10x + 4y$ provides a general statement of the value of your sales before tax.

a) What do the variables x and y represent?

b) How much money do you receive if you sell 6 video games and 11 books?

c) Write a new expression for selling DVDs at $7.25 and CDs at $5.

5.2 Equivalent Expressions, pages 182–189

13. Tom claims that 4 and $4x$ are like terms since they both contain 4. Do you agree? Explain.

14. For each expression, identify the coefficient, variables, and exponent for each variable.

a) $8xy^2$　　**b)** $-c^2$　　**c)** -4

15. Identify the like terms in each group.

a) $7r$　　$3s$　　$-s^2$　　7　　$4rs$　　$-8s$

b) $-2x^2$　　$3xy$　　x^2　　$5.3y$　　2　　$3xy$

16. Explain how you can tell like terms by looking at them. Give four different sets of examples with at least three like terms in each set.

17. The following diagrams represent terms in an expression. Draw a new diagram with like terms together and write an expression for the simplified answer.

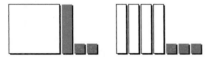

18. Use materials or diagrams to model each expression and show how to combine like terms. What is the simplified expression?

a) $3 - 2x + 1 + 5x$

b) $2x^2 - x + 4 - x^2 + 5x - 1$

19. Combine like terms.

a) $4a + 3 + 9a + 1$

b) $2b^2 - 5b - 4b^2 + 8b$

c) $1 - c + 4 + 2c - 3 + 6c$

20. Draw a shape with a perimeter represented by $(4x) + (3x - 1) + (x + 3) + (x - 2)$, where each quantity in parentheses represents the length of a side. Find a simpler expression for the perimeter by combining like terms.

21. Kara and Jasmine go to Splash-o-mania water park. The entrance fee is $20.00. Kara rents a locker for $1.50 per hour. Jasmine rents a tube for $3.00 per hour.

a) What is an expression that represents the cost for Kara?

b) What is an expression that represents the cost for Jasmine?

c) What is a simplified expression for the total cost for both Kara and Jasmine to stay at the water park together for any number of hours?

5.3 Adding and Subtracting Polynomials, pages 190–199

22. a) Simplify each of the algebraic expressions.

$(4x - 3) + (x - 1)$ $(4x - 3) - (x - 1)$

b) How are the processes similar? How are they different?

23. Is $2x^2 - 3x$ the opposite of $3x - 2x^2$? Show how you know.

24. For each of the following expressions, what is the opposite?

a) -3 **b)** $7 - a$ **c)** $x^2 - 2x + 4$

25. a) Show how to simplify the following addition. Use two different methods.

$(3p + 4q - 9) + (2 - 5q - p)$

b) Which method do you prefer? Why?

26. Combine like terms.

a) $(-p + 7) + (4p - 5)$

b) $(a^2 - a - 2) - (5 - 3a^2 + 6a)$

27. Complete the subtraction pyramid. Find the value in any box by subtracting the two expressions in the boxes immediately below it. Subtract in order from left to right.

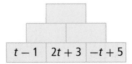

28. An end-of-year class party has a fixed cost of $140 to cover printing, decorations, and awards. In addition, it costs $12 to feed each person who attends.

a) What is an expression for the total cost of the party? What does your variable represent?

b) Create a short scenario to generate an addition or subtraction question with polynomials. Simplify by combining like terms.

Chapter 5 Practice Test

For #1 to #6, select the best answer.

1. Which polynomial is of degree 1?

 A $3 - 7x$ **B** $xy - 1$

 C $5x - 3xy$ **D** $x^2 - 5x + 2$

2. Which expression does not have zero as a constant term?

 A $-5x$ **B** $k + 8$

 C $y^2 - 2y$ **D** $ab + b - c$

3. Which of the following is not equivalent to $3x - 5 + 2 - 7x$?

 A $-4x - 3$

 B $3x - 7x - 5 + 2$

 C

 D

4. Which set of diagrams represents $3x - 2x^2 + 1$?

 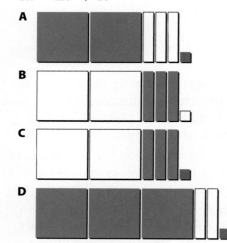

5. Which expression is a trinomial?

 A abc^3

 B $3mn$

 C $ef + g^2$

 D $-1 - x + c$

6. Which expression is the opposite of $-2k^2 + 3k - 1$?

 A $-1 - 3k + 2k^2$

 B $1 - 3k + 2k^2$

 C $1 - 3k - 2k^2$

 D $-1 - 3k - 2k^2$

Complete the statements in #7 and #8.

7. When you combine like terms, the expression $2t^2 - 5 - 8t^2 - 4$ becomes ▬.

8. In the monomial $-q^2$, the value of the coefficient is ■.

Short Answer

9. Draw a diagram to represent $x^2 - 2x$.

10. Create a single polynomial with
 • two terms
 • two variables
 • degree 2
 • a constant term

11. What is an expression, in simplest form, for the perimeter of the triangle?

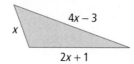

12. Write an expression to represent what the diagrams show. Then, simplify.

13. Simplify. Use models for at least one of the expressions. Show your work.

a) $(2x^2 - 8x + 1) + (9x^2 + 4x - 1)$

b) $(4 - 6w) - (3 - 8w)$

Extended Response

14. The number of peanuts two squirrels bury can be represented by $4n + 7$ and $5n - 1$, respectively.

a) Write and simplify an expression for the number of peanuts both squirrels bury.

b) What could the expression $(5n - 1) - (4n + 7)$ represent?

c) What is a simpler expression for $(5n - 1) - (4n + 7)$?

15. The cost for a birthday party at Big Fun Bowling is $100 for up to ten children, plus $5 per pair of bowling shoes. To rent the party room, the cost is $20, plus $4 per child for pizza.

a) What is an expression for the cost of bowling for up to ten children?

b) What is an expression for the cost of pizza in the party room for up to ten children?

c) What is a simplified expression for the total cost of up to ten children going bowling and having pizza in the party room?

d) Estimate, then calculate, the cost of nine children going bowling and having pizza in the party room.

Math Link: Wrap It Up!

You are an illusionist who is about to amaze your audience with a number trick. However, before you try the trick, you need to know how it works.

a) Try the trick, Guess a Number, several times. What do you notice about the middle digit of the number in step 4?

b) What do you notice about the other two digits?

c) How does the information from parts a) and b) help you to understand this number trick?

d) Make up a number-guessing trick. Show how algebra can help explain your number trick.

Guess a Number

Step 1 Tell someone to write down a three-digit number with no repeating digits. During the entire trick, do not look at what the person writes.

Step 2 Have the person arrange the digits in decreasing order.

Step 3 Ask the person to arrange the same three digits in increasing order.

Step 4 Tell the person to subtract the number in step 3 from the number in step 2.

Step 5 Ask the person to circle one number in the difference.

Step 6 Ask what the other two digits are. Identify the digit that was circled.

Challenges

Kayaks for Rent

You are the owner of a kayak rental shop. You offer 20 single-person kayaks and 10 two-person kayaks. You rent single-person kayaks for $35/day and two-person kayaks for $45/day.

The average cost to you for maintenance is $12/day for single-person kayaks and $18/day for two-person kayaks.

1. Develop an expression that can be used to calculate the maximum profit that you can generate over any number of days. Identify your variables.

2. What is your maximum profit for a 60-day period?

3. High demand allows you to increase your prices. You realize that you can make the same profit in #2 in 45 days. What changes would you make to your rental prices? Justify your new pricing structure.

4. You would like to expand your business and plan to buy some canoes and tents. However, you need to confirm your business plan first. You will charge $40/day for a canoe and $50/day for a large tent. You want to make a profit of at least $20 000/month from the canoes and tents. It costs you $17/day for maintenance and loan payments for a canoe, and $13/day for a tent. You have not yet decided how many of each you will buy. Develop an expression that allows you to meet your profit goal. Assume there are 30 days in a month.

What Have You Got to Hide?

Prime numbers have fascinated mathematicians for thousands of years. The earliest known reference to prime numbers dates to 500 B.C.E. At that time Pythagoras' school of Greek mathematicians discovered prime numbers and realized that these are the building blocks of whole numbers.

Prime numbers may be used to create encrypted data such as that used to hide personal information being sent on the internet. You be the cryptographer!

The following polynomials can be used to create prime numbers:
- $n^2 - n + 41$
- $n^2 + n - 1$
- $n^2 - n + 17$

Your challenge is to investigate whether the addition and/or subtraction of these polynomials can create prime numbers.

1. Test each polynomial using at least three possible n values. Show your testing process and the results of your test.

2. If decimals or fractions are substituted for n, are your results prime numbers? Show your testing process and results. What is your conclusion?

3. Add and/or subtract several combinations of the given polynomials. Test the resulting polynomials to see if they generate prime numbers when values are substituted in. Show your work.

6

Linear Relations

Some dimes have an image of *Bluenose*. This famous Canadian schooner is a symbol of Nova Scotia's prominence in the fishing industry and international trade. *Bluenose* was launched in 1921 in Lunenburg, Nova Scotia, as a racing ship and a fishing schooner.

A replica schooner, *Bluenose II*, has served as the floating ambassador for Nova Scotia since 1971.

The sailors who raced *Bluenose* had to think about factors such as length of a race, wind speed, and current. In racing, one factor is often related to another. For example, it takes longer to run a race if the current is strong. Sometimes the relationship between two factors can be represented mathematically in a linear relation.

Shipbuilders and sailors today continue to use linear relations to design, build, and operate vessels such as windsurf boards, racing sailboats, and supertankers.

What You Will Learn

- to represent pictorial, oral, and written patterns using linear expressions, equations, and graphs
- to interpret patterns in graphs
- to solve problems involving pictorial, oral, and written patterns by using linear equations and graphs

> **⬭ Did You Know?**
>
> From 1921 to 1938, *Bluenose* won the annual International Fishermen's Trophy for racing ships. After World War II, fishing schooners were retired. The undefeated *Bluenose* was sold to operate as a freighter in the West Indies. The ship sank in 1946.

Key Words

linear relation	constant
linear equation	interpolate
numerical coefficient	extrapolate
variables	

⦿ Literacy Link

A sequence chart can help you review terms and understand the order of concepts in this chapter. The chart is designed to be used throughout the chapter to help you connect new concepts.

Create a sequence chart in your math journal or notebook. As you work through the chapter, complete the chart.

- In the first box, define the term *linear relation*.
- In the second box, list the ways you learned to represent patterns.
- In the third box, show an example of how to solve a linear equation.
- In the fourth box, show how to describe a pattern using a linear equation.
- In the fifth box, explain how to interpolate values on a graph.
- In the sixth box, explain how to extrapolate values on a graph.
- In the seventh box, describe how to create a graph from a linear equation.

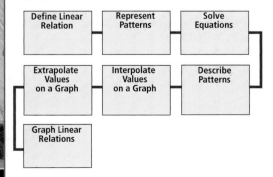

Define Linear Relation → Represent Patterns → Solve Equations

Extrapolate Values on a Graph ← Interpolate Values on a Graph ← Describe Patterns

Graph Linear Relations

Making the Foldable

Materials
- sheet of 11 × 17 paper
- ruler
- three sheets of 8.5 × 11 grid paper
- stapler
- sheet of 8.5 × 11 paper
- scissors

Step 1

Fold the long side of a sheet of 11 × 17 paper in half. Pinch it at the midpoint. Fold the outer edges of the paper to meet at the midpoint. Label it as shown.

Step 2

Fold the short side of a sheet of 8.5 × 11 paper in half. On half of the sheet, cut a straight line across the width every 3.5 cm, forming eight tabs. Label the tabs as shown.

Step 3

Stack two sheets of 8.5 × 11 grid paper so that the bottom edges are 2.5 cm apart. Fold the top edge of the sheets and align the edges so that all tabs are the same size. Staple along the fold. Label as shown.

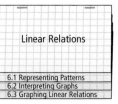

Step 4

Fold the short side of a sheet of 8.5 × 11 grid paper in half. Fold in two the opposite way. Make a cut through one thickness of paper, forming two tabs. Label the tabs as shown.

Step 5

Staple the booklets you made from Steps 2, 3, and 4 into the Foldable from Step 1, as shown.

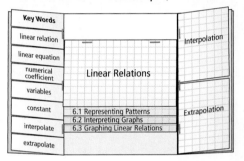

Using the Foldable

As you work through Chapter 6, define the Key Words, and record notes, examples, and Key Ideas in the appropriate section. Use the grid paper to show examples of interpolation and extrapolation.

Use the back of the Foldable to record your ideas for the Math Link: Wrap It Up!

On the front of the Foldable, keep track of what you need to work on. Check off each item as you deal with it.

Math Link

Marine Travel

You may never get to see a supertanker, even if you live on the coast, because they are too large to enter most ports. Supertankers can weigh 200 000 to 400 000 tonnes. The top speed of a supertanker when carrying a full load is only about 30 km/h. Once they are moving, they are hard to stop.

A crash stop manoeuvre from "full ahead" to "full reverse" can stop a loaded supertanker in about 15 min within approximately 3 km. The table of values shows the speed of a supertanker during a crash stop.

Time, t (min)	Speed, s (km/h)
0	30
3	24
6	18
9	12
12	6
15	0

1. **a)** What do you think the speed will be at 4 min? 5 min?
   b) Describe the pattern you see in the data. What do you notice about how the values change from one set of coordinate pairs to the next?

2. **a)** On a graph, plot the coordinate pairs in the table.
   b) Which variable did you plot on the horizontal axis? Why did you select that variable?
   c) Which variable did you plot on the vertical axis? Why did you select that variable?
   d) Does the graph match your pattern description? Explain.

3. Write an equation to model the data on the graph.

4. **a)** What value did you choose for the numerical coefficient and the constant?
   b) How did you determine each value?

5. A smaller tanker can stop in less time. The equation $s = -3t + 30$, where speed, s, in km/h, and time, t, in min, models stopping the smaller tanker.
   a) What would be the speed of the tanker at 7 min? How did you determine your answer?
   b) How much time would it take for the tanker to slow down to 8 km/h? Compare your solution with that of a classmate. Explain how you arrived at your answer.

In this chapter, you will explore mathematical relationships between variables, such as time and distance for different types of boats. At the end of the chapter, you will research and plan an adventure trip on water, showing mathematical relationships between variables.

Literacy Link

A metric tonne (t) is a measurement of mass that equals 1000 kg.

WWW Web Link

For more information about supertankers and other oil tankers, go to www.mathlinks9.ca and follow the links.

Representing Patterns

Emma Lake, Saskatchewan

Focus on...

After this lesson, you will be able to...
- represent pictorial, oral, and written patterns with linear equations
- describe contexts for given linear equations
- solve problems that involve pictorial, oral, and written patterns using a linear equation
- verify linear equations by substituting values

A skiff is a two-person sailing boat that can be used for racing. The carbon foam sandwich hull and multiple sails allow the boat to travel at speeds of 5 to 35 knots.

> ⊂⊃ **Did You Know?**
>
> A *knot* is a measure of a boat's speed. One knot is equal to 1.852 km/h. The term comes from the time when sailors measured the speed of a ship by tying knots an equal distance apart on a rope. The rope was gradually let out over the back of the ship at the same time that an hourglass was tipped. The sailors counted the number of knots that were let out until the sand ran out in the hourglass.

Materials
- ruler
- coloured pencils

Explore Patterns

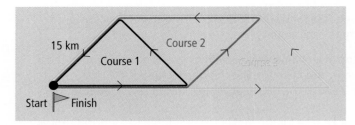

The first three racing courses are shown for a class of skiffs. Each leg of the course is 15 km.

How could you determine the total distance of each racing course? Describe different strategies you could use to solve this problem.

1. Draw what you think the next two courses might look like.

2. Organize the information for the first five courses so that you can summarize the results.

3. **a)** Describe the pattern in the race course lengths. Then, check that your Courses 4 and 5 fit the pattern.
   b) Describe the relationship between the course number and the length of the course.

4. Write an equation that can be used to model the length of the course in terms of the course number. Explain what your variables represent.

Reflect and Check

5. **a)** What are two methods you could use to determine the length of Course 9?
   b) Which method do you prefer? Explain why.

6. **a)** Determine which course is 135 km long.
   b) Determine the length of Course 23.
   c) How did you determine the answers to parts a) and b)?
   d) Discuss your solutions with a classmate.

Link the Ideas

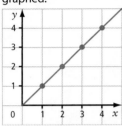
Example 1: Describe a Pictorial Pattern Using a Linear Equation

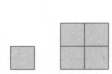 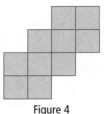

Figure 1   Figure 2   Figure 3   Figure 4

a) Describe the pattern.

b) Create a table of values to represent the linear relation between the number of squares and the figure number for the first four figures.

c) Write a linear equation to represent this pattern.

d) How many squares are in Figure 12?

e) Which figure number has 106 squares? Verify your answer.

Solution

a) The pattern is increasing. Each figure has three more squares than the previous figure. The squares have been added to the upper right corner of the previous pattern.

b)

Figure Number, n	Number of Squares, s
1	1
2	4
3	7
4	10

c) Add two columns to the table to help determine the pattern.

Figure Number, n	Number of Squares, s	Pattern	
		Multiply n by 3	Subtract 2 From Result
1	1	3	1
2	4	6	4
3	7	9	7
4	10	12	10

> The number of squares, s, increases by 3 for each figure number, n. Multiplying the figure number, n, by 3 results in 2 more than the number of squares. Therefore, subtracting 2 from $3n$ equals the number of squares, s.

The equation is $s = 3n - 2$.

d) Substitute $n = 12$ into the equation and solve for s.

$$s = 3(12) - 2$$
$$= 36 - 2$$
$$= 34$$

There are 34 squares in Figure 12.

e) Substitute $s = 106$ into the equation and solve for n.

$$106 = 3n - 2$$
$$106 + 2 = 3n - 2 + 2$$
$$108 = 3n$$
$$\frac{108}{3} = \frac{3n}{3}$$
$$36 = n$$

The solution is $n = 36$.

> How else could you solve the problem?

Check:

Left Side $= 106$ Right Side $= 3n - 2$
$$= 3(36) - 2$$
$$= 108 - 2$$
$$= 106$$

Left Side $=$ Right Side

The solution is correct. Figure 36 has 106 squares.

Show You Know

a) Write an equation to represent the number of circles in relation to the figure number.

Figure 1   Figure 2   Figure 3   Figure 4

b) How many circles are in Figure 71? Explain how you determined the answer.

c) Which figure number has 83 circles? How did you arrive at your answer?

Strategies

Use a Variable

Example 2: Describe a Written Pattern Using a Linear Equation

A bead design for a necklace has an arc shape:
- Row 1 has seven red beads.
- Row 2 has five additional beads and all the beads are green.
- Row 3 has five additional beads and all the beads are blue.
- The pattern repeats. Five beads are added to each successive row.

a) Draw the pattern for the first four rows.

b) Make a table of values showing the number of beads in relation to the row number.

c) What equation shows the pattern between the row number and the number of beads in the row?

d) How many beads are in Row 4? Explain how to check your answer.

e) How many beads are in Row 38?

f) If the bead pattern were continued, which row number would have 92 beads? How did you determine the answer?

Solution

Strategies

Draw a Diagram

a)

Row 1   Row 2   Row 3   Row 4

Strategies

Make an Organized List or Table

b)

Row Number, n	Number of Beads, b
1	7
2	12
3	17
4	22

c) Add two columns to the table to help determine the pattern.

Row Number, n	Number of Beads, b	Pattern	
		Multiply n by 5	Add 2 to Result
1	7	5	7
2	12	10	12
3	17	15	17
4	22	20	22

The equation is $b = 5n + 2$.

> Look at the diagram of the pattern. In the equation, what does the 5 mean? What does the 2 mean?

d) Count the number of beads in Row 4. There are 22 beads. You can check this by substituting $n = 4$ into the equation and solving for b.

$$b = 5n + 2$$
$$= 5(4) + 2$$
$$= 20 + 2$$
$$= 22$$

There are 22 beads in Row 4.

e) Substitute $n = 38$ into the equation and solve for b.

$$b = 5n + 2$$
$$= 5(38) + 2$$
$$= 190 + 2$$
$$= 192$$

There are 192 beads in Row 38.

> How else could you solve the problem?

> What colour are the beads in Row 38? Explain how you know.

f) Substitute $b = 92$ into the equation and solve for n.

$$92 = 5n + 2$$
$$92 - 2 = 5n + 2 - 2$$
$$90 = 5n$$
$$\frac{90}{5} = \frac{5n}{5}$$
$$18 = n$$

The solution is $n = 18$.

Check:

Left Side $= 92$ Right Side $= 5n + 2$
$$= 5(18) + 2$$
$$= 90 + 2$$
$$= 92$$

Left Side $=$ Right Side
The solution is correct. Row 18 has 92 beads.

Show You Know

In a banquet hall, a single rectangular table seats six people. Tables can be connected end to end as shown. Four additional people can be seated at each additional table of the same size.

a) What linear equation could represent this situation? Share with a classmate how you determined the equation.

b) How many tables connected together will seat 26 people?

Key Ideas

- Many pictorial and written patterns can be represented using a table of values or a linear equation.

  The pentagonal table can seat five people. The tables can be connected to form longer tables.

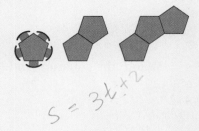

Number of Tables, t	Number of Sides, s	Pattern: Multiply t by 3 and Add 2
1	5	5
2	8	8
3	11	11

  The equation that models the pattern is $s = 3t + 2$.

- Linear equations can be verified by substituting values.

  Substitute $t = 3$ into the equation:
  $$s = 3(3) + 2$$
  $$= 9 + 2$$
  $$= 11$$
  The calculated value matches the value in the table.

Check Your Understanding

Communicate the Ideas

1. a) Explain how to develop a linear equation to represent this pattern.

b) What is the equation? Explain what each variable represents.

c) Compare your equation with one of a classmate's.

2. Christina and Liam work in a shoe store and earn a flat rate of $35/day plus $6.25 for every pair of shoes they sell. Each got a different value for how much they would earn after selling eight pairs of shoes.

Christina:
> I substituted $p = 8$ into the equation $w = 6.25p + 35$. When I solved for w, I got $85.

Liam:
> I substituted $p = 8$ into the equation $w = 6.25p$. When I solved for w, I got $50.

Who is correct? Explain how you know. What mistake did the other person make?

3. Describe to a partner how you could determine the ninth value in the following number pattern: 4, 7.5, 11, 14.5, 18, ...

Practise

For help with #4 to #6, refer to Example 1 on pages 212–213.

4. a) Describe the relationship between the number of regular octagons and the number of sides in this pattern.

b) Make a table of values showing the number of sides for each figure in relation to the number of octagons.

c) Write an equation to model the number of sides of each shape. Explain what each variable represents.

d) How many sides would a shape made up of 17 octagons have? 104

e) How many octagons are needed to make a figure with 722 sides?

5. a) Make a table of values to show the number of circles in relation to the figure number.

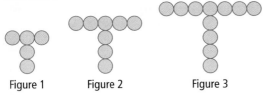

Figure 1   Figure 2   Figure 3

b) Describe the relationship between the number of circles and the figure number.

c) Develop an equation that can be used to determine the number of circles in each figure. Explain what each variable represents.

d) How many circles are in Figure 17?

e) Which figure number has 110 circles?

6. Laura used green and white tiles to create a pattern.

Figure 1   Figure 2   Figure 3

a) Make a table of values to show the number of green tiles in relation to the figure number.

b) Describe the relationship between the number of green tiles and the figure number.

c) Develop an equation to model the number of green tiles. Explain what each variable represents.

d) How many green tiles are in Figure 24?

e) Which figure number has 176 green tiles? Verify your answer.

For help with #7 to #9, refer to Example 2 on pages 214–215.

7. Matt created the following number pattern: 7, 16, 25, … .

a) Make a table of values for the first five terms.

b) Develop an equation that can be used to determine the value of each term in the number pattern.

c) What is the value of the 123rd term?

d) Which term has a value of 358?

8. The figure shows two regular heptagons connected along one side. Each successive figure has one additional heptagon. Each side length is 1 cm.

a) Draw the first six figures. Then, describe the pattern.

b) Make a table of values showing the perimeter for the first six figures.

c) What equation can be used to determine the perimeter of each figure? Identify each variable.

d) What is the perimeter of Figure 12?

e) How many heptagons are needed to create a figure with a perimeter of 117 cm?

Literacy Link

A regular heptagon has seven sides of equal length.

---

9. Jessica created a number pattern that starts with the term −5. Each subsequent number is 3 less than the previous number.

   a) Make a table of values for the first five numbers in the pattern.

   b) What equation can be used to determine each number in the pattern? Verify your answer by substituting a known value into your equation.

   c) What is the value of the 49th term?

   d) Which term has a value of −119? Verify your answer.

10. What linear equation models the relationship between the numbers in each table?

a)

x	y
0	13
1	16
2	19
3	22

b)

r	p
0	17
1	24
2	31
3	38

c)

k	t
1	−1.3
2	1.4
3	4.1
4	6.8

d)

f	w
1	−0.5
2	−4
3	−7.5
4	−11

Apply

11. Rob is in charge of arranging hexagonal tables for a parent-night presentation. The tables, which can seat six people, can be connected to form longer tables.

   a) Develop an equation to model the pattern. Identify each variable.

   b) How many parents can be seated at a row of five tables?

   c) Check your answer for part b). Show your work.

   d) A group of 30 people want to sit together. How many tables must be joined together to seat them?

12. A school pays a company $125 to design gym T-shirts. It costs an additional $15 to make each T-shirt.

   a) Copy and complete the table of values.

Number of T-Shirts	Cost ($)
0	125
5	200
10	
15	
35	
	950

   b) Develop an equation to determine the cost of the T-shirts. Explain the meaning of the numerical coefficient.

   c) What would it cost to make 378 T-shirts?

   d) If the school store has a budget of $2345 for T-shirts, how many T-shirts can be ordered?

13. An art store sells square picture frames with a border of tiles that each measure 2 cm by 2 cm. The smallest frame is 10 cm by 10 cm and requires 16 tiles.

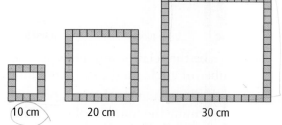

10 cm   20 cm   30 cm

   a) Develop an equation to determine the number of tiles required for each size of frame.

   b) How many tiles are needed to make a frame that is 30 cm by 30 cm?

   c) What are the dimensions of a square frame made with 196 tiles?

14. Edmund Halley, after whom Halley's comet was named, predicted that the comet would appear in 1758. The comet appears approximately every 76 years.

a) Use a table to show the years of the next six sightings after 1758.

b) When will Halley's comet appear in your lifetime?

c) Write an equation that can be used to predict the years when Halley's comet will appear.

d) Will Halley's comet appear in the year 2370? How did you arrive at your answer?

Science Link

A comet, which is made of frozen gas and dust, orbits around the sun. The dust tail of a comet can be up to 10 000 000 km long. This is 2.5 times as great as the average distance from Earth to the moon.

Extend

15. Find the pattern that expresses all the numbers that are 1 more than a multiple of 3.

a) What is the 42nd number?

b) How can your pattern test to see if 45 678 is 1 more than a multiple of 3?

16. a) A landscaper is planting elm trees along a street in a new subdivision. If elm trees need to be spaced 4.5 m apart, then how long is a row of n elm trees? Write the equation.

b) The street is 100 m long. If the landscaper wants to line the street on both sides with elm trees, how many trees will be needed? Will the trees be evenly spaced along the entire street?

17. A ball is dropped from a height of 2 m. The ball rebounds to $\frac{2}{3}$ of the height it was dropped from. Each subsequent rebound is $\frac{2}{3}$ of the height of the previous one.

a) Make a table of values for the first five rebound heights in the pattern.

b) What is the height of the fourth rebound bounce?

c) Is this a linear relation? Explain how you know.

Math Link

You are in charge of developing a racing course for a sailboat race on Lake Diefenbaker, in Saskatchewan. Five classes of sailboats will race on courses that are the same shape, but different lengths.

a) Design a racing course based on a regular polygon. The shortest course must be at least 5 km long. The longest course must be no longer than 35 km.
 • Draw and label a diagram of the racing course. Show at least the first four courses. Record the total length of each course.

b) Develop a linear relation related to your racing course.
 • Make a table of values.
 • Develop a linear equation that represents the relationship between the course number and the course distance.

c) Develop a problem related to your racing course. Provide the solution and verify it.

6.2

Interpreting Graphs

Focus on...

After this lesson, you will be able to...

- describe patterns found in graphs
- extend graphs to determine an unknown value
- estimate values between known values on a graph
- estimate values beyond known values on a graph

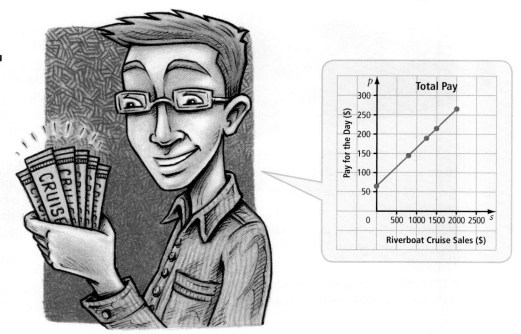

Richard is paid a daily salary and commission to sell riverboat cruises.

As a salesperson, he recognizes that it is important to know his sales in order to determine his commission. He is considering using a graph to calculate this amount. What do the variables p and s represent? What other information does the graph provide?

Explore Using a Graph to Solve Problems

Richard is paid \$64/day plus a commission of 10% of sales for selling riverboat cruises.

1. The table provides some information about his sales and daily pay.

Day	River Cruises Sold ($)	Pay for the Day ($)
Monday	1500	214
Tuesday	1250	
Wednesday	800	
Thursday	0	64
Friday	2010	

a) On the graph, locate the data points for each day.

b) How could you use the graph to estimate the missing values on the table? Try your method.

Literacy Link

Commission is a form of payment for services. Salespeople who earn commissions are paid a percent of their total sales. For example, a clothing store might pay a commission of 10% of sales.

Literacy Link

On the graph, the line joining the points shows that the data are *continuous*. This means that it is reasonable to have values between the given data points.

2. a) Estimate how much Richard must sell to earn $300 in one day. Describe your strategy.

   b) Estimate how much Richard would earn if he had sales of $1150. Describe your strategy.

3. The graph represents the linear equation $p = \dfrac{s}{10} + 64$. How could you use this information to determine the answers to #2? Explain why your strategy is effective.

Reflect and Check

4. a) Explain how your graph helped you to answer #2.

   b) Discuss your strategies with a classmate.

5. Work with a partner and use your graph.

   a) How much would Richard earn if he had sales of $2400?

   b) How much must Richard sell to earn $175 in one day?

6. a) List an advantage and a disadvantage of using a graph and an equation to determine values.

   b) Which method is more effective when
   - estimating pay given the sales?
   - determining sales given the pay?

Edmonton, Alberta

Link the Ideas

interpolate

- estimate a value between two given values
- interpolation should be used only when it makes sense to have values between given values. For example, 5.4 people does not make sense.

Example 1: Solve a Problem Using Interpolation

A weather balloon recorded the air temperature at different altitudes. The data approximately represent a linear relationship.

Altitude, a (m)	350	750	1000	1500	1800
Temperature, t (°C)	11.4	5.7	2.1	−5.0	−10.0

a) **Interpolate** the approximate value for the air temperature when the balloon was at a height of 600 m.

b) What was the approximate altitude of the balloon at an air temperature of −7.5 °C?

c) Is it possible to interpolate the precise value for the air temperature when the altitude is 1050.92 m? Explain.

Solution

Graph the data. Since temperature change is continuous, you can draw a straight line to connect the data points.

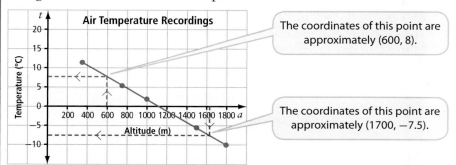

The coordinates of this point are approximately (600, 8).

The coordinates of this point are approximately (1700, −7.5).

a) On the graph, draw a vertical line from 600 to the point where the line intersects the graph. From the intersection point, draw a horizontal line to the y-axis. The value where the horizontal line meets the y-axis is approximately 8.

b) On the graph, draw a horizontal line from −7.5 to the point where the line intersects the graph. From the intersection point, draw a vertical line to the x-axis. The value where the vertical line meets the x-axis is approximately 1700.

c) No, you cannot interpolate a precise value. The temperature is related to altitude values to the nearest 50 m. There is too much uncertainty to accurately predict temperatures based on altitude measurements that have a precision of $\frac{1}{100}$ of a metre. You could, however, estimate the temperature for an altitude of between 1000 m and 1100 m.

Literacy Link

When describing variables on a graph, express the y-variable in terms of the x-variable. For example, the graph shows the relationship between temperature and altitude.

Tech Link

You can use a spreadsheet program to create the graph.

Strategies

Estimate and Check

This graph shows a plane's altitude as it lands. The relationship between altitude and time is approximately linear.

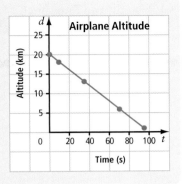

a) What was the plane's approximate altitude at 50 s?

b) At what time was the plane's altitude approximately 11 km?

c) Is it appropriate to join the points with a straight line? Explain.

Example 2: Solve a Problem Using Extrapolation

Anna is kayaking up the east coast of the Queen Charlotte Islands toward Graham Island.

Anna's course is shown by the red arrow on the map.

a) If Anna continues on her present course, **extrapolate** the values of the coordinates for latitude and longitude where she will land.

b) Could you use extrapolation to estimate where Anna sailed from? Explain.

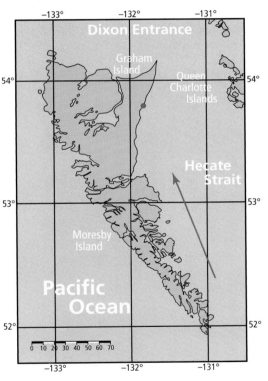

extrapolate

• estimate a value beyond a given set of values

• extrapolation should be used only when it makes sense to have values beyond given values

Did You Know?

The Queen Charlotte Islands or Haida Gwaii consist of two main islands off the northwest coast of British Columbia. In addition to Graham Island and Moresby Island, there are approximately 150 smaller islands.

Solution

a) Extend the line that represents the course until it touches land, and then read the coordinates of the point. From the map, the coordinates where Anna will land are approximately 53.8° north latitude and −131.8° west longitude.

b) No, the line extended in the direction that Anna sailed from does not strike land. This is evidence that this extended line does not show the place where she started.

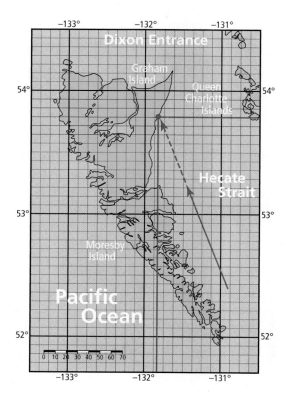

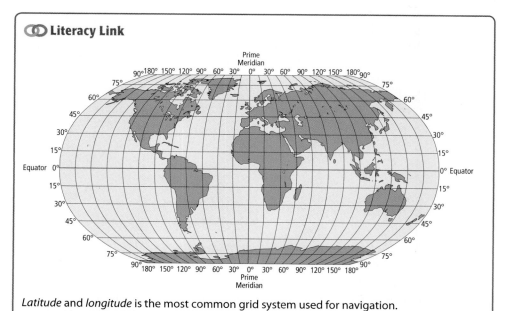

Literacy Link

Latitude and *longitude* is the most common grid system used for navigation.

- Each degree of latitude is approximately 111 km apart.
- Each degree of longitude varies from 0 to 111 km. A degree of longitude is widest at the equator and gradually decreases at the poles.

An example of a coordinate reading from a Canadian location might be 61° north latitude and −139° west longitude.

The value of a computer decreases over time. The graph shows the value of a computer after it was bought.

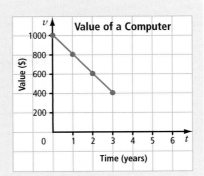

a) After what approximate period of time does the computer have no value?

b) When was the computer worth approximately $200?

c) Is it appropriate to join the points with a straight line? Explain.

Key Ideas

- On a graph, you can use a line to interpolate values between known values.
  - Start with a known value for x.

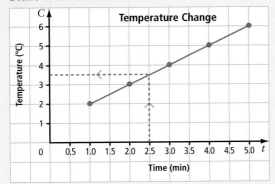

  - Start with a known value for y.

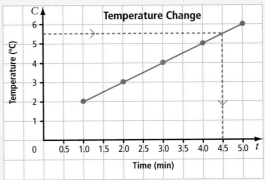

- On a graph, you can extend a line to extrapolate values beyond known values.
  - Use a dashed line to extend the line beyond the known x-value or y-value.
  - Start with a known value for x.
  - Start with a known value for y.

- Interpolation and extrapolation should be used only when it is reasonable to have values between or beyond the values on a graph.

Check Your Understanding

Communicate the Ideas

1. Josh asked you to help him understand interpolation and extrapolation. Use an example and a graph to help explain how interpolation and extrapolation are similar and how they are different.

2. Grace says it would be reasonable to interpolate values on these graphs. Is she correct? Explain.

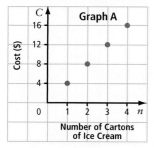 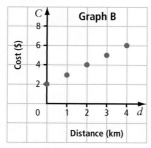

3. Develop a situation that involves a linear relation. Draw and label the corresponding graph. Develop a question and answer that requires extrapolating a value on the graph. Compare your work with that of a classmate.

Practise

For help with #4 to #7, refer to Example 1 on page 222.

4. The graph shows a linear relation between distance and time.

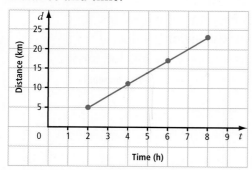

a) What is the approximate value of the d-coordinate when $t = 5$? Explain the method you used to determine the answer.

b) What is the approximate value of the t-coordinate when $d = 20$?

5. The graph shows a linear relation.

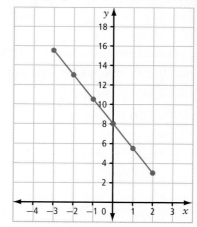

a) What is the approximate value of the y-coordinate when $x = -2.5$?

b) What is the approximate value of the x-coordinate when $y = 4$?

6. The graph shows a linear relation.

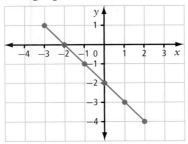

a) What is the approximate value of the y-coordinate when $x = 1.5$?

b) What is the approximate value of the x-coordinate when $y = 0.5$?

7. a) The table of values represents the distance that Sophie cycles in relation to time.

Time, t (h)	1	2	3	4	5	6
Distance, d (km)	12.5	25	37.5	50	62.5	75

a) Plot the linear relation on a graph.

b) From the graph, determine the approximate distance Sophie has cycled after 2.5 h.

c) From the graph, approximate how long it takes Sophie to cycle 44 km.

For help with #8 to #11, refer to Example 2 on pages 223–224.

8. The graph shows a linear relation between distance and time.

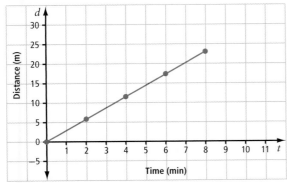

a) What is the approximate value of the d-coordinate when $t = 10$?

b) What is the approximate value of the t-coordinate when $d = 33$?

9. The graph shows a linear relation.

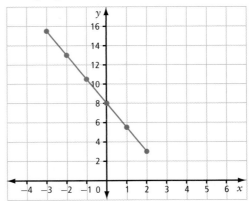

a) What is the y-coordinate when $x = -3$?

b) What is the x-coordinate when $y = 1$?

10. The graph shows a linear relation.

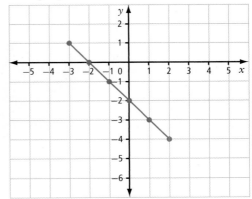

a) What is the approximate value of the y-coordinate when $x = -4$?

b) What is the approximate value of the x-coordinate when $y = -6$?

11. The table of values represents the drop in temperature after noon on a winter day.

Time, t (h)	1:00	2:00	3:00	4:00	5:00	6:00
Temperature, d (°C)	1	0	-1	-2	-3	-4

a) Plot the data on a graph.

b) From the graph, what is the approximate temperature at 6:30?

c) From the graph, determine the approximate time when the temperature is 2 °C.

Apply

12. a) In a bulk food store, trail mix costs $2.40 per 250 g. Plot the data on a graph.

Mass of Trail Mix, m (g)	250	500	750	1000	1250
Cost, C ($)	2.40	4.80	7.20	9.60	12.00

b) From the graph, approximate how much 2000 g of trail mix would cost.

c) From the graph, approximate how much trail mix you would get for $13.

13. The submarine HMCS *Victoria* can dive to a depth of 200 m.

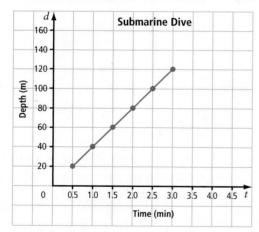

a) Is it reasonable to interpolate or extrapolate values on this graph? Explain.

b) How long does it take *Victoria* to reach a depth of 140 m?

c) What is the submarine's depth after 4 min?

14. A grade 9 class earns a profit of 53¢ for each program they sell for the school play.

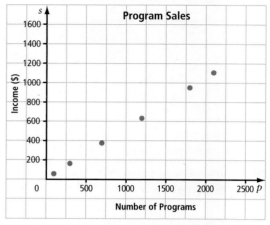

a) Is it reasonable to interpolate or extrapolate values on this graph? Explain.

b) If 500 programs were sold, how much profit would the students make? What strategy did you use to solve the problem?

c) Approximately how many programs would students need to sell in order to earn $2500?

15. Sean learned in his cooking class that the time it takes to cook a roast depends upon its mass. The graph shows the relationship between cooking time and the mass of a roast.

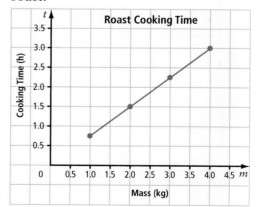

From the graph, determine the approximate cooking time for a roast with each given mass.

a) 1.25 kg   **b)** 2.25 kg   **c)** 4.2 kg

16. A cell phone company charges a $33.95 monthly fee and long-distance charges at a rate of $0.35 per minute. The graph shows the monthly cost of phone calls based on the number of long-distance minutes.

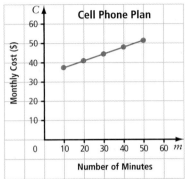

a) Is it reasonable to interpolate or extrapolate values on this graph? Explain.

b) What would be the approximate monthly bill for 60 min of long-distance calls?

c) Approximately how many minutes of long-distance calls could you buy for $50?

17. The graph represents the relationship between the cost of renting a power washer and rental time.

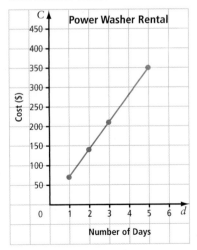

a) How much does it cost to rent a power washer for four days? What is the cost per day? How do you know?

b) How long could you rent the power washer if you had $420?

Extend

18. The table shows the relationship between stopping distance and speed of a vehicle.

Speed, s (km/h)	15	30	45	60	75
Stopping Distance, d (m)	6	15	28	42	65

a) Plot the data on a graph. Draw a line to join the data points to best approximate the trend.

b) What happens to stopping distance as speed increases?

c) Estimate the stopping distances for speeds of 5 km/h, 55 km/h, and 80 km/h.

d) Estimate the speed before a driver applied the brake for stopping distances of 10 m, 50 m, and 100 m.

e) About how much farther is the stopping distance at 50 km/h than it is at 30 km/h? at 70 km/h than at 50 km/h?

f) Why do you think the graph is not a straight line?

19. The speed of a falling skydiver is shown for the first 3 s.

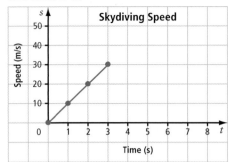

a) Approximately how long would it take for the skydiver to reach terminal velocity?

b) Approximately how far would the skydiver fall in that time?

c) Why do you think the graph is approximately a straight line?

> **Did You Know?**
>
> Terminal velocity is the maximum speed that a skydiver can reach when falling. Air resistance prevents most skydivers in free fall from falling any faster than 54 m/s.

Math Link

The area of the ocean called the Intertropical Convergence Zone (ITCZ) has little or no wind. Before propellers and motors, sailors used a relatively light anchor called a kedge to help them move across this region. The kedge anchor, which was attached to a line, was rowed out approximately 650 m ahead of the ship and dropped to the sea floor. A crew on the ship then grabbed the line and hauled it in to pull the ship to the anchor, a distance of 650 m. This process, called kedging, was repeated until the boat passed through the ITCZ.

a) Create a table of values showing the relationship between the number of kedges and the total distance travelled.

b) Plot the data on a graph. Label the graph.

c) Determine the value for how many kedges it would take to traverse the width of the ITCZ.

d) How did the skills you have learned in this chapter help you solve part c)?

> **Did You Know?**
>
> The ITCZ is located between 5° north and 5° south of the equator and is approximately 1100 km wide. Note how the position of the ITCZ moves during the year.

WWW Web Link

To learn more about the Intertropical Convergence Zone (ITCZ), go to www. mathlinks9.ca and follow the links.

Graphing Linear Relations

Focus on...

After this lesson, you will be able to...

- graph linear relations
- match equations of linear relations with graphs
- solve problems by graphing a linear relation and analysing the graph

Tina is in charge of ordering water supplies for a cruise ship. She knows the amount of water required per day for each passenger and crew member as well as the amount of water reserves that the ship carries. She decides to use her knowledge of linear relations to draw a graph representing the relationship between the amount of water needed and the length of a cruise.

If Tina were to develop an equation, how could she determine if the graph and the equation represent the same relationship?

Explore Graphs of Linear Relations

On a cruise, the average person requires a minimum of 4 L of water per day. The cruise ship has capacity for 1500 passengers and crew. The ship also carries a reserve of 50 000 L of water in case of emergency.

1. a) Use a method of your choice to determine how much water will be needed each day of a seven-day cruise.

b) On grid paper, plot the data and label your graph. Compare your graph with that of a classmate.

Materials
- grid paper
- ruler

> What values will you plot along the horizontal axis? along the vertical axis?

2. a) Predict how much water is needed for a ten-day cruise.

b) What linear equation represents the litres of water needed per day?

c) How could you verify your answer for part a)? Try out your strategy.

Reflect and Check

3. Do your graph and the equation represent the same relationship? Explain.

4. Discuss with a partner if it would be appropriate to interpolate or extrapolate values using a fraction of a day. Explain why or why not.

5. a) If the cruise ship used 152 000 L of water, approximately how long did the trip last? Compare the method you used with a classmate's.

b) Is there more than one way to answer part a)? Explain. Which method seems more efficient?

Link the Ideas

Example 1: Graph a Linear Equation

The world's largest cruise ship, *Freedom of the Seas*, uses fuel at a rate of 12 800 kg/h. The fuel consumption, *f*, in kilograms, can be modelled using the equation $f = 12\,800t$, where *t* is the number of hours travelled.

a) Create a graph to represent the linear relation for the first 7 h.

b) Approximately how much fuel is used in 11 h? Verify your solution.

c) How long can the ship travel if it has approximately 122 000 kg of fuel? Verify your solution.

Solution

Method 1: Use Paper and Pencil

a) Create a table of values. Graph the coordinate pairs.

> Describe the connection between the equation and the graph.

Time, *t* (h)	Fuel Consumption, *f* (kg)
0	0
1	12 800
2	25 600
3	38 400
4	51 200
5	64 000
6	76 800
7	89 600

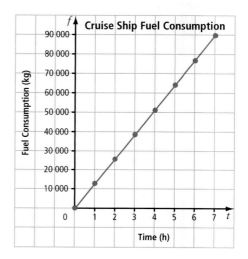

b) Draw a straight line to connect the data points. Extend the line past the last data point.

Approximately 140 000 kg of fuel are used in 11 h.

> What different methods might you use to represent and then solve the problem?

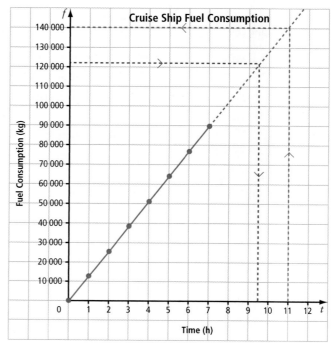

Check:
Substitute the value $t = 11$ into the equation $f = 12\,800t$.
$$f = 12\,800(11)$$
$$= 140\,800$$
The approximate solution is correct.

c) The fuel will last approximately 9.5 h.

Check:
Substitute $f = 122\,000$ into the equation and solve for t.
$$122\,000 = 12\,800t$$
$$\frac{122\,000}{12\,800} = t$$
$$t \approx 9.53$$
The approximate solution is correct.

Method 2: Use a Spreadsheet

a) In the spreadsheet, cell A1 has been labelled Time, t. Cell B1 has been labelled Fuel Consumption, f.

Enter the first eight values for t in cells A2 to A9. Then, enter the formula for the equation into cell B2. Use an = sign in the formula and * for multiplication. The value for t comes from cell A2.

	A	B
1	Time, t(h)	Fuel Consumption, f(kg)
2	0	=12800*A2
3	1	12800
4	2	25600
5	3	38400
6	4	51200
7	5	64000
8	6	76800
9	7	89600

Tech Link

You could use a graphing calculator to graph this linear relation. To learn about how to do this go to www.mathlinks9.ca and follow the links.

Use the cursor to select cells B2 down to B9.

Then, use the **Fill Down** command to enter the formula in these cells. The appropriate cell for t will automatically be inserted. For example, =12800*A6 will be inserted into cell B6.

Use the spreadsheet's graphing command to graph the table of values. Note that different spreadsheets have different graphing commands. Use your spreadsheet's instructions to find the correct command.

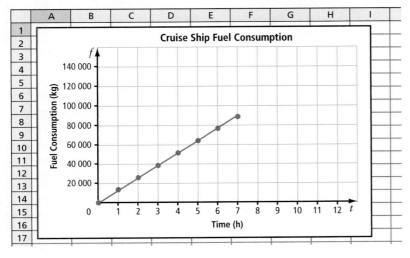

b) and **c)** From the menu, select **Add Trendline** to draw a straight line from the first data point to the last one. Extend the line past the last data point.

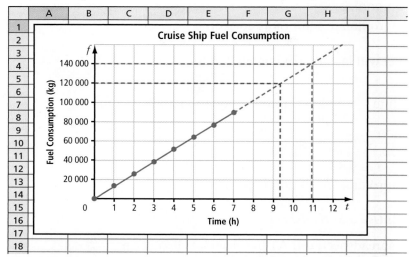

For part b), approximately 140 000 kg of fuel are used in 11 h.
For part c), the fuel will last approximately 9.5 h.

Show You Know

a) Graph the linear relation $y = 2x - 5$.
b) Use the graph to estimate the value of y if $x = 8$.
c) Use the graph to estimate the value of x if $y = -4$.

Example 2: Determine a Linear Equation From a Graph

Great Slave Lake, which is located in the Northwest Territories, is the deepest lake in North America. It has a maximum depth of 614 m. Sam decided to check the depth using his fish finder. He collected the following data up to a depth of 180 m, which was the maximum depth that his fish finder could read.

Distance From Shore, d (m)	Water Depth, w (m)
0	0
10	−35
20	−70
30	−105
40	−140
50	−175

Literacy Link

A depth, such as 35 m, is expressed in different ways. In a table and a graph, use the negative value, −35. In a sentence, say "35 m below surface."

Sam used a spreadsheet to graph the data.

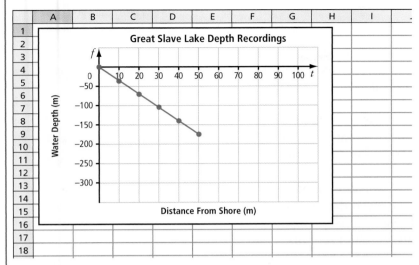

a) What linear equation does this graph represent? How do you know the equation matches the graph?

b) If this pattern continues, how far from shore would Sam be when the water is 614 m deep?

c) At what rate is the depth of the water decreasing?

d) Is it appropriate to interpolate or extrapolate values on this graph? Explain.

Solution

a) Add a column to the table to help determine the pattern.

Distance From Shore, d (m)	Water Depth, w (m)	Pattern: Multiply d by −3.5
0	0	0
10	−35	−35
20	−70	−70
30	−105	−105
40	−140	−140
50	−175	−175

The water depth, w, decreases by 3.5 m for each 1-m increase in the distance from shore, d. The equation is $w = -3.5d$.

Check by substituting a known coordinate pair, such as (30, 105), into the equation.

Left Side = −105   Right Side = −3.5(30)
                                                = −105

          Left Side = Right Side
The equation is correct.

> What is the connection between the graph and the equation?

b) Substitute $w = 614$ into the equation and solve for d.

$$-614 = -3.5d$$
$$\frac{-614}{-3.5} = d$$
$$d \approx 175.4$$

> How else could you solve this problem?

Sam would be approximately 175.4 m from shore when the water is 614 m deep.

c) The depth is decreasing at a rate of 3.5 m for each metre away from shore. The rate at which the water depth is decreasing is the coefficient of d in the equation.

d) Yes, it is reasonable to interpolate or extrapolate values between and beyond the given data points since the values for distance and depth exist. However, it is unreasonable to extrapolate values beyond the maximum depth of 614 m.

Show You Know

Identify the linear equation that represents the graph.

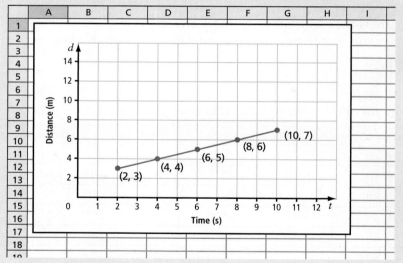

In the left margin:

Strategies
Solve an Equation

Example 3: Graph Horizontal and Vertical lines

For each table of values, answer the following questions:

Table 1

Time, t (s)	Distance, d (m)
0	6
30	6
60	6
90	6
120	6

Table 2

Distance, x (m)	Height, y (m)
1.5	2.5
1.5	3.0
1.5	3.5
1.5	4.0
1.5	4.5

a) Draw a graph to represent the table of values.

b) Describe a situation that the graph might represent.

c) Write the equation. Explain how you know the graph represents the equation.

Solution

a)

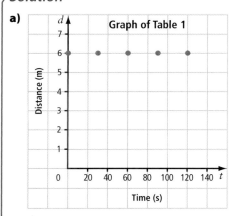
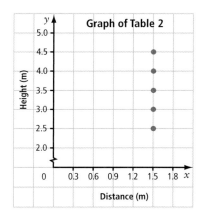

b) Table 1: The graph could show the relationship between distance and time when a pedestrian is waiting for a traffic light to change. The distance from the pedestrian to the opposite side of the road is constant.

Table 2: The graph could show the relationship between the height of a ladder and its distance from the wall where it is placed. The distance of the base of the ladder from the wall is constant as the ladder is extended.

> Think of a different situation to represent each graph.

c) Table 1: The distance, d, remains constant for each interval of time. The equation is $d = 6$.
For each value of t in the table and the graph, the value of d is 6.

Table 2: The distance, x, remains constant for each interval of height. The equation is $x = 1.5$.
For each value of y in the table and the graph, the value of x is 1.5.

a) Write the linear equation that represents the graph.

b) Explain how you know the graph matches the equation.

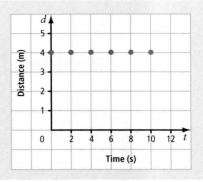

Key Ideas

- You can graph a linear relation represented by an equation.
  - Use the equation to make a table of values.
  - Graph using the coordinate pairs in the table. The graph of a linear relation forms a straight line.

$$k = \frac{j}{5} - 9$$

j	k
0	−9.0
1	−8.8
2	−8.6
3	−8.4
4	−8.2
5	−8.0

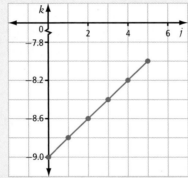

  - The graph of a linear relation can form a horizontal or a vertical line.
- You can use graphs to solve problems by interpolating or extrapolating values.

Check Your Understanding

Communicate the Ideas

1. You are given a linear equation. Describe the process you would follow to represent the equation on a graph. Use an example to support your answer.

2. Use examples and diagrams to help explain how horizontal and vertical lines and their equations are similar and how they are different.

3. a) Describe a real-life situation to represent the data on this graph.

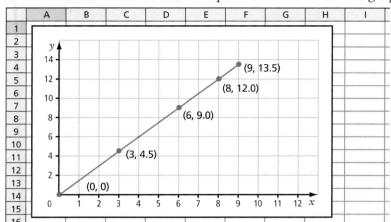

WWW Web Link

For practice matching graphs and linear equations, go to www.mathlinks9.ca and follow the links.

b) Explain how you would determine the equation that represents the graph. Give your explanation to a classmate.

c) Can you interpolate or extrapolate values on this graph? Explain your thinking.

Practise

For help with #4 to #7, refer to Example 1 on pages 232–234.

4. Ian works part-time at a movie theatre. He earns \$8.25/h. The relationship between his pay, p, and the time he works, t, can be modelled with the equation $p = 8.25t$.

a) Show the relationship on a graph.

b) Explain how you know the graph represents the equation.

c) Ian works 8 h in one week. Use two methods to determine his pay.

5. Andrea is travelling by bus at an average speed of 85 km/h. The equation relating distance, d, and time, t, is $d = 85t$.

a) Show the relationship on a graph.

b) How long does it take Andrea to travel 300 km?

6. Choose the letter representing the graph that matches each linear equation.

a) $y = 5x$

b) $y = -2x + 3$

c) $y = -\dfrac{x}{4} + 6$

A

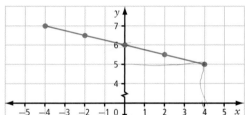

B

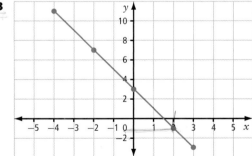

C

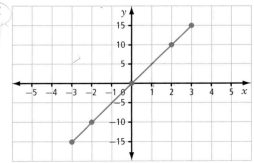

7. Create a table of values and a graph for each linear equation.

a) $x = 4$

b) $r = -3s + 4.5$

c) $m = \dfrac{k}{5} + 13$

For help with #8 to #11, refer to Example 2 on pages 234–236.

8. The graph shows the relationship between the cost, C, in dollars and the mass, m, in kilograms of pears.

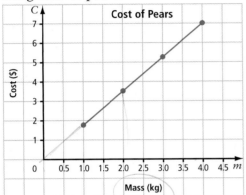

a) What is the linear equation?

b) How much could you buy for $5?

c) Is it appropriate to interpolate or extrapolate values on this graph? Explain.

9. The graph represents the relationship between the height of water in a child's pool, h, and the time, t, in hours as the pool fills.

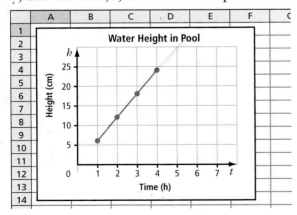

a) Determine the linear equation.

b) What is the height of the water after 5 h?

c) Is it appropriate to interpolate or extrapolate values on this graph? Explain.

10. Determine the linear equation that models each graph.

a)

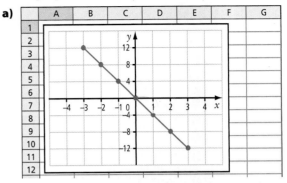

b)

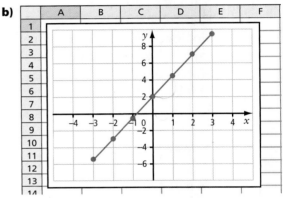

11. What linear equation does each graph represent?

a)

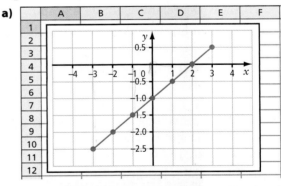

b)

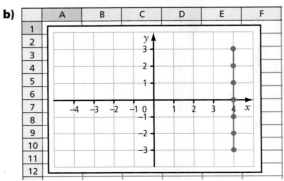

12. Create a graph and a linear equation to represent each table of values.

a)

x	y
−3	−10
−2	−7
−1	−4
0	−1
1	2
2	5
3	8

b)

r	t
−3	−2.5
−2	−1.0
−1	0.5
0	2.0
1	3.5
2	5.0
3	6.5

c)

f	z
−3	−3
−2	−3
−1	−3
0	−3
1	−3
2	−3
3	−3

d)

h	n
−3	−0.75
−2	−0.5
−1	−0.25
0	0
1	0.25
2	0.5
3	0.75

Apply

13. The graph represents the altitude of a hot-air balloon the first 20 min after it was released.

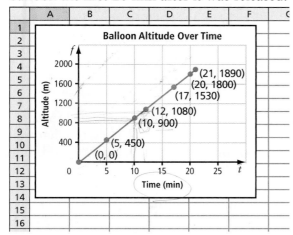

Balloon Altitude Over Time

(21, 1890)
(20, 1800)
(17, 1530)
(12, 1080)
(10, 900)
(5, 450)
(0, 0)

a) What was the approximate altitude of the balloon after 15 min?

b) Estimate how long it took for the balloon to rise to an altitude of 1 km.

c) What linear equation models the graph?

d) How fast is the balloon rising?

14. Sanjay conducted an experiment to determine how long it takes to heat water from 1 °C to its boiling point at 100 °C. He plotted his data on a graph.

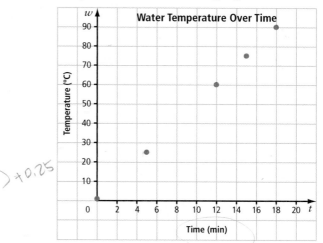

Water Temperature Over Time

a) Approximately how long did it take for the water to reach boiling point? Explain your reasoning.

b) What was the temperature of the water after 10 min?

c) At what rate did the water temperature increase? Explain your reasoning.

15. Paul drives from Edmonton to Calgary. He uses a table to record the data.

Time, t (h)	Distance, d (km)
0.5	55.0
0.9	99.0
1.2	132.0
1.5	165.0
2.3	253.0
2.7	297.0

a) Graph the linear relation.

b) How far did Paul drive in the first 2 h?

c) How long did it take Paul to drive 200 km?

d) Write the equation that relates time and distance.

e) What was Paul's average driving speed? What assumptions did you make?

WWW Web Link

To learn about using a graphing calculator to enter data on a table and plot the data on a graph, go to www.mathlinks9.ca and follow the links.

16. The relationship between degrees Celsius (°C) and degrees Fahrenheit (°F) is modelled by the equation $F = \frac{9}{5}C + 32$.

a) Graph the relationship for values between −50 °C and 120 °C.

b) Water boils at 100 °C. What is this temperature in degrees Fahrenheit?

c) Water freezes at 0 °C. How did you represent this on your graph?

d) At what temperature are the values for °C and °F the same?

17. Scuba divers experience an increase in pressure as they descend. The relationship between pressure and depth can be modelled with the equation $P = 10.13d + 102.4$, where P is the pressure, in kilopascals, and d is the depth below the water surface, in metres.

a) Graph the relationship for the first 50 m of diving depth.

b) What is the approximate pressure at a depth of 15 m? Verify your answer.

c) The maximum pressure a scuba diver should experience is about 500 kPa. At what depth does this occur? Verify your answer.

d) What does "+ 102.4" represent in the equation? How is it represented on the graph?

Did You Know?

After deep or long dives, scuba divers need to undergo decompression. They do this by ascending to the surface slowly in order to avoid decompression sickness, also known as the bends.

Extend

18. The graph shows the normal range of length for girls from birth to age 36 months.

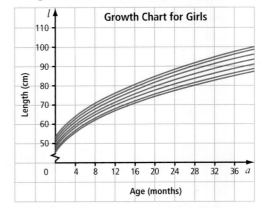

a) For what age range does girls' growth appear to represent a linear relation?

b) For what age range, does girls' growth appear to represent a non-linear relation?

19. Janice left the school at 12 noon riding her bike at 20 km/h. Flora left school at 12:30 riding her bike at 24 km/h.

a) Draw a distance–time graph to plot the data for both cyclists during the first four hours. Use a different colour for each cyclist.

b) How can you tell from the graph that Flora has caught up to Janice?

c) About what time did Flora catch up to Janice?

d) If Janice and Flora continued to ride at their respective speeds, at what time would they again be apart by a distance of 2 km?

20. An online music download site offers two monthly plans. Plan A offers $10 plus $1 per download and Plan B offers $1.50 per download.

a) Graph both linear relations on the same grid.

b) Explain the conditions under which each deal is better.

21. Simple interest is paid according to the formula $I = p \times r \times t$, where p is the principal, r is the rate of interest per year, and t is the time in years. The interest is not added to the principal until the end of the time period. Canada Savings Bonds offer a simple interest bond payable at 3.5% per year up to a maximum of ten years.

a) Create a table of values to show the interest earned on a $1000 bond for the ten-year period.

b) Use a graph to show the interest earned over ten years.

c) How many years would it take to earn $100 interest? $200 interest?

d) If you could leave the principal beyond the ten-year period, estimate the number of years it would take to earn $500 interest.

Math Link

The world's fastest submarines can reach speeds of 74 km/h in 60 s, starting from rest. If a submarine is already moving, then the time to reach its top speed will differ.

a) Choose four different starting speeds up to a maximum of 74 km/h. For each speed, assume that the acceleration is the same. For each speed include:
• a table of values
• a linear equation and a graph to represent the relationship between speed and time

b) Describe each graph. Identify any similarities and differences you observe between the graphs and the equations.

Did You Know?

A student team from the University of Québec set a new world speed record for the fastest one-person, non-propeller submarine. In 2007, the submarine, *OMER 6*, reached a speed of 4.642 knots (8.6 km/h) in the International Submarine Races.

Chapter 6 Review

Key Words

For #1 to #5, unscramble the letters for each term. Use the clues to help you.

1. R A N E I L   R A I N E T L O
   a pattern made by a set of points that lie in a straight line when graphed

2. P L E X A T R O T E A
   estimate values beyond known data

3. T S T O N C A N
   in $y = 4x + 3$, the number 3 is an example

4. E L I N A R   Q U E I O N A T
   an equation that relates two variables in such a way that the pattern forms a straight line when graphed

5. T R I P O L E N E A T
   estimate values between known data

6.1 Representing Patterns, pages 210–219

6. a) Make a table of values for the toothpick pattern.

   Figure 1   Figure 2   Figure 3

   b) Describe the pattern.

   c) Develop an equation relating the number of toothpicks to the figure number.

   d) How many toothpicks are in Figure 10? Verify your answer.

   e) How do the numerical values in the equation represent the pattern?

7. Derek has $56 in his bank account. He plans to deposit $15 every week for a year.

   a) Create a table of values for his first five deposits.

   b) What equation models this situation?

   c) How much money will Derek have in his account after 35 weeks?

   d) How long will it take him to save $500?

8. Taylor works at a shoe store. She makes $50 per day plus $2 for every pair of shoes she sells.

   a) Create a table of values to show how much she would earn for selling up to ten pairs of shoes in one day.

   b) Develop an equation to model this situation.

   c) How much money will Taylor make in a day if she sells 12 pairs of shoes? Use two methods for solving the problem.

6.2 Interpreting Graphs, pages 220–230

9. Many tree planters are paid according to how many trees they plant. The following graph shows the daily wages earned at a rate of $0.09 per tree planted.

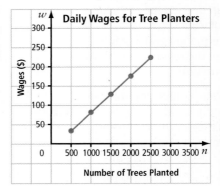

a) Approximately how much would a tree planter who planted 750 trees earn in one day?

b) In order to earn $250 in one day, approximately how many trees would a planter need to plant?

10. The graph shows the relationship between air pressure, in kilopascals, and altitude, in metres.

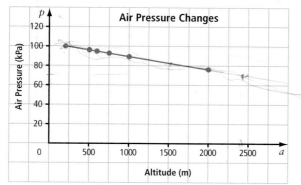

Air Pressure Changes

(Air Pressure (kPa) vs. Altitude (m))

a) What is the approximate air pressure at an altitude of 1500 m? 2400 m?

b) Approximately at what altitude is the air pressure 90 kPa? 60 kPa?

c) Does it make sense to interpolate or extrapolate values on this graph? Explain.

11. There are 15 schools in an urban school district. The table shows data about the student and teacher populations for eight of the schools.

Students	100	250	300	450	700	150	1025	650
Teachers	9	15	17	23	33	11	46	31

a) Graph the relationship between the number of students and teachers.

b) How many teachers might be in a school that has 850 students? 1200 students?

c) How many students might attend a school that employs 30 teachers? 50 teachers?

6.3 Graphing Linear Relations, pages 231–243

12. The cost of renting a snowboard can be calculated using the equation $C = 40 + 20d$, where C is the rental cost, in dollars, and d is the number of rental days.

a) Graph the linear relation for the first five days.

b) From the graph, what is the approximate cost of renting the snowboard for one day? seven days?

c) If buying a snowboard costs $300, use your graph to approximate how many days you could rent a board before it becomes cheaper to buy it.

d) Describe another method you could use to solve parts b) and c).

13. Graph the linear relation represented in the table of values.

Time (h)	Distance (km)
0.5	52.5
1.0	105.0
1.5	157.5
2.0	210.0
2.5	262.5
3.0	315.0
3.5	367.5
4.0	420.0

a) Describe a situation that might lead to these data.

b) Develop a linear equation to model the data.

c) What do the numerical coefficients and constants in the equation tell you?

14. A parking lot charges a flat rate of $3.00 and $1.75 for each hour or part of an hour of parking.

a) Create a table of values for the first 8 h of parking.

b) Graph the linear relation.

c) Use the graph to approximate how much it would cost to park for 4 h.

d) Using the graph, approximately how long could you park if you had $15.25?

e) What equation models this situation?

Chapter 6 Practice Test

For #1 to #3, select the best answer.

Use the pattern below to answer #1 and #2.

  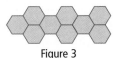

Figure 1   Figure 2   Figure 3

1. Which table of values best represents the pattern?

A

Figure Number (*f*)	1	2	3	4
Number of Sides (*s*)	18	36	54	72

B

Figure Number (*f*)	1	2	3	4
Number of Sides (*s*)	18	28	38	48

C

Figure Number (*f*)	1	2	3	4
Number of Sides (*s*)	12	20	28	36

D

Figure Number (*f*)	1	2	3	4
Number of Sides (*s*)	12	24	36	48

2. Which equation represents the pattern?

A $s = 12f$
B $s = 8f + 4$
C $s = 10f + 8$
D $s = 18f$

3. Which equation represents this graph?

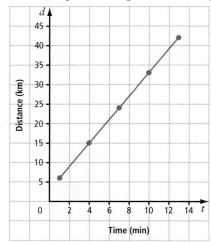

A $d = 2t + 4$
B $d = 4t - 1$
C $d = 3t + 3$
D $d = t + 5$

Complete the statements in #4 and #5.

4. When $x = 1.5$ on the graph, the approximate y-coordinate is ■.

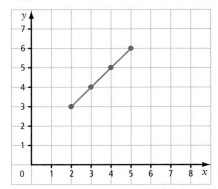

5. When $y = -8$ on the graph, the approximate x-coordinate is ■.

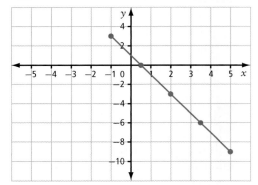

Short Answer

6. A number pattern starts with the number -2. Each number is 4 less than the previous number.

a) Make a table of values for the first five numbers in the pattern.

b) What equation can be used to determine each number in the pattern? Verify your answer.

c) What is the value of the 11th number in the pattern?

7. A cheese party pizza costs $21.25. The graph shows the cost of adding additional toppings.

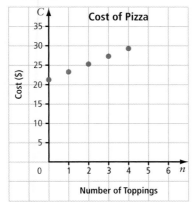

a) What is the approximate cost of a party pizza with five toppings?

b) Is it reasonable to interpolate values on this graph? Explain.

8. Create a table of values and a graph for each equation.

a) $y = -2x + 6$ **b)** $y = 2x - 6$

c) $y = 6$

9. How are the graphs in #8 similar? How are they different?

Extended Response

10. A cross-country ski park contains five different trails. The diagram shows the trails, with each trail being successively larger.

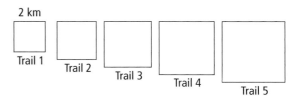

Each side length of the shortest trail is 2 km. The side length of each consecutive trail is 0.5 km longer than the previous one.

a) Construct a table of values to show the relationship between the trail number and the total distance of each trail.

b) What equation represents the relationship?

c) Graph the linear relation.

d) If a sixth trail were added, what would be its total distance?

Math Link: Wrap It Up!

You are planning a canoe trip with some friends. Where are you going? How long will your trip be? How many people are going?

You are in charge of ordering food supplies to meet the energy requirements of your group. For the trip, the amount of food energy required by a canoeist can be modelled by the equation $a = \dfrac{C}{100} - 17$, where a represents the person's age and C represents the number of calories.

Use the Internet, travel brochures, or other sources to find information about your trip.

a) Write a paragraph describing your trip.

b) Create a table of values for your data about total food energy requirements for the group.

c) Graph the linear relation.

d) Develop a problem based on your graph that also includes interpolation and extrapolation and provide a solution. Show your work.

Waterton Park, Alberta

Challenges

Hot-Air Ballooning

On January 15, 1991, the Pacific Flyer completed the longest flight ever made by a hot air balloon. The balloon flew 7671.91 km from Japan to northern Canada.

The balloon is designed to fly in the transoceanic jet streams. The Pacific Flyer hitched a ride on these strong winds and was swept high above the ocean.
The balloon reached a ground speed of 394 km/h. This is the fastest ground speed ever achieved by a hot-air balloon!

Thousands of Canadians enjoy a far less extreme ballooning experience each year. The following altitudes were recorded for two hot-air balloons at the indicated times.

	Time	Altitude	Time	Altitude
Hot-Air Balloon 1	8:00 a.m.	100 m	9:00 a.m.	5100 m
Hot-Air Balloon 2	8:15 a.m.	8100 m	8:45 a.m.	6600 m

Assume that each balloon is ascending or descending at a steady rate.

Justify your answers to each the following questions.

1. How far did Balloon 1 ascend between 8 a.m. and 9 a.m.? Based on your answer, calculate the speed of ascent in metres per hour. Show your calculations.

2. How far did Balloon 2 descend between 8:15 a.m. and 8:45 a.m.? Based on your answer, calculate the speed of descent in metres per hour. Show your calculations.

3. **a)** At what time will both balloons be at the same altitude?
   b) What is the altitude?

4. What is the altitude of each balloon at 8:20 a.m.?

5. At what time would you expect Hot Air Balloon 1 to reach 8100 m?

WWW Web Link

For more information about hot-air balloon records, go to www.mathlinks9.ca and follow the links.

Opening a Fitness Club

You and a friend are planning to open a new fitness club. You have researched two clubs that offer the services you would like to provide. These clubs offer the following membership plans if you join for a year:

> **Workout Club**
> one month free,
> then $35 per month

> **Get Fit Club**
> initial fee of $200,
> then $25 per month

1. Develop a membership plan that will make the fees for your club competitive. The plan should attract members and generate more income than at least one of the other club plans.

   a) What is your plan?

   b) Explain how your plan will attract members.

   c) Explain how your plan may result in earning more profit than the other clubs.

2. Suppose a potential member has $1000 to spend. Which club offers the best deal? Show your work.

Multiplying and Dividing Polynomials

Polynomials have been used for centuries to explore and describe relationships. These expressions are useful in everyday life. For example, a landscape designer might use a polynomial to help with calculating the cost of a landscaping project. The landscaper can calculate a number of different possible costs using a polynomial expression. This saves a lot of time. For what other jobs might polynomials be helpful?

What You Will Learn

- to multiply and divide polynomials using models and symbols
- to simplify polynomial expressions by combining like terms

Key Words

monomial	binomial
polynomial	distributive property

 Literacy Link

A spider map can help you understand and connect new terms and concepts. This spider map is designed to be used throughout the chapter.

Create a spider map in your math journal or notebook. As you work through the chapter, complete the map.

- After completing section 7.1, beside each heading on the upper left and upper right legs, provide your own examples and methods for multiplying monomials and dividing monomials.
- After completing section 7.2, beside each heading on the lower left leg, provide your own examples and methods for multiplying polynomials by monomials.
- After completing section 7.3, beside each heading on the lower right leg, provide your own examples and methods for dividing polynomials by monomials.

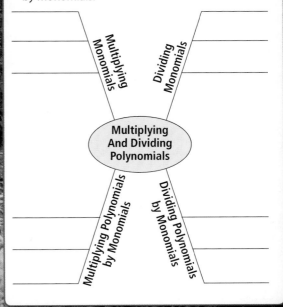

FOLDABLES™

Study Tool

Making the Foldable

Materials
- sheet of 11 × 17 paper
- two sheets of 8.5 × 11 paper
- scissors
- three sheets of 8.5 × 11 grid paper
- ruler
- stapler

Step 1

Fold the long side of a sheet of 11 × 17 paper in half. Pinch it at the midpoint. Fold the outer edges of the paper to meet at the midpoint. Label it as shown.

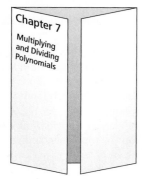

Chapter 7
Multiplying and Dividing Polynomials

Step 2

Fold the short side of a sheet of 8.5 × 11 paper in half. Fold in half the opposite way. Make a cut as shown through one thickness of paper, forming a two-tab book. Repeat Step 2 to make another two-tab book. Label them as shown.

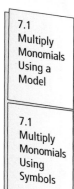

7.1 Multiply Monomials Using a Model

7.1 Divide Monomials Using a Model

7.1 Multiply Monomials Using Symbols

7.1 Divide Monomials Using Symbols

Step 3

Stack three sheets of grid paper so that the bottom edges are 2.5 cm apart. Fold the top edge of the sheets and align the edges so that all tabs are the same size. Staple along the fold. Label as shown.

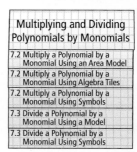

Multiplying and Dividing Polynomials by Monomials

7.2 Multiply a Polynomial by a Monomial Using an Area Model
7.2 Multiply a Polynomial by a Monomial Using Algebra Tiles
7.2 Multiply a Polynomial by a Monomial Using Symbols
7.3 Divide a Polynomial by a Monomial Using a Model
7.3 Divide a Polynomial by a Monomial Using Symbols

Step 4

Staple the three booklets you made into the Foldable from Step 1 as shown.

Using the Foldable

As you work through the chapter, write the Key Words in the remaining space in the centre panel, and provide definitions and examples. Beneath the tabs in the left, right, and centre panels, provide examples, show work, and record main concepts.

On the front of the right flap of the Foldable, record ideas for the Wrap It Up! On the back of the Foldable, make notes under the heading What I Need to Work On. Check off each item as you deal with it.

Math Link

Landscape Design

Gardeners and landscapers are often required to calculate areas when designing a landscape for a backyard, commercial property, or park. When determining how much soil, sand, gravel, mulch, and seed they need for a project, landscape designers also calculate volumes. Here is a landscape design created for a property.

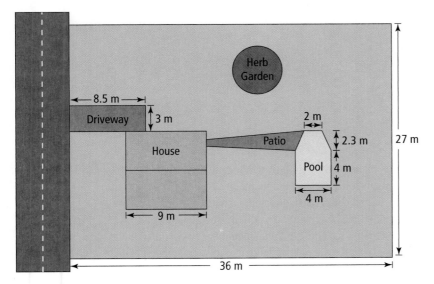

1. **a)** The circular herb garden has a radius of 4.5 m. What is the area of the herb garden?
   b) If the herb garden must have soil that is 0.5 m deep, what volume of soil is needed?
   c) What is the difference between the units used to measure the area and the units used to measure the volume of the herb garden?

2. The house is square. What fraction of the property does the house take up? Show two ways to express the answer.

3. The pool is in the shape of a square with a trapezoid attached to it. For the water in the pool to have a depth of 1.7 m, what volume of water is needed? Describe how you calculated the volume.

4. **a)** The patio has a surface area of 18 m². If it takes 48 paving stones to cover 1 m², how many paving stones are needed for the patio?
   b) Does your answer need to be exact? Explain.

5. What total area is grass? Explain how you calculated the area.

In this chapter, you will explore how to multiply and divide polynomials to help you create a landscape design for a park. What types of materials will you use?

Multiplying and Dividing Monomials

Focus on...

After this lesson, you will be able to…

- multiply a monomial by a monomial
- divide a monomial by a monomial

The band council would like to design a Medicine Wheel similar to the one shown above for a square area of the new school courtyard. According to the design, the edges of the outer circular pathway will just touch the edges of the square. The outer radius of the circle can be represented by $2x$. How could you determine the relationship between the area of the circle and the area of the square?

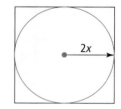

Literacy Link

A *monomial* has one term. For example, 5, $2x$, $3s^2$, $-8cd$, and $\dfrac{n^4}{3}$ are all monomials.

Explore Multiplying and Dividing Monomials

1. What is the side length of the square in terms of x?

2. a) Write an expression for the area of the circle.

  b) Write an expression for the area of the square.

3. Show how to compare the two areas using a ratio expressed in lowest terms.

> Do not use an approximate value for π. Leave π in the ratio.

4. How does the area of the square compare to the area of the circle?

Reflect and Check

5. Would this relationship be the same for any circle inscribed in a square? Explain.

6. a) How would you multiply the monomials $4x$ and $3x$?

  b) How would you divide the monomial $10x^2$ by the monomial $5x$?

Link the Ideas

Example 1: Multiply Monomials

Determine each product.
a) $(5x)(2x)$ **b)** $(3x)(2y)$

Solution

a) *Method 1: Use a Model*
You can use x-tiles and x^2-tiles to model $(5x)(2x)$.

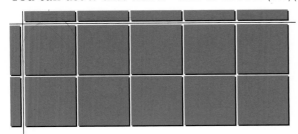

Each square has an area of $(x)(x) = x^2$. There are 10 positive x^2-tiles.
So, $(5x)(2x) = 10x^2$.

Method 2: Algebraically
Multiply the numerical coefficients.
Then, multiply the variables.
$$(5x)(2x)$$
$$= (5)(2)(x)(x)$$
$$= 10x^2$$

> How can you use the exponent laws to help you multiply the variables?

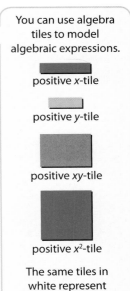

> You can use algebra tiles to model algebraic expressions.
>
> positive x-tile
>
> positive y-tile
>
> positive xy-tile
>
> positive x^2-tile
>
> The same tiles in white represent negative quantities.

b) *Method 1: Use a Model*
You can use x-tiles, y-tiles, and xy-tiles to model $(3x)(2y)$.

Each grey rectangle has an area of $(x)(y) = xy$.
There are 6 positive xy-tiles. So, $(3x)(2y) = 6xy$.

Method 2: Algebraically
$$(3x)(2y)$$
$$= (3)(2)(x)(y)$$
$$= 6xy$$

Show You Know

Determine each product in two different ways.
a) $(4x)(2y)$ **b)** $(-x)(7x)$

Example 2: Apply Monomial Multiplication

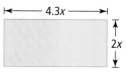

What is an expression for the area of the rectangle?

Solution

You can calculate the area, A, of a rectangle by multiplying the length by the width.
$A = (4.3x)(2x)$
$A = (4.3)(2)(x)(x)$
$A = (8.6)(x^2)$
$A = 8.6x^2$
An expression for the area of the rectangle is $8.6x^2$.

Show You Know

Calculate each product.

a) $(11a)(2b)$ b) $(-5x)(3.2)$

Example 3: Divide Monomials

Determine each quotient.

a) $\dfrac{-10x^2}{2x}$ b) $\dfrac{8xy}{4x}$

Solution

Strategies

Model It

a) *Method 1: Use a Model*
You can divide using algebra tiles.

Model $\dfrac{-10x^2}{2x}$ by representing the numerator with 10 negative x^2-tiles.

Arrange the 10 tiles into a rectangle so that one of the sides is 2 x-tiles long.

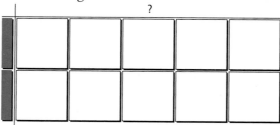

The unknown side length of the rectangle is made up of 5 negative x-tiles.

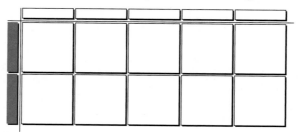

$$\dfrac{-10x^2}{2x} = -5x$$

Method 2: Algebraically

You can divide the numerator and the denominator by $2x$.

$$\frac{-10x^2}{2x}$$

> How can you use the exponent rules to help you divide the variables?

$$= \frac{\overset{-5x}{\cancel{-10x^2}}}{\underset{1}{\cancel{2x}}}$$

$$= -5x$$

b) *Method 1: Use a Model*

Model $\dfrac{8xy}{4x}$ by representing the numerator with 8 xy-tiles. Arrange the 8 tiles into a rectangle so that one of the sides is 4 x-tiles long.

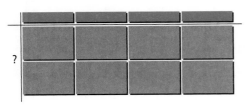

The unknown side length of the rectangle is made up of 2 y-tiles.

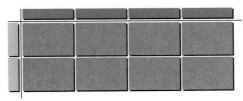

$$\frac{8xy}{4x} = 2y$$

Method 2: Algebraically

Divide common factors in the numerator and denominator.

$$\frac{8xy}{4x}$$

$$= \frac{\overset{2}{\cancel{8}}xy}{\underset{1}{\cancel{4}}x}$$

$$= 2y$$

Show You Know

Determine each quotient.

a) $\dfrac{12xy}{3y}$

b) $\dfrac{-14x^2}{-2x}$

Example 4: Apply Monomial Division

The area of a triangle is given by the expression $18x^2$. The base of the triangle is represented by $4x$. What is the height of the triangle in terms of x?

Strategies

Draw a Diagram

Solution

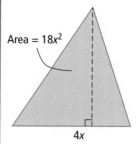

Area $= 18x^2$

$4x$

The area of a triangle can be calculated by multiplying the base by the height, then dividing by 2.

Area = base × height ÷ 2

So, if the area and base are known, then

Height $= 2 \times \dfrac{\text{area}}{\text{base}}$

Height $= \dfrac{(2)(18x^2)}{4x}$

Height $= \dfrac{36x^2}{4x}$

Divide the numerical coefficients.
Then, divide the variables.

Height $= 9x$

The height of the triangle is $9x$.

Show You Know

Calculate each quotient.

a) $\dfrac{18x^2}{3x}$

b) $14y \div (-2)$

c) $\dfrac{-18.6mn}{-3n}$

Key Ideas

- You can represent the multiplication and division of monomials using a model.

  $(2x)(-3x)$
  There are 6 negative x^2-tiles.
  $(2x)(-3x) = -6x^2$

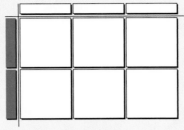

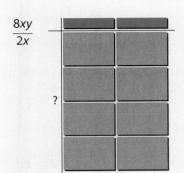

$\dfrac{8xy}{2x}$

?

The unknown side length of the rectangle is made up of 4 positive y-tiles.

$\dfrac{8xy}{2x} = 4y$

- To multiply monomials algebraically, you can multiply the numerical coefficients and use the exponent rules to multiply the variables.
- To divide monomials algebraically, you can divide the numerical coefficients and use the exponent rules to divide the variables.

Check Your Understanding

Communicate the Ideas

1. Explain to a partner at least two ways you could find the product of $(3x)$ and $(5x)$.

2. Laurie used the following method to divide $16n^2$ by $2n$.

   $\dfrac{16n^2}{2n}$

   $= (16 - 2)(n^2 - n)$

   $= 14n$

   Does Laurie's method have any errors? If so, what are her errors and what is the correct solution?

Practise

For help with #3 to #8, refer to Example 1 on page 255.

3. What multiplication statement is represented by each set of algebra tiles?

a)

b)

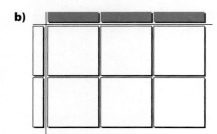

c)

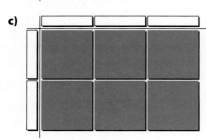

4. Determine the multiplication statement shown by each set of algebra tiles.

a)

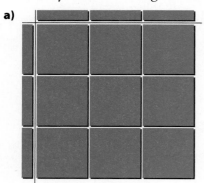

b)

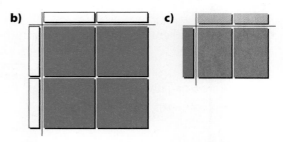

c)

5. Model and complete each multiplication statement.

a) $(2x)(4x)$ **b)** $(-4x)(2x)$
c) $(-4x)(-2x)$ **d)** $(-2x)(4x)$

6. Represent each multiplication statement with a model. Then, give the product.

a) $(3x)(5x)$ **b)** $(x)(-6x)$
c) $(-3x)(2x)$ **d)** $(-x)(x)$

For help with #7 to #10, refer to Example 2 on page 256.

7. Find the product of each pair of monomials.

a) $(2y)(5y)$ **b)** $(3a)(-6b)$
c) $(-q)(-9q)$ **d)** $\left(\dfrac{2}{3}x\right)(3x)$
e) $(-3r)(-2t)$ **f)** $(1.5p)(-3p)$

8. Multiply each pair of monomials.

a) $(3n)(2n)$ **b)** $(-4k)(-7k)$
c) $(-4w)(2.5w)$ **d)** $\left(\dfrac{-3}{5}x\right)(15x)$
e) $(8m)(-0.5n)$ **f)** $(t)(-7t)$

9. A rectangle has a width of $3.9x$ and a length of $5x$. What is an expression for the area of the rectangle?

10. A parallelogram has a base of $8.1z$ and a height of $4.2z$. What is an expression for the area of the parallelogram?

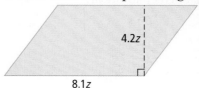

For help with #11 to #16, refer to Example 3 on pages 256-257.

11. Write the division statement represented by each set of algebra tiles.

a)

b)

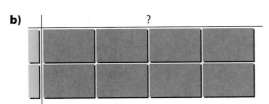

c)

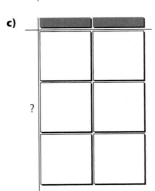

12. Determine the division statement shown by each set of algebra tiles.

a)

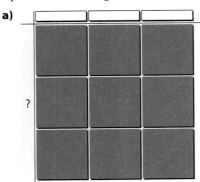

b)

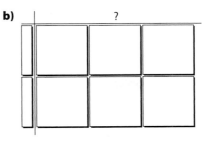

c)

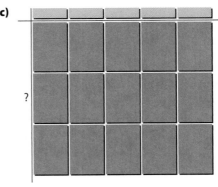

13. Model and complete each division.

a) $\dfrac{8x^2}{2x}$

b) $\dfrac{5xy}{5y}$

c) $\dfrac{-12x^2}{4x}$

d) $\dfrac{2x^2}{-x}$

14. Model and complete each division.

a) $\dfrac{-15x^2}{3x}$

b) $\dfrac{10xy}{2x}$

c) $\dfrac{12x^2}{-3x}$

d) $\dfrac{-9x^2}{-3x}$

15. Find the quotient of each pair of monomials.

a) $\dfrac{7x^2}{x}$

b) $\dfrac{25st}{5s}$

c) $\dfrac{125t}{5}$

d) $\dfrac{-8m}{-2m}$

e) $\dfrac{81rs}{3rs}$

f) $\dfrac{4.5p^2}{-3p}$

16. Divide.

a) $12.4x^2 \div x$

b) $-15r \div (-4r)$

c) $0.6t^2 \div 0.2t^2$

d) $-18pn \div 3n$

e) $k \div 4k$

f) $\dfrac{2}{3}x^2 \div 2x$

Apply

17. Find an expression for the area of each figure.

a)

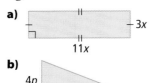

$3x$

$11x$

b)

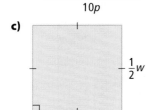

$4p$

$10p$

c)

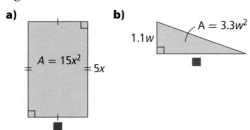

$\frac{1}{2}w$

18. What is the missing dimension in each figure?

a)

$A = 15x^2$

$5x$

b)

$A = 3.3w^2$

$1.1w$

■

19. The area of a rectangle is $72d^2$ and its length is $20d$. What is an expression for its width?

20. Claire wants to build a patio outside her café. The rectangular space outside of Claire's café is three times as long as it is wide. The area of the space is 48 m². Claire would like to build a patio with dimensions 3.5 m by 12.5 m in this space. Will it fit? Explain.

21. The diagram shows that x is the radius of the large circle and the diameter of the small circle. Write the ratio of the area of the large circle to the area of the small circle. Simplify the expression.

x

22. A circle is inscribed in a square as shown.

r

In terms of the radius, r, determine each of the following ratios.

a) the area of the square to the area of the circle

b) the perimeter of the square to the circumference of the circle

---

⊕ Literacy Link

An *inscribed circle* fits exactly into another figure so that the edges of the two figures touch, but do not intersect.

---

23. Jonasie and Elisa are taking two tourists on a trip to photograph caribou. The visitors will be travelling by dogsled. The dogsled's length is 4 times its width. The sled has a rectangular base area of 3.2 m². The equipment to be loaded on the sled measures 0.8 m wide by 3.5 m long. Will the equipment fit on the sled as it is presently packed? Explain your answer.

Extend

24. A rectangular prism has a volume in cubic centimetres expressed as the monomial $60xy$. The length and width of the prism, in centimetres, are $4x$ and $3y$ respectively.

a) Determine the height.

b) Write an expression for the surface area of the rectangular prism.

25. How is determining $\dfrac{9n}{3n^2}$ similar to and different from determining $\dfrac{9n^2}{3n}$?

26. A and B represent monomials. When A is multiplied by B, the result is A. When A is divided by B, the result is A. What is the monomial B?

27. A contractor needs to order the glass for a window. The window is in the shape of an isosceles triangle and the height of the window is 2.5 times the base width.

a) Determine an expression for the area of the window in terms of the width of its base.

b) If the width of the base must be 85 cm, what is the largest window area the contractor can use?

Math Link

Landscape designs for gardens may include rectangular and circular areas for flower beds, lawns, patios, and pools. As a landscape designer, you sometimes need to:

- calculate the volume of material, such as soil, gravel, water, or mulch, needed to fill these areas to a certain depth
- calculate the area that a known volume of material will cover

The following are the formulas for these calculations:

Volume = area × depth

$$\text{Area} = \frac{\text{volume}}{\text{depth}}$$

- Draw a rectangle and circle that might be used in landscaping. Label the design element that each shape represents.
- Use variables for the dimensions of the shapes.
- Create an area formula for each shape.
- For each shape, tell what type of material you will use to fill it. Also, tell what the depth of the material will be.
- Create a volume formula for each shape.
- Along with each formula, include an explanation concerning any coefficients you use. For example, you may have to convert centimetre measurements to metres.

> You may wish to create a spreadsheet that allows you to enter the values to calculate areas and volumes.

> How do these coefficients relate to your landscape design?

Multiplying Polynomials by Monomials

In the 1880s, braking a train was a tough job. The engineer "whistled down" for brakes and reversed his engine. Two people were responsible for the brakes. One rode in the cab on the engine and the other rode in the caboose. These people would run toward each other over the swaying, rocking car tops, tightening each car's brake control wheel as they went.

Physics Link

Air brakes on trains became commonplace in the 1900s, making the task of stopping a train much easier. Air brakes use compressed air in a piston to push the brake shoe onto the train wheel. The system works like a bicycle brake.

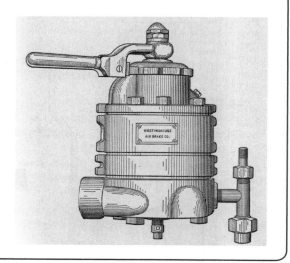

Explore Multiplying a Polynomial by a Monomial

When a train's brakes are applied, the train travels a distance before it stops. After t seconds, the distance, in metres, that the train travels is given by the polynomial $2t(20 - t)$.

1. What part of the diagram does $2t(20 - t)$ represent?

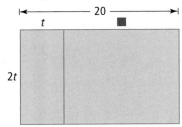

2. What polynomial represents the unknown length in the diagram? How did you determine this polynomial?

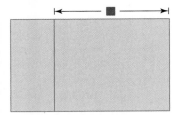

3. Find three rectangles in the diagram. What is an expression for the area of the largest rectangle? What is an expression for the area of the smallest rectangle?

4. What is the difference in area between the largest and smallest rectangles? Show two ways to find your answer.

5. Calculate the area of the medium-sized rectangle using the dimension you determined in #2.

Reflect and Check

6. Describe the steps you used in #5 to calculate the area of the medium-sized rectangle.

7. How is the area of the medium-sized rectangle related to the areas of the large rectangle and the small rectangle?

8. How far does the train travel in 10 s? Show how you arrived at your answer.

Literacy Link

A polynomial is made up of terms connected by addition or subtraction.

Examples:
$x + 5$
$2d - 2.4$
x
$3s^2 + 5s - 6$
$\dfrac{h^2}{2} - \dfrac{h}{4}$

Link the Ideas

Strategies

Draw a Diagram

Example 1: Multiply a Polynomial by a Monomial Using an Area Model

Determine the product.
$(3x)(2x + 4)$

Solution

Draw a rectangle with side dimensions that represent $3x$ and $2x + 4$.

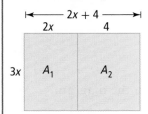

Calculate the area of each rectangle.
$A_1 = (3x)(2x)$
$A_1 = 6x^2$

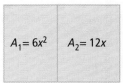

$A_2 = (3x)(4)$
$A_2 = 12x$
The total area is $A_1 + A_2 = 6x^2 + 12x$.

Show You Know

Calculate each product.

a) $(2x)(x + 3)$ **b)** $(2 + c)(c)$

Example 2: Multiply a Polynomial by a Monomial Using Algebra Tiles

Find the product.
$(2x)(3x - 5)$

Solution

You can use x-tiles and negative 1-tiles to model $2x$ and $3x - 5$.

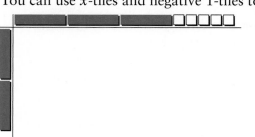

Use x^2-tiles and negative x-tiles to model $(2x)(3x - 5)$.

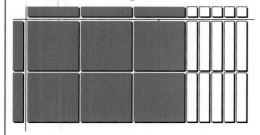

There are 6 positive x^2-tiles and 10 negative x-tiles.

So, $(2x)(3x - 5) = 6x^2 - 10x$.

Show You Know

Find each product.

a) $(2 + 3x)(3x)$ **b)** $(4x)(2x - 1)$

Example 3: Multiply a Polynomial by a Monomial Algebraically

The dimensions of a rectangular gym floor are represented by the expressions $4x$ and $5x - 3$. What is a polynomial expression for the area of the gym floor? Write the expression in simplified form.

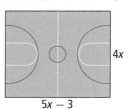

$4x$

$5x - 3$

Solution

You can calculate the area of a rectangle, A, by multiplying the width by the length.

$A = (4x)(5x - 3)$

You can apply the distributive property. Multiply $4x$ by each term in the binomial $5x - 3$.

$A = (4x)(5x - 3)$
$A = (4x)(5x) - (4x)(3)$
$A = (4)(5)(x)(x) - (4)(3)(x)$
$A = 20x^2 - 12x$

A simplified expression for the area of the gym floor is $20x^2 - 12x$.

> **Literacy Link**
>
> The *distributive property* allows you to expand algebraic expressions. Multiply the monomial by each term in the polynomial.
>
> $a(b + c) = ab + ac$

> **Literacy Link**
>
> A *binomial* is a polynomial with two terms, such as $6y^2 + 3$ and $2x - 5$.

Show You Know

Calculate each product.

a) $(-3x)(2x + 5)$ **b)** $(5y)(11 - x)$

Key Ideas

- You can represent the multiplication of a polynomial by a monomial using models.

  - area model

    $\overset{\longleftarrow\ 2x + 2\ \longrightarrow}{}$

	$2x$	2
$3x$	$A_1 = 6x^2$	$A_2 = 6x$

    $(3x)(2x + 2)$
    The product is represented by $A_1 + A_2$.
    $(3x)(2x + 2) = 6x^2 + 6x$

  - algebra tiles

    $(2x)(-2x + 3)$
    There are 4 negative x^2-tiles and 6 positive x-tiles.
    $(2x)(-2x + 3) = -4x^2 + 6x$

- To multiply a polynomial by a monomial algebraically, you can expand the expression using the distributive property. Multiply each term of the polynomial by the monomial.

  $(-1.2x)(3x - 7)$
  $= (-1.2x)(3x) - (-1.2x)(7)$
  $= -3.6x^2 + 8.4x$

Check Your Understanding

Communicate the Ideas

1. Describe two methods you could use to multiply polynomials by monomials.

2. Sara is going to simplify the expression $(3x)(2x + 4)$. Can she add the terms in the brackets and then multiply? Explain.

3. Mahmoud used the following method to expand the expression $(5x)(2x + 1)$.

   $(5x)(2x + 1) = 10x^2 + 1$

   a) Show that Mahmoud's solution is incorrect.
   b) How would you correct his solution?

Practise

For help with #4 to #7, refer to Example 1 on page 266.

4. What multiplication statement is represented by each area model?

a)

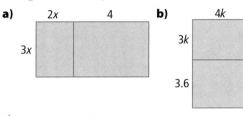

2x   4

3x

b)

4k

3k

3.6

c)

3.2k   5.1

k

5. Determine the multiplication statement shown by each area model.

a)

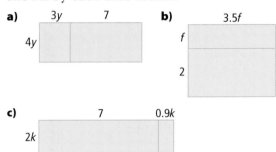

3y   7

4y

b)

3.5f

f

2

c)

7   0.9k

2k

6. Expand each expression using an area model.

a) $(3.2r + 1)(4r)$ **b)** $\left(\dfrac{1}{2}a\right)(3a + 6)$

7. Use an area model to expand each expression.

a) $(2x)(4x + 2)$ **b)** $(6k + 2)(4.5k)$

For help with #8 to #11, refer to Example 2 on pages 266-267.

8. What multiplication statement is represented by the algebra tiles?

a)

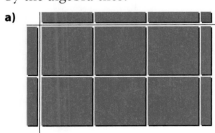

b)

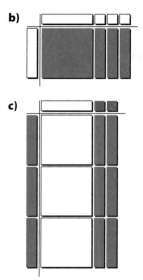

c)

9. Determine the multiplication statement shown by the algebra tiles.

a)

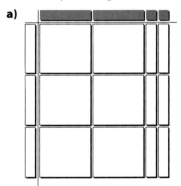

b)

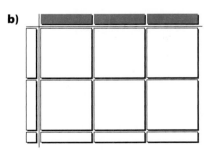

c)

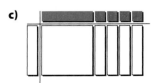

10. Expand each expression, using algebra tiles.

  a) $(x - 5)(3x)$ **b)** $(2x)(-2x + 3)$

11. Use algebra tiles to expand each expression.

  a) $(4x + 2)(-3x)$ **b)** $(-4x)(3x - 1)$

For help with #12 and #13, refer to Example 3 on page 267.

12. Expand using the distributive property.

  a) $(2x)(3x - 1)$

  b) $(3p)(2p - 0.8)$

  c) $(0.5m)(7 - 12m)$

  d) $\left(\frac{1}{2}r - 2\right)(-r)$

  e) $(2n - 7)(8.2)$

  f) $(3x)(x + 2y + 4)$

13. Multiply.

  a) $(4j)(2j - 3)$

  b) $(-1.2w)(3w - 7)$

  c) $(6x)(4 - 2.4x)$

  d) $\left(\frac{3}{7}v + 7\right)(-1)$

  e) $(3 - 9y)(y)$

  f) $(-8a - 7b - 2)(8a)$

Apply

14. A rectangular Kwakiutl button blanket has a width of $3x$ and a length of $4x - 3$.

  a) What is an expanded expression for the area of the blanket?

  b) What is a simplified expression for the perimeter of the blanket?

15. Lee has decided to build a shed on a square concrete slab. The shed has the same width, w, as the slab. Its length is 2 m shorter than the width of the slab.

  a) What is an expression for the area of the shed?

  b) If the width, w, of the slab is 4 m, what is the area of the shed?

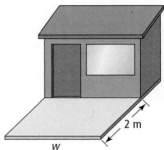

16. The basketball court for the Jeux de la Francophonie is 5.5 m longer than 1.5 times the width.

  a) What is an expression for the area of the basketball court?

  b) If the length is 28 m, what is the area of the basketball court?

Did You Know?

The Jeux de la Francophonie are games for French-speaking people. They are held every four years in different locations around the world. The games include sports and artistic events. Canada is represented by three teams: Québec, New Brunswick, and a third team representing the rest of Canada.

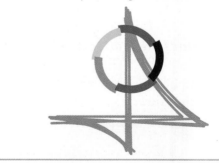

17. A rectangular field is $(4x + 2)$ m long. The width of the field is 2 m shorter than the length. What is an expression for the area of the field?

18. A rectangular skateboard park is $(3x)$ m long. Its width is 4 m less than the length.

   a) What is an expression for the area of the park?

   b) If $x = 15$, what is the area of the park?

Extend

19. A rectangluar packing crate has the dimensions shown, in metres.

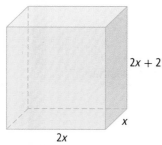

   a) What is an expression for the total surface area of the crate?

   b) What is an expression for the volume of the crate?

20. The surface area, SA, of a cylinder is $SA = 2\pi r^2 + 2\pi rh$, where r is the radius and h is the height. The formula for the volume, V, of a cylinder is $V = \pi r^2 h$. What is the surface area of a cylinder that has a height of 5 cm and a volume of 80π cm³?

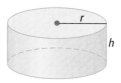

21. A rectangle measuring $(12n)$ m by 8 m has a square of side length 2 m cut out in the four corners. The cut-out shape forms an open box when the four corners are folded and taped.

   a) Draw the box and label its dimensions.

   b) What is the surface area of this open box?

   c) What is the capacity of this box?

Math Link

You are drawing up plans for a landscape design. You are going to include one of the following design elements, which will be in the shape of a rectangle:
- swimming pool
- concrete patio
- hockey rink
- beach volleyball pit

The rectangular shape is 2 m longer than twice the width. You must choose an appropriate depth for your design element.

   a) Create a formula for calculating the volume of material needed to fill your design element.

   b) Use your formula to calculate the volume of material needed for widths of 2 m, 3 m, 4 m, and 5 m. Which width would you prefer for your design element? Why?

> For example, a swimming pool may have a depth of 1.5 m.

> Is a pool filled right to the top with water? How might this affect your formula?

Dividing Polynomials by Monomials

Focus on...

After this lesson, you will be able to...
- divide a polynomial by a monomial

When you are buying a fish tank, the size of the tank depends on the size and habits of the fish. A tank for a jaguar cichlid, or *Parachromis managuensis*, should have the minimum dimensions shown, in metres.

The volume of the rectangular tank can be represented by the polynomial expression $7.5w^2 - 3w$. How could you determine a polynomial expression that represents the length of the tank in terms of w?

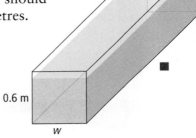

0.6 m

w

Materials
- algebra tiles

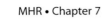

Explore Dividing a Polynomial by a Monomial

A rectangular solid has a width of $2x$, a height of 3, and an unknown length. The area of the base of the solid is represented by the polynomial $2x^2 + 4x$.

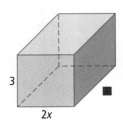

3

2x

1. Show that the volume of the solid shown can be represented by the polynomial $6x^2 + 12x$.

2. Use algebra tiles to represent the area of the rectangular base.

3. Count the number of x-tiles and 1-tiles required for the missing dimension of the rectangle. What expression represents the missing dimension?

Reflect and Check

What happens if you multiply your expression by the width of the rectangular solid?

4. Show that your expression for the missing dimension in #3 is correct.

5. Describe the steps you would take to find an expression for the ratio of the volume to the side measuring $2x$.

Link the Ideas

Example 1: Divide a Polynomial by a Monomial Using a Model

Determine the quotient.

$$\frac{6x^2 - 8x}{2x}$$

Solution

You can use algebra tiles.
Use 6 positive x^2-tiles and
8 negative x-tiles to represent
the polynomial $6x^2 - 8x$.

The vertical side of the rectangle
represents the monomial divisor, $2x$.

Strategies

Model It

Count the number of positive x-tiles
and negative 1-tiles required to
complete the horizontal side of the
rectangle.

There are 3 positive x-tiles and
4 negative 1-tiles, or $3x - 4$. This
expression represents the result of
dividing the polynomial, $6x^2 - 8x$,
by the monomial, $2x$.

$$\frac{6x^2 - 8x}{2x} = 3x - 4$$

Check:
Multiply the quotient, $3x - 4$, by the divisor, $2x$.

$$(2x)(3x - 4)$$
$$= (2x)(3x) - (2x)(4)$$
$$= 6x^2 - 8x$$

> You can also determine
> the quotient
> algebraically.
> $$\frac{6x^2 - 8x}{2x}$$
> $$= \frac{6x^2}{2x} - \frac{8x}{2x}$$
> $$= \frac{\overset{3x}{\cancel{6x^2}}}{\underset{1}{\cancel{2x}}} - \frac{\overset{4}{\cancel{8x}}}{\underset{1}{\cancel{2x}}}$$
> $$= 3x - 4$$

> How do you know
> that the answer is
> correct?

Show You Know

Determine each quotient.

a) $\dfrac{3x^2 + 6x}{3x}$

b) $\dfrac{8x^2 - 2x}{2x}$

Example 2: Dividing a Polynomial by a Monomial Algebraically

> The formula for the surface area of a cylinder is $2\pi r^2 + 2\pi rh$.

a) What is the ratio of the surface area to the radius of the cylinder? Write the ratio in simplified form.

b) If the height, h, of the cylinder is the same as the radius, r, what is the ratio of the surface area to the radius? Write the ratio in simplified form.

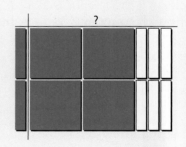

Solution

a) $\dfrac{\text{surface area}}{\text{radius}} = \dfrac{2\pi r^2 + 2\pi rh}{r}$

The expression can be broken down into two parts.

$$\frac{\text{surface area}}{\text{radius}}$$

$$= \frac{2\pi r^2}{r} + \frac{2\pi rh}{r}$$

$$= \frac{2\pi \overset{r}{\cancel{r^2}}}{\underset{1}{\cancel{r}}} + \frac{2\pi \overset{1}{\cancel{r}}h}{\underset{1}{\cancel{r}}}$$

$$= 2\pi r + 2\pi h$$

b) Substitute $h = r$ into the ratio from part a).

$$\frac{\text{surface area}}{\text{radius}}$$
$$= 2\pi r + 2\pi h$$
$$= 2\pi r + 2\pi (r)$$
$$= 2\pi r + 2\pi r$$
$$= 4\pi r$$

Show You Know

Determine each quotient.

a) $\dfrac{15x^2 - 12x}{3x}$

b) $\dfrac{-2t^2 + 4t}{2t}$

Key Ideas

- You can divide a polynomial by a monomial using a model.

  $\dfrac{4x^2 - 6x}{2x}$

  The unknown side length of the rectangle is made up of $2x - 3$ tiles.

  $\dfrac{4x^2 - 6x}{2x} = 2x - 3$

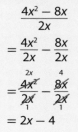

- When you divide a polynomial by a monomial algebraically, you can divide the numerical coefficients and apply the exponent laws to the variables.

  $$\frac{4x^2 - 8x}{2x}$$

  $$= \frac{4x^2}{2x} - \frac{8x}{2x}$$

  $$= \frac{\overset{2x}{\cancel{4x^2}}}{\underset{1}{\cancel{2x}}} - \frac{\overset{4}{\cancel{8x}}}{\underset{1}{\cancel{2x}}}$$

  $$= 2x - 4$$

Check Your Understanding

Communicate the Ideas

1. Explain how you would perform the following division: $\dfrac{3x^2 + 6x}{2x}$.

2. Anita used the following method to simplify an expression:

a) Show that Anita's solution is incorrect.

b) How would you correct her solution?

$$\dfrac{9k^2 - 3k}{3}$$
$$= \dfrac{9k^2}{3} - \dfrac{3k}{3}$$
$$= 3k - 1$$

3. Use a model to show a polynomial division statement with a quotient of $3x + 2$.

Practise

For help with #4 to #7, refer to Example 1 on page 273.

4. What division statement is represented by the algebra tiles? Determine the quotient.

a)

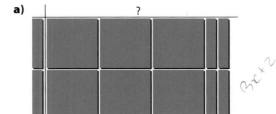

$3x+2$

b)

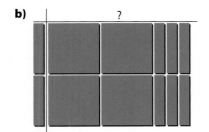

$2x+3$

c)

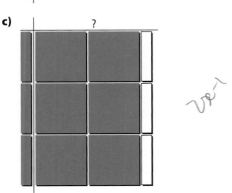

$2x-1$

5. Determine the division statement represented by the algebra tiles and give the quotient.

a)

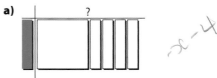

$x-4$

b)

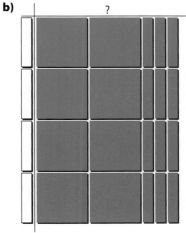

$2x-3$

c)

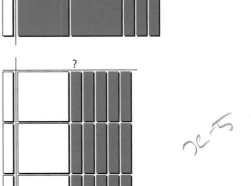

$x-5$

6. Divide each expression, using a model.

a) $\dfrac{5x^2 - 10x}{5x}$

b) $\dfrac{4x^2 + 12x}{2x}$

7. Use a model to divide each expression.

a) $\dfrac{-8x^2 - 4x}{4x}$

b) $\dfrac{-3x^2 + 5x}{-x}$

For help with #8 and #9, refer to Example 2 on page 274.

8. Divide.

a) $\dfrac{2y^2 + 4.2y}{2y}$

b) $\dfrac{12m^2 - 6.2m + 24}{2}$

c) $\dfrac{-18y^2 - 6y}{-6y}$

d) $\dfrac{3cv - 2.7c}{3c}$

9. Determine each quotient.

a) $\dfrac{2.7c^2 + 3.6c}{3c}$

b) $\dfrac{2x^2 + 8xy}{x}$

c) $\dfrac{-s^2 - 1.5st}{5s}$

d) $\dfrac{-14w^2 - 7w + 0.5}{0.5}$

Apply

10. A dump truck holds 10 m³ of soil. You are filling a rectangular space in a yard with the dimensions of $(2x + 3)$ by $5x$ by 2, in metres. What polynomial expression represents the number of truck loads of soil you will need?

11. A rectangular fish tank has the dimensions shown, in metres. The volume of the tank can be represented by $7.5w^2 - 3w$.

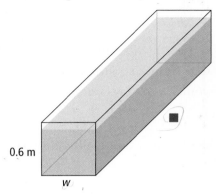

0.6 m

w

a) What polynomial expression represents the area of the base of the tank?

b) What polynomial expression represents the length of the tank?

c) What is the length of the tank if the width is 0.6 m? What is the volume of the tank?

12. For their Valentine's Day dance, the grade 9 students want to decorate the end wall of the gym with red poster paper. The area of the wall is given by the polynomial $45x^2 + 20x$. One sheet of poster paper covers an area given by the monomial $5x$. What polynomial expression represents the number of sheets of paper the students will need to cover the wall?

13. A rectangle has an area of $9x^2 - 3x$ square units. The width of the rectangle is $3x$ units. What is the length?

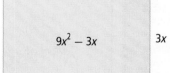

$9x^2 - 3x$ $3x$

14. The formula used to predict the distance an object falls is $d = 4.9t^2 + vt$. In the formula, d is the distance, in metres, t is the time, in seconds, and v is the starting velocity of the object, in metres per second.

a) The average speed of a falling object is calculated as $s = \dfrac{d}{t}$, where s is the average speed, in metres per second. Use this information to develop a formula for the average speed of a falling object in terms of t and v.

b) What is the average speed of an object that falls for 5 s, if it starts from a resting position?

Extend

15. Divide.

a) $\dfrac{3.6gf + 0.93g}{0.3g}$

b) $\dfrac{\frac{2}{3}b^2 - \frac{1}{3}ab + \frac{1}{3}b}{\frac{1}{3}b}$

c) $\dfrac{-4.8x^2 + 3.6x - 0.4}{0.2}$

16. Two rectangles have common sides with a right triangle, as shown. The areas and widths of the rectangles are shown. What is a simplified expression for the area of the triangle?

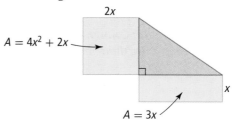

17. What is the ratio of the area of the shaded rectangle to the area of the large rectangle?

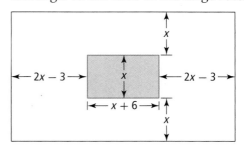

18. If a rectangle has length $2xy$ and area $12x^2y + 6xy^2$, what is its perimeter?

Math Link

You are designing a park that includes a large parking lot that will be covered with gravel.

a) Design two different-shaped parking lots using any single shape or combination of regular shapes. Include the dimensions on a drawing of each parking lot design. Note that you will need to be able to calculate the area of your parking lots. Each area should be a different shape. Make them no less than 200 m² and no greater than 650 m².

b) A truck with dimensions similar to those shown in the picture will deliver the gravel. Write an expression for the approximate area that a single load of gravel will cover to a depth of 5 cm.

c) There are three sizes of trucks that can deliver the gravel. The widths are 1.5 m, 2 m, and 3 m. Approximately how many truckloads would it take for each truck size to deliver the required amount of gravel for each of your parking lots? You will cover each parking lot to a depth of 5 cm. Show your work.

d) Which truck size do you think would be the most efficient to use for each of your parking lots? Explain your reasoning.

Chapter 7 Review

Key Words

For #1 to #4, match the polynomial in Column A with an equivalent polynomial in Column B. Polynomials in Column B may be used more than once or not at all.

Column A

1. $\dfrac{8xy}{2x}$

2. $\dfrac{12x^2 - 6x}{3x}$

3. $(-2x + 1)(-2x)$

4. $\dfrac{12xy - 6x}{3}$

Column B

A $4xy - 2x$

B $4x^2 - 2x$

C $4y$

D $2x^2 - 2x$

E $4xy$

F $4x - 2$

7.1 Multiplying and Dividing Monomials, pages 254–263

5. Use a model to complete each monomial multiplication statement.

   a) $(3x)(5x)$

   b) $(4x)(-5y)$

6. Find each product.

   a) $(-3.2x)(-2.7y)$

   b) $\left(\dfrac{3}{7}a\right)(-14a)$

7. Use a model to complete each monomial division statement.

   a) $\dfrac{6x^2}{2x}$

   b) $15a^2 \div (-3a)$

8. Determine each quotient.

   a) $\dfrac{-4.8r^2}{-1.2r}$

   b) $2xy \div 2x$

9. A rectangle is four times as long as it is wide. If the area of the rectangle is 1600 cm², what are its dimensions?

10. A square is inscribed in a circle with radius r as shown. What is the ratio of the area of the square to the area of the circle?

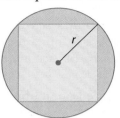

7.2 Multiplying Polynomials by Monomials, pages 264–271

11. What polynomial multiplication statement is represented by each area model?

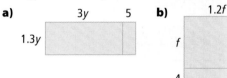

12. What polynomial multiplication statement is represented by the algebra tiles?

   a)

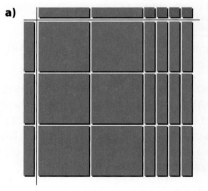

   b)

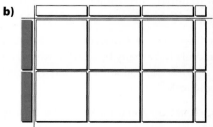

13. Expand.

a) $(20x)(2.3x - 1.4)$

b) $\left(\frac{2}{3}p\right)\left(p - \frac{3}{4}\right)$

14. The length of a piece of rectangular cardboard in centimetres is $6x + 3$.

The width is 1 cm less than $\frac{1}{3}$ of the length.

What is an expression for the area of the cardboard?

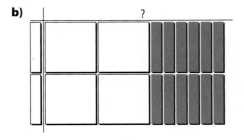

6x + 3

7.3 Dividing Polynomials by Monomials, pages 272-277

15. Determine the division statement represented by the algebra tiles. Give the quotient.

a)

b)

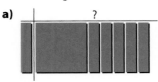

16. Divide.

a) $\dfrac{12n^2 - 2n}{2n}$

b) $\dfrac{15x - 3x^2}{1.5x}$

17. A triangle has an area represented by $3x^2 + 6x$. If the base of the triangle is $3x$, what is the height?

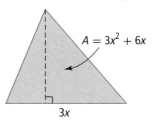

$A = 3x^2 + 6x$

3x

18. A rectangular wall has a circular window. The area of the wall can be represented by $32x^2 + 16x$. The length of the wall is $8x$. The diameter of the circular window has a measurement that is half the width of the wall. What is the radius of the window written as an expression in terms of x?

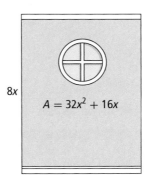

8x

$A = 32x^2 + 16x$

19. Naullaq is cutting ice blocks from the lake for her mother's drinking water tank. The cylindrical tank has a volume of $4x^2\pi$. Once each block has melted, it will have a volume of $3x^2$. How many blocks does she need to cut so that her mother's tank will be filled when the ice melts? Give your answer to the nearest whole block. Explain your answer.

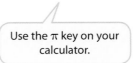

Use the π key on your calculator.

Chapter 7 Practice Test

For #1 to #6, select the best answer.

1. Which monomial multiplication statement is represented by the algebra tiles?

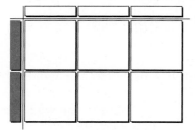

A $(3x)(-2x) = -6x^2$

B $(2x)(-3x) = -6x^2$

C $(2x)(3x) = 6x^2$

D $(-2x)(-3x) = 6x^2$

2. What is the product of $3y$ and $2.7y$?

A $0.9y$ **B** $8.1y$

C $0.9y^2$ **D** $8.1y^2$

3. Which monomial division statement is represented by the algebra tiles?

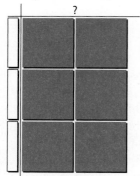

A $\dfrac{-6x^2}{-3x} = -2x$

B $\dfrac{-6x^2}{-3x} = 2x$

C $\dfrac{6x^2}{-3x} = -2x$

D $\dfrac{6x^2}{-3x} = 2x$

4. Which is equivalent to $-27q^2 \div 9q$?

A $3q^2$ **B** $3q$

C $-3q$ **D** $-3q^2$

5. Which is equivalent to $\left(\dfrac{2}{3}x\right)(-3x - 6)$?

A $-2x^2 - 4x$ **B** $-2x - 4$

C $2x - 4$ **D** $2x^2 - 4x$

6. Calculate $\dfrac{15y^2 - 10y}{-5y}$.

A $-3y - 2$ **B** $-3y + 2$

C $3y - 2$ **D** $3y + 2$

Complete the statements in #7 and #8.

7. The expression $\dfrac{-24x^2 + 8xz}{4x}$ is equivalent to ▇▇▇.

8. A polynomial multiplication expression that is equivalent to $24d^2 - 12d$ is ▇▇▇.

Short Answer

For #9 to #11, show all of the steps in your solutions.

9. Calculate $(2.4x)(4y)$.

10. What is the product of $12h$ and $\dfrac{-3}{4}h + 2$?

11. Simplify $\dfrac{2x^2 + 3x}{-3x}$.

12. Paula is building a rectangular patio. It will have a square flower bed in the middle. The rest will have paving stones. The patio will have a length of $4x$ and a width of $3.1x$. The area of the flower bed will be $3.5x^2$. What area of the patio will need paving stones?

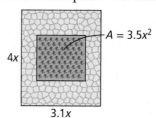

$A = 3.5x^2$

$4x$

$3.1x$

13. A sports field is 15 m longer than twice its width. What is an expression for the area of the field in terms of its width, w? Expand the expression.

14. The area of a rectangular sandbox can be expressed as $24xy + 36x$. The width of the sandbox is $6x$. What is the perimeter of the sandbox?

A = 24xy + 36x

6x

Extended Response

15. a) What error did Karim make when completing the division statement shown?

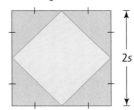

$$\frac{-18d^2 - 6d}{3d}$$
$$= \frac{-18d^2}{3d} + \frac{6d}{3d}$$
$$= -6d + 2$$

b) Show the correct method.

16. A square with a side length of $2s$ has a smaller square inscribed. The vertices of the smaller square are at the midpoints of the sides of the larger square. What is the ratio of the area of the larger square to the area of the smaller square? Express your answer in its simplest form.

2s

Math Link: Wrap It Up!

You have been hired to create a landscape design for a park. The park is rectangular and covers an area of 500 000 m². The park includes the following features:
- a play area covered with bark mulch
- a sand area for playing beach volleyball
- a wading pool

The features in your design include the following shapes:
- a circular area
- a rectangular area
- a parallelogram-shaped area with the base three times the height

The features of your park have varying depths.

Include the following in your design:
- a scale drawing showing the layout of each of the required features
- a list showing the area of each feature and the volume of each material (mulch, sand, and water) required to complete the park
- a polynomial expression for the area and volume of each feature, using a variable for one of the dimensions

Challenges

Design a Card Game

You are a game designer. You are going to create a skill-testing card game that involves the multiplication and division of polynomial expressions.

Materials
• at least 30 index cards per pair of students , or heavy paper for cutting out cards

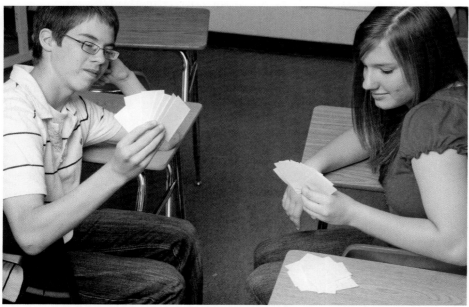

Work with a partner. You will create at least 15 pairs of cards, using the following guidelines:
• For each pair, on one card write a polynomial expression that involves multiplication or division. On the other card write an equivalent expression.
• Include the types of polynomial expressions found in each section of Chapter 7.
• Use a variety of constants, monomials, and polynomials.

> One card might be $(5x)(4x)$, and the equivalent card might be $20x^2$.

1. Create a list of the pairs of expressions for your game.

2. Create the cards.

3. Write the rules for your game. Your game should be suitable for two or more players.

4. Exchange your cards and rules with another set of partners. Play the game.

Polynomial Puzzle

Materials
- sample polynomial puzzle per student
- scissors

1. Try the nine-piece puzzle below.

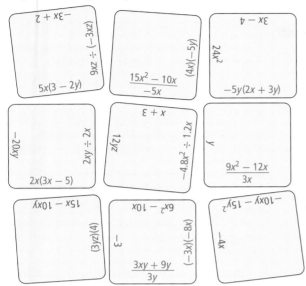

a) Cut out the pieces of a copy of the puzzle.

b) Solve the puzzle. Polynomial expressions involving multiplication or division are red. Matching equivalent expressions are blue. Match each multiplication or division expression with its equivalent expression. The diagram shows how a solved nine-piece puzzle would look.

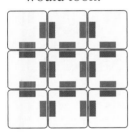

2. Design your own 16-piece puzzle.

a) Draw 16 equal-sized squares on a piece of paper.

b) Write your own matching expressions. Place them the same way as in the small diagram above so that each expression and its equivalent are across from each other.
- Include the types of polynomial expressions found in Chapter 7.
- Include a variety of constants, monomials, and polynomials.
- Cover a variety of difficulty levels.

c) Cut out your sixteen puzzle pieces. Mix them up.

d) Exchange your puzzle with a classmate's. Solve your classmate's puzzle.

Chapters 5–7 Review

Chapter 5 Introduction to Polynomials

1. The following diagram of algebra tiles models a backyard.

   a) What is an expression for the perimeter of the backyard?
   b) What is an expression for the area of the backyard?

2. Use materials or diagrams to show the collection of like terms in each expression.
   a) $8c + 3 - 5c + 1$
   b) $-1 + x - 1 - x + 1$
   c) $g^2 - g + 5 + 2g - 4g^2$

3. Write the following expressions in simplest form.
   a) $(2m - 3) + (5m + 1)$
   b) $(w^2 - 4w + 7) + (3w^2 + 5w - 3)$
   c) $(9y^2 - 6.8) + (4.3 - 9y - 2y^2)$

4. Write a simpler expression.
   a) $(-7z + 3) - (-4z + 5)$
   b) $(3d - 2d - 7) - (d^2 - 5d + 6cd - 2)$
   c) $(2x^2 + 3xy) - (-xy + 4x^2)$

5. The Better Buys antique shop sells comic books for $10, hardcover books for $8, and paperback novels for $3.

   a) Write an algebraic expression for the antique shop's total income from the sale of comics, hardcover books, and paperbacks. Tell what each variable represents.
   b) Use your expression to show the total income after the sale of 15 comics, 7 hardcover books, and 5 paperbacks.
   c) One day, the store sold $100 worth of comics, hardcovers, and paperbacks. What number of each item did the store sell? Show that more than one answer is possible.

6. A park is divided equally into three square sections. Each section will have a side measurement of $2n + 4$. The park will have fencing built as shown. Each opening has length n and does not need any fencing. What is the total length of fencing needed to complete the job?

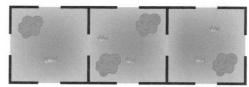

Chapter 6 Linear Relations

7. a) Describe the relationship between the figure number and the number of tiles.

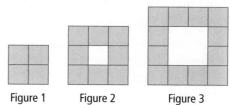

   Figure 1   Figure 2   Figure 3

   b) Develop a linear equation to model the pattern.
   c) If the pattern were continued, how many squares would be in Figure 8?

8. Monika is saving money for a ski trip. She starts with $112 in her bank account. She decides to deposit $25 every week until she has enough money to pay for the trip.

a) Create a table of values for the first five deposits.

b) What linear equation models this situation?

c) If Monika needs at least $450 for her trip, for how many months does she need to deposit money into her bank account?

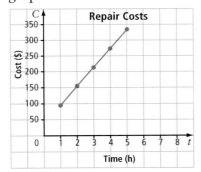

9. A car mechanic charges a $35 base fee for labour plus an hourly rate of $60. The graph shows this linear relation.

a) Approximately how much would the mechanic charge after working on a vehicle for 8 h?

b) Approximately how many hours would a mechanic work to charge $225 in labour costs?

c) Another mechanic charges at the same rate, but in half-hour increments. What would be the cost of a repair that took 9.5 h to complete?

10. A computer salesperson earns a monthly salary plus a 10% commission on each sale. The sales, commission, and earnings are shown in the table.

Sales ($)	Commission ($)	Earnings ($)
0	0	2000
5 000	500	2500
10 000	1000	3000
15 000	1500	3500
20 000	2000	4000
25 000	2500	4500

a) Draw a graph showing the linear relation between sales and earnings.

b) The salesperson earns $3750 in one month. What are the approximate total sales for that month?

c) The salesperson earns $5500 the next month. What are the approximate total sales for that month?

d) Approximately how much would the salesperson have to sell in order to earn $4250 in one month?

11. Draw the graph that represents this table of values.

Time (h)	0.25	0.50	0.75	1.00	1.25	1.50	1.75
Cost ($)	0.5	1.0	1.5	2.0	2.5	3.0	3.5

a) Describe a situation to represent the data on the graph.

b) Write an equation to model the data.

c) What is the cost for 3.25 h?

Chapter 7 Multiplying and Dividing Polynomials

12. Find the product of each pair of monomials.

a) $(3x)(4x)$

b) $(2.5y)(-4y)$

c) $(s)(-0.5s)$

d) $\left(\dfrac{t}{5}\right)(10t)$

13. Divide.

a) $8.4x^2 \div x$

b) $(-12h^2) \div 2h$

c) $(-0.6n^2) \div (-0.2n)$

d) $\dfrac{4.8p^2}{-1.2p}$

14. Use an area model to expand each expression.

a) $(3x)(2x + 1)$

b) $(5w + 3)(1.5w)$

15. If a foosball table is 3 cm longer than twice its width, what is an expression for the area of the foosball table? Express your answer in expanded form.

16. Determine each quotient.

a) $\dfrac{12g^2 + 8g}{4g}$

b) $\dfrac{-6x^2 + 3xy}{3x}$

c) $(9.3ef^2 - 62e) \div (-3.1e)$

d) $(24n^2 + 8n) \div (0.5n)$

17. A rectangle has an area represented by the expression $10x^2 - 5x$. If the length of the rectangle is $5x$, what is an expression for the width, w, of the rectangle in terms of x?

w

$5x$

Choosing a Television to Suit Your Room

You want to find a television that
• best suits your needs, and
• considers your room size and the location for the television.

Materials
• measuring tape
• grid paper

Does a standard or high-definition television (HDTV) make the most sense for your room? How large of a screen should you get?

1. The following table gives you the best viewing distance for the screen size for two types of TVs.

Screen Size (cm)	Viewing Distance (cm)	
	Standard TV	**HDTV**
68.8	205.7	172.7
81.3	243.8	203.2
94.0	281.9	233.7

   a) Given this information, what size of television would be best for your classroom? Make a sketch of your classroom, including where you plan to place the TV and the best place for a student to view it from.

   b) If the television is 320 cm away from your seat, how large of a standard TV would be best?

   c) How will your answer for part b) change if you have a HDTV?

2. The diagram shows the viewing angles for various types of televisions. Calculate the viewing area of the TV type and size of your choice.

3. What type and size of TV would be best for a room in your home? Justify your response.

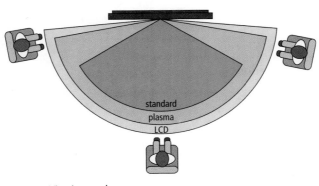

standard
plasma
LCD

Viewing angle:
standard: 120°
plasma: 160°
LCD: 170°

8

Solving Linear Equations

A balanced diet is one of the keys to good health, physical and mental development, and an active life. Making healthy food choices requires knowledge of your nutritional needs and of the nutrients found in foods. There are resources to help you. An example is Canada's Food Guide. It stresses the importance of eating a variety of food such as vegetables, fruits, and whole grains. It is also important to control your intake of fat, sugar, and salt.

WWW Web Link

To get a copy of Canada's Food Guide, go to www.mathlinks9.ca and follow the links. The links also provide useful resources on how to use the food guide. These resources include "Eating Well with Canada's Food Guide" and "Eating Well with Canada's Food Guide—First Nations, Inuit and Métis."

What You Will Learn

• to model problems using linear equations
• to solve problems using linear equations

Key Words

equation	constant
variable	opposite operation
numerical coefficient	distributive property

⊂⊃ Literacy Link

A concept map can help you visually organize your understanding of math concepts.

Create a concept map in your math journal or notebook. Make each oval large enough to write in. Leave enough space to attach additional ovals to each strategy shown. As you work through the chapter, complete the concept map.

For each strategy
• develop an example
• list the steps for solving the equation

Discuss your strategies with a classmate. You may wish to add to or correct what you have written.

with multiplication and division — with two operations — Solving Equations — with grouping symbols — with variables on both sides

Making the Foldable

Materials
- sheet of 11 × 17 paper
- ruler
- four sheets of 8.5 × 11 paper
- scissors
- stapler
- index cards

Step 1

Fold the long side of a sheet of 11 × 17 paper in half. Pinch it at the midpoint. Fold the outer edges to meet at the midpoint. Label it as shown.

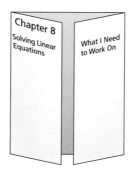

Step 2

Fold the short side of a sheet of 8.5 × 11 paper in half. Pinch it at the midpoint. Fold the outer edges to meet at the midpoint. Fold in three the opposite way. Make four cuts as shown through one thickness of paper, forming six tabs.

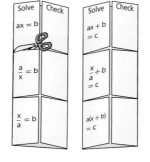

Repeat Step 2 to make another shutter-fold booklet. Label them as shown.

Step 3

Fold the long side of a sheet of 8.5 × 11 paper in half. Pinch it at the midpoint. Fold the outer edges of the paper to meet at the midpoint. Fold in three the opposite way. Make four cuts through one thickness of paper, forming six tabs. Label the tabs as shown.

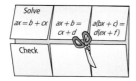

Step 4

Use half a sheet of 8.5 × 11 paper to create a pocket for storing Key Words and examples of linear equations.

Step 5

Staple the three booklets and the pocket you made into the Foldable from Step 1 as shown.

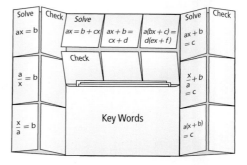

Using the Foldable

As you work through Chapter 8, use the shutter-fold booklets on the left and right panels to check your understanding of the concepts. Write an equation below the left tab, in the form indicated. Write the solution to the equation under the right tab. Use the centre shutterfold in a similar manner, writing the equation under the top tab and the solution under the bottom tab.

Use the back of the Foldable to record your ideas for the Math Link: Wrap It Up!

On the front of the Foldable, make notes under the heading What I Need to Work On. Check off each item as you deal with it.

Math Link

Solve Problems Involving Nutrition

Some problems that involve nutrition can be modelled using linear equations. In this chapter, you will use linear equations of different forms to model problems involving various foods.

1. Model each problem with an equation. Then, solve the equation. Share your method with your classmates.

   a) The mass of carbohydrate in a medium-sized peach is 5 g less than the mass of carbohydrate in a medium-sized orange. The peach contains 10 g of carbohydrate. What mass of carbohydrate is in the orange?

   b) Half a pink grapefruit contains 47 mg of vitamin C. What mass of vitamin C does a whole pink grapefruit contain?

   c) One litre of skim milk contains 1280 mg of calcium. What is the mass of calcium in one 250-mL serving of skim milk?

   d) A 250-mL serving of baked beans in tomato sauce contains 11 g of fibre. This mass of fibre is 1 g more than the mass of fibre in two 85-g servings of whole wheat pasta. What mass of fibre is in one 85-g serving of whole wheat pasta?

   e) The mass of potassium in a medium-sized apple, including the skin, is about 160 mg. This mass is 10 mg more than one third of the mass of potassium in an average-sized banana. What mass of potassium is in the banana?

   f) One serving of a snack contains 250 mL of dried apricots and 125 g of low-fat, plain yogurt. Three servings of this snack contain 36 g of protein. If 125 g of yogurt provides 7 g of protein, how much protein is in 250 mL of dried apricots?

2. **a)** Develop two different problems involving nutrition that can be modelled using linear equations. Use the Internet or the library to research the nutritional information. Make sure you can solve the problems you create.

   b) Ask a classmate to solve your problems. Verify your classmate's solutions.

WWW Web Link

To learn more about nutrition, healthy eating, and the nutritional values of different foods, go to www.mathlinks9.ca and follow the links

8.1

Solving Equations: $ax = b, \dfrac{x}{a} = b, \dfrac{a}{x} = b$

Focus on...

After this lesson, you will be able to...
- model problems with linear equations that can be solved using multiplication and division
- solve linear equations with rational numbers using multiplication and division

Steve Nash is arguably the most successful basketball player that Canada has produced. He grew up in Victoria, British Columbia. In high school, he led his team to the provincial championship and was the province's player of the year. He has since become one of the top players in the National Basketball Association (NBA).

One year, Steve scored 407 points for the Phoenix Suns in 20 playoff games. If the equation $20x = 407$ represents this situation, what does x represent? What operation could you use to determine the value of x?

Did You Know?

A Canadian, Dr. James Naismith, invented the game of basketball in 1891. At the time, he was teaching in Springfield, Massachusetts.

Explore Equations Involving Multiplication and Division

1. a) Each paper clip represents the variable x. Each circle represents a cup viewed from above. How does the diagram model the linear equation $2x = 0.12$?

> What other combination of coins could you use to represent 0.12?

b) How does the diagram model the solution to the equation in part a)? What is the solution?

c) Explain how the second part of the diagram in part b) can also model the equation $0.06y = 0.12$. What is the solution? Explain.

WWW Web Link

To learn more about Steve Nash's life, his career, and his work in communities, go to www.mathlinks9.ca and follow the links.

Materials

- coins
- paper cups or small containers
- paper clips

2. Work with a partner to explore how to model the solutions to the following equations using manipulatives or diagrams. Share your models with other classmates.

a) $3x = 0.6$

b) $0.05y = 0.25$

3. a) How does reversing the second part of the diagram from #1b) model the solution to the equation $\frac{n}{2} = 0.06$?

b) What is the solution? Explain.

c) Describe how the diagram in part a) can also model the solution to the equation $\frac{0.12}{k} = 0.06$. What is the solution? Explain.

4. Work with a partner to explore how to model the solutions to the following equations using manipulatives or diagrams. Share your models with other classmates.

a) $\frac{x}{3} = 0.05$

b) $\frac{0.33}{c} = 0.11$

Reflect and Check

5. a) How can you model solutions to equations of the form $ax = b$, $\frac{x}{a} = b$, and $\frac{a}{x} = b$ using manipulatives or diagrams?

b) Think of other ways to model the solutions. Explain how you would use them.

6. a) When a basketball player takes the ball away from an opposing player, it is called a *steal*. In his first nine seasons in the NBA, Steve Nash averaged 0.8 steals per game. Write and solve an equation that can be used to determine how many games it took, on average, for Steve to achieve four steals.

b) Use at least one other method to solve the problem. Share your solutions with your classmates.

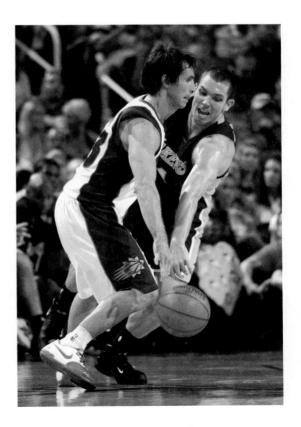

Link the Ideas

Example 1: Solve One-Step Equations With Fractions

Solve each equation.

a) $2x = \dfrac{3}{4}$ **b)** $\dfrac{m}{3} = -\dfrac{2}{5}$ **c)** $-2\dfrac{1}{2}k = -3\dfrac{1}{2}$

Solution

a) You can solve the equation $2x = \dfrac{3}{4}$ using a diagram or algebraically.

Strategies

Draw a Diagram

Method 1: Use a Diagram

Model the equation $2x = \dfrac{3}{4}$ on a number line.

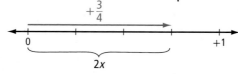

The length of the curly bracket represents $2x$, so half of this length represents x.

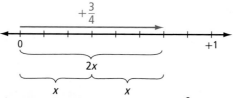

> Why were the divisions on the number line changed from quarters to eighths?

The diagram shows that $x = \dfrac{3}{8}$.

Method 2: Solve Algebraically

Solve by applying the opposite operation.

$$2x = \dfrac{3}{4}$$
$$2x \div 2 = \dfrac{3}{4} \div 2$$
$$x = \dfrac{3}{4} \times \dfrac{1}{2}$$
$$= \dfrac{3}{8}$$

> Why do you divide both sides by 2?

> To divide $\dfrac{3}{4}$ by 2, why do you multiply by $\dfrac{1}{2}$?

Check:

Left Side $= 2x$ Right Side $= \dfrac{3}{4}$

$= 2\left(\dfrac{3}{8}\right)$

$= \dfrac{6}{8}$

$= \dfrac{3}{4}$

Left Side $=$ Right Side

The solution, $x = \dfrac{3}{8}$, is correct.

Literacy Link

An *opposite operation* "undoes" another operation. Examples of opposite operations are:

- addition and subtraction
- multiplication and division

Opposite operations are also called *inverse operations*.

b) You can solve the equation $\frac{m}{3} = -\frac{2}{5}$ using a diagram or algebraically.

Method 1: Use a Diagram
Model the equation $\frac{m}{3} = -\frac{2}{5}$ on a number line.

The length of the curly bracket represents $\frac{m}{3}$, so use three of these to represent m.

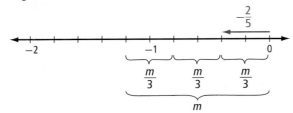

The diagram shows that $m = -\frac{6}{5}$, or $-1\frac{1}{5}$.

Method 2: Solve Algebraically
Solve by applying the opposite operation.

$$\frac{m}{3} = -\frac{2}{5}$$

$$3 \times \frac{m}{3} = 3 \times \left(-\frac{2}{5}\right)$$

$$m = \frac{3}{1} \times \frac{-2}{5}$$

$$= \frac{-6}{5} \text{ or } -\frac{6}{5} \text{ or } -1\frac{1}{5}$$

> What is the opposite operation of dividing by 3?

> $3 \times \left(-\frac{2}{5}\right) \approx 3 \times \left(-\frac{1}{2}\right)$ **M E**
> $\approx -1\frac{1}{2}$

> $-1\frac{1}{5}$ is close to the estimate, so this answer is reasonable.

Check:

Left Side $= \frac{m}{3}$ Right Side $= -\frac{2}{5}$

$$= \frac{-\frac{6}{5}}{3}$$

$$= -\frac{6}{5} \div 3$$

$$= \frac{-6}{5} \times \frac{1}{3}$$

$$= \frac{-6}{15}$$

$$= \frac{-2}{5} \text{ or } -\frac{2}{5}$$

Left Side $=$ Right Side

The solution, $m = -\frac{6}{5}$, is correct.

c) Isolate the variable by applying the opposite operation.

$$-2\frac{1}{2}k = -3\frac{1}{2}$$

$$-2\frac{1}{2}k \div \left(-2\frac{1}{2}\right) = -3\frac{1}{2} \div \left(-2\frac{1}{2}\right)$$

$$k = -\frac{7}{2} \div \left(-\frac{5}{2}\right)$$

$$= \frac{-7}{2} \div \frac{-5}{2}$$

$$= \frac{-7}{-5}$$

$$= \frac{7}{5} \text{ or } 1\frac{2}{5}$$

> What is the sign of the quotient when a negative is divided by a negative?

> $-4 \div (-3) = \frac{4}{3}$ **M**⊙**E**

> One way to divide fractions with the same denominator is to simply divide the numerators. How else could you divide these fractions?

Check:

Left Side $= -2\frac{1}{2}k$ Right Side $= -3\frac{1}{2}$

$$= -2\frac{1}{2}\left(1\frac{2}{5}\right)$$

$$= -\frac{5}{2}\left(\frac{7}{5}\right)$$

$$= -\frac{35}{10}$$

$$= -\frac{7}{2} \text{ or } -3\frac{1}{2}$$

Left Side $=$ Right Side

The solution, $k = \frac{7}{5}$, is correct.

Show You Know

Solve.

a) $3x = -\frac{2}{3}$

b) $\frac{x}{2} = \frac{5}{6}$

c) $-1\frac{1}{4}y = 1\frac{3}{4}$

Example 2: Solve One-Step Equations With Decimals

Solve each equation. Check each solution.

a) $-1.2x = -3.96$ **b)** $\dfrac{r}{0.28} = -4.5$

Solution

a) Solve by applying the opposite operation.

$$-1.2x = -3.96$$
$$\frac{-1.2x}{-1.2} = \frac{-3.96}{-1.2}$$
$$x = 3.3$$

$-4 \div -1 = 4$ **M**•**E**

C 3.96 +⇄− ÷ 1.2 +⇄− = 3.3

Check:

Left Side $= -1.2x$ Right Side $= -3.96$
$$= -1.2(3.3)$$
$$= -3.96$$

C 1.2 +⇄− × 3.3 = -3.96

Left Side $=$ Right Side

The solution, $x = 3.3$, is correct.

b) Isolate the variable by applying the opposite operation.

$$\frac{r}{0.28} = -4.5$$
$$0.28 \times \frac{r}{0.28} = 0.28 \times (-4.5)$$
$$r = -1.26$$

$0.28 \times 4.5 \approx 0.3 \times 4$
≈ 1.2 **M**•**E**

C 0.28 × 4.5 +⇄− = -1.26

> What is the sign of the product when a positive is multiplied by a negative?

Check:

Left Side $= \dfrac{r}{0.28}$ Right Side $= -4.5$

$$= \frac{-1.26}{0.28}$$
$$= -4.5$$

C 1.26 +⇄− ÷ 0.28 = -4.5

Left Side $=$ Right Side

The solution, $r = -1.26$, is correct.

Show You Know

Solve and check.

a) $\dfrac{u}{1.3} = 0.8$

b) $5.5k = -3.41$

Example 3: Apply Equations of the Form $\frac{a}{x} = b$

The formula for speed is $s = \frac{d}{t}$,

where s is speed, d is distance, and t is time. The length of a Canadian football field, including the end zones, is 137.2 m. If a horse gallops at 13.4 m/s, how much time would it take the horse to gallop the length of the field? Express your answer to the nearest tenth of a second.

Solution

Substitute the known values into the formula.

$$s = \frac{d}{t}$$

$$13.4 = \frac{137.2}{t}$$

$$t \times 13.4 = t \times \frac{137.2}{t}$$

> Why do you multiply by t?

$$t \times 13.4 = 137.2$$

$$\frac{t \times 13.4}{13.4} = \frac{137.2}{13.4}$$

$$t \approx 10.2$$

> $130 \div 13 = 10$ M E

C **137.2** ÷ **13.4** = `10.23880597`

The horse would take approximately 10.2 s to gallop the length of the field.

Check:
For a word problem, check your answer by verifying that the solution is consistent with the information given in the problem.

Calculate the speed by dividing the distance, 137.2 m, by the time, 10.2 s.

C **137.2** ÷ **10.2** = `13.45098039`

Because the time was not exactly 10.2 s, this calculated speed of about 13.45 m/s is not exactly the same as the speed of 13.4 m/s given in the problem. But since these speed values are close, the answer is reasonable.

Show You Know

If a musher and her dog-team average 23.5 km/h during a dogsled race, how long will it take to sled 50 km? Express your answer to the nearest tenth of an hour.

Example 4: Write and Solve Equations

Winter Warehouse has winter jackets on sale at 25% off the regular price. If a jacket is on sale for $176.25, what is the regular price of the jacket?

Solution

Let p represent the regular price of the jacket.

The sale price is 75% of the regular price. So, the sale price is $0.75p$.

> How do you know that the sale price is 75% of the regular price?

Since the sale price is $176.25, an equation that represents the situation is

$$0.75p = 176.25$$

$$\frac{0.75p}{0.75} = \frac{176.25}{0.75}$$

$$p = 235$$

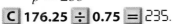 $200 \div 1 = 200$ M E

C 176.25 ÷ 0.75 = 235.

The regular price of the jacket is $235.

Check:
The price reduction is 25% of $235.

$0.25 \times \$235 = \$58.75$

The sale price is $235 − $58.75.

$\$235 − \$58.75 = \$176.25$

The calculated sale price agrees with the value given in the problem, so the answer, $235, is correct.

Show You Know

Winter Warehouse is selling mitts at 30% off the regular price. If the sale price is $34.99, what is the regular price of the mitts?

Key Ideas

- You can solve equations in various ways, including
  - using diagrams

    $$\frac{g}{2} = \frac{2}{3}$$

    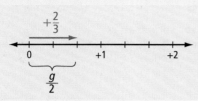

    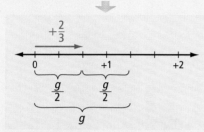

    $$g = \frac{4}{3} \text{ or } 1\frac{1}{3}$$

  - using concrete materials

    $$2x = 0.10$$

    $$x = 0.05$$

  - using an algebraic method

    $$\frac{-1.4}{p} = -0.8$$

    $$p \times \left(\frac{-1.4}{p}\right) = p \times (-0.8)$$

    $$-1.4 = p \times (-0.8)$$

    $$\frac{-1.4}{-0.8} = \frac{p \times (-0.8)}{-0.8}$$

    $$1.75 = p$$

- You can check solutions by using substitution.

  Left Side $= \dfrac{-1.4}{p}$ Right Side $= -0.8$

  $$= \frac{-1.4}{1.75}$$

  | C | 1.4 | +ᶜ− | ÷ | 1.75 | = | -0.8 |

  $$= -0.8$$

  Left Side = Right Side

  The solution, $p = 1.75$, is correct.

- To check the solution to a word problem, verify that the solution is consistent with the facts given in the problem.

Check Your Understanding

Communicate the Ideas

1. To solve the equation $\frac{y}{2} = \frac{5}{3}$, John first multiplied both sides by 3.

a) Do you think that John's first step is the best way to isolate the variable y? Explain.

b) How would you solve the equation?

2. When Ming solved $0.3g = 0.8$, her value for g was $2.666\ldots$. She expressed this to the nearest tenth, or 2.7. When Ming checked by substitution, she found that the left side and the right side did not exactly agree.

Left Side $= 0.3g$ Right Side $= 0.8$
$ = 0.3(2.7)$
$ = 0.81$

a) How could Ming make the left side and right side agree more closely?

b) Did Ming's check show that the solution was correct? Explain.

3. The length of Shamika's stride is 0.75 m. Both Amalia and Gustav were trying to calculate how many strides it would take Shamika to walk 30 m from her home to the bus stop.

a) Amalia represented the situation with the equation $0.75p = 30$. Explain her thinking.

b) Gustav represented the situation with the equation $\frac{30}{p} = 0.75$. Explain his thinking.

c) Whose equation would you prefer to use? Explain.

Practise

4. Write an equation that is represented by the model shown. Then, solve it.

For help with #5 to #7, refer to Example 1 on pages 294–296.

5. Model the solution to the equation $4x = \frac{3}{4}$ using a number line.

6. Solve.

a) $2v = \frac{-5}{6}$ **b)** $\frac{x}{2} = \frac{2}{5}$

c) $\frac{4}{3} = -1\frac{1}{4}a$ **d)** $-1\frac{1}{2}x = -2\frac{1}{4}$

7. Solve.

a) $\frac{3}{5} = \frac{x}{4}$ **b)** $2y = -\frac{6}{5}$

c) $-\frac{7}{6} = -\frac{4}{3}n$ **d)** $2\frac{2}{3}w = 1\frac{1}{6}$

For help with #8 and #9, refer to Example 2 on page 297.

8. Solve and check.

a) $-5.6x = 3.5$ **b)** $\frac{e}{-2.2} = -0.75$

9. Solve.

a) $\frac{h}{4.1} = 3.6$ **b)** $1.472 = 0.46c$

For help with #10 and #11, refer to Example 3 on page 298.

10. Solve and check.

a) $-5.5 = \dfrac{1.1}{a}$

b) $\dfrac{4.8}{m} = 6.4$

11. Solve. Express each solution to the nearest hundredth.

a) $\dfrac{2.02}{n} = 0.71$

b) $-7.8 = \dfrac{-4.3}{x}$

Apply

12. The average speed of a vehicle, s, is represented by the formula $s = \dfrac{d}{t}$ where d is the distance driven and t is the time.

a) If Pablo drove at an average speed of 85 km/h for 3.75 h, what distance did he drive?

b) If Sheila drove 152 km at an average speed of 95 km/h, how much time did her trip take?

13. A roll of nickels is worth $2.00. Write and solve an equation to determine the number of nickels in a roll.

14. Write and solve an equation to determine the side length, s, of a square with a perimeter of 25.8 cm.

15. Without solving the equation $-\dfrac{5}{d} = -1.3$, predict whether d is greater than or less than 0. Explain your reasoning.

16. The diameter, d, of a circle is related to the circumference, C, by the formula $\dfrac{C}{d} = \pi$. Calculate the diameter of a circle with a circumference of 54.5 cm. Express your answer to the nearest tenth of a centimetre.

17. A regular polygon has a perimeter of 34.08 cm and a side length of 5.68 cm. Identify the polygon.

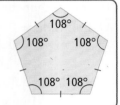

> **⬭ Literacy Link**
>
> A *regular polygon* has equal sides and equal angles. For example, a regular pentagon has five equal sides. Each angle measures 108°.

18. One year, a student council sold 856 copies of a school yearbook. Four fifths of the students at the school bought a copy. How many students did not buy a yearbook?

19. A score of 17 on a math test results in a mark of 68%. What score would give you a mark of 100%?

20. The area of Nunavut is about $4\dfrac{3}{8}$ times the area of the Yukon Territory. Nunavut covers 21% of Canada's area. What percent of Canada's area does the Yukon Territory cover?

Lewis Lake, Yukon

21. Dianne spends 40% of her net income on rent and 15% of her net income on food. If she spends a total of $1375 per month on rent and food, what is her net monthly income?

22. Ellen and Li play on the same basketball team. In one game, Ellen scored one tenth of the team's points and Li scored one fifth of the team's points. Together, Ellen and Li scored 33 points. How many points did the team score altogether?

23. Sailaway Travel has a last-minute sale on a Caribbean cruise at 20% off. Their advertisement reads, "You save $249.99." What is the sale price of the cruise?

24. Organizers of the Canadian Francophone Games hope to attract 500 volunteers to help host the games. The organizers predict that there will be about three and half times as many experienced volunteers as first-time volunteers. About how many first-time volunteers do they expect to attract?

25. A square piece of paper is folded in half to make a rectangle. The perimeter of the rectangle is 24.9 cm. What is the side length of the square piece of paper?

Extend

26. Solve.

a) $\dfrac{1}{3} + \dfrac{1}{6} = \dfrac{5}{6}x$

b) $-\dfrac{0.45}{1.8} = -\dfrac{0.81}{z}$

c) $\dfrac{y}{4} - \dfrac{y}{3} = -\dfrac{1}{10}$

d) $\dfrac{f}{0.55} = 2.6 - 3.5$

27. Solve. Express each solution to the nearest hundredth.

a) $0.75 + 1.23 = -3.9t$

b) $\dfrac{6.3}{h} = 2(-4.05)$

28. Solve and check.

a) $x \div \dfrac{1}{2} = -\dfrac{3}{4}$

b) $t \div \left(-\dfrac{2}{3}\right) = -\dfrac{1}{2}$

c) $\dfrac{5}{6} \div y = \dfrac{2}{3}$

d) $-\dfrac{2}{5} \div g = \dfrac{3}{10}$

29. a) A jar contains equal numbers of nickels and dimes. The total value of the coins is $4.05. How many coins are in the jar?

b) A jar contains a mixture of nickels and dimes worth a total of $4.75. There are three times as many nickels as dimes. How many dimes are there?

30. A cyclist is travelling six times as fast as a pedestrian. The difference in their speeds is 17.5 km/h. What is the cyclist's speed?

Math Link

Solve parts a) and b) in at least two different ways. Write and solve an equation as one of the methods for each part. Share your solutions with your classmates.

Three dried figs contain about 1.2 mg of iron.

a) What is the mass of iron in one dried fig?

b) Teenagers need about 12 mg of iron per day. How many dried figs would you have to eat to get your recommended daily amount of iron?

c) Write a formula that relates the mass of iron to the number of figs. Use your equation to calculate the mass of iron in eight figs.

d) Use your formula in part c) to determine the number of figs that contain 1.8 mg of iron.

Solving Equations:
$$ax + b = c, \frac{x}{a} + b = c$$

Focus on...

After this lesson, you will be able to...

- model problems with linear equations involving two operations
- solve linear equations with rational numbers using two operations

@ **WWW Web Link**

To learn more about waterfalls in Canada and around the world, go to www.mathlinks9.ca and follow the links.

Two of Canada's highest measured waterfalls are in British Columbia. Takakkaw Falls, is in Yoho National Park, 27 km west of Lake Louise. Its height is 254 m. This is 34 m more than half the height of Della Falls in Strathcona Park on Vancouver Island.

Choose a variable to represent the height of Della Falls. Then, write and solve an equation to find the height of Della Falls.

Della Falls, Vancouver Island

Materials
- coins
- cups or small containers
- paper clips

Explore Equations With Two Operations

1. a) How does the diagram model the solution to the equation $2x + 0.30 = 0.50$?

b) What is the solution?

2. a) Explain how the second part of the diagram in #1 can model the equation $0.10y + 0.30 = 0.50$. What is the solution? Explain.

b) How does the second part of the diagram in #1 also model the solution to the equation $\frac{z}{10} + \frac{3}{10} = \frac{1}{2}$? What is the solution?

3. Describe how you would use manipulatives or diagrams to model the solution to each of the following.

a) $3x + 0.05 = 0.26$

b) $0.01x + 0.05 = 0.08$

c) $\frac{x}{4} + \frac{1}{5} = \frac{7}{10}$

4. Work with a partner to explore how to model the solution to the equation $2x - 0.11 = 0.15$. Share your models with other classmates.

Reflect and Check

5. a) How can you model solutions to equations of the form $ax + b = c$ and $\frac{x}{a} + b = c$ using manipulatives or diagrams?

b) Think of other ways to model the solutions. Explain how you would use them.

6. The tallest waterfall in the world is Angel Falls in Venezuela, with a height of about 0.8 km. This height is 0.08 km less than twice the height of Della Falls. Write and solve an equation to determine the height of Della Falls in kilometres. Check that your answer agrees with the height in metres you determined at the beginning of this section.

Angel Falls, Venezuela

> **Did You Know?**
>
> Canada's tallest free-standing structure is the CN Tower, with a height of about 550 m. This is about 250 m less than the height of Angel Falls.

Link the Ideas

Example 1: Solve Two-Step Equations With Fractions

Solve and check.

a) $2x + \dfrac{1}{10} = \dfrac{3}{5}$

b) $\dfrac{k}{3} - \dfrac{1}{2} = -1\dfrac{3}{4}$

Solution

a)

$$2x + \dfrac{1}{10} = \dfrac{3}{5}$$

> To isolate the variable in a two-step equation, use the reverse order of operations. Add or subtract first, and then multiply or divide.

$$2x + \dfrac{1}{10} - \dfrac{1}{10} = \dfrac{3}{5} - \dfrac{1}{10}$$

$$2x = \dfrac{3}{5} - \dfrac{1}{10}$$

$$2x = \dfrac{6}{10} - \dfrac{1}{10}$$

$$2x = \dfrac{5}{10}$$

$$2x \div 2 = \dfrac{1}{2} \div 2$$

> $\dfrac{1}{2} \div \dfrac{2}{1} = \dfrac{1}{2} \times \dfrac{1}{2}$

$$x = \dfrac{1}{4}$$

Check by modelling the equation $2x + \dfrac{1}{10} = \dfrac{3}{5}$ on a number line.

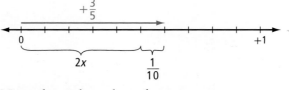

> This diagram models the original equation $2x + \dfrac{1}{10} = \dfrac{3}{5}$. How does it show that $2x = \dfrac{5}{10}$?

Now show the value of x.

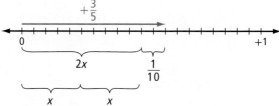

The second diagram shows that $x = \dfrac{5}{20}$ or $\dfrac{1}{4}$.

The solution, $x = \dfrac{1}{4}$, is correct.

b) $\frac{k}{3} - \frac{1}{2} = -1\frac{3}{4}$

$\frac{k}{3} - \frac{1}{2} = -\frac{7}{4}$

You may prefer to work with integers than to perform fraction operations. Change from fractions to integers by multiplying by a common multiple of the denominators.

$$12 \times \frac{k}{3} - 12 \times \frac{1}{2} = 12 \times \left(-\frac{7}{4}\right)$$

$$4k - 6 = -21$$
$$4k - 6 + 6 = -21 + 6$$
$$4k = -15$$

$$\frac{4k}{4} = \frac{-15}{4}$$

$$k = -\frac{15}{4}$$

> A common multiple of the denominators 3, 2, and 4 is 12.

Check:

Left Side $= \frac{k}{3} - \frac{1}{2}$ Right Side $= -1\frac{3}{4}$

$$= -\frac{15}{4} \div 3 - \frac{1}{2}$$

$$= \frac{-15}{4} \times \frac{1}{3} - \frac{1}{2}$$

$$= \frac{-5}{4} - \frac{1}{2}$$

$$= \frac{-5}{4} - \frac{2}{4}$$

$$= \frac{-7}{4} \text{ or } -1\frac{3}{4}$$

Left Side = Right Side

The solution, $k = -\frac{15}{4}$, is correct.

Show You Know

Solve and check.

a) $2y + \frac{1}{2} = \frac{3}{4}$

b) $\frac{n}{2} - \frac{3}{4} = 2\frac{3}{8}$

Example 2: Solve Two-Step Equations With Decimals

Solve $\frac{a}{2.8} - 2.5 = -3.7$ and check the solution.

Solution

$$\frac{a}{2.8} - 2.5 = -3.7$$

$$\frac{a}{2.8} - 2.5 + 2.5 = -3.7 + 2.5$$

$$\frac{a}{2.8} = -1.2$$

$$2.8 \times \frac{a}{2.8} = 2.8 \times (-1.2)$$

$$a = -3.36$$

> $2.8 \times (-1.2) \approx 3 \times (-1)$ **M E**
> ≈ -3

Check:

Left Side $= \dfrac{a}{2.8} - 2.5$ Right Side $= -3.7$

$= \dfrac{-3.36}{2.8} - 2.5$

$= -1.2 - 2.5$

$= -3.7$

Left Side $=$ Right Side

The solution, $a = -3.36$, is correct.

Show You Know

Solve $\dfrac{h}{1.6} + 3.3 = 1.8$ and check the solution.

Example 3: Apply Two-Step Equations With Decimals

Colin has a long-distance telephone plan that charges 5¢/min for long-distance calls within Canada. There is also a monthly fee of $4.95. One month, Colin's total long-distance charges were $18.75. How many minutes of long-distance calls did Colin make that month?

Solution

Let m represent the unknown number of minutes.

The cost per minute is 5¢ or $0.05.
The cost of the phone calls, in dollars, is $0.05m$.
The total cost for the month is the cost of the calls plus the monthly fee, or $0.05m + 4.95$.
The total cost for the month is $18.75.

An equation that represents the situation is $0.05m + 4.95 = 18.75$.
$0.05m + 4.95 - 4.95 = 18.75 - 4.95$
$$0.05m = 13.80$$
$$\frac{0.05m}{0.05} = \frac{13.80}{0.05}$$
$$m = 276$$

$$\frac{13.80}{0.05} \approx \frac{15}{0.05}$$
$$\approx 300$$

Colin made 276 min of long-distance calls that month.

Check:
The cost for 276 min at 5¢/min is $\$0.05 \times 276$.
$0.05 \times 276 = 13.80$
The total cost for the month is $\$13.80 + \$4.95$, which equals $\$18.75$.
This total cost agrees with the value stated in the problem.

Show You Know

Suppose that Colin changes to a cheaper long-distance plan. This plan charges 4¢/min for long-distance calls within Canada, plus a monthly fee of $\$3.95$. For how many minutes could he call long distance in a month for the same total long-distance charge of $\$18.75$?

Key Ideas

- You can determine or check some solutions by using a model.

$3u + \dfrac{1}{8} = \dfrac{7}{8}$

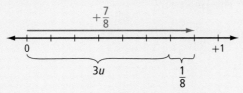

$3u = \dfrac{6}{8}$

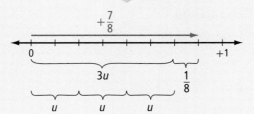

$u = \dfrac{2}{8}$ or $\dfrac{1}{4}$

- To isolate the variable in a two-step equation, use the reverse order of operations. Add or subtract first, and then multiply or divide.

$$0.4w - 1.5 = 0.3$$
$$0.4w - 1.5 + 1.5 = 0.3 + 1.5$$
$$0.4w = 1.8$$
$$\frac{0.4w}{0.4} = \frac{1.8}{0.4}$$
$$w = 4.5$$

- To solve two-step equations involving fractions, you may prefer to rewrite the equation and work with integers than to perform fraction operations.

$$\frac{w}{5} - \frac{3}{2} = \frac{1}{10}$$

To work with integers, multiply all terms by a common multiple of the denominators. For the denominators 5, 2, and 10, a common multiple is 10.

$$10 \times \frac{w}{5} - 10 \times \frac{3}{2} = 10 \times \frac{1}{10}$$
$$2w - 15 = 1$$
$$2w - 15 + 15 = 1 + 15$$
$$2w = 16$$
$$\frac{2w}{2} = \frac{16}{2}$$
$$w = 8$$

- You can check solutions by using substitution.

$$\text{Left Side} = \frac{w}{5} - \frac{3}{2} \qquad \text{Right Side} = \frac{1}{10}$$
$$= \frac{8}{5} - \frac{3}{2}$$
$$= \frac{16}{10} - \frac{15}{10}$$
$$= \frac{1}{10}$$

Left Side = Right Side

The solution, $w = 8$, is correct.

- To check the solution to a word problem, verify that the solution is consistent with the facts given in the problem.

Check Your Understanding

Communicate the Ideas

1. Explain how the diagrams model the equation $\frac{x}{2} + \frac{1}{4} = \frac{5}{8}$ and its solution. What is the solution?

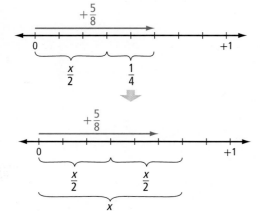

2. Ryan solved $2r + 0.3 = 0.7$ as follows. Do you agree with his solution? Explain.

$$\frac{2r}{2} + 0.3 = \frac{0.7}{2}$$
$$r + 0.3 = 0.35$$
$$r + 0.3 - 0.3 = 0.35 - 0.3$$
$$r = 0.05$$

3. Jenna did not want to perform fraction operations to solve the equation $\frac{x}{2} - \frac{1}{9} = \frac{5}{6}$, so she first multiplied both sides by 54. Is this the common multiple you would have chosen? Explain.

4. a) Milos solved $0.05x - 0.12 = 0.08$ by multiplying both sides by 100 and then solving $5x - 12 = 8$. Show how he used this method to determine the correct solution.

b) When Milos was asked to solve $\frac{x}{0.05} - 0.12 = 0.08$, he reasoned that he could determine the correct solution by solving $\frac{x}{5} - 12 = 8$. Do you agree with his reasoning? Explain.

Practise

5. Write an equation that is modelled by the following. Then, solve it.

6. Model the equation $3x + 0.14 = 0.50$ using concrete materials. Solve using your model.

For help with #7 and #8, refer to Example 1 on pages 306–307.

7. Solve.

a) $4y - \frac{2}{5} = \frac{3}{5}$ **b)** $2d - \frac{1}{2} = \frac{5}{4}$

c) $\frac{n}{2} + 1\frac{2}{3} = \frac{1}{6}$ **d)** $\frac{4}{5} - 2\frac{1}{2}r = \frac{3}{10}$

8. Solve.

a) $1\frac{1}{2} = 4h + \frac{2}{3}$ **b)** $\frac{4}{3}x + \frac{3}{4} = \frac{1}{2}$

c) $\frac{3}{4} - \frac{d}{3} = \frac{3}{8}$ **d)** $-4\frac{2}{5} = -3\frac{1}{5} + \frac{7}{10}g$

For help with #9 and #10, refer to Example 2 on page 308.

9. Solve and check.

a) $\frac{x}{0.6} + 2.5 = -1$

b) $0.38 = 6.2 - \frac{r}{1.2}$

10. Solve.

a) $-0.02 - \frac{n}{3.7} = -0.01$

b) $\frac{k}{-0.54} + 0.67 = 3.47$

For help with #11 and #12, refer to Example 3 on pages 308–309.

11. Solve and check.

a) $2 + 12.5v = 0.55$

b) $-0.77 = -0.1x - 0.45$

12. Solve.

a) $0.074d - 3.4 = 0.707$

b) $67 = 5.51 + 4.3a$

Apply

13. The cost of a pizza is $8.50 plus $1.35 per topping. How many toppings are on a pizza that costs $13.90?

14. Hiroshi paid $34.95 to rent a car for a day, plus 12¢ for each kilometre he drove. The total rental cost, before taxes, was $55.11. How far did Hiroshi drive that day?

15. On Saturday morning, Marc had a quarter of his weekly allowance left. He spent a total of $6.50 on bus fares and a freshly squeezed orange juice on Saturday afternoon. He then had $2.25 left. How much is his weekly allowance?

16. Nadia has a summer job in an electronics store. She is paid $400 per week, plus 5% commission on the total value of her sales.

a) One week, when the store was not busy, Nadia earned only $510.30. What was the total value of her sales that week?

b) Nadia's average earnings are $780 per week. What is the average value of her weekly sales?

17. Benoit was helping his family build a new fence along one side of their yard. The total length of the fence is 28 m. They worked for two days and completed an equal length of fence on each day. On the third day, they completed the remaining 4.8 m of fence. What length of fence did they build on each of the first two days?

18. The perimeter of a regular hexagon is 3.04 cm less than the perimeter of a regular pentagon. The perimeter of the regular hexagon is 21.06 cm. What is the side length of the regular pentagon?

19. The greatest average annual snowfall in Alberta is on the Columbia Icefield. The greatest average annual snowfall in Manitoba is at Island Lake. An average of 642.9 mm of snow falls on the Columbia Icefield in a year. This amount of snow is 22.5 mm less than twice the annual average at Island Lake. What is the average annual snowfall at Island Lake?

Columbia Icefield

20. During a camping trip, Nina was making a lean-to for sleeping. She cut a 2.5-m long post into two pieces, so that one piece was 26 cm longer than the other. What was the length of each piece?

21. The average monthly rainfall in Victoria in July is 2.6 mm less than one fifth of the amount of rain that falls in Edmonton in the same period. Victoria averages 17.6 mm of rainfall in July. What is the average monthly rainfall in Edmonton in July?

22. The temperature in Winnipeg was 7 °C and was falling by 2.5 °C/h. How many hours did it take for the temperature to reach −5.5 °C?

23. Max and Sharifa are both saving to buy the same model of DVD player, which costs $99, including tax. Max already has $31.00 and decides to save $8.50 per week from now on. Sharifa already has $25.50 and decides to save $10.50 per week from now on. Who can pay for the DVD player first? Explain.

24. A cylindrical storage tank that holds 375 L of water is completely full. A pump removes water at a rate of 0.6 L/s. For how many minutes must the pump work until 240 L of water remain in the tank?

25. The average distance of Mercury from the sun is 57.9 million kilometres. This distance is 3.8 million kilometres more than half the average distance of Venus from the sun. What is the average distance of Venus from the sun?

26. Create an equation of the form $\frac{x}{a} + b = c$ with each given solution. Compare your equations with your classmates' equations.

a) $\frac{2}{3}$

b) -0.8

27. Write a word problem that can be solved using an equation of the form $ax + b = c$. Include at least one decimal or fraction. Have a classmate solve your problem.

Extend

28. Solve.

a) $\frac{3}{2} + \frac{w}{4} = \frac{5}{6} - \frac{1}{2}$

b) $\frac{3}{4}\left(-\frac{2}{9}\right) = 4\frac{1}{2}x + \frac{1}{3}$

29. Solve. Express each solution to the nearest hundredth.

a) $0.75 + 0.16y + 0.2y = 0.34$

b) $\frac{-1.85}{0.74} = 2.22 - 0.57s$

30. Solve.

a) $\frac{0.2}{x} + 0.8 = 1.2$

b) $\frac{1}{2} - \frac{4}{n} = -\frac{1}{4}$

c) $-\frac{3.52}{h} - 1.31 = 1.19$

d) $4\frac{5}{6} = 3\frac{1}{3} - \frac{3}{y}$

31. Determine the value of x.

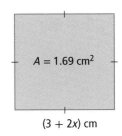

$A = 1.69$ cm²

$(3 + 2x)$ cm

32. A freight train passes through a 750-m long tunnel at 50 km/h. The back of the train exits the tunnel 1.5 min after the front of the train enters it. What is the length of the train, in metres?

Revelstoke, British Columbia

Math Link

A slice of canned corned beef contains about 0.21 g of sodium. This much sodium is 0.01 g more than the mass of sodium in four slices of roast beef. What is the mass of sodium in a slice of roast beef?

a) Write an equation that models the situation.

b) Solve the equation in two different ways.

c) Which of your solution methods do you prefer? Explain.

Solving Equations: $a(x + b) = c$

Did You Know?

Farms account for only about 7% of the land in Canada. About 80% of Canada's farmland is located in the Prairie Provinces: Alberta, Saskatchewan, and Manitoba.

Each year, Canada's Prairie Provinces produce tens of millions of tonnes of grains, such as wheat, barley, and canola. The growth of a grain crop partly depends on the quantity of heat it receives. One indicator of the quantity of heat that a crop receives in a day is the *daily average temperature*. This is defined as the average of the high and low temperatures in a day.

How can you calculate the daily average temperature on a day when the high temperature is 23 °C and the low temperature is 13 °C? If the low temperature is 10 °C, how could you determine the high temperature that would result in a daily average temperature of 15 °C?

What equations can you use to represent these situations?

Materials
- coins
- paper cups or small containers
- paper clips

Explore Equations With Grouping Symbols

1. Explain how the diagram models the solution to the equation $2(x + 0.10) = 0.30$. What is the solution?

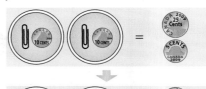

2. Work with a partner to explore how to model the solutions to the following equations using manipulatives or diagrams. Share your models with other classmates.

a) $2(x + 0.25) = 0.54$

b) $3\left(x + \dfrac{1}{20}\right) = \dfrac{9}{10}$

Reflect and Check

3. a) How can you model solutions to equations of the form $a(x + b) = c$ using manipulatives or diagrams?

b) Think of other ways to model the solutions. Explain how you would use them.

4. Stefan works on a farm in the Fraser Valley of British Columbia. Two of the fields are square. The perimeter of the larger field is 2.4 km. The side length of the larger field is 0.1 km more than the side length of the smaller field. Create a labelled drawing of this situation. Suggest ways of determining the side length of the smaller field. Include a suggestion for solving an equation of the form $a(x + b) = c$. Share your ideas with your classmates.

Link the Ideas

Example 1: Solve Equations With Grouping Symbols

Solve and check.

a) $3(d + 0.4) = -3.9$

b) $\dfrac{t - 1}{5} = \dfrac{3}{2}$

Solution

a) *Method 1: Use the Distributive Property First*
Use the distributive property to remove the brackets.

$$3(d + 0.4) = -3.9$$
$$(3 \times d) + (3 \times 0.4) = -3.9$$
$$3d + 1.2 = -3.9$$
$$3d + 1.2 - 1.2 = -3.9 - 1.2$$
$$3d = -5.1$$
$$\dfrac{3d}{3} = \dfrac{-5.1}{3}$$
$$d = -1.7$$

> **Literacy Link**
>
> The *distributive property* is:
>
> $a(b + c) = ab + ac$

Method 2: Divide First

$$3(d + 0.4) = -3.9$$

$$\frac{3(d + 0.4)}{3} = \frac{-3.9}{3}$$

$$d + 0.4 = -1.3$$

$$d + 0.4 - 0.4 = -1.3 - 0.4$$

$$d = -1.7$$

Why do you divide both sides by 3?

Check:

Left Side $= 3(d + 0.4)$ Right Side $= -3.9$

$\quad\quad\quad = 3(-1.7 + 0.4)$

$\quad\quad\quad = 3(-1.3)$

$\quad\quad\quad = -3.9$

Left Side $=$ Right Side

The solution, $d = -1.7$, is correct.

b)
$$\frac{t - 1}{5} = \frac{3}{2}$$

$$10 \times \frac{t - 1}{5} = 10 \times \frac{3}{2}$$

$$2(t - 1) = 15$$

$$2t - 2 = 15$$

$$2t - 2 + 2 = 15 + 2$$

$$2t = 17$$

$$\frac{2t}{2} = \frac{17}{2}$$

$$t = \frac{17}{2}$$

Why do you multiply both sides by 10? Is there a different way to solve the equation?

> **Literacy Link**
>
> A *fraction bar* acts as a grouping symbol and as a division symbol.
> The expression $\dfrac{t - 1}{5}$ can be written as $\dfrac{1}{5}(t - 1)$ or as $(t - 1) \div 5$.

Check:

Left Side $= \dfrac{t - 1}{5}$ Right Side $= \dfrac{3}{2}$

$\quad\quad\quad = \left(\dfrac{17}{2} - 1\right) \div 5$

$\quad\quad\quad = \left(\dfrac{17}{2} - \dfrac{2}{2}\right) \div 5$

$\quad\quad\quad = \dfrac{15}{2} \div \dfrac{5}{1}$

$\quad\quad\quad = \dfrac{15}{2} \times \dfrac{1}{5}$

$\quad\quad\quad = \dfrac{3}{2}$

Left Side $=$ Right Side

The solution, $t = \dfrac{17}{2}$, is correct.

Show You Know

Solve and check.

a) $2(e - 0.6) = 4.2$

b) $\dfrac{c + 2}{3} = -\dfrac{5}{2}$

Example 2: Apply Equations With Grouping Symbols

On a typical February day in Whitehorse, Yukon Territory, the daily average temperature is −13.2 °C. The low temperature is −18.1 °C. What is the high temperature?

Solution

Let the high temperature be T degrees Celsius. The daily average temperature, in degrees Celsius, is the average of the high and low temperatures, or $\dfrac{T + (-18.1)}{2}$. The daily average temperature is −13.2 °C.

> How could you estimate the high temperature?

An equation that represents this situation is $\dfrac{T + (-18.1)}{2} = -13.2$.

Isolate the variable, T.

$$\frac{T + (-18.1)}{2} = -13.2$$

$$2 \times \frac{T + (-18.1)}{2} = 2 \times (-13.2)$$

$$T - 18.1 = -26.4$$

$$T - 18.1 + 18.1 = -26.4 + 18.1$$

$$T = -8.3$$

The high temperature is −8.3 °C.

Check:

The average of the high and low temperatures is $\dfrac{-8.3 + (-18.1)}{2}$.

$$\frac{-8.3 + (-18.1)}{2} = \frac{-26.4}{2}$$

$$= -13.2$$

The calculated average of −13.2 °C agrees with the daily average temperature given in the problem.

Show You Know

On a typical day in October in Churchill, Manitoba, the daily average temperature is −1.5 °C. The high temperature is 1.3 °C. Estimate and then calculate the low temperature.

Barren Lands, Churchill, Manitoba

Key Ideas

- To isolate the variable in an equation of the form $a(x + b) = c$, you can

  - use the distributive property first

    $$4(r - 0.6) = -3.2$$
    $$4r - 2.4 = -3.2$$
    $$4r - 2.4 + 2.4 = -3.2 + 2.4$$
    $$4r = -0.8$$
    $$\frac{4r}{4} = \frac{-0.8}{4}$$
    $$r = -0.2$$

  - divide first

    $$4(r - 0.6) = -3.2$$
    $$\frac{4(r - 0.6)}{4} = \frac{-3.2}{4}$$
    $$r - 0.6 = -0.8$$
    $$r - 0.6 + 0.6 = -0.8 + 0.6$$
    $$r = -0.2$$

- To solve equations involving grouping symbols and fractions, you can rewrite the equation and work with integers instead of performing fraction operations.

$$\frac{q - 1}{2} = \frac{3}{4}$$
$$4 \times \frac{q - 1}{2} = 4 \times \frac{3}{4}$$
$$2(q - 1) = 3$$
$$2q - 2 = 3$$
$$2q - 2 + 2 = 3 + 2$$
$$2q = 5$$
$$\frac{2q}{2} = \frac{5}{2}$$
$$q = \frac{5}{2}$$

- You can check solutions by using substitution.

$$\text{Left Side} = \frac{q - 1}{2} \qquad\qquad \text{Right Side} = \frac{3}{4}$$
$$= \left(\frac{5}{2} - 1\right) \div 2$$
$$= \left(\frac{5}{2} - \frac{2}{2}\right) \div 2$$
$$= \frac{3}{2} \times \frac{1}{2}$$
$$= \frac{3}{4}$$

Left Side = Right Side
The solution, $q = \dfrac{5}{2}$, is correct.

- To check the solution to a word problem, verify that the solution is consistent with the facts given in the problem.

Check Your Understanding

Communicate the Ideas

1. Mario solved the equation $2(n + 1.5) = 4.5$ as follows.

$$2(n + 1.5) = 4.5$$
$$2n + 3 = 9$$
$$2n = 6$$
$$n = 3$$

a) What is the error in his reasoning? Explain.

b) Write the correct solution.

2. Cal and Tyana solved the equation $3(k - 4.3) = -2.7$ in different ways. Cal used the distributive property first, while Tyana divided first.

a) Show both of their methods.

b) Whose method do you prefer? Explain.

c) If the equation was $3(k - 4.3) = -2.5$, which method would you use? Explain.

3. Renée and Paul used different methods to solve $\dfrac{x + 1}{2} = \dfrac{3}{5}$.

a) Renée first multiplied both sides by a common multiple.
$$10 \times \dfrac{x + 1}{2} = 10 \times \dfrac{3}{5}$$
Show the rest of her solution.

b) Paul first rewrote the equation as $\dfrac{1}{2}(x + 1) = \dfrac{3}{5}$ and used the distributive property. Show the rest of his solution.
$$\dfrac{1}{2}x + \dfrac{1}{2} = \dfrac{3}{5}$$

c) Which solution do you prefer? Explain.

4. Viktor and Ashni were solving the following problem together.

A square with a side length of $x + 1$ has a perimeter of 18.6 units. What is the value of x?

They disagreed over how to model the situation with an equation.

Viktor's Equation   *Ashni's Equation*
$4(x + 1) = 18.6$ $4x + 1 = 18.6$

a) Which equation is correct? Explain.

b) What is the value of x?

c) How can you check whether your value for x is correct?

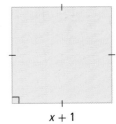

$x + 1$

Practise

5. Write an equation that is represented by the following. Then, solve the equation.

For help with #6 to #9, refer to Example 1 on pages 315–316.

6. Solve and check.

a) $2(x + 1.5) = 7.6$

b) $-2.8 = -1(c - 0.65)$

c) $-3.57 = 3(a + 4.51)$

d) $-3.6(0.25 - r) = 0.18$

7. Solve. Express each solution to the nearest hundredth.

a) $3(u - 12.5) = -3.41$

b) $14.01 = -7(1.93 + m)$

c) $6(0.15 + v) = 10.97$

d) $-9.5(x - 4.2) = 7.5$

8. Solve and check.

a) $\dfrac{n + 1}{2} = -\dfrac{3}{4}$

b) $\dfrac{5}{2} = \dfrac{1}{3}(x - 2)$

c) $\dfrac{3}{4}(w + 2) = 1\dfrac{1}{3}$

d) $\dfrac{7}{6} = \dfrac{2(5 - g)}{3}$

9. Solve.

a) $\dfrac{1-y}{3} = \dfrac{2}{5}$

b) $-\dfrac{1}{2}(q+4) = 2\dfrac{1}{4}$

c) $-\dfrac{7}{10} = \dfrac{e+3}{5}$

d) $\dfrac{2(p-3)}{3} = \dfrac{1}{2}$

For help with #10 and #11, refer to Example 2 on page 317.

10. Solve and check.

a) $\dfrac{x+4.1}{3} = 2.5$

b) $19.8 = \dfrac{4.2+k}{-3}$

c) $\dfrac{q-6.95}{2} = -4.61$

d) $-2.1 = \dfrac{4.6-a}{-5}$

11. Solve.

a) $-0.25 = \dfrac{q-1.6}{2}$

b) $\dfrac{y+0.385}{-1} = -0.456$

c) $\dfrac{7.34+n}{4} = 1.29$

d) $7.56 = \dfrac{p-15.12}{-2}$

Apply

12. The mean of two numbers is 3.2. One of the numbers is 8.1. What is the other number?

13. Two equilateral triangles differ in their side lengths by 1.05 m. The perimeter of the larger triangle is 9.83 m. Determine the side length of the smaller triangle by

a) representing the situation with an equation of the form $a(x+b) = c$, and solving the equation.

b) using a different method of your choice. Explain your reasoning.

14. The regular pentagon has a perimeter of 18.8 units. What is the value of x?

$x - 3$

15. On a typical January day in Prince Rupert, British Columbia, the daily average temperature is −0.2 °C. The low temperature is −3.7 °C. What is the high temperature?

16. A regular hexagon has a perimeter of 41.4 units. The side length of the hexagon is represented by the expression $2(3-d)$. What is the value of d?

17. Henri bought three jars of spaghetti sauce. He used a coupon that reduced the cost of each jar by $0.75. If he paid $6.72 altogether, what was the regular price of each jar?

18. Luisa bought five concert tickets. She paid a $4.50 handling fee for each ticket. The total cost, before tax, was $210.00. What was the cost of each ticket, excluding the handling fee?

19. Mary wants to make her family kamiks, which are boots made from seal or caribou skin. She usually pays $80 for each skin, but Lukasie offers her a discount if she buys five skins. If Mary pays $368, how much did Lukasie reduce the price of each skin?

20. The area of a trapezoid can be found using the formula

$A = \dfrac{1}{2}(a+b) \times h$, where a and b are the lengths of the two parallel sides, and h is the distance between them.

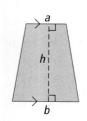

Determine each of the following.

a) h when $A = 27.3$ cm², $a = 2.3$ cm, and $b = 4.7$ cm

b) a when $A = 4.8$ m², $b = 1.9$ m, and $h = 3$ m

Literacy Link

A *trapezoid* is a quadrilateral with exactly two parallel sides.

21. A square picture frame is made from wood that is 1.6 cm wide. The perimeter of the outside of the frame is 75.2 cm. What is the side length of the largest square picture that the frame will display?

1.6 cm

22. For a fit and healthy person, the maximum safe heart rate during exercise is approximately related to their age by the formula $r = \frac{4}{5}(220 - a)$. In this formula, r is the maximum safe heart rate in beats per minute, and a is the age in years. At what age is the maximum safe heart rate 164 beats/min?

Extend

23. Solve and check.

a) $2(x + 3) + 3(x + 2) = 0.5$

b) $4(y - 3) - 2(y + 1) = -4.2$

c) $1.5(4 + f) + 2.5(5 - f) = 15.7$

d) $-5.3 = 6.2(t + 6) - 1.2(t - 2)$

24. Solve.

a) $4(d + 3) - 3(d - 2) = 1.2$

b) $-10.5 = 5(1 - r) + 4(r - 3)$

c) $3.9 = 2.5(g - 4) + 1.5(g + 5)$

d) $-1.8(h + 3) - 1.3(2 - h) = 1$

25. The area of the trapezoid is 1.5 square units. What are the lengths of the parallel sides?

3x – 2
4
2x – 1

26. If $1.5(x + 1) + 3.5(x + 1) = 7.5$, determine the value of $-10(x + 1)$ without determining the value of x. Explain your reasoning.

27. Tahir is training for an upcoming cross-country meet. He runs 13 km, three times a week. His goal is to increase his average speed by 1.5 km/h, so that he can complete each run in $1\frac{1}{4}$ h. How long does he take to complete each run now, to the nearest tenth of a minute? Solve this problem in two different ways.

28. a) Solve $x(n - 3) = 4$ for n by dividing first.

b) Solve $x(n - 3) = 4$ for n by using the distributive property first.

c) Which method do you prefer? Explain.

Math Link

One serving of a breakfast mixture consists of 200 mL of a corn bran cereal and 250 mL of 2% milk. Two servings of the mixture provide 1.4 mg of thiamin. If 250 mL of 2% milk provides 0.1 mg of thiamin, what mass of thiamin is in 200 mL of the cereal?

a) Write an equation that models the situation.

b) Solve the equation in two different ways.

c) Which of your solution methods do you prefer? Explain.

Did You Know?

Thiamin is another name for vitamin B_1. The body needs it to digest carbohydrates completely. A lack of thiamin can cause a loss of appetite, weakness, confusion, and even paralysis. Sources of thiamin include whole grains, liver, and yeast.

Solving Equations: $ax = b + cx$, $ax + b = cx + d$, $a(bx + c) = d(ex + f)$

Laura is playing in the park with her greyhound, Dash. Laura picks up the ball and starts to run. When Dash starts chasing her, Laura is 20 m away from him and is running away at 5 m/s. Dash runs after her at 15 m/s. Suppose Dash chases Laura for t seconds. What situation does the equation $15t = 5t + 20$ represent? What does the expression on each side of the equal sign represent? If you solved this equation, what would the value of t indicate?

Explore Equations With Variables on Both Sides

1. Explain how the diagrams model the solution to the equation $3x = 0.10 + x$. What is the solution?

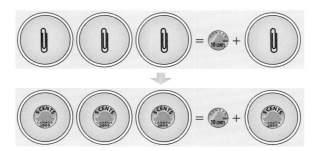

2. Work with a partner to explore how to model the solutions to the following equations using manipulatives or diagrams. Share your models with other classmates.

   a) $3x + 0.10 = 2x + 0.15$

   b) $2(x + 0.50) = 3(x + 0.25)$

Reflect and Check

3. a) How can you model solutions to equations with variables on both sides using manipulatives or diagrams?

b) Explain other ways that you could model the solutions.

4. Laura and her greyhound, Dash, went home along a trail. Laura strolled at 2 km/h along the shortest route. Dash trotted along at 3 km/h but covered 0.50 km of extra distance by zigzagging. Suggest methods for determining the length of time they took to reach home together. Share your ideas with your classmates.

Link the Ideas

Example 1: Apply Equations of the Form $ax = b + cx$

In a jar of coins, there are 30 fewer quarters than dimes. The value of the dimes equals the value of the quarters. How many dimes are in the jar?

Solution

Let d represent the number of dimes.
The number of quarters is $d - 30$.
The value of the dimes is $0.10d$ dollars.
The value of the quarters is $0.25(d - 30)$ dollars.
The value of the dimes equals the value of the quarters.
An equation that represents the situation is $0.10d = 0.25(d - 30)$.

$$0.10d = 0.25(d - 30)$$
$$0.10d = 0.25d - 7.5$$
$$0.10d - 0.25d = 0.25d - 7.5 - 0.25d$$
$$-0.15d = -7.5$$
$$\frac{-0.15d}{-0.15} = \frac{-7.5}{-0.15}$$
$$d = 50$$

There are 50 dimes in the jar.

> $$\frac{-7.5}{-0.15} \approx \frac{-8}{-0.2}$$ **M E**
> $$\approx 40$$

> You could use fractions of dollars and write the equation as
> $$\frac{1}{10}d = \frac{1}{4}(d - 30).$$
> You could also use cents and write the equation as $10d = 25(d - 30)$

Check:
There are 30 fewer quarters than dimes.
$50 - 30 = 20$
There are 20 quarters in the jar.
Value of dimes: $50 \times \$0.10 = \$5.00$
Value of quarters: $20 \times \$0.25 = \$5.00$
The dimes and quarters have equal values, as stated in the problem.

Show You Know

In a jar of coins, there are 20 more nickels than quarters. The value of the nickels equals the value of the quarters. How many quarters are in the jar?

Example 2: Apply Equations of the Form $ax + b = cx + d$

Alain has \$35.50 and is saving \$4.25/week. Eva has \$24.25 and is saving \$5.50/week. In how many weeks from now will they have the same amount of money?

Solution

Let the number of weeks from now be w.
In w weeks, Alain will have $35.50 + 4.25w$ dollars.
In w weeks, Eva will have $24.25 + 5.50w$ dollars.
In w weeks, Alain and Eva will have the same amount of money.
An equation that describes the situation is
$35.50 + 4.25w = 24.25 + 5.50w$.

Isolate the variable.

$$35.50 + 4.25w = 24.25 + 5.50w$$
$$35.50 + 4.25w - 4.25w = 24.25 + 5.50w - 4.25w$$
$$35.50 = 24.25 + 1.25w$$
$$35.50 - 24.25 = 24.25 + 1.25w - 24.25$$
$$11.25 = 1.25w$$
$$\frac{11.25}{1.25} = \frac{1.25w}{1.25}$$
$$9 = w$$

> Try a different first step than subtracting 4.25w from both sides. Complete your solution and check that you can get the correct final answer.

Alain and Eva will have the same amount of money in nine weeks.

Check:
In nine weeks, Alain will have \$35.50 + 9 × \$4.25, or \$73.75.
In nine weeks, Eva will have \$24.25 + 9 × \$5.50, or \$73.75.
So, they will have the same amount of money in nine weeks from now.
The solution is correct.

Show You Know

One Internet café charges \$1 for 15 min and \$0.20 per page for printing. A second Internet café charges \$2 per hour and \$0.25 per page for printing. Suppose you want to use the Internet for one hour. How many pages would you need to print in order to make the two cafés equal in price?

Example 3: Solve Equations of the Form $a(bx + c) = d(ex + f)$

Solve $\frac{1}{3}(2x - 1) = \frac{1}{2}(3x + 1)$ and check.

Solution

$$6 \times \frac{1}{3}(2x - 1) = 6 \times \frac{1}{2}(3x + 1)$$
$$2(2x - 1) = 3(3x + 1)$$
$$4x - 2 = 9x + 3$$
$$4x - 2 - 4x = 9x + 3 - 4x$$
$$-2 = 5x + 3$$
$$-2 - 3 = 5x + 3 - 3$$
$$-5 = 5x$$
$$\frac{-5}{5} = \frac{5x}{5}$$
$$-1 = x$$

Check:

Left Side $= \frac{1}{3}(2x - 1)$ Right Side $= \frac{1}{2}(3x + 1)$

$\qquad = \frac{1}{3}[2(-1) - 1]$ $\qquad = \frac{1}{2}[3(-1) + 1]$

$\qquad = \frac{1}{3}(-2 - 1)$ $\qquad = \frac{1}{2}(-3 + 1)$

$\qquad = \frac{1}{3}(-3)$ $\qquad = \frac{1}{2}(-2)$

$\qquad = -1$ $\qquad = -1$

$\qquad\qquad$ Left Side $=$ Right Side

The solution, $x = -1$, is correct.

Show You Know

Solve $\dfrac{3f + 1}{4} = \dfrac{3 + 2f}{2}$ and check.

Key Ideas

- You can solve and check equations with variables on both sides by applying the algebraic techniques learned in earlier sections.

$$3(0.5t + 1.3) = 2(0.4t - 0.85)$$
$$1.5t + 3.9 = 0.8t - 1.7$$
$$1.5t + 3.9 - 0.8t = 0.8t - 1.7 - 0.8t$$
$$0.7t + 3.9 = -1.7$$
$$0.7t + 3.9 - 3.9 = -1.7 - 3.9$$
$$0.7t = -5.6$$
$$\frac{0.7t}{0.7} = \frac{-5.6}{0.7}$$
$$t = -8$$

Check:

Left Side $= 3(0.5t + 1.3)$ Right Side $= 2(0.4t - 0.85)$

$\qquad = 3[0.5(-8) + 1.3]$ $\qquad = 2[0.4(-8) - 0.85]$

$\qquad = 3(-4 + 1.3)$ $\qquad = 2(-3.2 - 0.85)$

$\qquad = 3(-2.7)$ $\qquad = 2(-4.05)$

$\qquad = -8.1$ $\qquad = -8.1$

$\qquad\qquad$ Left Side $=$ Right Side

The solution, $t = -8$, is correct.

Check Your Understanding

Communicate the Ideas

1. Ken solved the equation $\frac{r}{2} = 3(r + 0.5)$ as shown. Is Ken's solution correct? If not, identify any errors and determine the correct solution.

$$\frac{r}{2} = 3(r + 0.5)$$
$$2 \times \frac{r}{2} = 2 \times 3(r + 0.5)$$
$$r = 6(2r + 1)$$
$$r = 12r + 6$$
$$-11r = 6$$
$$r = -\frac{6}{11} \text{ or } -0.545\,4...$$

2. Helga and Dora were solving the following problem together.

A boat left Kyuquot and headed west at 15.5 km/h. A second boat left Kyuquot half an hour later and headed west at 18 km/h. For how many hours did the first boat travel before the second boat overtook it?

Both girls used t to represent the time taken by the first boat. However, they disagreed on the equation to model the situation.

Helga's Equation   *Dora's Equation*
$15.5t = 18(t + 0.5)$ $15.5t = 18(t - 0.5)$

a) Explain what the expression on each side of each equation represents.

b) Which equation is correct? Explain.

c) What is the solution to the problem?

Did You Know?

Kyuquot is a village on the west coast of Vancouver Island. The village is the home of the northernmost of the Nuu-chah-nulth First Nations bands. The Nuu-chah-nulth people were formerly known as the Nootka.

3. a) Pierre decided to try solving $0.5(2x + 3) = 0.2(4x - 1)$ by guess and check. Do you think that this is a good method for solving the equation? Explain.

b) What method would you use to solve the equation?

Practise

4. Write an equation that is modelled by the diagram. Then, solve it.

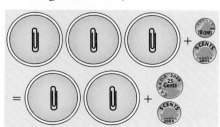

5. Model the equation $3(x + 0.15) = 2(x + 0.50)$. Then solve it.

For help with #6 and #7, refer to Example 1 on page 323.

6. Solve and check.

a) $0.5x = 1.6 + 0.25x$

b) $\frac{1}{3}y - \frac{1}{2} = \frac{1}{6}y$

c) $7.52 + 3.2a = -6.2a$

d) $-g = 2\frac{1}{2}g - 3$

7. Solve.

a) $\frac{1}{2}n = \frac{2}{5} + \frac{1}{5}n$

b) $-0.2w - 1.1 = 0.3w$

c) $5.1 - 3.5p = -2.3p$

d) $\frac{1}{2}(1 - e) = 1\frac{1}{6}e$

e) $\frac{3}{4}(d + 2) = \frac{2}{3}d$

For help with #8 and #9, refer to Example 2 on page 324.

8. Solve and check.

a) $2.6 + 2.1k = 1.5 + 4.3k$

b) $\frac{1}{6}p - 5 = \frac{1}{2}p + 2$

c) $4.9 - 6.1u = -3.2u - 3.8$

d) $4 + \frac{3}{5}h = -1\frac{2}{5}h - 1$

9. Solve.

a) $0.25r - 0.32 = 0.45r + 0.19$

b) $15.3c + 4.3 = 16.9 - 16.2c$

c) $-\frac{7}{8}k + 2 = 1 - \frac{3}{4}k$

d) $1\frac{1}{2}p + \frac{1}{4} = 2\frac{1}{4}p - \frac{5}{2}$

For help with #10 to #12, refer to Example 3 on page 325.

10. Solve and check.

a) $2(q - 0.1) = 3(0.3 - q)$

b) $\frac{1}{2}(x + 1) = \frac{1}{3}(x - 1)$

c) $0.2(4y + 3) = 0.6(4y - 1)$

d) $\frac{2x - 1}{2} = \frac{2x + 1}{3}$

11. Solve.

a) $4(s + 1.6) = -3(s - 1.2)$

b) $6.2(2g - 3) = 4.2(2g + 3)$

c) $\frac{3}{4}(x + 2) = \frac{2}{3}(x + 3)$

d) $\frac{6m - 3}{5} = \frac{4m - 1}{3}$

12. Solve. Express each answer to the nearest hundredth.

a) $1.2c - 7.4 = 3.4c$

b) $0.59n = 3.2(4 - n)$

c) $4.38 - 0.15x = 1.15x + 2.57$

d) $-0.11(3a + 5) = 0.37(2a - 1)$

Apply

13. A jar contains 76 more pennies than nickels. The total value of the pennies equals the total value of the nickels.

a) How many nickels are there?

b) What is the total value of all the coins in the jar?

14. Atu now has $28.50 and is saving $8.75/week. Beth now has $104.75 and is spending $6.50/week from her savings. In how many weeks from now will they have the same amount of money?

15. The two rectangles have equal perimeters. What are the dimensions of each rectangle?

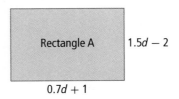
Rectangle A   1.5d − 2
0.7d + 1

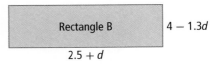
Rectangle B   4 − 1.3d
2.5 + d

16. a) Determine the value of x so that the two triangles have equal perimeters.

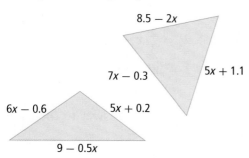

b) Check your solution by evaluating the perimeter of each triangle.

17. Sarah and Rachel are sisters. They leave a park at the same time on their bicycles and ride home along the same bicycle path. Sarah is in a hurry, so she cycles at 15 km/h. Rachel has time to spare, so she cycles at 11 km/h. Sarah gets home 12 min before Rachel. How long did Sarah take to ride home from the park?

18. The two rectangles have equal areas. Determine the area of each rectangle.

19. Elda walked from her home to her friend Niabi's house at 4.5 km/h. When Elda returned home along the same route, she strolled at 3.5 km/h. Elda took a total of 40 min to walk to Niabi's house and back again.

a) How many minutes did Elda take to walk from her home to Niabi's house?

b) How far is it from Elda's home to Niabi's house?

20. Alan's height is $\frac{4}{5}$ of his father's height. Alan's older brother, Ben, is 6 cm taller than Alan. Ben's height is $\frac{5}{6}$ of their father's height. How tall is their father?

21. Members of a cinema club pay $10 to see a movie instead of paying the regular price of $12.50. Annual membership in the club costs $30. What is the least number of movies you would need to see in a year in order to save money by buying a membership?

22. In still water, Jana's motorboat cruises at 16.5 km/h. On the river, the boat travels faster downstream than upstream, because of the current. The boat takes 5 h for a trip upstream, but only 2 h to cover the same distance on the return trip downstream. Determine the speed of the current.

23. Is each a true statement? Explain your reasoning.
  a) $1.2(0.5x - 1.8) = 0.8(0.75x - 2.7)$
  b) $-0.7(0.45y + 0.6) = -0.5(0.63y + 0.84)$

24. Describe a situation that could be modelled by the equation $3.5x + 1.2 = 4x + 0.9$.

25. Write a problem that can be modelled by an equation with the same variable on both sides. Have a classmate solve your problem.

Extend

26. Solve.
  a) $0.25x + 0.75x = 0.8x + 3.5$
  b) $\dfrac{y}{2} - \dfrac{y}{3} = \dfrac{y}{5} + 1$
  c) $0.5(4d + 3) - 2.6 = 1.5d$
  d) $2.6(j - 1) + 0.7 = 1.2(3 - j) + 0.2$

27. Solve.
  a) $15.3 - 8.9 - 1.3a = 4.3a + 0.1$
  b) $3 - \dfrac{1}{2}(4 - s) = 2 + \dfrac{1}{4}(5 + s)$
  c) $\dfrac{1}{3} + \dfrac{2}{3}(q - 2) = \dfrac{4}{3}(q + 2) - \dfrac{5}{3}$
  d) $1.5z - 2.1(2z + 3) = 4.2z + 0.3(z + 9)$

28. Solve $2(x + 5) = 3(x + k)$ for k and check the solution.

29. If $m = -0.8$ is a solution to the equation $2(1.8n + m) = m(5 - 2n)$, what is the value of n?

30. Solve.
  a) $\dfrac{2x + 1}{2} + \dfrac{4x - 5}{3} = -1$
  b) $\dfrac{3y + 4}{5} - \dfrac{y + 2}{2} = \dfrac{4y - 1}{10}$

Math Link

The mass of riboflavin in one small serving (75 g) of raw almonds is 0.87 mg less than the mass of riboflavin in $2\dfrac{1}{2}$ small servings of raw almonds. What is the mass of riboflavin in one small serving of raw almonds?

a) Write an equation that models the situation.

b) Solve the equation using guess and check.

c) Solve the equation by isolating the variable.

d) Which of these solution methods do you prefer? Explain why.

> **Did You Know?**
>
> Riboflavin is another name for vitamin B_2. It helps our digestion and our immune system. A lack of riboflavin can cause skin and eye irritation. Sources of riboflavin include milk, yeast, and eggs.

Chapter 8 Review

Key Words

For #1, fill in each blank by selecting from the terms provided. Terms can be used more than once.

1. In the ▬▬ $\frac{2}{3}k + \frac{1}{2} = -\frac{5}{6}$,
   - k is a ▬▬,
   - $\frac{2}{3}$ is a ▬▬,
   - $\frac{1}{2}$ is a ▬▬, and
   - $-\frac{5}{6}$ is a ▬▬.

   A numerical coefficient

   B variable

   C constant

   D equation

For #2 and #3, unscramble the letters to complete the statements using key words. Explain the meanings of the key words.

2. Subtraction is the ▬▬ ▬▬ to addition.

   N O I S I E T O P O P A T E R O P

3. When solving equations, you can remove brackets using the ▬▬ ▬▬.

   O P P R I S I T E T R U B E D Y V I R T

8.1 Solving Equations: $ax = b$, $\frac{x}{a} = b$, $\frac{a}{x} = b$, pages 292–303

4. Model the solution to the equation $\frac{x}{2} = -0.4$ on a number line. What is the solution?

5. Solve and check.
   a) $4d = -\frac{2}{5}$
   b) $2.68 = \frac{y}{3}$
   c) $\frac{3.5}{h} = -0.2$
   d) $-7.6u = -14.44$

6. Solve. Express each solution to the nearest tenth.
   a) $67.5 = -14.3w$
   b) $-\frac{68.3}{k} = -7.6$

7. The density of an object, D, in grams per cubic centimetre, is defined by $D = \frac{m}{V}$. In this formula, m is the mass, in grams, and V is the volume, in cubic centimetres. The density of pure iron is 7.87 g/cm³.
   a) What is the mass of a piece of pure iron with a volume of 5.5 cm³?
   b) What is the volume of a piece of pure iron with a mass of 98.375 g?

8. Raj and Tom are the top scorers on their soccer team. One season, Raj scored one quarter of their team's goals and Tom scored one sixth of their team's goals. Raj and Tom scored a total of 25 goals. How many goals did their team score?

8.2 Solving Equations: $ax + b = c$, $\frac{x}{a} + b = c$, pages 304–313

9. Model the solution to the equation $2x + \frac{1}{12} = \frac{3}{4}$ on a number line. What is the solution?

10. Nona solved the equation $-3.3g + 1.5 = -8.4$ as shown.

    $$-3.3g + 1.5 = -8.4$$
    $$-3.3g + 1.5 - 1.5 = -8.4 - 1.5$$
    $$-3.3g = -9.9$$
    $$\frac{-3.3g}{3.3} = \frac{-9.9}{3.3}$$
    $$g = -3$$

    a) What mistake did Nona make?
    b) What is the correct solution?

11. Solve and check.

a) $\dfrac{t}{1.6} + 5.9 = -3.2$

b) $2.05 = 0.9x - 6.5$

c) $\dfrac{2}{5} = \dfrac{2}{3} - \dfrac{r}{5}$

d) $2\dfrac{1}{2} + 1\dfrac{1}{6}v = -\dfrac{5}{6}$

12. Oksana paid a $14.00 handling charge to buy four Leela Gilday concert tickets on the Internet. The total cost of her order, including the handling charge, was $153.80. What was the cost of each ticket?

> **Did You Know?**
>
> Leela Gilday was born and raised in Yellowknife, Northwest Territories. She is a singer/songwriter from the Dene Nation. Leela started singing at an early age, and her performing career began at the Folk on the Rocks Music Festival when she was eight years old. Leela now performs across Canada and abroad with her band.

13. The sun takes 25.38 Earth days to rotate once about its axis. This time is 3.92 Earth days less than half the time that Mercury takes to rotate once about its axis. How many Earth days does Mercury take to rotate once about its axis?

8.3 Solving Equations: $a(x + b) = c$, pages 314–321

14. Solve and check.

a) $3(5.8 + e) = -2.7$

b) $-\dfrac{5}{6} = \dfrac{r - 4}{3}$

c) $10.1 = \dfrac{0.9 + h}{-2}$

d) $-\dfrac{4}{5}(q + 1) = -1\dfrac{1}{2}$

15. Solve $0.11 = -3(1.93 + m)$. Express the solution to the nearest hundredth.

16. An equilateral triangle has a perimeter of 17.85 m. The side length of the triangle, in metres, is $2k - 0.5$. What is the value of k?

17. Lorna took three of her friends to visit the zoo. The bus fares cost $5.50 per person. The cost of admission to the zoo was the same for each person in the group. Lorna spent $109 altogether on fares and admission. What was the cost of each admission?

8.4 Solving Equations: $ax = b + cx$, $ax + b = cx + d$, $a(bx + c) = d(ex + f)$, pages 322–329

18. Solve and check.

a) $\dfrac{1}{5}n + \dfrac{3}{2} = \dfrac{3}{10}n$

b) $-0.25f = 0.35 - 0.45f$

c) $12.4g + 34.3 = 9.5 - 3.1g$

d) $1.4(2h + 3) = 0.9(3h - 2)$

e) $\dfrac{3v + 2}{3} = \dfrac{2v - 1}{4}$

19. The square and the equilateral triangle have equal perimeters.

$3a + 0.6$ $2a + 4.6$

a) What is the value of a?

b) What is the perimeter of each shape?

20. The perimeter of a rectangle is 3.5 times the length. The width is 2.5 cm less than the length. What is the width?

Chapter 8 Practice Test

For #1 to #4, select the correct answer.

1. What is the solution to the equation
$\frac{1}{3} - \frac{3}{2}x = -\frac{1}{6}$?

  A $-\frac{1}{9}$ **B** $\frac{1}{9}$

  C $\frac{3}{1}$ **D** $\frac{1}{3}$

2. What is the solution to the equation
$\frac{-5.2}{t} = -3.25$?

  A 1.6   **B** −1.6

  C 0.625   **D** −0.625

3. What is the solution to the equation
$0.45 - 0.3g = 0.85 + 0.2g$?

  A 0.8   **B** −0.8

  C 1.25   **D** −1.25

4. Which equation does not have the
solution $y = -2$?

  A $\frac{y}{4} + 1 = \frac{1}{2}$

  B $\frac{7}{8} - \frac{1}{y} = 1\frac{3}{8}$

  C $\frac{2y - 1}{4} = \frac{5y - 4}{8}$

  D $\frac{2}{3}y + \frac{3}{2} = -\frac{1}{12}y$

Complete the statements in #5 and #6.

5. To solve a linear equation, you isolate
the ▬.

6. For $2.43 = -0.38v$, the solution expressed
to the nearest hundredth is $v = $ ■.

Short Answer

7. Model the solution to the equation $\frac{x}{2} = -\frac{3}{4}$
on a number line. What is the solution?

8. **a)** Describe the steps you would use to solve
the equation $1.5(x + 3) = 0.5(x - 1)$.

  b) How would the steps in part a) be
different from those you would use
to solve $1.5x + 3 = 0.5x - 1$?

9. Solve and check.

  a) $\frac{a + 1}{2} = \frac{2a - 1}{5}$

  b) $2.8(3d - 2) = -12.32$

10. Solve. Express each solution to the nearest
tenth.

  a) $-13.9x = 5.7 - 12.5x$

  b) $0.8(2s + 3) = -0.6(5s - 2)$

11. Precipitation is moisture that falls in the
form of rain or snow. The relationship
between the depth of rain, r, and the
depth of snow, s, that results from equal
quantities of precipitation is $\frac{r}{s} = 0.1$.

  a) If a storm delivers 15.5 cm of snow,
what depth of rain would result from
the same amount of precipitation on a
warmer day?

  b) If a storm delivers 2.7 cm of rain, what
depth of snow would result from the
same amount of precipitation on a
colder day?

12. Nav is working part time. She pays a
monthly fee of $5.95 for her bank account,
plus $0.75 for each deposit or withdrawal.
One month, the total cost of her account
was $12.70. How many deposits or
withdrawals did she make that month?

13. Two computer technicians both charge a fee for a home visit, plus an hourly rate for their work. Dana charges a $64.95 fee, plus $45/h. Tom charges a $79.95 fee, plus $40/h. For what length of service call do Dana and Tom charge the same amount?

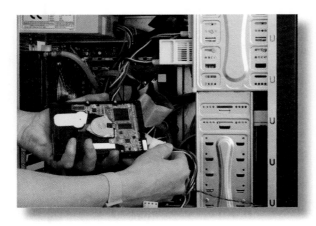

14. The square and the regular pentagon have equal perimeters. What is the perimeter of each shape?

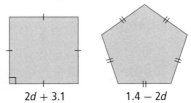

$2d + 3.1$ $1.4 - 2d$

Extended Response

15. a) Identify the error in the following solution.

$$-3.1(2n + 3) = 12.3$$
$$-6.2n + 3 = 12.3$$
$$-6.2n + 3 - 3 = 12.3 - 3$$
$$-6.2n = 9.3$$
$$\frac{-6.2n}{-6.2} = \frac{9.3}{-6.2}$$
$$n = -1.5$$

b) Correct the error in part a) to determine the correct solution. Express your answer to the nearest tenth.

Math Link: Wrap It Up!

The table shows the energy content, in megajoules, of single servings of some common foods.

Food	Serving Size	Energy (MJ)
Brazil nuts (raw)	125 mL	2.03
Buttermilk	250 mL	0.44
Canola oil	15 mL	0.52
Cheddar cheese	45 g	0.76
Corn (boiled)	1 ear	0.35
Lentils (cooked, drained)	250 mL	1.02
Mango (peeled)	1 mango	0.48
Potato (baked)	1 potato	0.94
Salmon (canned)	95 g	0.81

Use data from the table to write a word problem that can be solved using each of the following types of linear equations. Show the complete solutions to your own problems.

Have a classmate check your solutions. Modify your problems or correct your solutions, if necessary.

a) an equation of the form $ax = b$

b) an equation of the form $\frac{x}{a} = b$

c) an equation of the form $ax + b = c$

d) an equation that includes a grouping symbol

e) an equation with the same variable on both sides

Challenges

School Store

A school store is a convenience to both students and teachers. But a school store is also a great opportunity for you. If you volunteer to work in the school store, it gives you real job training.

You be the store worker. How can you use your knowledge of linear equations to help you make business decisions?

1. The wholesale price of a case of 36 fruit bars is $20. If the bars are sold in the store for $0.75/bar, write and solve an equation to determine the amount of profit for the sale of one case of fruit bars.

2. The student leadership team has volunteered to work and promote sales in the store for one week. The profit made during that week from the sale of granola and fruit bars, chocolate milk, and frozen milk treats will be donated to charity. The price and average sales of these items are provided in the table.

Product	Price/Case	Number in Each Case	Average Weekly Sales
Granola bars	$26.40	48	115
Fruit bars	$20.00	36	160
Chocolate milk	$43.20	90	156
Frozen milk treats	$17.98	18	88

a) Determine a price per item so that the store makes a profit of at least $150 during the week. Show your thinking for determining the price for each item.

b) Plan an advertisement that includes price per item.

> **Did You Know?**
> In business, many managers use a spreadsheet to solve this type of problem.

> **Literacy Link**
> *Wholesale price* is the price charged for products when you buy large numbers of them from someone who sells to the owners of stores.
>
> *Profit* refers to the difference between selling price of goods and what it costs to buy and sell them.

Pair Up, Create, and Solve

In this game, you will solve various equations that you and your partner will make together.

Materials
• scissors
• blank paper

1. Cut a piece of paper into 19 equal-sized cards. You may find it easiest to cut the paper into 20 pieces and discard one. Label the cards as shown.

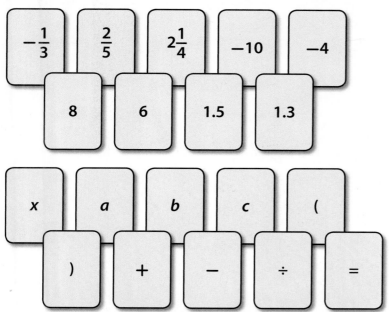

Turn the cards in the first two rows face down on the table in a random fashion so that the numbers are hidden. Keep the cards in the second two rows face-up.

2. Using the cards in the second two rows, one partner will lay out an equation on the table in one of the following forms:
$$ax = b \quad \frac{x}{a} = b \quad ax + b = c \quad \frac{x}{a} + b = c \quad a(x + b) = c$$

3. The second partner randomly selects from the overturned cards to replace a, b, and/or c with numerical values, and then solves the resulting equation. Work together to check the answer.

4. Replace the cards in their rows, and switch roles. Repeat this process until you have tried all five equation forms.

9

Linear Inequalities

Would you dare to ride the Mindbender, the world's largest indoor, triple-loop roller coaster? You can find this roller coaster at West Edmonton Mall.

Many people around the world seek the thrills that amusement parks can offer on rides that are action-packed, scary, or fast and fun. Amusement park operators consider types of rides, as well as the costs of operating and maintaining the rides. They compare these costs to the money they expect to collect from ticket sales. Sometimes they analyse situations by comparing quantities using linear inequalities.

What You Will Learn

- to represent linear inequalities verbally, algebraically, and graphically
- to determine and verify solutions of linear inequalities
- to generalize and apply rules for solving linear inequalities
- to compare and explain the processes for solving linear equations and linear inequalities
- to compare and explain solutions of linear equations and linear inequalities
- to solve problems involving linear inequalities

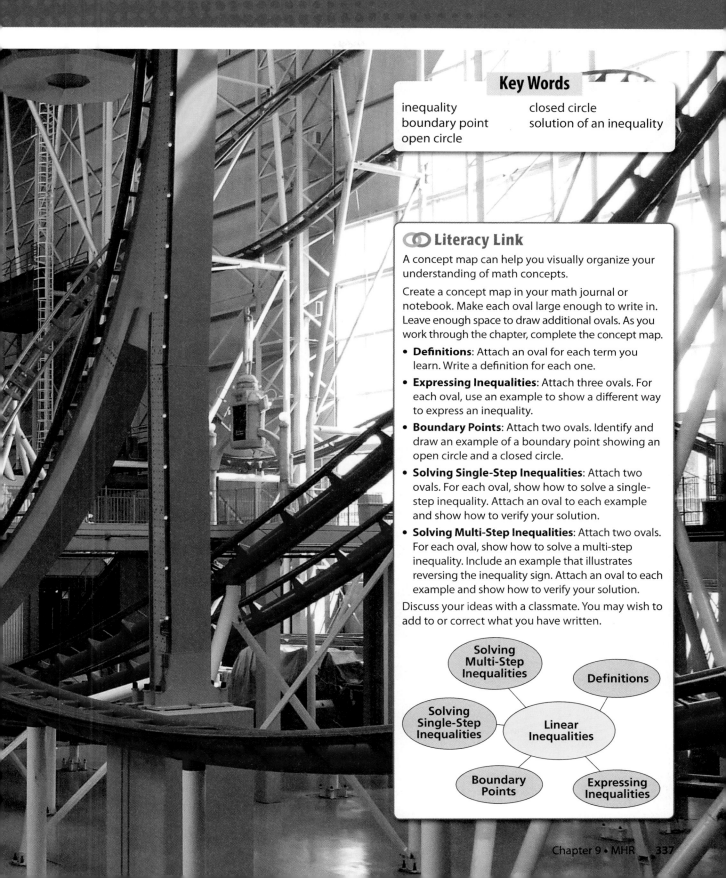

Key Words

inequality
boundary point
open circle

closed circle
solution of an inequality

◯◯ Literacy Link

A concept map can help you visually organize your understanding of math concepts.

Create a concept map in your math journal or notebook. Make each oval large enough to write in. Leave enough space to draw additional ovals. As you work through the chapter, complete the concept map.

- **Definitions**: Attach an oval for each term you learn. Write a definition for each one.
- **Expressing Inequalities**: Attach three ovals. For each oval, use an example to show a different way to express an inequality.
- **Boundary Points**: Attach two ovals. Identify and draw an example of a boundary point showing an open circle and a closed circle.
- **Solving Single-Step Inequalities**: Attach two ovals. For each oval, show how to solve a single-step inequality. Attach an oval to each example and show how to verify your solution.
- **Solving Multi-Step Inequalities**: Attach two ovals. For each oval, show how to solve a multi-step inequality. Include an example that illustrates reversing the inequality sign. Attach an oval to each example and show how to verify your solution.

Discuss your ideas with a classmate. You may wish to add to or correct what you have written.

Making the Foldable

Materials
- sheet of 11 × 17 paper
- four sheets of 8.5 × 11 paper
- stapler
- ruler
- scissors
- glue

Step 1

Fold the long side of a sheet of 11 × 17 paper in half. Pinch it at the midpoint. Fold the outer edges of the paper to meet at the midpoint. Label it as shown.

Step 2

Fold the short side of a sheet of 8.5 × 11 paper in half. Fold in three the opposite way. Make two cuts as shown through one thickness of the paper, forming three tabs. Label the tabs as shown.

Step 3

Fold the short side of a sheet of 8.5 × 11 paper in half. Fold in two the opposite way. Make a cut through one thickness of paper, forming two tabs. Label the tabs as shown.

Step 4

Fold the short side of two sheets of 8.5 × 11 paper in half. Cut along the folds, so that you will end up with four pages. Label the top sheet as shown.

Step 5

Staple the sheets from Step 4 to the inside of the Foldable as shown. Staple or glue the two booklets you made into the Foldable from Step 1, as shown.

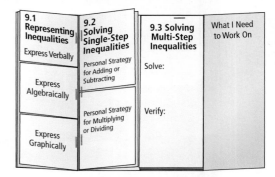

Using the Foldable

As you work through Chapter 9, make notes about the Key Words and record examples of inequalities. Record your notes and Key Ideas in the appropriate section. For section 9.1, use examples to show each form of expression. For section 9.2, use an example to demonstrate your personal strategy for each operation. For section 9.3, solve inequalities and verify the solutions for sample problems.

Use the back of the Foldable to record your ideas for the Wrap It Up! On the inside right flap of the Foldable, keep track of what you need to work on. Check off each item as you deal with it.

Math Link

Amusement Park Rides

In 1893, the first-ever Ferris wheel became the landmark at the World's Fair in Chicago. The wheel had 36 school-bus size gondolas that could each hold up to 60 people. People got a 20-min ride during which the wheel made two revolutions. During the first revolution, the wheel made six stops for loading and unloading passengers. During the second, it made one revolution without stopping.

The original Ferris wheel was demolished in 1906. Today there are many Ferris wheels at amusement parks, fairs, and carnivals throughout the world.

1. Using the term *less than or equal to*:
   a) describe the restriction on the number of people in each gondola of the first Ferris wheel
   b) describe the restriction on the total number of people that the first Ferris wheel could carry

2. a) Research a modern Ferris wheel. Find at least two facts about its design and capacity.
   b) Describe a restriction on a modern Ferris wheel. Use a term such as *greater than or equal to* or *less than or equal to*.

3. Think about other amusement park rides you may have seen.
   a) What reasons might designers have for restricting the number of people on a ride at one time?
   b) What other types of restrictions might designers put in place?
   c) Describe a restriction in more than one way.

In this chapter, you will explore some factors involved in operating rides and managing an amusement park. At the end of the chapter, you will develop a plan for operating an amusement park.

Did You Know?

Designed by George W. G. Ferris, a bridge builder, the wheel was 26 storeys tall. The radius of the wheel was about 38 m. The centre of the wheel was about 40 m off the ground.

Did You Know?

The world's tallest Ferris wheel is the Singapore Flyer, located in Singapore. At 165 m tall, it opened to the public in 2008.

WWW Web Link

For information about the history of Ferris wheels and the tallest ones in the world, go to www.mathlinks9.ca and follow the links.

Representing Inequalities

Did You Know?

Zdeno Chara is the tallest person who has ever played in the NHL. He is 206 cm tall and is allowed to use a stick that is longer than the NHL's maximum allowable length.

The official rule book of the NHL states limits for the equipment players can use. One of the rules states that no hockey stick can exceed 160 cm.

What different ways can you use to represent the allowable lengths of hockey sticks?

Explore Inequalities

1. a) Show how you can use a number line to graph lengths of hockey sticks in centimetres. Use a convenient scale for the range of values you have chosen to show. Why did you select the scale you chose?

   b) Mark the maximum allowable length of stick on your line.

2. a) Consider the NHL's rule about stick length. Identify three different allowable stick lengths that are whole numbers. Identify three that are not whole numbers. Mark each value on your number line.

   b) Think about all the possible values for lengths of sticks that are allowable. Describe where all of these values are located on the number line. How could you mark all of these values on the number line?

3. a) Give three examples of stick lengths that are too long. Where are these values located on the number line?

b) Discuss with a partner how to state the possible length of the shortest illegal stick. Is it reasonable to have a minimum length for the shortest illegal stick? Why or why not?

Reflect and Check

4. The value of 160 cm could be called a boundary point for the allowable length of hockey sticks.

a) Look at the number line and explain what you think the term *boundary point* means.

b) In this situation, is the boundary point included as an allowable length of stick? Explain.

5. The allowable length of hockey sticks can be expressed mathematically as an **inequality**. Since sticks must be less than or equal to 160 cm in length, the linear inequality is $l \leq 160$, where l, in centimetres, represents the stick length.

Write an inequality to represent the lengths of illegal sticks. Discuss your answer with a classmate.

inequality

- a mathematical statement comparing expressions that may not be equal
- can be written using the symbol $<, >, \leq, \geq,$ or $\neq$

Link the Ideas

Reading an inequality depends on the inequality symbol used.

Inequality	Meaning
$a > b$	a is greater than b
$a < b$	a is less than b
$a \geq b$	a is greater than or equal to b
$a \leq b$	a is less than or equal to b
$a \neq b$	a is not equal to b

> **⊙⊙ Literacy Link**
>
> Inequalities can be expressed three ways:
> - *Verbally* using words. For example, "all numbers less than or equal to 0.75."
> - *Graphically* using visuals, such as diagrams and graphs. For example,
>
>
>   0   0.75 1
> - *Algebraically* using mathematical symbols. For example, $x \leq 0.75$.

Example 1: Represent Inequalities

Many jobs pay people a higher rate for working overtime. Reema earns overtime pay when she works more than 40 h a week.

a) Give four possible values that would result in overtime pay.

b) Verbally express the amount of time that qualifies for overtime as an inequality.

c) Express the inequality graphically.

d) Express the inequality algebraically.

e) Represent the amount of time that does not qualify for overtime as an inequality. Express the inequality verbally, graphically, and algebraically.

Solution

a) Reema does not qualify for overtime if she works exactly 40 h. She qualifies only if she works more than 40 h. Some examples include 40.5 h, 42 h, 46.25 h, and 50 h.

b) In order to qualify for overtime, Reema needs to work more than 40 h.

c) Draw a number line to represent the inequality graphically. Display the value 40 and values close to 40. The value 40 is a **boundary point**. This point separates the regular hours from the overtime hours on the number line. Draw an open circle at 40 to show the boundary point. Starting at 40, draw an arrow pointing to the right to show that the possible values of t are greater than but not equal to 40.

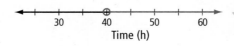
Time (h)

> The open circle shows that the value 40 is not a possible value for the number of hours that qualify for overtime.

> **boundary point**
> - separates the values less than from the values greater than a specified value
> - may or may not be a possible value in a solution
> - an open circle shows that the boundary point is not included in the solution
>
>   boundary point
>
>   7   8   9
> - a closed circle shows that the boundary point is included in the solution
>
>   boundary point
>   4   4.6   5

d) The inequality is $t > 40$, where t represents the amount of time, in hours, that Reema works in a week.

> Which of the three representations of an inequality do you prefer?

e) Verbally: Reema does not qualify for overtime if the number of hours she works is less than or equal to 40 h.

Graphically: Draw a closed circle at 40. Draw an arrow pointing to the left of 40 to show the possible values of t less than or equal to 40.

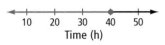

> The closed circle shows that 40 is a possible value for the number of hours that do not qualify for overtime.

Algebraically: Using t to represent the amount of time, in hours, that Reema works, $t \leq 40$.

Show You Know

In many provinces, you must be at least 16 years of age to get a driver's licence.

a) Sketch a number line to represent the situation.

b) Represent the situation algebraically.

Example 2: Express Inequalities

a) Express the inequality shown on the number line verbally and algebraically.

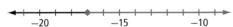

b) Express the inequality shown on the number line algebraically.

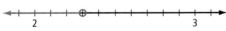

c) Express the inequality $x \geq -\dfrac{4}{7}$ graphically.

d) Express the inequality $35 < n$ graphically.

Solution

a) The number line shows a closed circle on -17 and an arrow to the right. This means values are the same as or larger than -17.

> What does the arrow to the right represent? What does the closed circle represent?

Verbally: The number line indicates all the values greater than or equal to -17.

Algebraically: Using x as the variable, $x \geq -17$.

b) The space between 2 and 3 is divided into ten intervals, so each one represents 0.1 or $\frac{1}{10}$.

The number line shows an open circle on 2.3 and an arrow to the left. This indicates the values less than 2.3 but not including 2.3.

Using x as the variable, $x < 2.3$ or $x < 2\frac{3}{10}$ or $x < \frac{23}{10}$.

c) The inequality represents values greater than or equal to $-\frac{4}{7}$.

The boundary point is between -1 and 0.
Draw a number line with -1 and 0 labelled.
Divide the space between -1 and 0 into seven intervals.

> Why do you divide into seven intervals?

Draw a closed circle at $-\frac{4}{7}$. Draw an arrow to the right

to indicate values that are greater than or equal to $-\frac{4}{7}$.

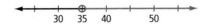

d) In this inequality, the variable is on the right. You can read the inequality as "35 is less than n." This is the same as saying n is larger than 35. Draw a number line showing an open circle on 35 and an arrow pointing to the right.

Show You Know

a) Express the inequality shown on the number line algebraically.

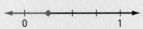

b) Represent the inequality $n < -12$ on a number line.

c) Write an inequality for the values shown on the number line. Describe a real-life scenario that the inequality might represent.

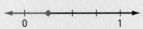

d) Show the possible values for x on a number line, if $-7 \geq x$. What is a different way to express $-7 \geq x$ algebraically?

Example 3: Represent a Combination of Inequalities

Many real life situations can be described by a combination of two inequalities. Represent the situation described in the newspaper headline using inequalities. Show it verbally, graphically, and algebraically.

Average Daily Water Use
From 327 L to 343 L Per Person

Solution

The newspaper headline describes two inequalities.

Verbally: Daily water use was greater than or equal to 327 L and daily water use was less than or equal to 343 L.

Graphically: Draw a closed circle at 327 and a closed circle at 343. Draw a line segment joining the two circles. This graph represents values that are greater than or equal to 327, and less than or equal to 343.

Daily Water Usage (L)

The values represented by the situation are between and including the boundary points.

Algebraically: Use w to represent the number of litres of water used. You can represent this situation with two inequalities.
$w \geq 327$ and $w \leq 343$

The values that satisfy both inequalities represent the situation.

Show You Know

The most extreme change in temperature in Canada took place in January 1962 in Pincher Creek, Alberta. A warm, dry wind, known as a chinook, raised the temperature from −19 °C to 22 °C in one hour. Represent the temperature during this hour using inequalities. Express the inequalities verbally, graphically, and algebraically.

Key Ideas

- A linear inequality compares linear expressions that may not be equal.

    $x \geq -3$ means that x is greater than or equal to -3.

- Situations involving inequalities can be represented verbally, graphically, and algebraically.

    - Verbally: Use words.

    - Graphically: Use visuals, such as diagrams and graphs.

    - Algebraically: Use mathematical symbols, such as numbers, variables, operation signs, and the symbols $<$, $>$, $\leq$, and $\geq$.

A person must be under twelve years of age to qualify for a child's ticket at the movies. Let a represent the age of the person.

The values of a are less than 12.

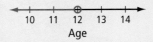
Age

The inequality is $a < 12$.

- An inequality with the variable on the right can be interpreted two ways.

    $8 < x$ can be read "8 is less than x." This is the same as saying "x is greater than 8."

Check Your Understanding

Communicate the Ideas

1. Consider the inequalities $x > 10$ and $x \geq 10$.
    a) List three possible values for x that satisfy both inequalities. Explain how you know.
    b) Identify a number that is a possible value for x in one but not both inequalities.
    c) How are the possible values for inequalities involving $>$ or $<$ different than for inequalities involving $\geq$ or $\leq$? Give an example to support your answer.

2. On a number line, why do you think an open circle is used for the symbols $<$ and $>$, and a closed circle for the symbols $\leq$ and $\geq$?

3. Tiffany and Charles have each written an inequality to represent numbers that are not more than 15. Their teacher says that both are correct. Explain why.

    Charles: $15 \geq x$ Tiffany: $x \leq 15$

4. Consider the inequality $x \neq 5$.
    a) List at least three possible values for x.
    b) How many values are not possible for x? Explain.
    c) Explain how you would represent the inequality on a number line.

Practise

For help with #5 to #9, refer to Example 1 on pages 342–343.

5. Write the inequality sign that best matches each term. Use an example to help explain your choice for each.

   a) at least

   b) fewer than

   c) maximum

   d) must exceed

6. For which inequalities is 4 a possible value of x? Support your answer using two different representations.

   a) $x > 3$

   b) $x < 4$

   c) $x > -9$

   d) $x \geq 4$

7. Write a word statement to express the meaning of each inequality. Give three possible values of y.

   a) $y \geq 8$

   b) $y < -12$

   c) $y \leq 6.4$

   d) $y > -12.7$

8. At the spring ice fishing derby, only fish 32 cm or longer qualify for the prize categories.

   a) Draw a number line to represent the situation.

   b) Write a statement to represent the sizes of fish that qualify for prizes.

For help with #9 to #12, refer to Example 2 on pages 343–344.

9. Write a word statement to express each inequality.

   a)

   b)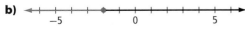

   c)

10. Express each inequality algebraically in two different ways.

   a)

   b)

   c)

11. Sketch a number line to show each inequality.

   a) $x > 3$

   b) $x < 12$

   c) $x \geq -19$

   d) $-3 \geq x$

12. Represent each inequality graphically.

   a) $y \leq 10.7$

   b) $y \geq -5.3$

   c) $y < -\dfrac{4}{5}$

   d) $4.8 > x$

For help with #13 to #15, refer to Example 3 on page 345.

13. For each combination of inequalities, show the possible values for x on a number line.

   a) $x > 12$ and $x < 17$

   b) $x \geq -5$ and $x \leq 0$

   c) $x \geq 1\dfrac{3}{4}$ and $x \leq 4$

   d) $x < -4\dfrac{1}{2}$ and $x > -11$

14. a) Represent the possible values for y graphically, if $y > -9.3$ and $y < -6.7$.

   b) Mark any three values on the number line. For each one, explain whether it is a possible value for y.

15. Represent the values shown in red on each number line by a combination of inequalities.

   a)

   b)

   c)

Apply

16. The manager of a clothing store has set goals for her sales staff. Express each goal algebraically.

a) The monthly total sales, m, will be a minimum of $18\,000.

b) At month end, the total time, t, spent counting store inventory will be at most 8 h.

c) The value of total daily sales, d, will be more than $700.

17. If Emily keeps a daily balance of at least $1500 in her bank account, she will pay no monthly fees.

a) Draw a number line to represent the situation.

b) If x represents her daily balance, write an inequality that represents the possible values for x when she will pay no fees.

18. Paul is training for a race and hopes to beat the record time. The number line represents the finishing times that will allow him to beat the record.

40   42
Finishing Time (s)

a) Write a statement to express the finishing times that will let Paul beat the record.

b) Express the inequality algebraically.

19. a) Develop a problem that could be represented by an inequality. Express the inequality verbally.

b) Graph the inequality.

c) Express the inequality algebraically.

20. Owen has a coupon for a restaurant.

Buy one meal and get the second meal of equal or lesser value for free!

a) Owen buys a meal for $10.75. If m is the cost of his second meal, write an inequality to represent the possible values of m that will allow him to use the coupon.

b) Represent the inequality graphically.

21. Shanelle is buying insurance for a car to drive to and from work. The cost of insurance will be higher if she works farther than 15 km from home.

a) Verbally express the inequality that represents the possible values for the distance for which Shanelle will have to pay more insurance.

b) Sketch a number line to represent the inequality.

22. During winter, ice roads allow access to remote places in northern communities. The ice road to Aklavik, NWT is made through the Mackenzie River Delta. The ice road to Tuktoyuktuk travels up the Mackenzie River and out onto the sea ice. Ice roads are made by flooding the existing ice on a river or lake until it reaches the required thickness.

For safety reasons, there are restrictions such as the ones shown.

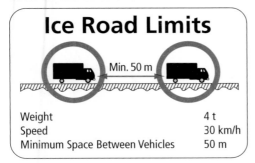

Ice Road Limits

Min. 50 m

Weight	4 t
Speed	30 km/h
Minimum Space Between Vehicles	50 m

Represent each restriction

a) graphically

b) algebraically

Extend

23. a) If the inequalities $x \geq 6$ and $x \leq 6$ are both true, describe the possible values for x.

b) What would a number line showing possible values of x look like for this situation? Justify your answer.

24. Bluesky is building a wooden puzzle triangle. She has cut two sides that measure 30 cm and 80 cm, respectively. The longest side of the triangle is 80 cm. Write inequalities to represent the possible lengths for the third side of the triangle.

25. What values of x would each of the following combinations of inequalities represent? Explain verbally and show graphically.

a) $x > 4$ and $x < 7$ **b)** $x < 4$ and $x < 7$

c) $x > 4$ and $x > 7$ **d)** $x < 4$ and $x > 7$

Math Link

For safety reasons, some amusement park rides have age and height restrictions for riders.

a) Choose an amusement park ride that you have seen or design one of your own. Describe your ride.

b) For your ride, consider the safety restrictions or conditions that you might impose on riders. List at least three restrictions. Use terms of your choice.

c) Represent each restriction algebraically using a different variable for each.

d) Sketch a sign. Use words and graphics that clearly inform riders about each of your restrictions.

Solving Single-Step Inequalities

Focus on...

After this lesson, you will be able to...

- solve single-step linear inequalities and verify solutions
- compare the processes for solving linear equations and linear inequalities
- compare the solutions of linear equations and linear inequalities
- solve problems involving single-step linear inequalities

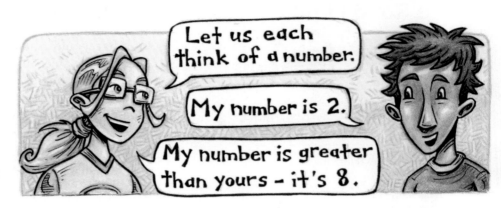

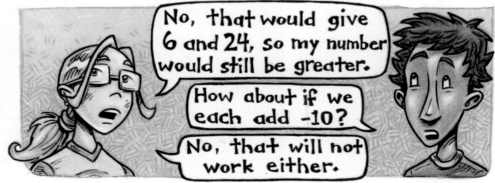

How might you solve Katie's puzzle?

Consider the mathematical operations of addition, subtraction, multiplication, and division. What operations (+, −, ×, ÷), if any, will reverse the situation so that Joe has the greater number?

Explore Mathematical Operations and Linear Inequalities

Materials
- long strip of paper or number line
- ruler
- two different-coloured tokens or markers

1. On a long strip of paper, draw a number line that shows integers from −20 to 20.

2. a) Work with a partner. Each partner needs to choose an even, positive whole number that is less than 10. Do not choose the same number. Use a different token to show the position of each partner's starting number on the number line.

b) Record an inequality that compares the starting numbers. Note the direction of the inequality symbol and who has the greater number.

c) Choose the same mathematical operation to perform on each partner's number. Move the markers to show the resulting numbers. If necessary, extend your number line.

Whose resulting number is greater? Record an inequality that compares these numbers.

Subtract 4.
Move the counters.

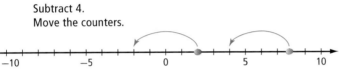

d) Starting each time with your original numbers and inequality, take turns to choose a different mathematical operation and perform it. Each time, move the counters. Whose number is greater? Record the resulting inequality.

e) Try different operations until you are able to predict which operations will reverse an inequality symbol and which ones will keep it the same. Organize your observations and results.

Strategies

Identify All Possibilities

3. a) Conduct a new trial by choosing one negative and one positive number. Use these starting numbers to test your predictions in #2e).

b) Model each operation using the number line and markers. Record your results.

Reflect and Check

4. Consider how the markers moved on the number line.

a) What mathematical operations changed the direction of the inequality symbol? Explain.

b) What operations kept the inequality symbol the same? Explain.

c) Develop an example to support your explanation for parts a) and b).

5. Review your strategy for solving Katie's puzzle. What advice would you give about an operation that would make Joe's number greater than Katie's?

Link the Ideas

Example 1: Solve Inequalities

Solve each inequality.

a) $-2x < 8$ **b)** $x - 3 \geq 2$ **c)** $-5 > \dfrac{x}{3}$

Solution

a) *Method 1: Use a Model*
You can model the inequality $-2x < 8$ using blocks.

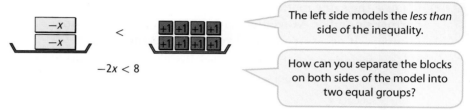

The left side models the *less than* side of the inequality.

How can you separate the blocks on both sides of the model into two equal groups?

$-2x < 8$

The model shows the inequality with two negative x-blocks on the left side and eight positive unit blocks on the right side. In order for the left side to be less than the right side, each negative x-block must be less than four positive unit blocks.

$-x < 4$

What values of x will make this inequality true?

The inequality $-x < 4$ will be true for $x > -4$. Notice that each side has changed its sign and the inequality symbol is reversed. Represent this solution using blocks. The side with the positive x-block is now greater than the right side.

$x > -4$

Why is the following true?
$-x < 4$
$= -x + x - 4 < 4 + x - 4$
$= -4 < x$

The solution to the inequality $-2x < 8$ is $x > -4$.

Method 2: Isolate the Variable
$$-2x < 8$$
$$\frac{-2x}{-2} > \frac{8}{-2}$$
$$x > -4$$

When dividing by a negative number on both sides, why do you reverse the inequality symbol?

The solution to the inequality is $x > -4$.

b) Isolate the variable.

$$x - 3 \geq 2$$
$$x - 3 + 3 \geq 2 + 3$$
$$x \geq 5$$

> When adding a positive number to both sides, what happens to the inequality symbol?

The solution to the inequality is $x \geq 5$.

c) Isolate the variable.

$$-5 > \frac{x}{3}$$
$$(-5) \times 3 > \frac{x}{3} \times 3$$
$$-15 > x$$
$$x < -15$$

> How does multiplying by a positive number on both sides affect the inequality symbol?

The solution to the inequality is $x < -15$.

Show You Know

Solve each inequality.

a) $x - 1.6 \leq -5.6$ **b)** $-10 > 4x$ **c)** $\dfrac{x}{-8} > 3$

Example 2: Verify Solutions to Inequalities

Trevor was asked to solve the inequality $-2x \geq 11$. He represented his solution, $x \geq -5.5$, on a number line. Verify whether Trevor's **solution of the inequality** is correct.

> What values might you use to verify the solution?

solution of an inequality

• a value or set of values that satisfies an inequality
• can contain many values

Solution

Substitute some possible values of x into the original inequality:
• Check that the value of the boundary point is correct.
• Check that the inequality symbol is correct.

If the number line is correct, the boundary point of -5.5 should make the two sides of the inequality the same.

Substitute -5.5 into the inequality.

Check:

$$-2x = 11$$
$$-2(-5.5) = 11$$
$$11 = 11$$

True statement

Strategies

Guess and Check

The two sides are equal.
Therefore, -5.5 is the correct boundary point.

If the number line is correct, any value greater than -5.5 should make a true statement.

Substitute one or more values greater than -5.5, such as -5 and 0, into the inequality.

Choose numbers that are easy to work with.

Check:

$-2x \geq 11$	$-2x \geq 11$
$-2(-5) \geq 11$	$-2(0) \geq 11$
$10 \geq 11$	$0 \geq 11$
False statement	False statement

The values -5 and 0 are non-solutions since they result in false statements.

Substituting numbers greater than -5.5 does not result in true statements.

Trevor has drawn the arrow facing the wrong way on the number line. He should have changed the direction of the inequality symbol in his solution. The solution should be $x \leq -5.5$.

Verify the correct solution by substituting one or more values less than -5.5, such as -8 and -6, into the inequality.

Check:

$-2x \geq 11$	$-2x \geq 11$
$-2(-8) \geq 11$	$-2(-6) \geq 11$
$16 \geq 11$	$12 \geq 11$
True statement	True statement

The values -8 and -6 are specific solutions since they result in true statements.

Trevor's solution is not correct.
He forgot to reverse the inequality sign when dividing by a negative number.

Show You Know

Verify the solution for each inequality.
If incorrect, what is the solution?

a) For the inequality $x - 12 \leq 20$, the solution is $x \leq 32$.

b) For the inequality $-5x < 30$, the solution is $x < -6$.

Example 3: Model and Solve a Problem

A games store is offering games on sale for $12.50, including tax. Sean has set his spending limit at $80. How many games can Sean buy and stay within his limit?

a) Write an inequality to model the problem.
b) Solve the inequality and interpret the solution.

Solution

a) If n represents the number of games that Sean can buy, the cost of n games is 12.5 times n. Sean must spend no more than $80.

The situation can be modelled with the inequality $12.5n \leq 80$.

b)
$$12.5n \leq 80$$
$$\frac{12.5n}{12.5} \leq \frac{80}{12.5}$$
$$n \leq 6.4$$

> $12 \times 6 = 72$ $12 \times 7 = 84$ **M E**
> The number of games Sean can buy is between 6 and 7.

> Since it is not possible to buy part of a game, 6.4 is not a solution to the original problem, even though it is a solution to the inequality $12.5n \leq 80$. Only a whole number is a possible solution for this situation.

Sean can buy up to and including six games and stay within his spending limit.

Show You Know

Yvonne is planting trees as a summer job. She gets paid $0.10 per tree planted. She wants to earn at least $20/h. How many trees must she plant per hour in order to achieve her goal?

a) Write an inequality to model the number of trees Yvonne must plant to reach her goal.
b) Will the solution be a set of whole numbers or a set of integers? Explain.
c) Solve the inequality and interpret the solution.

> **Did You Know?**
> *Piecework* is work paid by the amount done, not by the time it takes. For example, tree planters are paid by the number of trees they plant.

Key Ideas

- The solution to an inequality is the value or values that makes the inequality true.

    $5x > 10$

    A specific solution is any value greater than 2. For example, 2.1, 3, or 22.84.
    The set of all solutions is $x > 2$.

- You can solve an inequality involving addition, subtraction, multiplication, and division by isolating the variable.

$x - 3 \leq 5$	$8x \leq 24$	$\dfrac{x}{-2} > 6$
$x - 3 + 3 \leq 5 + 3$	$\dfrac{8x}{8} \leq \dfrac{24}{8}$	$\dfrac{x}{-2} \times -2 < 6 \times -2$
$x \leq 8$	$x \leq 3$	$x < -12$

    > Reverse the inequality symbol when multiplying or dividing both sides by a negative number.

- To verify the solution to an inequality, substitute possible values into the inequality:
    - Substitute the value of the boundary point to check if both sides are equal.
    - Substitute specific value(s) from the solution to check that the inequality symbol is correct.

        Check if $x \geq -3$ is the solution to $-8x \leq 24$.

Substitute the boundary point -3.	Substitute a value greater than the boundary point -3.
$-8x = 24$	$-8x \leq 24$
$-8(-3) = 24$	$-8(0) \leq 24$
$24 = 24$	$0 \leq 24$
The two sides are equal. Therefore, -3 is the correct boundary point.	Substituting a value greater than -3 results in a true statement. Therefore, the inequality symbol is correct.

Check Your Understanding

Communicate the Ideas

1. Maria and Ryan are discussing the inequality $2x > 10$.

    Maria: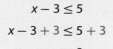
    > The solution to the inequality is 6. When I substitute 6 for x, a true statement results.

    Ryan:
    > I agree that 6 is a solution but it is not the whole solution.

    What does Ryan mean?

2. Explain how the process for verifying a solution is different for a linear inequality than for a linear equation. Discuss your answer with a classmate.

3. What process would you use to solve the inequality $-15x \leq 90$?

4. Represent on a number line
   • the linear equation $6x = 18$
   • the linear inequality $6x \geq 18$
   Compare the solutions. How are they the same? How are they different?

Practise

For help with #5 to #8, refer to Example 1 on pages 352–353.

5. Solve each inequality.

   a) $x - 7 \geq 22$ **b)** $4 < x + 11$

   c) $8.6 + x > -5.2$ **d)** $100 \leq x + 65$

6. Solve each inequality.

   a) $6y \geq 54$ **b)** $29 > -2y$

   c) $3.1y \leq -12.4$ **d)** $-1.6y < -10$

7. Solve each inequality.

   a) $\dfrac{x}{5} > 30$ **b)** $\dfrac{x}{-4} \geq -9$

   c) $2 \geq \dfrac{x}{1.2}$ **d)** $-\dfrac{1}{6}x < 5$

8. Look at the following operations. For each one, does the inequality symbol need to be reversed when the operation is performed on both sides of an inequality? Why or why not?

   a) Subtract 5.

   b) Multiply by 6.

   c) Add -15.

   d) Divide by -3.

   e) Multiply by -19.7.

   f) Divide by 0.3.

For help with #9 to #13, refer to Example 2 on pages 353–354.

9. Verify whether the specific solution is correct for each inequality.

   a) $x - 2.5 \leq 10; x = 12$

   b) $3x \geq 21; x = 8$

   c) $-4x < 20; x = -3$

   d) $-\dfrac{1}{5}x \leq 3; x = -20$

10. Verify whether the specific solution satisfies each inequality.

   a) $y - 10.2 \geq 18; y = 30$

   b) $-6y \leq 36; y = -7$

   c) $\dfrac{-2}{3}y \geq 10; y = 10$

   d) $\dfrac{1}{2}y < 13; y = -2$

11. Show whether $x < 4$ is the solution for each inequality.

   a) $-3x > -12$

   b) $10 + x > 14$

   c) $1 > \dfrac{x}{4}$

   d) $-x > -4$

12. Verify that the solution shown on each number line is correct.

   a) $x + 10 > 14$

   b) $-3.2 < \dfrac{x}{5}$

13. Verify each solution represented graphically.

   a) $-10 \geq x - 1$

   b) $-5x \geq -62$

For help with #14 and #15, refer to Example 3 on page 355.

14. The Super Fencing Company builds cedar fences for homes at a cost of $85 per section of fence, including tax. How many sections of fence could you buy if you could spend no more than $1400?

a) Model the problem using an inequality.

b) Solve the inequality.

c) Is the boundary point a reasonable solution for the number of fence sections? Explain.

15. Megan is competing in a series of mountain bike races this season. She gets 6 points for each race she wins. If she gets more than 50 points in total, she will move up to the next racing category. How many race wins this season will allow her to move up to the next category?

a) Use an inequality to represent the problem.

b) Determine the solution and use it to solve the problem.

c) Is the boundary point a reasonable solution for the number of race wins? Explain.

Apply

16. For each of the following inequalities, state three values that are specific solutions and three values that are non-solutions.

a) $-5 + x < -10$

b) $-3x < 24$

17. Colin's teacher asked him to solve the inequality $-5x \geq -15$. His solution was $x \leq 3$. He explained that he reversed the inequality symbol because of the negative number. Write a more accurate explanation.

18. A local sports complex offers the following options for sharpening skates.

Skate Sharpening Rates
Standard Rate: $5.75 per pair of skates
Special: $49 per month for unlimited sharpening

a) Estimate at what point the special would be the better option. Show the process you used. Why do you think your method provides a reasonable estimate?

b) Model and solve the problem using an inequality. Compare the answer to your estimate.

19. The owner of a craft store donates 3% of her profits to a local charity every month. If she wants to donate at least $250 this month, how much profit will the business need to earn?

a) Model and solve the problem using an inequality.

b) Verify your solution. Show your work.

20. Andrew's family is driving from Winnipeg to Saskatoon. Before leaving, they fill the gas tank with 57 L of fuel. The car uses fuel at an average rate of 8.4 L/100 km for highway driving. How many kilometres can they drive on this amount of fuel? What assumptions did you make?

21. Natalie is entering the 3200-m event at an upcoming meet. Each lap of the track is 400 m. Her goal is to beat the current record of 9 min 23 s. How fast must she run each lap, on average, to beat the record?

a) Explain why the situation can be modelled using the inequality $8x < 563$.

b) Solve the problem and verify your solution. Show your work.

22. Fiona has a rewards card that gives her a reward point for every $5 she spends. If she earns at least 120 points in a year, she gets a bonus. How much does she need to spend to get at least 120 points?

Extend

23. Chris has a weekend business building doghouses. Each doghouse takes 4 h to build and is sold for $115. Chris wants to earn at least $1000 per month. He wants to work no more than 50 h on his business per month.

a) Write two inequalities to model the situation.

b) Solve each inequality.

c) What possible numbers of doghouses can he build each month and stay within his guidelines?

24. Solve and check the inequality $-\frac{2}{5}x < \frac{1}{3}$. Show the solution on a number line.

25. If $-2x > 22$ and $-4x < 60$, determine the possible values of x that satisfy both inequalities. Show your solution on a number line.

26. A food company that is developing a new energy bar has not decided on the size of the bar. The recipe includes 9% protein and 13% fat. The company wants the bar to contain at least 6 g of protein and no more than 10 g of fat. Use two inequalities to determine the possible range of masses for the bar.

27. Consider the inequality $ax \leq 5a$.

a) Solve the inequality if $a > 0$.

b) Solve the inequality if $a < 0$.

28. Solve each combination of inequalities.

a) $-5 \leq x + 9$ and $x + 9 \leq 8$

b) $-2 < 2x$ and $2x < 12$

c) $-15 \leq -6x$ and $-6x < 9$

Math Link

Some amusement parks offer single-ride tickets, where you pay each time you ride, and all-day passes, where you pay once for unlimited rides. The prices for both types of tickets need to be high enough for the amusement park to earn a profit but low enough that people decide to come.

Search various media, such as newspapers, magazines, and the Internet. Look for information about ticket prices at amusement parks.

a) Choose a price for single-ride tickets and a price for all-day passes. Explain why your choices are reasonable.

b) Use an inequality to determine the number of rides that make one option a better deal than the other.

c) Your friends plan on going on seven rides in your amusement park. Which is the better option for them? Show your work.

Solving Multi-Step Inequalities

Bryan's grandmother gave him $60 to spend at the go-cart track. Each lap at the track costs $3.50. How many laps can he buy if he wants to have at least $20 left over to buy lunch for himself and his grandmother?

Describe different strategies you could use to solve this problem.

Explore Multi-Step Inequalities

1. a) Estimate the number of laps Bryan can buy.

   b) How can your strategy help you set up and solve an inequality?

2. Develop an inequality that can be used to determine the number of laps Bryan can buy.

3. a) Outline a strategy for solving your inequality.

   b) Use your strategy to determine the solution. Show your steps.

   c) How can you use the solution to solve the problem?

Reflect and Check

4. a) Is the solution to the problem a single value? Or is it a set of several possible values? Explain.

   b) What words in the problem indicate that you could model it using an inequality? Explain.

5. a) Compare the strategy you used to solve the multi-step inequalities with that of a classmate. Which strategy do you prefer? Explain.

   b) How did your knowledge of solving linear equations help you solve these inequalities?

Link the Ideas

Example 1: Solve Multi-Step Inequalities

a) Solve $\frac{x}{4} + 3 > 8$. Show your solution algebraically and graphically.

Verify the solution.

b) Solve $-3x - 10 \le 5x + 38$, and verify the solution.

c) Solve $-2(x + 3) \le 10x + 18$, and verify the solution.

Solution

a) Use the same process to solve a multi-step inequality as for solving a linear equation.

$$\frac{x}{4} + 3 > 8$$

$$\frac{x}{4} + 3 - 3 > 8 - 3$$

$$\frac{x}{4} > 5$$

$$\frac{x}{4} \times 4 > 5 \times 4$$

$$x > 20$$

> What steps would you follow to isolate the variable?

The number line shows the solution.

Verify the solution:
Substitute the boundary point 20 to check that both sides are equal.

$$\frac{x}{4} + 3 = 8$$

$$\frac{20}{4} + 3 = 8$$

$$5 + 3 = 8$$

$$8 = 8$$

Substitute a value greater than 20. If a true statement results, then the inequality symbol is correct.

$$\frac{x}{4} + 3 > 8$$

$$\frac{24}{4} + 3 > 8$$

$$6 + 3 > 8$$

$$9 > 8$$

Since both statements are true, the solution $x > 20$ is correct.

b) Isolate the variable.

Isolate the Variable on the Left Side

$$-3x - 10 \leq 5x + 38$$
$$-3x - 10 + 10 \leq 5x + 38 + 10$$
$$-3x \leq 5x + 48$$
$$-3x - 5x \leq 5x + 48 - 5x$$
$$-8x \leq 48$$
$$\frac{-8x}{-8} \geq \frac{48}{-8}$$
$$x \geq -6$$

Isolate the Variable on the Right Side

$$-3x + 3x - 10 \leq 5x + 38 + 3x$$
$$-10 \leq 8x + 38$$
$$-10 - 38 \leq 8x + 38 - 38$$
$$-48 \leq 8x$$
$$\frac{-48}{8} \leq \frac{8x}{8}$$
$$-6 \leq x$$

Verify the solution:

Substitute the boundary point -6 to check that both sides are equal.
$$-3x - 10 = 5x + 38$$
$$-3(-6) - 10 = 5(-6) + 38$$
$$18 - 10 = -30 + 38$$
$$8 = 8$$

Substitute a value greater than -6. If a true statement results, then the inequality symbol is correct.
$$-3x - 10 \leq 5x + 38$$
$$-3(0) - 10 \leq 5(0) + 38$$
$$0 - 10 \leq 0 + 38$$
$$-10 \leq 38$$

Since both statements are true, the solution $x \geq -6$ is correct.

c) *Method 1: Use the Distributive Property*
$$-2(x + 3) \leq 10x + 18$$
$$-2x - 6 \leq 10x + 18$$
$$-2x - 6 - 10x \leq 10x + 18 - 10x$$
$$-12x - 6 \leq 18$$
$$-12x - 6 + 6 \leq 18 + 6$$
$$-12x \leq 24$$
$$\frac{-12x}{-12} \geq \frac{24}{-12}$$
$$x \geq -2$$

Method 2: Divide First
You can divide first by -2.
$$-2(x + 3) \leq 10x + 18$$
$$\frac{-2(x + 3)}{-2} \geq \frac{10x + 18}{-2}$$
$$x + 3 \geq -5x - 9$$
$$x + 5x + 3 \geq -5x - 9 + 5x$$
$$6x + 3 \geq -9$$
$$6x + 3 - 3 \geq -9 - 3$$
$$6x \geq -12$$
$$\frac{6x}{6} \geq \frac{-12}{6}$$
$$x \geq -2$$

Verify the solution:
Substitute the boundary point −2.
$$-2(x + 3) = 10x + 18$$
$$-2((-2) + 3) = 10(-2) + 18$$
$$-2(1) = -20 + 18$$
$$-2 = -2$$

Substitute a value greater than −2, such as 0.
$$-2(x + 3) \leq 10x + 18$$
$$-2(0 + 3) \leq 10(0) + 18$$
$$-2(3) \leq 0 + 18$$
$$-6 \leq 18$$

> Choose numbers you find easy to work with.

Since both statements are true, the solution $x \geq -2$ is correct.

WWW Web Link

To practise solving inequalities using multiplication and division, go to www.mathlinks9.ca and follow the links.

Show You Know

Solve each inequality and verify the solution.
a) $4x + 11 > 35$ b) $5 - 2x > 10x + 29$ c) $4(x - 2) \geq 5x - 12$

Example 2: Solve a Problem Using Inequalities

Sarah has offers for a position as a salesperson at two local electronics stores. Store A will pay a flat rate of $55 per day plus 3% of sales. Store B will pay a flat rate of $40 per day plus 5% of sales. What do Sarah's sales need to be for store B to be the better offer?
a) Write an inequality to model the problem.
b) Solve the inequality and interpret the solution.

> **Did You Know?**
>
> Sales people often work on *commission*, which is a form of payment based on the amount of their sales.

Solution

a) Let s represent the value of Sarah's sales for a particular day.
   Determine s when the pay for store B is greater than the pay for store A.
   Pay for store B > Pay for store A
   $$40 + 5\% \text{ of sales} > 55 + 3\% \text{ of sales}$$
   $$40 + 0.05s > 55 + 0.03s$$

> What do 0.03 and 0.05 represent in the inequality?

b)
$$40 + 0.05s > 55 + 0.03s$$
$$40 + 0.05s - 40 > 55 + 0.03s - 40$$
$$0.05s > 15 + 0.03s$$
$$0.05s - 0.03s > 15 + 0.03s - 0.03s$$
$$0.02s > 15$$
$$\frac{0.02s}{0.02} > \frac{15}{0.02}$$
$$s > 750$$

Sarah's pay will be higher at store B when her sales are greater than $750. If she thinks that her sales will be more than $750 on most days, then store B is the better offer.

Show You Know

Danny started his own computer repair business. He offers his customers two payment options. Option A has a base fee of $40 plus $8 per hour. Option B has no base fee but costs $15 per hour. How many hours does a repair job have to take in order for option B to be less expensive?

a) Model the problem using an inequality.

b) After how many hours will option B be less expensive?

Key Ideas

- To solve a multi-step inequality, isolate the variable.
$$-3(x - 5) \leq 3x + 9$$
$$-3x + 15 \leq 3x + 9$$
$$-3x + 15 - 3x \leq 3x + 9 - 3x$$
$$-6x + 15 \leq 9$$
$$-6x + 15 - 15 \leq 9 - 15$$
$$-6x \leq -6$$
$$\frac{-6x}{-6} \geq \frac{-6}{-6}$$
$$x \geq 1$$

> Remember to reverse the inequality symbol, when multiplying or dividing by a negative number.

- Problems that involve comparing different options can often be modelled and solved using inequalities.

Check Your Understanding

Communicate the Ideas

1. Describe the similarities and differences between the process for solving a multi-step linear equation and a multi-step linear inequality. Discuss your answer with a classmate.

2. Consider the inequality $3x + 10 > 5x + 22$. Lindsay started to solve the inequality by subtracting $5x$ from both sides. Victoria told her to start by subtracting $3x$ from both sides.

   a) Use Lindsay's approach to solve the inequality.

   b) Use Victoria's approach to solve the inequality.

   c) Are the solutions the same? Explain.

   d) Explain why you think Victoria gave her advice. Is her reasoning helpful in solving the inequality? Explain.

   e) Which method of solving the inequality do you prefer? Explain why.

Practise

For help with #3 to #7, refer to Example 1 on pages 361–363.

3. Solve each inequality and verify the solution.

   a) $5x - 19 < 36$

   b) $27 + 2x > -13$

   c) $3 \leq \frac{x}{5} - 7$

4. Determine the solution of each inequality.

   a) $-5y + 92 \geq 40$

   b) $2.2 > 10.6 + 4y$

   c) $\frac{y}{-6} - 2 < 16$

   d) $\frac{3}{2}x + 6 \leq 10\frac{4}{5}$

5. a) Verify that $x \geq 8$ is the correct solution to the inequality $3x + 11 \geq 35$.

   b) Verify that $x < -3$ is the correct solution to the inequality $24 - 5x > 39$.

6. Solve each inequality and verify the solution.

   a) $7x < 2x + 30$

   b) $10x - 22 \geq 8x$

   c) $-12x + 10 > 19 - 4x$

   d) $\frac{1}{2}(x + 5) > 22$

7. Determine each solution.

   a) $-2y > 8y - 20$

   b) $9y - 17 \leq 8 + 6.5y$

   c) $3.4 - 1.3y < 0.5y - 2.2$

   d) $\frac{3}{4}y - 1 \geq -\frac{1}{4}(1 - 2y)$

For help with #8 and #9, refer to Example 2 on pages 363–364.

8. For each situation
   - choose a variable and explain what it represents
   - write an inequality

   a) A basketball team wants to buy new jerseys. Uniforms R Us charges $50 per jersey. Jerseys Unlimited charges $40 per jersey plus $80 for a logo design. How many jerseys does the team need to buy for Jerseys Unlimited to be the better option?

   b) Ann uses her cell phone to send text messages. The monthly charge for text messaging is currently $15 plus $0.05 per message sent. The company is offering a new plan that costs a flat rate of $0.12 per text message. How many text messages does Ann need to send in order for the new plan to be the better option?

9. John is considering two paper delivery jobs. The *Advance* will pay $10 plus $0.05 for each paper delivered daily, and the *Times* will pay $15 plus $0.04 for each paper delivered daily. How many papers delivered each day would make the *Advance* the better offer?

a) Write an inequality to model the problem.

b) Solve the inequality and interpret the solution.

@ **Web Link**

To learn how to solve inequalities using a graphing calculator, go to www.mathlinks9.ca and follow the links.

Apply

10. Kim is comparing the rates at two car rental companies for a one-day rental. She wants to determine how many kilometres she would need to drive for ABC Rentals to be the better rental option.

> **ABC Rentals**
> $25 per day plus $0.14 per kilometre

> **It's a Deal Rentals**
> $55 per day

a) Estimate the number of kilometres that would make ABC Rentals the better option.

b) Represent the situation using an inequality.

c) Solve the inequality and interpret the solution.

d) Compare the solution with your estimate.

11. Kevin is comparing job offers at two stores. Dollar Deal offers $8/h plus 10% commission. Great Discounts offers $18/h with no commission. What do Kevin's weekly sales need to be in order for Dollar Deal to pay more? Assume that he works an 8-h day five days per week.

12. The student council is considering two different companies to print the school's yearbooks. Great Graphics charges $250 plus $12.25 per book. Print Express charges $900 plus $9.50 per book. How many orders for yearbooks would make Print Express the better option?

13. Greenway Golf Course offers two plans for paying for buckets of balls at the driving range. How many buckets of balls used per month make the members' plan the better deal?

Greenway Golf Course Rates
Standard Plan: $6 per bucket
Member's Plan: $98 monthly fee plus $1.50 per bucket

14. Molly has a business making candles. Her business costs are $200 plus $0.70 per candle made. She charges her customers $3.50 for each candle. If she sells all of the candles she makes, how many candles sold would allow her to make a profit?

15. Two full water storage tanks are being drained for maintenance. The first tank holds 800 L of water and drains at a rate of 18 L/min. The second tank holds 500 L of water and drains at a rate of 7 L/min. Use an inequality to determine when the first tank will contain less water than the second tank.

16. Rob and Ashley are riding their bicycles uphill. Currently, Rob is 5.7 km from the top and climbing at 0.24 km/min. Ashley is 4.5 km from the top and riding at 0.17 km/min.

   a) Estimate when Rob will be closer to the top than Ashley.

   b) Use an inequality to determine when Rob will be closer to the top than Ashley.

Extend

17. Solve $\frac{2}{3}(2x - 5) < \frac{1}{2}(x + 2)$.

Show the solution on a number line.

18. If $2x + 5 > 10$ and $5x - 4 < 20$, determine the possible values of x. Show your solution on a number line.

19. Lauren charges $12 to cut lawns for neighbours. It takes her 25 min to cut each lawn and 40 min per month to maintain her lawn mower. She wants to earn $400 each month without working more than 16 h cutting lawns. How many lawns can Lauren cut in a month and stay within her guidelines? Use two inequalities to determine the range for the number of lawns that she can cut.

20. Ella's teacher asked which is greater, x or $-x$? Ella said that x is always greater than $-x$.

   a) Write an inequality to represent Ella's response and solve it. When, if ever, is Ella correct?

   b) Ella's teacher explained that her response is correct for some values of x only. For what values of x is Ella incorrect? Give one specific solution where Ella is correct and one where she is incorrect.

21. Solve $-13 \leq 5 - 2x$ and $5 - 2x \leq 9$.

22. Given that $b < 0$, solve the inequality $3 > bx + 3$.

Math Link

An amusement park manager needs to ensure that the park is profitable. For the park to make a profit, the total revenue needs to be more than the total expenses.

There are fixed expenses and revenues that remain the same. There are also variable expenses and revenues that depend on the number of visitors.

The manager estimates operating expenses and revenues for the park per visitor. These are shown in the table. Assuming the park offers ten rides, fill in the missing information.

a) What is the total of the variable expenses per visitor? What are the total fixed costs? Write an expression to represent the total expenses.

b) What is the total of the variable revenues per visitor? What are the total fixed revenues? Write an expression to represent the total revenues.

c) Develop and solve an inequality to determine the number of visitors needed per day to make a profit. Justify your solution mathematically.

Daily Expenses	
Total variable operating costs per visitor	$15
Total fixed costs ($5000 + $1200 per ride)	
Daily Revenues	
Admission (includes ride pass) per visitor	$38
Food per visitor	$25
Souvenirs per visitor	$10
Parking per visitor	$10
Total variable revenues per visitor	
Fixed revenue from sponsorship	$2500

Chapter 9 Review

Key Words

For #1 to #6, write the term from the list that completes each statement.

algebraically   boundary point
closed circle   graphically
inequality   open circle
solution

1. A mathematical statement comparing expressions that may not be equivalent is called an ▮▮▮ .

2. Inequalities can be represented ▮▮▮ on a number line or ▮▮▮ using symbols.

3. On a number line, a(n) ▮▮▮ ▮▮▮ indicates that the boundary point is not a possible solution.

4. For the inequality $x > 5$, the value of 7 is a specific ▮▮▮ .

5. On a number line, the value that separates solutions from non-solutions is called the ▮▮▮ ▮▮▮ .

6. On a number line, a(n) ▮▮▮ ▮▮▮ indicates that the boundary point is a possible solution.

9.1 Representing Inequalities, pages 340–349

7. An Internet business is preparing a flyer to advertise a sale. Express each statement as an inequality.

   a) Savings of up to 40%!

   b) Free shipping for purchases of $500 or more!

   c) Over 80 major items on sale!

8. Road racers use bicycles that are designed to go as fast as possible. Cycling organizations place restrictions on bicycle design to ensure fairness and rider safety. Express each restriction as an inequality.

   a) The minimum allowable road racing bicycle mass is 6.8 kg.

   b) A road racing bicycle can be no more than 185 cm in length.

9. Verbally and algebraically express the inequality represented on each number line.

   a)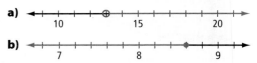

   b)

10. Sketch a number line to represent each inequality.

   a) $r > -4$ b) $s \leq 7$

   c) $9.5 > t$ d) $v \leq -\dfrac{5}{4}$

11. For each inequality in #10, state one value that is a solution and one value that is a non-solution.

9.2 Solving Single-Step Inequalities, pages 350–359

12. Solve each inequality.

   a) $d - 7 > -10$ b) $2.7 < a - 2.7$

   c) $-11 \geq \dfrac{b}{3}$ d) $-\dfrac{1}{5}c > 3.2$

13. Verify that the solution shown on each number line is correct. If a number line is incorrect, explain why.

a) $-5x \geq -40$

b) $-10 > 4x$

14. Tim earns $14.50/h working for his parents' business during the summer. His goal is to earn at least $600 each week. How many hours will Tim need to work each week to achieve his goal?

a) Write an inequality to model the problem.

b) Solve the inequality and interpret the solution.

15. Danielle is treating her friends to ice cream. Each scoop of ice cream costs $2.25. She wants to spend less than $30. How many scoops of ice cream can she buy and stay within her limit?

9.3 Solving Multi-Step Inequalities, pages 360–367

16. Verify whether the number line shows the correct solution for $11 - 3x > 17$. If the number line is incorrect, explain why.

17. a) Verify whether $x \geq 5$ is the correct solution for $5x + 4 \leq 6x - 1$.

b) Describe a second method to verify the solution.

18. Solve each inequality and verify the solution.

a) $\frac{x}{3} - 5 < 10$

b) $9x + 30 > 13x$

c) $3x \leq 8x + 5$

d) $5x + 8 < 4x - 12$

e) $17 - 3x \leq 7x + 3$

f) $2(3x + 4) > 5(6x + 7)$

19. A student committee is planning a sports banquet. The cost of the dinner is $450 plus $24 per person. The committee needs to keep the total costs for the dinner under $2000. How many people can attend the banquet?

20. Greg is considering two different plans for music downloads. How many tracks purchased would make plan A the better option?

Plan A

$0.97 per track purchased plus $10.00/month unlimited PC streaming plus $15.00/month for downloading songs to an MP3 player

Plan B

$0.99 per track purchased plus $9.00/month unlimited PC streaming plus $144.00/year for downloading songs to an MP3 player

Chapter 9 Practice Test

For #1 to #5, select the best answer.

1. Karen told her mother that she would be out for no more than 4 h. If t represents the time in hours, which inequality represents this situation?

A $t < 4$ **B** $t \leq 4$

C $t > 4$ **D** $t \geq 4$

2. Which inequality does the number line represent?

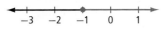

A $x < -1$ **B** $x \leq -1$

C $x > -1$ **D** $x \geq -1$

3. Which number is not a specific solution for the inequality $y - 2 \geq -4$?

A -6 **B** -2

C 2 **D** 6

4. Solve: $5 - x < 2$

A $x < 3$ **B** $x > 3$

C $x < 7$ **D** $x > 7$

5. What is the solution of $5(x - 3) \leq 2x + 3$?

A $x \leq -6$ **B** $x \geq -6$

C $x \leq 6$ **D** $x \geq 6$

Complete the statements in #6 and #7.

6. The number line representing the inequality $x < 5$ would have a(n) ▰▰▰ circle at 5 and an arrow pointing to the ▰▰▰ .

7. The solution to $-4x < 16$ is x ▰ than ▰ .

Short Answer

8. Represent each inequality on a number line.

a) $-3 < x$

b) $x \leq 6.8$

9. Verify whether $x > -3$ is the correct solution to the inequality $8 - 5x < 23$. Show your thinking. If the solution is incorrect, explain why.

10. Christine is researching a career as an airline pilot. One airline includes the following criteria for pilots. Express each of the criteria algebraically as an inequality.

a) Pilots must be shorter than 185 cm.

b) Pilots must be at least 21 years old.

11. Solve and graph each inequality.

a) $-6 + x \geq 10$

b) $2.4x - 11 > 4.6$

c) $12 - 8x < 17 - 6x$

12. Represent each situation algebraically as an inequality.

a) Luke earns \$4.75 per item sold and must earn over \$50.

b) It takes Nicole 3 h to sew beads on a pair of mitts. She has no more than 40 h of time to sew beads on all the mitts she plans to give to her relatives as presents.

Extended Response

13. Consider the inequality $6x - 4 > 9x + 20$.

   a) Solve the inequality algebraically.

   b) Represent the solution graphically.

   c) Give one value that is a specific solution and one that is a non-solution.

   d) To solve the inequality, Min first subtracted $6x$ from both sides. Alan first subtracted $9x$ from both sides. Which method do you prefer? Explain why.

14. The Lightning Soccer Club plans to buy shirts for team members and supporters. Pro-V Graphics charges a $75 set-up fee plus $7 per shirt. BT Designs has no set-up fee but charges $10.50 per shirt. How many shirts does the team need to order for Pro-V Graphics to be the better option?

15. Dylan is organizing a curling tournament. The sports complex charges $115/h for the ice rental. Dylan has booked it for 6 h. He will charge each of the 14 teams in the tournament an entrance fee. How much must he charge each team in order to make a profit?

Math Link: Wrap It Up!

You are an amusement park manager who has been offered a job planning a new park in a different location.

a) Give your park a name and choose a location. Explain how you made your choice. State the population of the area around the park that you chose.

b) Choose a reasonable number of rides for your park. Assume that the fixed costs include $5000 in addition to maintenance and wages. Assume maintenance and repairs cost $400 per ride and that it takes eight employees to operate and supervise each ride. Conduct research and then decide:
  • the number of hours that rides will be open
  • the average hourly wage for employees

> What might be the problem if you choose too few or too many rides?

c) Organize your estimates about operating expenses and revenues for the park. You can use the table in the Math Link on page 367 as a reference.

d) Write an expression to represent each of the following for the number of rides you chose:
  • expenses per visitor
  • revenue per visitor

e) For the number of rides you chose, how many visitors will be needed for the park to make a profit? Show all your work. Justify your solution mathematically.

f) Assume that you have now opened your park. You find that 0.1% of the people in the area come to the park per day, on average. Using this information, will your park earn a profit? If not, explain what changes you could make. Show all your work and justify your solution.

Challenges

Not for Profit

Your school has created a fundraising committee to raise money for charity. You are the committee manager. Use your knowledge of writing and solving inequalities to help make pricing decisions for items that will be sold to raise money.

1. You have decided to sell T-shirts and posters.

   a) The cost to make each T-shirt is $10. You estimate that you will sell 50 shirts. If you want to make a profit of at least $250, what price will you charge for these T-shirts? Show your solution in two different ways.

   b) A printing company will print posters for 40% of the profits you make from the sale of them. The printing company will provide 150 posters. If you sell them all, what should you sell the posters for to make a profit of at least $75? Write and solve an inequality to determine possible selling prices. Explain why your price is reasonable.

2. Choose a different profit goal for either the T-shirt or the poster. Determine a price structure that will allow you to achieve your new profit. Write and solve an inequality to determine your new prices.

The Inequalities Game

Materials
- deck of playing cards (face cards and jokers removed)
- set of four game boards per student pair

1. Play the Inequalities Game with a partner. These are the rules:
   - Each player draws one card from the card deck. The player with the higher card chooses whether to be Player 1 or 2.
     - Player 1's solution target is all positive integers.
     - Player 2's solution target is all negative integers.
   - Player 1 shuffles and deals ten cards to each player face down. Players can look at their own cards. The remaining cards are kept in a pile face down called the mystery pile.
     - Red cards are positive numbers and black cards are negative numbers.
     - Use Game Board A or B the first time you play the game.
   - For each turn, players choose one of their own cards to cover a card space on the game board.
     - For each hand, take turns playing first. Start with Player 2.
   - When both spaces on the game board are covered, mentally solve the inequality. If the solution to the inequality contains
     - only positive integers, Player 1 wins the hand
     - only negative integers, Player 2 wins the hand
     - some positive and some negative integers, neither player wins the hand
   - When you win a hand, take the cards from the game board and keep them in your scoring pile.
   - The player with the most cards in the scoring pile after ten hands is the winner. If there is a tie, play more hands by randomly placing the top two cards in the mystery pile on the game board until one player wins a hand.

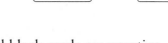

$x >$

> $-2x > 5$
> For the solution, x must be a negative integer. The solution consists of negative integers only.

> The solution is x > 5.
> I win the hand.

> The solution is x < −4.
> I win the hand.

> The solution is x > −2 or x < 3. Neither player wins the hand.

2. Play the game again using the other Game Board (A or B).

3. Play the game again using Game Board C or D. These game boards have space for three cards. Each player covers a space on the game board as in #1, and then the third space is covered using the top card from the mystery pile.

4. Create your own game board and use it to play the game. Is the game board you developed fair for each player or does one player have an advantage? Explain.

10

Circle Geometry

The pathways of the model airplane and the satellite shown are both circular. There are forces that are acting on these two objects to keep them in their circular orbits. What would happen to these objects if these forces were instantly removed? What direction would the airplane and the satellite move in relation to the circles?

In this chapter, you will explore some properties of circles and use them to solve a variety of problems.

What You Will Learn

- to apply properties of circles to determine the measures of unknown angles and line segments
- to solve problems involving properties of circles

⬤⬤ History Link

Euclid was a Greek mathematician who lived around 300 B.C. He is considered the "father of geometry." In his book *Elements* he clearly presented the fundamental principles of geometry and provided logical proofs of these principles. *Elements* was one of the first books to be published after the invention of the printing press in the fifteenth century. It is considered the oldest textbook. For more information about Euclid, go to www.mathlinks9.ca and follow the links.

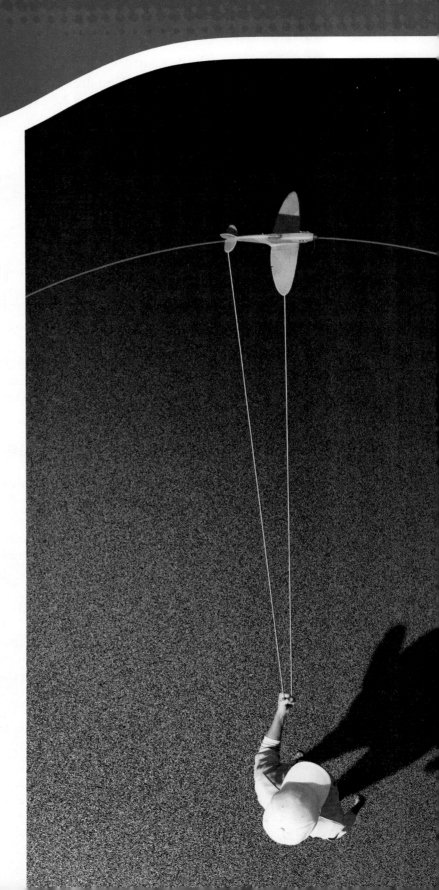

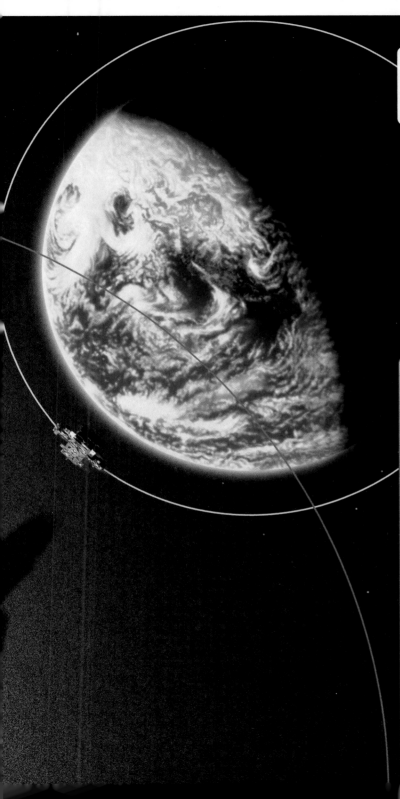

Key Words

chord	arc
central angle	perpendicular bisector
inscribed angle	tangent

⬤⬤ Literacy Link

A web can help you create connections among ideas. It helps you understand how new ideas are related.

Create a web in your math journal or notebook. As you work through the chapter, complete the web by defining each term.

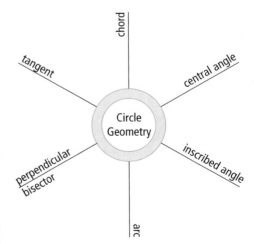

After you complete the web, use a compass to draw a large circle below the web. On your circle, draw the parts of the circle that you defined in the web. Beside the web, add a legend. Use a colour code to identify each different part of the circle.

Making the Foldable

Materials
- sheet of 11 × 17 paper
- compass
- six sheets of 8.5 × 11 paper
- scissors
- stapler
- ruler

Step 1

Fold the long side of a sheet of 11 × 17 paper in half. Pinch it at the midpoint. Fold the outer edges of the paper to meet at the midpoint. Use a compass to draw a circle and label it as shown. Add the chapter title.

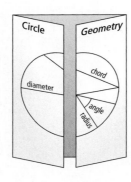

Step 2

Fold the short side of a sheet of 8.5 × 11 paper in half. Fold in three the opposite way. Make two cuts as shown through one thickness of paper, forming three tabs. Label the tabs as shown.

Step 3

Fold the short side of a sheet of 8.5 × 11 paper in half. Fold in three the opposite way. Make two cuts as shown through one thickness of paper, forming three tabs. Label the tabs as shown.

Step 4

Stack four sheets of 8.5 × 11 paper and staple at the four corners. Use a compass to draw a circle with a radius of 7.5 cm on the top sheet. Cut around the circle through all four thicknesses of paper. Fold the four circles in half. Title every second page of the booklet with a section title. The first page is shown.

Step 5

Staple the booklets from Steps 2 and 3 into the Foldable from Step 1. Staple the booklet from Step 4 along the fold line into the Foldable.

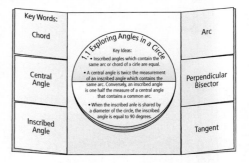

Using the Foldable

As you work through the chapter, write definitions of the Key Words beneath the tabs on the left and the right. In the centre booklet, there are two pages for each chapter section. Record the Key Ideas on the first page, and examples on the second page. There is one extra circle at the end for additional notes.

On the back of the centre panel of the Foldable, make notes under the heading What I Need to Work On. Check off each item as you deal with it.

Math Link

Geometry in Design

Architects, engineers, graphic designers, and many artists rely on their understanding of geometric principles in their work.

For Aboriginal people, the circle is a very important shape. The medicine wheel, where spiritual teachings occurred, was frequently framed in a circle using large rocks.

Work with a partner to complete the activity and questions.

1. On tracing paper, construct a circle that has a diameter of at least 5 cm.

2. a) Fold the paper so that the circle is folded exactly in half. Then, reopen the tracing paper. Along the fold, draw a line segment that has both endpoints on the circle.
   b) What is the mathematical term for this line segment?

3. a) Fold the circle in half again, making a different crease. Draw a line segment along this crease.
   b) What is the mathematical term for the intersection of the two line segments created?

4. a) Estimate the measure of each of the four angles you created.
   b) Measure the four angles with a protractor. How did your estimates compare?
   c) What is the sum of the four central angles?

5. An environmental club is considering using the logo shown. What kind of triangle is used in the diagram? Explain your reasoning. How could you create this logo?

6. Experiment with drawing different regular polygons (with six or fewer sides), outside or inside a circle, so that each side or vertex of the polygon touches the circle. What difficulties did you have?

7. Brainstorm some businesses that have circles in their advertisements.

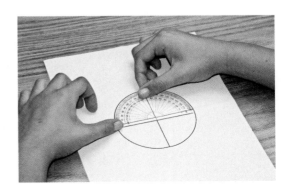

In this chapter, you will design a two-dimensional blueprint for a piece of art, a logo, or an advertisement. You will learn some geometric properties that can assist you with creating designs involving circles.

10.1

Exploring Angles in a Circle

Focus on...

After this lesson, you will be able to...

- describe a relationship between inscribed angles in a circle
- relate the inscribed angle and central angle subtended by the same arc

Maddy, Jennifer, and Nia are each about to shoot at the empty net. If they are each equally accurate with their shot, who do you think is most likely to score?

Materials

- compass or circular geoboard with elastic bands
- protractor
- ruler

---

chord

- a line segment with both endpoints on a circle

---

central angle

- an angle formed by two radii of a circle

---

inscribed angle

- an angle formed by two chords that share a common endpoint

---

arc (of a circle)

- a portion of the circumference

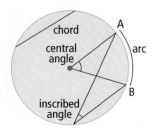

Explore Relationships Between Angles in a Circle

1. Construct a large circle and label its centre C. Construct a **chord** AB and a **central angle** ∠BCA. Measure ∠BCA.

2. Create the **inscribed angle** ∠BDA. What is the measure of ∠BDA?

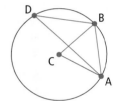

3. How do the measures of ∠BCA and ∠BDA compare?

4. Create a second inscribed angle ∠BEA. What is the measure of ∠BEA?

5. Choose another point on the circle between D and E. Create one more inscribed angle that has its arms touching the endpoints of the **arc** AB. What is the measure of this inscribed angle?

6. Repeat steps 1 to 5 for a different sized circle, and a different sized chord AB.

Reflect and Check

7. **a)** What is the relationship between a central angle and an inscribed angle that stands on the same arc?

   b) What is the relationship between all the inscribed angles that stand on the same arc?

8. Predict which hockey player in the opening paragraph is most likely to score on the empty net. Explain.

Link the Ideas

You can use properties related to angles in a circle to solve problems.

Inscribed Angles
The inscribed angles *subtended* by the same arc are congruent.

Central and Inscribed Angles
The measure of the central angle is equal to twice the measure of the inscribed angle subtended by the same arc.

Example 1: Determine Angle Measures in a Circle

Point C is the centre of the circle. ∠AEB = 35°

a) What is the measure of ∠ADB?
Justify your answer.

b) What is the measure of ∠ACB?
Justify your answer.

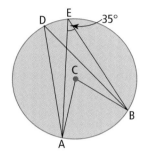

Literacy Link

An angle that *subtends* an arc or a chord is an angle that "stands on" or is formed by the endpoints of the arc or chord.

Solution

a) The inscribed angles, ∠ADB and ∠AEB, are equal because they are subtended by the same arc, AB.

Therefore, ∠ADB = 35°.

b) The central angle ∠ACB is subtended by the same arc AB as the inscribed angle ∠AEB. A central angle is twice the measure of an inscribed angle that is subtended by the same arc.
∠ACB = 2∠AEB
= 2 × 35°
= 70°

Therefore, ∠ACB = 70°.

WWW Web Link

You may wish to explore these geometric properties on a geoboard or on a computer. Go to www. mathlinks9.ca and follow the links.

Show You Know

Point C is the centre of the circle. ∠DAB = 55°.
What are the measures of angles ∠DEB and ∠DCB?
Justify your answers.

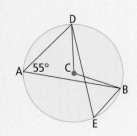

Example 2: Use Central and Inscribed Angles to Recognize Relationships

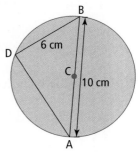

Point C is the centre of the circle.
diameter AB = 10 cm
chord BD = 6 cm

a) What is the measure of ∠ADB?
Explain your reasoning.
b) What is the length of the chord AD?
Justify your answer.

Solution

a) The diameter AB divides the circle into two semicircles. Since AB is a straight line, the central angle ∠ACB is 180°. Then, ∠ADB must be half of 180° because it is an inscribed angle that is subtended by the same arc, AB. The measure of ∠ADB is 90°.

b) Since ∠ADB = 90°, △ABD is a right triangle.
The Pythagorean relationship can be used to find the length of AD.
$$AD^2 + BD^2 = AB^2$$
$$AD^2 + 6^2 = 10^2$$
$$AD^2 + 36 = 100$$
$$AD^2 = 64$$
$$AD = \sqrt{64}$$
$$AD = 8$$

Therefore, AD = 8 cm.

Show You Know

Point C is the centre of the circle. AB is the diameter.
chord AD = 12 cm
chord BD = 5 cm
a) What is the measure of ∠ADB? Explain your reasoning.
b) What is the length of the diameter AB?

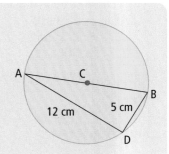

Example 3: Use Central and Inscribed Angles to Solve Problems

Jamie works for a realtor. One of his jobs is to photograph houses that are for sale. He photographed a house two months ago using a camera lens that has a 70° field of view. He has returned to the house to update the photo, but he has forgotten his original lens. Today he only has a telephoto lens with a 35° field of view.

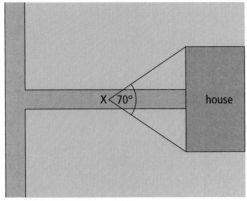

From what location(s) could Jamie photograph the house, with the telephoto lens, so that the entire house still fills the width of the picture. Explain your choices.

Solution

Draw a circle with the centre located at the vertex of the 70° angle. Use one arm of the angle as the radius of the circle. Construct any number of different inscribed angles that each contains the front of the house. Any of these points are locations from which Jamie could take the photo. The measure of each of these inscribed angles will be half the measure of the central angle.

Strategies

Draw a Diagram

Identify all Possibilities

$70° \div 2 = 35°$

Each inscribed angle will measure 35°, which corresponds to the field of view for Jamie's telephoto lens. Depending on access, and whether there are any trees or a garden in the way, any point on the major arc that is outside of the house will work.

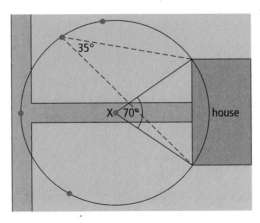

⚭ Literacy Link

A *major arc* is more than a semicircle. A *minor arc* is less than a semicircle.

Show You Know

A flashlight has a field of view measuring 25°, and a camera has a field of view measuring 50°. How can you position the camera and flashlight so that the camera will capture the same area as the flashlight illuminates?

Key Ideas

- Inscribed angles subtended by the same arc of a circle are equal. ∠DEB = ∠DAB
- A central angle is twice the measure of an inscribed angle subtended by the same arc. ∠DCB = 2∠DAB
- An inscribed angle is one half the measure of a central angle subtended by the same arc. ∠DAB = $\frac{1}{2}$∠DCB
- When the inscribed angle is subtended by a diameter of the circle, the inscribed angle is equal to 90°.

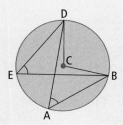

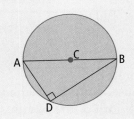

Check Your Understanding

Communicate the Ideas

1. In the diagram, ∠BDA measures half of ∠BCA. Does the rule for inscribed angles hold true for ∠BEA? Explain your reasoning.

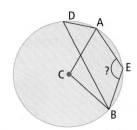

2. Manny constructed a circle using a compass. He used a straight edge to draw a diameter. Then, he constructed an inscribed angle that shared endpoints with the diameter. What is the measure of the inscribed angle he constructed? How do you know?

Practise

For help with #3 to #5, refer to Example 1 on page 379.

3. What are the measures of ∠ADB and ∠AEB? Justify your answers.

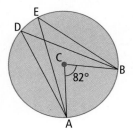

4. a) What is the measure of ∠FJG? Explain your reasoning.

   b) What is the measure of ∠FCG? Justify your answer.

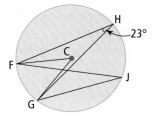

5. Draw a circle with a central angle that measures 60°. Draw and label the measure of two inscribed angles that are subtended by the same arc as the central angle.

For help with #6 and #7, refer to Example 2 on page 380.

6. Point C is the centre of the circle.
diameter AD = 17 cm
chord BD = 15 cm

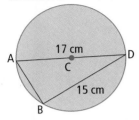

a) What is the measure of ∠ABD? Explain.

b) What is the length of the chord AB?

7. The circle has centre C and a radius of 8 cm.
∠FEG = 45°.

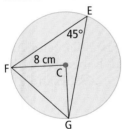

a) What is the measure of ∠FCG?

b) What is the length of the chord FG? Express your answer to the nearest tenth of a centimetre.

For help with #8 and #9, refer to Example 3 on page 381.

8. After a power outage, Jacob helps his mother by shining a flashlight beam at the breaker panel while she locates the tripped breakers. His flashlight projects light through an angle of 15°, while his mother's flashlight projects light through an angle of 30°. Use a diagram to show a good place for Jacob to stand so that his flashlight will illuminate the same area of the breaker panel as his mother's flashlight does.

9. For a high school drama production, three spotlights are positioned on an arc at the back of the theatre, just above the audience. Each spotlight projects light through an angle of 22° and fills the rectangular front of the stage. Use a diagram to identify an ideal location to take a photo of the performance using a camera with a lens that has a field of view of 44°.

Apply

10. In the diagram, C is the centre of the circle and ∠ABD = 38°. For each of the following questions, justify your answer.

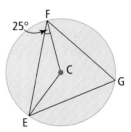

a) What is the measure of ∠ACD?

b) What type of triangle is △ACD?

c) What is the measure of ∠CAD?

11. Point C is the centre of the circle and ∠CFE = 25°. Justify each of your answers to the following questions.

a) What is the measure of ∠ECF?

b) What is the measure of ∠EGF?

12. If ∠KJM = 15°, ∠JML = 24°, and point C is at the centre of the circle, what is the measure of each of the following angles?

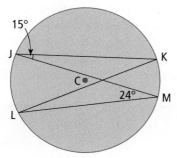

15°

J   K

C

24° M

L

a) ∠KLM   **b)** ∠JKL
c) ∠JCL   **d)** ∠KCM

48   30.

13. In the diagram, ∠BAD = 34° and ∠ADE = 56°.

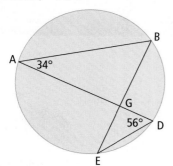

B

A 34°

G

56° D

E

a) What is the measure of ∠ABE?
b) What is the measure of ∠AGB?
c) What type of triangle is △ABG?
d) What is the measure of ∠DGE?

14. After looking at the diagram of the circle, Amanda decides to use the Pythagorean relationship to calculate the length of chord AB. Will this method work? Explain.

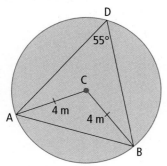

D

55°

C

A 4 m
4 m

B

15. Find the unknown angle measures, x and y, in each diagram. Where C is labelled, it is the centre of the circle.

a)
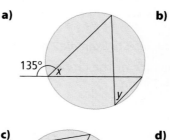

135° x

y

b)
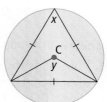

x

C

y

c)
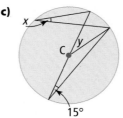

x

C y

15°

d)
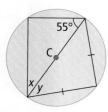

55°

C

x y

16. Design a geometry question involving a given central angle for which the answer is an inscribed angle measuring 30°. Include a diagram with your question.

17. A circle with centre C has a diameter AB. The inscribed angle ∠ADE measures 14°. What are the measures of ∠ACE and ∠ABE? Draw a diagram.

Extend

18. Find the unknown angle measures, x and y, in each diagram, given that C is the centre of the circle.

a)
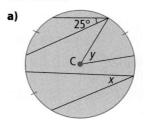

25°

C y

x

b)
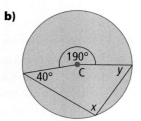

190°

40° C y

x

19. A hole has a diameter of 20 cm. What is the maximum side length of a square that will fit into the hole?

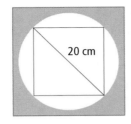

20 cm

20. For each of the following diagrams, calculate the value of x.

a)

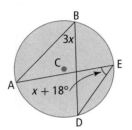

b)

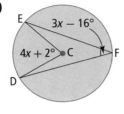

21. In the semicircle, $\angle HBE = 27°$. C is on the diameter and is the midpoint of AB.

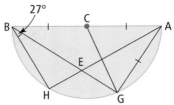

Determine the measure of each angle, justifying your work mathematically.

a) $\angle BHA$

b) $\angle BEH$

c) $\angle AEG$

d) $\angle ACG$

e) $\angle BCG$

Math Link

a) Design a piece of art using one circle and any number of inscribed and central angles.

b) Describe how the angles and line segments in your design are related.

⊙⊙ Tech Link

Inscribed and Central Angles

In this activity, you will use dynamic geometry software to explore inscribed and central angles in a circle. To use this activity, go to www.mathlinks9.ca and follow the links.

Explore

1. a) What is the measure of the central angle?

   b) What is the measure of the inscribed angle?

   c) What is the measure of the minor arc BC?

2. Drag point A around the circle. What happens to the measure of the two angles $\angle BOC$ and $\angle BAC$? Why does this happen?

3. Drag either point B or point C around the circle. Record at least four measurements of the inscribed angle and the central angle from different locations on the circle.

4. Describe any relationships between the central angle $\angle BOC$ and the inscribed angle $\angle BAC$ subtended by the same arc.

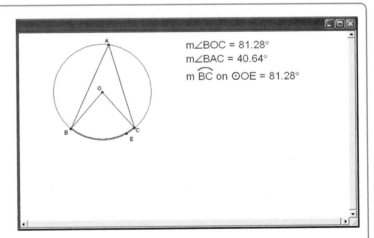

$\angle$BAC	$\angle$BOC

10.2

Exploring Chord Properties

Focus on...

After this lesson, you will be able to...
- describe the relationship among the centre of a circle, a chord, and the perpendicular bisector of the chord

An archeologist found an edge piece of a broken Aztec medallion. If she assumes it is circular, how might she determine the circumference of the whole medallion?

Explore Chords in a Circle

Materials
- compass
- tracing paper
- ruler

1. Construct a large circle on tracing paper and draw two different chords.

2. Construct the perpendicular bisector of each chord.

3. Label the point inside the circle where the two perpendicular bisectors intersect.

> What methods could you use to do this construction?

Literacy Link

A *perpendicular bisector* passes through the midpoint of a line segment at 90°.

4. Share your construction method with another classmate.

Reflect and Check

5. a) What do you notice about the point of intersection of the two perpendicular bisectors in step 3?

    b) Do you think that this will be true for any chord and any circle? How could you test your prediction?

WWW **Web Link**

You may wish to explore these geometric properties on a computer. Go to www.mathlinks9.ca and follow the links.

6. How could the archeologist use perpendicular bisectors to determine the circumference of the Aztec medallion?

Link the Ideas

You can use properties related to chords in a circle to solve problems.

> **Perpendicular Bisector of a Chord**
> A line that passes through the centre of a circle and is perpendicular to a chord bisects the chord.

Example 1: Bisect a Chord With a Radius

Radius CD bisects chord AB. Chord AB measures 8 cm. The radius of the circle is 5 cm. What is the length of line segment CE? Justify your solution.

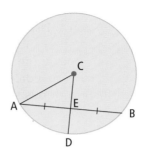

Solution

Since CD is a radius that bisects the chord AB, then CD is perpendicular to AB and $\angle AEC = 90°$.

The length of AE is 4 cm because CD bisects the 8-cm chord AB. The radius AC is 5 cm. Using the Pythagorean relationship in $\triangle ACE$,

$$CE^2 + AE^2 = AC^2$$
$$CE^2 + 4^2 = 5^2$$
$$CE^2 + 16 = 25$$
$$CE^2 = 9$$
$$CE = \sqrt{9}$$
$$CE = 3$$

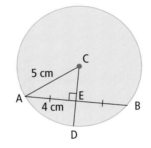

Strategies

Organize, Analyse, Solve

Therefore, CE measures 3 cm. This is the shortest distance from the chord AB to the centre of the circle.

Show You Know

Radius CH bisects chord FG. Chord FG measures 12 cm. The radius of the circle measures 10 cm. What is the length of CJ?

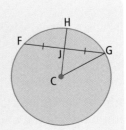

Example 2: Use Chord Properties to Solve Problems

Louise would like to drill a hole in the centre of a circular table in order to insert a sun umbrella. Use a diagram to explain how she could locate the centre.

Solution

Draw two chords. Locate the midpoint of each chord. Use a carpenter's square to draw the perpendicular bisectors of each chord. Locate the point of intersection of the two perpendicular bisectors. The point of intersection is the centre of the table.

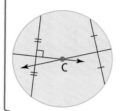

Did You Know?

A *carpenter's square* is used in construction to draw and confirm right angles.

Show You Know

Mark would like to plant a cherry tree in the centre of a circular flower bed. Explain how he could identify the exact centre using circle properties.

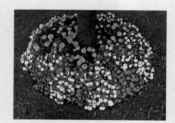

Key Ideas

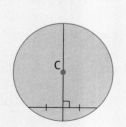

- The perpendicular bisector of a chord passes through the centre of the circle.
- The perpendicular bisectors of two distinct chords intersect at the centre of the circle.
- If a bisector of a chord in a circle passes through the centre, then the bisector is perpendicular to the chord.
- If a line passes through the centre of a circle and intersects a chord at right angles, then the line bisects the chord.
- The shortest path between the centre of a circle and a chord is a line that is perpendicular to the chord.

Check Your Understanding

Communicate the Ideas

1. Describe how you know that the diameter of the circle forms a right angle with the chord at their point of intersection.

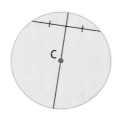

2. Explain how you could locate the centre of the circle using the two chords shown.

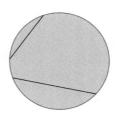

3. Amonte was explaining the properties of perpendicular bisectors to his friend Darius.

"There are three important properties of perpendicular bisectors of chords in circles:
- The line bisector cuts the chord in two equal line segments.
- The line intersects the chord at right angles; they are perpendicular.
- The line passes through the centre so it contains the diameter.
If any two of these properties are present, then the third property exists."

Is Amonte's explanation correct? What does he mean by the last statement?

Practise

For help with #4 and #5, refer to Example 1 on page 387.

4. CD bisects chord AB. The radius of the circle is 15 cm long. Chord AB measures 24 cm. What is the length of CE? Explain your reasoning.

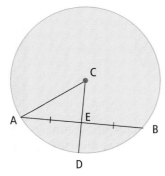

5. The radius CF bisects chord HJ. CG measures 4 mm. Chord HJ measures 14 mm. What is the radius of the circle, expressed to the nearest tenth of a millimetre? Justify your answer.

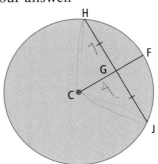

6. Hannah wants to draw a circular target on her trampoline. Explain, using diagrams, how she could locate the centre of the trampoline.

Apply

7. The radius of the circle is 17 m. The radius CD is perpendicular to the chord AB. Their point of intersection, E, is 8 m from the centre C. What is the length of the chord AB? Explain your reasoning.

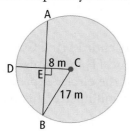

8. The radius of the circle is 11.1 cm, the radius CM is perpendicular to the chord LK, and MQ measures 3.4 cm. What is the length of the chord LK? Express your answer to the nearest tenth of a centimetre.

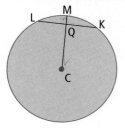

9. Calculate the unknown length, x. Give each answer to the nearest tenth.

a)

b)

10. The circular cross section of a water pipe contains some water in the bottom. The horizontal distance across the surface of the water is 34 cm. The inner diameter of the pipe is 50 cm. What is the maximum depth of the water? Express your answer to the nearest centimetre.

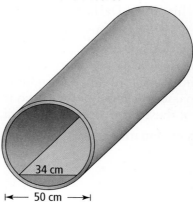

11. If you know that the radius CD = 5 cm, and BC = 3 cm, what is the area of △ABD?

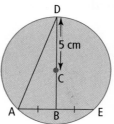

12. A circle has a diameter of 50 mm. A chord is 14 mm long. What is the shortest distance from the centre of the circle, C, to the chord? Include a diagram with your solution.

13. How could you locate the centre of a regular octagonal table using chord properties? Include a diagram in your explanation.

14. Your classmate used a compass to draw a circle with a radius of 8 cm. He felt the circle was inaccurate and tore it into small pieces. How could you use the following piece to check his accuracy?

15. In this circle, the diameter AE = 20 cm, the chord DE = 16 cm, AF = 7.2 cm, and ∠BFE = 90°.

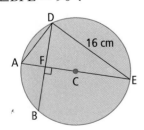

Determine the following measures and justify your answers. Express lengths to the nearest tenth of a centimetre.

a) ∠ADE   **b)** AD

c) DF   **d)** BD

16. Point E is the midpoint of the chord MP. HJ is a diameter of the circle. C is the centre of the circle, and ∠HCP = 130°.

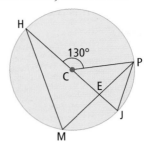

Determine the following angle measures. Justify your answers.

a) ∠HMP   **b)** ∠HEM

c) ∠MHJ   **d)** ∠MPJ

e) ∠PCE   **f)** ∠CPE

17. A helicopter pilot surveys the water level in an aqueduct in a remote section of the country. From the air, the pilot measures the horizontal width of the water to be 7.3 m. The aqueduct is a hemisphere and has an inner diameter of 12 m. What is the depth of the water? Express your answer to the nearest tenth of a metre.

18. Gavyn was asked to find the length of the chord AB. He was told that the radius of the circle is 13 cm, radius CD is perpendicular to chord AB, and chord AB is 5 cm from the centre C.

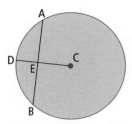

Determine the mistakes that Gavyn made and find the correct length of AB.

Gavyn's Solution

Draw the radius AC, which is the hypotenuse of right triangle △AEC.

By the Pythagorean relationship,

$$EC^2 + AC^2 = AE^2$$
$$13^2 + 5^2 = AE^2$$
$$169 + 25 = AE^2$$
$$194 = AE^2$$
$$AE = \sqrt{194}$$
$$AE \approx 13.9$$

Since CD is a radius and it is perpendicular to AB, then CD bisects the chord AB.

$$AB \approx 2 \times 13.9$$
$$AB \approx 27.8$$

Therefore, AB is approximately 27.8 m.

19. Some plastic tubing is moulded with an I-beam on the inside to provide extra strength. The length of each of two parallel chords is 10 mm, and the perpendicular distance between these two chords is 12 mm. What is the diameter of the circular tubing? Express your answer to the nearest tenth of a millimetre.

Extend

20. a) How do you know that △FGH is a right triangle?

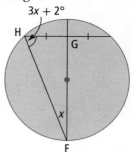

b) Solve for x algebraically and determine the measures of both acute angles in △FGH.

21. Line segment OC is a bisector of chords AB and DE. If O is the centre of the circle on the left and C is the centre of the circle on the right, explain how you know that AB is parallel to DE.

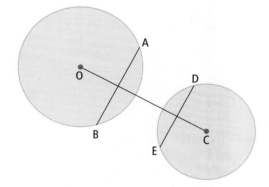

The North American Plains Indians and Tibetan Buddhists create mandalas. A mandala is a piece of art framed within a circle. The design draws the viewer's eyes to the centre of the circle. Mandalas have spiritual significance for their creators. The photo shows a Buddhist monk using coloured sand to create a mandala.

a) Refer to the portion of the sand mandala shown in the picture. Design a mandala with a similar pattern but your own design. For example, you could create a mandala to celebrate the work of a famous mathematician. Your design should show only part of the mandala.

b) If you want to display your mandala, you will need to know how much room the entire design will take up. What is a reasonable estimate for the circumference of your mandala? Explain your reasoning.

c) How do you think the monks ensure symmetry in their mandalas? How could you use your knowledge of circle properties to help you?

WWW Web Link

For more information about sand mandalas, go to www.mathlinks9.ca and follow the links.

Tech Link

Perpendicular Lines to a Chord

In this activity, you will use dynamic geometry software to explore perpendicular lines from the centre of a circle to a chord. To use this activity, go to www.mathlinks9.ca and follow the links.

AC = 2.61 cm
BC = 2.61 cm
m∠OCB = 90°

Explore

1. a) What is the measure of ∠OCB?

   b) What is the measure of line segment AC?

   c) What is the measure of line segment BC?

2. Drag point A to another location on the circle.

   a) Describe what happens to the measure of ∠OCB when you drag point A to a different location on the circle.

   b) What happens to the measures of the line segments AC and BC? Explain.

3. Drag point B around the circle.

   a) What effect does this have on the measure of ∠OCB?

   b) What effect does this have on the lengths of line segment AC and line segment BC?

4. What conclusions can you make about ∠OCB, the angle formed by the segment from the centre of the circle to the midpoint of the chord?

5. What conclusions can you make about the relationship between line segment AC and line segment BC?

Tangents to a Circle

When a car turns, the wheels are at different angles in relation to the car. Each wheel is turning through its own circle. What is the relationship between the four circles where the tires turn?

Materials
• Turning Circle diagram

• protractor
• ruler

Explore Circles and Their Tangents

1. Find the midpoint of each line segment that represents a tire.

2. Draw a perpendicular line from each midpoint toward the inside of the turning circle.

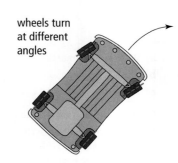

wheels turn at different angles

Reflect and Check

3. What do you notice about the intersection of these perpendicular lines?

4. a) Each wheel of a car travels through a different circular path. What do these circles have in common?

b) Based on your observations, what is the measure of the angle between a **tangent** to a circle and the radius at the point of tangency?

---

tangent (to a circle)

• a line that touches a circle at exactly one point
• the point where the line touches the circle is called the point of tangency

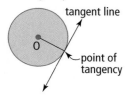

tangent line

0

point of tangency

WWW Web Link

You may wish to explore these geometric properties on a computer. Go to www.mathlinks9.ca and follow the links.

Link the Ideas

You can use properties of tangents to a circle to solve problems.

Tangent to a Circle
A tangent to a circle is perpendicular to the radius at the point of tangency.

Tangent Chord Relationship
A chord drawn perpendicular to a tangent at the point of tangency contains the centre of the circle, and is a diameter.

Example 1: Determine Angle Measures in a Circle With a Tangent Line

In the diagram shown, AB is tangent to the circle at point D, BE contains the diameter FE, and $\angle ABE = 50°$.

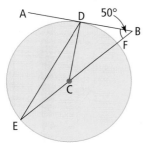

a) What is the measure of $\angle BDC$? Justify your answer.
b) What is the measure of central angle $\angle DCE$? Explain your reasoning.
c) What type of triangle is $\triangle CDE$? Justify your answer.
d) What is the measure of $\angle DEC$? Explain your reasoning.

Solution

a) Since AB is tangent to the circle at point D, then radius CD is perpendicular to line segment AB. Therefore, $\angle BDC = 90°$.

b) The sum of the angles in a triangle is 180°.
In $\triangle BCD$, $\angle DCB = 180° - 90° - 50°$
$\angle DCB = 40°$

Since $\angle DCE$ and $\angle DCB$ form a straight line, they are supplementary.
$\angle DCE + \angle DCB = 180°$
$\angle DCE + 40° = 180°$
$\angle DCE = 180° - 40°$
$\angle DCE = 140°$

> **Literacy Link**
> *Supplementary angles* add to 180°.

c) Triangle CDE is an isosceles triangle because CD and CE are radii of the circle and radii are equal in length.

d) *Method 1: Use Angles in a Triangle*

The sum of the angles in a triangle is 180°. ∠DCE = 140°. Since △CDE is an isosceles triangle, then the angles opposite the equal sides are equal. ∠DEC = $\frac{1}{2}$ × 40° or 20°.

∠DEC = 20°.

Method 2: Use Inscribed Angles

∠DEF is the same as ∠DEC because the points F and C lie on the same line. This is an inscribed angle subtended by the same arc as the central angle, ∠DCF. Since an inscribed angle is one half the measure of a central angle subtended by the same arc, then ∠DEC = $\frac{1}{2}$ × 40° or 20°.

∠DEC = 20°

Show You Know

Line segment AF is tangent to the circle at point E. Line segment DF contains the diameter DB, and ∠CFE = 34°. What are the measures of angles ∠CEF, ∠ECF, and ∠EDF? Explain your reasoning.

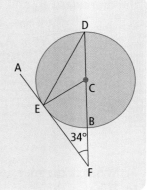

Example 2: Use the Tangent Chord Relationship

In the diagram, AB is tangent to the circle at point B. BD is a diameter of the circle. AB = 7 mm, AD = 25 mm, and △BCE is an equilateral triangle.

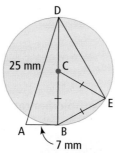

a) What is the length of diameter BD? Justify your answer.
b) What is the length of chord BE? Explain your reasoning.
c) What is the measure of the inscribed angle ∠BED?
d) What is the length of chord DE? Justify your answer and express your answer to the nearest millimetre.

Solution

a) Diameter BD is perpendicular to tangent AB because B is the point of tangency on the circle. Therefore, $\angle ABD = 90°$ and $\triangle ABD$ is a right triangle.

Use the Pythagorean relationship in $\triangle ABD$.
$$AB^2 + BD^2 = AD^2$$
$$7^2 + BD^2 = 25^2$$
$$49 + BD^2 = 625$$
$$BD^2 = 576$$
$$BD = \sqrt{576}$$
$$BD = 24$$

The length of diameter BD is 24 mm.

b) BC and CE are radii of the circle. Since $\triangle BCE$ is an equilateral triangle, side BE is equal the length of the radius, or one half of the diameter.
$$\frac{1}{2}(24) = 12$$

The length of chord BE is 12 mm

c) The inscribed angle $\angle BED$ is subtended by a diameter, so it is a right angle. $\angle BED = 90°$.

The inscribed angle $\angle BED = 90°$.

d) Use the Pythagorean relationship in $\triangle BDE$.
$$BE^2 + DE^2 = BD^2$$
$$12^2 + DE^2 = 24^2$$
$$144 + DE^2 = 576$$
$$DE^2 = 576 - 144$$
$$DE^2 = 432$$
$$DE = \sqrt{432}$$
$$DE \approx 21$$

The length of chord DE is 21 mm, to the nearest millimetre.

Show You Know

In the diagram shown, PQ is tangent to the circle at point Q. QR is a diameter of the circle. Line segment PQ = 9 mm, PR = 41 mm, and $\triangle QCS$ is an equilateral triangle.

a) What is the length of diameter QR? Justify your answer.

b) What is the length of chord QS? Explain your reasoning.

c) What is the length of chord RS? Justify your answer and express your answer to the nearest millimetre.

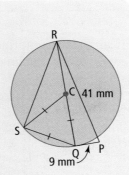

Science Link

An object that is moving in a circular path will move in a straight line tangent to that circle if the force pulling the object toward the centre is suddenly removed. This force is known as *centripetal force*.

Example 3: Solve Problems With Tangents to Circles

A speed skater is practising on a circular track with a radius of 40 m. He falls and slides off the track in a line tangent to the circle. If he slides 22 m, how far is he from the centre of the rink? Express your answer to the nearest tenth of a metre. Include a diagram in your explanation.

Solution

In the diagram, the speed skater fell at point A and slid to point B.

Since the line segment AB is tangent to the circle, then it will be perpendicular to radius AC. The Pythagorean relationship can be used to calculate the distance BC, which represents how far the speed skater is from the centre of the rink.

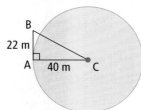

$$BC^2 = AB^2 + AC^2$$
$$BC^2 = 22^2 + 40^2$$
$$BC^2 = 484 + 1600$$
$$BC^2 = 2084$$
$$BC = \sqrt{2084}$$
$$BC \approx 45.7$$

After sliding 22 m, the speed skater is approximately 45.7 m from the centre of the rink.

Sports Link

Jeremy Wotherspoon from Red Deer, Alberta, is one of Canada's best speed skaters. He has set several records at the 500-m distance.

Show You Know

Callan is attempting to land his model airplane when the wire breaks just before touchdown. If the length of the control wire is 10 m and the plane stops at a location 74 m from Callan, how far does the plane travel after the wire breaks. Express your answer to the nearest tenth of a metre.

Key Ideas

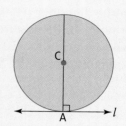

- A line that touches a circle at exactly one point is tangent to the circle.
- Point A is known as the point of tangency.
- A line *l* that is tangent to a circle at point A is perpendicular to the radius AC.
- A chord drawn perpendicular to a tangent line at the point of tangency contains the centre of the circle, and is a diameter.

Check Your Understanding

Communicate the Ideas

1. Raven and Elliott are discussing the diagram shown.

   Elliott claims that line segment AB is a tangent to the circle because it touches the circle in one place. Raven disagrees. Who is correct, and why?

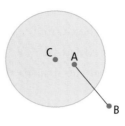

2. If BC is a radius of the circle, is AB tangent to the circle? Explain how you know.

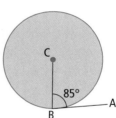

Practise

For help with #3 and #4, refer to Example 1 on pages 395–396.

3. In the diagram, AB is tangent to the circle at point D, BE contains the diameter EF, and ∠ABE = 60°.

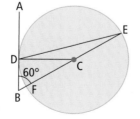

   Explain your reasoning when answering each of the following questions.

   a) What is the measure of ∠BDC?

   b) What is the measure of central angle ∠DCE?

   c) What type of triangle is △CDE?

   d) What is the measure of ∠DEC?

4. Line segment JK is tangent to the circle at point H. GH is a diameter and ∠CGL = 10°.

   Justify your answers to the following questions.

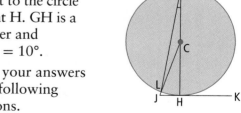

   a) What type of triangle is △CGL?

   b) What is the measure of ∠GCL?

   c) What is the measure of ∠JCH?

   d) What is the measure of ∠JHG?

   e) What is the measure of ∠CJK?

For help with #5 and #6, refer to Example 2 on pages 396–397.

5. In the diagram, AB is tangent to the circle at point B. BD is a diameter of the circle, AB = 6 m, AD = 10 m, and △BCE is an equilateral triangle.

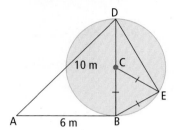

Justify your answers to the following questions.

a) What is the length of the diameter BD?

b) What is the length of chord BE?

c) What is the measure of the inscribed angle ∠BED?

d) What is the length of chord DE, to the nearest metre?

6. In the diagram, FG is tangent to the circle at point G. GH is a diameter, CJ = 5 mm, FG = 7 mm, and △CGJ is an equilateral triangle.

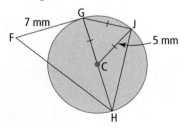

a) What is the length of the diameter? Justify your answer.

b) Is △GHJ a right triangle? Justify your answer.

c) What is the length of chord HJ? Explain your reasoning. Express your answer to the nearest tenth of a millimetre.

d) What is the measure of angle ∠FGH? Justify your answer.

e) What is the length of FH? Explain your reasoning. Express your answer to the nearest tenth of a millimetre.

For help with #7, refer to Example 3 on page 398.

7. A dog is tied on a leash to the clothesline pole in the backyard. The leash is 5 m long and the pole is a perpendicular distance of 5 m from the edge of the house. What is the distance from the pole to the cat door? How close to the cat door can the dog get? Express your answers to the nearest tenth of a metre.

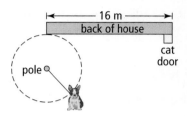

Apply

8. Find the length of x in each diagram. Line *l* is tangent to the circle. Express your answer to the nearest tenth, where necessary.

a)

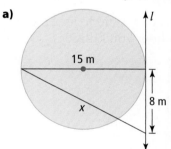

b)

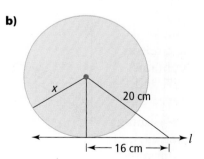

9. Find the measure of the angle θ in each diagram. Line *l* is tangent to the circle.

a)

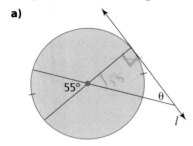

b)

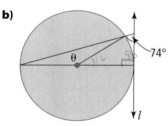

Literacy Link

The Greek letter θ is *theta*. It is often used to indicate the measure of an unknown angle.

---

10. Both circles are identical in size. They are tangent to each other and to line *l*.

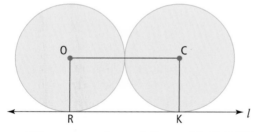

a) What type of quadrilateral is ROCK? Explain your reasoning.

b) If the radius of each circle is 5 cm, what is the perimeter of ROCK?

11. Line segment AB is tangent to a circle at point A. The diameter AD of the circle is 7.3 cm. If the length of AB is 4.2 cm, determine the length of BD. Include a diagram in your solution. Express your answer to the nearest tenth of a centimetre.

12. In the diagram, △ABD is an isosceles triangle. AD is a tangent to the circle at point D, and BD is a diameter of the circle.

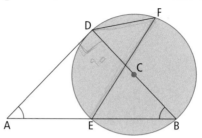

Justify your answers for each question.

a) What is the measure of ∠ADB?

b) What is the measure of ∠DBE?

c) What is the measure of ∠DFE?

13. Answer each question, given the following information.

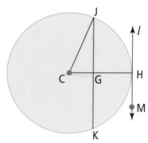

- The line *l* is tangent to the circle at point H.
- The line *l* is parallel to the chord JK.
- The radius of the circle measures 9.1 cm.
- The chord JK measures 17 cm.

Explain your reasoning for each answer.

a) What is the measure of ∠CHM?

b) What is the measure of ∠CGJ?

c) What is the length of JG?

d) What is the length of CG? Express your answer to the nearest tenth of a centimetre.

14. If JG is a tangent to the circle, what is the value of x and and the measure of $\angle$JGH?

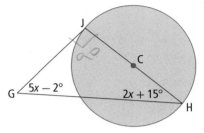

15. Line l is tangent to the circle as shown. Use properties of inscribed and central angles to find the value of angle θ. Explain your reasoning.

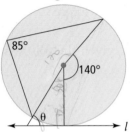

16. The aerial picture represents farmland. The circular green areas represent fields that are watered using a centre-pivot watering system. Design a question and solution using the relationship between tangents and radii of circles.

17. Two concentric circles have their centres at point C. The radius of the smaller circle is 8 cm. The length of chord AB is 26 cm and is tangent to the smaller circle. What is the circumference of the larger circle? Express your answer to the nearest centimetre.

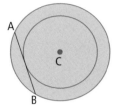

18. Three congruent circles are tangent to one another as shown. Circle A is tangent to both the x-axis and the y-axis. Circle B is tangent to the x-axis. The centre of circle A has coordinates (2, 2). What are the coordinates of the centres of circles B and C?

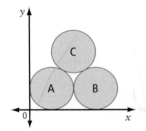

Extend

19. A steel centre square is used in woodwork to locate the centre of a wooden cylinder. Sketch the picture in your notebook and identify the edge(s) that most closely resemble a tangent to a circle. How do you think the centre square is used to locate the centre of the cylinder?

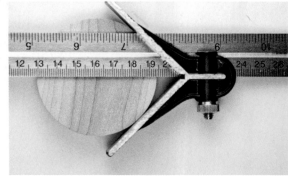

20. Two poles with radii of 18 cm and 7 cm are connected by a single metal band joining their centres and points of their outer edges. This is shown below. Determine the length of the metal band that is needed, if AB is tangent to both poles.

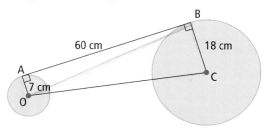

21. A rubber ball with a diameter of 6 cm is found on a frozen pond with only 2 cm sticking above the ice surface at its highest point. What is the circumference of the circle where the ball touches the ice surface? Express your answer to the nearest tenth of a centimetre.

22. A length of chain is attached to a suncatcher with a diameter of 20 cm. The chain is attached at points E and B such that the segments BD and ED are tangent to the circle. What is the total length of chain needed to hang the suncatcher on a nail at point D? Show your reasoning.

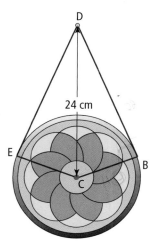

Math Link

a) Design a piece of art or a company logo using at least one circle. Incorporate at least one tangent. Remember that two circles can be tangent to each other.

b) Determine the measures of any chords, radii, diameters, or tangent lines in your design.

⬤ Tech Link

Tangents to a Circle

In this activity, you will use dynamic geometry software to explore tangent lines to a circle. To use this activity, go to www.mathlinks9.ca and follow the links.

Explore

1. What is the measure of ∠BAC?

2. a) Describe what happens to the measure of ∠BAC as you drag point A to different locations on the circle.

 b) What conclusion can you make?

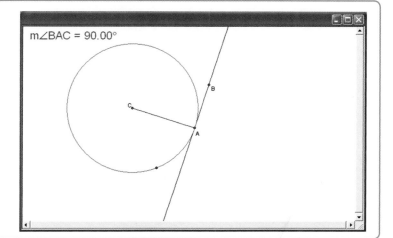

Key Words

Unscramble the letters for each puzzle in #1 to #4.
Use the clues to help you solve the puzzles.

1. I R U S D A

the distance from the centre to any point
on the circle

2. I S C B D E I N R E A G L N

an angle formed by two chords that share
a common endpoint

3. R O C H D

a line segment that has both endpoints on
the same circle

4. C R P P D E E N L A U R I S I T C R O B E

a line or line segment that passes through
the midpoint of a line segment at 90°

10.1 Exploring Angles in a Circle, pages 378–385

5. Determine the measure of each angle.

  a) ∠ABD

  b) ∠ACD

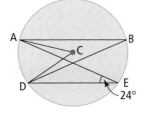

6. What are the measures of unknown angles x and y?

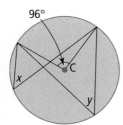

7. Parmjeet explains that if an inscribed angle in a circle has a measure of 13.5°, the central angle subtended by the same arc will also measure 13.5°. Do you agree with her thinking? Why or why not?

8. What is the measure of each central angle on the dartboard?

9. What is the measure of ∠EFG?

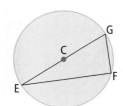

10. What is the measure of ∠BAD in the semicircle?

10.2 Exploring Chord Properties, pages 386–393

11. Explain how you know that the line *l* must pass through the centre of the circle.

12. Andrea tries to find the centre of a wooden table top by placing a string across the top and finding its midpoint. She misses the centre by 1 cm. What went wrong? How might she have found the centre more accurately?

13. What is the length of chord AE? Explain how you determined your answer.

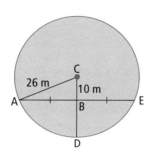

14. Archaeologists have found a broken piece of a wagon wheel as shown. Show how they can determine the circumference of the entire wheel from this broken piece.

15. If chord FG has a length of 18 cm and the diameter of the circle is 22 cm, what is the shortest distance between FG and the centre of the circle? Express your answer to the nearest tenth of a centimetre.

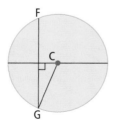

10.3 Tangents to a Circle, pages 394–403

16. What is the measure of ∠FCG if DE is tangent to the circle?

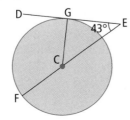

17. If AB is tangent to the circle at B, what is the length of the radius?

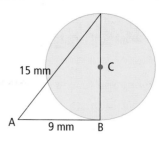

18. Jasmine was flying a remote-control airplane in a circle with a radius of 50 m. The signal was lost by the airplane which then flew along a tangent from the circle until it crashed 140 m from Jasmine's location. How far did the airplane travel horizontally along the tangent? Include a diagram in your answer. Calculate the distance to the nearest metre.

19. Line segment AF is tangent to the circle at E, and ∠AFD = 48°. Find the measure of each angle. Justify your answers.

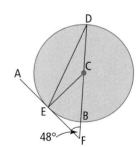

a) ∠CEF   b) ∠ECF
c) ∠ECD   d) ∠DEC
e) ∠AED   f) ∠EDB

20. Line segment AB is tangent to the circle at E. Determine the measure of the requested angles.

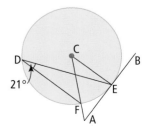

a) ∠ACE
b) ∠CAB

Chapter 10 Practice Test

For #1 and #2, choose the best answer.

1. Which statement is true?

   A A central angle is smaller than an inscribed angle subtended by the same arc.

   B Two inscribed angles are never equal in size.

   C An inscribed angle subtended by a diameter of the circle is always 90°.

   D An inscribed angle in a semicircle can be larger than 90°.

2. What is the measure of the inscribed angle?

   A 25°   **B** 50°

   C 100°   **D** 200°

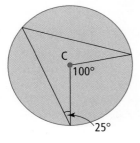

Complete the statements in #3 and #4.

3. The length of EF is ■.

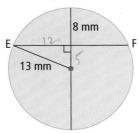

4. If AB is tangent to the circle, the measure of ∠BCD is ■.

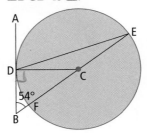

Short Answer

5. What is the length of radius x? Express your answer to the nearest tenth of a centimetre.

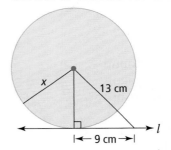

6. Find the measure of angle θ. Line l is tangent to the circle.

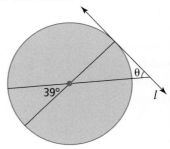

Extended Response

7. What are the measures of ∠ADB and ∠ACB? Explain your reasoning.

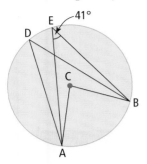

8. The diagram represents the water level in a pipe. The surface of the water from one side of the pipe to the other measures 20 mm, and the inner diameter of the pipe is 34 mm. What is the shortest distance from the centre of the pipe to the water level, rounded to the nearest millimetre? Explain your reasoning.

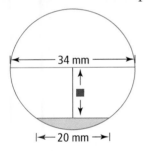

9. The Namdaemun gate, a two-storey, pagoda-style wooden building on a stone base, was Korea's premier national treasure. This 600-year-old structure in Seoul was destroyed in a fire in 2008.

To rebuild the gate, square beams were cut from logs. What is the largest dimension of square that can be cut from a log with a diameter of 40 cm?

Math Link: Wrap It Up!

Design a piece of art or a logo using at least two circles.

- Incorporate each circle property that you have studied into your design, and label where you use these properties.

- You may wish to use some or all of the designs that you created in the Math Link revisits throughout the chapter.

Challenges

Dream Catcher

The legend of the Dream Catcher exists in varying forms among Aboriginal Peoples. In the design, the Dream Catcher is formed into a loop. Its centre is woven in a web-like pattern.

It is said that the night air contains good dreams and bad dreams. According to the legend, the good dreams go through the web into the sleeper. The bad dreams become hopelessly entangled in the web and perish at the first light of dawn.

The number of points connected to the ring is often eight, in honour of the spider. The webbing is made of sinew. The web can be adorned with natural objects such as stones, beads, shells, bark, and feathers. A bloodstone is often hung in the centre.

You be the artist. In this challenge, you are going to draw a Dream Catcher and explore how its construction relates to circle geometry.

1. **a)** Draw a circle with a minimum radius of 8 cm. Place eight equally spaced markings on the circle.

   b) What are two different ways to determine the placement of the markings?

Materials
- compass
- ruler
- protractor

2. Draw the first row of webbing by joining each pair of consecutive markings with a straight line.

   a) What are two different measures of the central angle made between the first and seventh markings and the circle centre? Show your thinking.

   b) What is the measure of the inscribed angle subtended by the same arc as the central angle you found in 2a)?

3. Draw the second row of webbing. How do the central and inscribed angles of the layers compare? Show your thinking.

4. Continue drawing the rows of webbing until an opening of approximately 5 cm in diameter is in the centre. How many rows did you need?

5. Compare your drawing to an actual Dream Catcher or pictures of Dream Catchers. How does your design differ from the actual constructed ones?

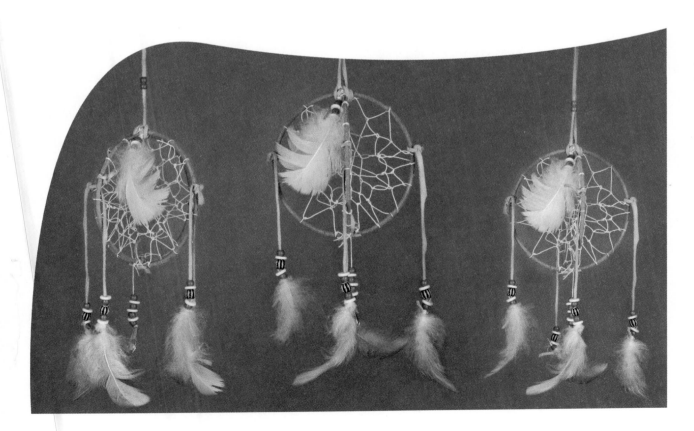

11

Data Analysis

Research involves asking questions, collecting information, and analysing the data to draw conclusions. Businesses and governments use research-based statistics to inform and persuade people. Park wardens use statistics to predict birth rates, death rates, and migration patterns of plant and animal populations. They also use statistics to predict the size of populations such as elk.

In this chapter, you will learn about factors that influence the collection of data. You will learn about how to reduce the chances of invalid results from a survey. You will collect and display data, and draw conclusions based on the results.

What You Will Learn

- to identify factors that can affect the collection of data
- to identify the difference between a population and a sample
- to decide whether to use the population or a sample
- to identify different types of samples
- to use data for making predictions
- to develop and carry out a research project
- to assess your research project

> **Did You Know?**
>
> The Cree name for elk is *wapiti*.

Key Words

population
sample
convenience
  sample
random sample

stratified sample
systematic sample
voluntary response
  sample
biased sample

🔗 Literacy Link

A concept map can help you visually organize your understanding of math concepts.

Create a concept map in your math journal or notebook. Make each oval large enough to write in. Leave enough space to draw additional ovals. As you work through the chapter, complete the concept map.

Organize each term you learn by determining which of the three blue ovals it relates to. Then, attach and label an oval for the term and define it.

Discuss your ideas with a classmate. You may wish to add to or correct what you have written.

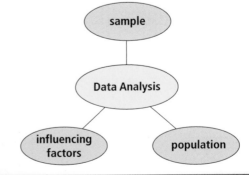

Materials

- sheet of 11 × 17 paper
- ruler
- seven sheets of 8.5 × 11 paper
- scissors
- stapler

Step 1

Fold the long side of a sheet of 11 × 17 paper in half. Pinch it at the midpoint. Fold the outer edges of the paper to meet at the midpoint. Label it as shown.

Step 2

Fold the short side of a sheet of 8.5 × 11 paper in half. On one side, use a ruler to draw a line 4 cm from the top. Then, draw six more lines at 4-cm intervals. Cut along the lines through one thickness of paper, forming eight tabs. Label the tabs as shown.

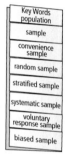

Step 3

Staple five sheets of 8.5 × 11 paper together along the top edge. Draw a line 15 cm from the bottom of the top sheet. Cut across the entire width of the page at this mark. Make a line 12 cm up from the bottom of the second sheet and cut across the width of the page at this mark. Similarly, cut off 9 cm from the third page, 6 cm from the fourth page, and 3 cm from the fifth page. Label as shown.

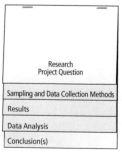

Step 4

Use a quarter sheet of 8.5 × 11 paper to create a pocket for storing additional terms. Staple the pocket to the inside right flap of the Foldable as shown below. Use index cards or cut strips of notebook paper to fit inside the pocket.

Step 5

Staple the booklets from Steps 2 and 3 into the Foldable from Step 1 as shown.

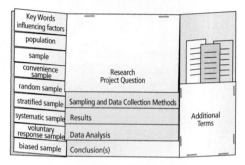

Using the Foldable

As you work through the chapter, define the Key Words beneath the tabs on the left panel. Record notes about the research project under the tabs on the centre panel. Use the pocket to store the definitions for additional terms related to data analysis.

Use the back of your Foldable to create a flow chart to track your progress on the research project. On the front of the Foldable, keep track of what you need to work on. Check off each item as you deal with it.

Math Link

Protecting and Managing Wildlife

Elk Island National Park in Alberta is Canada's largest fully enclosed park. It is home to the densest population of ungulates in Canada. These ungulates include plains bison, wood bison, moose, deer, and elk.

Park wardens and naturalists play an important role in studying, monitoring, and managing the wildlife in the park.

Val decided to study the population of the ungulates in Elk Island National Park. The table shows the data she collected from the park warden.

1. **a)** Use at least two different methods to display the data that Val collected.
   b) Explain why you chose each method to display the data.

2. What is the most common ungulate in the park? Explain.

3. Elk Island National park has an area of 194 km². What is the mean number of elk per square kilometre? Show your thinking.

4. What percent of the ungulate population do bison represent?

Ungulate	Approximate Total Park Count (2007 Fall Count)
Plains bison	425
Wood bison	400
Elk	605
Moose	300
Deer	558

Literacy Link

An *ungulate* is a mammal with hooves. One example is a bison. Most ungulates use the tips of their hooves to hold their body weight as they move.

Did You Know?

Population density is a measure of the number of individuals living in a defined area. The population density of ungulates in Elk Island National Park is second only to the density in the Serengeti Plains of Africa.

Throughout this chapter, you will study an issue related to wildlife protection and management. As you do, you will develop your own research project. Your project will involve collecting, displaying, and analysing your data. You might study birth rates, death rates, or migration patterns of an animal population. Or, you might consider the effects of tourism, recreation, or environmental factors, such as pollution, on a population.

You might study a wildlife issue in a park. If so, what park will you choose? Where is the park located? What issue interests you? Research at least two areas of interest.

WWW Web Link

For more information about national parks, go to www.mathlinks9.ca and follow the links.

Factors Affecting Data Collection

Focus on...

After this lesson, you will be able to...

- identify how bias, use of language, ethics, cost, time and timing, privacy, and cultural sensitivity may influence the collection of data
- write and analyse appropriate survey questions

A Super Food employee provides samples of Bob Brat Sausages to customers between 5:00 p.m. and 5:30 p.m. for one day.

Store employees asked customers who buy Bob Brat Sausages the following question.

> Did you buy Bob Brat Sausages because they are delicious, quick to prepare, or both delicious and quick to prepare?

The table shows the results from the survey.

Bob Brat Sausages	
Delicious	‖‖	
Quick to prepare	‖‖
Both delicious and quick to prepare	‖‖ ‖|

A few weeks later, a store flyer made this advertising claim.

Over 90% of shoppers love Bob Brat Sausages because they taste great and save time!

What factors might have influenced the survey responses? How accurate do you think the advertising claim is? Explain.

Literacy Link

A *survey* is used to collect opinions and/or information.

Literacy Link

An *advertising claim* gives information about the performance of a product or service. The claim is designed to encourage you to buy. The claim may be true, false, or a little of both.

Explore Factors That Affect Survey Responses

1. From the store's point of view, did Super Foods promote Bob Brat sausages well? Explain.

2. a) Did the survey ask a fair question? Explain your reasoning.
   b) Did the survey sample represent the whole population of shoppers? Explain.

3. Some people who read the flyer said the advertisement was misleading. Do you agree with them? Explain why or why not. Discuss your ideas with your group.

Reflect and Check

4. Imagine you are hired as the store's public relations consultant.
   a) What factors do you need to address to make the data collected about the sausages more accurate?
   b) Develop a survey question you would ask about Bob Brat Sausages. Who would you ask?

Link the Ideas

Several *influencing factors* affect how data are collected or how responses are obtained.

These include:
- *bias*: Does the question show a preference for a specific product?
- *use of language*: Is the question presented in such a way that people understand what is being asked?
- *ethics*: Does the question refer to inappropriate behaviour?
- *cost*: Does the cost of the study outweigh the benefits?
- *time and timing*: Does the time the data were collected influence the results? Is the timing of the survey appropriate?
- *privacy*: Do people have the right to refuse to answer? Are the responses kept confidential?
- *cultural sensitivity*: Might the question offend people from different cultural groups?

> **Literacy Link**
>
> *Ethics* involves judgments of right and wrong. For example, cheating on a test is wrong.

Example 1: Identify Factors Affecting Data Collection

Helen and Andre are reviewing the data collection methods used by a marketing company. For each situation, help them identify any influencing factors. Explain your reasoning.

a) A sales representative stands in front of a display of different kinds of toothpaste. He asks every person buying toothpaste the following question.

> What is your favourite brand of toothpaste? For what reason(s)?

b) Free samples of sunscreen are sent to every home in fall and winter. A mail reply card asks people if they would use the product again.

c) A grocery store employee conducts a telephone survey of people living within 10 km of the store. To help determine what meat products to sell, she asks what type of red meat people prefer.

d) A sales representative conducts a telephone survey. As she poses the question, a person receiving the call says, "I am not interested, thank you." The sales representative responds, "Why not? Your input provides useful information." She begins to repeat the survey question.

e) Your school is under construction and is quite dusty and dirty. A survey is conducted about the environmental health of your school. The survey is done every four years.

f) A sales representative sets up an online survey. The survey offers a free MP3 file of a song that was downloaded from the Internet to everyone who completes the survey. The company has not bought the rights to the song.

Solution

a) There is no bias. Standing in front of a toothpaste display allows the sales representative to survey people who are buying toothpaste.

b) Fall and winter sun is less intense than spring and summer sun. People may be less likely to wear sunscreen during fall and winter. Therefore, these seasons are not likely the best choice for testing sunscreen. Sending sunscreen products during fall and winter is very costly for the company. In addition, asking people if they would use the product again assumes that they did use it. This may confuse people who have not tested the product. The language is unclear.

c) The question is biased. It assumes that all people eat red meat, which is not true. Red meat is not acceptable to some people. For these people, this may be a culturally sensitive question.

d) The sales representative does not respect the individual's right to refuse to participate in the survey. In addition, any responses obtained under pressure may not truly represent the person's opinion.

e) This survey is poorly timed. When a school is under construction, some routines may be disturbed. People may express frustration with the temporary changes. This would reflect in a negative way on the survey.

f) Offering a reward to participants in the survey is ethically wrong. In addition, it is not ethical to download music from the Internet without buying it. When people do this, musicians are not being paid for their work.

Example 2: Write Survey Questions Free of Influencing Factors

A steel milling company conducts a survey.

a) Does the survey question influence the results? Explain.

b) Rewrite the question so that it is free of influencing factors.

> The proposed mill will produce 250 jobs and economic benefits for your community. Are you in favour of having a forward-thinking steel mill in your community?   YES   NO

Solution

a) Yes, the wording in the question may lead people to answer in a specific way. It implies that due to the economic benefits the company can offer, people should vote in favour of the mill.

b) A better way to ask the question is, "Are you in favour of having a steel mill in your community?"

Key Ideas

- Survey questions should be worded so they are free from factors influencing the responses.

  The survey questions ask about purchases made at a school cafeteria.

  > 1. Do you buy food at the school cafeteria?   YES   NO
  > 2. If you responded NO, what reason best explains why you do not buy food at the cafeteria? Circle one.
  >   A The quality of the food is poor.
  >   B I do not like the food choices.
  >   C The cafeteria is in an inconvenient location.
  >   D The prices are too high.
  >   E Other (Please explain.) _____

- Influencing factors include bias, use of language, ethics, cost, time and timing, privacy, and cultural sensitivity.

  Which box shows better survey questions? Why?

  > 1. In the past year, how many times did you buy food items at the cafeteria? _____

  > 1. In the past week, did you buy any food items at the cafeteria?   YES   NO
  >
  > 2. If you responded YES, how many times did you buy each of the following food items?
  > soup or salad _____   main course _____   drink _____   snack _____

Check Your Understanding

Communicate the Ideas

1. Your friend is unclear what the term *bias* means. Develop an example to help explain the term.

2. Explain how influencing factors affect the collection of data. Give an example.

3. Shunta and Susan are discussing how to choose the top five lunch specials for the cafeteria menu. Each develops a different survey question. They decide to survey all the students.

   Shunta:
   > What are your top five favourite lunch specials?

   Susan:
   > Which are your top five favourite lunch specials from this menu? Circle your choices.
   >
   > | LUNCH SPECIALS | |
   > | --- | --- |
   > | tomato soup and salad | grilled cheese |
   > | hamburger | chicken salad sandwich |
   > | vegetable lasagna | turkey hot dog |
   > | vegetarian chili | pepperoni pizza |

   Which survey question do you prefer? Explain why.

Practise

For help with #4 and #5, refer to Example 1 on pages 416-417.

4. In each case, identify and describe any factors that may affect the collection of data.

   a) Survey members of the soccer team about new uniforms for the volleyball team.

   b) At a truck rally, ask drivers what type of vehicle they prefer to drive.

   c) Provide samples of a new granola bar at all conferences and conventions in your community. Ask people who attend the following question.

   > What is your favourite among the new granola bars you tried in the past month?

   d) Ask customers in a sports store the following question.

   > Invincible Bikes are the most sturdy and expertly designed bikes on the market. What brand will you buy?

5. For each situation, identify whether there is bias. If so, identify the bias. Then, rewrite the statement to correct it.

   a) Ask all horse owners if they are willing to pay higher horse-boarding fees.

   b) Ask owners of horses boarded in a stable in the city centre if this location is annoying.

   c) Ask horseback riders if they would support building a public park on the site of their stable.

For help with #6 to #8, refer to Example 2 on page 417.

6. In each case, describe the effect of any influencing factors on the collection of data. Then, write an improved survey question.

   a) A sales representative asks the following question.

   > Which do you prefer?
   > A   Cola
   > B   Diet Cola

   b) An opposition party member asks the following question.

   > Is the current prime minister not the best prime minister in Canadian history?
   > YES   NO

   c) A small business develops the following question.

   > Do you know about the Hands-On Repair Company and the maintenance your appliances and tools need?
   > YES   NO

   d) Jennifer asks students the following question.

   > What is your parents' total income?

7. Rewrite each survey question without any influencing factors.

a) Sam asks riders of all-terrain vehicles the following question.

> Do you support closing some riding trails to save some endangered animals?
> YES   NO

b) A marketer surveys all the people entering a movie theatre.

> Who is your favourite male movie star?
> A   Brad Pitt
> B   Keanu Reeves
> C   Matt Damon
> D   Other _____

c) A student asks people at an airport the following question.

> Do you think flying is still the cheapest way to travel a long distance?
> YES   NO

8. Rewrite each survey question so there are no influencing factors.

a)
> Do you like to watch hockey, the only great sport?
> YES   NO

b)
> Most people choose chocolate, but what is your favourite flavour of ice cream?

c)
> A recent survey shows that 42% of teens use the Internet to watch TV. What TV shows do you watch most often online?

Apply

9. For each situation, write two different survey questions that may have resulted in each conclusion.

a) Most juice lovers prefer apple and orange.

b) Yellow is the most popular shirt colour.

c) Four out of five doctors surveyed strongly support a healthy, natural-food diet.

10. Write a survey question for each situation. Identify who you would ask to participate in the survey.

a) You want to find out which sport teens like best.

b) You want to find out if price or brand is more important when buying a cell phone.

c) You want to find out which media source people trust most to give them accurate information.

11. Rewrite each survey question so that it collects more helpful data.

a)
> If you are a juice drinker, would you consider switching to Crystal Juice?
> YES   NO

b)
> Which of the following cough medicines have you tried?
>
> Brand X   Brand Y   Brand Z

c)
> Would you run if you came across a moose?
> YES   NO

d)
> Are you satisfied with your Internet access? Circle one response.
> A   Excellent
> B   Good
> C   Poor

12. For each case, identify the influencing factors that may affect the collection of data. Then, write a survey question that is free of influencing factors and is clearly written.

  a) Teens are asked about which clothing items they have bought at an expensive store in the past year.

  b) The members of a golf club are asked if they are in favour of a proposed highway. It will reduce traffic jams by going through the golf course.

Extend

13. a) Write two survey questions that relate to a topic of your choice, such as sports, fashion, movies, or games.
  • Develop a question that contains bias.
  • Develop a different question that is free of influencing factors.

  b) Use the first question to survey 20 friends or classmates. Use the second question to survey 20 different friends or classmates.

  c) Compare the results. Identify the bias in the first question. Explain how its wording may have affected the results.

14. a) You have been hired to develop Arctic adventure tours. Develop three survey questions to help determine the activities that appeal to tourists.

  b) Exchange your questions with a classmate. Critique each other's questions for clarity and the presence of any influencing factors.

  c) Based on the feedback, revise your survey questions so they are clearly written and free of influencing factors.

15. When interpreting the results of a political poll, why is it important to know the source of the poll?

Math Link

For your research project, select a wildlife protection or management topic.

a) Use a graphic organizer such as the concept map shown here to help you organize ideas for your topic. Record subtopics and connecting details and facts.

b) Choose a subtopic to study.

c) Consider what data you need to obtain related to your topic. Then, write three possible research questions.

d) Exchange your questions with a classmate to check that they are free of influencing factors. Revise your questions if necessary.

I am interested in the effects of climate change on Arctic mammals, in particular, the beluga whale.

Climate Change — melting sea ice — walrus — threatened Arctic mammals — narwhal — polar bear — beluga whale — habitat loss — shifts in food supply — rising water temperature

WWW Web Link

For information about national and provincial parks in Canada, go to www.mathlinks9.ca and follow the links.

Research Questions: How does melting sea ice threaten Arctic mammals? Which Arctic mammals are most threatened by melting sea ice? What are the population trends for beluga whales in Canada?

Collecting Data

Focus On ...

After this lesson you will be able to...

- identify the difference between a population and a sample
- identify different types of samples
- justify using a population or a sample for given situations
- determine whether results from a sample can be applied to a population

Do Internet forums accurately reflect the opinions of all their readers? Do these people share the same opinions as those who do not read the forums?

How can you reduce the chances of making inaccurate predictions from a survey?

Explore Using Survey Data to Make Predictions

Work as a class. Develop a question to determine the opinions of students at your school about a topic of your choice. For a topic, you might choose favourite foods, sports, actors, or musicians.

1. Write and edit your survey question.

2. Survey everyone in your class.

3. **a)** Organize the results.

   b) Based on the results of the class survey, predict the whole school's response to your question.

4. Does your prediction accurately reflect the opinions of all students in your school? Explain.

Reflect and Check

5. Is your class a **population** or a **sample**? Explain.

6. How else might you choose people for your survey to reflect the opinions of all students in your school?

7. How can you reduce the chances of making inaccurate predictions using a survey?

Link the Ideas

There are several different types of samples.

convenience sample
- a sample created by choosing individuals from the population who are easy to access

random sample
- a sample created by choosing a specific number of individuals randomly from the whole population. *Random* means that each individual has an equal chance of being chosen. As a result, a random sample is likely to represent the whole population. Data from a random sample can be used to make predictions about the population. Stratified samples and systematic samples are types of random samples.

stratified sample
- a sample created by dividing the whole population into distinct groups, and then choosing the same fraction of members from each group

systematic sample
- a sample created by choosing individuals at fixed intervals from an ordered list of the whole population

voluntary response sample
- a sample created by inviting the whole population to participate

population
- all of the individuals in the group being studied
- for example, the population in a federal election is all eligible voters

sample
- any group of individuals selected from the population
- for example, a sample of the population in a federal election might be 100 individuals chosen from each province or territory

Example 1: Identify the Population

Identify the population for each situation. Then, state whether you would survey the population or a sample of the population. Explain your reasoning.

a) A bicycle store owner wants to know which brand of mountain bike her customers prefer.

b) The school board wants to know how many hours of homework students do each day.

c) A candle manufacturer wants to know how many of its candles are made with flaws.

Solution

a) The population is the store's customers. It depends on the size of the store. A small store might survey all of its customers. A large, busy store would likely survey a sample of customers. For them it would be time-consuming and costly to survey all of the customers.

b) The population is students in schools within the school board. The school board would likely survey a stratified sample of its students. They would want to include the same fraction of students at various grade levels because the amount of homework done varies from grade to grade.

c) The population is all candles made by the company. A small company might check each candle made. A large company might check every tenth candle. It would be costly and time-consuming to check every item.

Show You Know

For each scenario, identify the population. Then, indicate whether you would survey the population or a sample. Explain your reasoning.

a) The Royal Garden restaurant needs to know which main dish its customers favour.

b) Stephan wants to find out if teachers in Canada prefer to wear glasses or contact lenses.

c) A junior hockey team wants to find out why some people who bought season tickets last year are not buying them this year.

Example 2: Identify a Sample

For each situation, describe how the sample could be selected. Identify the type of sample.

a) A teacher wishes to get feedback from her class about the school dance. She plans to survey 5 students out of a class of 30.

b) A telephone company wants to determine whether a fitness centre would be well used by its 3000 employees. The company plans to survey 300 employees.

c) A chain store is trying to decide whether to open a store in Camrose, Alberta. The company decides to survey people in Camrose and three nearby towns. The population of each location is shown in the table.

Location	Population
Camrose	16 000
Bashaw	825
Tofield	1 876
Daysland	876

d) A marketing research company mails surveys to all of the adult residents in a town. The survey asks about brands of consumer products. The residents are asked to mail their responses in a prepaid envelope.

e) A restaurant owner wants to know the favourite pizza topping of his customers. He plans to survey every customer who orders a pizza in his restaurant between 5:00 p.m. and 10:00 p.m. one evening.

Solution

You can use different types of samples in a survey. These are some possible solutions.

a) The teacher could put all the students' names in a box and draw five names. This is a *random sample*.

b) The company plans to survey 300 out of their 3000 employees. To ensure that the sample fairly represents the population, the company might interview every tenth person on the payroll list. This is a *systematic sample*. This type of sample is time and cost efficient.

c) Since the city has more people who use the company's products than the nearby towns, the company could survey 25% of the population in each location. This is a *stratified sample*. Since 25% of each group is surveyed, the same proportion of each town is represented in the sample. In this case, the company would survey 4000 people from Camrose, 206 people from Bashaw, 469 people from Tofield, and 219 people from Daysland.

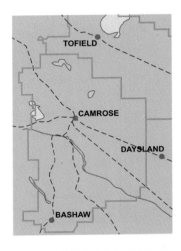

d) The marketing research company is inviting all residents to participate. This is a *voluntary response sample*. This sample may not represent the population because only those who are interested will respond.

e) This is a *convenience sample*. It is not random since only customers who order pizza are surveyed. However, the sample does target customers who will provide useful input. These customers are easily accessible. The sample provides the owner with information right away and costs no extra money.

> For each situation, is there a different type of sample that might be used? If so, explain what type of sample and how you would organize it.

Show You Know

a) For each scenario, what type of sample would you use? How would you select the sample?
- A marketing firm plans to conduct a telephone survey in a city of 800 000 people. The survey asks whether there is interest in a new art gallery.
- A student wants to know the most popular cell phone provider that grade 9 students use.

b) In each case, identify the type of sample.
- A coach puts the names of all of the basketball players into a hat and draws one name for a free basketball.
- A questionnaire is sent to every ninth person on an alphabetical list of a store's credit card customers.
- The student council invites all students to provide ideas for activities.

Key Ideas

- A population is the whole group of individuals being studied. It is not always practical or cost effective to survey everyone in a large population. You might survey a sample of the population.
- A sample is any part of the population.
- A random sample ensures that all people have an equal chance of being selected for a study. You can use data from a random sample to make predictions about the population. Systematic samples and stratified samples are types of random samples.
- Voluntary response samples and convenience samples are types of non-random samples.

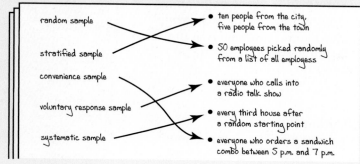

Check Your Understanding

Communicate the Ideas

1. Your friend sends you this e-mail. Write your response.

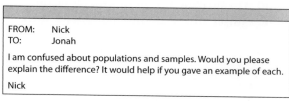

> FROM: Nick
> TO: Jonah
>
> I am confused about populations and samples. Would you please explain the difference? It would help if you gave an example of each.
>
> Nick

2. A group can be the population or a sample, depending on the survey question. Do you agree? Give examples to support your opinion.

3. Kim and Scott want to know how many people took public transit to come to the sold-out concert. The seating capacity at the venue is 18 000 people.

Kim: I plan to ask the first 20 people who arrive.

Scott: I plan to ask the first 200 people.

   a) Whose sample would provide a more accurate representation of the population? Explain why.

   b) Recommend a different type of sample that would give more accurate results. Explain your reasoning.

Practise

For help with #4 and #5, refer to Example 1 on pages 423-424.

4. Identify the population for each survey question. Indicate whether the population or a sample should be used for the survey. Justify your choice.

a)
> Which band rocks like no other?

b)
> Who will be next year's grade 10 representative on student council?

c)
> Which styles of soccer shirts should be sold at Sports R Us?

d)
> What brand of shampoo do you prefer?

5. In each case, identify the population. State whether you would survey the population or a sample of the population. Justify your choice.

a) A newspaper wants to know the online activities of Internet users at home.

b) The principal wants to know if people associated with the school are in favour of school uniforms.

c) An electronics store needs to find out whether its customers are satisfied with the repairs and services department.

d) The municipal government wants to determine if bus transit is needed for people with special needs.

For help with #6 and #7, refer to Example 2 on pages 424-425.

6. For each situation in #5, what type of sample would you use? How would you select the sample?

7. For each context, identify and describe the sample you would select for a survey.

a) A radio talk-show host wants listeners' views on a proposed by-law about watering lawns and gardens.

b) A province wants to select 25 schools to participate in a new physical education program.

c) A marketing firm wants to know teens' favourite magazines.

d) A reporter wants to ask people downtown about their plans to participate in the Big Valley Jamboree.

> **Did You Know?**
>
> The Big Valley Jamboree, which is held in Camrose, Alberta, is Canada's biggest country music show. It was voted the Canadian Country Music Association's Country Music Event of the Year in 2006.

Apply

8. For each context, would you recommend surveying the population or a sample? Justify your choice.

a) You want to determine the air quality in hospitals in Edmonton, Alberta.

b) You want to know post-secondary plans of grade 9 students.

c) You want to test the quality of parachutes.

d) You want to test the quality of bike tires.

9. Kristi wants to create a menu for a family picnic that will appeal to adults, teens, and children. Her family includes 20 adults, 8 teens, and 12 children. If she has time to talk to only 10 people, how should she choose her sample? Explain.

10. Jason, a member of the Graduation Committee, plans to ask each student who enters the cafeteria the following questions.

> What is your favourite paint colour for the cafeteria walls? _____
>
> Should the cafeteria be used for graduation?   YES   NO

a) Identify the population.

b) Identify the sample.

c) Will the results of his survey accurately represent the population? Explain.

d) Is Jason correct in using the same sample for both questions? Explain your thinking.

11. The student council plans to survey students about how best to spend the budget for activities. Enzo prefers to spend the money on baseball equipment. He decides to randomly survey students at a baseball game.

a) Is there a bias in Enzo's sample? If so, what is the bias?

b) Describe a sample that would reflect the overall opinion of students. Explain your thinking.

12. Anita and Cindi are asked to find out what type of mural to paint in the entrance of their office tower. There are 1400 employees. Cindi proposes using a random sample of 20 employees. Anita suggests using a stratified sample to get input from every department. Whose sampling method is better? Explain your reasoning.

13. Erin plans to survey her friends to determine the average number of children per household in Canada. Is this a random sample? Explain your reasoning.

14. Ben asked 50 people at random in a mall the following question.

> Are you allergic to any of these animals?
> A   cats
> B   dogs
> C   birds
> D   gerbils
> E   hedgehogs

His results are displayed.

Animal Allergy	Frequency	Total
Cats		26
Dogs		12
Birds		8
Gerbils		4
Hedgehogs		0

a) Ben made the following predictions based on his data. Do you agree with each prediction? Explain.
  - Almost 25% of the population is allergic to dogs.
  - Hedgehogs do not cause allergies.

b) Improve the survey question. Explain your reasoning.

Extend

15. Search various media for information about a recent survey. Use sources such as magazine and newspaper articles, or radio, television, and Internet reports.

a) Identify and comment on the population and the sample.

b) Are the predictions valid for the population? Explain your reasoning.

c) Was the survey well conducted? What improvements, if any, would you recommend?

16. Five firefighters conducted a survey to assess how well the fire department is performing. They asked local residents the following question.

> Which of the following choices best describes your opinion of how well the fire department is doing?
> A   Excellent
> B   Very Good
> C   Good
> D   Poor

A week later, the local paper has the headline as shown.

THE DAILY NEWS

Survey Reveals Majority Very Satisfied With Fire Department

a) How might the wording of the question affect the collection of data? Rewrite the question to produce more accurate responses.

b) What else may have influenced the collection of data? Describe how to conduct a survey that would reflect opinions more accurately.

Math Link

For your research project, choose one of the research questions you wrote for the Math Link on page 421.

a) What is your question?

b) Write a hypothesis that clearly states what you want to prove or disprove.

c) Identify and describe the population for your question.

d) To answer your question, you will need to find data from studies and surveys that have already been done. You will do the research in the Math Link on page 439. What sampling methods do you think would be used to collect data related to your question? Explain your reasoning.

An example is shown.

> **Literacy Link**
>
> A *hypothesis* is a statement put forward to guide an investigation.

Research Question: What are the population trends for beluga whales in Canada?

We predict that all beluga whale populations in Canada are threatened.

We hypothesize that there are few differences in the population trends for the whale populations in Canada.

Beluga whale, Somerset Island, Nunavut

The beluga whale populations in Canada can be organized into seven groups.

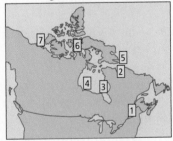

1. St. Lawrence
2. Ungava Bay
3. Eastern Hudson Bay
4. Western Hudson Bay
5. Cumberland Sound
6. High Arctic
7. Beaufort Sea

We expect that studies will use samples of beluga whale populations since there are large numbers of whales spread out over large areas.

Probability in Society

When planning an outdoor event, knowing the probability of a rain shower or a thunderstorm can be helpful. Forecasters often use probability to express their degree of certainty in the chance of a weather event occurring. For example, a 30% probability of rain today means that there are 3 chances in 10 that you will get wet today.

To produce a probability forecast, the forecaster studies the current weather situation, including wind and moisture patterns and determines how these patterns will change over time. What assumptions might a weather forecaster make when making a probability forecast?

Explore Making Decisions Based on Probability

You are a town planner and need to know if people want walking trails or bike paths along the nearby river. There are 15 000 people in the town. You decide to survey 1500 people.

1. Identify the population.

2. Describe how you might select the sample and how you could conduct the survey.

3. a) As a result of the survey, suppose 60% of people prefer bike paths. What prediction would you make about the preference of the town's population?

 b) What assumptions did you make in your prediction?

Reflect and Check

4. a) Exchange your sample with the one of a classmate. Does your classmate's sample represent the population? Explain your reasoning.

 b) Based on the sample, what decision will you make about walking trails or bike paths?

Link the Ideas

Example 1: Use a Sample to Make a Prediction About the Population

Ruth wants to determine the most common eye colour of students. All grade 12 students in five of seven high schools in a city recorded their eye colour. A total of 2300 students were surveyed. The results are shown in the table.

Eye Colour	Total
Brown	1656
Blue	483
Green	115
Other	46

a) From the results, predict how many of the 7200 students at the local college will have brown eyes. Show your thinking.

b) Is your prediction reasonable? Explain why or why not.

WWW Web Link

For information about gene types that determine eye colour, go to www.mathlinks9.ca and follow the links.

Solution

a) Of the 2300 students surveyed, 1656 students have brown eyes.

$$\text{Percent with brown eyes} = \frac{1656}{2300} \times 100$$
$$= 72$$

Calculate 72% of 7200.
$0.72 \times 7200 = 5184$

Based on the results, approximately 5200 students at the local college will have brown eyes.

Strategies
Estimate and Check

Over half of the surveyed students have brown eyes. This means that at least 3600 students at the college have brown eyes.

b) No, not necessarily. An assumption was made that the high school sample represents the college population.

The sample represents the local grade 12 population by surveying all students in five out of seven schools. The sample may not represent the college student population. A college often has many students who come from other parts of the province or territory, and other provinces and countries. In this case, the sample could be a **biased sample**. As a result, the prediction may not be valid for the college population.

You can be more confident that the prediction is reasonable by revising the prediction statement to include a limitation. "If the student population in the high schools and the college are similar, based on the results, there are approximately 5200 college students who have brown eyes."

biased sample
• does not represent the population
• can make survey results inaccurate

Literacy Link

To *generalize* means to make a broad statement from known facts.

Did You Know?

Advertising and marketing agencies often generalize results from a sample that does not represent the population. They do this in order to promote a product or service. Consumers need to consider advertising claims carefully.

Show You Know

Use the information in Example 1 to help answer the following.

a) Predict how many of the local college students have blue eyes or green eyes. Show your work.

b) Can you generalize the results from the sample to the local college population? Explain.

c) What limitation might you include to make your prediction more accurate?

Example 2: Avoid Making a False Prediction

Mr. Krutz gave an assignment worth 30 marks. After marking the first five papers, he was concerned that the students did not understand the assignment. He predicted most students would not do well.

a) Based on Mr. Krutz's sample, predict the "average" mark for the whole class on the assignment as a percent.

b) The scores for all 30 students in the class are:

20	15	18	19	18	16	17	23	24	30
22	24	21	20	24	25	19	24	15	28
27	28	22	24	19					
13	28	22	24	20					

Why does Mr. Krutz's sample lead him to make a false prediction?

Solution

a) To predict the average mark, Mr. Krutz could use the measures of central tendency.

Mean:

$$\text{Mean} = \frac{20 + 15 + 18 + 19 + 18}{5}$$

$$= 18$$

The mean is 18.

Median:
The median is 18.

Mode:
The mode is 18.

The mean, median, and mode for the sample scores are 18. Based on the sample statistics, the "average" mark on the assignment is predicted to be

$\frac{18}{30} \times 100$ or 60%.

Strategies

Organize, Analyse, and Solve

b) The mean, median, and mode for the class population are 22, 22, and 24, respectively.

How did Mr. Krutz determine these values?

Mr. Krutz assumed that the sample consisting of the first five papers was representative of the entire class. This is false. The mean score in the sample is 60%. The mean score in the population is approximately 73%. The most frequent score is 80%.

Mr. Krutz may have considered too few members of the class. The sample does not represent the population.

Show You Know

Use the data in Example 2.

What if Mr. Krutz had marked the last five papers first?

Do they give a more reasonable prediction of the class average? Explain.

Example 3: Make a Decision Based on Probability

A youth association surveys its 400 members about their preferred activity. There are 100 members in each of four groups. The activities were chosen from a youth activities resource. The table displays the survey results.

Group	Swimming	Rock Climbing	Watching Movies	Bowling	Total
Red	14	9	40	37	100
Blue	11	19	59	11	100
Green	27	12	57	4	100
Yellow	13	24	44	19	100

a) What is the probability that a member of any group will choose swimming? Based on this, predict how many of the 400 members will choose swimming.

b) What assumptions did you make?

c) Based on the survey results, predict the probability that a member will choose swimming.

d) Compare your answers for parts a) and c). Explain any differences.

Solution

a) The theoretical probability of choosing any one of the four activities is equally likely.

$P(\text{swimming}) = \dfrac{1}{4}$ or 25%

The probability that a member of any group will choose swimming is $\dfrac{1}{4}$.

Since there are 400 members, 100 will probably choose swimming.

b) The assumptions are as follows:
- Every activity has an equal chance of being selected.
- Members have an equal level of interest in each activity.

c) The survey results reflect the experimental probability.

$$P(\text{swimming}) = \dfrac{14 + 11 + 27 + 13}{400}$$

$$= \dfrac{65}{400}$$

$\dfrac{65}{400} = 16.25\%$

The experimental probability that a member will choose swimming is 16.25%.

d) 25% > 16.25%. The theoretical probability is greater than the experimental probability. Watching movies has the greatest probability. The group of students who answered this survey appear to prefer watching movies to swimming, rock climbing, or bowling. The experimental probability gives a truer reflection of the youths' interests.

Refer to the information in Example 3.

a) Based on the survey results, what is the probability that a member will choose watching movies? bowling?

b) If you were the youth coordinator planning the activities, how would you determine the favourite activity? Explain your reasoning.

Key Ideas

- A biased sample can make survey results inaccurate.
- When a sample represents the population, you can generalize the results to the population.
- You can use experimental probability and theoretical probability to help make decisions based on probability.

> A biased sample may result when a large percent of individuals in a sample refuse to participate in a survey.

Check Your Understanding

Communicate the Ideas

1. Kelly is confused about the difference between a sample that represents the population and one that does not. Use an example to help explain the difference to him.

2. Use the cartoon to explain how a sample might result in a false prediction.

3. How might you use experimental probability and theoretical probability to help make a decision about what flavours of ice cream to offer at a sport tournament?

Practise

For help with #4 and #5, refer to Example 1 on page 431.

4. A light bulb factory samples light bulbs as they come off the assembly line. A random sample shows that 1 bulb out of every 20 is defective. In a run of 1380 bulbs, the quality manager predicts that 69 bulbs will be defective. What assumptions did the quality manager make in his prediction?

5. A toothpick factory samples every 100th toothpick for damage. The sample shows a 0.17% probability of damage. How many toothpicks would you predict to be damaged in the daily production of 2.4 million toothpicks? Include any assumptions you made in your prediction.

For help with #6 and #7, refer to Example 2 on pages 432-433.

6. A cafeteria supervisor asked three students who are vegetarians about their preference for a lunch menu. All three chose garden salad, tomato soup, and garlic bread. The supervisor plans to serve their menu choice the next day, thinking that it will sell well.

   a) Did the sample lead the supervisor to make a false prediction? Explain.

   b) If the prediction is false, explain how you might make a more accurate one.

7. A manufacturer makes the following claim about the mass of its health bars.

   Each bar has a mass of at least 50 g.

   Erika and Brett weighed ten health bars to check the claim. Three bars had a mass less than 50 g and one bar had a mass of exactly 50 g. The students predicted that 30% of the health bars made by the company would not meet the claim.

   a) Did the sample lead the students to make a false prediction? Explain.

   b) If the prediction is false, explain how you might make a more accurate one.

For help with #8 and #9, refer to Example 3 on page 434.

8. Greenville, a town with 4000 people, is having an election for mayor. A reporter polled 40 people and found 53% chose Candidate A, 23% chose Candidate B, and the rest chose Candidate C.

   a) How many people polled chose Candidate C?

   b) What is the theoretical probability that a voter will choose Candidate A? What assumptions did you make?

   c) Compare the experimental and theoretical probabilities of Candidate A winning.

   d) The reporter predicts that Candidate A will win the election. Do you agree with his prediction? Explain your reasoning.

9. A movie rental company has five types of movies. They are drama, comedy, horror, action, and science fiction/fantasy movies.

   a) What is the theoretical probability that a person will choose a comedy?

   b) What assumptions did you make?

   c) The table displays the movie preferences from a random survey of 50 customers. Predict the probability that a customer will choose a comedy movie.

Movie Type	Responses
Drama	15
Comedy	10
Horror	12
Action	11
Science fiction/Fantasy	2

   d) Compare your answers for parts a) and c). Explain any differences.

   e) About how many rentals out of a total of 2000 movies will be drama movies?

Apply

10. Miya received the following scores from ten judges in a skating competition. Skating performances are given a score out of 10.

Judge	1	2	3	4	5	6	7	8	9	10
Score	8.5	6	6.5	6.5	6.5	7	6	6.5	4.5	7

    a) Calculate Miya's mean score based on all ten judges.

    b) Use the first three judges' scores as a sample. Calculate the mean.

    c) Use the last three judges' scores as a sample. Calculate the mean.

    d) Compare the mean from each sample to the mean for all judges. Are the samples a good predictor for Miya's overall score? Explain.

11. Jack wants to know the weekly earnings of grade 9 students who work part-time in the summer. He surveyed five grade 9 students. Here are the results: $75, $120, $45, $250, and $85.

  a) Is this a biased sample? Explain your reasoning.

  b) Jack concluded that grade 9 students earn an average of $115 per week. Do you agree with his conclusion? Explain.

12. Colin read an article that claims that more girls are born than boys. Colin predicted that a couple has a 50% chance of having a boy. He tested the prediction by tossing a coin 100 times for each of 10 trials. Here are the results.

Trial	Boys	Girls
1	40	60
2	43	57
3	50	50
4	46	54
5	48	52
6	58	42
7	50	50
8	49	51
9	50	50
10	53	47

Do these experimental results confirm Colin's prediction or the article's claim? Show your thinking.

13. The graph shows the number of collision claims per 100 vehicles insured for male drivers in Alberta, in 2004.

Number of Collision Claims Per 100 Vehicles Insured

Many insurance companies charge drivers under the age of 25 higher insurance premiums based on the probability of accidents. Find information about car insurance costs based on the probability of collision. Paste the article into your notebook.

a) In the article, what are the assumptions associated with each probability? Is each probability accurate? Explain.

b) In your opinion, is there a bias against young drivers? Explain your reasoning.

c) "Decisions about car insurance costs are based on a combination of experimental probability, theoretical probability, and biased judgment." Do you agree or disagree with this statement? Explain your reasoning.

WWW Web Link

For information about road safety, risk factors, and factors affecting car insurance rates, go to www.mathlinks9.ca and follow the links.

14. Cathy and John are waiting for the bus. John predicts that one of the next five vehicles to pass the bus stop will be a minivan. Cathy predicts two of the next five vehicles will be minivans. John made his prediction based on five types of vehicles on the road: cars, sport utility vehicles (SUVs), buses, minivans, and trucks.

  a) How do you think John and Cathy made their predictions?

  b) John and Cathy decided to test their predictions by conducting a survey. They observed vehicles passing the bus stop for 1 h at the same time each day for five days. The table shows their results.

Type	Day 1	Day 2	Day 3	Day 4	Day 5
Car	30	28	25	27	25
SUV	20	25	18	22	18
Bus	4	4	3	4	4
Minivan	8	10	12	9	7
Truck	10	7	11	8	10

From the results, whose prediction was more accurate? Explain.

  c) In one day, 800 vehicles passed the bus stop. Based on the survey results, predict the number of trucks.

15. The Jackson family is celebrating the coming birth of triplets. They currently have two boys. Mrs. Jackson is hoping for three girls.

a) What is the theoretical probability that she will have three girls? Show your thinking.

b) The Jacksons used a random number generator to simulate the situation. They decide that 1 indicates a girl and 0 indicates a boy. The table shows the results for ten trials. What is the experimental probability of three girls?

Trial	Experimental Results		
1	0	0	0
2	0	1	1
3	0	1	0
4	1	0	1
5	1	0	1
6	1	1	0
7	1	0	0
8	1	1	0
9	0	0	0
10	0	1	0

c) Compare the experimental probability and the theoretical probability.

d) The boys predict that their mother will have three more boys. Do you agree with their prediction? Justify your answer.

e) What assumptions did you make?

Extend

16. A random sample of 160 students out of 2100 participants in a summer youth program responded to a survey.

	Yes	No
Do you play a musical instrument?	40	120
Do you play on a sports team?	25	135

a) Does the sample represent the population? Explain.

b) Based on the data, what is the probability that a participant, chosen at random, will play a musical instrument?

c) Of the 160 students interviewed, 20 students played a musical instrument and were on a sports team. Predict how many of the 2100 youth group members do not play a musical instrument or play on a sports team.

d) What assumptions did you make in part c)?

17. Search magazines, newspapers, or the Internet. Look for an article that uses probability to make a prediction for a population.

a) Identify the assumptions associated with the probability.

b) Explain the limitations of each assumption.

c) In your opinion, is the prediction accurate? Justify your answer.

18. Search magazines, newspapers, or the Internet for an issue of personal interest.

a) Take a stand on the issue. Write an argument that includes a probability statement to support your stand. Use methods of your choice to display your data.

b) Take the opposite stand. Using the same data, or new data, write an argument that includes a probability statement to support your new stand.

c) Present your arguments to a classmate. Have your classmate point out the strengths and weaknesses of both arguments.

Math Link

For your research project, collect data from studies and surveys that have been done. Use sources such as scientific publications and the Internet. Depending on the data that you find, you may need to revise your research question.

a) Describe the data you will look for. Where will you look?

b) Record notes for at least three studies related to your question. Include the following information for each study:
- Describe the sampling method used. Did it involve the population or a sample?
- For a study involving a sample, discuss whether the results can be generalized to the population.
- Describe the method used to collect the data.
- Summarize the results.
- Describe any assumptions that were made. Explain the limitations of each assumption.
- Discuss the accuracy of any predictions made about the population.
- Provide complete source information.

A summary of a whale population study is shown.

We researched a study done by the Committee on the Status of Endangered Wildlife in Canada. The table shows the estimated whale populations.

Beluga Whale Population	Estimated Population (2004)	Population Compared to Pre-Whaling	Trend
St. Lawrence	950	low	• endangered • stable or increasing
Ungava Bay	too small to estimate	very low, or may no longer exist	• may no longer exist
Eastern Hudson Bay	2000	low	• decreasing rapidly
Western Hudson Bay	23 000	large	• unknown
Cumberland Sound	1500	low	• endangered • stable or increasing
High Arctic	20 000	unknown	• unknown
Beaufort Sea	39 000	large	• not threatened • increasing

Smith, T. G. "COSEWIC Assessment and Update Status Report on the Beluga Whale *Delphinapterus leucas* in Canada." 2004. Committee on the Status of Endangered Wildlife in Canada. Ottawa. 20 Oct 2008 <http://dsp-psd.pwgsc.gc.ca/Collection/CW69-14-170-2004E.pdf>.

11.4

Developing and Implementing a Project Plan

Focus on...

After this lesson, you will be able to...

- develop a research project plan
- complete a research project according to a plan, draw conclusions, and communicate findings
- self-assess a research project by applying a rubric

Developing and carrying out a research project requires careful planning. During the Math Links on pages 421, 429, and 439, you worked on Step 1, as shown in the flow chart. Use your work to continue to develop your project plan. In this section, you will also develop a rubric, carry out your plan, and then assess your project using your rubric.

Use the flow chart to help organize your research project and carry out your plan.

Step 1: Develop the project plan.
- ✔ Write the research question.
- ✔ Write the hypothesis.
- ✔ Describe the population.
- ✔ Describe how you will collect data.
- ✔ Record notes for at least three studies related to the research question.

Step 2: Create a rubric to assess your project.

Step 3: Continue to develop the project plan.
- ✔ Describe how you will display the data.
- ✔ Describe how you will analyse the data.
- ✔ Describe how you will present your findings.

Step 4: Complete the project according to your plan.
- ✔ Display the data.
- ✔ Analyse the data.
- ✔ Draw a conclusion or make a prediction.
- ✔ Evaluate the research results.

Step 5: Present your findings.

Step 6: Self-assess your project.

Materials

- blank Research Project Rubric

Step 1

Complete the research for your project.

Develop a rubric so that you know what is expected. Use the following example and a copy of the blank Research Project Rubric to help develop your own.

- List the criteria in column 1. You may find it useful to order the criteria according to the sequence of the project.

- For each criterion, record an indicator for each of four levels of performance. See how the first row in the example below is completed to give you ideas for your own rubric.
  - Level 1 reflects work that shows little evidence of expected results.
  - Level 2 reflects work that meets the minimum expected standard.
  - Level 3 reflects work that meets the expected standard.
  - Level 4 reflects work that is beyond the expected standard.

Criteria	Level 1	Level 2	Level 3	Level 4
Planning • question and hypothesis • description of population	• not clear and not related • limited or missing	• fairly clear but not related • some description	• mostly clear and related • adequate description	• very clear, concise, and related • detailed description
Performing • research and data collection				
Recording • data display				
Analysing • analysis • conclusion(s)				
Presenting • project plan and evaluation of results				

Step 3

Continue to develop the project plan.

a) Describe how you will organize and display your data. Select only data that help you answer your question.

b) Describe your method for analysing the data from the studies you find. Consider the following ideas.
- Describe any assumptions that were made. Explain the limitations of each assumption.
- Discuss the accuracy of any predictions made about the population.

c) Describe how you will present your findings.

Step 4

Complete the project.

a) Display the data.

b) Analyse the data. Draw a conclusion or a prediction you can make from the data.

c) Evaluate your research results. Consider using the following questions.
- Do the data answer your question or do you need to do further research?
- Do the data support your hypothesis? Explain.
- Are the data biased? Explain.
- What questions could you ask as a result of your research?
- What other sampling methods could have been considered?
- Troubleshoot any problems you may have encountered, such as the following: Did you use too few resources? Was your research question too broad? How well was the data collected? Were there influencing factors on the collection of data?

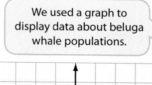

We used a graph to display data about beluga whale populations.

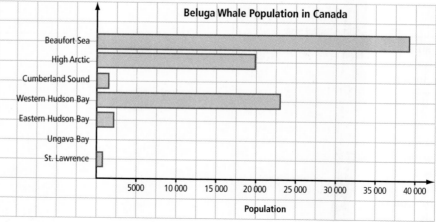

The data show significant differences in the size and population trends for the beluga populations in Canada. We would need to do further research to find the reasons for the differences.

The data do not support our hypothesis.

We had difficulty finding population counts. The estimates for whale populations range widely from a total of 72 000 to 144 000 belugas in Canadian waters.

There are problems in conducting whale counts using boat and aerial surveys. These methods are limited because they can count whales only near the surface. Studies that use satellite tracking, time-depth recording of animals, and aerial surveys are the most promising for future research.

There may have been a bias in the data due to the web sites we were able to access.

As a result of our research we could ask these questions:
- What factors affect the beluga whale population in each Canadian location?
- Conservation efforts for the St. Lawrence population appear to have helped maintain the numbers. Why have they not helped the Ungava Bay population?
- What are the trends for the populations of beluga whales in other locations in the world?

Step 5

Present your findings in a format of your choice. You might choose a written or oral report, use technology, or use a combination of formats.

Your presentation needs to outline your project plan and your conclusions. It should include:

- a title that indicates the purpose of your project
- a research question and a hypothesis
- a description of the population
- for the studies researched,
  - the sampling methods used
  - the methods used to collect data
  - the results and conclusions
- your display of the data and data sources
- your conclusion to answer your research question
- your evaluation of the research results
- a bibliography of all sources

Math Link: Wrap It Up!

You have arrived at the final step of your research project. You will assess your project.

Step 6

a) Use the rubric you developed to assess your research project. Identify your project's strengths and weaknesses.

b) Identify two things you liked about your project. Identify one thing you would do differently next time.

c) Have a classmate who read or watched your presentation assess your project using the rubric. Ask for constructive feedback on how to improve the project.

Chapter 11 Review

Key Words

For #1 to #9, choose the letter representing the term that best matches each description.

1. an example is every tenth person in a line-up

2. privacy and cost are examples that affect data collection

3. an example is polling 2 students out of 100 students about who will win an election

4. an example is the first 30 people entering the gates at a football game

5. a sample in which all members of a population have an equal chance of being selected

6. any group selected from a population

7. the whole group of people being studied

8. an example is dividing the population into males and females and then randomly selecting a proportional number from each group

9. an example is a population invited to call in a response to a radio talk show

A convenience sample

B population

C influencing factors

D sample

E biased sample

F voluntary response sample

G random sample

H systematic sample

I stratified sample

11.1 Factors Affecting Data Collection, pages 414–421

10. For each situation, identify and describe any influencing factors that affect a survey.

   a) Ask the first 40 people entering a park office if they are willing to pay increased rates to help offset increased costs.

   b) Ask ten people selected at random in a grocery store if they like store-bought bread.

   c) Ask 15 juice drinkers if they would support replacing the juice in the vending machine with bottled water.

11. Identify any factors that may influence data collection. Then, write an improved survey question.

   a) Which do you prefer: chocolate cheesecake or strawberry cheesecake?

   b) Everybody loves The Rockets, but who is your favourite rock group?

   c) A recent survey shows that 45% of Internet users download music. What music did you download in the past month?

11.2 Collecting Data, pages 422–429

12. Identify the population for each situation. Then, describe how you would select a sample for each.

   a) the spending habits of teens in Canada

   b) the popularity of different kinds of music in your school

   c) the cost of gasoline in your community

13. For each situation, identify the type of sample. Identify any bias in each sample.

   a) The first 20 shoppers to enter the north entrance of a mall are surveyed.

   b) Youth conference delegates are divided into groups according to the western province or territory where they live. Then, 20 youths from each group are randomly selected.

   c) The area supervisor for a fast-food chain selects employees at one store location.

14. What type of sample do you recommend for each situation? Explain why.

    a) a survey of doctors, nurses, and hospital administrators to determine whether the hospital needs an additional wing

    b) a survey of customers to determine the favourite sundae topping

15. To check the spread of a disease among trees in a forest, a forester wants to inspect 10% of the trees. Identify each of the following types of samples the forester could use.

    a) Sample 10% of the trees closest to the logging road.

    b) Divide the forest into sections and randomly select 10% of the trees in each section.

    c) Give each tree a number. Randomly select a starting tree and then select every tenth tree after the starting number.

11.3 Probability in Society, pages 430–439

16. A biologist captures, tags, and releases 85 bull trout in a stream. A month later, she returns and captures 100 bull trout and notes that 28 of them have tags.

    a) Based on this result, predict how many bull trout fish are in the stream.

    b) What assumptions did you make?

    c) What could the biologist do differently to make the prediction more accurate?

> **Did You Know?**
>
> Bull trout, lake trout, and Arctic char belong to a subgroup of the salmon family. Bull trout that live in lakes can grow to more than 9 kg. Those that live in streams rarely grow to more than 2 kg.
>
>
> Bull trout, Oldman River, Alberta

17. Nancy is running for treasurer on student council. She surveys 20 people in her class about who they will vote for. Based on her survey results, Nancy predicts that 75% of the 328 grade 9 students will vote for her.

    a) Is her prediction reasonable? Explain.

    b) Explain how she could ensure a more accurate prediction.

18. Students in two grade 9 classes in a school were asked what item they spend most money on. The results are posted here.

Item	Number of Students
Movies	11
Cell phone	13
Music	11
Clothes	6
Other	7

The students were divided into four groups and asked to make a prediction for all grade 9 students based on the results.

Group 1: Grade 9s like buying other items more than clothes.

Group 2: Cell phones are more important to grade 9s than any other form of entertainment.

Group 3: Of the 500 grade 9 students in the city, it is likely that 135 will have cell phones.

Group 4: It is likely that a grade 9 student will spend his or her money on either movies or music.

Explain why you agree or disagree with each prediction.

Chapter 11 Practice Test

For #1 to #4, choose the best answer.

1. Linda and Matt each survey 20 people about the carving in front of the post office. Linda was in the mall entrance and Matt was in the entrance to the fine arts centre. When they compared their results, the responses were very different. What influencing factor(s) may have caused the difference?

   A cultural sensitivity

   B timing

   C use of language

   D all of the above

2. Diana wants to survey grade 9 students about their favourite flavour of soft drink. Which question is most appropriate?

   A Is cola your favourite type of soft drink?

   B Do you like soft drinks?

   C What is your favourite flavour of soft drink?

   D What brand of soft drink do you prefer?

3. An eco-tourism company is researching how to expand its tours. They divide the western provinces into eight areas. Then, they survey 10% of the population in each area. Which sampling method is this?

   A convenience sample

   B stratified sample

   C systematic sample

   D voluntary response sample

Bull River East Kootenay, British Columbia

4. A business sends questionnaires to 50% of its employees randomly selected from a list. Which sampling method is this?

   A convenience sample

   B stratified sample

   C systematic sample

   D voluntary response sample

Complete the statements in #5 to #7.

5. A small group that represents a population is a ▉▉▉▉ .

6. Choosing members of the population at fixed intervals from a membership list describes a ▉▉▉▉ .

7. A web site that asks browsers to fill out an online survey is using a ▉▉▉▉ .

Short Answer

8. Cheyenne wants to survey students in her high school about types of music for a school dance. They can choose from rap, alternative, rock, and country.

   a) What is the population for this study?

   b) Write a survey question that is clearly stated and free from influencing factors.

   c) Describe two sampling methods she could use for her survey.

9. Read the survey question.

   > Do you think students should take Physical Education in school?
   > YES   NO

   a) The school sports coaches are randomly surveyed. Is this sample biased? Explain.

   b) The school sports teams are randomly surveyed. Is this sample biased? Explain.

   c) Describe a sample that is free from bias.

10. For each situation, decide if you would survey the population or a sample. Give a reason.

a) A truck loaded with fresh produce arrives for inspection.

b) Are the smoke detectors in the office tower working?

c) How much exercise do students get?

11. On an assembly line for cell phones, a random sample shows 3% of the units are defective. How many are likely to be defective in a run of 3248 cell phones? Include any assumptions you made in your prediction.

Extended Response

12. Paul knew the theoretical probability of getting heads when he tossed a coin was 50%. After conducting an experiment of ten trials, his experimental probability of getting heads was 60%. He concluded that the more times he tosses the coin, the more likely he will get heads. Do you agree? Why or why not?

13. Greg is researching to what extent programs are successful in protecting burrowing owls. Burrowing owls are considered endangered in Canada. In 1977, there were about 2000 breeding pairs of burrowing owls in Canada. By 2003, the population was reduced to less than 500 pairs. Greg found data from the Manitoba Wildlife Branch that has been monitoring and protecting these owls since 1982.

The graph shows data about the burrowing owl population in Manitoba since 1989.

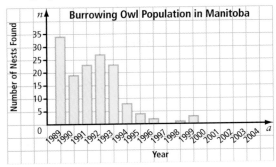

Based on the data, Greg concludes that programs in place to protect burrowing owls are not successful in increasing the population. Provide feedback to Greg about his question, data, and conclusion. What conclusion might you suggest to Greg? What further advice might you give?

Challenges

Global Warming

Tornados, floods, droughts, tsunami, killer heat waves, and other extreme weather events often make headlines. Many climate scientists have linked extreme weather events to global warming.

You be the climate scientist. Collect and analyse weather data to help you determine whether or not there is a warming trend in your area.

1. Collect climate data such as air temperature or ocean temperature for an area of your choice. Critique the quality of your data. Possible questions to consider include:
   • What sources did you use?
   • How was the data collected?
   • How far back in time does the data go?

2. Graph your data.

3. a) Is there a warming trend in the area you analysed? Justify your answer.
   b) What are the limitations of your data?
   c) Do your findings support global warming? Explain.

4. Exchange your data and graph(s) with those of a classmate. Assess the limitations of the data.

Did You Know?

Climate scientists or climatologists measure weather patterns and how they change over time in order to forecast the weather. They analyse and interpret maps, charts, photographs, and other data that include temperature, rain and snowfall, and wind.

WWW Web Link

For Environment Canada's climate data for specific locations and dates going back to 1840, go to www.mathlinks9.ca and follow the links.

Probability in Society

Read these headlines.

THE DAILY NEWS
60% of Audience Loves Movie

THE DAILY NEWS
54% of Canadian households have a water-saving showerhead.

Almost half of the people did not like this movie. No way that I will watch it!

Most people liked this movie. I want to watch this one!

This is terrible. Almost half of all Canadians do not care about conserving water.

We are doing well. More than half of all Canadians are conserving water.

Headlines such as these can be used to support different points of view. You be the researcher. Search newspapers, magazines, or the Internet for two different headlines that include a probability statement.

1. For each headline, state whether you think experimental probability or theoretical probability is involved. Explain your thinking.

2. **a)** Identify the assumptions associated with each probability.
   b) Describe the limitations of each assumption.

3. **a)** Use the probability statement from one headline to develop two opposing positions you could take.
   b) Write an argument to support each position.
   c) Identify one strength and one weakness of each argument.

WWW Web Link

For sources of online headlines, go to www.mathlinks9.ca and follow the links.

For online newspapers, go to www.mathlinks9.ca and follow the links.

Chapters 8–11 Review

Chapter 8

1. For each equation:
- Without solving, predict whether the value of x is greater than 1 or less than 1. Explain your reasoning.
- Solve to verify your prediction.

a) $8x = \dfrac{2}{5}$ **b)** $\dfrac{x}{9} = \dfrac{5}{6}$

c) $\dfrac{7}{x} = \dfrac{1}{4}$ **d)** $\dfrac{1}{x} = \dfrac{5}{2}$

2. The formula for the area of a triangle is $A = \dfrac{1}{2}bh$, where b is the length of the base and h is the altitude. A triangle has an area of 10.54 m² and a base length of 6.2 m. What is the altitude of the triangle?

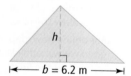

3. Bruno bought four identical boxes of granola. He received $6.04 in change from a $20.00 bill. How much did he pay for each box of granola?

4. Two electricians both charge a fee for a service call, plus an hourly rate for their work. Theo charges a $49.95 fee plus $40.00 per hour. Vita charges a $69.95 fee plus $32.00 per hour. For what length of service call do Theo and Vita charge the same amount?

5. The equilateral triangle and the square have equal perimeters. What is the side length of the square?

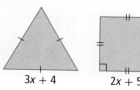

Chapter 9

6. What is the algebraic form of the inequality represented on each number line?

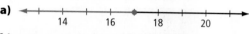

a)

b)

7. Represent each inequality graphically.

a) $x < -6$ **b)** $2.4 \leq x$

8. Write an inequality to represent each election promise that a politician made.

a) At least eight new highways projects will be started.

b) There will be a budget surplus of over 1.3 million this year.

c) Unemployment will be no more than 3.7%.

d) Taxes will be lowered by as much as 10%.

9. Solve each inequality. Express the solution algebraically and graphically.

a) $15 > x + 6.2$ **b)** $-25x < 40$

c) $\dfrac{x}{5} \geq -10$ **d)** $20 - x \leq 8$

10. Solve each inequality and verify the solution.

a) $4x + 17 \geq 35$

b) $8 < \dfrac{x}{4} + 3$

c) $5x + 30 > 8x - 9$

d) $2(3 - 4x) \leq 3(8 - 2x)$

11. Linda needs to hire a rubbish removal service to clean up a construction site. The Junk King charges $325 plus $110/t. The Clean Queen charges $145/t. How many tonnes of rubbish would make The Junk King the better option?

12. Lori is going to rent a climbing wall for a school fun night. The rental charge for the wall is $145/h. She has at most $800 to spend.

a) What is an inequality that can be used to model the situation?

b) For how many hours could Lori rent the wall and stay within her spending limit?

13. A company uses two different machines to make items they sell. The first machine has made 2000 items so far and produces new items at a rate of 25/h. The second machine has made 1200 items so far and produces new items at a rate of 45/h. When will the second machine have made more items than the first machine?

Chapter 10

14. Point C is the centre of the circle. ∠DAB = 47°. What are the measures of angles ∠DEB and ∠DCB? Justify your answers.

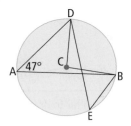

15. In the diagram, CD bisects chord AB. The radius of the circle is 7 cm, and chord AB = 9 cm. What is the length of CE? Express your answer to the nearest tenth of a centimetre.

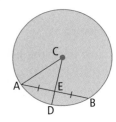

16. The radius of the circle shown is 25 mm. The radius CG is perpendicular to the chord EF. Chord EF is 7 mm from the centre at C. What is the length of the chord EF?

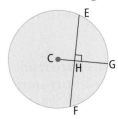

17. Point C is the centre of two concentric circles. The radius of the smaller circle is 9 cm. The length of chord FG is 40 cm and it is tangent to the smaller circle. What is the circumference of the larger circle? Express your answer to the nearest centimetre.

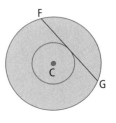

Chapter 11

18. For each survey question:
- Describe any influencing factor(s).
- Rewrite the question so it is clearly stated and free from influencing factors.

a)

> Do you like to play cards, the greatest indoor game?
> YES   NO

b)

> What type of milk do you prefer to drink?

19. You decide to survey students about their online activities.

a) What is the population?

b) Describe two different sampling methods you could use.

20. Identify the population and describe a sample for each situation. Justify your choice.

a) A television talk-show host asks the audience their views on a media story.

b) An author plans to survey people in a bookstore about whether they have read his book.

c) The sports coordinator at a school needs to find out how to improve services for students.

21. A marketer conducting a survey randomly selects 40 departments in 20 city stores in western Canada. From the 40 departments, she randomly selects 20 department managers and 6 sales associates.

a) Describe the population.

b) Describe the sampling method.

c) Is there more than one possible sample? Explain your thinking.

22. The grade 9 students organized a barbecue for kindergarten to grade 9 students. All grade 9 students were surveyed about the menu. Based on the survey, the students decided on the following menu.

hamburgers and pop for junior high students

hot dogs and juice for elementary students

At the barbecue, the elementary students were served before the junior high students. By the time that the junior high students were served, there were no hamburgers or pop left. They had to eat hot dogs and drink juice.

a) How did the sampling method used lead to a false prediction?

b) Describe a sampling method that would allow students to make an accurate prediction. Explain how you would conduct the survey.

23. A quiz has ten true/false questions.

a) What is the theoretical probability of answering each question correctly by guessing?

b) What assumptions have you made?

c) Model an experiment of ten trials to represent the quiz. Describe your model and complete the trials. Record your data.

d) What is your experimental probability of getting five out of ten questions correct?

e) Can you use these results to predict how well a student who guesses will do on the quiz? Explain.

Chapter 1

1.1 Line Symmetry, pages 12–15

4. a)

b)

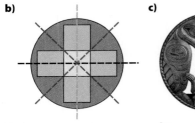

c)

5. a)

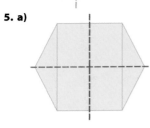

b)

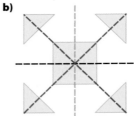

c)

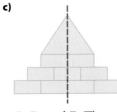

6. B, D, and E. They can be folded in two different ways so that they overlap exactly. Each of the other figures has more than two lines of symmetry.

7. a)   **b)**

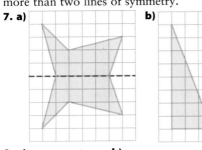

8. a)   **b)**

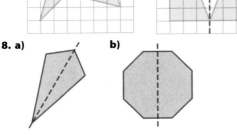

9. a)

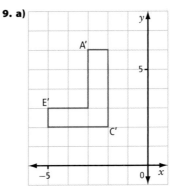

b) A′(−3, 6), C′(−2, 2), E′(−5, 3)   **c)** Yes, the original image and the reflected image show line symmetry. However, each individual figure does not show line symmetry within itself.

10. Example: **a)**

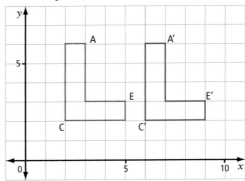

b) A′(7, 6), C′(6, 2), E′(9, 3)   **c)** No. The image was not reflected and does not contain line symmetry within itself.   **d)** No. See explanation in 10c).

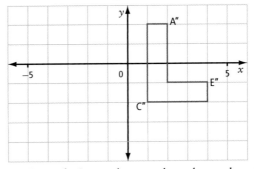

11. Example: I agree because these shapes show horizontal and/or vertical line symmetry within themselves, a horizontal or vertical translation of the shape results in line symmetry between the original and new images. A figure with only vertical line symmetry within itself will show line symmetry after a horizontal translation only.

12. a) Yes, the flag has horizontal line symmetry. If folded from bottom to top through the middle of the horizontal blue stripe, the upper and lower halves will overlap.
b) Moving the vertical blue and white stripes to the centre of the flag would give it two lines of symmetry.
13. a) one horizontal **b)** one vertical **c)** two: one horizontal and one vertical **d)** four: one horizontal, one vertical, and two oblique
14. Example:

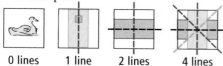

0 lines   1 line   2 lines   4 lines

15. a) B, C, D, E, H, I, K, O, X
b) A, H, I, M, O, T, U, V, W, X, Y **c)** H, I, O, X
16. a) Example:

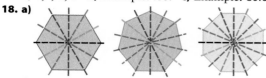

b) Example: HI H **c)** Example: WHO W
            I   H
                                    O

17. a) 0, I, 3, 8 **b)** Example: IOOI **c)** Example: 80I08
18. a)

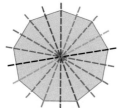

b) The number of equal, interior angles equals the number of lines of symmetry. **c)** Yes. As the number of interior angles increases, you approach a circle shape, which is symmetrical from all angles.

19. a) A **b)** Different colours mean that figure B becomes a non-symmetric figure. **c)** Figure A has five lines of symmetry.
20.

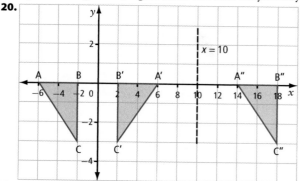

Triangle A″B″C″ is the result of a horizontal translation 20 units to the right.
21. a) If the two-dot separator in the digital clock is ignored, then both clocks show line symmetry at some time.

b) The digital clock can show horizontal line symmetry at 8:08, 8:38, 3:03 (not 1:01 or 10:10, etc., because of the shape of the number 1); the analogue clock can show line symmetry at any time when the line of symmetry bisects the angle between the hands and bisects the squares representing the numbers or when the time is 6:00 or 12:00.
22.

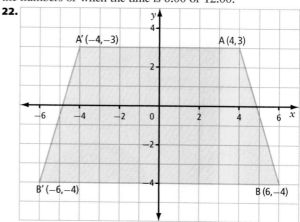

70 square units
23.

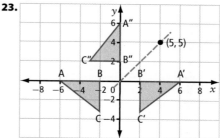

Triangle A″B″C″ is the image created by rotating the original triangle 90° about the origin.
24. Example: Yes, a three-dimensional object such as a cube is symmetric because all faces and edges are of equal size. A plane cutting the cube parallel to a face and through the centre will create two identical rectangular prisms.

1.2 Rotation Symmetry and Transformations, pages 21–25

4. a) order of rotation = 4, angle of rotation = 90°, fraction of a turn = $\frac{1}{4}$, centre of rotation is at centre of figure. **b)** order of rotation = 2, angle of rotation = 180°, fraction of a turn = $\frac{1}{2}$, centre of rotation is at centre of figure. **c)** order of rotation = 2, angle of rotation = 180°, fraction of a turn = $\frac{1}{2}$, centre of rotation is between 9 and 6.
5. a) Yes; angle of rotation = 90° **b)** Yes; angle of rotation = 120° **c)** Yes; angle of rotation = 180°
6. a) number of lines of symmetry = 6, order of rotation = 6
b) number of lines of symmetry = 2, order of rotation = 2
c) number of lines of symmetry = 2, order of rotation = 2

7. a) number of lines of symmetry = 3, angle of rotation = 120° **b)** number of lines of symmetry = 5, angle of rotation = 72°

8. a)

b) Rotate the original figure 180° and join the two figures. Translate the new figure to the right so it does not overlap. Join the two figures. Now join this new figure with the original one on the right.

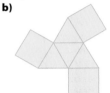

9. a) 3

b)

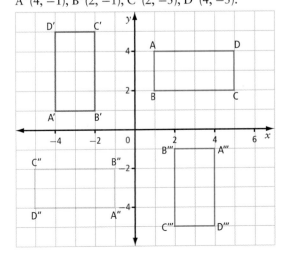

c) No, because the image does not show line symmetry.
10. a) Example: line symmetry: pu, pa; rotation symmetry: ki, ku;

11. a) Both. Lines of symmetry: the vertical black line with three red squares to its left and to its right in each row; the horizontal black line with two red squares above it and below it in each column. The centre of rotation is located where the two lines of symmetry intersect.
b) Neither. There would be a vertical line of symmetry through the noses of the centre column of faces if the face colours on each side of the line matched each other.
c) Neither. There would be 180° rotation symmetry if the pink and blue dolphins were the same colour.
d) Rotation symmetry only of order 4. The centre of rotation is at the centre of the figure.
12. a) The vertices of the images are:
A′(−4, 1), B′(−2, 1), C′(−2, 5), D′(−4, 5);
A″(−1, −4), B″(−1, −2), C″(−5, −2), D″(−5, −4);
A‴(4, −1), B‴(2, −1), C‴(2, −5), D‴(4, −5).

b) Each image is oriented with the longer dimension along the horizontal and the order of labelling switches between clockwise and counter-clockwise.

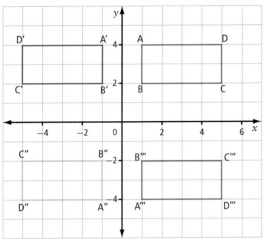

13. a) order of rotation = 4, angle of rotation = 90°
b) No; the rotation of the design makes line symmetry impossible.
14. a) There are eight lines of symmetry; the angle between the lines is 22.5°
b) order of rotation = 8, angle of rotation = 45°
15. Example:

16. a)

b)

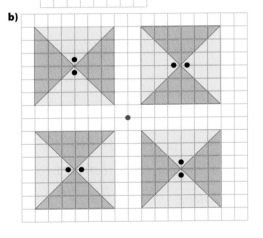

17. a) order of rotation = 5, angle of rotation = 72°
b) order of rotation = 7, angle of rotation = 51.4°
c) order of rotation = 6, angle of rotation = 60°
d) order of rotation = 12, angle of rotation = 30°
18. a) Example: Some parts of the diagram appear to be rotated and projected five times, whereas others (such as the interior bolts) appear four times. Depending on which part is chosen, the order of rotation may seem different.
b) Adding another bolt so that the total on the inside rim is five would give this diagram rotation symmetry.
19. a) The top half of the card, along with the K symbol, is rotated 180° (rotation order 2). **b)** Cards are designed so they can be read while being held from either end.
c) No; attempting to fold the card along any line does not result in an overlap.
20. Rachelle is correct. Although there are 20 wedges on the board, the alternating red and green colours must be grouped together and then rotated to reproduce the image.
21. a) H, I, N, O, S, X, Z **b)** 0, I, 8 **c)** Example: X08OI
22. Example: A hexagon-shaped sign, a six-sided snowflake, or other object.
23. a) A: no symmetry because of the variation in overlap of green and blue circles in pairs of opposite rays;
B: rotational symmetry of order 4 and line symmetry
b) Example: The logo of Sun Microsystems shows rotational symmetry, and UNESCO shows vertical line symmetry.
24. a) $m = 12$. The letter m represents the number of teeth in the gear. **b)** $n = 16$ **c)** 4.5 turns **d)** 6 turns
e) $\dfrac{(x)(m)}{y} = \text{number of turns}_B$
25. a) All of the objects have at least one example of line symmetry. All of Group A show multiple lines of symmetry. Only the left object in Group B does not show rotation symmetry.
b) Example: A cube has many lines of symmetry because the edges are all of equal length.
26.

The shape made would be a hexagon. The order of rotation for the shape is 6.

1.3 Surface Area, pages 32–35

4. a) Estimate the total surface area of a solid, $2 \times 4 \times 5$ rectangular prism. The total surface area of the object is 72 cm². **b)** Estimate the total surface area of a solid, $4 \times 4 \times 6$ prism. The total surface area of the object is 112 cm².
5. a) 216 cm² **b)** 256 cm²
6. a) 12 cm² **b)** 214 cm²

7. a) 17 cm by 9 cm by 11 cm **b)** The surface area with the cutout is the same as the surface area without the cutout (4750 cm²).
8. a) For one box: width = 2 cm, height = 1 cm, depth = 3 cm **b)** 96 cm² **c)** one box: 22 cm²; six boxes: 132 cm². The ratio of the surface area for the six combined boxes to the surface area for six separate boxes is 8:11.
9. a) 4320 cm² **b)** 54 720 cm² **c)** Only three surface areas need to be calculated (shelf, side, back).
10. a) 36 cm² **b)** Example: A 1 cm × 2 cm × 5 cm rectangular prism has a surface area of 34 cm², while a 1 cm × 1 cm × 10 cm rectangular prism has a surface area of 42 cm².
11. Example: Surface area is important to consider when painting a building, icing a cake, and packaging items.
12. a) 0.06 m. This allows rainwater to flow away from the house, off the roof to the ground below.
b) 57.89 m²; You must assume that there is no bottom included in this calculation, all angles are 90°, the garage door is to be included, and an average height of 2.4 m.
13. a) left mug: 286.5 cm²; right mug: 298.6 cm²
b) The left mug has better heat-retaining properties. It has less surface area exposed to the air resulting in lower heat loss.
14. 1.92 m²
15. a) The object's top and bottom faces, left and right faces, and front and back faces are symmetrical.
b) 324.57 cm²
16. a) You must use the Pythagorean theorem three times.
b) 51.7 m² **c)** 33 bundles of shingles for a cost of $889.35
17. a) The two flues are each 24 cm wide and 20 cm tall.
b) 4672 cm²
18. 392 cm²; To calculate the surface area of the inside of the box, you must assume the metal has zero thickness.
19. a)

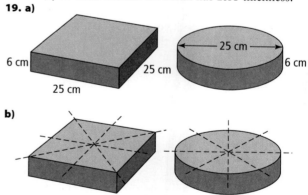

c) square cake: 1850 cm²; 8 square-cake slices: 3270.8 cm²; round cake: 1452.3 cm²; 8 round-cake slices: 2651.9 cm²; surface area increase of square cake: 1448.6 cm²; surface area increase of round cake: 1200 cm²; For both cakes, the eight equal slices increase the total surface area by almost double compared to the unsliced cakes.

20. The rice with the small grains has a smaller surface area per grain than the rice with larger grains. This means that more rice per cup can come into contact with the hot water with the smaller grains, meaning it can cook faster.

21. Example: Elephants' ears are very thin, but large, giving them a large surface area. This allows more skin to be exposed to air, and allows more skin to be cooled or warmed by the air, regulating the elephant's body temperature.

22. 12 201.95 cm²

23. 391 m²

Chapter 1 Review, pages 36–37

1. E
2. A
3. D
4. B
5. F
6. C
7. a) 4; vertical, horizontal, two oblique
b) 6; vertical, horizontal, four oblique
8. a) **b)**

9. a) A′(5, 3), B′(5, 2), C′(1, 2), D′(1, 4), E′(3, 4), F′(3, 3). This shows a vertical line of symmetry with the original image. **b)** A″(1, 0), B″(1, −1), C″(5, −1), D″(5, 1), E″(3, 1), F″(3, 0). This does not show symmetry with the original image.
10. a) order of rotation = 4; angle of rotation = 90°, one quarter turn **b)** order of rotation = 8; angle of rotation = 45°, one eighth turn
11. There is an oblique line of symmetry from the top left corner to the bottom right corner.
12. a)

b) Example: The letter H in the image would make both line symmetry and rotation symmetry. Other possible answers include A, I, M, O, T, V, W, X, and Y.
13. The design has rotation symmetry only with an order of rotation of 3. Because of the colouring and overlapping, there is no line symmetry.
14. a) P′(−2, −4), Q′(−5, −4), R′(−5, −1), U′(−3, −1), V′(−3, −3), W′(−2, −3). Yes, the two images are related by rotation symmetry. **b)** P″(2, −4), Q″(5, −4), R″(5, −1), U″(3, −1), V″(3, −3), W″(2, −3). Yes, the two images are related by horizontal line symmetry.

c) P‴(−5, 4), Q‴(−2, 4), R‴(−2, 1), U‴(−4, 1), V‴(−4, 3), W‴(−5, 3). No, the images are not related by symmetry.

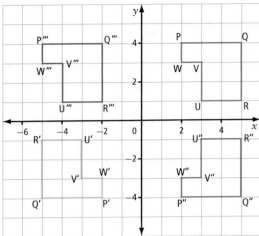

15. 35.1 cm²
16. a) top: 444 cm²; bottom: 1088 cm² **b)** 1244 cm²
17. a) 38 cm² **b)** 42 cm² **c)** 72 cm²

Chapter 2

2.1 Comparing and Ordering Rational Numbers, pages 51–54

4. a) D **b)** C **c)** A **d)** E **e)** B
5. a) W **b)** Y **c)** Z **d)** V **e)** X
6.

7. a) $4.\overline{1}$ **b)** $-\dfrac{4}{5}$ **c)** $5\dfrac{3}{4}$ **d)** $-\dfrac{9}{8}$
8. $-1\dfrac{2}{3}, -\dfrac{1}{5}, -0.1, 1\dfrac{5}{6}, 1.9$
9. $1.\overline{8}, \dfrac{9}{5}, -\dfrac{3}{8}, -\dfrac{1}{2}, -1$
10. Example: **a)** $\dfrac{-4}{10}$ **b)** $\dfrac{5}{3}$ **c)** $\dfrac{-3}{4}$ **d)** $\dfrac{8}{-6}$
11. Example: **a)** $\dfrac{-2}{6}$ **b)** $\dfrac{4}{5}$ **c)** $-\dfrac{5}{4}$ **d)** $\dfrac{-7}{2}$
12. a) $\dfrac{1}{3}$ **b)** $\dfrac{7}{10}$ **c)** $-\dfrac{1}{2}$ **d)** $-2\dfrac{1}{8}$
13. a) $\dfrac{4}{7}$ **b)** $-\dfrac{5}{3}$ **c)** $-\dfrac{7}{10}$ **d)** $-1\dfrac{4}{5}$
14. Example: **a)** 0.7 **b)** −0.5625 **c)** 0.1 **d)** −0.825
15. Example: **a)** 1.6 **b)** −2.4 **c)** 0.6 **d)** −3.015
16. Example: **a)** $\dfrac{1}{4}$ **b)** $\dfrac{-1}{20}$ **c)** $-\dfrac{3}{4}$ **d)** $\dfrac{-21}{40}$
17. Example: **a)** $1\dfrac{4}{5}$ **b)** $1\dfrac{1}{4}$ **c)** $-3\dfrac{7}{20}$ **d)** $-2\dfrac{1}{50}$

18. a) +8.2; Example: An increase suggests a positive value. **b)** +2.9; Example: A growth suggests a positive value. **c)** −3.5; Example: Below sea level suggests a negative value. **d)** +32.5; Example: Earnings suggest a positive value. **e)** −14.2; Example: Below freezing suggests a negative value.

19. a) helium and neon **b)** radon and xenon
c) helium (−272.2), neon (−248.67), argon (−189.2), krypton (−156.6), xenon (−111.9), radon (−71.0)
d) radon (−61.8), xenon (−107.1), krypton (−152.3), argon (−185.7), neon (−245.92), helium (−268.6)

20. a) Example: −2 is to the left of −1 on the number line, so $-2\frac{1}{5}$ is to the left of $-1\frac{9}{10}$ and therefore, it is smaller. **b)** Example: Since both mixed numbers are between −1 and −2 on the number line, Naomi needed to examine the positions of $-\frac{1}{4}$ and $-\frac{2}{7}$. Since $-\frac{2}{7}$ is to the left of $-\frac{1}{4}$, $-1\frac{1}{4}$ is greater.

21. a) 6.1 (Penticton), 5.4 (Edmonton), 3.9 (Regina), 0.6 (Whitehorse), −0.1 (Yellowknife), −5.1 (Churchill), −14.1 (Resolute) **b)** Yellowknife

22. a) = **b)** > **c)** = **d)** < **e)** > **f)** >

23. Yes. Example: Zero can be expressed as the quotient of two integers as long as the dividend is zero, and the divisor is any number except zero.

24. Example: **a)** $\frac{2}{5}$ **b)** $\frac{3}{-4}$ **c)** $\frac{-10}{3}$ **d)** $\frac{5}{-4}$

25. −3, −2, −1, 0, 1, and 2

26. a) 0.44 **b)** $0.\overline{3}$ **c)** −0.7 **d)** −0.66; Example: To determine which pair is greater, write each pair of fractions in an equivalent form with the same positive denominator and compare the numerators.

27. $\frac{-1}{3}, \frac{-2}{3}, \frac{-3}{3}, \frac{-4}{3}$, and $\frac{-5}{3}$

28. None. Example: $\frac{2}{3}$ and $0.\overline{6}$ are equivalent numbers.

29. a) −2; Yes, any integer less than −2 also makes the statement true. **b)** +9; No **c)** −1; No **d)** 0; No **e)** 4; Yes, 0, 1, 2, and 3 will also make the statement true. **f)** −1; No **g)** −26; No **h)** −1; Yes, −2, −3, −4, −5, −6, −7, −8, −9, −10, and −11 also make the statement true.

30. a) 8 **b)** −2 **c)** −3 **d)** 25

2.2 Problem Solving With Rational Numbers in Decimal Form, pages 60–62

4. a) −2, −1.93 **b)** 2, 2.3 **c)** −10, −9.98 **d)** 6, 5.34
5. a) −2.25 **b)** 1.873 **c)** 0.736 **d)** −12.94
6. a) −9, −8.64 **b)** −1, −1.3 **c)** 36, 30.25 **d)** 4, 4.6
7. a) 3.6 **b)** 9.556 **c)** −22.26 **d)** −1.204 **e)** 0.762 **f)** −0.833
8. a) −13.17 **b)** 2.8 **c)** −3.08
9. a) 1.134 **b)** −1.4 **c)** −5.2
10. 38.7 °C
11. a) +7.7 °C **b)** +1.54 °C/h

12. a) 3.8 − (−2.3) **b)** 6.1 m
13. a) 85.5 m **b)** 19 min
14. a loss of $16.25
15. a) −8.2 °C **b)** 1.9 °C
16. a) 2.2 **b)** Example: Use hundredths instead of tenths.
17. 2.06 m
18. a) −2.37 **b)** 1.75
19. a) loss of $1.2 million per year
b) profit of $3.6 million
20. Example: If the cost of gasoline is $1.30/L, then the difference would be $13.65.
21. 11 min
22. 2080 m
23. −0.6 °C
24. a) −5.3 **b)** −4.4 **c)** 2.1 **d)** −2.5
25. Example: At 16:00 the temperature in Calling Lake, Alberta, started decreasing at the constant rate of −1.1 °C/h. At 23:00 the temperature was −19.7 °C. What was the temperature at 16:00? The answer is −12 °C.
26. 2.88
27. a) −25.8 **b)** −3.3
28. a) 2.6 **b)** −0.35 **c)** −0.45
29. a) 3.5 × (4.1 − 3.5) − 2.8 = −0.7
b) [2.5 + (−4.1) + (−2.3)] × (−1.1) = 4.29
c) −5.5 − (−6.5) ÷ [2.4 + (−1.1)] = −0.5

2.3 Problem Solving With Rational Numbers in Fraction Form, pages 68–71

5. a) $0, \frac{1}{2}$ **b)** $1, 1\frac{1}{12}$ **c)** $-1, \frac{-5}{6}$ **d)** $0, \frac{5}{6}$
e) $-\frac{1}{2}, -\frac{1}{2}$ **f)** $\frac{1}{2}, \frac{5}{8}$

6. a) $0, \frac{-1}{12}$ **b)** $\frac{-2}{3}, \frac{-5}{9}$ **c)** $-1, \frac{-17}{20}$ **d)** $-\frac{1}{2}, \frac{-1}{8}$
e) $-1, \frac{-3}{4}$ **f)** $\frac{-1}{2}, \frac{-7}{20}$

7. a) $1, \frac{24}{25}$ **b)** $6, 5\frac{5}{6}$ **c)** $0, \frac{-1}{20}$ **d)** $1, 1\frac{1}{8}$
e) $-2\frac{1}{2}, -2$ **f)** $0, \frac{-4}{15}$

8. a) $0, \frac{1}{12}$ **b)** $1, 1\frac{1}{15}$ **c)** $-\frac{1}{2}, -\frac{15}{28}$ **d)** $-2, -1\frac{7}{10}$
e) $\frac{-1}{2}, \frac{-14}{33}$ **f)** $\frac{2}{3}, \frac{3}{5}$

9. $19.50
10. He is short 6.4 m.
11. 120 jiffies
12. a) $2\frac{1}{2}$ h **b)** $13\frac{1}{2}$ h
c) Tokyo is $3\frac{1}{4}$ h ahead of Kathmandu.
d) Chatham Islands are $16\frac{1}{4}$ h ahead of St. John's.
e) Kathmandu, Nepal
13. a) $\frac{1}{50}$ **b)** 2400 km
14. a) Ray **b)** $\frac{1}{24}$ of a pizza **c)** $1\frac{1}{8}$ of a pizza

15. a) $1\frac{5}{8}, 2\frac{1}{4}, 2\frac{7}{8}$ **b)** $-\frac{1}{24}, \frac{1}{48}, -\frac{1}{96}$

16. a) $108.80 **b)** $44.80

17. a) Example: $-\frac{2}{3}$ is a repeating decimal, so she would need to round before adding. **b)** Example: Find a common denominator, change each fraction to an equivalent form with a common denominator, and then add the numerators.

18. 9.5 m

19. a) $\frac{-5}{4}$ **b)** $1\frac{1}{10}$ **c)** $\frac{8}{13}$ **d)** $-1\frac{1}{2}$

20.

$-\frac{1}{2}$	$-2\frac{1}{6}$	$\frac{1}{6}$
$-\frac{1}{6}$	$-\frac{5}{6}$	$-1\frac{1}{2}$
$-1\frac{5}{6}$	$\frac{1}{2}$	$-1\frac{1}{6}$

21. a) $\frac{4}{15}$ **b)** $\frac{9}{20}$ **c)** $-2\frac{1}{4}$

22. a) 1 large scoop + 1 medium scoop − 1 small scoop or 2 large scoops − 1 medium scoop **b)** 1 large scoop − 2 small scoops or 2 medium scoops − 3 small scoops

23. Example: $-2\frac{1}{6} - \blacksquare = -\frac{4}{3}$. Find the rational number to replace $\blacksquare$. The answer is $\frac{-5}{6}$.

24. Yes. Example: If the two rational numbers are both negative, the sum would be less.
Example: $\frac{-1}{4} + \frac{-5}{6} = \frac{-13}{12}$

25. Example: **a)** $\left[-\frac{1}{2} + \left(-\frac{1}{2}\right)\right] + \left[-\frac{1}{2} - \left(-\frac{1}{2}\right)\right] = -1$

b) $\left[-\frac{1}{2} - \left(-\frac{1}{2}\right)\right] + \left[-\frac{1}{2} - \left(-\frac{1}{2}\right)\right] = 0$

c) $\left[\left(-\frac{1}{2}\right) \times \left(-\frac{1}{2}\right)\right] + \left[-\frac{1}{2} - \left(-\frac{1}{2}\right)\right] = \frac{1}{4}$

d) $\left(-\frac{1}{2}\right) \div \left(-\frac{1}{2}\right) \div \left(-\frac{1}{2}\right) \div \left(-\frac{1}{2}\right) = 4$

e) $\left[-\frac{1}{2} + \left(-\frac{1}{2}\right)\right] + \left[\left(-\frac{1}{2}\right) \times \left(-\frac{1}{2}\right)\right] = -\frac{3}{4}$

f) $\left(-\frac{1}{2}\right) \div \left(-\frac{1}{2}\right) \div \left(-\frac{1}{2}\right) - \left(-\frac{1}{2}\right) = -1\frac{1}{2}$

26. $\frac{-3}{8}$

27. $-\frac{1}{2}$ and 2

History Link, page 71

1. Example: **a)** $\frac{1}{5} + \frac{1}{10}$ **b)** $\frac{1}{2} + \frac{1}{7}$ **c)** $\frac{1}{4} + \frac{1}{5}$ **d)** $\frac{1}{2} + \frac{1}{9}$

2. Example: A strategy is to work with factors of the denominator.

3. Example: **a)** $\frac{1}{28} + \frac{1}{4}$ **b)** $\frac{1}{18} + \frac{1}{6}$ **c)** $\frac{1}{66} + \frac{1}{6}$

4. Example: **a)** $\frac{1}{8} + \frac{1}{4} + \frac{1}{2}$ **b)** $\frac{1}{24} + \frac{1}{12} + \frac{1}{3}$

c) $\frac{1}{12} + \frac{1}{6} + \frac{1}{2}$

2.4 Determining Square Roots of Rational Numbers, pages 78–81

5. Example: 12

6. Example: 0.55

7. a) 9, 9.61 **b)** 144, 156.25 **c)** 0.36, 0.3844
d) 0.09, 0.0841

8. a) 16 cm², 18.49 cm² **b)** 0.0016 km², 0.001 225 km²

9. a) Yes, 1 and 16 are perfect squares. **b)** No, 5 is not a perfect square. **c)** Yes, 36 and 100 are perfect squares. **d)** No, 10 is not a perfect square.

10. a) No **b)** Yes **c)** No **d)** Yes

11. a) 18 **b)** 1.7 **c)** 0.15 **d)** 45

12. a) 13 m **b)** 0.4 mm

13. a) 6, 6.2 **b)** 2, 2.12 **c)** 0.9, 0.933 **d)** 0.15, 0.148

14. a) 0.92 m **b)** 7.75 cm

15. 1.3 m

16. a) 3.16 m **b)** 6.16 m **c)** 4.2 L

17. a) $3504 **b)** The cost will not be the same.
c) The cost of fencing two squares each having an area of 60 m² is $4960.

18. No. Example: Each side of the picture is 22.36 cm. This is too large for the frame that is 30 cm by 20 cm.

19. 2.9 cm

20. 3.8 m

21. 27.4 m

22. 14.1 cm

23. 12.5 cm; Assume the 384 square tiles are all the same size.

24. a) 7.2 km **b)** 4.6 km **c)** 252.4 km

25. 35.3 cm

26. 12.2 m

27. 4.1 cm

28. a) 2.53 s **b)** 3.16 s **c)** 1.41 s

29. 30 m/s greater

30. 12.3 s

31. a) 59.8 cm² **b)** 34.7 cm²

32. 36 cm

33. 25.1 cm²

34. 3.6 m

35. 1.8 cm by 5.4 cm

36. 4

Chapter 2 Review, pages 82–83

1. OPPOSITES

2. RATIONAL NUMBER

3. PERFECT SQUARE

4. NON-PERFECT SQUARE

5. $\frac{3}{24}, \frac{-10}{-6}, \frac{-6}{4}, \frac{82}{-12}$

6. a) = **b)** < **c)** > **d)** = **e)** > **f)** >

7. a) Example: Axel wrote each fraction in an equivalent form so both fractions had a common denominator of 4. He then compared the numerators to find that $-6 < -5$, so $-1\frac{1}{2} < -1\frac{1}{4}$. **b)** Example: Bree wrote $-1\frac{1}{2}$ as -1.5 and $-1\frac{1}{4}$ as -1.25. She compared the decimal portions to find that $-1.5 < -1.25$. **c)** Example: Caitlin compared $-\frac{2}{4}$ and $-\frac{1}{4}$ and found that $-\frac{2}{4} < -\frac{1}{4}$. **d)** Example: Caitlin's method is preferred because it involves fewer computations.

8. Example: $-\frac{5}{6}$ and $\frac{5}{-7}$

9. a) -0.95 **b)** 1.49 **c)** -8.1 **d)** 1.3

10. a) -0.6 **b)** 8.1 **c)** -6.5 **d)** 5.3

11. 1.6 °C/h

12. $1.3 million profit

13. a) $-\frac{2}{15}$ **b)** $-1\frac{1}{8}$ **c)** $-1\frac{9}{10}$ **d)** $4\frac{7}{12}$

14. a) $\frac{4}{9}$ **b)** $-\frac{20}{21}$ **c)** $-12\frac{5}{6}$ **d)** $1\frac{17}{22}$

15. The quotients are the same. Example: The quotient of two rational numbers with the same sign is positive.

16. 420 h

17. $\frac{9}{10}$

18. a) Yes, both 64 and 121 are perfect squares.
b) No, 7 is not a perfect square.
c) Yes, 49 and 100 are perfect squares.
d) No, 10 is not a perfect square.

19. Example: The estimate is 14.8.
220 is between the perfect square numbers 196 and 225. The square roots of 196 and 225 are 14 and 15. Since 220 is closer to 225, the value in the tenths place should be close to 8 or 9.

20. 0.0225

21. a) 3.6 **b)** 0.224

22. a) Example: When the number is greater than 1. The square root of 49 is 7.
b) Example: When the number is smaller than 1. The square root of 0.16 is 0.4.

23. a) 1.5 cm; Example: One method is to find the square root of 225, and divide by 10. A second method is to divide 225 by 100, then find the square root of the quotient. **b)** 21.2 cm

24. a) 2.5 cans **b)** 6.6 m by 6.6 m

25. 15.7 s

Chapter 3

3.1 Using Exponents to Describe Numbers, pages 97–98

4. a) $7^2 = 49$ **b)** $3^3 = 27$ **c)** $8^5 = 32\ 768$
d) $10^7 = 10\ 000\ 000$

5. a) 1^4; 1 is the base and 4 is the exponent
b) 2^5; 2 is the base and 5 is the exponent
c) 9^7; 9 is the base and 7 is the exponent
d) 13^1; 13 is the base and 1 is the exponent

6. a) 25 **b)** 27 **c)** 1024

7. a) 512 **b)** 64 **c)** 1

8.

	Repeated Multiplication	Exponential Form	Value
a)	$6 \times 6 \times 6$	6^3	216
b)	$3 \times 3 \times 3 \times 3$	3^4	81
c)	7×7	7^2	49
d)	11×11	11^2	121
e)	$5 \times 5 \times 5$	5^3	125

9. No, because $4^3 = 64$ and $3^4 = 81$

10. a) 81 **b)** -125 **c)** -128

11. a) -64 **b)** -1 **c)** 2187

12.

	Repeated Multiplication	Exponential Form	Value
a)	$(-3) \times (-3) \times (-3)$	$(-3)^3$	-27
b)	$(-4) \times (-4)$	$(-4)^2$	16
c)	$(-1) \times (-1) \times (-1)$	$(-1)^3$	-1
d)	$(-7) \times (-7)$	$(-7)^2$	49
e)	$(-10) \times (-10) \times (-10)$	$(-10)^3$	-1000

13. No, because $(-6)^4 = 1296$ and $-6^4 = -1296$

14. $3 \times 3 \times 3 = 3^3$

15. a)

Month	Body Length (cm)
Beginning	1
1	2
2	4
3	8
4	16
5	32
6	64
7	128
8	256
9	512
10	1024

b) $2^5 = 32$ cm **c)** After 6 months.

16. 1^{22}, 2^5, 7^2, 4^3, 3^4

17. $2^{15} = 32\ 768$

18. a) 3^2 **b)** $(-3)^2$

19. Example: Multiplication is repeated addition. For example, $3 \times 5 = 3 + 3 + 3 + 3 + 3$
$= 15$
Powers are a way to represent repeated multiplication. For example, $3^5 = 3 \times 3 \times 3 \times 3 \times 3$
$= 243$

20.

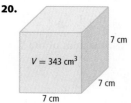

$V = 343$ cm³, 7 cm, 7 cm, 7 cm

21. Example: 12×12, $2 \times 6 \times 2 \times 6$, $2 \times 2 \times 3 \times 2 \times 2 \times 3$

22.

Exponential Form	Value
5^3	125
5^4	625
5^5	3 125
5^6	15 625
5^7	78 125
5^8	390 625
5^9	1 953 125
5^{10}	9 765 625

a) An even exponent has 625 as its last three digits. An odd exponent has 125 as its last three digits. **b)** 625

23.

Exponential Form	Value
3^1	3
3^2	9
3^3	27
3^4	81
3^5	243
3^6	729
3^7	2 187
3^8	6 561
3^9	19 683
3^{10}	59 049
3^{11}	177 147
3^{12}	531 441

a) Example: The units digit follows a pattern of 3, 9, 7, 1 **b)** Example: I predict that the units digit will be a 7. The cycle is of length 4. So, with an exponent of 63, the cycle would go through 15 times, with a remainder of 3. That means that the units digit would be the third number in the cycle, which is a 7.

3.2 Exponent Laws, pages 106–107

5. a) $4^7 = 16\ 384$ **b)** $7^6 = 117\ 649$ **c)** $(-3)^7 = -2187$
6. a) $5^5 = 3125$ **b)** $(-6)^6 = 46\ 656$ **c)** $8^3 = 512$
7. a) $4^3 \times 4^4 = 4^7$ **b)** $2^5 \times 2^2 = 2^7$ **c)** $9^4 \times 9^7 = 9^{11}$
8. $3 \times 3 \times 3 \times 3 \times 3 \times 3 \times 3 \times 3 \times 3 = 3^9$
9. a) $5^2 = 25$ **b)** $3^4 = 81$ **c)** $(-4)^4 = 256$
10. a) $7^3 = 343$ **b)** $(-8)^2 = 64$ **c)** $(-2)^1 = -2$
11. a) $\dfrac{6^4}{6^3} = 6^1$ **b)** $\dfrac{3^8}{3^2} = 3^6$ **c)** $\dfrac{5^7}{5^1} = 5^6$

12. $\dfrac{(-5)^7}{(-5)^2}$

13. $\dfrac{(6^2)^3}{6^3} = 6^3$

14. a) $3^8 = 6561$ **b)** $7^4 \times (-3)^4 = 194\ 481$
c) $\dfrac{5^4}{6^4} = \dfrac{625}{1296}$

15. a) $-4^6 = -4096$ **b)** $3^4 \times 4^4 = 20\ 736$ **c)** $\dfrac{4^3}{5^3} = \dfrac{64}{125}$

16. $[(2)^2]^4$

17.

Expression	Repeated Multiplication	Powers
a) $[2 \times (-5)]^3$	$2 \times (-5) \times 2 \times (-5) \times 2 \times (-5)$	$2^3 \times (-5)^3$
b) $(9 \times 8)^2$	$9 \times 8 \times 9 \times 8$	$9^2 \times 8^2$
c) $\left(\dfrac{2}{3}\right)^4$	$\dfrac{2}{3} \times \dfrac{2}{3} \times \dfrac{2}{3} \times \dfrac{2}{3}$	$\dfrac{2^4}{3^4}$

18. a) 1; Example: $2^4 = 16$
$$2^3 = 8$$
$$2^2 = 4$$
$$2^1 = 2$$
$$2^0 = 1$$
b) $\dfrac{2^4}{2^4} = \dfrac{16}{16}$ and $\dfrac{2^4}{2^4} = 2^{4-4}$
$$= 1 \qquad\qquad = 2^0$$
Therefore, $2^0 = 1$.

19. a) $-4^0 = -1$ because $4^0 = 1$, so $-(1) = -1$ **b)** -1
20. a) $\dfrac{20^2}{50^2}$ **b)** $\left(\dfrac{2}{5}\right)^2$
21. a) 3^{11} **b)** $(-4)^3$
22. Example: Jenny multiplied the exponents in step 2. She should have added the exponents.
23. Example: $4^1 \times 4^4$, $4^2 \times 4^3$, $4^0 \times 4^5$
24. Example: Place 3 in the numerator and 5 in the denominator.
25. Example: **a)** $81^3 = 27^4$ **b)** $81^6 = 27^8$
26. a) 121 **b)** 33

3.3 Order of Operations, pages 111–113

5. a) 128 **b)** 63 **c)** -1250 **d)** -12
6. a) $4 \times 2^4 = 64$ **b)** $3 \times (-2)^3 = -24$
c) $7 \times 10^5 = 700\ 000$ **d)** $-1 \times 9^4 = -6561$
7. Example: **a)** $4 \times 3^2 = 36$ **b)** $-5 \times 4^3 = -320$
8. a) 18 **b)** 70 **c)** 535 **d)** 73
9. a) -11 **b)** 58 **c)** 1 **d)** 44
10. a) $3(2)^3 = 24$, and $2(3)^2 = 18$, so $3(2)^3$ is greater by 6.
b) $(3 \times 4)^2 = 144$, and $3^2 \times 4^2 = 144$, so the expressions are equal. **c)** $6^3 + 6^3 = 432$, and $(6 + 6)^3 = 1728$, so $(6 + 6)^3$ is greater by 1296.
11. In step 3, Justine should have multiplied 4 by 9. The correct answer is -27.
12. In step 1, Katarina should have squared 4 correctly to obtain 16. The correct answer is 76.
13. $9^3 - 7^3 = 386$ cm^3
14. a) 49 **b)** 2401 **c)** $7^1 + 7^2 + 7^3 + 7^4 = 2800$
15. $6^2 - 5^2 = 11$ cm^2
16. $10^2 - 8^2 = 36$ cm^2
17. 1 953 125
18. a) Question 2: $12 500, question 3: $50 000, question 4: $200 000
b) 6 questions **c)** The 8th question.
d) $3125(4^0) + 3125(4^1) + 3125(4^2) + 3125(4^3) = 265\ 625$
19. a) 48 **b)** 3×2^4 **c)** Example: It represents the number of coaches who made the first six calls.
d) It represents the round number of the calls.
e) $3 \times 2^6 = 192$ **f)** $5 \times 2^3 = 40$
20. 2^{2^2}

3.4 Using Exponents to Solve Problems, pages 118–119

3. 216 cm³

4. Area of square: $14^2 = 196$ cm²; Surface area of cube: $6(6)^2 = 216$ cm². The surface area of the cube is larger.

5. a) 60 **b)** 14 580 **c)** $20(3^n)$

6. a) 400 **b)** 1600 **c)** 819 200

7. a) Example: If an assumption that she needs 100 cm² of overlap is made, she would need 12 796 cm² of paper.

8. 9×10^{13} joules

9. a) It represents the number of questions.

b) It represents the possible answers for each question.

c) TTTT, TTTF, TTFT, TFTT, TTFF, TFTF, TFFT, FFFF, FFFT, FFTF, FTFF, FFTT, FTFT, FTTF, FTTT

d) $2^{10} = 1024$

10. $60^3 = 216\ 000$

11. a) 37.5 m **b)** 180 m

c) Example:

$$\boxed{\text{C}}\ \boxed{0.75}\ \boxed{\times}\ \boxed{60}\ \boxed{\times}\ \boxed{(}\ \boxed{2000}\ \boxed{\div}\ \boxed{1000}\ \boxed{)}\ \boxed{x^2}\ \boxed{=}\ 180.$$

12. a) The term "googol" was created by nine year old Milton Sirotta, the nephew of the American mathematician Edward Kasner who was investigating very large numbers at the time. The Latin word for "a lot" is "googis". Google™ possibly used that name to suggest the enormous amount of information their search engine could be used to investigate. **b)** 100 zeros. **c)** The time to write a googol as a whole number is the time it would take to write a 1 followed by 100 zeros, a total of 101 digits. If two digits could be written per second, it would take $101 \div 2$ or about 51 s.

13. a) Same base, different exponent: $3^7 \div 3^5 = 3^{7-5}$
$$= 3^2$$
$$= 9$$

Rule: Divide the larger power by the smaller power and evaluate. This will indicate how many times as large the larger power is compared to the smaller power.

Different base, same exponent: $6^4 \div 5^4 = \left(\dfrac{6}{5}\right)^4$
$$= \dfrac{1296}{625}$$

Rule: Divide the larger power by the smaller power, express as a single power with a fractional base, then evaluate. This will indicate how many times as large the larger power is compared to the smaller power.

b) $32^4 = (2^5)^4$ $64^3 = (2^6)^3$ $2^{20} \div 2^{18} = 2^2$
$\ = 2^{20}\qquad\quad = 2^{18}\qquad\qquad\quad = 4$
So 32^4 is four times as large as 64^3.

Chapter 3 Review, pages 120–121

1. coefficient

2. exponential form

3. base

4. power

5. exponent

6. a) 2^3 **b)** $(-3)^4$

7. a) $4 \times 4 \times 4 \times 4 \times 4 \times 4$ **b)** $6 \times 6 \times 6 \times 6$

c) $(-5) \times (-5) \times (-5) \times (-5) \times (-5) \times (-5) \times (-5)$

d) $-(5 \times 5 \times 5 \times 5 \times 5 \times 5 \times 5)$

8. Area = 25 square units

9. $4 \times 4 \times 4 = 4^3$
$= 64$
$V = 64$ cm³

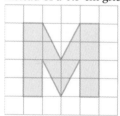

A = 25   5

5

10. $-3^4, 9, 2^5, 7^2, 4^3$

11. a) $3 \times 3 \times 5 \times 5 \times 5 \times 5$

b) $(-3) \times (-3) \times (-3) \times 2 \times 2 \times 2 \times 2 \times 2 \times 2$

12. a) $2^3 \times 2^2 = 2^5$ **b)** $\dfrac{4^2 \times 4^4}{4^3} = 4^3$

13. a) $(-5) \times (-5) \times (-5) \times (-5) \times (-5) \times (-5) \times (-5) = (-5)^7$ **b)** $3^2 \times 3^2 \times 3^2 \times 3^2 = 3^8$

14. a) $6^3 \times 4^3$ **b)** $7^5 \times (-2)^5$

15. a) $\dfrac{4^2}{5^2}$ **b)** $\dfrac{2^4}{7^4}$

16. a) -16 **b)** 1 **c)** 243

17. Example: **a)** $(-2)^2 + (-2)^3 = -4$

b) $(2^3)^2 - 4 \times 6^0 = 60$

c) $(-3)^4 - (-3)^3 + (2 \times 4)^2 = 172$

18. a) 47 **b)** 9 **c)** 1 **d)** $1\dfrac{16}{25}$

19. In step 2, the error is that Ang added $81 + 7$ when he should have multiplied 7 and 8.

20. 150 m²

21. a) 80 **b)** 640

22. a) 4.9 m **b)** 19.6 m **c)** 176.4 m

Chapter 4 Scale Factors and Similarity

4.1 Enlargements and Reductions, pages 136–138

4. a) Use a 1-cm grid instead of a 0.5 cm grid.

b) Use a 1-cm grid instead of a 0.5 cm grid.

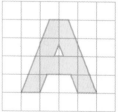

5. Use a 2-cm grid instead of a 0.5 cm grid.

France

6. a) Use a 0.5-cm grid instead of a 1 cm grid.

b) Use a 0.5-cm grid instead of a 1 cm grid.

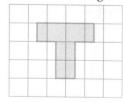

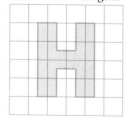

7. a) greater than 1   **b)** equal to 1   **c)** less than 1

8.

Sierra Leone

9. a) enlargement   **b)** 100. The lens makes all dimensions of the original image appear to be enlarged by 100 times.

10. Examine the font used in both posters. Mia's font is 0.5 cm high, and Hassan's is 0.25 cm high. Mia's font is twice the height of Hassan's, so the scale factor is 2.

11. Example: Measure the width of the sunglasses in both images. Determine the scale factor. Then, see if the scale factor applies to another pair of corresponding parts (e.g. the width of the mouth).

12. a) width = 27 cm, length = 54 cm
b) width = 4.5 cm, length = 9 cm

13.

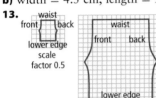

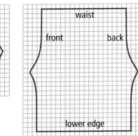

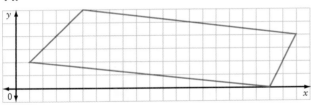

14.

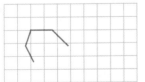

15. Example: You could reduce the image with a scale factor of $\frac{1}{4}$. Then, width = 10.5 cm, height = 7.5 cm, depth = 2.5 cm

17. a)

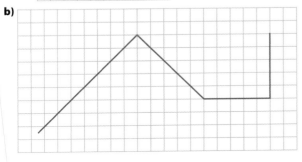

b)

4.2 Scale Diagrams, pages 143–145

4. a) Divide 144 by 3.   **b)** Divide 117 by 5.2.
5. a) 13   **b)** 126
6. a) 1210 cm or 12.1 m   **b)** 16 mm
7. a) 38.9 m   **b)** 14 m
8. a) 0.15   **b)** 1.68
9. a) 0.02   **b)** 0.5
10. 0.02
11. 0.04
12. $\dfrac{1}{16\ 000\ 000}$

13. a) 6.3 cm   **b)** Yes, an actual egg could have a length of approximately 6.3 cm.

14. a) $\dfrac{1}{15}$ **b)** The length of the footprint image is approximately 3.4 cm. With the scale factor of $\dfrac{1}{15}$, the actual length of the footprint is approximately 51 cm.   **c)** Example: The span of a human hand to the footprint could be approximately 1 : 2.1. The footprint is approximately 2 times as large as a human hand span.

15. 50 000

16. Yes, it will fit. The model will measure 2.5 m in height, giving it a 0.5 m clearance.

17. length = 17.4 m, height = 4.35 m

18. a) 2   **b)** 3   **c)** 1.5   **d)** $\dfrac{1}{3}$ **e)** $\dfrac{2}{3}$

19. a) $\dfrac{1}{1800}$ **b)** 2700 cm or 27 m

20. a)

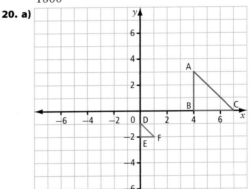

b) Yes, the sides of the larger triangle are 3 times the length of the sides of the smaller triangle.   **c)** $\dfrac{1}{3}$ **d)** 3
e) Area of △ABC is 4.5 square units; area of △DEF is 0.5 square units.   **f)** 1 : 0.1; 1 : 9   **g)** The scale factor of the area is 3 times larger than the scale factor of the sides (when comparing △DEF : △ABC)

21. a) 2.6 m   **b)** 5.2 m

22. a) 2.5, $\dfrac{2}{5}$ **b)** Example: Scale factors between a smaller object and a larger one are often easier to use.

4.3 Similar Triangles, pages 150–153

4. Corresponding angles: ∠P and ∠T, ∠Q and ∠U, ∠R and ∠V.
Corresponding sides: PQ and TU, PR and TV, QR and UV.
5. Corresponding angles: ∠A and ∠Y, ∠B and ∠W, ∠C and ∠X.
Corresponding sides: AB and YW, BC and WX, AC and YX.
6. Yes, the triangles are similar because the sides are the proportional; the sides are related by a scale factor of 5.
7. No, the triangles are not similar because the sides are not proportional.
8. △ABC, △EFG, and △KLM are similar.

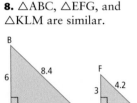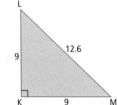

9. $x = 56$
10. $x = 10$
12. 2.0 m
13. 4.0 m
14. 7.68 m
15. $x = 76.25$ cm
16. Peter is taller. Michael is 149.3 cm tall.

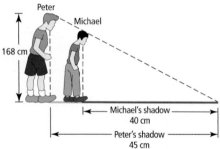

17. Example: Two buildings, A and B, stand side by side. Building A casts a shadow of 120 m and is 60 m tall. Building B has a shadow of 60 m. Using the diagram, find the height of Building B.

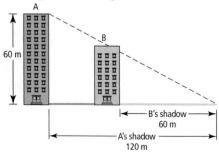

$$\frac{60}{120} = \frac{x}{60}$$
Building B is 30 m tall.

18. a) $x = 420.48$ m   **b)** The shadow may not reach the street level due to surrounding buildings.
19. a) No, the corresponding angles are not equal. The angle measures of one triangle are: 50°, 60°, and 70°. The angle measures of the other triangle are: 50°, 50°, and 80°. **b)** Yes, the triangles are similar because they both have angle measures of 45°, 60°, and 75°.
20. a) 13.3 cm and 16.0 cm   **b)** 1:2.67
21. First, measure your height, and the length of the building's shadow. After measuring your own shadow, find the ratio of your shadow to the building's shadow. Then, divide your height by that value to find the height of the building.
22. ZY = 4.9 cm
23. The area is 150 cm².

4.4 Similar Polygons, pages 157–159

3. a) Similar   **b)** Not similar
4.

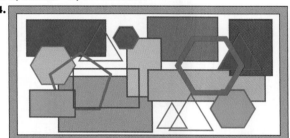

5. $x = 4$
6. $x = 2.8$ m
7. No. The corresponding angles must be the same.
8. a)

similar   dissimilar

b) The two similar hexagons are similar to the photo because the interior angles are the same and the side lengths are related by a scale factor. The two dissimilar hexagons do not have these properties.
9. The side length of the game board will be 15.0 cm.
10. a) 7.5 m   **b)** 1080°. Example: An octagon can be divided into six non-overlapping triangles.
11. a) The final enlargement should be 6 times the size of the original diagram.   **b)** The corresponding angles are equal, and the dimensions are all enlarged by the same proportion.
12. 39.3 cm
13. 14.1 cm

14. a) $\frac{1}{20}$ **b)**

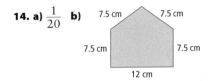
7.5 cm   7.5 cm
7.5 cm   7.5 cm
12 cm

c) length$_{model}$ = 15 cm, width$_{model}$ = 12 cm

15. 19 250 L

16. The ratio of areas to the ratio of corresponding side lengths in similar polygons is equal to the scale factor comparing side lengths squared.

17. The volume ratio is the same as the side ratio cubed.

18. a) The similar polygons have 7 sides, so they are heptagons.   **b)** Example: Each heptagon is a reduction of the centre heptagon, with the scale factor decreasing with distance from the centre.

Chapter 4 Review, pages 160–161

1. POLYGON
2. SIMILAR
3. SCALE FACTOR
4. PROPORTION
5. a)

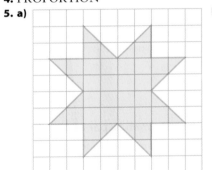

b)

6. The vertical height of the drawing is 3 cm. The enlarged egg will have a vertical height of 9 cm.

7. The vertical height of the drawing is 3 cm. The reduced drawing will have a vertical height of 1.5 cm.

8. a)

b)

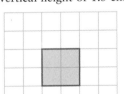

c)

9. $\frac{2}{13}$

10. a) 14 cm   **b)** 13.9 cm

11. 8.7 cm

12. $\frac{1}{10\ 000\ 000}$

13. No. The corresponding sides are not proportional.

14. $x = 10$

15. $x = 3$
16. No. They are not similar.
17. 10.1 cm
18. $x = 7.2$; $y = 9.6$

Chapters 1–4 Review, pages 166–168

1. a)

b)

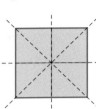

2. Example: The shape could be traced and cut out, then flipped over the dashed line and traced as the reflected image or each point could be reflected over the dashed line and connected to create the shape.

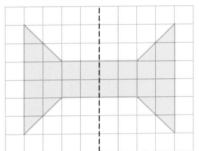

3.

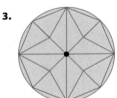

a) Example: There are four lines of symmetry, 1 vertical, 1 horizontal and 2 oblique. **b)** Example: 4
c) 90°, $\frac{1}{4}$ revolution

4. a) Example: Diameter of circular cake and side length of square cake are 25 cm. Height of both cakes is 10 cm. Square: 1625 cm², circle: 1276.5 cm²
b) Example: Square: 2625 cm², an increase of 61.5%. Circle: 2276.3, an increase of 78.3%.

5. a)

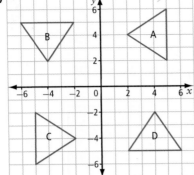

b)

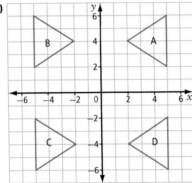

6. a) 11 250 cm² **b)** 10 000 cm², a decrease in surface area of 1250 cm²

7. $-2\frac{3}{4}$, -0.9, $-\frac{4}{5}$, $-\frac{2}{3}$, $0.\overline{6}$, 2.7

8. $-6\frac{7}{20}$

9. a) -1, -0.68 **b)** 4, 3.6 **c)** 4, 4.6 **d)** -1, -1.07
e) -2, -2.03 **f)** -20, -22.26 **g)** 4, 3.41 **h)** 1, 1

10. a) $2, 2\frac{1}{5}$ **b)** $-1\frac{1}{3}, -1\frac{1}{15}$ **c)** $-\frac{25}{12}, -\frac{19}{12}$
d) $-\frac{1}{3}, -\frac{7}{24}$ **e)** $-\frac{3}{70}, -\frac{3}{70}$ **f)** $\frac{5}{6}, \frac{5}{6}$ **g)** $-2, -1\frac{17}{18}$
h) $6, 6\frac{1}{4}$

11. a) 2 cm, 1.6 cm **b)** 0.1 km, 0.1 km
c) 0.2 mm, 0.22 mm **d)** 1 km, 1.01 km

12. 6.8 m

13. 4^{17}

14. 3

15. $(-4)^9$, $-262\ 144$

16. $21 \times 21 \times 21 \times 21$, $3^4 \times 7^4$

17. a) 1600 **b)** 25 600

18.

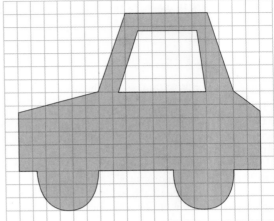

19. a) 12 **b)** 18.5 **c)** 0.414
20. $x = 1$
21. 647 km; assuming the distance on the diagram measures 4.2 cm
22. Rectangles B and D and rectangles A and F are similar.
23. a) hexagons, triangles, heptagons **b)** The hexagons are similar, the triangles are similar, and the heptagons are similar. Example: Each triangle shares two edges with hexagons and one edge with a heptagon. The similar shapes decrease in size with distance from the centre.

Chapter 5

5.1 The Language of Mathematics, pages 179–182

5. a) 3, trinomial **b)** 1, monomial **c)** 4, polynomial
d) 1, monomial
6. a) 1, monomial **b)** 3, trinomial **c)** 1, monomial
d) 2, binomial
7. a) $6x$ and -15 **b)** $7 + a + b$ **c)** $3x - y$ and $4c^2 - cd$
8. a) degree 1, 2 terms **b)** degree 2, 2 terms
c) degree 2, 3 terms
9. a) degree 2, 2 terms **b)** degree 2, 3 terms
c) degree 0, 1 term
10. a) $2 + p$ and $2x^2 - y^2$
b) $3b^2$, $4st + t - 1$, and $2x^2 - y^2$
c) b **d)** $2 + p$ and $4st + t - 1$
11. a) $2x - 3$ **b)** $x^2 - 2x + 1$ **c)** $-x^2 + 3x - 2$
12. a) $2x^2 + 4$ **b)** $-x^2 - 2x - 4$ **c)** 4

13. a) 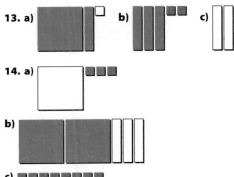 **b)** **c)**

14. a)

b)

c)

15. a) Example: $x + 2$ **b)** Example: $3x$

c) Example: $9x^2$

d) Example: $x^2 + x + y + 3$

16. a) Example: Both tiles share a common dimension of 1 unit. **b)** $x + 3$
17. a) $6x$ **b)** $2x + 3$ **c)** $x^2 + 4x$
18. Example: The expression $x^2 + 3x + 2$ is a trinomial of degree 2.

19. a) 2 **b)** 6 **c)** 1 **d)** 2 **e)** −5
20. a) $3x^2 - 2x + 1$
b) Example: $d^2 - 5d + 2$

21. a) $8 + x$, x represents the unknown number
b) $x + 5$, x represents the amount of money **c)** $w + 4$, w represents the width of the page **d)** $5x + 2$, x represents the unknown number **e)** $3n - 21$, n represents the number of people
22. a) Example: The Riggers scored 5 more than triple the number of goals scored by the Raiders. **b)** Example: The number of coins remaining from a purse containing 10 coins after an unknown number of coins were removed

23. a) a represents the number of adults and c represents the number of children
b) $215
c) $23a + 17c$
24. $10a + 5s$, where a represents the number of adults and s represents the number of students.
25. a) $2w + s$ **b)** w represents the number of wins and s represents the number of shoot-out losses **c)** 4
d) 28 **e)** Two possible records for Team B are: 8 wins, 12 shoot-out losses, and 0 losses in regulation time ($2 \times 8 + 12 = 28$); 10 wins, 8 shoot-out losses, and 2 losses in regulation time ($2 \times 10 + 8 = 28$).
26. a) binomial of degree 1 **b)** Example: 5 could be the charge per person, 75 could be the cost of renting the room. **c)** $825
27. a) Example: $2c - w$, where c represents the number of correct answers and w represents the number of wrong answers. **b)** All 25 questions correct would result in a maximum score of 50 points. All 25 questions wrong would result in a minimum score of −25.
c)

Number Correct	Number Wrong	Number Unanswered	Score
20	5	0	35
20	4	1	36
20	3	2	37
20	2	3	38
20	1	4	39
20	0	5	40

28. 2
29. a) $6x + 6$ **b)** $x + 3 = 2x$ **c)** $x + 3 = 2x$, subtract x from both sides, $3 = x$
30. Example: $xz + 4y + 3$
31. a) Example: $d = st$, where d represents distance, s represent speed, and t represents time.
b)

Part of Race	Distance (km)	Speed (km/h)	Time (h)
swim	d_1	1.3	$\dfrac{d_1}{1.3}$
cycle	d_2	28.0	$\dfrac{d_2}{28}$
run	d_3	12.0	$\dfrac{d_3}{12}$

c) $\dfrac{d_1}{1.3} + \dfrac{d_2}{28} + \dfrac{d_3}{12}$ **d)** 3.416 h, assuming that Deidra races at her average pace **e)** 12.868 h

5.2 Equivalent Expressions, pages 187–189

5. a) coefficient: -3; number of variables: 1
b) coefficient: 1; number of variables: 1
c) coefficient: 0; number of variables: 0
6. a) coefficient: 4; number of variables: 1
b) coefficient: -1; number of variables: 3
c) coefficient: -8; number of variables: 2
7. a) x^2 and xt　**b)** $-ts$ and xt　**c)** $3x$ and $4t$　**d)** $-ts$
8. a) $2a$ and $-7.1a$　**b)** $3m$ and $\frac{4}{3}m$
c) -1.9 and 5; $6p^2$ and p^2
9. a) $-2k$ and $104k$　**b)** $\frac{1}{2}ab$ and ab
c) -5 and 5; $13d^2$ and d^2
10. a) $-4x^2 + 4x$　**b)** $-3n - 1$　**c)** $-q^2 - q$　**d)** $c - 4$
e) $5h^2 - h$　**f)** $-j^2 + 5j - 6$
11. a) $-2d^2 - 3d$　**b)** $-y^2 + 3y$　**c)** $p^2 + p - 2$
d) $4m + 2$　**e)** $3q^2 - 4q$　**f)** $-3w^2 + 3w - 4$
12. B, C, and E
13. Example: Yes. 2 m and 1 m are expressed in the same unit of measurement, so they can be considered like terms. Their sum is 3 m. 32 cm and 63 cm are expressed in the same unit of measurement, so they can be considered like terms. Their sum is 95 cm.
14. a) Example: The amount of liquid in a can is reduced by 3 mL.　**b)** Example: The number of coloured markers is 5 more than twice the number of pens.
15. a) Example: $p^2 + p^2 - 6p + 3p + 5 - 3$
b) Example: $10x^2 - 13x^2 + x + 4x - 10 + 6$
c) $r^2 + r^2 + 2r^2 - 7q^2 + 5q^2 - 3qr$
16. a) $10d + 3$　**b)** $4w + 18$
17. a)　　　　　　　　　　**b)** $9s + 4$

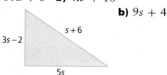

18. a) $5n - 700$, where n represents the number of students　**b)** $550　**c)** Example: estimate: 150; actual: 141
19. a) $60n + 54$　**b)** $174
c) $60n + 54 + \dfrac{60n + 54}{2}$; $90n + 81$
20. a) $3000 + 16b$　**b)** $12\ 600　**c)** $21　**d)** $19
21. a) Raj combined $3x - 5x$ incorrectly; it should be $-2x$. He also combined $-8 + 9$ incorrectly; it should be 1.
b) $-2x + 1$
22. a) $x + 3x + 7 + 2x - 5$　**b)** $6x + 2$
23. When $y = w$. Example: Assign a value to x, such as $x = 10$. Substitute this value into the two expressions. The first expression becomes $y + 13$. The second expression becomes $w + 13$. If the two expression are equal, then $y = w$.

24. a)

Wholesale Price ($)	Expression for Retail Price	Retail Price ($)
8.00	$8 + (0.4)(8)$	11.20
12.00	$12 + (0.4)(12)$	16.80
30.00	$30 + (0.4)(30)$	42.00
x	$x + 0.4x$	$1.4x$

b) Example: $x + 10 + (0.4)(x + 10) = x + 10 + 0.4x + 4$
$$= 1.4x + 14$$
Or multiply 1.4 by x, which yields $1.4x$, and multiply 1.4 by 10, which yields 14.
25. a) Zip: $100 + 2p$, where p represents the number of posters; Henry: $150 + p$, where p represents the number of posters　**b)** Zip: $350; Henry: $275
c) Total cost is $850. Add Zip's price to Henry's price: $500 + $350 = $850. Or add like terms: $100 + 2p + 150 + p = 250 + 3p$, and then substitute $p = 200$. Simplify to $850.

5.3 Adding and Subtracting Polynomials, pages 196–199

5. C
6. a) $5x - 7$　**b)** $-5a^2 - a + 2$　**c)** $10p$　**d)** $2y^2 + 6y - 6$
7. a) $3x + 4$　**b)** $-n + 3$　**c)** $b^2 - 1$　**d)** $a^2 - a - 1$
8. a) $-3x + 1$ **b)** $x^2 - 2x - 3$

9. a) $x - 1$　　　**b)** $-2x^2 + 1$

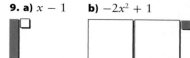

10. a) $9x$　**b)** $-5d - 6$　**c)** $2x^2 - 3x + 5$
11. a) $-3x + 7$　**b)** $-4g^2 + 4g - 2.5$　**c)** $-v^2 - 8v + 1$
12. B
13.

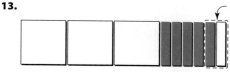

Remove $-2x^2 - x$.

14. a) $-3x - 2$　**b)** $-5b^2 - 9b$　**c)** $-3w + 7$
d) $-m^2 + m$
15. a) $13c - 3$　**b)** $-4r^2 - 3r - 6$　**c)** $2y^2 - 7y$
d) $8j^2 - 4j + 8$
16. a) the perimeter　**b)** $6x$　**c)** 30; Example: The expression in part b) was used because it involved fewer steps.

17.

18. a) $399d + 160$; d represents the number of days the backhoe is rented. **b)** $550d + 160$ **c)** $949d + 160$
d) $151d$
19. a) $-x + 5 + 3x + 1$ **b)** A: $(-x + 5) - (4x - 3) = -5x + 8$;
B: $(3x + 1) - (4x - 3) = -x + 4$
20. a) $17n + 2150$ **b)** \$12 350 **c)** The expression represents the difference in the cost of printing and the cost of shipping; $13n + 1850$
21. The second line should be $4p^2 - p + 3 - p^2 - 3p + 2$, and the result of $(-p - 3p)$ is not $-3p$, so the answer should be $3p^2 - 4p + 5$.
22. a) $10x - 12$ **b)** $2a^2 - a - 4$ **c)** $5t^2 - 6t + 9$
d) $-2.3x + 0.4$
23. a) $3x^2 + 5x - 3$

b) $x^2 - 5x - 3$

24. $4x^2 + 2x$
25. a) Example: Assume you also pay \$0.12 for punctuation. For St. Mary's High School,
$C = (25)(0.12)(31) + (25)(0.12)(19)$
b) Example: For St. Mary's High School,
$C = (25)(0.12)(31) + (25)(0.12)(19) + (25)(17.95)$
c) Example: $C = (25)(17.95) + (25)(0.12)(n)$, where n represents the number of letters.
d) $(3n + 448.75) + (3n + 448.75) = 6n + 897.5$
26. a) \$37 **b)** \$35 **c)** $7l + 5s + 38$, assuming at least one large print and at least one small print.
27. $w + 23 + w + 8 + w + 23 + w + 8 = 4w + 62$
28. a) $(-n^2 + 3600n) - (-3n^2 + 8600)$
$= 2n^2 + 3600n - 8600$ **b)** profit; Example: Replacing n with 20 in the expression $2n^2 + 3600n - 8600$ yields a positive answer of \$64 200.
29. $1004x$
30. $8w + 142$

Chapter 5 Review, pages 200–201

1. D
2. E
3. D
4. A
5. C
6. B
7. a) 4 terms, polynomial **b)** 2 terms, binomial
c) 1 term, monomial **d)** 3 terms, trinomial
8. a) This is a degree 2 polynomial because the term with the highest degree ($6x^2$) has a degree of 2.

b) This is a degree 2 polynomial because the term with the highest degree (ab) has a degree of 2.
c) This is a degree 1 polynomial because the term with the highest degree (y) has a degree of 1.
9. a) Example: $3y - 11$ **b)** Example: $a + 2b - 7c$
c) $m^2 - 4$ **d)** 18
10. a)

b)

11. a) $x^2 - 3x + 2$ **b)** $-2x^2 + x$ **c)** $-3x + 2$
12. a) x represents the number of video games sold and y represents the number of books sold. **b)** \$104
c) $7.25d + 5c$, where d represents the number of DVDs and c represents the number of CDs
13. One term has the variable x; the other does not have the variable x. So, the two terms cannot be like terms.
14. a) coefficient: 8, variables: x and y, exponent: 2
b) coefficient: -1, variable: c, exponent: 2
c) There are no coefficients or variables because this term is a constant.
15. a) $3s$ and $-8s$ **b)** $-2x^2$ and x^2, $3xy$ and $3xy$
16. Example: Like terms must be identical except for the coefficients. Four sets of examples that contain at least three like terms are:
a) $16z, x, 2z, -z, y$ **b)** $-ab, a, 4b, 6ab, -2ba$
c) $m, m^2, -m, m^3, 6m$ **d)** $xy, 4yx, -11yx, 10s^2, -4yx$
17. $-x^2 - 3x + 5$

18. a) $4 + 3x$

b) $x^2 + 4x + 3$

19. a) $13a + 4$ **b)** $-2b^2 + 3b$ **c)** $7c + 2$
20. Perimeter = $9x$

4x

$x - 2$ $x + 3$

$3x - 1$

21. a) $20 + 1.50n$, where n represents the number of hours renting the locker **b)** $20 + 3n$, where n represents the number of hours renting the tube **c)** $40 + 4.5n$

22. a) $5x - 4$, $3x - 2$ **b)** Example: The processes
are similar in that the like terms were combined. The
processes are different in that one involved addition and
the other involved subtraction.
23. Yes. Example: The opposite term of $2x^2$ is $-2x^2$ and
the opposite term for $-3x$ is $3x$.
24. a) 3 **b)** $-7 + a$ **c)** $-x^2 + 2x - 4$
25. a) Example: Group together the like terms:
$(3p - p) + (4q - 5q) + (-9 + 2) = 2p - q - 7$.
Another method is to change the order of the terms and
line up the polynomials vertically. $3p + 4q - 9$
$$\begin{array}{r} -p - 5q + 2 \\ \hline 2p - q - 7 \end{array}$$
b) Example: The first method is preferred because the
terms are grouped horizontally.
26. a) $3p + 2$ **b)** $4a^2 - 7a - 7$
27.

		$-4t - 2$	
	$-t - 4$	$3t - 2$	
$t - 1$	$2t + 3$	$-t + 5$	

28. a) $140 + 12n$, where n represents the number of
people attending **b)** Example: Another class decides
to spend more on food and refreshments for their
party and less on printing, decorations, and awards.
Their cost for food is \$15/person and \$100 for the
other items. The sum of the costs for both classes is
$(140 + 12n) + (100 + 15n) = 240 + 27n$. The difference
of the costs is $(140 + 12n) - (100 + 15n) = 40 - 3n$.

Chapter 6

6.1 Representing Patterns, pages 217–219

4. a) Example: Every time an octagon is added the
number of sides increases by 6.

b)

Number of Octagons, n	Number of Sides, s
1	8
2	14
3	20
4	26

c) $s = 6n + 2$; s represents number of sides, n represents
number of octagons **d)** 104 **e)** 120

5. a)

Figure Number, n	Number of Circles, c
1	5
2	8
3	11

b) Example: Three circles are added for each subsequent
figure. **c)** $c = 3n + 2$; c represents number of circles, n
represents figure number **d)** 53 **e)** 36

6. a)

Figure Number, n	Number of Green Tiles, t
1	8
2	12
3	16

b) Example: Four green tiles are added for each
subsequent figure. **c)** $t = 4n + 4$; t represents number of
green tiles, n represents figure number **d)** 100 **e)** 43

7. a)

Term, t	Value, v
1	7
2	16
3	25
4	34
5	43

b) $v = 9t - 2$ **c)** 1105 **d)** 40
8. a) Each subsequent term has one additional heptagon.

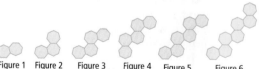

Figure 1 Figure 2 Figure 3 Figure 4 Figure 5 Figure 6

b)

Figure Number, n	Perimeter, P (cm)
1	12
2	17
3	22
4	27
5	32
6	37

c) $P = 5n + 7$; P represents perimeter in centimetres, n
represents figure number **d)** 67 cm **e)** 22

9. a)

Term, t	Value, v
1	-5
2	-8
3	-11
4	-14
5	-17

b) $v = -3t - 2$ **c)** -149 **d)** 39
10. a) $y = 3x + 13$ **b)** $p = 7r + 17$ **c)** $t = 2.7k - 4$
d) $w = -3.5f + 3$
11. a) $s = 4t + 2$, s represents number of seats,
t represents number of tables **b)** 22 **c)** Example:
Substitute $t = 5$ into the equation and solve for s. **d)** 7

12. a)

Number of T-Shirts, n	Cost, C (\$)
0	125
5	200
10	275
15	350
35	650
55	950

b) $C = 15n + 125$; C represents cost, n represents
number of T-shirts. The numerical coefficient is the cost
for each additional T-shirt. **c)** \$5795 **d)** 148
13. a) $t = 2s - 4$; t represents number of tiles,
s represents size of frame **b)** 56 **c)** 100 cm by 100 cm

14. a)

Sighting Number, n	Year, y
1	1758
2	1834
3	1910
4	1986
5	2062
6	2138
7	2214

b) 2062   **c)** $y = 76n + 1682$; y represents year, n represents sighting number   **d)** No. By substituting $y = 2370$ into the equation and solving for n, a decimal answer results. Therefore, the comet will not appear in 2370.

15. a) 127   **b)** Substitute $y = 45\ 678$ into the equation $y = 3x + 1$, and solve for x. If x is a whole number, then $45\ 678$ is 1 more than a multiple of 3.

16. a) $l = 4.5(n - 1)$; l represents length of row, n represents number of trees   **b)** 46 trees will not be evenly spaced because the number of trees has a decimal in the answer.

17. a)

Number of Rebounds, n	Rebound Heights, h (m)
0	2
1	$1\frac{1}{3} \approx 1.33$
2	$\frac{8}{9} \approx 0.89$
3	$\frac{16}{27} \approx 0.59$
4	$\frac{32}{81} \approx 0.39$
5	$\frac{64}{243} \approx 0.26$

b) 0.39 m   **c)** No, this relation is not linear. The rebound heights do not decrease at a constant rate with each bounce.

6.2 Interpreting Graphs, pages 226–230

4. a) 14 km, interpolation   **b)** 7 h
5. a) 14   **b)** 1.5
6. a) −3.5   **b)** −2.5
7. a)

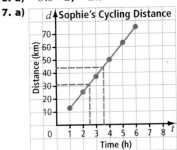

b) 31 km   **c)** 3.5 h
8. a) 29 m   **b)** 10.2 min
9. a) approximately 15.5   **b)** approximately 2.6
10. a) 2   **b)** 4

11. a)

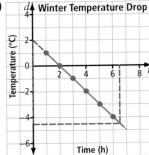

b) −4.5 °C   **c)** 12 noon

12. a)

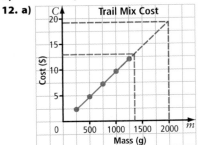

b) $19   **c)** 1400 g
13. a) It is reasonable to interpolate and extrapolate the graph. The submarine can be underwater for a fraction of a minute, and the graph shows a linear relationship.
b) 3.5 min   **c)** 160 m
14. a) Yes, the graph is linear, and it is reasonable to determine the income from the number of programs as long as the number of programs is a whole number.
b) $250, interpolation   **c)** 5000
15. a) 1 h   **b)** 1.8 h   **c)** 3.2 h
16. a) Yes, the graph is linear, and it is reasonable to determine the cost from the number of minutes used.
b) $55   **c)** 45 min
17. a) The cost for renting four days is $280. The cost per day is $70. Divide the cost for four days by the number of days.   **b)** 6 days
18. a) 5.3 s   **b)** 143 m   **c)** The skydiver is accelerating at a constant rate.
19. a)

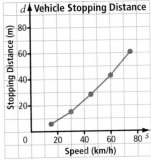

b) As the speed increases the stopping distance also increases.
c) Example: 2 m, 36 m, 80 m   **d)** Example: 20 km/h, 65 km/h, 85 km/h   **e)** Example: 17 m, 26 m   **f)** The graph is not a straight line because the rate of deceleration of the car is different for different speeds of the car.

6.3 Graphing Linear Relations, pages 239–243

4. a)

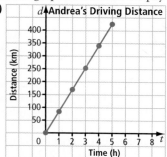

b) The graph represents the equation because his pay increases at a rate of $8.25 for each hour worked. The rate at which his pay increases is the coefficient in the equation.
c) $66; substitute $t = 8$ into the equation and solve for p, or use the graph to estimate his pay using extrapolation.

5. a)

b) 3.5 h
6. a) C **b)** B **c)** A
7. a)

x	y
4	0
4	1
4	2
4	3
4	4

b)

s	r
−2	10.5
−1	7.5
0	4.5
1	1.5
2	−1.5

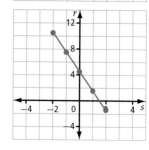

c)

k	m
−10	11
−5	12
0	13
5	14
10	15

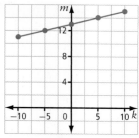

8. a) $C = 1.75m$ **b)** approximately 2.9 kg **c)** Yes, because the values exist beyond and between the points. However, a cost or mass value less than zero does not exist.
9. a) $h = 6t$ **b)** 30 cm **c)** Yes, because the values exist beyond and between the points. However, a height or time value less than zero does not exist.
10. a) $y = -4x$ **b)** $y = 2.5x + 2$
11. a) $y = 0.5x - 1$ **b)** $x = 4$
12. a) $y = 3x - 1$ **b)** $t = 1.5r + 2$

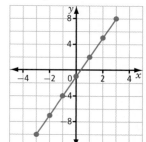

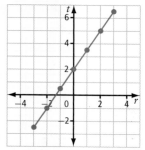

c) $z = -3$ **d)** $n = 0.25h$

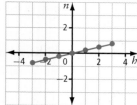

13. a) 1350 m **b)** 11 min **c)** $A = 90t$ **d)** 90 m/min
14. a) $t = 20$ min **b)** T = 50 °C **c)** 5 °C/min
15. a)

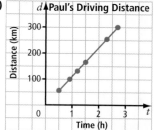

b) 220 km **c)** 1.8 h **d)** $d = 110t$ **e)** 110 km/h

16. a)

Temperature (°C)	Temperature (°F)
−50	−58
−40	−40
−30	−22
−20	−4
−10	14
0	32
10	50
20	68
30	86
40	104
50	122
60	140
70	158
80	176
90	194
100	212
110	230
120	248

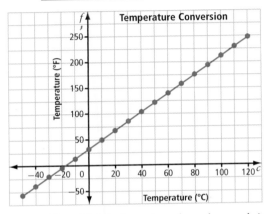

b) 212 °F **c)** This is the point where the graph intersects the y-axis. **d)** −40°

17. a)

Depth, d (m)	Pressure, P (kPa)
0	102.4
10	203.7
20	305.0
30	406.3
40	507.6
50	608.9

Scuba Diving Pressure Change

b) 250 kPa is the approximate pressure using interpolation **c)** 39.25 m **d)** 102.4 kPa is the air pressure at sea level ($d = 0$).

18. a) Girls' growth appears to be linear at greater than 24 months of age. **b)** Girls' growth appears to be non-linear prior to 24 months of age.

19. a)

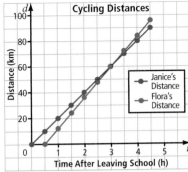

Time, t (h)	Janice's Distance, j (km)	Flora's Distance, f (km)
0	0	n/a
0.5	10	0
1	20	12
1.5	30	24
2	40	36
2.5	50	48
3	60	60
3.5	70	72
4	80	84
4.5	90	96

b) This is where the two lines intersect. **c)** At 3:00 p.m. or after 3 h **d)** At 3:30 p.m. or after 3.5 h

20. a)

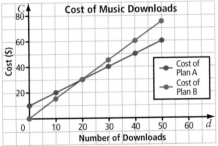

Number of Downloads, d	Cost of Plan A, A ($)	Cost of Plan B, B ($)
0	10	0
10	20	15
20	30	30
30	40	45
40	50	60
50	60	75

b) If you purchase fewer than 20 songs per month, Plan B is a better deal. If you purchase more than 20 songs per month, Plan A is a better deal.

21. a)

Year, y	Interest, I ($)
0	0
1	35
2	70
3	105
4	140
5	175
6	210
7	245
8	280
9	315
10	350

b) $350

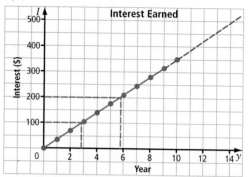

c) 2.85 years, 5.7 years   **d)** approximately 14 years

Chapter 6 Review, pages 244–245

1. linear relation
2. extrapolation
3. constant
4. linear equation
5. interpolate
6. a)

Figure Number, n	Number of Toothpicks, T
1	4
2	7
3	10
4	13
5	16
6	19

b) Three toothpicks or one square is added in each figure.
c) $T = 3n + 1$ **d)** 31   **e)** The numerical coefficient of n is 3. This is the number of additional toothpicks in each subsequent figure. The constant is 1 and this represents the difference between the number of toothpicks in Figure 1 and the number of toothpicks added each time.

7. a)

Time, t (weeks)	Savings, s ($)
0	56
1	71
2	86
3	101
4	116
5	131

b) $s = 15t + 56$ **c)** $581   **d)** 29.6 or 30 weeks
8. a)

Pairs of Shoes Sold, s	Earnings, E ($)
0	50
1	52
2	54
3	56
4	58
5	60
6	62
7	64
8	66
9	68
10	70

b) $E = 2s + 50$ **c)** $74; You can extrapolate using a graph, or substitute and solve using the equation.
9. a) $70   **b)** 2800 trees

10. a) 84 kPa, 70 kPa   **b)** 825 m, 3000 m
c) Yes, because values of air pressure and altitude both exist beyond and between points on the graph.
11. a)

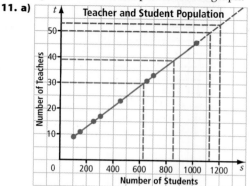

b) 38 teachers, 54 teachers
c) 600 students, 1100 students
12. a)

Number of Days, d	Cost, C ($)
0	40
1	60
2	80
3	100
4	120
5	140

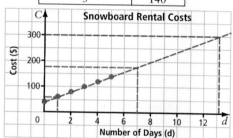

b) $60, $180   **c)** A snowboard would become cheaper to buy after 13 days.   **d)** Substitute the known value into the equation and solve for the unknown value.
13.

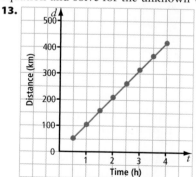

a) Example: You are driving from Toronto to Ottawa at a speed of 105 km/h.   **b)** Example: $d = 105t$
c) The numerical coefficient in this equation is 105. This represents the speed at which the car is travelling per hour. The constant is zero.

14. a)

Number of Hours, t	Cost, C ($)
0	3.00
1	4.75
2	6.50
3	8.25
4	10.00
5	11.75
6	13.50
7	15.25
8	17.00

b)

c) $10.00   **d)** 7 h   **e)** $C = 1.75t + 3$

Chapter 7

7.1 Multiplying and Dividing Monomials, pages 260–263

3. a) $(2x)(3x) = 6x^2$ **b)** $(-2x)(3x) = -6x^2$
c) $(-2x)(-3x) = 6x^2$
4. a) $(3x)(3x) = 9x^2$ **b)** $(-2x)(-2x) = 4x^2$
c) $(2y)(x) = 2xy$
5. a) $8x^2$

b) $-8x^2$

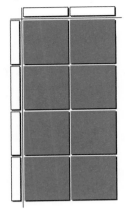

c) $8x^2$

d) $-8x^2$

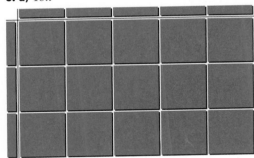

6. a) $15x^2$

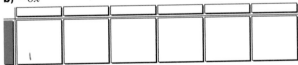

b) $-6x^2$

c) $-6x^2$

d) $-x^2$

d) $-2x$

7. a) $10y^2$ **b)** $-18ab$ **c)** $9q^2$ **d)** $2x^2$ **e)** $6rt$ **f)** $-4.5p^2$
8. a) $6n^2$ **b)** $28k^2$ **c)** $-10w^2$ **d)** $-9x^2$ **e)** $-4mn$ **f)** $-7t^2$
9. $19.5x^2$
10. $34.02z^2$

11. a) $\dfrac{6x^2}{3x} = 2x$ **b)** $\dfrac{8xy}{2y} = 4x$ **c)** $\dfrac{-6x^2}{2x} = -3x$

12. a) $\dfrac{9x^2}{-3x} = -3x$ **b)** $\dfrac{-6x^2}{-2x} = 3x$ **c)** $\dfrac{15xy}{5y} = 3x$

13. a) $4x$

14. a) $-5x$

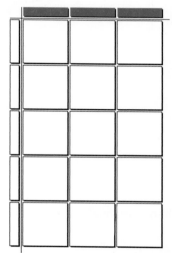

b) x

c) $-3x$

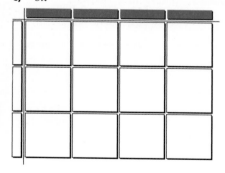

b) $5y$

c) $-4x$

d) $3x$

15. a) $7x$ **b)** $5t$ **c)** $25t$ **d)** 4 **e)** 27 **f)** $-1.5p$

16. a) $12.4x$ **b)** 3.75 **c)** 3 **d)** $-6p$ **e)** 0.25 **f)** $\frac{x}{3}$

17. a) $33x^2$ **b)** $20p^2$ **c)** $\frac{w^2}{4}$

18. a) $3x$ **b)** $6w$

19. a) $3.6d$

20. No, it will not fit. If x represents the width of Claire's space, then the length is $3x$ and the area is $x(3x) = 3x^2$. So $3x^2 = 48$, and by solving the equation, $x = 4$. The width of Claire's space is 4 m. The length is then 12 m, which is not long enough for a 12.5 m patio.

21. 4

22. a) $\frac{4}{\pi}$ **b)** $\frac{4}{\pi}$

23. If x represents the width of the dogsled, then the length is $4x$ and the area if $x(4x) = 4x^2$. So $4x^2 = 3.2$, and by solving the equation, $x \approx 0.89$. The width of the dogsled is about 0.89 m and the length is about 3.56 m. This is just barely long and wide enough for the equipment to fit.

24. a) 5 cm **b)** $SA = 24xy + 40x + 30y$

25. Example: They are similar because you have to divide 9 by 3 in each one. However, they differ because you get a fraction in the quotient for one, but not the other.

26. 1

27. a) $1.25x^2$ **b)** 9031.25 cm^2

7.2 Multiplying Polynomials by Monomials, pages 269–271

4. a) $(3x)(2x + 4) = 6x^2 + 12x$
b) $(4k)(3k + 3.6) = 12k^2 + 14.4k$
c) $(k)(3.2k + 5.1) = 3.2k^2 + 5.1k$
5. a) $(4y)(3y + 7) = 12y^2 + 28y$
b) $(3.5f)(f + 2) = 3.5f^2 + 7f$
c) $(2k)(7 + 0.9k) = 14k + 1.8k^2$
6. a) $12.8r^2 + 4r$ **b)** $\frac{3}{2}a^2 + 3a$

 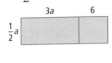

7. a) $8x^2 + 4x$ **b)** $27k^2 + 9k$

 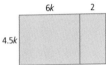

8. a) $(2x)(3x + 1) = 6x^2 + 2x$
b) $(-x)(-x - 3) = x^2 + 3x$
c) $(3x)(-x + 2) = -3x^2 + 6x$
9. a) $(-3x)(2x + 2) = -6x^2 - 6x$
b) $(3x)(-2x - 1) = -6x^2 - 3x$
c) $(-x)(x + 4) = -x^2 - 4x$
10. a) $3x^2 - 15x$

b) $-4x^2 + 6x$

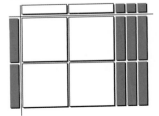

11. a) $-12x^2 - 6x$

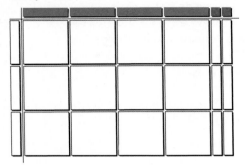

b) $-12x^2 + 4x$

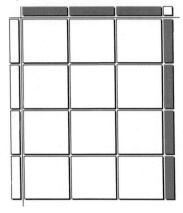

12. a) $6x^2 - 2x$ **b)** $6p^2 - 2.4p$ **c)** $3.5m - 6m^2$
d) $-0.5r^2 + 2r$ **e)** $16.4n - 57.4$ **f)** $3x^2 + 6xy + 12x$
13. a) $8j^2 - 12j$ **b)** $-3.6w^2 + 8.4w$ **c)** $24x - 14.4x^2$
d) $-\dfrac{3}{7}v - 7$ **e)** $3y - 9y^2$ **f)** $-64a^2 - 56ab - 16a$
14. a) $12x^2 - 9x$ **b)** $P = 3x + 3x + 4x - 3 + 4x - 3$
$$P = 14x - 6$$
15. a) $w^2 - 2w$ **b)** 8 m²
16. a) $1.5w^2 + 5.5w$ **b)** 420 m²
17. $16x^2 + 8x$
18. a) $9x^2 - 12x$ **b)** 1845 m²
19. a) $16x^2 + 12x$ **b)** $4x^3 + 4x^2$
20. $SA = 226.19$ cm²
21. a)

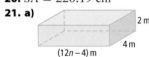

b) $(96n - 16)$ m² **c)** $(96n - 32)$ m³

7.3 Dividing Polynomials by Monomials, pages 275–277

4. a) $\dfrac{(6x^2 + 4x)}{2x} = 3x + 2$ **b)** $\dfrac{4x^2 + 6x}{2x} = 2x + 3$
c) $\dfrac{(6x^2 - 3x)}{3x} = 2x - 1$

5. a) $\dfrac{-x^2 - 4x}{x} = -x - 4$ **b)** $\dfrac{8x^2 + 12x}{-4x} = -2x - 3$
c) $\dfrac{-3x^2 + 15x}{-3x} = x - 5$
6. a) $x - 2$

b) $2x + 6$

7. a) $-2x - 1$

b) $3x - 5$

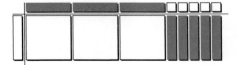

8. a) $y + 2.1$ **b)** $6m^2 - 3.1m + 12$ **c)** $3y + 1$ **d)** $v - 0.9$
9. a) $0.9c + 1.2$ **b)** $2x + 8y$ **c)** $-0.2s - 0.3t$
d) $-28w^2 - 14w + 1$
10. $2x^2 + 3x$
11. a) $A = 12.5w^2 - 5w$ **b)** $l = 12.5w - 5$
c) $l = 2.5$ m, $V = 0.9$ m^3
12. $9x + 4$
13. The length is $(3x - 1)$ units.
14. a) $s = 4.9t + v$ **b)** 24.5 m/s
15. a) $12f + 3.1$ **b)** $2b - a + 1$ **c)** $-24x^2 + 18x - 2$
16. $3x + 1.5$
17. $x + 6 : 15x$
18. $12x + 4xy + 6y$

Chapter 7 Review, pages 278–279

1. C
2. F
3. B
4. A
5. a) $15x^2$

b) $-20xy$

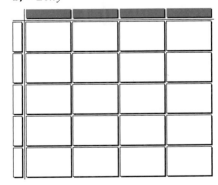

6. a) $8.64xy$ **b)** $-6a^2$
7. a) $3x$

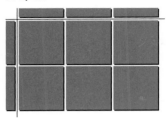

b) $-5a$

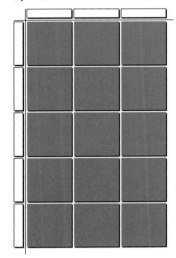

8. a) $4r$ **b)** y
9. 20 cm by 80 cm
10. $2 : \pi$
11. a) $(1.3y)(3y + 5) = 3.9y^2 + 6.5y$
b) $(1.2f)(f + 4) = 1.2f^2 + 4.8f$
12. a) $(3x)(2x + 4) = 6x^2 + 12x$
b) $(2x)(-3x - 1) = -6x^2 - 2x$
13. a) $46x^2 - 28x$ **b)** $\frac{2}{3}p^2 - \frac{1}{2}p$
14. $12x^2 + 6x$
15. a) $\frac{x^2 + 5x}{x} = x + 5$ **b)** $\frac{-4x^2 + 12x}{-2x} = 2x - 6$
16. a) $6n - 1$ **b)** $10 - 2x$
17. $2x + 4$
18. $x + \frac{1}{2}$
19. Naullaq will need 5 blocks of ice to fill the drinking tank. The answer must be rounded up because 4 blocks will not fill the tank and Naullaq is only cutting full blocks.

1. a) Perimeter $= 2(x + 1) + 2(x + 3)$
b) Area $= x^2 + 4x + 3$
2. a) $3c + 4$

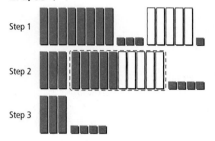

Step 1

Step 2

Step 3

b) $-x$

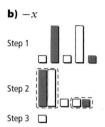

Step 1

Step 2

Step 3

c) $3g^2 + g + 5$

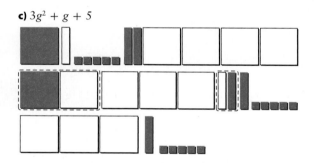

3. a) $7m - 2$ **b)** $4w^2 + w + 4$ **c)** $7y^2 - 9y - 2.5$
4. a) $-3z - 2$ **b)** $-d^2 - 6cd + 6d - 5$ **c)** $2(-x^2 + 2xy)$
5. a) Example: $I = 10c + 8h + 3p$, where I represents the shop's income, c represents the number of comic books sold, h represents the number of hardcover books sold and p represents the number of paperback books sold.   **b)** 221 **c)** Example: 70 comic books, 3 hardcover books, 2 paperback books or 3 comic books, 5 hardcover books, 10 paperback books.
6. $10(n + 4)$
7. a) Starting with 4 tiles, add 4 tiles for each new figure
b) $t = 4n$, where t is the number of tiles and n is the figure number.   **c)** 32

8. a)

Week	Savings ($)
0	112
1	137
2	162
3	187
4	212
5	237

b) $s = 112 + 25w$, where s is Monika's savings and w is the number of weeks.   **c)** 13.52 weeks or 3.38 months
9. a) $515   **b)** 3.2 h   **c)** $605
10. a)

b) $17 500   **c)** $35 000   **d)** $22 500
11. a) Example:

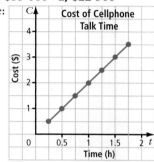

A cell phone company charges $0.50 for every 0.25 h of talk-time purchased.   **b)** $C = 2t$, where C is the cost of talk-time and t is the talk-time purchased, in hours.
c) $6.50
12. a) $12x^2$ **b)** $-10y^2$ **c)** $-0.5s^2$ **d)** $2t^2$
13. a) $8.4x$ **b)** $-6h$ **c)** $3n$ **d)** $-4p$
14. a)

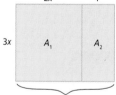

$A_1 + A_2 = 6x^2 + 3x$

b)

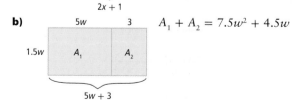

$A_1 + A_2 = 7.5w^2 + 4.5w$

15. $w(2w + 3)$
16. a) $3g + 2$ **b)** $-2x + y$ **c)** $-(3f^2 - 20)$ **d)** $48n + 16$
17. $2x - 1$

Chapter 8

8.1 Solving Equations: $ax = b$, $\frac{x}{a} = b$, $\frac{a}{x} = b$, pages 301–303

4. $3x = 0.27$, $x = 0.09$

5. $x = \frac{3}{16}$

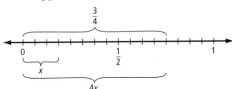

6. a) $v = -\frac{5}{12}$

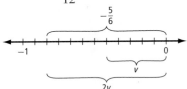

b) $x = \frac{4}{5}$ or 0.8

c) $a = -\frac{16}{15}$ **d)** $x = \frac{3}{2}$

7. a) $x = \frac{12}{5}$ **b)** $y = -\frac{3}{5}$ **c)** $n = \frac{7}{8}$ **d)** $w = \frac{7}{16}$

8. a) $x = -0.625$ **b)** $e = 1.65$

9. a) $h = 14.76$ **b)** $c = 3.2$

10. a) $a = -0.2$ **b)** $m = 0.75$

11. a) $n = 2.85$ **b)** $x = 0.55$

12. a) $d = 318.75$ km **b)** $t = 1.6$ h

13. $0.05n = 2.00$, $n = 40$

14. $s = 6.45$ cm

15. d is greater than zero because the value of $-\frac{5}{d}$ is negative. Therefore, d must be positive.

16. $d = 17.4$ cm

17. $n = 6$, hexagon

18. 214 students did not buy the yearbook.

19. A score of 25 would give a mark of 100%.

20. The Yukon Territory covers 4.8% of Canada.

21. Her net monthly income is $2500.

22. The team scored 110 points together.

23. The sale price was $999.96.

24. They expect to attract about 111 new volunteers.

25. The side length is 8.3 cm.

26. a) $x = \frac{3}{5}$ **b)** $z = 3.24$ **c)** $y = \frac{6}{5}$ **d)** $f = -0.495$

27. a) $t = -0.51$ **b)** $h = -0.78$

28. a) $x = -\frac{3}{8}$ **b)** $t = \frac{1}{3}$ **c)** $y = \frac{5}{4}$ **d)** $g = -\frac{4}{3}$

29. a) There are 54 coins in the jar.
b) There are 19 dimes.
30. The cyclist's speed is 21 km/h.

8.2 Solving Equations: $ax + b = c$, $\frac{x}{a} + b = c$, pages 311–313

5. $x = 0.20$
6. $x = 0.12$

7. a) $y = 0.25$ **b)** $d = \frac{7}{8}$ **c)** $n = -3$ **d)** $r = \frac{1}{5}$

8. a) $h = \frac{5}{24}$ **b)** $x = -\frac{3}{16}$ **c)** $d = \frac{9}{8}$ **d)** $g = -\frac{12}{7}$

9. a) $x = -2.1$ **b)** $r = 6.984$
10. a) $n = -0.037$ **b)** $k = -1.512$
11. a) $v = -0.116$ **b)** $x = 3.2$
12. a) $d = 55.5$ **b)** $a = 14.3$
13. four toppings
14. 168 km
15. $35
16. a) $2206 **b)** $7600
17. 11.6 m
18. 4.82 cm
19. 332.7 mm
20. 112 cm or 1.12 m, 138 cm or 1.38 m
21. 101 mm
22. 5 h
23. Sharifa. It will only take 7 weeks for her to save enough money.
24. 3.75 min
25. 108.2 million km

26. a) Example: $\frac{x}{2} + 1 = \frac{4}{3}$ **b)** Example: $\frac{x}{0.4} + 1 = -1$

27. Example: John is 2.5 years older than twice his brother's age. John is 12.5 years old. How old is his brother?
$2b + 2.5 = 12.5$, $b = 5$
John's brother is 5 years old.

28. a) $w = -\frac{14}{3}$ **b)** $x = -\frac{1}{9}$

29. a) $y = -1.14$ **b)** $s = 8.28$

30. a) $x = 0.5$ **b)** $n = \frac{16}{3}$ **c)** $h = -1.408$ **d)** $y = -2$

31. $x = -0.85$
32. 500 m

8.3 Solving Equations: $a(x + b) = c$, pages 319–321

5. $3(x + 0.05) = 0.60$, $x = 0.15$
6. a) $x = 2.3$ **b)** $c = 3.45$ **c)** $a = -5.7$ **d)** $r = 0.3$
7. a) $u = 11.36$ **b)** $m = -3.93$ **c)** $v = 1.68$ **d)** $x = 3.41$

8. a) $n = -\frac{5}{2}$ **b)** $x = \frac{19}{2}$ **c)** $w = -\frac{2}{9}$ **d)** $g = \frac{13}{4}$

9. a) $y = -\frac{1}{5}$ **b)** $q = -\frac{17}{2}$ **c)** $e = -\frac{13}{2}$ **d)** $p = \frac{15}{4}$

10. a) $x = 3.4$ **b)** $k = -63.6$ **c)** $q = -2.27$
d) $a = -5.9$
11. a) $q = 1.1$ **b)** $y = 0.071$ **c)** $n = -2.18$ **d)** $p = 0$
12. $x = -1.7$
13. a) $3(x + 1.05) = 9.83$, $x = 2.2$
14. $x = 6.76$
15. 3.3 °C
16. $d = -0.45$
17. $2.99
18. $37.50
19. $6.40/skin
20. a) $h = 7.8$ cm **b)** $a = 1.3$ m
21. 15.6 cm
22. 15 years old
23. a) $x = -2.3$ **b)** $y = 4.9$ **c)** $f = 2.8$ **d)** $t = -8.98$
24. a) $d = -16.8$ **b)** $r = 3.5$ **c)** $g = 1.6$ **d)** $h = -18$
25. The longer side is 0.5 units and the shorter side
is 0.25 units.
26. -15
27. 1 h 27.6 min
28. a) $n = \frac{4}{x} + 3$ **b)** $n = \frac{4}{x} + 3$

c) Divide first, because it involves fewer steps.

8.4 Solving Equations: $ax = b + cx$, $ax + b = cx + d$, $a(bx + c) = d(ex + f)$, pages 326–329

4. $3x + 0.15 = 2x + 0.30$, $x = 0.15$
5. $x = $0.55

6. a) $x = 6.4$ **b)** $y = 3$ **c)** $a = -0.8$ **d)** $g = \frac{6}{7}$

7. a) $n = \frac{4}{3}$ **b)** $w = -2.2$ **c)** $p = 4.25$ **d)** $e = \frac{3}{10}$
e) $d = -18$

8. a) $k = 0.5$ **b)** $p = -21$ **c)** $u = 3$ **d)** $h = -\frac{5}{2}$

9. a) $r = -2.55$ **b)** $c = 0.4$ **c)** $k = 8$ **d)** $p = \frac{11}{3}$

10. a) $q = 0.22$ **b)** $x = -5$ **c)** $y = 0.75$ **d)** $x = \frac{5}{2}$

11. a) $s = -0.4$ **b)** $g = 7.8$ **c)** $x = 6$ **d)** $m = -2$
12. a) $c = -3.36$ **b)** $n = 3.38$ **c)** $x = 1.39$ **d)** $a = -0.17$
13. a) 19 nickels **b)** $1.90
14. 5 weeks
15. Rectangle A: 2.5 units by 3.1 units;
Rectangle B: 0.1 units by 5.5 units
16. a) $x = 1.4$ **b)** The perimeter of each triangle is
23.3 units.
17. 33 min
18. Each rectangle has an area of 13.68 square units.
19. a) 17.5 min **b)** 1.3125 km
20. $f = 180$ cm
21. 12 movies/year

22. The speed of the current is 7.07 km/h.
23. a) Yes. When the distributive property is applied to
both sides of the expression, the result is two identical
expressions. **b)** Yes. When the distributive property is
applied to both sides of the expression, the result is two
identical expressions.
24. Example: My dad always tells the same story about
how hard he worked when he first came to Canada. He
said he worked after school as a server in a restaurant
earning $x/h. One day, he worked 3.5 h and had
$1.2 in tips. Another day, he worked 4 h and had
$0.90 in tips. Both days, he earned the same amount of
money. How much was my dad getting per hour?
25. Example: One video store charges a $5 annual
membership fee and $4 per movie. Another store charges
no membership fee, but $5 per movie. How many movies
per year would you have to rent for the cost to be the
same at both stores? Let m represent the number of
movies. $4m + 5 = 5m$, $m = 5$ movies.
26. a) $x = 17.5$ **b)** $y = -30$ **c)** $d = 2.2$ **d)** $j = 1.5$
27. a) $a = 1.125$ **b)** $s = 9$ **c)** $q = -3$ **d)** $z = -1.25$
28. $k = \dfrac{10 - x}{3}$
29. $n = -1.2$
30. a) $x = \dfrac{1}{14}$ **b)** $y = -\dfrac{1}{3}$

Chapter 8 Review, pages 330–331

1. D, B, A, C, C
2. opposite operation
3. distributive property
4. $x = -0.8$

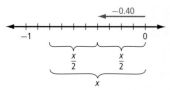

5. a) $d = -\dfrac{1}{10}$ **b)** $y = 8.04$ **c)** $h = -17.5$ **d)** $u = 1.9$
6. a) $w = -4.7$ **b)** $k = 9.0$
7. a) $m = 43.3$ g **b)** $v = 12.5$ cm³
8. 60 goals
9. $x = \dfrac{1}{3}$

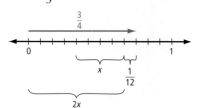

10. a) She should have divided by -3. **b)** $g = 3$

11. a) $t = -14.56$ **b)** $x = 9.5$ **c)** $r = \dfrac{4}{3}$ **d)** $v = -\dfrac{20}{7}$

12. $34.95

13. 58.6 Earth days

14. a) $e = -6.7$ **b)** $r = 1.5$ **c)** $h = -21.1$ **d)** $q = \dfrac{7}{8}$

15. $m = -1.97$

16. $k = 3.225$ m

17. $21.75

18. a) $n = 15$ **b)** $f = 1.75$ **c)** $g = -1.6$ **d)** $h = -60$

e) $v = -\dfrac{11}{6}$

19. a) $a = 1.9$ **b)** $P = 25.2$ units

20. $w = 7.5$ cm

Chapter 9

9.1 Representing Inequalities, pages 347–349

5. a) Example: $x \geq 3$ **b)** Example: $x < 7$
c) Example: $x \leq -13$ **d)** Example: $x > -1.5$
6. a) Yes; 4 is greater than 3.

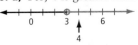

b) No; 4 is not less than 4.

c) Yes; 4 is greater than −9.

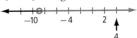

d) Yes; 4 is greater than or equal to 4.

7. a) Example: All values greater than or equal to 8.
Three possible values are 11, 15, and 22.
b) Example: All values less than −12. Three possible
values are −14, −21.5, and −100.
c) Example: All values less than or equal to 6.4. Three
possible values are 1, 3, and 6.4.
d) Example: All values that exceed −12.7. Three possible
values are −11, 0, and 33.
8. a)

b) $p \geq 32$
9. a) All values greater than 4.   **b)** All values less than or
equal to −2.   **c)** All values greater than or equal to −13.
10. a) Example: $x < 12.7$ or $12.7 > x$
b) Example: $y > 4.65$ or $4.65 < y$
c) Example: $y \leq -24.3$ or $-24.3 \geq y$
11. a)

b)

c)

d)

12. a)

b)

c)

d)

13. a)

b)

c)

d)

14. a)

b) Example: The values of −10.0 and −9.8 are both less
than −9.3, so they are not possible values. Conversely,
−9.0 is larger than −9.3 so it is a possible value.

15. a) The value is greater than or equal to 20, and
less than or equal to 27; $20 \leq x$ and $x \leq 27$ **b)** The
value is less than 2, and greater than −6; $-6 < x$ and
$x < 2$ **c)** The value is less than −8, and greater than or
equal to −9.2; $-9.2 \leq x$ and $x < -8$
16. a) $m \geq 18\ 000$ **b)** $t \leq 8$ **c)** $d > 700$
17. a)

b) $x \geq 1500$
18. a) Paul will beat the record if he finishes the race in
less than 41.5 s. **b)** $t < 41.5$
19. a) Example: A school environmental awareness club
hopes to recycle at least 650 cans each month.
b)

c) $c \geq 650$
20. a) $m \leq 10.75$ **b)**

21. a) Shanelle will have to pay more insurance if the
distance between her home and workplace is farther than
15 km. **b)**

22. a)

b) $w \leq 4$; $s \leq 30$; $m \geq 50$
23. a) $x = 6$ **b)** Since the only possible value for x that
satisfies both inequalities is 6, there will be a single solid
dot on the number line at 6.
24. $50 < s \leq 80$
25. a) All values greater than 4 and less than 7

b) All values less than 4

c) All values greater than 7

d) All values less than 4 and greater than 7

9.2 Solving Single-Step Inequalities, pages 357–359

5. a) $x \geq 29$　**b)** $-7 < x$　**c)** $x > -13.8$　**d)** $35 \leq x$
6. a) $y \geq 9$　**b)** $-14.5 < y$　**c)** $y \leq -4$　**d)** $y > 6.25$
7. a) $x > 150$　**b)** $x \leq 36$　**c)** $2.4 \geq x$　**d)** $x > -30$
8. a)–c) No, the inequality is not changed because there is no multiplication or division by a negative number.
d) Yes, the direction of the inequality is changed because there is division by a negative number.
e) Yes, the direction of the inequality is changed because there is multiplication by a negative number.
f) No, the inequality is not changed because there is no multiplication or division by a negative number.
9. a) yes　**b)** yes　**c)** yes　**d)** no
10. a) yes　**b)** no　**c)** no　**d)** yes
11. a) yes　**b)** no　**c)** yes　**d)** yes
12. a) yes　**b)** No; the correct answer is $x > -16$, not $x > 16$.
13. a) No; the correct solution is $-9 \geq x$, not $-11 \geq x$.
b) yes
14. a) $85f \leq 1400$　**b)** $f \leq 16.47$　**c)** No, the boundary value is not a positive integer, which is required when discussing the number of fence sections.
15. a) $6w > 50$　**b)** $w > 8.\overline{3}$. Megan must win 9 or more races to move up to the next racing category.　**c)** No, the number of races won will be a non-negative integer.
16. a) Example: Three solutions are -6, -20.2, and -10. Three non-solutions are 0, -4, and 8.6.
b) Example: Three solutions are 0, -2, and 5.5. Three non-solutions are -11, -8, and -16.
17. Example: The inequality sign is reversed because each side was divided by a negative number, -5.
18. a) Example: The single sharpening cost is about $6. When this is divided by 48, the answer is 8. So, if the skates need to be sharpened more than 8 times, the monthly charge would be a better option.
b) $5.75s > 49$; $s > 8.52$. It would be better to take advantage of the monthly special if the skates were sharpened more than 8 times. The estimate and solution to the inequality are the same.
19. a) $0.03p \geq 250$; $p \geq 8333.\overline{3}$. The owner would need to make a profit of at least $8333.33 in order to donate at least $250 to the local charity.　**b)** Example: Check the boundary point, $8333.\overline{3}$, and then check that both sides of the inequality are equal: $0.03(8333.\overline{3}) = 250$. Check a number that is larger than the boundary value (9000) and see that it is a solution: $0.03(9000) = 270$. Since 270 is larger than 250, then 9000 is a solution to the inequality.
20. $0.084k \leq 57$; $k \leq 678.57$; They can travel no more than 678.57 km, assuming the car consumes the average amount of fuel.
21. a) Natalie must run 8 laps in order to complete the 3200-m distance: $3200 \div 400 = 8$. The total time of 9 min 23 s is equivalent to 563 s: $9 \times 60 + 23 = 563$. The expression $8x$ represents her total time, where x is her average time per lap. Consequently, her total time must be less than the current record of 563 s: $8x < 563$.
b) $x < 70.375$

22. $\frac{s}{5} \geq 120$; $s \geq 600$. She will have to spend at least $600 to get at least 120 points.
23. a) $115d \geq 1000$; $4d \leq 50$　**b)** $d \geq 8.70$; $d \leq 12.5$
c) Chris can build between 9 and 12 doghouses and stay within his guidelines.
24. $x > -\dfrac{5}{6}$
25.

26. The mass of the energy bar must be between 66.67 g and 76.92 g.
27. a) $x \leq 5$　**b)** $x \geq 5$
28. a) $-14 \leq x$ and $x \leq -1$　**b)** $-1 < x$ and $x < 6$
c) $\dfrac{5}{2} \geq x$ and $x > -\dfrac{3}{2}$

9.3 Solving Multi-Step Inequalities, pages 365–367

3. a) $x < 11$　**b)** $x > -20$　**c)** $50 \leq x$
4. a) $y \leq 10.4$　**b)** $-2.1 > y$　**c)** $y > -108$　**d)** $x \leq 3\dfrac{1}{5}$
5. a) Check the boundary value: $3(8) + 11 = 35$. Check another number in the solution set, $x = 10$: $3(10) + 11 = 41$. Since 41 is greater than 35, the solution is correct.　**b)** Solve the inequality: $24 - 5x - 24 > 39 - 24$. Finally, simplify $\dfrac{-5x}{-5} < \dfrac{15}{-5}$ to get the solution, $x < -3$.
6. a) $x < 6$　**b)** $x \geq 11$　**c)** $x < -\dfrac{9}{8}$　**d)** $x > 39$
7. a) $y < 2$　**b)** $y \leq 10$　**c)** $y > \dfrac{28}{9}$　**d)** $y \geq 3$
8. a) Example: Let j represent the number of jerseys; $40j + 80 < 50j$　**b)** Example: Let n represent the number of text messages sent in one month; $0.12n < 0.05n + 15$
9. a) $0.05p + 10 > 0.04p + 15$　**b)** John will have to deliver more than 500 papers to make the *Advance* the better offer.
10. a) Example: ABC Rentals would be a better deal if you travel less than 200 km per day ($30 \div 0.15$).
b) $0.14k + 25 < 55$　**c)** ABC Rentals will be the better option if Kim travels less than 214.3 km per day.
11. Kevin's weekly sales must be at least $4000 for Dollar Deal to pay more.
12. Print Express would be the better option if more than 236 yearbooks are ordered.
13. The member's plan is a better deal when 22 or more buckets of balls are used per month.
14. Molly must sell at least 72 candles in order to make a profit.
15. The first tank will contain less water after $27\dfrac{3}{11}$ minutes have passed.
16. a) Example: Estimate: 20 min　**b)** Rob will be closer to the top after 17.14 min have passed.
17. $x < 5.2$;

18.

19. Lauren can cut 34, 35, or 36 lawns per month and stay within her guidelines.
20. a) Ella is correct when $x > 0$.
b) Ella is incorrect when $x \le 0$. Example: Ella is correct when $x = 2$, but she is incorrect when $x = -11.2$.
21. $9 \ge x$ and $x \ge -2$
22. $x > 0$

Chapter 9 Review, pages 368–369

1. inequality
2. graphically; algebraically
3. open circle
4. solution
5. boundary point
6. closed circle
7. a) Example: Savings $\le 40\%$
b) Example: Free shipping for purchases $\ge \$500$
c) Example: Number of items on sale > 80
8. a) Example: The bicycle must be at least 6.8 kg in mass.

b) Example: The bicycle must be less than or equal to 185 cm.

9. a) $x > 13$; A number greater than 13.
b) $x \le 8.6$. A number less than or equal to 8.6.
10. a)
b)
c)
d)
11. Example:

Linear Inequality	One Solution Value	One Non-solution Value
$r > -4$	3	-10
$0 \le s \le 7$	3.4	11
$9.5 > t$	8	22
$v \le -\dfrac{5}{4}$	-2	0

12. a) $d > -3$ **b)** $5.4 < a$ **c)** $-33 \ge b$ **d)** $c < -16$
13. a) No, the solution is incorrect. The boundary value of 8 is correct but the direction is incorrect.
b) The solution is correct.
14. a) $14.5t \ge 600$ **b)** Tim must work at least 41.4 h per week to achieve his goal.
15. Danielle can buy a maximum of 13 scoops of ice cream and stay within her budget.
16. No, the solution is incorrect. The boundary value is correct but the direction is incorrect.
17. a) Yes, the solution is correct. **b)** Example: First, check that the boundary value creates an equation. Then, check a solution value in the original inequality and see if it results in a true inequality statement.

18. a) $x < 45$ **b)** $7.5 > x$ **c)** $x \ge -1$ **d)** $x < -20$
e) $1.4 \le x$ **f)** $x < -\dfrac{9}{8}$
19. The maximum number of people that can attend the banquet is 64.
20. Greg would need to purchase at least 201 tracks per month to make Plan A the better option.

Chapter 10

10.1 Exploring Angles in a Circle, pages 382–385

3. ADB and AEB are inscribed angles that are subtended by the same arc as the central ACB. The measure of ACB is 82°. Therefore, ADB and AEB have measures that are half the measure of ACB. Half of 82 is 41. So, the measure of ADB is 41° and the measure of AEB is 41°.
4. a) 23°. Example: The inscribed angles subtended by the same arc of a circle are equal. **b)** 46° Example: A central angle is twice the measure of an inscribed angle subtended by the same arc.
5.

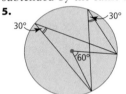

6. a) 90°. Example: $\angle ABD$ is an inscribed angle subtended by the diameter of the circle. **b)** 8 cm
7. a) 90° **b)** 11.3 cm
Example: Since $\triangle CFG$ is a right triangle, by the Pythagorean relationship,
$$8^2 + 8^2 = FG^2$$
$$64 + 64 = FG^2$$
$$128 = FG^2$$
$$\sqrt{128} = FG$$
$$11.3 \approx FG$$
8. Example: Jacob could place his flashlight anywhere on the major arc MN.

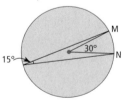

9. Example: In the diagram, X is the ideal location.

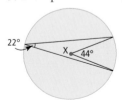

10. a) 76°. Example: ∠ACD is a central angle subtended by the same arc as the inscribed angle ∠ABD. Its measure is twice the inscribed angle's measure. **b)** △ACD is an isosceles triangle because the sides AC and DC are radii of the same circle and are therefore equal. **c)** 52°. Subtract the measure of ∠ACD, 76°, from 180° and divide by 2.

11. a) 130° **b)** 65°. △FCE is an isosceles triangle since sides FC and EC are radii of the same circle. Therefore, the measure of ∠ECF = 180° − 2(25°) = 130°. ∠EGF is an inscribed angle subtended by the same arc as the central angle ∠EGF and is therefore one half its measure.

12. a) 15° **b)** 24° **c)** 48° **d)** 30°

13. a) 56° **b)** 90° **c)** a right triangle **d)** 90°

14. No. Example: Neither △ADB or △ACB are right triangles. The Pythagorean relationship can only be used with right triangles.

15. a) $x = 45°$, $y = 45°$ **b)** $x = 60°$, $y = 120°$ **c)** $x = 15°$, $y = 30°$ **d)** $x = 35°$, $y = 45°$

16. In the diagram, find the measure of ∠PMQ.

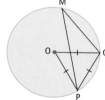

17. The measure of ∠ACE = 28° and the measure of ∠ABE = 14°.

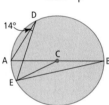

18. a) $x = 25°$, $y = 50°$ **b)** $x = 95°$, $y = 55°$

19. 14.14 cm

20. a) 9° **b)** 17°

21. a) 180° ÷ 2 = 90° **b)** 180° − 90° − 27° = 63° **c)** 63°. ∠AEG is opposite ∠BEH and therefore equal. **d)** 60° **e)** 120°

10.2 Exploring Chord Properties, pages 389–393

4. 9 cm. Example: Since △ACE is a right triangle, by the Pythagorean relationship,
$$12^2 + CE^2 = 15^2$$
$$144 + CE^2 = 225$$
$$CE^2 = 81$$
$$CE = \sqrt{81}$$
$$CE = 9$$

5. 8.1 mm. Example: Draw radius HC to form a right triangle. By the Pythagorean relationship,
$$4^2 + 7^2 = CH^2$$
$$16 + 49 = CH^2$$
$$65 = CH^2$$
$$\sqrt{65} = CH$$
$$8.1 \approx CH$$

6. Example: Hannah should draw any two chords on the circle. She should then locate and draw the perpendicular bisectors of each chord. The intersection of the perpendicular bisectors is the centre of the trampoline.

7. 30 m. Example: Find the length of EB by using the Pythagorean relationship.
$$8^2 + EB^2 = 17^2$$
$$64 + EB^2 = 289$$
$$EB^2 = 225$$
$$EB = \sqrt{225}$$
$$EB = 15$$
Double the length of EB to obtain the length of AB. 2(15) = 30. The length of AB is 30 m.

8. 16 cm

9. a) 5.2 **b)** 5.6

10. 7 cm

11. 16 cm²

12. 24 mm

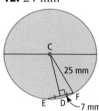

13. Example: Locate and draw the perpendicular bisectors of any two sides of the octagon. The point where the two perpendicular bisectors intersect is the centre of the octagon.

14. Example: Draw any two chords. Locate and draw the perpendicular bisectors of the two chords. The point of intersection of the two perpendicular bisectors is the centre of the circle. Measure the distance from the centre of the circle to the endpoint of any chord. If the measurement is 8 cm, his diagram was accurate.

15. a) 90°. An inscribed angle that subtends a diameter has a measure of 90°. **b)** 12 cm. △ADE is a right triangle. By using the Pythagorean relationship,
$$16^2 + AD^2 = 20^2$$
$$256 + AD^2 = 400$$
$$AD^2 = 144$$
$$AD = \sqrt{144}$$
$$AD = 12$$

c) 9.6 cm. △DFE is a right triangle. By using the Pythagorean relationship,

$$12.8^2 + DF^2 = 16^2$$
$$163.84 + DF^2 = 256$$
$$DF^2 = 92.16$$
$$DF = \sqrt{92.16}$$
$$DF \approx 9.6$$

d) 19.2 cm. The length of BD = twice the length of DF.

$$BD = 2DF$$
$$BD = 2(9.6)$$
$$= 19.2$$

16. a) 65°. ∠HMP subtends the same arc as the central angle that has a measure of 130°. Therefore, the measure of ∠HMP is half of 130°. **b)** 90°. Segment CJ is the perpendicular bisector of chord MP. Therefore ∠HEM is 90°. **c)** 25°. ∠HEM is 90°. Therefore, △HME is a right triangle, so 180° − 90° − 65° = 25°. **d)** 25°. ∠MPJ is an inscribed angle subtending the same arc as the inscribed angle of 25°. **e)** 50°. ∠HCP and ∠PCE are supplementary angles. **f)** 40°. △CEP is a right triangle, so 180° − 90° − 50° = 40°.

17. 1.2 m

18. Example: Gavyn made two mistakes. The first mistake is that the diagram is labelled incorrectly: segment AC should be labelled as 13 cm. The second mistake is that segment AC is the hypotenuse, not a leg. So, by the Pythagorean relationship, EC² + AE² = AC². The correct length of AB is 24 cm.

19. 15.6 mm

20. a) If a bisector of a chord passes through the centre of a circle, then the bisector is perpendicular to the chord. **b)** 22° and 68°

21. Since the bisectors of chords AB and DE pass through the centres of their respective circles, the bisectors are perpendicular to chords AB and DE. Two line segments perpendicular to the same segment are parallel.

10.3 Tangents to a Circle, pages 399–403

3. a) 90°. ∠BDC is 90° because segment AB is tangent to the circle at point D and segment DC is a radius. **b)** 150°. ∠DCB = 30° because triangle DBC is a right triangle and 180° − 90° − 60° = 30°. Since ∠DCB and ∠DCE are supplementary angles, ∠DEC = 180° − 30° = 150° **c)** △CDE is an isosceles triangle since two sides are radii of the circle and are therefore equal. **d)** 15°. ∠DEC is an inscribed angle subtending the same arc as central angle ∠DCB, which is 30°. Therefore, ∠DEC = $\frac{1}{2}$ the measure of ∠DCB.

4. a) △CGL is an isosceles triangle since two sides are radii of the circle and are therefore equal. **b)** 160°. Since △CGL is isosceles, 180° − 10° − 10° = 160°. **c)** 20°. Since ∠JCH is a central angle subtending the same arc as ∠JGC, which is 10°, the measure of ∠JCH is twice the measure of ∠JGC.

d) 90°. Since segment JH is tangent to the circle at point H, it is perpendicular to the radius CH. **e)** 70°. Since triangle CJH is a right triangle and ∠JCH = 20°, 180° − 90° − 20° = 70°.

5. a) 8 m. Since triangle ABD is a right triangle, by using the Pythagorean relationship,

$$6^2 + BD^2 = 10^2$$
$$36 + BD^2 = 100$$
$$BD^2 = 64$$
$$BD = \sqrt{64}$$
$$BD = 8$$

b) 4 m. Since chord BE is the same measure as a radius and the diameter is 8 m, the measure of chord BE is 4 m. **c)** 90°. ∠BED is a right angle because it is an inscribed angle subtending a diameter. **d)** 7 m. Since △DEB is a right triangle, by using the Pythagorean relationship,

$$4^2 + DE^2 = 8^2$$
$$16 + DE^2 = 64$$
$$DE^2 = 48$$
$$DE = \sqrt{48}$$
$$DE \approx 7$$

6. a) 10 mm. The diameter is twice the measure of the radius. **b)** Yes. Since inscribed angle ∠GJH subtends the diameter GH, it is therefore a right angle. **c)** 8.7 mm. Since △GHJ is a right triangle, by using the Pythagorean relationship,

$$5^2 + HJ^2 = 10^2$$
$$25 + HJ^2 = 100$$
$$HJ^2 = 75$$
$$HJ = \sqrt{75}$$
$$HJ \approx 8.7$$

d) 90°. Since segment FG is tangent to the circle at point G and segment CG is a radius of the circle, angle FGH = 90°. **e)** 12.2 mm. Since △FGH is a right triangle, by using the Pythagorean relationship,

$$7^2 + 10^2 = FH^2$$
$$49 + 100 = FH^2$$
$$149 = FH^2$$
$$\sqrt{149} = FH$$
$$12.2 \approx FH$$

7. 16.8 m, 11.8 m

8. a) 17 m **b)** 12 cm

9. a) 35° **b)** 164°

10. a) Rectangle. Example: It is a rectangle because opposite sides are equal and all angles are 90°. **b)** 30 cm

11. 8.4 cm. Since △ABD is a right triangle, by using the Pythagorean relationship,
$$4.2^2 + 7.3^2 = DB^2$$
$$17.64 + 53.29 = DB^2$$
$$70.93 = DB^2$$
$$\sqrt{70.93} = DB$$
$$8.4 \approx DB$$

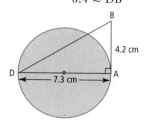

12. a) 90°. Since segment AD is tangent to the circle at point D and DB is a diameter, a right angle is formed at the point of tangency.   **b)** 45°. Since △ADB is an isosceles right triangle, $(180° - 90°) \div 2 = 45°$.
c) 45°. ∠DFE is an inscribed angle subtending the same arc as inscribed angle, ∠DBA which is 45°.
13. a) 90°. Since line l is tangent to the circle at point H and CH is a radius, a right angle is formed.   **b)** 90°. Since chord JK is parallel to line l and line l is perpendicular to segment CH, segment JK is perpendicular to segment CH.
c) 8.5 cm. Since a line passing through the centre of a circle that is perpendicular to a chord bisects the chord.
d) 3.2 cm. Since △CGJ is a right triangle, by using the Pythagorean relationship,
$$8.5^2 + CG^2 = 9.1^2$$
$$72.25 + CG^2 = 82.81$$
$$CG^2 = 10.56$$
$$CG = \sqrt{10.56}$$
$$CG \approx 3.2$$
14. $x = 11$, ∠JGH $= 53°$
15. 40°. Example: The inscribed angle of 85° subtends the same arc as a central angle. Therefore, the measure of the central angle is twice the measure of the inscribed angle, or 170°. One of the angles of the right triangle has a measure of $170° - 140° = 30°$.
So, $180° - (90° + 30°) = 60°$.

16. Example: The four congruent circles represent watered regions of the square field. The circles are tangent to the sides of the square. If the area of the field is 400 m², what is the area of the field that is not watered?

Answer: The side length of the square is the square root of the area of the square, or 20 m. The radius of each circle is 5 m. To find the area of the unwatered region, subtract the area of the four circles from the area of the square field.
$$400 - 4\pi r^2 \approx 400 - 314.16$$
$$\approx 85.8$$
The area of the unwatered region is 85.8 m²
17. 96 cm
18. B has coordinates (6, 2). C has coordinates (4, 6).
19.

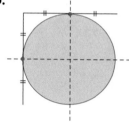

20. 146 cm
21. 17.6 cm
22. 43.6 cm

Chapter 10 Review, pages 404–405

1. radius
2. inscribed angle
3. chord
4. perpendicular bisector
5. a) 24°   **b)** 48°
6. $x = 48°$, $y = 48°$
7. No, the central angle inscribed by the same arc as the inscribed angle has a measure that is twice as large.
8. 18°
9. 90°
10. 28°
11. Example: The perpendicular bisector of a chord passes through the centre of the circle.
12. Example: She should have found the perpendicular bisector of her string and the perpendicular bisector of a second string. The intersection of the two perpendicular bisectors would be the location of the centre of the table.

13. 48 m. Since △ACB is a right triangle, by using the Pythagorean relationship,

$$10^2 + AB^2 = 26^2$$
$$100 + AB^2 = 676$$
$$AB^2 = 576$$
$$AB = \sqrt{576}$$
$$AB = 24$$

The radius is 24 m. The diameter AE is twice the radius, or 48 m.

14. Example: Two chords should be drawn. Then the perpendicular bisector of each chord should be drawn. The intersection of the two perpendicular bisectors is the centre of the circle. Next, find the measure from the centre to a point on the circle. This distance is the radius, which would be used to find the circumference.

15. 6.3 cm

16. 133°

17. 6 mm

18. The horizontal distance was 131 m. The variable, d, represents the horizontal distance.

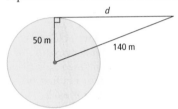

19. a) 90°. The line that is tangent to a circle at a point of tangency is perpendicular to the radius at that point. **b)** 42°. △CEF is a right triangle, so 180° − 90° − 48° = 42° **c)** 138°. ∠ECD and ∠ECF are supplementary angles, so 180° − 42° = 138°. **d)** 21°. △DEC is an isosceles triangle, so ∠DEC = (180° − 138°) ÷ 2 = 21°. **e)** 69°. ∠AED + ∠DEC + ∠CEF = 180°, so 180° − 90° − 21° = 69°. **f)** 21°. ∠EDB is an inscribed angle that subtends the same arc as the central angle ∠ECF, which is 42°, and is therefore one half its measure.

20. a) 42° **b)** 48°

Chapter 11

11.1 Factors Affecting Data Collection, pages 419–421

4. Example: **a)** The responses would be biased. The soccer team would have no interest in uniforms for the volleyball team. **b)** The responses would be biased. Truck drivers would probably respond that they prefer to drive trucks. **c)** The cost of the survey would be high and may outweigh the benefits of the study. **d)** The influencing factor is use of language. The positive descriptions of "most sturdy" and "expertly designed" could prompt them to choose Invincible Bikes.

5. Example: **a)** No bias. **b)** The bias is asking only owners of boarding horses and using the negative word "annoying". Rewrite: "Where should the stable be located?" **c)** The bias is asking only riders and including "on the site of the stable." Rewrite: "Where should a public park be built?"

6. Example: **a)** The influencing factor is the use of language. The respondent may not prefer either of the two choices. Rewrite: "What soda do you prefer?" **b)** The influencing factor is asking the opposition party member. Rewrite: "Who do you think is the best prime minister in Canadian history?" **c)** The person responding may be confused by the question. Rewrite: "Do your appliances and tools need any maintenance? If yes, do you know about the Hands-On-Repair Company?" **d)** This is private information. Students may not know their parents' income. No suggestion for a rewrite.

7. Example: **a)** "Which riding trails would you support closing?" **b)** "Who is your favourite male movie star?" **c)** "What is the cheapest way to travel a long distance?"

8. Example: **a)** "What sport do you like to watch?" **b)** "What is your favourite flavour of ice cream?" **c)** "Do you use the Internet to watch TV? If yes, what shows do you watch most often online?"

9. Example: **a)** "What juice flavour is your favourite?" or "Which of the following is your favourite juice flavour? a) apple, b) orange, c) pineapple, d) grapefruit, e) other" **b)** "What is your favourite shirt colour?" or "Which of the following is your favourite shirt colour? a) yellow, b) black, c) white, d) red, e) other" **c)** "What kind of diet do you support?" or "Which type of diet do you support? a) natural food, b) high protein, c) low carbohydrates, d) low fat, e) other"

10. Example: **a)** Ask people ages 13 to 19; "What sport do you like best?" **b)** Ask cell-phone owners; "What is most important consideration when buying a cell phone?" **c)** Ask people who use a media source; "What media source do you trust the most?"

11. Example: **a)** "Have you tried Crystal Juice? If yes, would you consider buying it as your regular juice?" **b)** "Do you use cough medicines? If yes, which brands do you use?" **c)** "If you were hiking in the bush and came across a moose, what would you do?" **d)** "Do you have Internet access? If yes, how satisfied are you with the level of service you receive?"

12. Example: **a)** The use of "expensive store" in the question makes the question biased. Rewrite: "Where have you purchased clothing items within the past year?" **b)** Asking members of the golf club makes the question biased. Rewrite: "Are you in favour of the proposed highway?"

13. Example: **a)** Biased question: "Do you prefer mindless computer games or mind stimulating board games like chess?" Rewrite: "What kind of games do you prefer to play?"

14. Example: **a)** Question 1: "Would you consider going on an Arctic adventure tour? If yes, what activities would appeal to you?" Question 2: "If you were going on an Arctic adventure tour, which of the following activities would interest you? a) dogsledding, b) white-water rafting, c) mountain climbing, d) big game hunting" Question 3: "Have you ever gone on a trip to the Arctic? If yes, what activities did you participate in?"

c) The use of language is the influencing factor that creates the bias. The words "mindless" and "mind stimulating" could sway a participant's answer to the survey question.

15. Example: If the source of the poll is a political party, the survey question may contain influencing factors that would affect the outcome.

11.2 Collecting Data, pages 427–429

4. Example: **a)** The population would be people who listen to rock bands. Since this population size could be quite large, a sample would be the most time- and cost-effective. **b)** The population would be this year's grade 9 students. A sample or population could be used, depending on the number of grade 9 students. **c)** The population would be customers of the store who buy soccer shirts. A sample or population could be used, depending on the number of customers. **d)** The population would be people who use shampoo. Since most people use shampoo, the population would be too large. A sample would be more appropriate.

5. Example: **a)** The population would be people who use the Internet at home. Since the population would be very large, a sample would be less time-consuming and more cost-effective. **b)** The population would be people associated with the school. A sample would be less time-consuming. **c)** The population would be customers of an electronics store who use the repairs and service department. A sample or population could be used, depending on the number of customers. **d)** The population would be people with special needs. A sample would be appropriate. It would be difficult to find and ask all people with special needs.

6. Example: **a)** Voluntary response; place an ad in the newspaper asking people to respond. **b)** Stratified; count the number of people in different categories of people associated with the school: students, parents, and staff. Ask a proportional number of people from each group. **c)** Systematic; ask every 10th repair/service customer. **d)** Voluntary response; place an ad in the newspaper asking people with special needs to respond.

7. Example: **a)** Ask people listening to the show to volunteer to phone-in their opinions. This is a voluntary response sample. **b)** Take a random sample by assigning each school a number, and have a random number generator select 25 numbers. **c)** Take a convenience sample by asking the first 50 teenagers who enter the mall on a Saturday. **d)** Take a convenience sample by asking the first 50 people who enter a coffee shop downtown.

8. Example: **a)** Population; there are not that many hospitals. **b)** Sample; it would be too costly and time-consuming to ask all grade 9 students. **c)** Population; all parachutes should be tested because their use involves life or death. **d)** Sample; it would be too costly and time-consuming to test all bike tires.

9. Adults represent 50% of the population, teens represent 20% of the population, and children represent 30% of the population. Kristi could stratify by asking 5 adults, 2 teens, and 3 children.

10. a) The population is the students of the school. **b)** The sample is students who use the cafeteria. **c)** For the first question, yes, students who use the cafeteria would have an opinion about paint colours for the walls. For the second question, no, students who do not use the cafeteria should also be included in the survey regarding the use of the cafeteria for graduation. **d)** No, he should not use the same sample for each question. Even though both questions refer to the cafeteria, the two questions are unrelated. Students who use the cafeteria would have an opinion about paint colours for the walls. But students who do not use the cafeteria should be included in the survey regarding the use of the cafeteria for graduation.

11. a) Yes, there is a bias in Enzo's sample. The bias is surveying people at a baseball game regarding spending the budget on baseball equipment. **b)** A random sample of ten students from each class would reflect the overall opinion of the students.

12. There could be 20 different responses from either method. The sample is too small to yield a conclusive result. If Anita uses a stratified sample that is larger, then her method would be better due to more people being involved. Also, the stratified sample would ensure that all departments are represented.

13. Example: She must have enough friends to make a large sample. Her friends' families must represent the population of Canadian households.

14. Example: **a)** Yes; $\frac{12}{50}$ is 24%, so 24% of the people in the survey are allergic to dogs. No; The fact that none of the 50 people surveyed are allergic to hedgehogs does not mean that no people are allergic to hedgehogs. **b)** "Are you allergic to any animals? If yes, what animal are you allergic to?" There may be other animals that are not on the list that people are allergic to. Some people may not have allergies to any animals.

16. Example: a) The survey assumes everyone surveyed is aware of what the fire department is doing. Rewrite: "Have you had the fire department perform a service for you? If yes, how would you rate the service?"
b) Influencing factors: Who was asked? When were they asked? How were they asked? It could have been a convenience sample that asked people who lived around the fire station. It may have been a voluntary response sample, where people were asked to mail in a response to a survey question that was placed in their mailbox. A random, stratified, or systematic survey would reflect opinions more accurately.

11.3 Probability in Society, pages 435–439

4. He assumed that the random sample was large enough to represent the entire population of light bulbs.
5. If the sample is accurate, 4080 toothpicks would be damaged. Assumption: The sample was random and large enough to represent the population of toothpicks.
6. a) Yes, only vegetarians were sampled. Assuming that there are non-vegetarians in the school population, the supervisor made a false prediction.
b) Example: Ask a larger sample of students, stratifying vegetarian and non-vegetarian students.
7. a) The prediction may be correct, but a larger sample would be more accurate. **b)** Use a larger sample.
8. a) 10 people **b)** The theoretical probability is $33\frac{1}{3}\%$. This assumes each of the three candidates has the same chance of winning. **c)** The experimental probability of 53% is greater than the theoretical probability of $33\frac{1}{3}\%$.
d) If the winner receives the greatest number of votes and the poll represents the population of voters, Candidate A will win.
9. a) 20% **b)** Assumption: Each movie type has the same chance of being selected. **c)** 20%
d) The probabilities are the same. **e)** 600 movies
10. a) 6.5 **b)** 7 **c)** 6 **d)** The samples are close indicators because they were off by 0.5 from the mean of all ten judges.
11. a) The sample is too small, so it may not represent the population of grade 9 students who work part-time. It could be biased. **b)** No, since the sample could be biased.
12. The experimental probability of having a boy is 48.7%. Since this is slightly less than the theoretical probability of 50%, the results confirm the article's claim.
14. a) John used theoretical probability assuming that each vehicle has an equal chance of passing the bus stop. Cathy used an experimental probability method based on her past experience. **b)** John's prediction was 20%. Cathy's was 40%. The experimental probability was about 13%. John was closer.
c) 105 trucks.

15. a) The theoretical probability of giving birth to a girl is $\frac{1}{2}$. So, the theoretical probability of having three girls is $\frac{1}{2} \times \frac{1}{2} \times \frac{1}{2} = \frac{1}{8}$. **b)** 0% **c)** The theoretical probability is 12.5% or $\frac{1}{8}$ and the experimental probability is 0%.
d) No, both the theoretical and experimental probabilities are very low. **e)** Assumption: The probability that a newly-born child is a boy is 50%.
16. a) Example: Yes, the sample was random and sufficiently large. **b)** 25% **c)** 1509 students
d) Assumption: The proportion in the general population is the same as the proportion in the sample.

Chapter 11 Review, pages 444–445

1. H
2. C
3. E
4. A
5. G
6. D
7. B
8. I
9. F
10. Example: a) The wording is an influencing factor. The use of the word "increased" will tend to make people respond negatively. **b)** The wording is confusing, "What is store-bought bread?" **c)** The sample is biased. Only juice drinkers are asked the survey question.
11. Example: a) The influencing factor is the use of language. The question assumes that respondents like cheesecake. Rewrite: "Do you like cheesecake? If yes, what is your favourite flavour?" **b)** The influencing factor is a bias by stating that "everyone loves the Rockets." Rewrite: "Do you like rock music? If yes, who is your favourite rock group?" **c)** The influencing factor is ethics, assuming respondents download music from the Internet. Rewrite: "Do you download music from the Internet? If yes, what music did you download in the past month?"
12. Example: a) The population is teens in Canada. Take a stratified sample by categorizing teens by where they live: rural, city, small town. **b)** The population is students in your school. Take a random sample by systematically choosing every 10th student from an alphabetical list. **c)** The population is the gas station retailers in the community. Take a random sample by placing the name of each retailer in a box, and drawing ten names.

13. a) This is a convenience sample. This sample may not typify the average mall shopper.   **b)** This is a type of stratified sample. But unless the population of each province or territory is the same, selecting 20 youths from each group is not a proportional selection.   **c)** This is a convenience sample. Selecting employees from one store location may not typify the average employee of a fast-food chain.

14. Example: **a)** A stratified sample of the doctors, nurses, and hospital administrators would be representative of the hospital's needs.   **b)** A systematic sample of every 10th customer who buys a sundae would give a representative random sample.

15. a) convenience   **b)** stratified   **c)** systematic

16. a) Approximately 304 trout   **b)** Assumptions: All fish are equally easy to catch. None of the fish died and none were born. The stream is a closed system and the fish cannot "escape" into a lake or ocean.   **c)** Example: Wait less time, but long enough to ensure a thorough mixing of the fish. Perhaps four or five days would give more accurate results.

17. Example: **a)** No. Her sample is biased since all the sample members were also members of her class.   **b)** She could take a systematic sample by obtaining an alphabetical list of all the grade 9 students and asking every 10th student on the list.

18. Assumption: The sample represents the population of grade 9 students.
Group 1: I agree with this statement because only 12.5% indicated they spent the most money on clothes.
Group 2: I disagree with this statement because only 27% chose cell phones. Cell phones are more expensive than many other forms of entertainment. This may lead students to spend more money on them, but they could attend movies or buy music more often.
Group 3: I agree with this statement because 27% of 500 is 135.
Group 4: I disagree with this statement because less than half of the sample spent money on these items.

Chapters 8–11 Review, pages 450–452

1. a) $x < 1$, since 8 times x is less than 8. $x = \dfrac{1}{20}$

b) $x > 1$, since x divided by 9 is close to 1, x must be close to 9. $x = 7.5$ **c)** $x > 1$, since 7 divided by x is less than 1, x must be greater than 7. $x = 28$

d) $x < 1$, since for x to fit into 1 almost 3 times, x must be less than 1. $x = \dfrac{2}{5}$

2. 3.4 m

3. $3.49

4. 2.5 h

5. 21

6. a) $x \le 17$ **b)** $-6.6 \le x < -5$

7. a) $x < -6$

b) $2.4 \le x$

8. a) $8 \le x$ **b)** 1.3 million $< x$ **c)** $x \le 3.7\%$ **d)** $x \le 10\%$

9. a) $x < 8.8$

b) $x > -\dfrac{8}{5}$

c) $-50 \le x$

d) $12 \le x$

10. a) $4.5 \le x$ **b)** $20 < x$ **c)** $13 > x$ **d)** $-9 \le x$

11. More than approximately 9.29 t

12. a) $145t \le 800$ **b)** 5.5 or fewer hours

13. after 40 h

14. $\angle DEB = 47°$, $\angle DCB = 94°$

15. CE = 5.4 cm

16. EF = 48 mm

17. 138 cm

18. Example: **a)** The wording leads the respondents to choose cards. Rewrite: "Do you play cards?"   **b)** People surveyed may not drink milk. Rewrite: "Do you drink milk? If yes, what type do you prefer to drink?"

19. Example: **a)** The population is students.   **b)** A convenience sample could be used, in which you ask your friends. A systematic sample could be used, in which you obtain an alphabetical list of students in your school, and ask every 10th student on the list.

20. Example: a) The population is the audience of the talk show. A voluntary sample of people watching the show could be used. **b)** The population is the people in the book store. The author could use a convenience sample by asking the first 50 people who enter the store.
c) The population is the students of the school. The sample could be a systematic sample of every 20th student on the school roster.

21. Example: a) The population is department managers and sales associates. **b)** The sampling method is random. **c)** Yes; there is a random sample of 20 stores, a random sample of 40 departments, and a random sample of department managers and sales associates.

22. Example: a) Since the grade 9 students were the only ones sampled, they assumed they knew what the elementary students would want to eat for the barbecue. **b)** A stratified sample would work best. Group the school by grades, and take a proportional sample of each grade.

23. a) 50% **b)** The assumption is that there is an equal chance of each answer being either correct or incorrect.
c) Example: Flipping a coin could be used to model this experiment. **e)** An experiment of only ten trials may not be enough to accurately predict the outcome.

Glossary

A

acute angle An angle that is between 0° and 90°.

angle of rotation (for symmetry) The minimum size of the angle needed to turn a shape or design onto itself. The angle may be measured in degrees or fractions of a turn.

arc (of a circle) A portion of the circumference of a circle. A minor arc is less than a semicircle, and a major arc is more than a semicircle.

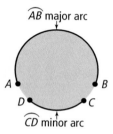

$\overset{\frown}{AB}$ major arc

$\overset{\frown}{CD}$ minor arc

area The number of square units contained in a two-dimensional region.

assumption Something taken for granted, as though it were true.

B

base (of a power) The number used as a factor for repeated multiplication. In 4^6, the base is 4.

biased sample Does not represent the population, and can make survey results inaccurate.

binomial An expression with two terms, such as $6y^2 + 3$ and $2x - 5y$.

bisect Divide into two equal parts.

bisector A line or line segment that cuts an angle or line segment into two equal parts.

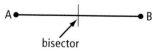

bisector

boundary point

boundary point The point that separates the values less than from the values greater than a specified value. If it is a possible value, it is shown with a closed circle on a number line. If it is not a possible value, the circle is open. For example, the boundary points for the inequality $-4 \le x < 4$ are -4 (closed circle) and 4 (open circle).

closed circle   open circle

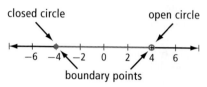

boundary points

C

central angle An angle formed by two radii of a circle. The vertex of the angle is at the centre of the circle, and the endpoints are on the circle.

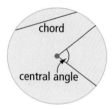

chord

central angle

centre of rotation The point about which the rotation of an object or design turns.

chord A line segment joining two points on the circumference of a circle.

circumference The boundary of or distance around a circle. This is a linear measurement. It is often represented by the variable C.

coefficient See numerical coefficient.

common denominator A common multiple of the denominators of a set of fractions. A common denominator for $\frac{1}{2}$ and $\frac{1}{3}$ is 6 because a common multiple of 2 and 3 is 6.

common multiple A common multiple is a number that is a multiple of two or more numbers. For example, common multiples of 3 and 5 include 0, 15, and 30.

composite object An object made from two or more separate objects.

congruent Identical in shape and size.

constant A known value in an equation or an expression. In the equation $s = 3n - 2$, -2 is a constant.

convenience sample A group of individuals that is chosen because its members are easy to access.

coordinate grid A grid made of intersecting vertical and horizontal lines. Also called a Cartesian plane.

coordinate pair(s) See coordinates.

coordinate(s) An ordered pair, (x, y), is a pair of numbers used to locate a point on a coordinate grid. Coordinates are the values in an ordered pair. The x-coordinate is the distance from the vertical or y-axis. The y-coordinate is the distance from the horizontal or x-axis.

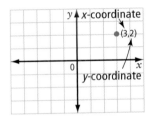

corresponding angles Angles that have the same relative position in two geometric figures.

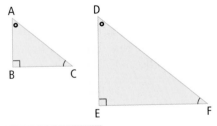

corresponding sides Sides that have the same relative position in two geometric figures.

D

degree of a polynomial The degree of the highest-degree term in a polynomial. For example, the polynomial $7a^2 - 3a$ has a degree of two.

degree of a term The sum of the exponents on the variables in a single term. For example, the degree of $3x^3z^2$ is 5. A variable with no exponent has a degree of one.

diagonal A line joining two non-adjacent vertices of a polygon.

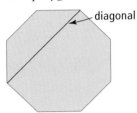

diameter The distance across a circle through its centre. Represented by the variable d.

distributive property The rule that states $a(b + c) = ab + ac$ for all real numbers a, b, and c.

E

enlargement An increase in the dimensions of an object by a constant factor. The enlargement can be 2-D or 3-D.

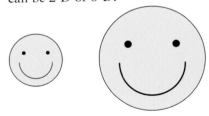

equation A statement that two mathematical expressions are equal and have the same value.

equilateral triangle A triangle with three equal sides.

ethics Involves judgments of right and wrong behaviour. For example, cheating on a test is wrong, or unethical.

experimental probability The probability of an event occurring based on experimental results.

exponent The number of times you multiply the base in a power by itself. For example, in 2^3, 3 is the exponent, so the base is multiplied by itself three times: $2 \times 2 \times 2 = 8$.

exponential form A shorter way of writing repeated multiplication, using a base and an exponent. For example, $5 \times 5 \times 5$ in exponential form is 5^3.

extrapolate To estimate a value beyond a given set of values.

G

generalize To infer a general principle or make a broad statement from known facts.

H

heptagon A 2-D shape with seven sides.

hypotenuse The side opposite the right angle in a right triangle.

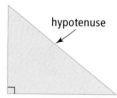

hypothesis A proposition put forward to guide an investigation.

I

inequality A mathematical statement comparing expressions that may not be equal. These can be written using the symbols less than ($<$), greater than ($>$), less than or equal ($\leq$), greater than or equal ($\geq$), or not equal ($\neq$).

inscribed angle An angle formed by two chords that share a common endpoint. The vertex and endpoints are on the circle.

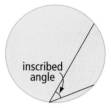

interior angle An angle that is formed inside a polygon by two sides meeting at a vertex.

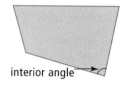

interpolate To estimate the value between two given values.

isosceles triangle A triangle with exactly two equal sides.

L

like terms Terms that have the same variable(s) raised to the same exponent(s). For example, $3x$ and $-2x$ are like terms.

line of symmetry A line running through the centre of an object or design such that the halves on each side of the line are mirror images. These lines can be vertical, horizontal, or oblique. A figure may have more than one line of symmetry. Also called a line of reflection.

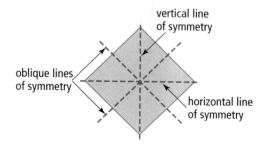

linear equation An equation whose graph is a straight line.

linear relation A relation that appears as a straight line when graphed.

M

mean A measure of central tendency calculated by finding the sum of a set of values divided by the number of values in the set. For example, for the set of values 6, 8, 5, 9, and 12,

$$\text{Mean} = \frac{6 + 8 + 5 + 9 + 12}{5}$$
$$= 8$$

median A measure of central tendency determined by the middle number in a set of data after the data have been arranged in order.

For the data 2, 5, 6, 8, and 9, the median is 6.
For the data 1, 3, 7, 7, 9, and 10, the median is 7.

mode A measure of central tendency determined by the most frequently occurring number in a set of data. There can be more than one mode.
For the data 3, 5, 7, 7, and 9, the mode is 7.
For the data 2, 2, 4, 6, 6, 8, and 11, the modes are 2 and 6.

monomial An algebraic expression with one term. For example, 5, $2x$, $3s^2$, $-8cd$, and $\frac{n^4}{3}$ are all monomials.

N

non-perfect square A rational number that cannot be expressed as the product of two equal rational factors. For example, you cannot multiply any rational number by itself and get an answer of 3, 5, 1.5, or $\frac{7}{8}$. The square root of a non-perfect square is a non-repeating, non-terminating decimal.

numerical coefficient A number that multiplies the variable. In $3n - 2$, the numerical coefficient is 3.

O

oblique Slanted, rather than vertical or horizontal.

octagon A 2-D shape with eight sides.

opposite operation Operations that "undo" other operations. Sometimes called "inverse operations." Examples of opposite operations are addition and subtraction, multiplication and division, and squaring and taking the square root.

opposites Two numbers or expressions with the same numeral, but different signs. For example, $+2$ and -2, and $3x + 2$ and $-3x - 2$, are opposites.

order of operations The correct sequence of steps for a calculation: Brackets, Exponents, Divide and Multiply in order from left to right, Add and Subtract in order from left to right.

order of rotation The number of times a shape or design fits onto itself in one turn. The order of rotation of this figure is 4.

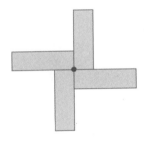

P

parallelogram A four-sided figure with opposite sides that are parallel and equal in length.

pentagon A 2-D shape with five sides.

perfect square A number that is the product of two identical factors.

$2 \times 2 = 4$, so 4 is a perfect square
$6 \times 6 = 36$, so 36 is a perfect square

perimeter The distance around the outside of a two-dimensional shape or figure.

perpendicular Describes lines that intersect at right angles (90°).

perpendicular bisector A line that divides a line segment in half and is at right angles to it.

plane A two-dimensional flat surface that extends in all directions.

polygon A two-dimensional closed figure made of three or more line segments.

polynomial An algebraic expression formed by adding or subtracting terms. For example,

$x + 5$, $2d - 2.4$, $3s^2 + 5s - 6$, and $\dfrac{h^2}{2} - \dfrac{h}{4}$

are all polynomials.

population All of the individuals that belong to a group being studied.

power An expression made up of a base and an exponent. For example, for the power 6^3, 6 is the base and 3 is the exponent.

prime factors Factors that are prime numbers. For example, the prime factors of 10 are 2 and 5.

probability The likelihood or chance of an event occurring. Probability can be expressed as a ratio, fraction, or percent.

proportion An equation that says that two ratios or two rates are equal. It can be written in fraction form as $\dfrac{1}{4} = \dfrac{5}{20}$, or in ratio form as $1:4 = 4:16$.

Pythagorean relationship The relationship between the lengths of the sides of a right triangle. The sum of the areas of the squares attached to the legs of the triangle equals the area of the square attached to the hypotenuse.

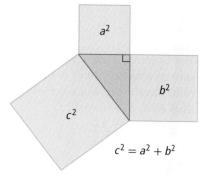

$$c^2 = a^2 + b^2$$

Q

quadrilateral A polygon that has four sides.

R

radius A line segment joining the centre of a circle to the outside edge. It can also refer to the length of this line segment and may be represented by the variable, r.

random An event in which every outcome has an equal chance of occurring.

random sample A sample of individuals chosen randomly from the whole population as a way of representing the whole population. Stratified samples and systematic samples are types of random samples.

ratio A comparison of two quantities with the same units.

rational number A number that can be expressed as the quotient of two integers, where the divisor is not zero. For example, 0.75, $\dfrac{3}{4}$, and -2 are rational numbers.

reciprocal The multiplier of a number to give a product of 1. For example, $\frac{3}{4}$ is the reciprocal of $\frac{4}{3}$ because $\frac{3}{4} \times \frac{4}{3} = 1$.

reduction A decrease in the dimensions of an object by a constant factor. For example, in the diagram, the second bulb is half as large as the first. A reduction can be 2-D or 3-D.

regular polygon A polygon with all sides equal and all interior angles equal.

repeating decimal A decimal number with a digit or group of digits that repeats forever. Repeating digits are shown with a bar: $0.\overline{4} = 0.444...$ and $-3.\overline{12} = -3.121212....$

right triangle A triangle containing a 90° angle.

rotation symmetry Occurs when a shape or design can be turned about its centre of rotation so that it fits onto its outline more than once in a complete turn. The design in the figure fits onto itself 10 times in one turn.

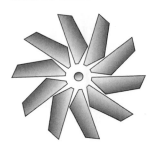

S

sample Any group of individuals selected from the population.

scale A comparison between the actual size of an object and the size of its image. This can be expressed as a ratio, as a fraction, as a percent, in words, or in a diagram. For example, a scale of 1 cm : 50 km on a map means that 1 cm on the map represents 50 km.

scale diagram A diagram that is similar to the actual figure or object. It may be smaller than or larger than the actual object, but must be in the same proportions.

scale factor The constant factor by which all dimensions of an object are enlarged or reduced in a scale drawing. The dimensions of this rectangle is multiplied by 3 so the scale factor is 3.

similar figures Figures that have the same shape, but different size. They have equal corresponding angles and proportional corresponding sides.

simulate To create a model that reflects a particular situation.

solution (of an inequality) A value or set of values that result in a true statement. The solution can contain a specific value or many values.

square root One of two equal factors of a number. The symbol is R. For example, 9 is the square root of 81 because 9×9 is 81.

stratified sample A sample that is created by dividing the whole population into distinct groups and then choosing the same fraction of members from each group.

subtended Lying opposite to. For example, in the figure, the arc AB subtends the angle, $\angle ACB$.

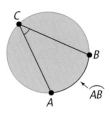

supplementary angles Angles that add to 180°.

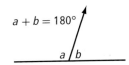

$a + b = 180°$

surface area The number of square units needed to cover a 3-D object. The sum of the areas of all the faces of an object.

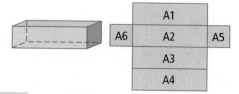

survey A question or questions asked of a sample of the population to gather opinions.

symmetry An object or image has symmetry if it is balanced and can fit onto itself either by reflection or rotation.

systematic sample A sample created by choosing individuals at fixed intervals from an ordered list of the whole population.

T

tangent (of a circle) A line that touches a circle at exactly one point. The line is perpendicular to the radius at that point. The point where the line touches the circle is called the point of tangency.

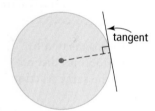

term A number or a variable, or the product of numbers and variables. The expression $5x + 3$ has two terms: $5x$ and 3.

terminating decimal A decimal number in which the digits stop. 0.4, 0.86, and 0.25 are terminating decimals.

tessellation A pattern or arrangement that covers an area or plane without overlapping or leaving gaps. Also called a tiling pattern.

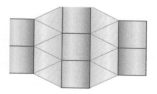

theoretical probability The expected probability of an event occurring. The ratio of the number of expected favourable outcomes to the total number of possible outcomes for an event.

transformation A change in a figure that results in a different position or orientation. Examples are translations, reflections, and rotations.

translation A slide along a straight line.

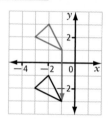

trapezoid A quadrilateral with one pair of parallel sides.

trinomial A polynomial with three terms. $x^2 + 3x - 1$ is a trinomial.

V

variable A letter that represents an unknown number.

vertex The point where two or more edges of a figure or object meet. The plural is *vertices*.

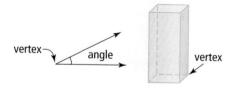

volume The amount of space an object occupies. Measured in cubic units.

voluntary response sample A sample where the whole population is invited to participate.

Index

A

addition
    decimals, 56, 58–59
    fractions, 63–64, 67
    polynomials, 191–193, 195
    rational numbers, 57
algebra, 174–175, 178
angle
    central, 378–382, 385, 396
    inscribed, 378–382, 385, 396
    supplementary, 395
arc, 378–382
area
    circle, 116
    square, 74, 116
    trapezoid, 320
    triangle, Heron's formula, 80
ascending order, 48
assumption, 430–431, 434–435

B

base (of exponent), 93, 96
    negative, 95
    positive, 94
bias, 415–416, 418
biased sample, 431, 435
binomial, 175–176, 178, 267
blueprint, 129
boundary point, 342

C

carpenter's square, 388
Celsius and Fahrenheit, 242
central angle, 378–382, 385, 396
centripetal force, 398
chord, 378–380, 387–388, 393, 395–397, 399
    perpendicular bisector, 386–388
    perpendicular line, 393
    tangent, 394–399
circle
    area, 116

circle geometry
    arc (of), 378–382
    central angle, 378–382, 385, 396
    chord, 378–380, 387–388, 393, 395–397, 399
    inscribed angle, 378–382, 385, 396
    perpendicular bisector, 386–388
    Pythagorean relationship, 380, 387, 397–398
    tangent, 394–399
circumference, 302
closed circle, 342
coefficient, 108, 110, 175, 184–186
commission, 220
composite object, 26
compound interest, 119
constant, 175–177, 212, 293
continuous data, 220
convenience sample, 423, 425–426
corresponding angles, 146–148, 150, 155–156
corresponding sides, 146–148, 150, 155–156
cost, 415–416, 418
cube, surface area, 115
cultural sensitivity, 415–416, 418
cylinder
    surface area, 27, 271, 274
    volume, 122, 271

D

data
    factors affecting collection, 415–418
decimals, 49
    addition, 56, 58–59
    division, 55, 57–59
    equations, 297, 300, 308–309
    multiplication, 55, 57–59
    order of operations, 58, 59

rational numbers, 47, 50, 55–59
    subtraction, 56, 59
degree of a polynomial, 176–178
degree of a term, 176–178
descending order, 48
distributive property, 267–268, 315
division
    decimals, 55, 57–59
    fractions, 65, 67
    monomials, 256–259
    polynomials by monomials, 273–274
    powers, 102, 104–105
    rational numbers, 55, 57–59, 65, 67
double inequality, 345

E

Einstein, Albert, 118
enlargement, 131–132, 135
equation, 293
    constant, 293
    decimals, 297, 300, 308–309
    fractions, 294–296, 300, 306–307, 309–310
    grouping $a(x + b) = c$, 315–318
    numerical coefficient, 293
    one–step $ax = b, \frac{x}{a} = b, \frac{a}{x} = b$, 294–300
    solving, *see* solving equations
    two–step $ax + b = c, \frac{x}{a} + b = c$, 306–310
    variable, 293
    variables on both sides, $ax = b + cx, ax + b = cx + d, a(bx + c) = d(ex + f)$, 293, 323–325
equivalent fractions, 49
ethics, 415, 417–418
Euclid, 93, 374

experimental probability,
434–435
exponent, 93, 96
base, 93, 96
laws, 101–105, 120
like terms, 184–186
order of operations, 109–110
powers, 93, 96, 101–103
problem solving, 115–117
terms, 175–178
zero, 104
exponential form, 93
extrapolate, 223–225

F

factored form, 101
Fahrenheit and Celsius, 242
fraction bar, 316
fractions
addition, 63–64, 67
ancient Egypt, 71
division, 65, 67
equations, 294–296, 300,
306–307, 309–310
multiplication, 65, 67
rational numbers, 47, 50,
63–67
subtraction, 63–64, 67

G

generalize, 432, 435
geometry, 374
graphic organizers
concept map, 171, 289, 337,
411
Frayer model, 43
sequence chart, 207
spider map, 89, 127, 251
thematic map, 3
web, 375
graphs
describing variables, 222
extrapolating, 223–225
horizontal and vertical lines,
237
interpolating, 222–223, 225
interpreting, 220–225

joining points, 212
linear equations, 232–234, 238
spreadsheets, 235

H

heptagon, 217
Heron of Alexandria, 81
Heron's formula, 80–81
hexagon, 158
horizontal line on graph,
237–238
hypothesis, 429

I

inequality, 341, 346
boundary point, 342, 356
double, 345–346
expressing, 342, 346
interpreting, 346
multi-step, 361–364
representing, also see number
lines, 342–346
single-step, 352–356
solution of, 353
solving, see solving inequalities
symbols, 342
influencing factors, 415
bias, 415–416, 418
cost, 415–416, 418
cultural sensitivity, 415–416,
418
ethics, 415, 417–418
privacy, 415, 418
time and timing, 415–416, 418
use of language, 415–418
inscribed angle, 378–382, 385,
396
inscribed circle, 262
interpolate, 222–223, 225
inverse operations, 294

J

Jeake, Samuel, 93

K

knot, 210

L

latitude, 224
like terms, 184–186
line of reflection, 5
line of symmetry, 6–14, 19, 20
linear equation, 212
determining from graph,
234–237
graphing, 232–234, 237–238
interpreting graphs, 222–225
patterns, 212, 214, 216
table of values, 212–216
linear inequality, 346
linear relation, 206
graphing, 232–234, 237–238
longitude, 224

M

magnification, 130
mean, 432–433
median, 432–433
mode, 432–433
monomial, 175–176, 178, 254
dividing polynomials, 273–274
division, 256–259
modelling, 255–257, 259
multiplication, 255–256, 259
multiplying polynomials,
266–268
Moore's Law, 107
Moore, Gordon, 107
multiplication
decimals, 55, 57–59
fractions, 65, 67
monomials, 255–256, 259
polynomials by monomials,
266–268
powers, 93–96, 101–103, 105
rational numbers, 55, 57–59,
65, 67

N

non perfect square, 77
number lines
boundary point, 342, 356
closed circle, 342
open circle, 342

Credits

Photo Credits

vi B.Lowry/IVY IMAGES; vii iStock; viii top B.Lowry/IVY IMAGES, Waltraud Ingerl/iStock; ix top Bill Ivy, THE CANADIAN PRESS/Actionpress, Rich Legg/iStock, James Brey/iStock; x, xi David Tanaka; xii Bill Ivy; xiii David Tanaka; xiv Miklos Voros/iStock; xvi David Tanaka; xvii C.Ivy/IVY IMAGES; p2–3 Bill Ivy; p5 top Robyn Roste/ResourceEye Services Inc., Bill Ivy; p7 Jean-Yves Benedeyt/iStock; p12 Raven Frog Panel courtesy of Douglas Reynolds Gallery. Used by permission of Don Yeomans, Haida artist; p16 Population Health Fund Later Life Component logo used by permission of Public Health Agency of Canada; p22 Dolphin tessellation used by permission Dr. Andrew Crompton, School of Architecture, Manchester University; p24 left group Bill Ivy, David Tanaka, right Nikolay Mikheev/iStock, bottom David Tanaka; p25 left Used by permission Saskatoon Shines Tourism Saskatoon, Canadian Broadcasting Corporation; p26 Micro Discovery/CORBIS; p27 Raymond Truelove/iStock; p29 Jay Spooner/iStock; p31 David Tanaka; p39 iStock; p41 top Marek Walica/iStock, middle left Bill Ivy, iStock, bottom left Micheal Rozanski/iStock, Thomas Moens/iStock; p42–43 David Tanaka; p45 David Tanaka; p46 O.Bierwagen/IVY IMAGES; p47 David Tanaka; p54 David Tanaka; p55 left B.Lowry/IVY IMAGES, THE CANADIAN PRESS/Paul Chiasson; p58 David Tanaka; p59 Yanik Chauvin/iStock; p61 David Tanaka; p63 THE CANADIAN PRESS/AP/Koji Sasahara; p66 David Tanaka; p69 NASA/JPL/Space Science Institute; p70 Bryan & Cherry Alexander Photography/Arcticphoto.com; p71 Helene Rogers/Alamy; p72 Roger Russmeyer/Corbis; p73 Kazuyoshi Nomachi/Corbis; p83 NASA; p84 THE CANADIAN PRESS/AP/David Longstreath; p86 Masterfile RF; p87 Bill Ivy; p88–89 B.Lowry/IVY IMAGES; p91 Calder, Alexander (1898–1976) © ARS, NY; Triple Gong, ca. 1948 Photo: Calder Foundation, New York, Art Resource, NY; p93 Bettman/Corbis; p96 GoGo Images/Alamy; p98 Visuals Unlimited/CORBIS; p99, 100 David Tanaka; p101 CartoonStock; p105 Vikram Raghuvanshi/iStock; p107 Dino Ablakovic/iStock; p109, 111 David Tanaka;

p114 David Tanaka, inset USFWS; p117 Linda Stewart/iStock; p118 David Tanaka; p119 top Brandon Laufenberg/iStock, Bill Ivy; p122 Jeff MacDonald/iStock; p123 iStock; p124 David J. Green/Alamy, Bernhard Classen/Alamy, vario images GmbH & Co. KG/Alamy; p125 top Chris Hepburn/iStock, Fred de Noyelle/Godong/Corbis; p126–127 Canadian Museum of Civilization Corporation; p130 top Perennou Nuridsany/Photo Researchers, Inc., Bruce Iverson; p136 top costint/iStock, Miklos Voros/iStock, Ruaridh Stewart/ZUMA/Corbis; p137 top Perennou Nuridsany/Photo Researchers, Inc., H.Kalen/IVY IMAGES; p138 THE CANADIAN PRESS/Chuck Stoody; p142 Maciej Noskowski/iStock; p143 top left clockwise Bill Ivy, Jocelyn Chillog, used by permission, Peter Oshkai/Alamy; p144 left David Tanaka, Norman Pogson/iStock; p145 left David Tanaka, Photo courtesy of Ron McKay, Cardinal River Operations, Teck Coal; p154, 158 Bill Ivy; p159 Tessa McIntosh; p162 USFWS; p163 Florin Tirlea/iStock; p165 top Used by permission of the Assembly of First Nations; The Trans Canada Trail, Ducks Unlimited, Canadian Blood Services; p167 Jacqui Hurst/CORBIS; p170–171 "The Forest Has Eyes" copyright 1984 Bev Doolittle, photo courtesy of The Greenwich Workshop, Inc.; p173 THE CANADIAN PRESS/Actionpress; p174 James Bray/iStock; p181 Jami Garrison/iStock; p182 THE CANADIAN PRESS/Penticton Herald/Mark Brett; p183 NASA; p190 David Lewis/iStock; p191 Tom Thaves; p199 left Jason Lugo/iStock, right Used by permission of the artists Annie Taipanak and Tobi Kreelak. Photos courtesy of WarkInuit.com; p201 Yellow Dog Productions/Getty Images; p203 Rich Legg/iStock; p204 T.Parker/IVY IMAGES; p205 Blue Lantern Studio/Corbis; p206–207 Bill Ivy; p209 B.Lowry/IVY IMAGES; p210 B.Lowry/IVY IMAGES; p211 219 top IVY IMAGES; Anne-Marie Scott; p221 InStock Photographic Ltd./iStock; p228 THE CANADIAN PRESS/AP/Ian Kershaw/Barrow Evening Mail; p229 Bill Ivy; p230 Martin McCarthy/iStock; p231 THE CANADIAN PRESS/Rex Features; p237 Judy Foldetta/iStock; p242 J.Mathias/IVY IMAGES; p243 Francois Legare/OMER 6; p244, p247 T.Parker/IVY IMAGES; p248 William Blacke/iStock;

p249 top Arne Trautmann/iStock, David Tanaka with permission of the Lethbridge YMCA Youth Fitness Group, Radu Razvan/iStock; p250–251 D. Trask/IVY IMAGES, inset Dennis MacDonald/Age FotoStock/Maxx Images; p254 Bighorn National Historic Park; p262 left W.Fraser/IVY IMAGES, B.Lowry/IVY IMAGES; p263 Bill Ivy; p264 top Robert Morton/iStock, wiki Creative Commons; p270 Christie's Images/CORBIS; p271 Arthur Kwiatkowski/iStock; p277 Inna Felker/iStock; p281 top Masterfile RF, Alistair Forrester/iStock; p282 David Tanaka; p285 top B.Marsh/IVY IMAGES, Chris Schmidt/iStock; p286 Bryan & Cherry Alexander/Arcticphotos.com; p287 Miklos Voros/iStock; p288–289 David Tanaka; p291 David Tanaka; p292 THE CANADIAN PRESS/AP/Matt York; p293 Barry Gossage/NBAE/Getty Images; p298 Cory Shannon, Used by permission of Karyn Drake; p299 iStock; p302 left David Tanaka, B.Lowry/IVY IMAGES; p303 David Tanaka; p304 wiki Creative Commons; p305 Birgit Prentner/iStock; p308 Bill Ivy; p312 left Masterfile RF, W.Ivy/IVY IMAGES; p313 Roy Ooms/Masterfile; p314 Steve McSweeney/iStock; p317, 321 B.Lowry/IVY IMAGES; p322 David Gilder/iStock; p326 David Wei/Alamy; p328 Bill Ivy; p331 left Amos Struck/iStock, David Tanaka; p333 top Andrew Howe/iStock, David Tanaka; p336–337 IVY IMAGES; p339 top Bettman/CORBIS, Roslan Rahman/Getty Images; p340 Andre Ringuette/NHLI via Getty Images; p341 Photo courtesy of britishcolumbia.com; p342 David Tanaka; p348 left Dennis MacDonald/PhotoEdit, First Light/Getty Images; p349 Dave Raboin/iStock; p355 David Tanaka; p358 T.Parker/IVY IMAGES; p359 top Alan & Sandy Carey/IVY IMAGES, Mark Tantrum/iStock; p360 David Tanaka; p363 Masterfile RF; p364 David Tanaka; p366 top brtPhoto/Alamy, David Tanaka, Otto Groning/iStock; p368 D.Johns/IVY IMAGES; p370 B.Lowry/IVY IMAGES; p371 D.Trask/IVY IMAGES; p374 inset JSL/NASA; p377 top Used by permission of the artist Michele Hardy "Circles #21" 2002 Michele Hardy, Provincial Museum of Alberta DkPf1-7, David Tanaka; p383 Rainer Schoditsch/Alamy; p388 top David Lewis/iStock, Bill Ivy; p390 Bill Ivy; p391 Baris Simsek/iStock; p393, 394 David Tanaka; p398 left THE CANADIAN PRESS/AP/Bas Czerwinski, B.Lowry/IVY IMAGES; p402 left IndexStock/Maxx Images, David Tanaka; p404 Nikolay Mikheev/

iStock; p405 top Bill Ivy, The Image Bank/Getty Images; p407 top wiki Creative Commons, David Tanaka; p408 Waltraud Ingerl/iStock; p409 Bill Ivy; p410–411 T.Parker/IVY IMAGES; p413 top Arco Images GmbH/Alamy, N.Lightfoot/IVY IMAGES; p416 John Lee/First Light/Getty Images; p419 Bill Ivy; p421 W.Towriss/IVY IMAGES; p423 Hamurishi/iStock; p427 Getty Images RF; p429 Norbert Rosing/National Geographic/Getty Images; p430 O.Bierwagon/IVY IMAGES; p431 Linda Tanaka; p436 THE CANADIAN PRESS/AP/Massimo Pinca; p438 Bill Ivy; p445 left Robert E Barber/Alamy, Hillary Fox/iStock; p446 T.Parker/IVY IMAGES; p447 Paul Tessier/iStock; p448 The Canadian Press/Brandon Sun/Bruce Bumstead; p449 David Tanaka; p451 Layne Kennedy/Corbis

Text Credits

p437 Data courtesy of Insurance Bureau of Canada

Illustration Credits

Ben Hodson: xviii, 51, 52, 74, 86, 92, 97, 108, 112, 121, 182, 189, 200, 220, 272, 324, 334, 345, 350, 351, 369, 372, 378, 386, 391, 414, 422, 428, 432, 435
www.mikecarterstudio.com: 22, 374–375

Technical Art

Brad Black, Tom Dart, Kim Hutchinson, and Adam Wood of First Folio Resource Group, Inc.